世界の幻想耽美

もくじ　　Contents

幻想耽美ダーク・ヒストリー　　海野 弘

〈幻想耽美〉の起源 ── ロマン主義

　不気味なアートがひそかに氾濫しつつある。そのスタイルは多様であるが、共通しているのは人体に対する強いこだわりである。美神に対して人体が犠牲に捧げられている。その儀式はあまりに残酷無惨なので秘儀として行われるか、私的な幻想として描かれるはずであった。しかしそれが流出しはじめ、パブリックな世界にあふれ出してきている。モダン・アートの歴史はそれを無視してきた。どうあつかうかとまどっているともいえる。だが、これだけあふれてくると、それをとりこむ新しい歴史を考えるべきではないだろうか。

　私は『ヨーロッパの幻想美術』、『ファンタジーと SF・スチームパンクの世界』（いずれも 2017年、パイ インターナショナル刊）を書いた。前者では 19世紀末の象徴主義を中心とし、後者ではゴシックとスチームパンクという 2つのコンセプトによってヴィクトリア期にさかのぼり、幻想美術の起源をロマン主義に置いた。

　これらの 2つの本であつかったアートが、いわゆる〈幻想耽美〉の起源として考えることができるのではないだろうか。もしそれなら、ロマン主義から〈幻想耽美〉までの系譜をたどってみたいと思った。

　ロマン主義は1790年から1850年にかけて興った運動で、安定した枠組みのある世界を目指す古典主義に反発し、不安の中を動揺し、秩序と論理に反対し、無限を追求しようとする。昼ではなく夜、生ではなく死、今ではなく過去（中世、ケルトなどへの回帰）を志向する。

　イギリスのロマン主義の起源の 1つとなったのはゴシック・リヴァイヴァルで、ゴシック趣味の中で、古城の幽霊がうごめく〈ホラー小説〉があらわれる。ウォルポールの『オトラント城奇譚』〈fig.1〉、ラドクリフの『ユードルフォの謎』〈fig.2〉などである。その系譜はドイツの E・T・A・ホフマン〈fig.3〉、アメリカのアラン・ポー〈fig.4〉などの怪奇と幻想の物語へとつづく。

　イギリス・ロマン主義はゴシック・リヴァイヴァルの中世趣味、怪奇趣味を受け継ぎ、メアリー・シェリーの『フランケンシュタイン』〈fig.5〉というホラー小説の傑作を残した。これは人間をつくろうとして怪物をつくってしまった話であり、現代の〈幻想耽美〉の 1つの源泉ではないだろうか。

　世紀末象徴主義において、ロマン主義が切り開いた夜の世界は、一気に逸脱とデカダンスを深め、百鬼夜行となる。私は『ヨーロッパの幻想美術』で、象徴主義美術を、「見たことのないもの、驚異、幻想、夢を描く」とした。

　1830 年代に写真が発明される。それによって、見たことのないものを描くという象徴主義の傾向は一層強まった。しかし面白いことに写真もまた象徴主義にライヴァル心を燃やし、幻想や夢を撮ることに取りつかれ、「心霊写真」が試

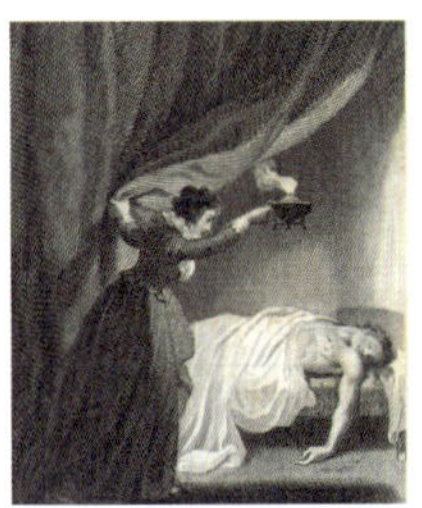

fig.1
書籍『オトラント城奇譚』挿絵
ホレース・ウォルポール著 / 1824 年版

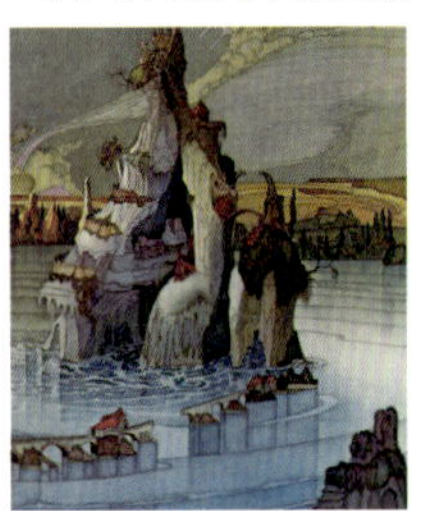

fig.2
書籍『ユードルフォの謎』挿絵
アン・ラドクリフ著 / 1806 年版

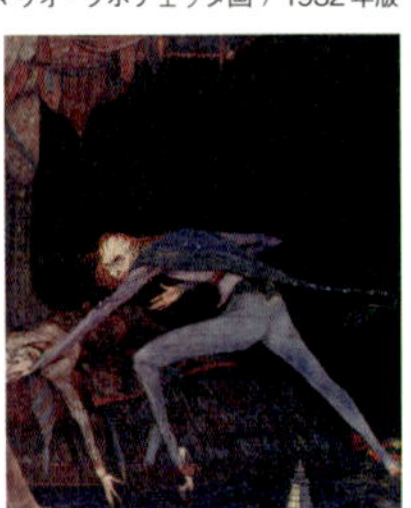

fig.3
書籍『ホフマン物語』挿絵
E・T・A・ホフマン著 /
マリオ・ラボチェッタ画 / 1932 年版

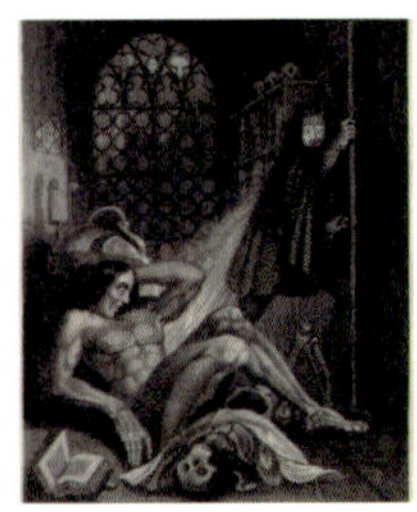

fig.4
書籍『ポー怪奇物語集』挿絵
エドガー・アラン・ポー著 /
ハリー・クラーク画 / 1923 年版

fig.5
書籍『フランケンシュタイン』挿絵
メアリー・シェリー著 / 1831 年版

みられる。今日の〈幻想耽美〉の写真はそこから発している。

　マリオ・プラーツのロマン派から世紀末にかけてのデカダンス文学論は『肉体と死と悪魔——ロマンティック・アゴニー』（1933）と題されている。肉体と死と悪魔こそ〈幻想耽美〉のテーマそのものなのである。

シュルレアリスム

　19世紀末の幻想美術（象徴主義、アール・ヌーヴォー）は20世紀のモダニスムによって排除される。それを復活させたのはシュルレアリスムである。

　シュルレアリスムには実は美術はないといわれる。それは詩人の運動であり、精神の転換を目指す、人生を変えるという倫理的な呼び掛けであるからだ。『シュルレアリスム宣言』（1924）では、論理の支配から脱出しようといっている。そして想像、夢、無意識、偶然を表現方法にとり入れた。

　あくまでことばの革命であったにもかかわらず、シュルレアリスムの表現方法に多くの画家が集まった。周辺にいた画家も含めるとかなりの数になる。〈シュルレアリスム〉というくくり方しかできないほど、その表現は多様であるが、マン・レイの写真〈fig.6〉、ルイス・ブニュエルの映画〈fig.7〉など、他の分野にも広がっている。

　シュルレアリスムの実験の1つに「甘美な死骸」という遊びがある。折った紙に、それぞれ他の人に知られないように詩の1行を書き、それを広げて、1つの詩をつくるといった遊びである。ことばではなく絵の場合は、人物像に構成するのが目標で、頭、上半身、腰、脚をそれぞれが勝手に書いて、合成する。

　1934年につくられた、ポール・エリュアール、ヴァランティーヌ・ユーゴー、アンドレ・ブルトン、ヌッシュ・エリュアールの合作した「甘美な死骸」〈fig.8〉がある。顔、上半身、腰、脚をそれぞれ4人が勝手につくる。人体を4つに切断し、また合成するのだ。

　「甘美な死骸」というのは〈幻想耽美〉にぴったりのことばではないだろうか。

　シュルレアリスムは1919年、アンドレ・ブルトン、フィリップ・スーポー、ルイ・アラゴンが雑誌『文学』を創刊したあたりからはじまる。

　1922年は「眠りの時代」といわれ、交霊術や催眠術によって、眠ったまま語ったりする実験をしている。この年、マン・レイやマックス・エルンスト〈fig.9〉が入ってくる。

　1924年、ブルトンは『シュルレアリスム宣言』を出し、機関誌『シュルレアリスム革命』を創刊する。シュルレアリスムは反体制的政治活動、革命運動へと向かい、1927年にはブルトンはフランス共産党に入るが、すぐに失望して離れる。シュルレアリスム内部で政治をめぐる対立が激しくなり、分裂する。

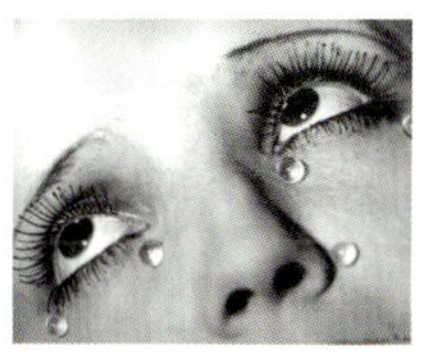

fig.6
「涙」
マン・レイ作 / 1932年

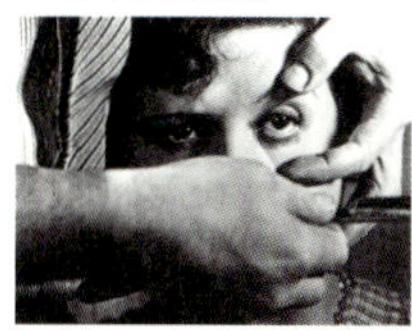

fig.7
映画「アンダルシアの犬」
ルイス・ブニュエル作 / 1929年

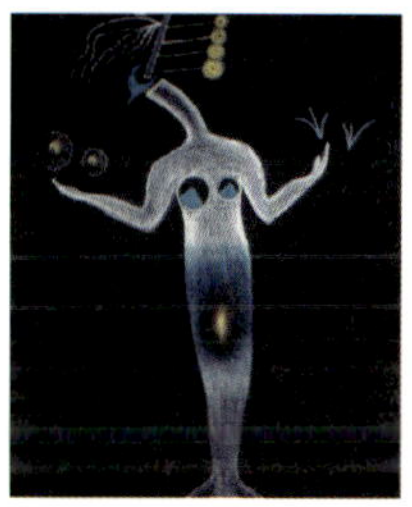

fig.8
「甘美な死骸」
ポール・エリュアール、ヴァンティーヌ・ユーゴー、
アンドレ・ブルトン、ヌッシュ・エリュアール作
 / 1934年

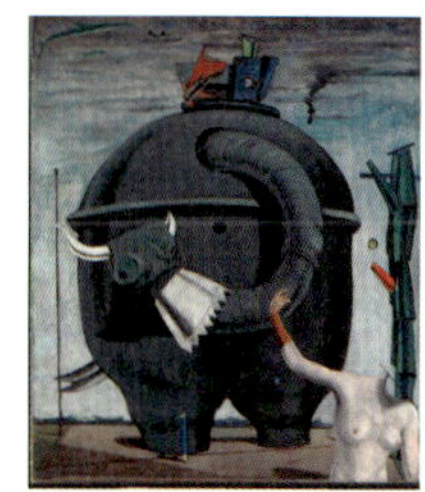

fig.9
「セレベスの象」
マックス・エルンスト画 / 1921年

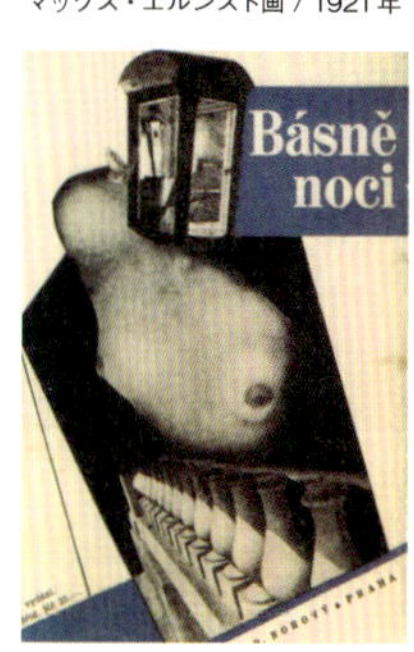

fig.10
書籍『夜の詩』表紙
ヴィーチェスラフ・ネズヴァル著
 / デザイン：カレル・タイゲ / 1938年版

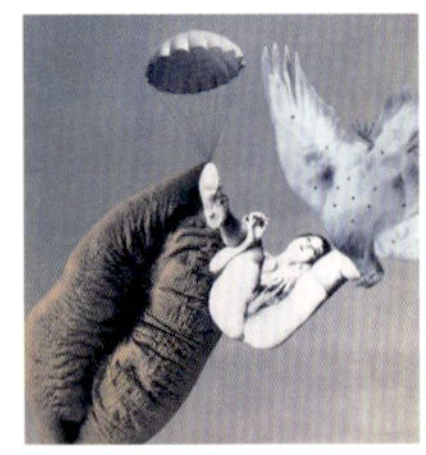

fig.11
「夢の中でエミリーは私のもとへ来る」
インジフ・シュティルスキー作 / 1933 年

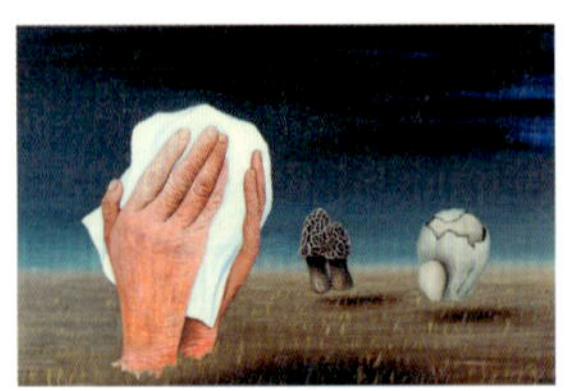

fig.12
「悲しい日」
トワイヤン画 / 1942 年

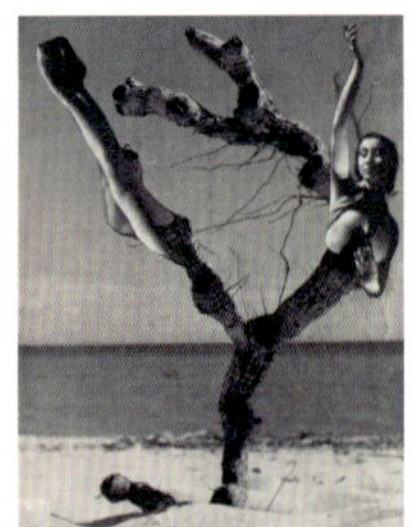

fig.13
「コラージュ」
カレル・タイゲ作 / 1948 年

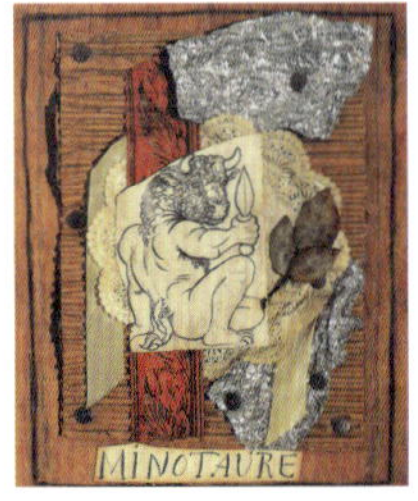

fig.14
雑誌『ミノトール』表紙
パブロ・ピカソ作 / 1933 年刊

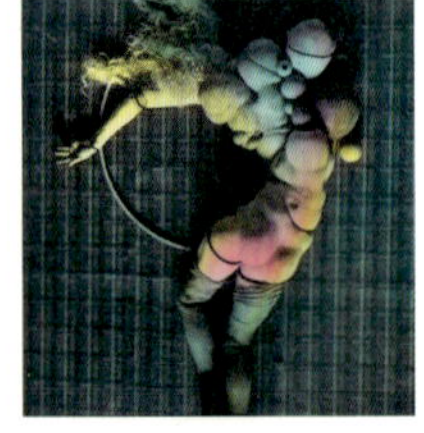

fig.15
書籍『人形の遊び』挿絵
ハンス・ベルメール作 / 1949 年刊

シュルレアリスムが豊かな実りを見せるのはそれからである。1929 年にはチェコスロヴァキアにシュルレアリスト集団ができる。ヴィーチェスラフ・ネズヴァル〈fig.10〉、インジフ・シュティルスキー〈fig.11〉、トワイヤン〈fig.12〉、カレル・タイゲ〈fig.13〉などである。シュルレアリスムは、パリからヨーロッパ全体に広がる。

1933 年に美術誌『ミノトール』〈fig.14〉が創刊される。1935 年にハンス・ベルメール〈fig.15〉が参加する。1937 年に東京で瀧口修造などの『アルバム・シュルレアリスト』が発刊された。瀧口は 1926 年頃、シュルレアリスムを知ったという。

1940 年、第 2 次世界大戦がはじまるとブルトンなど多くのシュルレアリストがアメリカなどに亡命した。大戦後もシュルレアリスムはつづいたが、多くの中心メンバーは亡くなり、運動は終わった。後期のシュルレアリスムで目立つのはベルメール、レオノール・フィニ〈fig.16〉、レオノーラ・カリントン〈fig.17〉、レメディオス・バロ〈fig.18〉、そしてチェコのシュルレアリスト、シュティルスキー、タイゲなどである。またシュルレアリストではないが彼らによって見出されたピエール・モリニエ〈fig.19〉、フェリックス・ラビッス〈fig.20〉もあげておこう。これらの画家はすべて〈幻想耽美〉の直接の源泉となっている。

ウィーン幻想派

第 2 次世界大戦後は、〈抽象美術〉の風が吹き荒れ、リアリズムも幻想美術もかすんでしまいそうであった。しかし幻想美術の系譜は途絶えることはなく、ウィーンに出現した。1950 年代に登場した 5 人組はやがて〈ウィーン幻想派〉と呼ばれることになる。くわしくは〈幻想的リアリズムのウィーン派〉である。5 人を育てたギュータースロー教授は〈ファンタスマゴリヤー〉（魔術師）とすべきだといったが使われなかった。〈シュルレアリスムのウィーン派〉ともいわれた。これは、5 人の 1 人ルドルフ・ハウズナー〈fig.21〉が「アート・クラブ」の仲間とシュルレアリスムのグループを 1946 年に結成したことによっている。直接的な接触はなかったが、シュルレアリスムの影響は意識していたのである。

敗戦後の荒廃したウィーンで彼らは出発した。ルドルフ・ハウズナー、ヴォルフガング・フッター〈fig.22〉、アリク・ブラウアー〈fig.23〉、アントン・レームデン〈fig.24〉、エルンスト・フックス〈fig.25〉の 5 人は「アート・クラブ」に属していた。「アート・クラブ」は国際的な美術組織で、ウィーン支部はギュータースローが指導していた。5 人のうちレームデンがチェコスロヴァキアの出身で、あとの 4 人はウィーン生まれであった。「アート・クラブ」でも 5 人は特に注目され、1 つのグループと見られ、まわりと対立するようになったので、5 人は 1951 年、「アート・クラブ」から独立して活動した。それぞれかなり画風はちがっていたが、ジャーナリズムによって〈ウィーン幻想派〉と呼ばれるようになった。

　〈ウィーン幻想派〉の特徴は、変形された人体、エロティシズムなどである。レームデンだけは風景が多いが、その風景自体、人間の体の一部であるかに見え、やはりエロティックである。

　〈ウィーン幻想派〉が世界的に注目されるのは 1970 年代である。日本では 1972 年に最初の展覧会が開かれている。おそらく現代の〈幻想耽美〉派が育つのはこの頃である。ロマン派、世紀末象徴派、シュルレアリスム、ウィーン幻想派と流れてきた地下水脈は、この時、日本に達していたのではないだろうか。

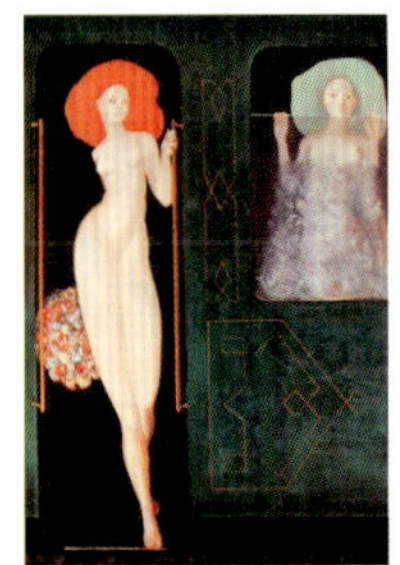

fig.16
「金星急行」
レオノール・フィニ画 / 1966 年

〈幻想耽美〉パンク ── 1970 年代

　幻想美術の系譜は、ウィーンから 1970 年代のロンドンに飛ぶ。エリート的な美術はそこで一気に解体され、大衆化し、サブカルチャー、アンダーグラウンド・アートへと転落（または進化）してゆく。幻想美術はパンクに吸収される。おそらくパンクが起こらなかったら、今日の〈幻想耽美〉はなかっただろう。

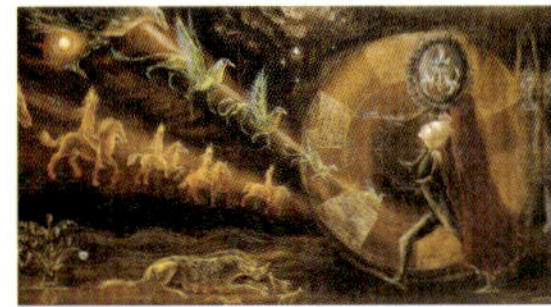

fig.17
「ル・グラン・アデュー」
レオノーラ・カリントン画 / 1958 年

　パンクのはじまりはセックス・ピストルズ〈fig.26〉であったといわれる。ビートルズなど初期のロッカーがエリート化した後の空白にあらわれたバンドで、社会に不満を持ち、今の社会を壊したいと思っていた。観客の怒りを買い、けんかになった。一方、自虐的であり、衣服を破き、ピンを体に刺したり、包帯を巻いてステージに出たりした。

　しかしパンクはロック・ミュージックだけにとどまらず、ファッションにも広がり、ヴィヴィアン・ウエストウッド〈fig.27〉がパンク・ファッションをつくり出した。パンクは一種のライフ・スタイルとなった。

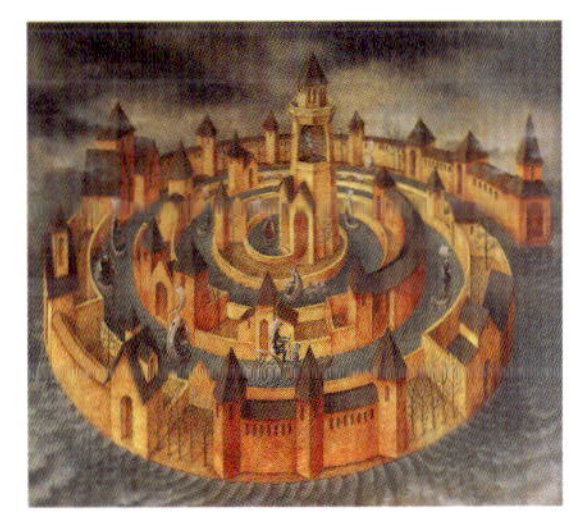

fig.18
「螺旋の運航」
レメディオス・バロ画 / 1958 年

　パンクの特徴の 1 つは DIY（ドゥ・イット・ユアセルフ）つまり手づくりの精神である。なんでも手当たりしだい、さらってきて、自分で組み立てるのだ。

　パンクの方法は、ディスク・ジョッキーがいくつものレコードを回しながら合成してゆくリミックスという方法に結びつく。やがてリミックスはインターネットの世界で使われる。世界中の画像が集められ、リミックスされる。

　リミックスこそ〈幻想耽美〉の方法である。まったく見たことのないおそろしい光景が描かれている。でもすべて見たことがないものだったら、混乱するだけだ。本当に恐いのは、それがデジャヴュ（既視感）を感じさせる時だ。私は以前にこれを見たことがある。ということは私もそこに関わっていたかもしれないのだ。それを感じさせるために、〈幻想耽美〉の作品には、古くなつかしいイメージが埋め込まれている。それは過去のイメージのリミックスなのである。

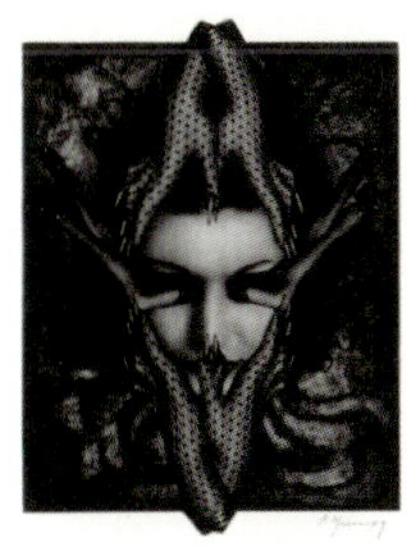

fig.19
フォトモンタージュ「子どもの男」
ピエール・モリニエ作 / 1969 年

　そのような現在と過去の重ね合わせが強く意識されるようになったのは、1970 年代のパンクにおいてであった。パンクはジェンダーの壁も壊した。女性のロッカーのバンドが本格的に登場するのはパンク以後である。

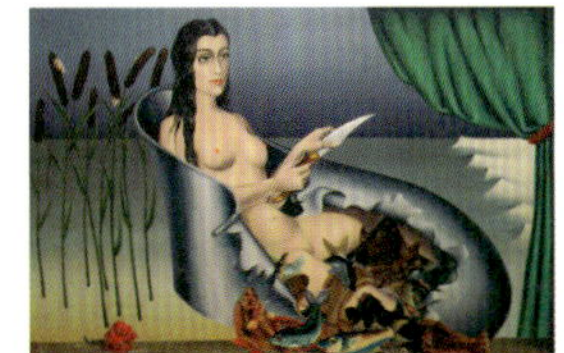

fig.20
「シャルロット・コルデー」
フェリックス・ラビッス画 / 1946 年

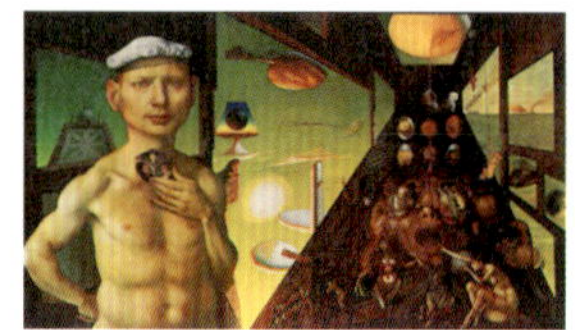

fig.21
「オデュッセウスの箱」
ルドルフ・ハウズナー画 / 1948-51、53-56 年

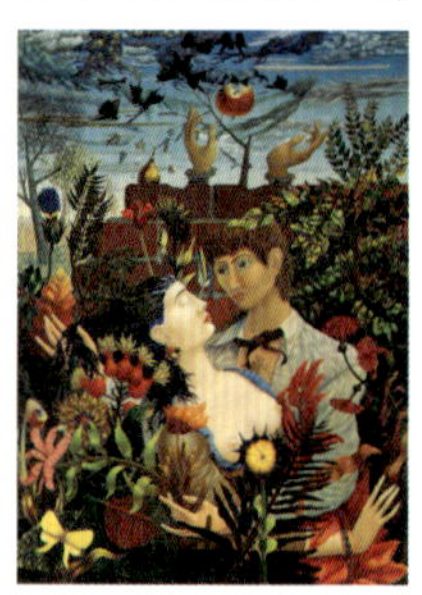

fig.22
「アダムとイヴ」
ヴォルフガング・フッター画 / 1955 年

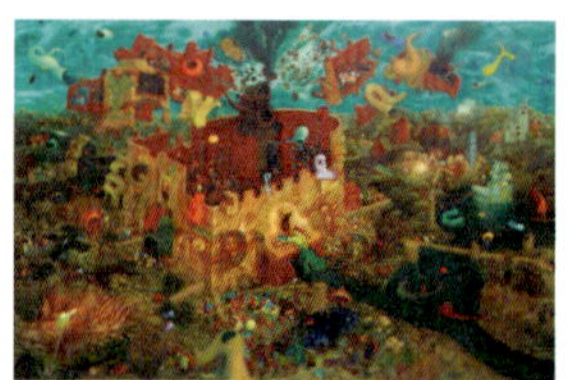

fig.23
「最後の晩」
アリク・ブラウアー画 / 1976 年

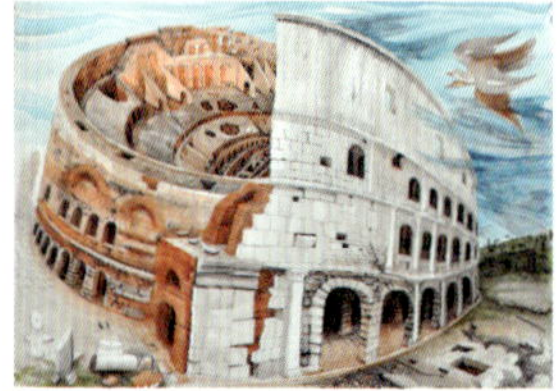

fig.24
「コロッセオ」
アントン・レームデン画 / 1973 年

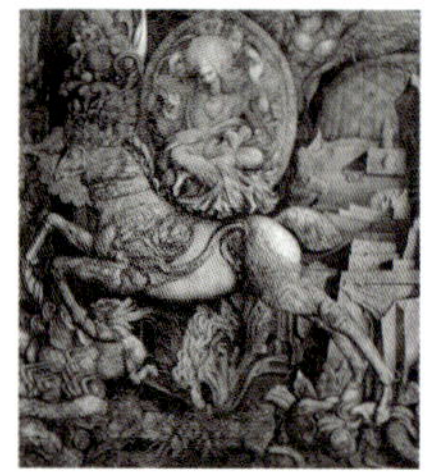

fig.25
「キリストの勝利」
エルンスト・フックス画 / 1965 年頃

　この時代がフェミニズムの時代であったことに注目しなければならない。魔女や女王への興味が復活した。マリオ・プラーツの『肉体と死と悪魔』はそれの先駆である。世紀末の〈ファム・ファタール〉が甦ってきた。

　パンクは一時的な現象と思われた。音楽としては短命であったが、芸術のさまざまな分野に広がった。文学ではSFと結びつき〈サイバーパンク〉というジャンルが生まれた。そこから未来へではなく過去へ、特にヴィクトリア期にタイムスリップする〈スチームパンク〉が生まれた。

　〈スチームパンク〉はスチーム（蒸気機関車）のメタリックな光に魅せられ、シャーロック・ホームズとともにロンドンを馬車で駆けてゆく。

　〈スチームパンク〉は一時の流行と見られたがまだつづいている。私は意外に重要な現代文化のキーワードではないかと思っている。そのことはすでに『ファンタジーとSF・スチームパンクの世界』で触れた。

　〈スチームパンク〉は〈幻想耽美〉の一端なのだ。そのヴィクトリア朝趣味、少女趣味、メタル趣味などはすべて、〈幻想耽美〉に織り込まれている。

〈幻想耽美〉ワールド

　〈幻想耽美〉は独自のものだろうか。独立しているのだろうか。いや、インターネットの時代にそんなことはあり得ない。〈幻想耽美〉的な作品はワールドワイドに存在し、この本はそのコレクションなのである。

　では、この領域を欧米ではどう見ているのだろう。さがしてみると 2008 年にベルリンで出された『アプセット──ヤング・コンテンポラリー・アート』があった。入っている絵のすべてが〈幻想耽美〉とはいえないがかなり重なっている。

　ペドロ・アロンソの「序論」を読んでみた。共通の表現スタイルは失われている。この混沌とした雲のような現象をどう読んだらいいのだろう。
「〈アプセット〉は絵画をメディアに選んで、形態的伝統と再現美術に図々しく回帰してゆく。」（同書）

　〈アプセット〉は日本的物に関わり、〈DIY〉で制作をしてゆく。〈アプセット〉は、ひっくりかえしという意味である。これまで〈アンダーグラウンド〉、〈ローブロー〉、〈ストリート・アート〉、〈グラフィティ〉などといわれてきたサブカルチャーとつながっている。

　さて、この本は、次のような分類をしている。まずは「ローブロー」。これは 1970 年代から「ハイブロー」に対立するコンセプトとなった。ここには、ミス・ヴァンなどが入っている。

　次はゴシックである。アヤ・カトウはここに入っている。

　3つ目は「リアリズム」。

4つ目は「イラストレーション」。ヴァーニャが入っている。

次が「キャラクター」。奈良美智はここに入っていた。

次は「アーバン・アート」。グラフィティ・アートはここに入る。

そして最後に「パターン」。

かなりのんびりした分類で体系性がないが、個々には面白い。

若者たちの雑多な表現は〈アプセット〉でくくって、地図をつくろうという試みは評価できる。

この本では、「ダーク・アート」と「フェティッシュ・アート」という分割を導入した。これはちょうど『ファンタジーとSF・スチームパンクの世界』で使った、ゴシックとスチームパンクにつながると思われる。〈ゴシック〉は18世紀末からリヴァイヴァルされ、19世紀には一方でウィリアム・モリスのモダン・デザインを刺激しつつ、一方で、ホラー、吸血鬼など、俗悪なサブカルチャーとして地下を流れつづける。破滅的な世界、世界の終末に憑かれたのが、「ダーク・アート」である。

「フェティッシュ・アート」は〈スチームパンク〉と関連づけられる。フェティシズムは、全体よりも、ある一部に固執することである。〈スチームパンク〉はメタリックなもの、時計のメカニズム、ヴィクトリア朝のアンティークに固執する。「ダーク・アート」は全体的な、あいまいな雰囲気を重視するが、「フェティッシュ・アート」はくっきりと見えることを求め、皮膚感覚による直接的な刺激を求める。

「ダーク」は見えないものに向かい、「フェティッシュ」は見えるものに向かう。あと、「ダーク・アート」の作品に見られるデカダンにも触れておかなければならない。そこには19世紀末の抑圧されたエロスがうごめいている。「ダーク・アート」には濃厚なエロスの香りがたちこめているが、そこには傷つけられ、快楽を楽しめない〈不快さ〉〈不気味さ〉が支配している。

少し具体的に見ていこう。ジェームス・ジーン（James Jean、P44-53）は台湾出身でロサンゼルスで活動している。画面の装飾的構成が見事だ。物語風の画面も面白い。絵の細部で楽しませる。

カミラ・デリコ（Camilla d'Errico、P54-57）は日本のマンガに影響を受けた。彼女は非常に組み合わせや構成力を得意としているようだ。

アレックス・グロス（Alex Gross、P58-65）はニューヨーク生まれで、ニューヨークらしいアメリカン・ライフを描いている。明るく、くっきりとすみずみまで。なにかおかしい。なにげない日常生活になにか別な世界が入ってきているのだ。

「アンドロイド」という作品のアンドロイドとは、娘の持っているスマホのことだが、ニューヨークのタイムズスクエアに羊があらわれている。フィリップ・K・ディックのSFの名作『アンドロイドは電気羊の夢を見るか？』を意識している。

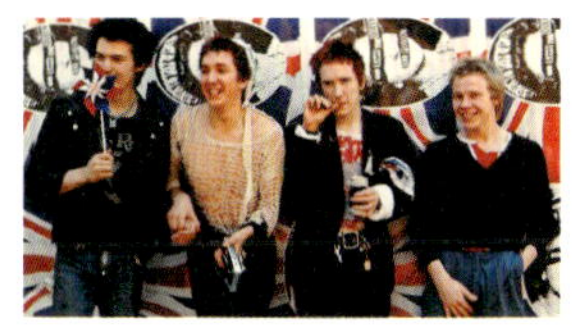

fig.26
セックス・ピストルズ

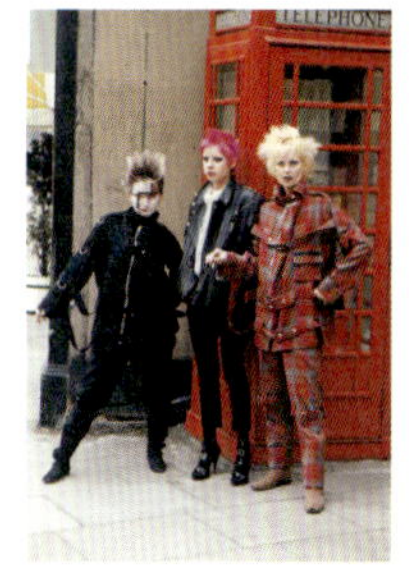

fig.27
1977年のヴィヴィアン・ウエストウッドの服

　ナオト・ハットリ（Naoto Hattori、P90-99）は、横浜生まれで、ニューヨークで活動している。細密なリアルな業者が完璧である。目玉が主なモチーフらしい。無数の目が私たちを見つめている。絵を見るのではなく、絵から見られている。

　ニコレッタ・チェッコリ（Nicoletta Ceccoli、P100-107）はサンマリノ共和国に生まれ、そこで活動している。彼女もアリス的世界に遊んでいる。フェティッシュ系にはアリス派が多いかもしれない。

　デヴィッド・ブレイ（David Bray、P118-125）は1950年代のピンナップ・ガールなどをもとにした女たちを描いている。通俗さ、俗悪さをおそれないのが〈幻想耽美〉である。

　グイド・クレパックス（Guido Crepax、P126-133）はフレンチ・コミックで活躍した。ヴァレンティーナのような人気キャラクターをつくった。ファッショナブルでマニアックでフェティッシュなクレパックスのコミックは、エロティックで、大衆漫画でありながら、悪書に入れられる。

　エリサ・アンコリ（Elisa Ancori、P142-149）はバルセロナ大学で美術を学んだ。人はかつて魚から進化した。そのイメージをもとにした「メタモルフィッシュ」は衝撃を与えた。ウロコを描き、魚のかぶりものをする。人間の肉体は切り刻まれ、魚へと変身、回帰してゆく。そのメカニックなプロセスの一方、ゴシックの水の女のイメージ、人魚姫の世界が浮かんでゆく。

　ゾーイ・ラケイ（Zoe Lacchei、P150-157）は、ローマ近郊の出身で、日本のマンガ、アニメなどが好きだった。豊満な肉体の妖女を描くが、彼女たちはしばしば縛られ、責めさいなまれている。かつては男のものであったSM画を女性も描くようになった。〈幻想耽美〉の1つの特徴は女性の参加ではないだろうか。パンクは、ポルノグラフィティを女性にも開放したのだ。

　クリスティン・シラーフ（Kristin Shiraef、P158-165）は、ヴィクトリア朝ゴシックである。アリスのように想像力の世界をめぐり、不思議なものたちに会う。

　では「ダーク・アート」を見ることにしよう。ベクシンスキー（Zdzisław Beksiński、P174-177）はポーランドのおくれてきたシュルレアリストである。彼はディストピア（反ユートピア）を描きつづける。死滅してゆく世界は祖国ポーランドの反映であろうか。彼の巧みな線によって、人体はまわりの物に侵食されていく。

　アレッサンドロ・ビアンキ（Alessandro Sicioldr Bianchi、P178-185）はトスカーナの作家である。イタリアのクラシックなスタイルを学んだ。その絵はまるで世紀末の象徴主義の絵画を見るかのようだ。

　ゴットフリート・ヘルンヴァイン（Gottfried Helnwein、P186-193）は、ウィーンで学んだ。その後、アイルランド、ロサンゼルスなどで広く活動している。彼の作品は、演劇的、心理サイコ・ドラマの1シーンを見ているかのようだ。

　サム・エクトプラズム（Sam Ectoplasm、P194-201）はフランス生まれで、カナダで活動している。彼女の作品では、白い皮膚がやぶけ、内臓やら化け物やらがあらわれる。残酷絵の極致である。ダーク系はそれを闇に包むが、サム・エクトプラズムは白日の下にさらけ出す。

　ハンナ・ヤタ（Hannah Yata、P202-209）は、アメリカ人と日本人の間に生まれた。美しい自然の中で育った。彼女の絵は、動物と人間の体のリミックスである。極彩色は女性の肉体と鳥などが1つになり、新しい人間となっている。

　アントワーヌ・ベルナール（Antoine Bernhart,P210-216）は、1968年〈ネオ・シュルレアリスト〉グループを結成している。パリが5月革命で学生たちがあふれていた頃だ。ベルナールの特徴は〈ポルノグラフィ〉である。彼は『SMスナイパー』などのイメージに魅せられたという。〈ローブロー〉がアートと一体化している。2009年パリのエロティシズム美術館で「地獄の地獄」展を開いている。〈地獄〉というのはパリの図書館でポルノグラフィティを保管する部屋のことだ。彼の絵は、性的に責められるシーンが多いが、明らかに日本のSM雑誌の挿絵に似ている。このようなエキセントリックな性の趣味には世界的なネットワークが発達している。〈幻想耽美〉はそのルートによって世界的に交流している。

　「ダーク・アート」と「フェティッシュ・アート」の後に、「アート写真」、「立体アート」の章を立てている。

　あり得ないもの、見えないものを、写真は撮れるだろうか。〈幻想耽美〉はそれに挑み、写真はそのための非常に有効なメディアであることがわかってきた。「アート写真」を見ると、その豊かさが伝わってくる。

　〈幻想耽美〉は、DIYというパンクの方法を受け継いでいる。使えるものはなんでも使ってつくり上げる。使えるイメージも手に入ればなんでも使う。

　セイコ・カトウ（Seiko Kato、P322-329）は日本のコラージュ作家でイギリスのブラントンに住む。唐草文でドクロを飾るといった作品をつくっている。フェティッシュで装飾的であり、スチームパンクとも言える。

　世界のニュー・アートは、こんなにも自由に多様になってきている。そこでは新しいテクニックも古いテクニックも使われている。そしてなにより、描くこと、そのテーマに枠はなく、好きなことを思いきり描けるようになってきている。かくされたもの、禁じられたものが描けるようになった。そのような解き放たれた、だが混沌として方向の見えない時代に私たちはいる。

The Dark History of the Fantasy Aesthetic

Hiroshi Unno

The Origins in Romanticism

A flood of uncanny art traveling underground permeates popular culture. It appears in many different styles, but shares common features. We see an obsessive interest in the human body. Human bodies are sacrificed on the altar of Beauty. Those merciless sacrifices are performed as secret rituals, depicted as private fantasies. But then they flow into public culture. Nonetheless, this stream has been ignored in the history of modern art. How, then, should it be treated? Since the art of fantasy has become so widespread, it is time, I have suggested, to write new history.

I have written two previous books on this topic: *The Art of Decadence: European Fantasy Art of the Fin-de-Siècle* and *The Art of Fantasy, Sci-fi and Steampunk,* both published by PIE International in 2017. The first examines late nineteenth century, fin-de-siècle Symbolism. The second traces the histories of Victorian Gothic and Steam Punk, discovering the origins of the Fantasy Aesthetic in Romanticism.

The art covered in those two books can be thought of as the origin of the Fantasy Aesthetic. Here I wish to consider the genealogy that links the Fantasy Aesthetic to Romanticism.

Romanticism was a movement that flourished between 1790 and 1850. Rebelling against Classicism, which sought a fixed and stable world, the Romantics were active in a period of instability, opposed to order and reason, and sought a world without limits. They were oriented towards night, not day, death, not life, and the past — the Medieval or Celtic worlds — not the present.

One of the origins of English Romanticism was Gothic Revival and the haunted castles depicted in horror stories. Such uncanny and fantastic tales as Horace Walpole's *The Castle of Otranto* and Ann Radcliff's *The Mysteries of Udolfo* emerged. Germany's E.T.A. Hoffman and America's Edgar Allen Poe should also be included in this genealogy.

English Romanticism continued the Gothic Revival's interest in the Medieval and the uncanny. Among its products was Mary Shelley's horror novel masterpiece *Frankenstein.* Its description of attempts to create a human being that resulted in creating a monster is one of the wellsprings of today's Fantasy Aesthetic.

In fin-de-siècle Symbolism, we find the night world opened up by Romanticism, suddenly became a parade of monsters in which tendencies to perversion and decadence deepened. In *European Fantasy Art*, I described Symbolist art as "work that depicted the unseen, the marvelous, fantasies, and dreams."

Following the invention of photography in the 1830s, the Symbolist tendency to describe the heretofore invisible became even stronger. What is particularly interesting is how photography's invention ignited a fierce spirit of rivalry between photography and Symbolism, leading to efforts to photograph illusions and dreams and experiments with "spirit photography." Today's photographs that embody the Fantasy Aesthetic can be traced to that source.

When Mario Praz titled his study tracing how fin-de-siècle Decadence developed from Romanticism *Flesh, Death, and the Devil—Romantic Agony* (1933), he was describing the major themes of the Fantasy Aesthetic.

Surrealism

The fin-de-siècle Fantasy Aesthetic, in Symbolism and Art Nouveau, was excluded from the canon of twentieth-century Modernism. It was then revived by Surrealism.

It is said that Surrealism is not, in fact, art. It was a movement composed of poets who sought a return to the spiritual, evoking ethical discourse that called for the transformation of human life. It was in this spirit that *The Surrealist Manifesto* (1924) proclaimed the need to escape the domination of theory and to include imagination, dreams, the unconscious, and the accidental in its methods of creative expression.

It hardly needs saying, however, that despite its being a revolution in the use of words, Surrealism, as an expressive method, attracted many artists. If we would include painters peripheral to Surrealism, they would sum up to a large number. Diverse forms of artistic expression were inextricably intertwined with Surrealism, and pervaded other categories of art such as Man Ray's photography and Louis Buñuel's films.

One of Surrealism's experiments was a game called "Exquisite Corpse." Individuals would write lines of poetry concealed from others on scraps of paper. These were then spread out to form a single poem. Pictures might be used instead of words, with offhand sketches of heads, torsos, waists, and legs combined to construct human images.

This *Exquisite Corps* was created by Paul Éluard, Valentine Hugo, André Breton, and Nusch Eluard in 1934. The four artists individually produced the sketches of the face, torso, waist, and legs, first tearing apart the human body and then reconstructing it in the final image. "Exquisite Corpse" is a perfect example of the Fantasy Aesthetic.

The start of the Surrealist movement was marked by the 1919 publication of the first issue of the magazine *Littérature* by André Breton, Philippe Soupault, and Louis Aragon.

During 1922, "the period of the sleeping fits," experiments were conducted using spiritualist and hypnotic techniques to induce speaking while still asleep. That was also the year in which Man Ray and Max Ernst joined the movement.

In 1924, Breton created *The Surrealist Manifesto* and published the first issue of the movement's magazine *La Révolution surréaliste* (The Surrealist Revolution). As a political movement, Surrealism opposed existing systems and aimed to become a revolutionary movement. In 1927 Breton joined the French Communist Party, but was quickly disappointed and left it. Torn apart by intense internal political battles, the Surrealist movement split.

The rich flowering of Surrealism came somewhat later. In 1929, a surrealist group was formed in Czechoslovakia. Its members included Vítězslav Nezval, Jindřich Štyrský, Toyen, and Karel Teige. The movement spread from Paris to the whole of Europe.

In 1933, the first issue of the art magazine *Minotaur* was published. In 1935, Hans Bellmer joined the movement, and in 1937, Shûzô Takiguchi published his *Album Surrealiste* in Tokyo. Takiguchi had learned about Surrealism in about 1926.

In 1940, following the outbreak of World War II, Breton and many other Surrealists fled to America. Surrealism continued after the war, but many of the core members had died. Notable figures from Surrealism's final phase included Bellmer, Leonor Fini, Leonora Carrington, Remedios Varo, and the Czech Surrealists Štyrský and Teige. We should also mention Pierre Molinier and Félix Labisse, who, while not Surrealists, were considered to be so. All of these artists were directly connected with the wellsprings of the Fantasy Aesthetic.

Fantastic Realism in Vienna

Following the end of World War II, Abstraction swept over the art world. Both Realism and the Fantasy Aesthetic seemed on the verge of disappearing. The Fantasy Aesthetic survived, however, appearing in a new form in Vienna. In the 1950s, a five-member group became known as Die Wiener Schule des Phantastischen Realismus (the Vienna School of Fantastic Realism). These five artists had been trained by Professor Albert Paris Gütersloh, an advocate, though not himself a practitioner, of Phantasmagoria. One of the five, Rudolph Hausner and four Art Club friends formed a Surrealist group in 1946. While not directly connected with the Surrealist movement, they were strongly influenced by Surrealism.

This group was launched amidst the devastation of postwar Vienna. The five included, besides Rudolph Hausner, Wolfgang Hutter, Arik Brauer, Anton Lehmden, and Ernst Fuchs, all affiliated with the Art Club, the Vienna branch of an international art organization led by Gütersloh. Of the five members, Lehmden was born in Czechoslovakia; the remaining four were born in Vienna. While all were members of the Art Club, they formed a distinct cluster, which in 1951 broke off to form an independent group. While each had his own characteristic painting style, journalists labeled them collectively the Vienna School of Fantastic Realism.

The distinctive features of Vienna Fantastic Realist art are its eroticism and use of deformed bodies. Lehmden painted mostly landscapes; but in his landscapes, parts of human bodies are always visible, and the paintings are erotic.

It was during the 1970s that the Vienna School of Fantastic Realism attracted global attention. The school's first exhibition in Japan was held in 1972. It was around this time, then, that the Fantastic Aesthetic began to appear in its contemporary forms. The underground currents connecting the Romantics, the fin-de-siècle Symbolists, Surrealism, and Vienna Fantastic Realism had reached Japan.

The Fantastic Aesthetic / Punk — the 1970s

During the 1970s, the genealogy of the Fantasy Aesthetic leaped from Vienna to London. It ceased to be elite art and suddenly collapses (or evolves) into a subculture, underground art. Punk breathed new life into, or least revived, it, producing today's Fantasy Aesthetic.

Punk is said to have started with the Sex Pistols. Punk appeared in the empty space created when the Beatles and other early rockers became elevated to the elite; that space was occupied by bands expressing dissatisfaction with contemporary society and a desire to destroy it. Audiences became enraged. Fights broke out. At the same time, masochism, torn clothing, sticking pins in the body, and bondage appeared on stage.

Punk was more than rock music. It spread to the fashion world, with Vivienne Westwood designing Punk fashion. Punk had become a lifestyle.

One of Punk's characteristics was DIY (Do-It-Yourself), an embrace of the handmade spirit. Use whatever is ready to hand, feel free to wear whatever you can throw together.

The Punk approach can also be linked to disk jockeys who play and remix multiple recordings. Remix permeates the Internet, where images from around the world are collected and combined.

Remix itself is a method employed by the Fantasy Aesthetic. Never before seen terrifying landscapes are created. However, not every element in them is original; they are only jumbled together. What is truly terrifying is when, looking at one of these landscapes, we experience déja-vu, the sense that somehow one has seen these things before and is somehow involved in what is going on there. To cause us to experience that feeling, works that embody the Fantasy Aesthetic are filled with images that evoke nostalgia. They remix the past.

It was in 1970s, Punk that this mixing and overlapping of past and present became most visible. Punk broke down walls created by gender. It was only after Punk that female rockers formed their own bands.

We must also note that it was the era of Feminism. Interest in witches and queens revived in a manner anticipated in Mario Praz's *Flesh, Death, and the Devil*. The fin-de-siècle femme fatale had been resurrected.

Punk was a transient phenomenon. As music it was short-lived. Its influence did, however, spread to many art genres. In fiction, Cyberpunk SF appeared. Then Steampunk was born, traveling through time not to the future but to a Victorian past.

In Steampunk, Sherlock Holmes and horse-drawn carriages are bathed in the metallic gleam of steam-powered engines.

Steampunk was viewed as another transient trend but has proved unexpectedly durable. To me, "Steam Punk" has become a concept central to understanding contemporary culture, as I mentioned in *The Art of Fantasy, Sci-fi and Steampunk*.

Steampunk is only one part of the Fantasy Aesthetic. Its fascination with the Victorian, little girls, and the metallic are, however, woven tightly into the Fantasy Aesthetic's fabric.

The Fantasy Aesthetic / World

Is the Fantasy Aesthetic its own thing? Is it a totally independent phenomenon? Of course not; in the Internet Era, that is impossible. Works that embody the Fantasy Aesthetic exist worldwide. This book is a collection of these works.

How, then, is this domain regarded in Europe and America? We searched and found *The Upset: Young Contemporary Art* catalogue produced in 2008 in Berlin. While not all of the works from this exhibition display the Fantasy Aesthetic, those played an important role.

I read Pedro Alonzo's introduction in the exhibition catalogue. There is no shared style to be found in these works displayed at this exhibition. They are instead a cloud-like, chaotic phenomenon. Alonzo wrote " The Upset comprises images that represent the return of diverse formal traditions and forms of reproduction."

To link *Upset* to Japanese things, I turn to DIY. "Upset" means to turn upside down. The use of this word connects it to earlier subcultures, including "Underground," "Low Brow," "Street Art," and "Graffiti."

This book is divided into sections focused on different types of art. First is Low Brow, a concept that emerged in the 1970s in opposition to "High Brow" art. Here we include works by street artist Miss Van.

Next comes Gothic, where we include work by Aya Kato.

The third section is devoted to Realism, the fourth to Illustration, including work by Vania Vatralova-Stankov.

Then comes Characters, including work by Yoshitomo Nara, followed by Urban Art, including graffiti.

The last section is Patterns.

The classification of works may be loose and unsystematic, but the individual works are interesting.

This attempt to link young artists' diverse forms of expression to Upset should be seen as an experiment in creating a global map.

This book is broadly divided info "Dark Art" and "Fetish Art." This division corresponds to "Gothic" and "Steampunk" in *The Art of Fantasy, Sci-fi and Steampunk*. The revival of Gothic in the end of the eighteenth century stimulated the nineteenth century's development of modern design by William Morris' and continued underground as a vulgar subculture devoted to horror, vampires, and other disturbing things. This subculture produced Dark Art obsessed with extinction and the end of the world.

Fetish Art is linked to Steampunk. "Fetishism" refers to obsession with parts of the body instead of the whole. Steampunk refers to obsession with the metallic, clockwork, and Victorian antiques. From an overall perspective, Dark Art emphasizes on an ambiguous atmosphere. In contrast, Fetish art strives for clarity and direct, tactile sensation.

"Dark" is oriented to the invisible, "Fetish" to what can be seen. We must also touch on the decadence visible in Dark Art. Here we discover traces of the suppressed Eros found in fin-de-siècle art. Dark Art is saturated with a rich, erotic fragrance; but this is dominated by wounds, unhappiness, the uncanny and the ominous.

Let us be a bit more concrete. James Jean (P44-53) was born in Taiwan but is active in Los Angeles. The decorative structure of his surfaces is outstanding. His storytelling surfaces are also outstanding. In both we enjoy the fine details.

Camilla d'Errico (P54-57) was influenced by Japanese manga. Her strength is an extraordinary ability to combine and compose.

Alex Gross (P58-65) was born in New York and paints scenes from American life characteristic of that city. They are bright and clear in every detail, but also have something odd. Something otherworldly appears in casual, everyday lives.

Grass's *Android* refers to his daughter's smartphone but with a sheep appearing in New York's Times Square, an allusion to Philip K. Dick's SF masterpiece *Do Androids Dream Of Electric Sheep?*

Born in Yokohama, Naoto Hattori (P90-99) is active in New York; he is a perfectionist who pursues the real in every detail, using the eyeball as his principal motif. Countless eyes stare at us. We are not seeing a painting; we are seen by the painting.

Nicoletta Ceccoli (P100-107) is active in her birthplace, the Republic of San Marino. The world in which she plays resembles that of *Alice* in *Wonderland*. Alice fans are numerous among those engaged in Fetish Art.

David Bray (P118-125) paints women like those in pin-up art from the 1950s. There is nothing common or vulgar about them, but the Fantasy Aesthetic is present.

Guido Crepax (P126-133) is a comic illustrator who has created a popular character who resembles the drag queen Valentina. Crepax's fetishistic character is both fashion-obsessed and erotic. She appears in pornographic as well as mass market manga.

Elisa Ancori (P142-149) studied art at the University of Barcelona. Her *Metamorfish*, which draws on the idea that human beings evolved from fish, is shocking. She depicts a goby, with the fish wearing a headdress. She slices open human bodies, transforming them into avatars of fish. Besides these mechanical processes, she produces gothic images of women in water, transporting us to a world of mermaid princesses.

Zoe Lacchei (P150-157), while born near Rome, loved Japanese manga and anime. When depicting voluptuous, enchanting women, she often shows them bound and tortured. Her work resembles the sadomasochistic images that were once the preserve of men. One distinctive feature of the Fantasy Aesthetic is the way in which women as well as men are involved. Punk opened up pornography to women.

Kristin Shiraef (P158-165) takes us back to the Victorian Gothic, to an imaginary, world like Alice's, where we encounter uncanny things.

Let us turn now to Dark Art. Zdzisław Beksiński (P174-177) might be called a Polish Surrealist who missed the Surrealist movement. He continues to paint dystopias (anti-utopias). Do his worlds on the verge of extinction reflect Poland, his ancestral home? His skillfully drawn lines depict human bodies being eroded by things around them.

Alessandro Sicioldr Bianchi (P178-185) is a Tuscan artist who has studied the Italian Classical style. His works remind us of paintings by the fin-de-siècle Symbolists.

Gottfried Helnwein (P186-193) studied art in Vienna. Since then, he has worked in many places, including Ireland and Los Angeles. His works can be seen as scenes from dramatic psychodramas.

Sam Ectoplasm (P194-201) was born in France and is now active in Canada. In her works, white skin is torn apart. Internal organs and monsters appear. The cruelty is extreme. Dark Art is usually enveloped in darkness, but in Sam Ectoplasm's work, darkness appears in the white light of day.

Hannah Yata (P202-209) is a half-American, half-Japanese raised in a beautiful natural setting. In her images, human and animal bodies are remixed. Women's bodies and birds are fused, using extreme colors to create new forms of humanity.

Antoine Bernhart (P210-216) formed the Neo-Surrealist group in 1968, a year in which student uprisings in May filled the streets of Paris. Bernhart's specialty is pornography. He is famous for such images as *SM Sniper*, in which Low Brow and art become one. In 2009, his work was presented in the *l'Enfer des Enfers* exhibition at the Musée de l'Erotisme in Paris. "Enfer (Hell) " referred to the rooms set aside for preserving pornography in Paris libraries. Many of his works depict erotic torture and resemble the illustrations in pornographic magazines in Japan. The Internet has spread interest in these eccentric sexual tastes worldwide, creating a channel for the Fantasy Aesthetic around the globe.

Following the sections devoted to Dark Art and Fetish Art are sections devoted to Art Photography and Tree-Dimensional Art.

Can photographs capture impossible, invisible things? For the Fantasy Aesthetic, photography is a highly effective medium through which to approach this challenge. The richness of this approach can be seen in Art Photography.

The Fantasy Aesthetic is heir to DIY Punk. Whatever comes to hand can be used. Anything and everything can be used to create the artist's image.

Seiko Kato (P322-329) is a Japanese collage artist who lives in Brighton in the UK. Her works are skulls decorated with arabesques. Fetishistic decoration: it could also be called Steampunk.

Around the world, New Art has proliferated freely and taken on many forms. Techniques both old and new are used. Most important of all, however, is the breaking free of established frameworks, to depict whatever the artist desires. Once hidden or forbidden things are depicted. With liberation from all restrictions, we find ourselves in a chaotic world in which new directions remain obscure.

Editorial Note

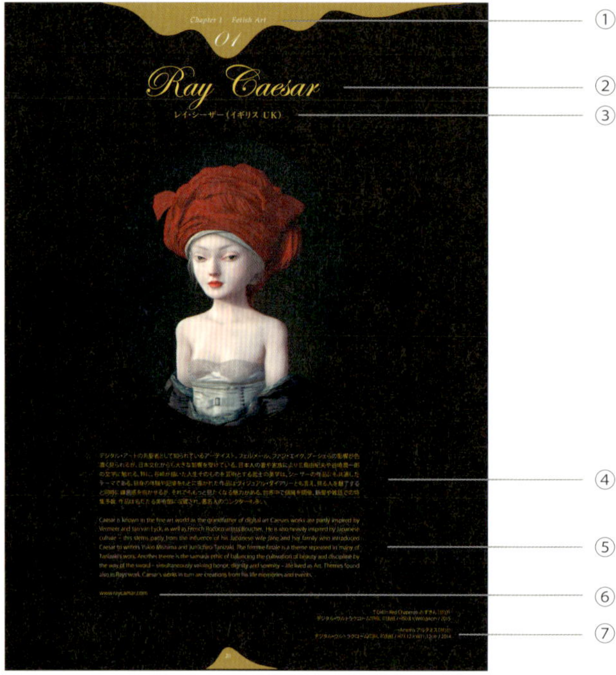

①
章、カテゴリー
Chapter and Category

②
作家名
Artist's Name

③
作家名（日本語）、国
Artist's Name (Japanese)，Country

④
作家プロフィール（日本語）
Artist's Profile (Japanese)

⑤
作家プロフィール（英語）
Artist's Profile (English)

⑥
作家ウェブサイト
Artist's Website

⑦
作品クレジット
Artwork Credits

作品タイトル（英語またはその他の言語、日本語）
画材・素材 / サイズ / 制作年
の順に掲載しております。
Artwork Title (English or other languages, Japanese)
Medium (Japanese) / Size (Hight × Width × Depth cm/pixel) / Year
are shown in each caption.

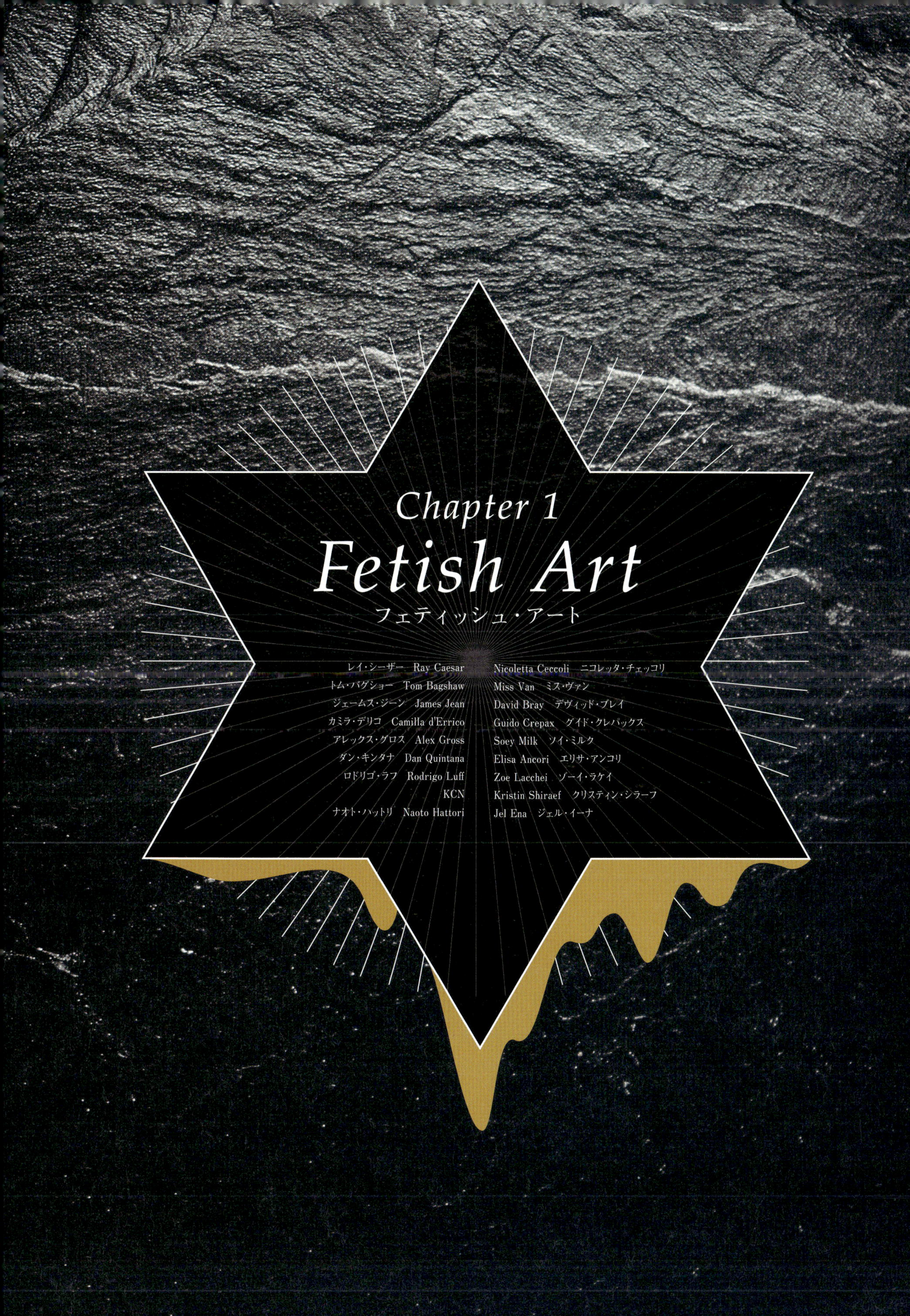

Chapter 1
Fetish Art
フェティッシュ・アート

レイ・シーザー　Ray Caesar
トム・バグショー　Tom Bagshaw
ジェームズ・ジーン　James Jean
カミラ・デリコ　Camilla d'Errico
アレックス・グロス　Alex Gross
ダン・キンタナ　Dan Quintana
ロドリゴ・ラフ　Rodrigo Luff
KCN
ナオト・ハットリ　Naoto Hattori

Nicoletta Ceccoli　ニコレッタ・チェッコリ
Miss Van　ミス・ヴァン
David Bray　デヴィッド・ブレイ
Guido Crepax　グイド・クレパックス
Soey Milk　ソイ・ミルク
Elisa Ancori　エリサ・アンコリ
Zoe Lacchei　ゾーイ・ラケイ
Kristin Shiraef　クリスティン・シラーフ
Jel Ena　ジェル・イーナ

01

Ray Caesar

レイ・シーザー（イギリス UK）

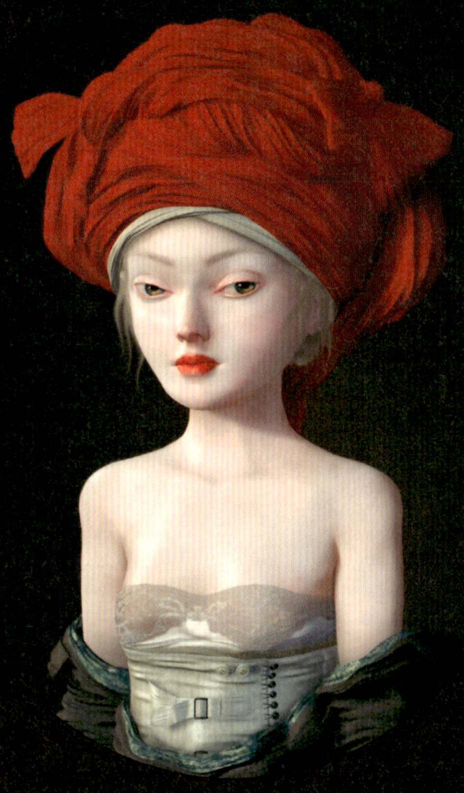

デジタル・アートの先駆者として知られているアーティスト。フェルメール、ファン・エイク、ブーシェらの影響が色濃く見られるが、日本文化からも大きな影響を受けている。日本人の妻や家族により三島由紀夫や谷崎潤一郎の文学に触れる。特に、谷崎が描いた人生そのものを芸術とする武士の美学は、シーザーの作品にも共通したテーマである。自身の体験や記憶をもとに描かれた作品はヴィジュアル・ダイアリーとも言え、見る人を魅了すると同時に嫌悪感を抱かせるが、それでももっと見たくなる魅力がある。世界中で個展を開催、新聞や雑誌での特集多数。作品は名だたる美術館に収蔵され、著名人のコレクターも多い。

Caesar is known in the fine art world as the grandfather of digital art Caesars works are partly inspired by Vermeer and Jan van Eyck, as well as French Rococo artists Boucher. He is also heavily inspired by Japanese culture – this stems partly from the influence of his Japanese wife Jane and her family who introduced Caesar to writers Yukio Mishima and Jun'ichiro Tanizaki. The femme fatale is a theme repeated in many of Tanizaki's work. Another theme is the samurai ethic of balancing the cultivation of beauty and discipline by the way of the sword – simultaneously valuing honor, dignity and serenity – life lived as Art. Themes found also in Rays work. Caesar's works in turn are creations from his life memories and events. His visual diaries captivate us and repel us, yet we always ache for more. His work has been exhibited extensively in solo shows internationally in Europe, the States, Canada and Asia as well as appearing in numerous prominent publications. Caesar works are collected by numerous venerated institutions as well as prominent collectors.

www.raycaesar.com

↑ Girl in Red Chaperon 赤ずきん（部分）
デジタル・ウルトラクローム印刷、印画紙 / H50.8×W40.64cm / 2015　Ray Caesar/Gallery House

→Artemis アルテミス（部分）
デジタル・ウルトラクローム印刷、印画紙 / H71.12×W71.12cm / 2014　Ray Caesar/Gallery House

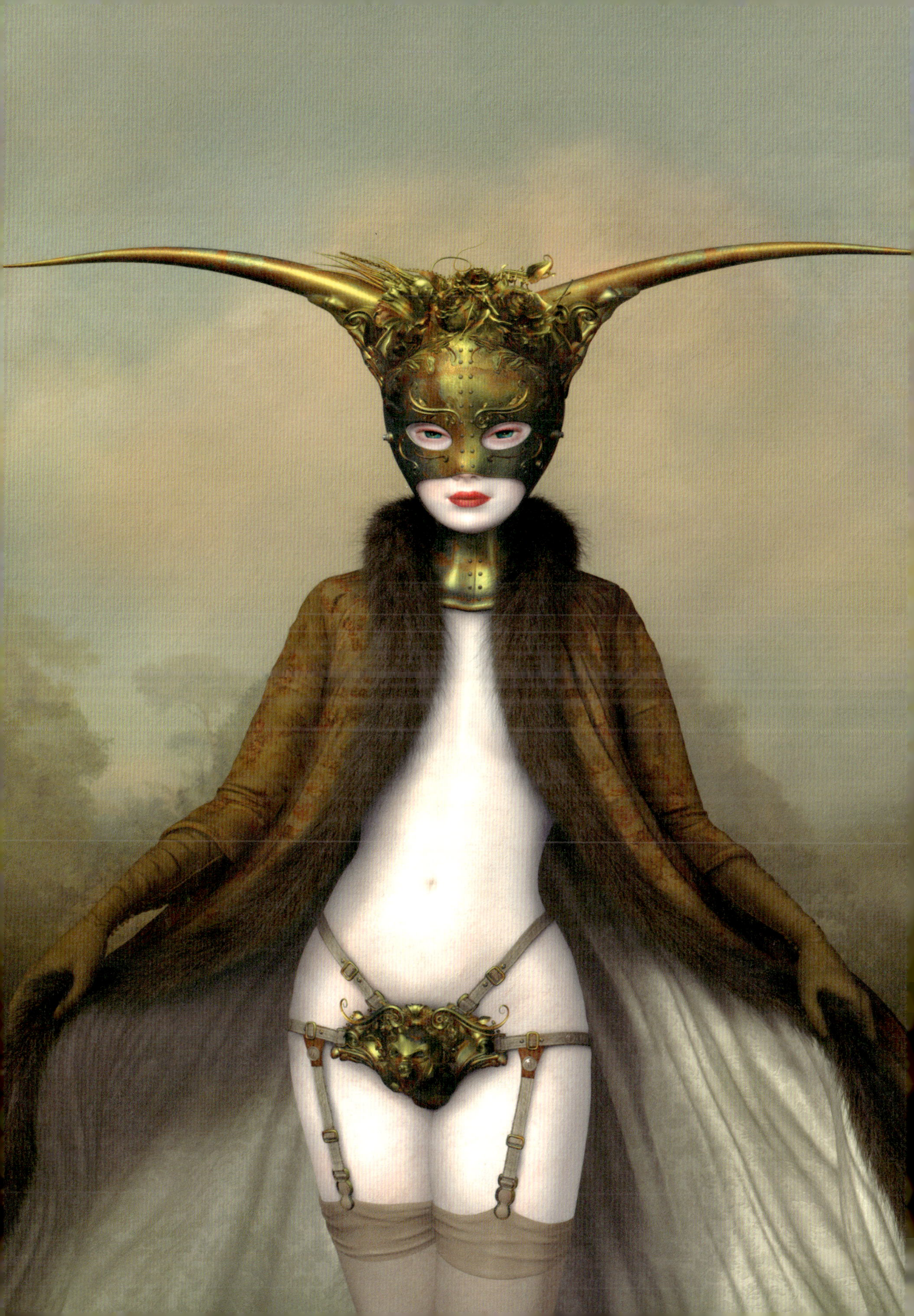

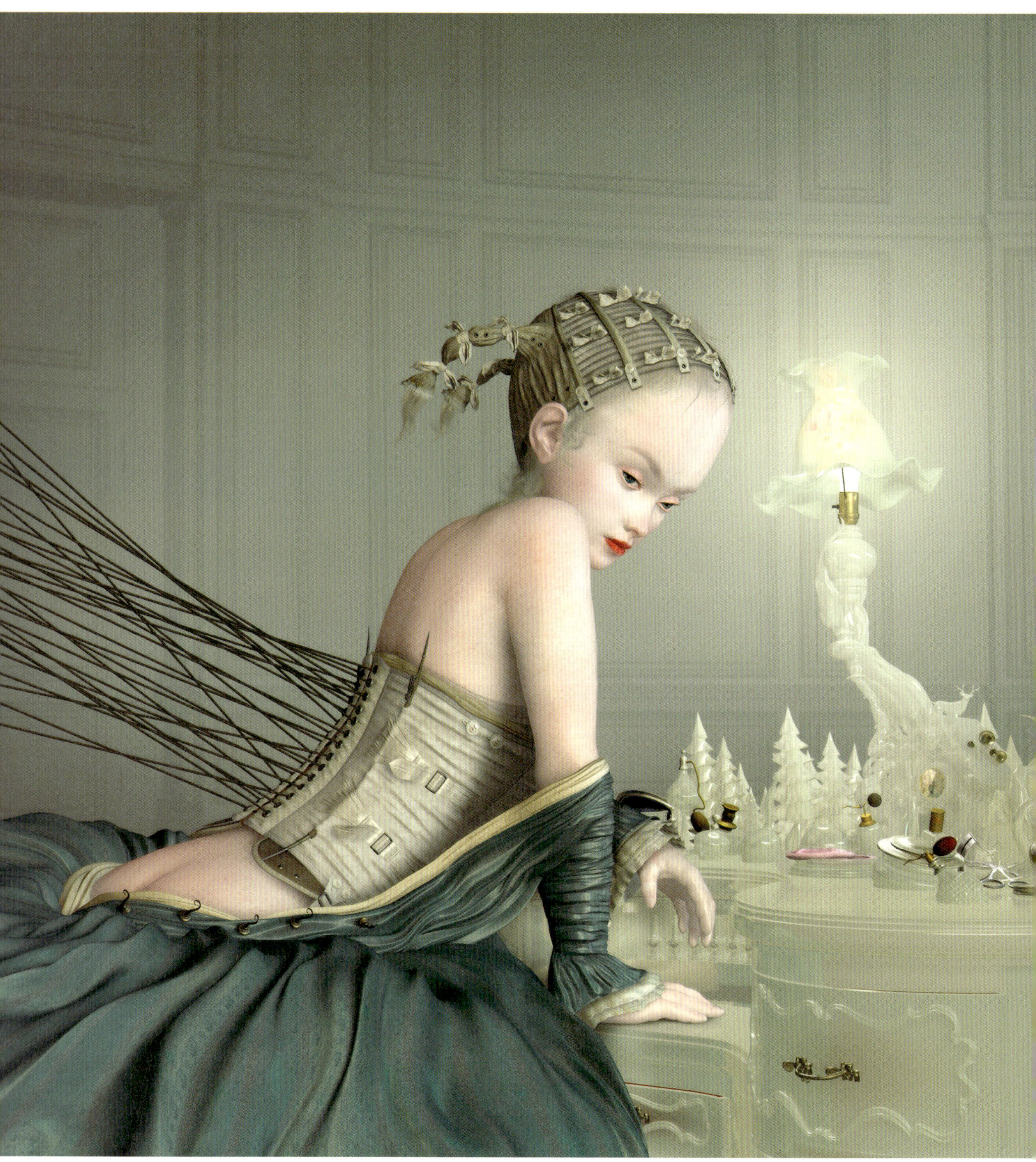

Bound 束縛
デジタル・ウルトラクローム印刷、印画紙 / H91.44×W91.44cm / 2014　Ray Caesar/Gallery House

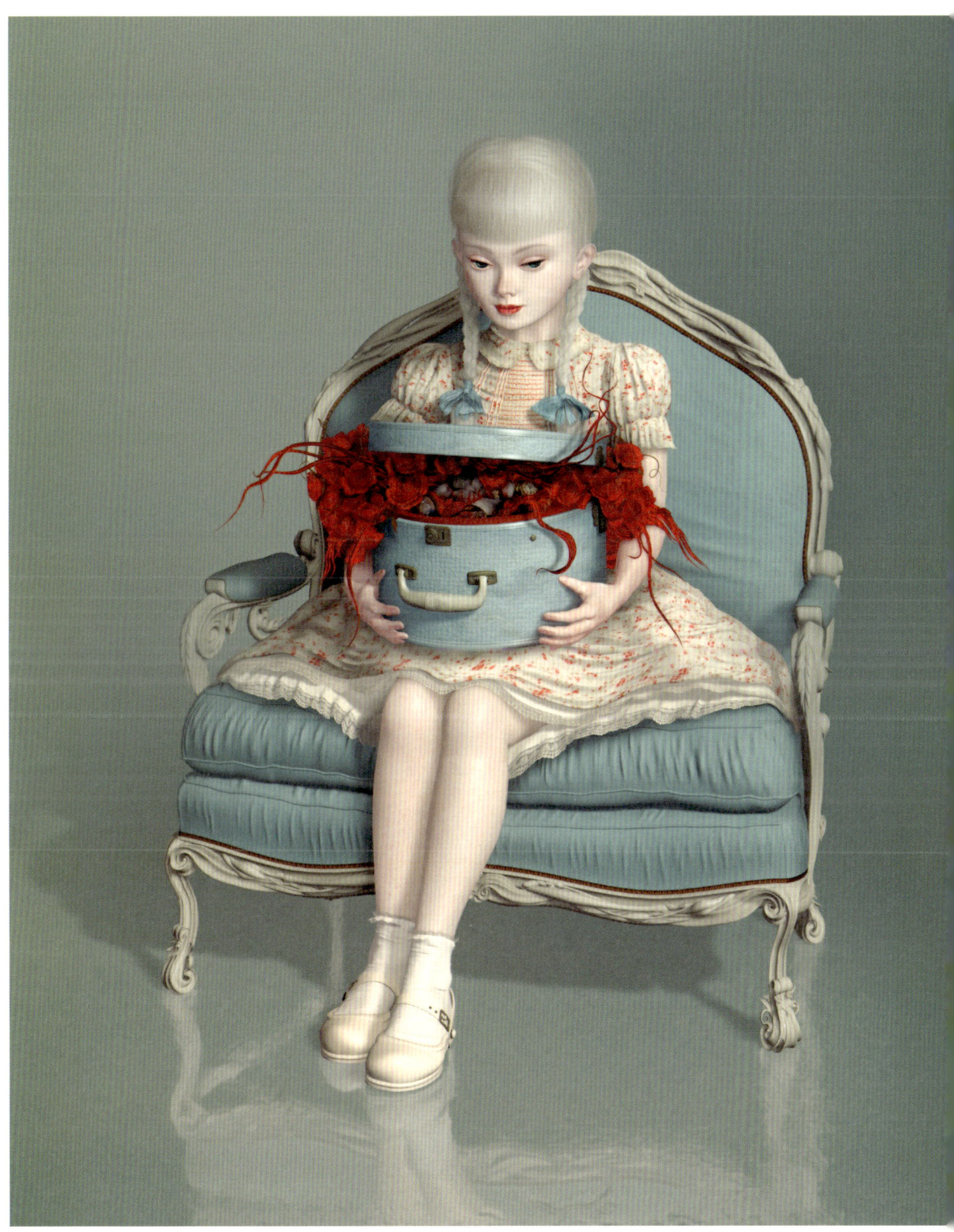

Keepsake 形見
アーカイバル・カラー印刷、印画紙 / H50.8×W40.64cm / 2016　Ray Caesar/Gallery House

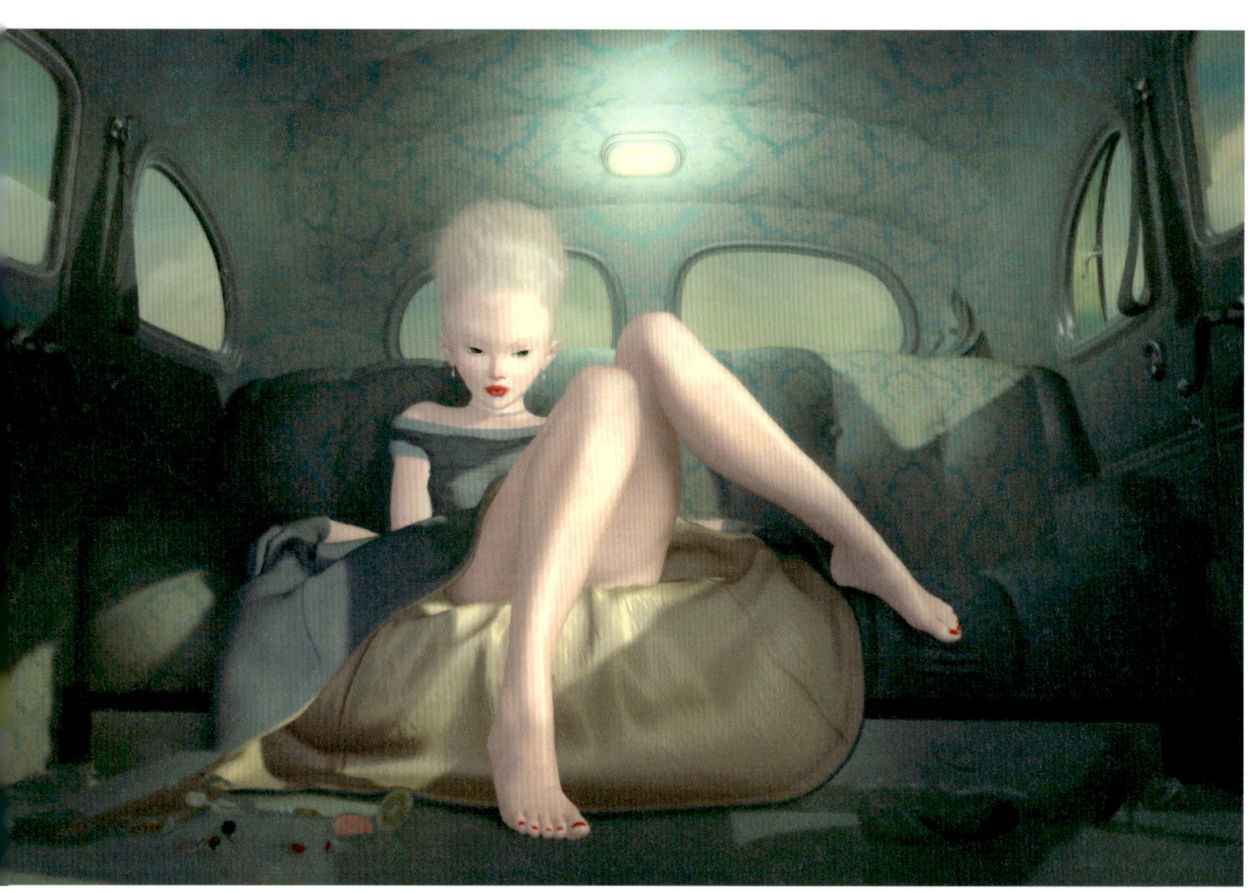

Day Trip 日帰りの旅
デジタル・ウルトラクローム印刷、印画紙 / H60.94×W91.44cm / 2011　Ray Caesar/Gallery House

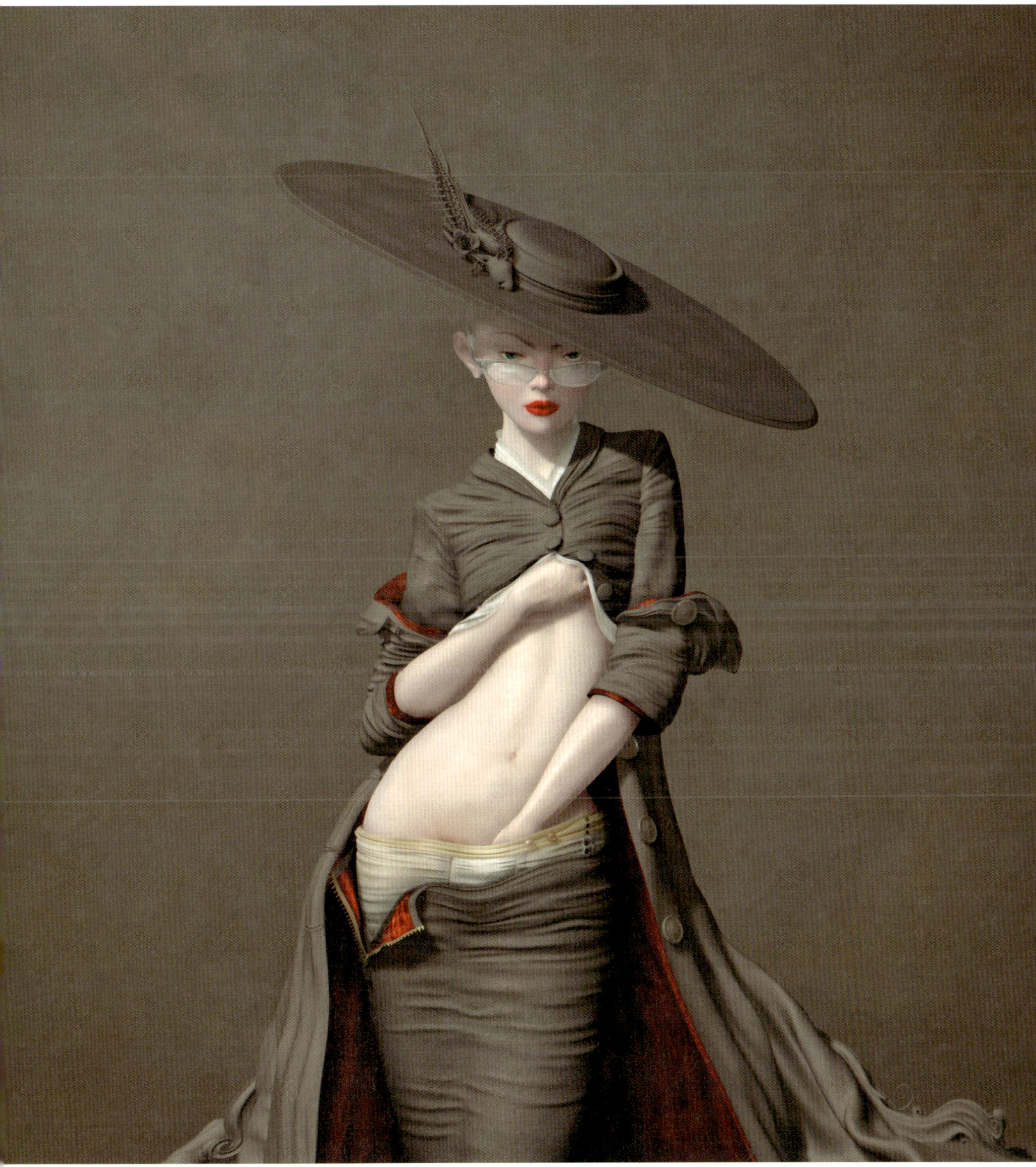

Self Examination 自省
デジタル・ウルトラクローム印刷、印画紙 / H76.2×W76.2cm / 2011　Ray Caesar/Gallery House

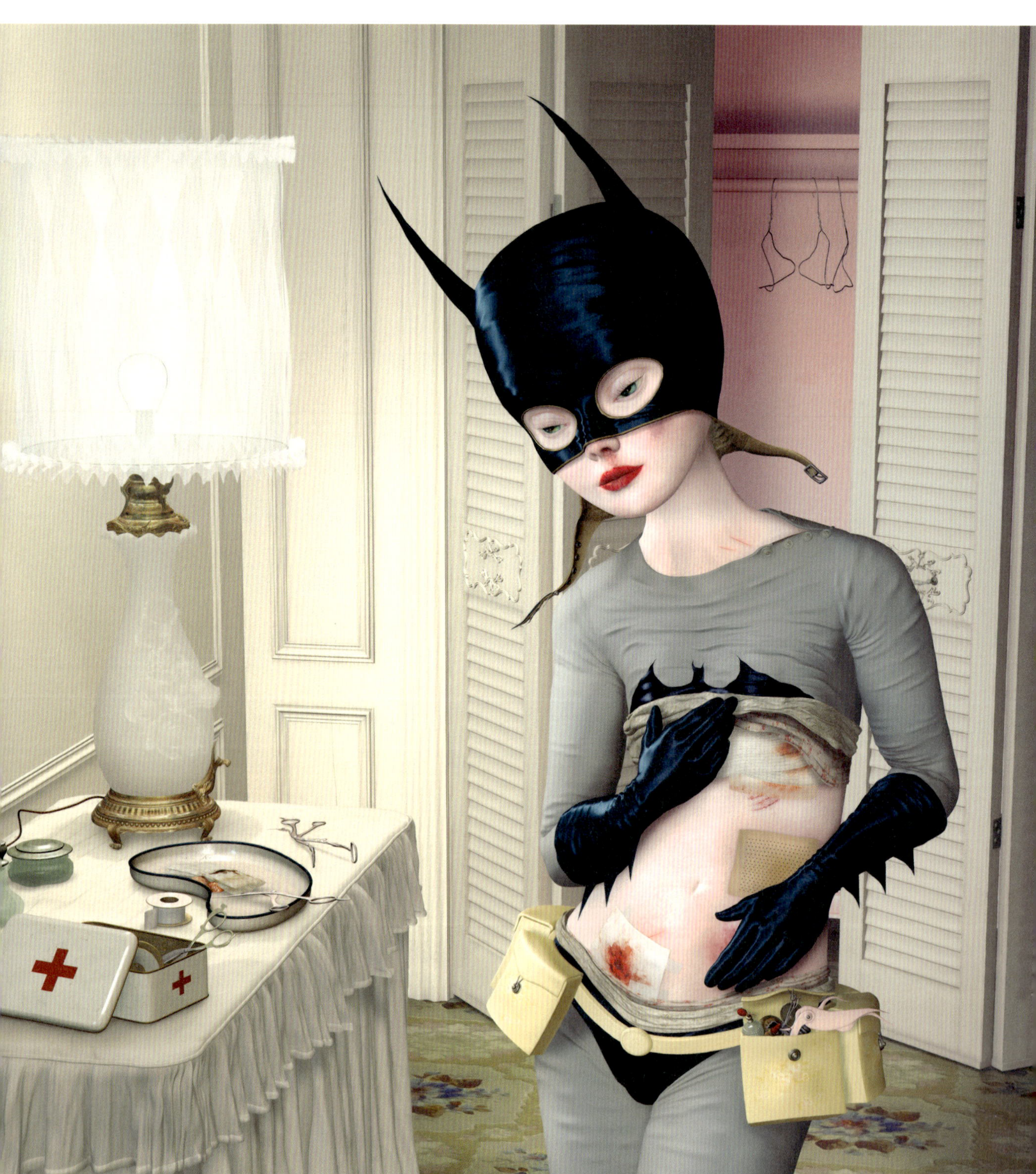

Old Wounds 古傷
デジタル・ウルトラクローム印刷、印画紙・マットインクジェット写真用紙 / H60.96×W60.96cm / 2015　Ray Caesar/Gallery House

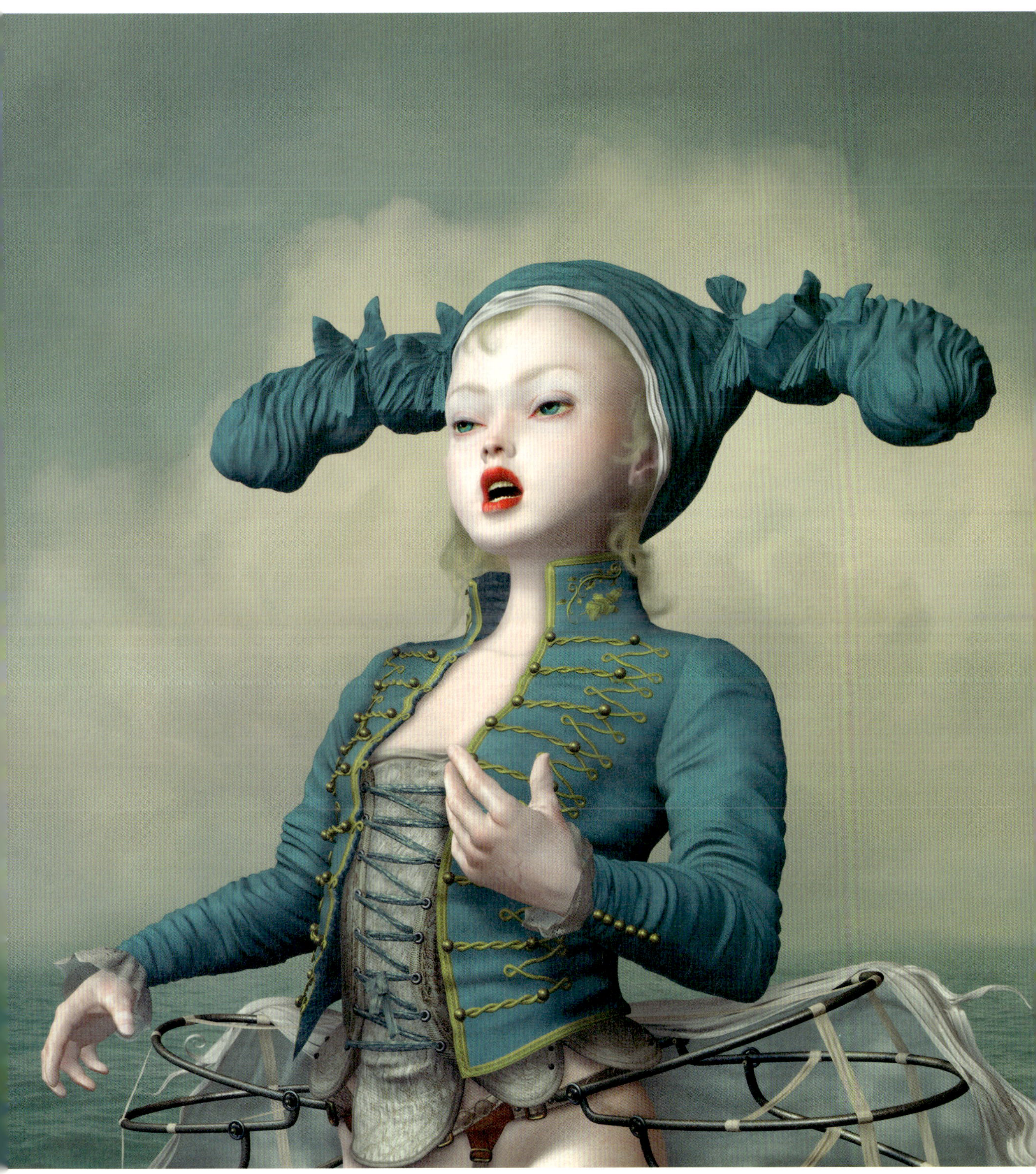

Song for the Dearly Departed 親愛なる故人に贈る歌
デジタル・ウルトラクローム印刷、印画紙 / H60.96×W60.96cm / 2015　Ray Caesar/Gallery House

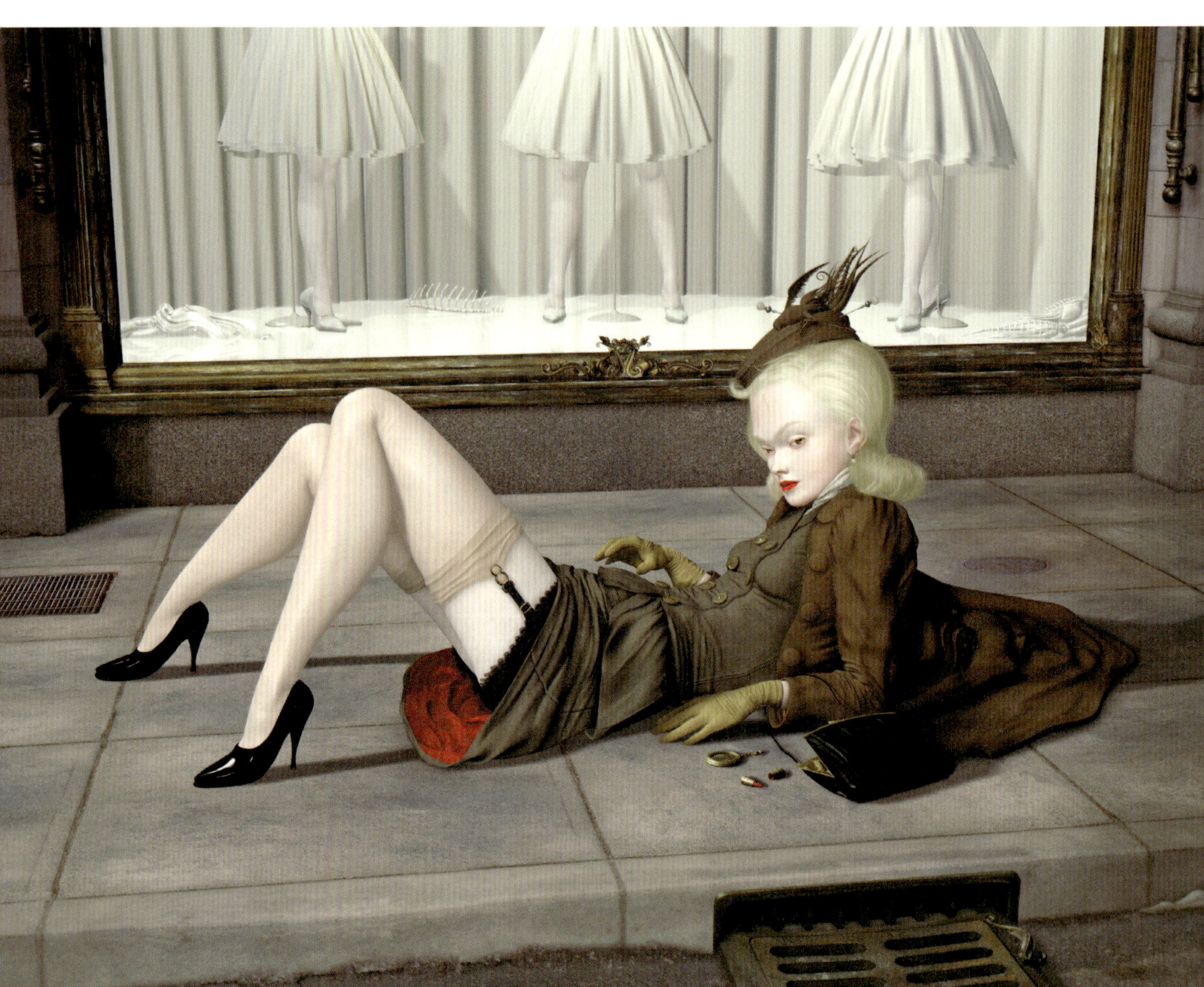

Fallen つまずいた女
デジタル・ウルトラクローム印刷、印画紙 / H76.2×W101.6cm / 2013　Ray Caesar/Gallery House

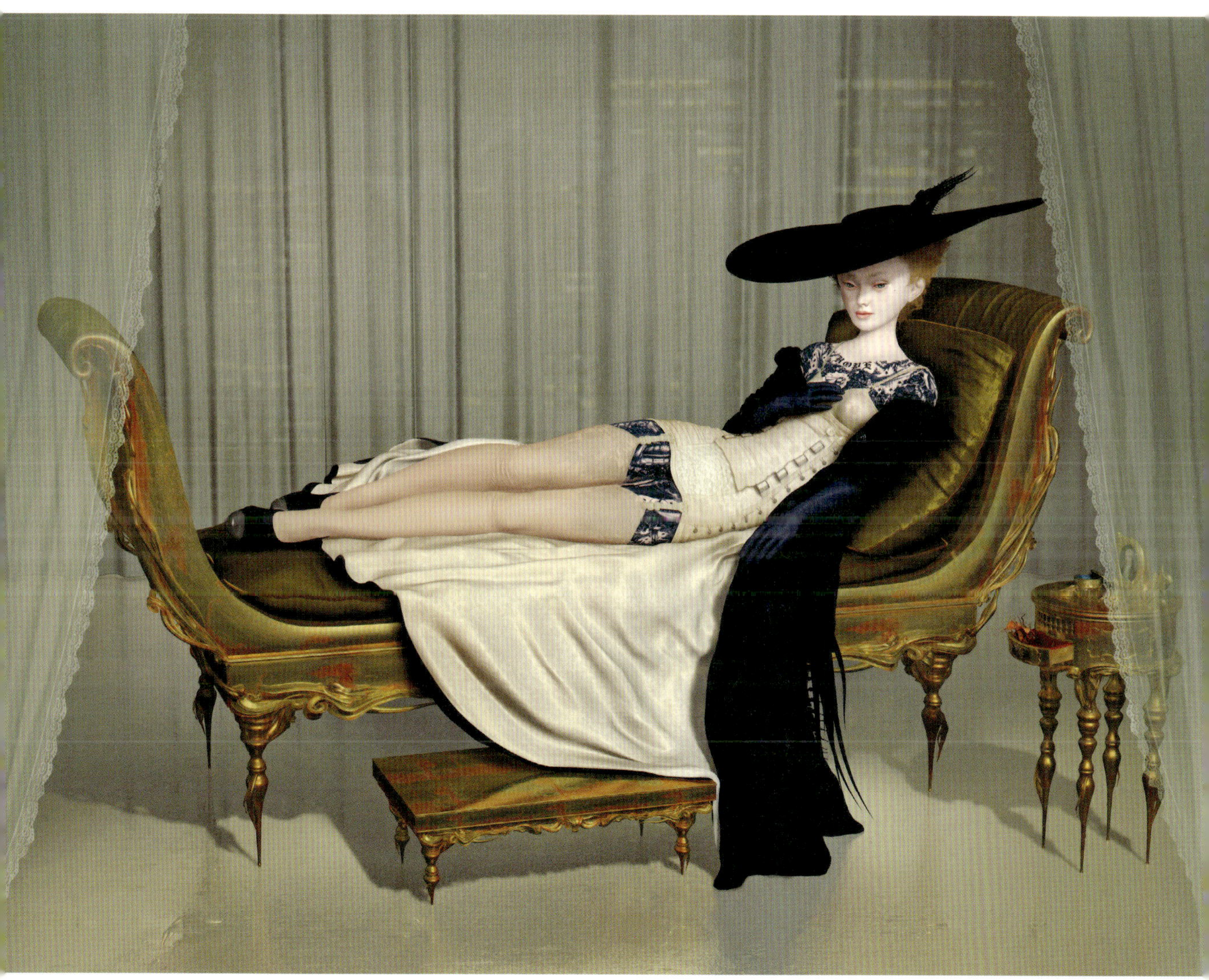

Madame R マダムR
デジタル・ウルトラクローム印刷、印画紙 / H76.2×W101.6cm / 2015　Ray Caesar/Gallery House

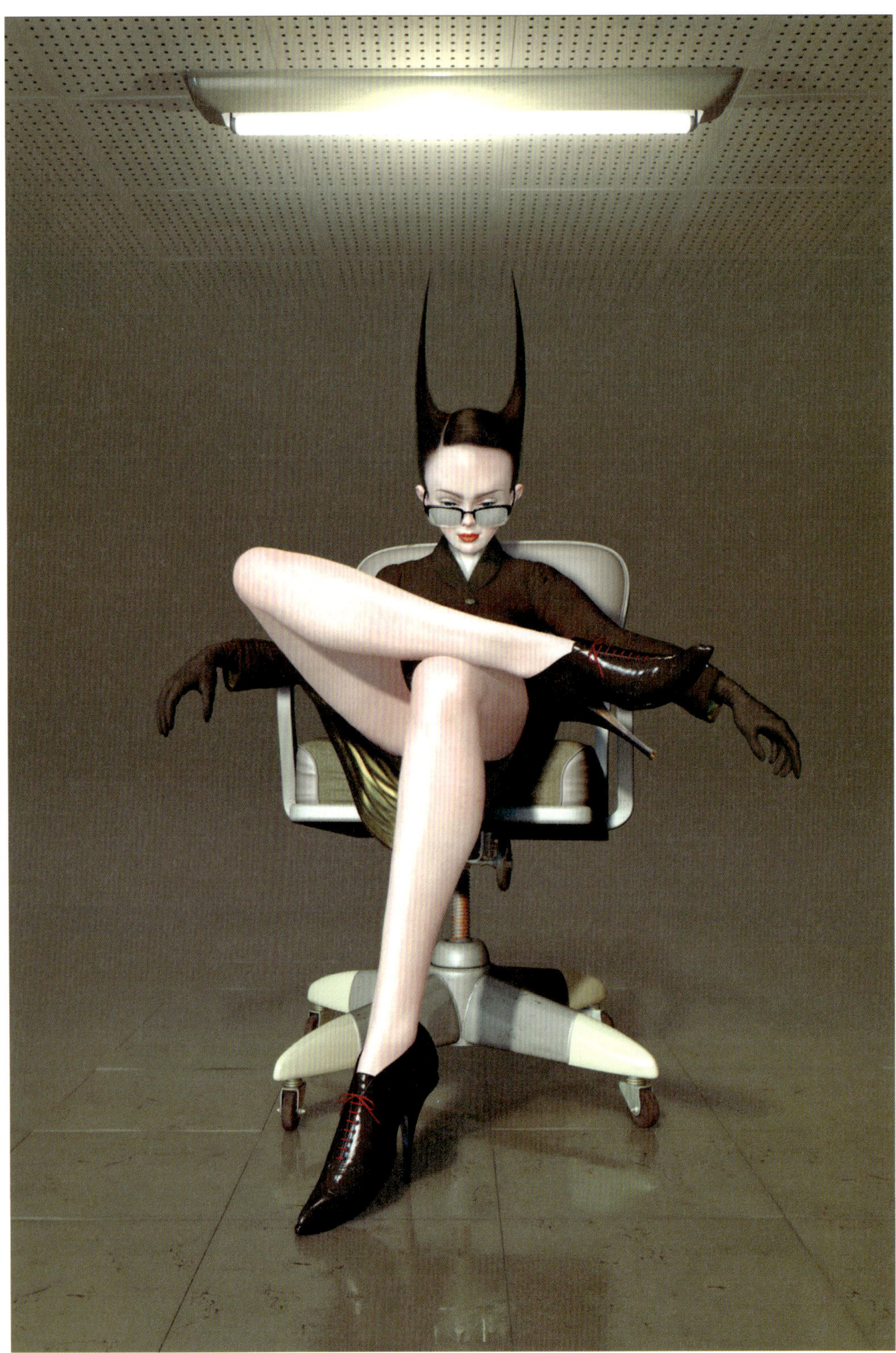

The Manager ザ・マネジャー
デジタル・ウルトラクローム印刷、印画紙 / H60.96×W91.44cm / 2012　Ray Caesar/Gallery House

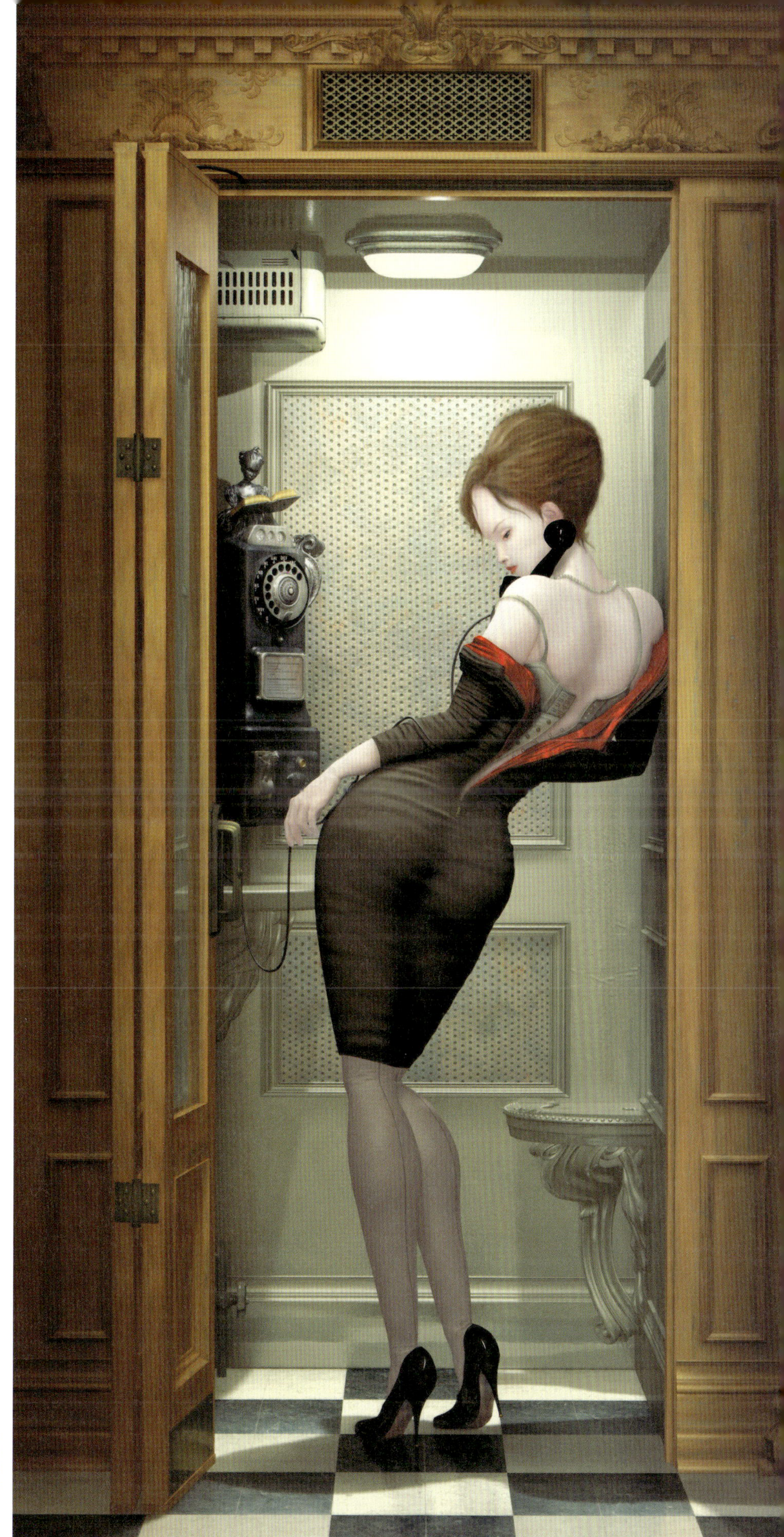

Night Call ナイト・コール
デジタル・ウルトラクローム印刷、印画紙 /
H50.8×W91.44cm / 2012
Ray Caesar/Gallery House

02

Tom Bagshaw

トム・バグショー（イギリス UK）

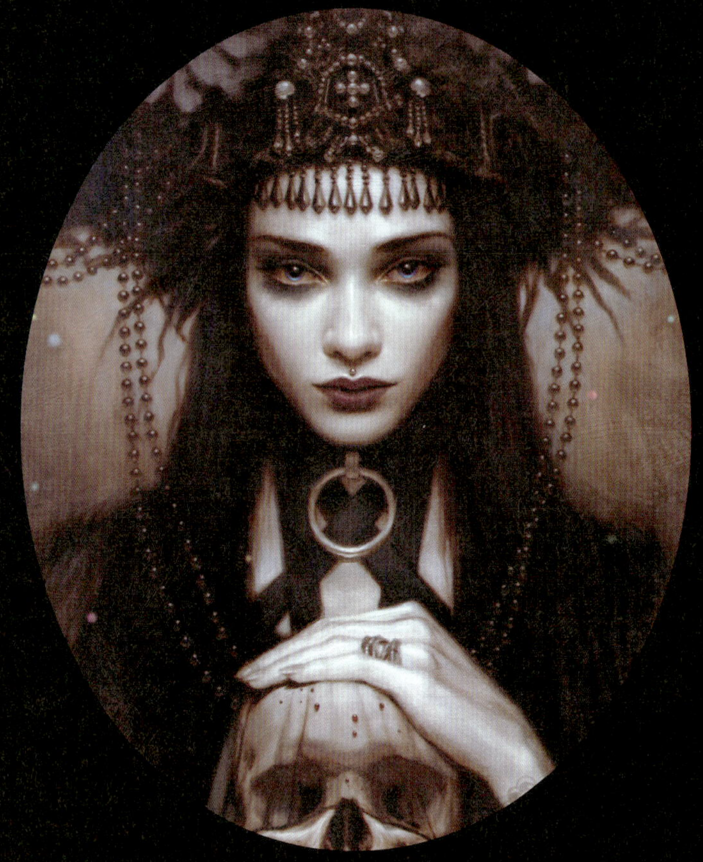

ジョージア王朝時代に栄えたイギリスのバースを拠点に活動するアーティスト。セントラル・イラストレーション・エージェンシー所属。Mostlywanted名義で商業イラストレーターとしても活動。ファッション、広告、出版業界から引っ張りだこで、顧客にはBBC、GQなど世界的な大企業が名を連ねる。アーティストとしてはデジタル・ペインティングを制作し、幻想的で美しく神秘的な女性を描く。見る者の想像力をかき立てるテーマを扱いながらも、その表現方法は写実主義に基づく。作品で中心的な役割を果たす女性は、決してか弱い乙女ではない。強く神秘的で見る人を惹きつける。世界中の多くのギャラリーで作品を紹介されている。

Based in the Georgian city of Bath, England, Tom Bagshaw works as a commercial illustrator under the moniker "Mostlywanted" and is represented by The Central Illustration Agency. His talents are sought after by clients in fashion, advertising, editorial and publishing, and include Sony, the BBC, GQ and more. For his personal work he has developed a highly rendered digital painting style through which he explores portraiture and figurative themes of fantasy, beauty and mysticism. While his work deals with imaginative content, it also aims for a strong level of realism in its presentation. Feminine beauty and portraiture play a central role in his work, but the women he depicts are never frail damsels in distress. More often than not they are strong, intriguing characters, with an air of mystery to them. His digital paintings have been shown in galleries all around the world.

www.mostlywanted.com

↑Wake 覚醒（部分）
デジタル彩色 / H25×W25cm / 2016

→Accismus アクシスムス（ほしいと思っているものを本心とは裏腹に拒否すること、部分）
デジタル彩色 / H38×W28cm / 2015

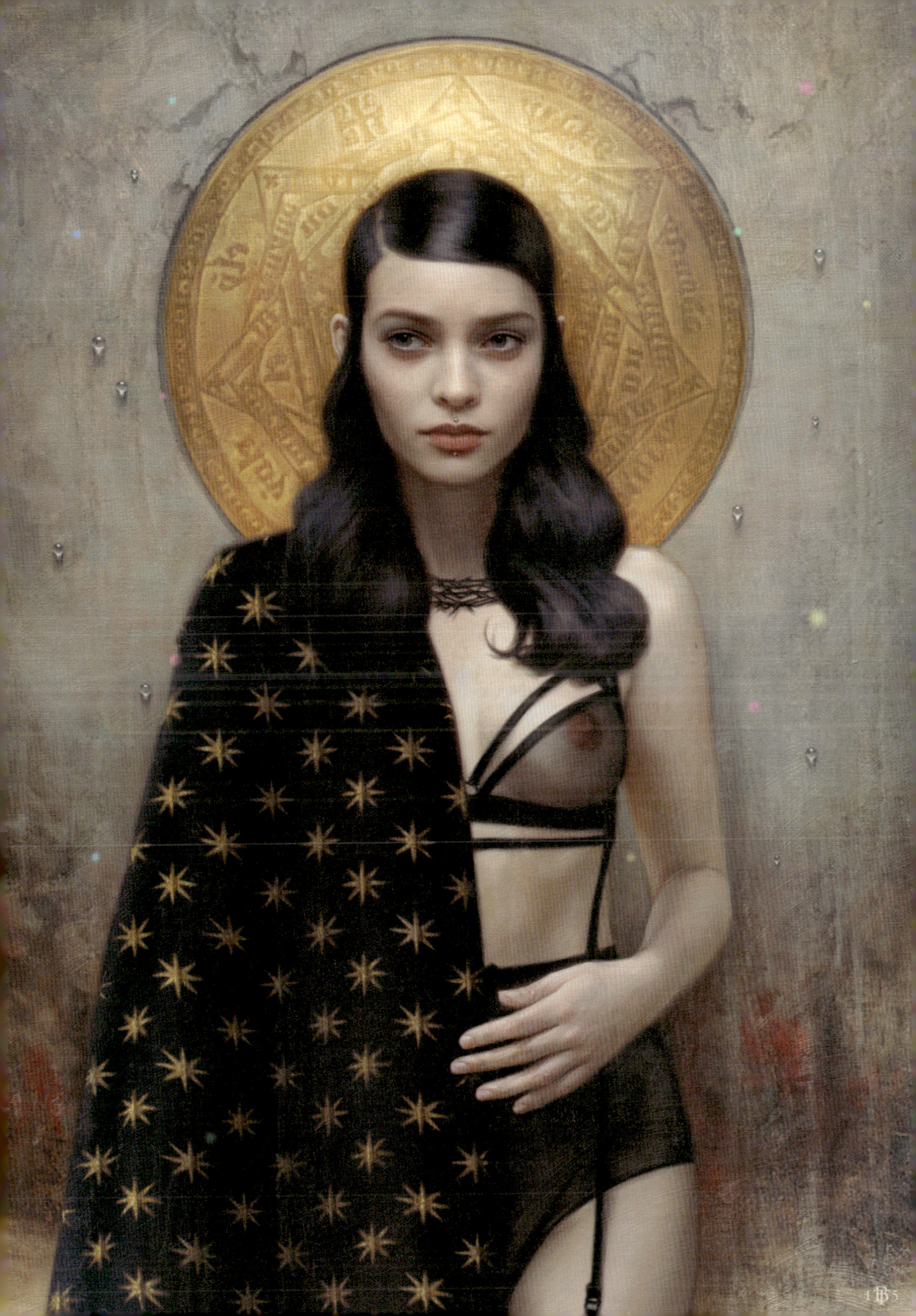

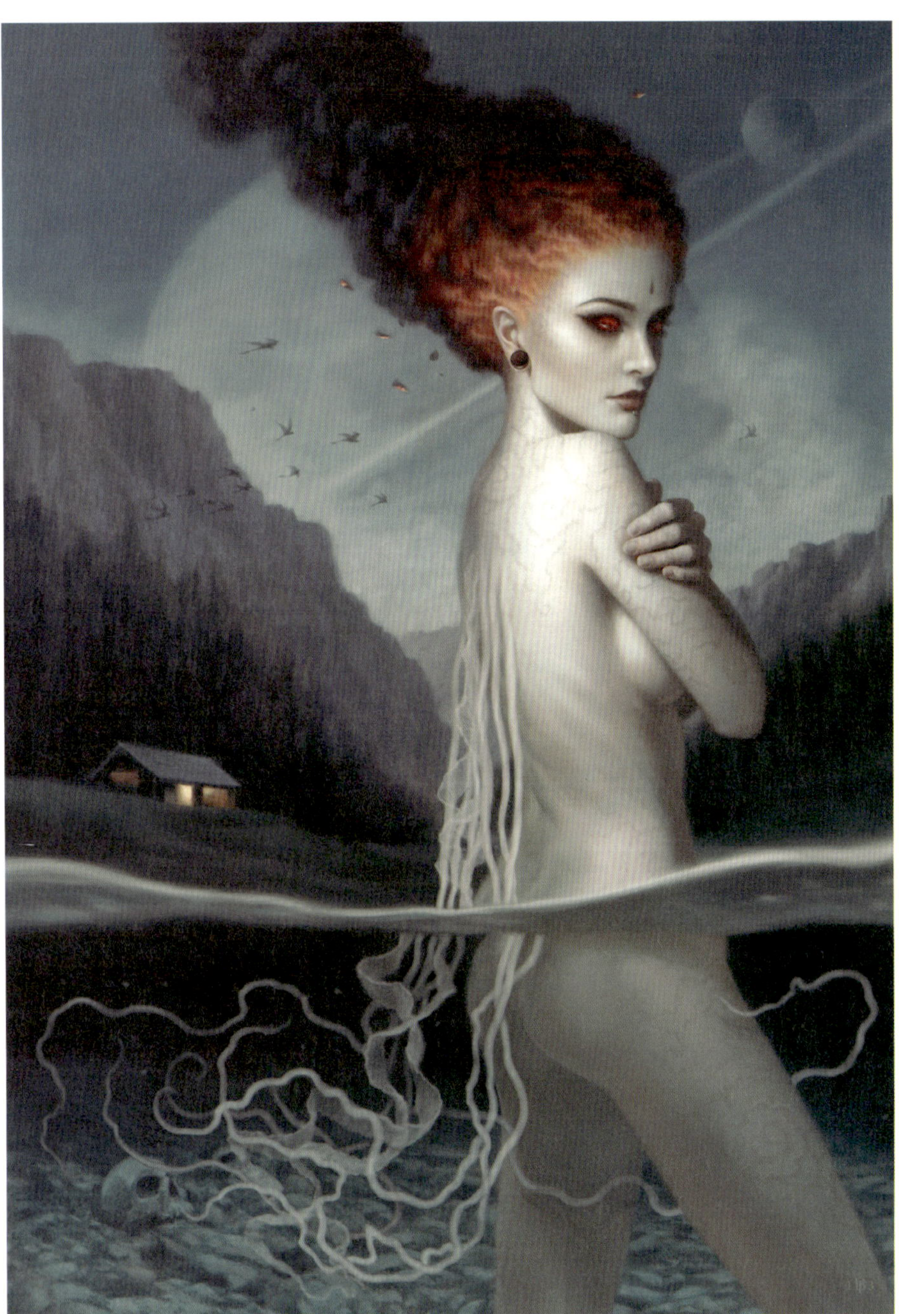

Night Swimming ナイス・スイミング
デジタル彩色 / H48×W35cm / 2013

Regrets 心残り
デジタル彩色 / H48×W38cm / 2011

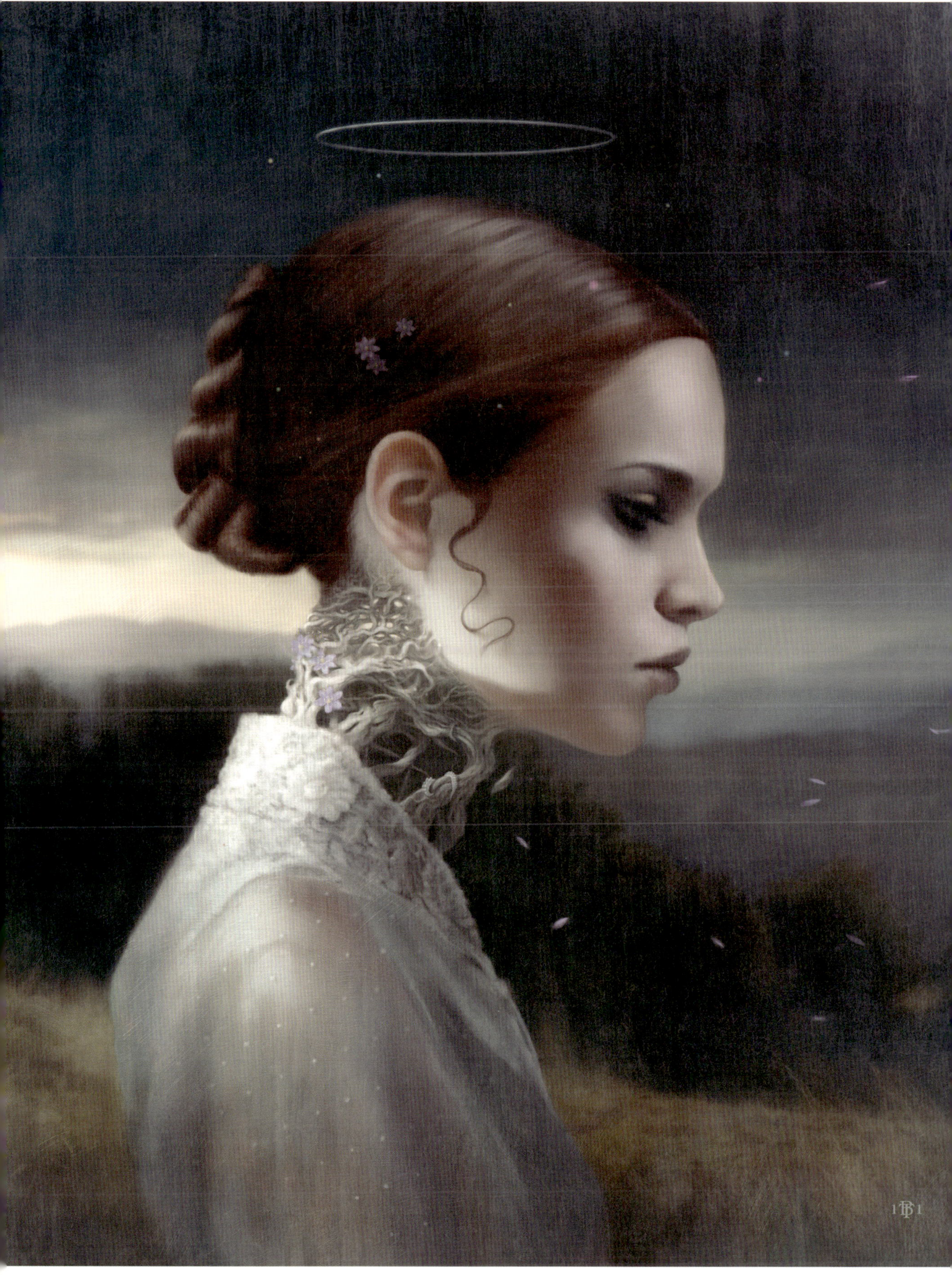

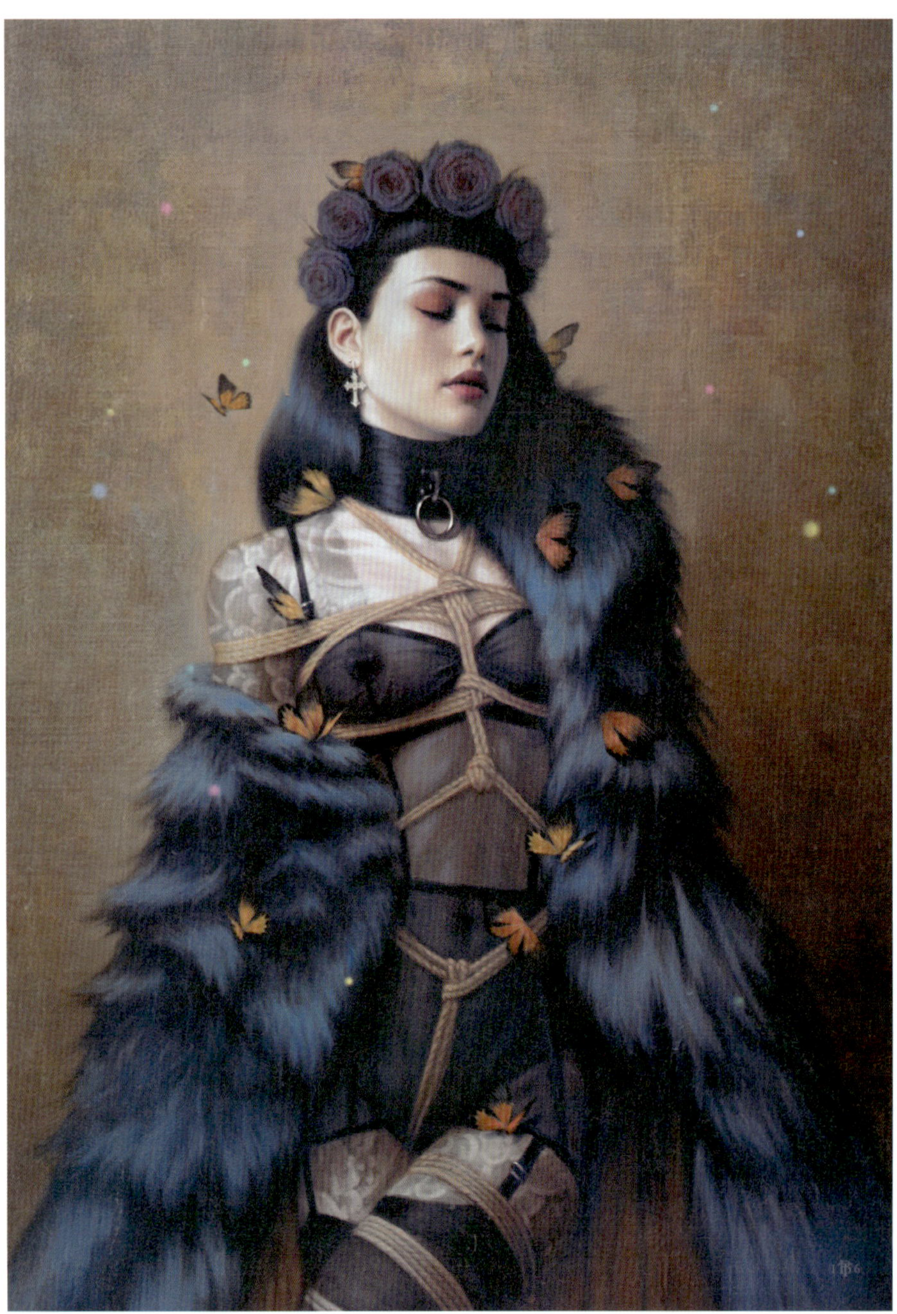

Anthesis 開花
デジタル彩色 / H40×W30cm / 2016

Better Angels 性善（部分）
デジタル彩色 / H40×W30cm / 2017

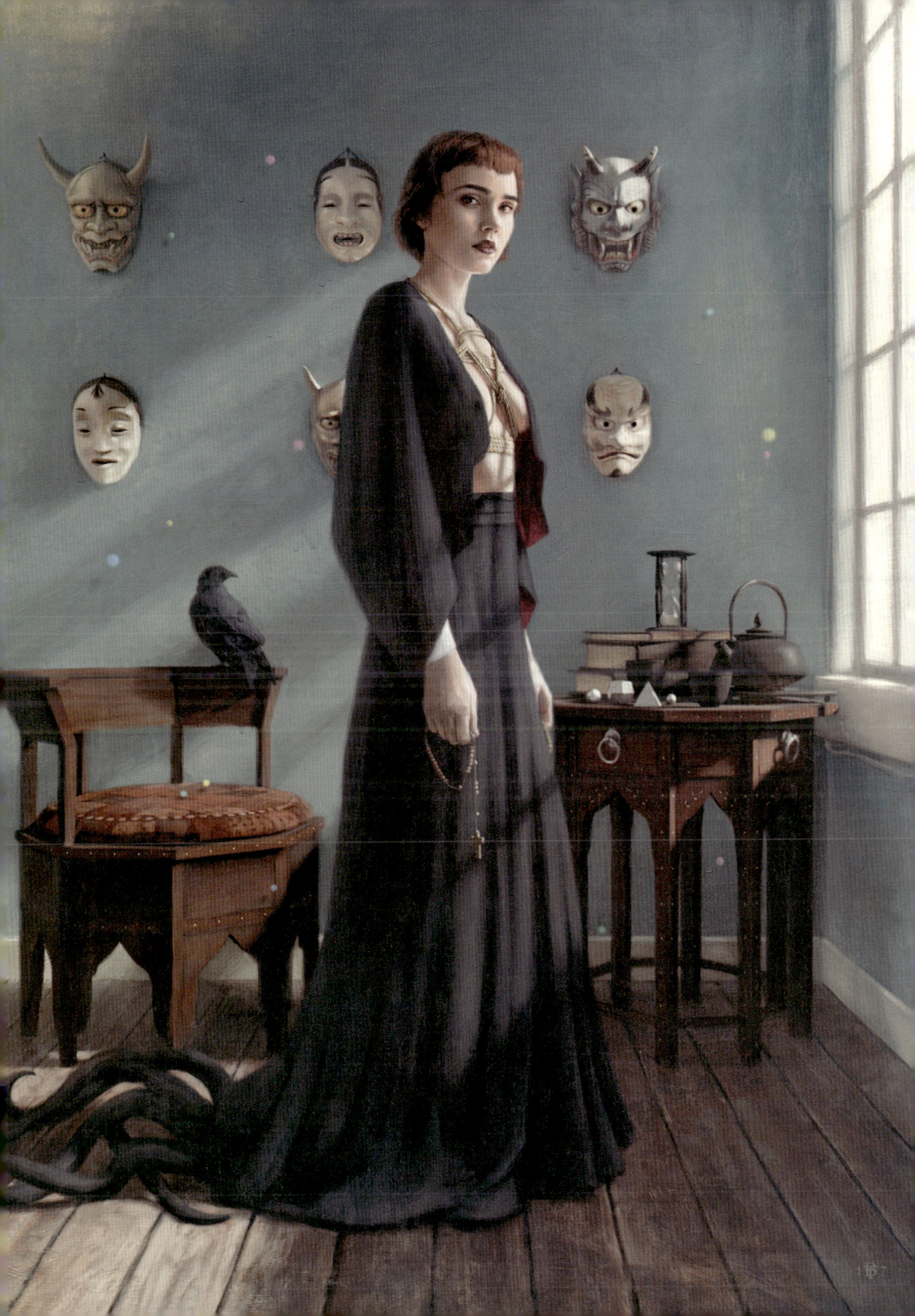

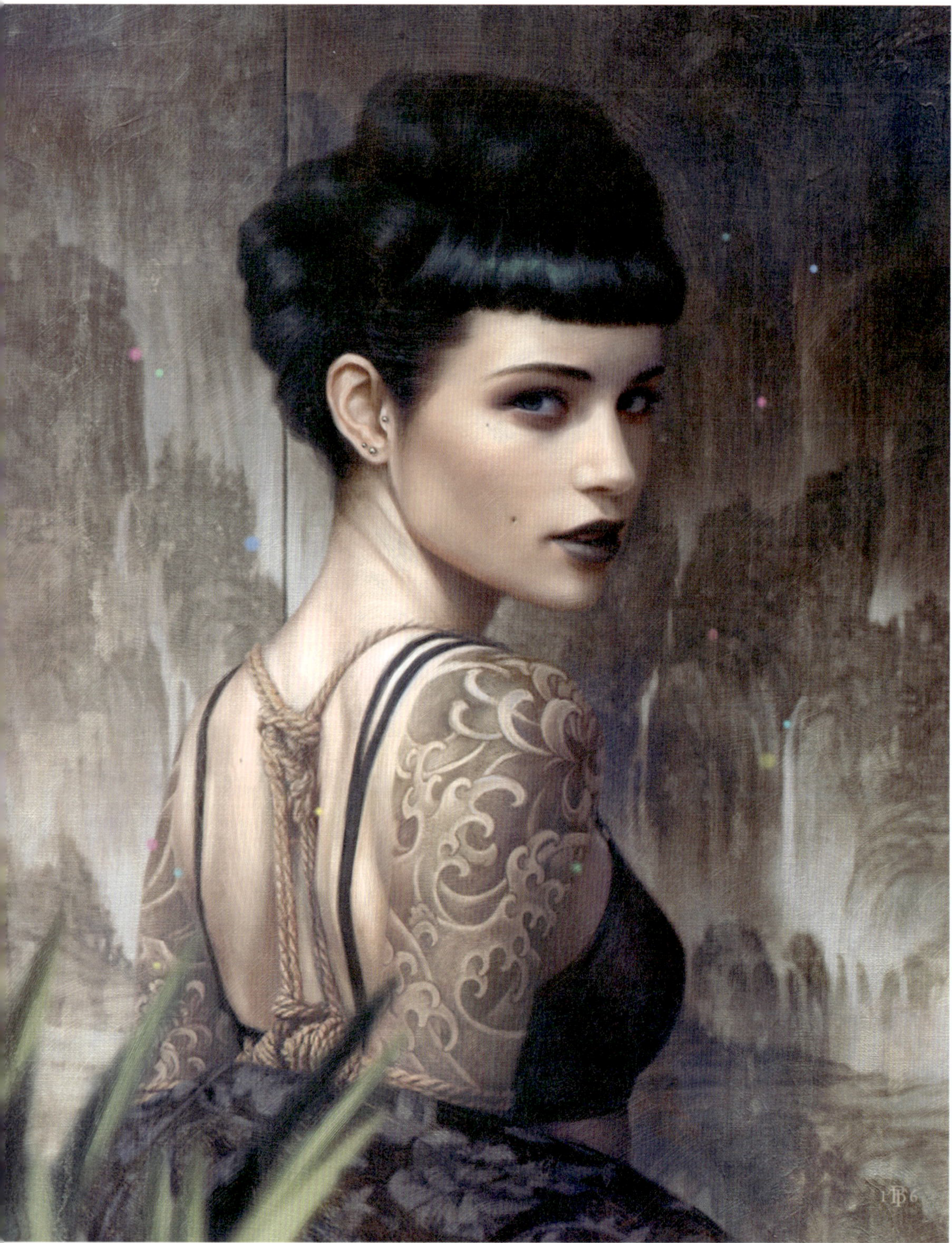

Deeper Water 深海
デジタル彩色 / H30×W25cm / 2016

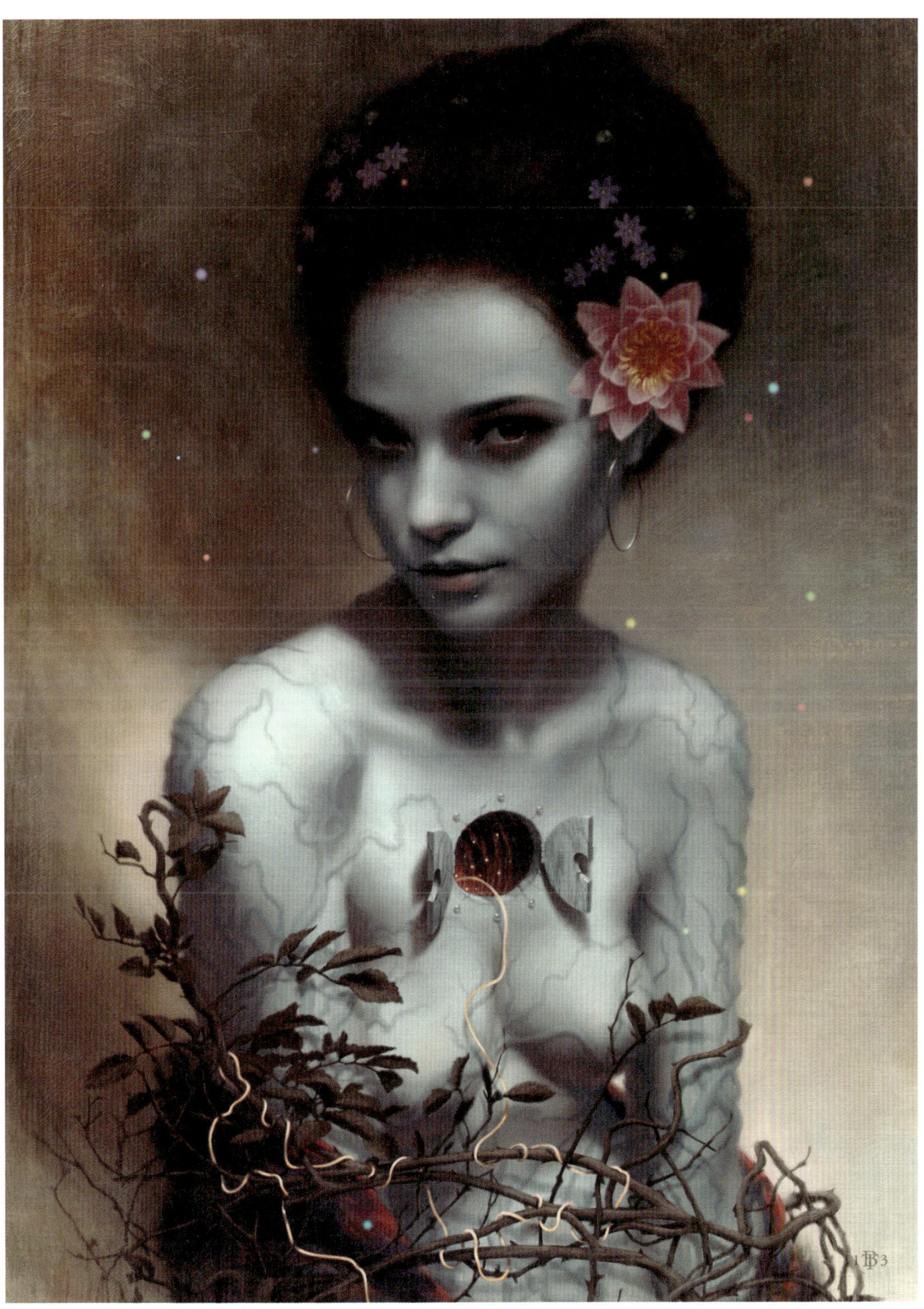

Neve ネヴェ
デジタル彩色 / H38×W28cm / 2013

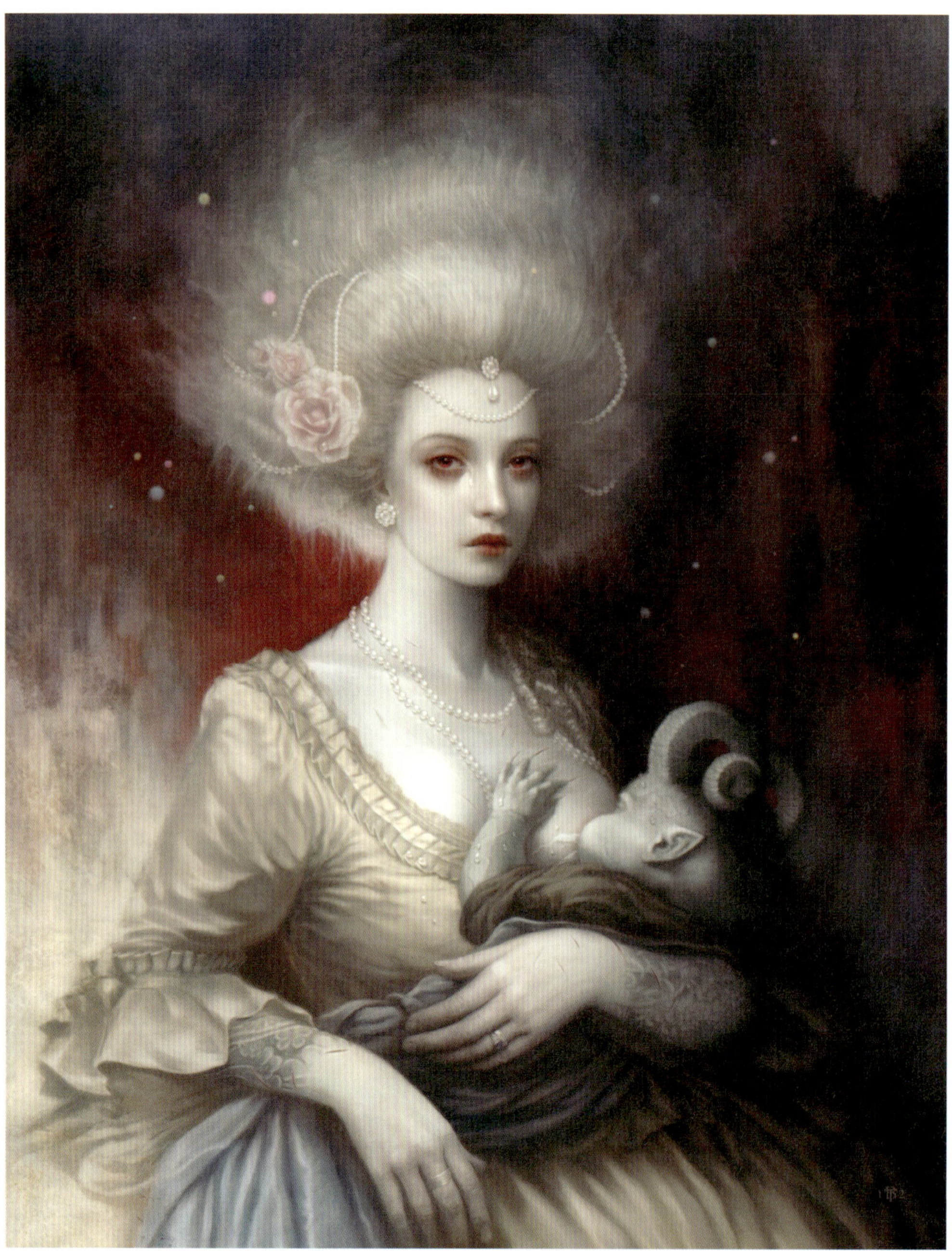

Lullaby 子守歌
デジタル彩色 / H50×W40cm / 2012

Pandora パンドラ
デジタル彩色 / H71×W50cm / 2010

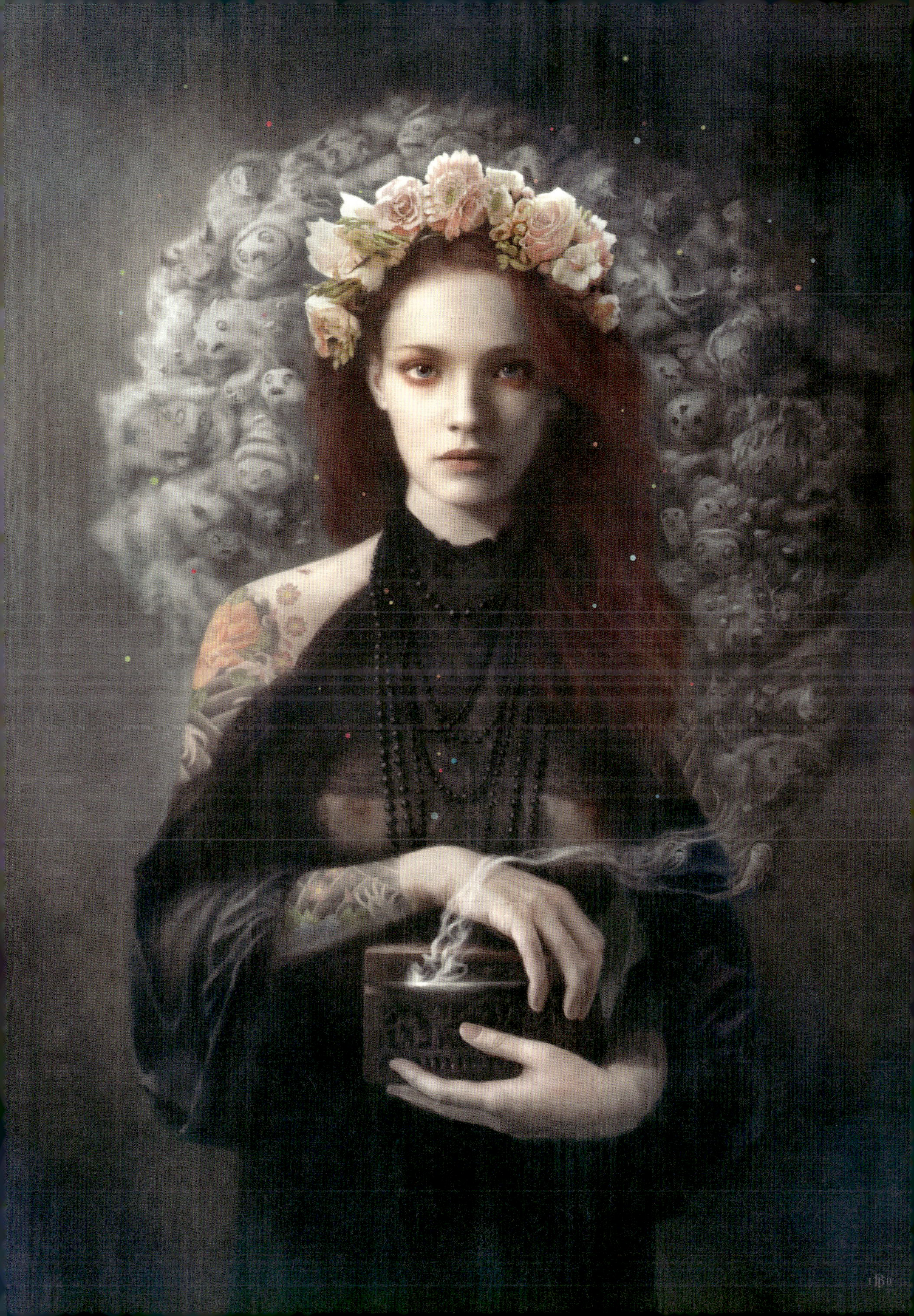

03

James Jean

ジェームス・ジーン（台湾 Taiwan）

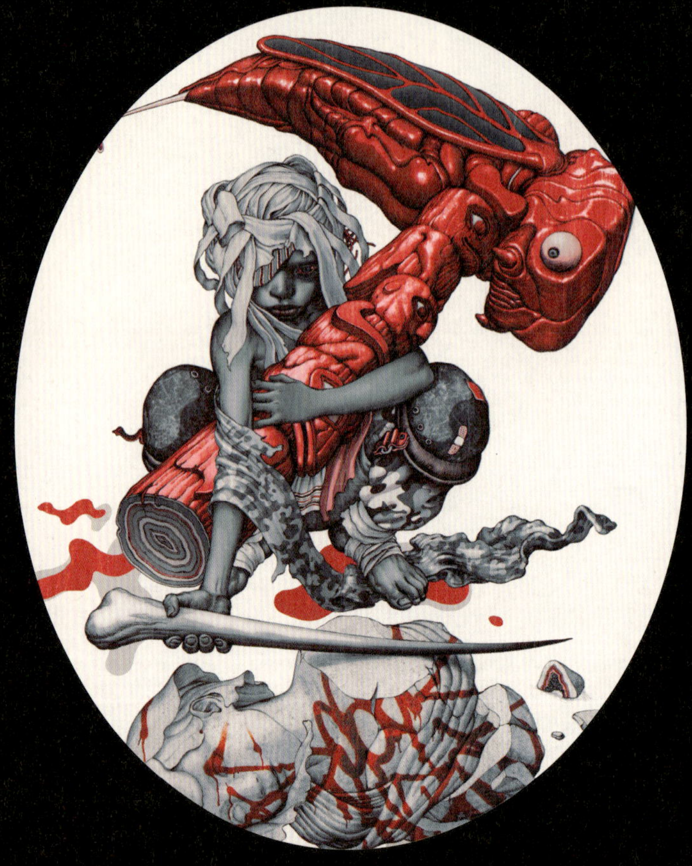

台湾出身。ニューヨークのスクール・オブ・ヴィジュアル・アーツ卒業。現在はロサンゼルス在住。多才で知られ、
様々な分野に活躍の場を広げている。ニューヨーク、ロサンゼルス、ロンドン、香港、東京と世界中で個展を開催。
伝統的な中国の掛け軸、日本の浮世絵、ルネッサンスの肖像画など異なるジャンルや時代の技法を実験的に試
み、個人と経験に焦点を当てた宇宙論的な世界を繊細で細密な筆致で描く。現代の文化、寓話からインスパイア
されたイメージを重ね合わせ、独自の神話の世界を創り出している。

James Jean was born in Taiwan and attended the School of Visual Arts in New York. He currently lives and
works Los Angeles. Renowned for his virtuosic ability to work across different genres with an imaginative and
multifaceted approach to image making, he has held exhibitions of his fine art in New York, Los Angeles,
London, Hong Kong and Tokyo. Jean fuses contemporary subjects with aesthetic techniques inspired by
traditional Chinese scroll paintings, Japanese woodblock prints, and Renaissance portraiture. By experiment-
ing with different styles and art-historical genres, Jean depicts detailed cosmological worlds that focus on
both individual and universal experiences. Layered with imagery drawn from contemporary culture and
age-old allegories, he imagines a collective realm of mythological proportions.

www.jamesjean.com

↑Manguch マングク（部分）
インク、デジタル彩色 / H22.86×W30.48cm / 2014

→Ama II アマ II（アッカドの出産・誕生の女神、部分）
アクリル、カンヴァス / H101.6×W76.2cm / 2017

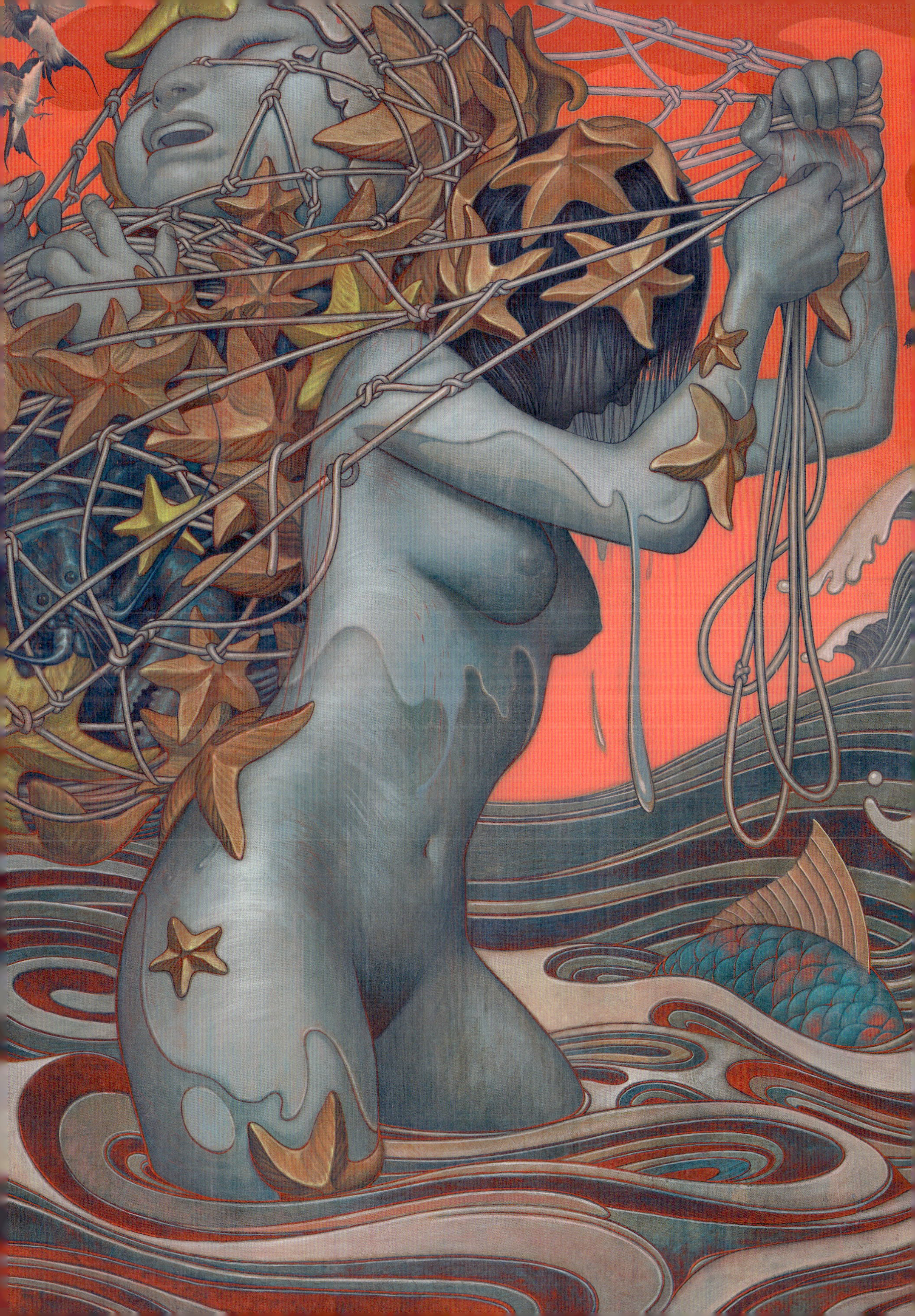

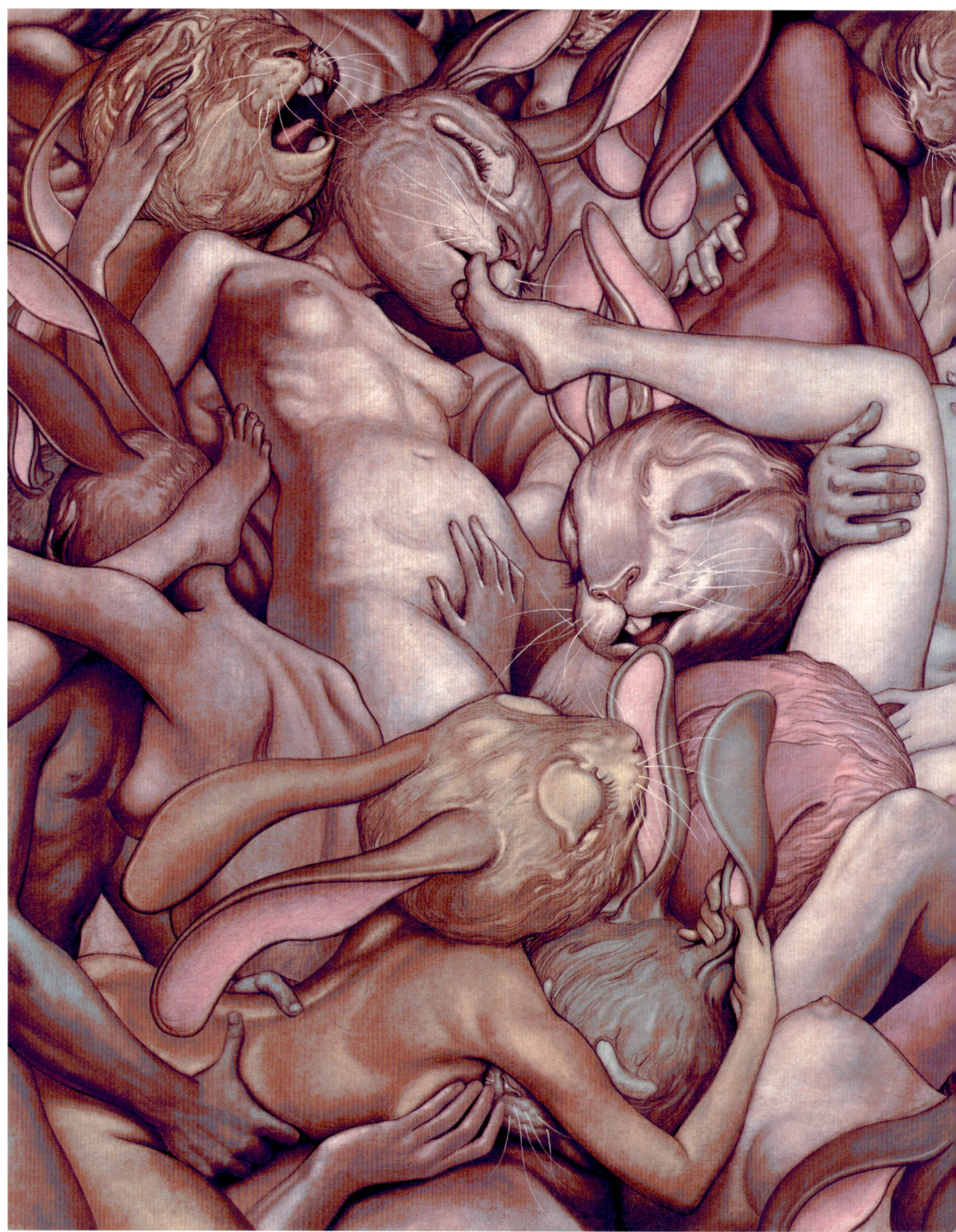

Aides Lapin エイド・ラパン
デジタル / H6000×W9539pixel / 2016

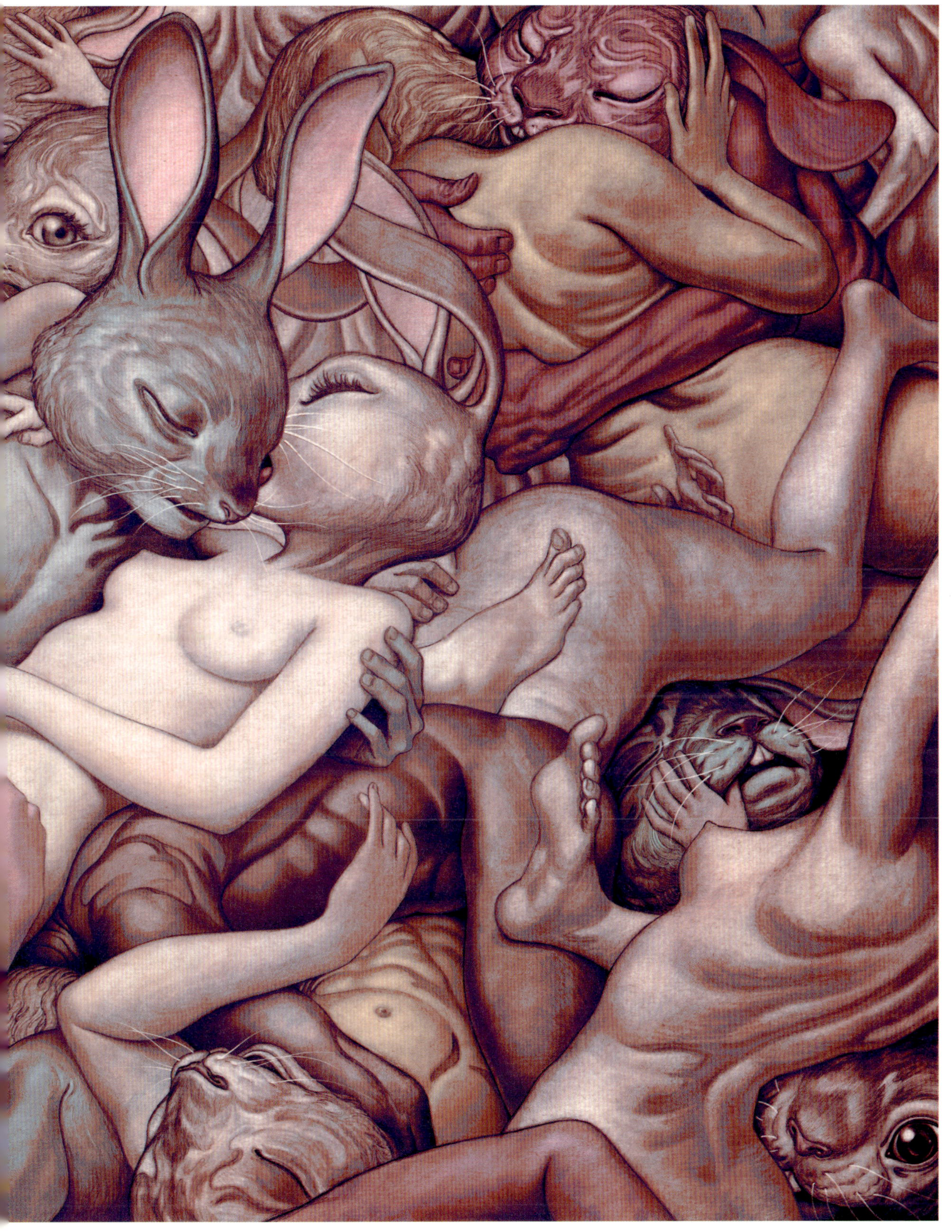

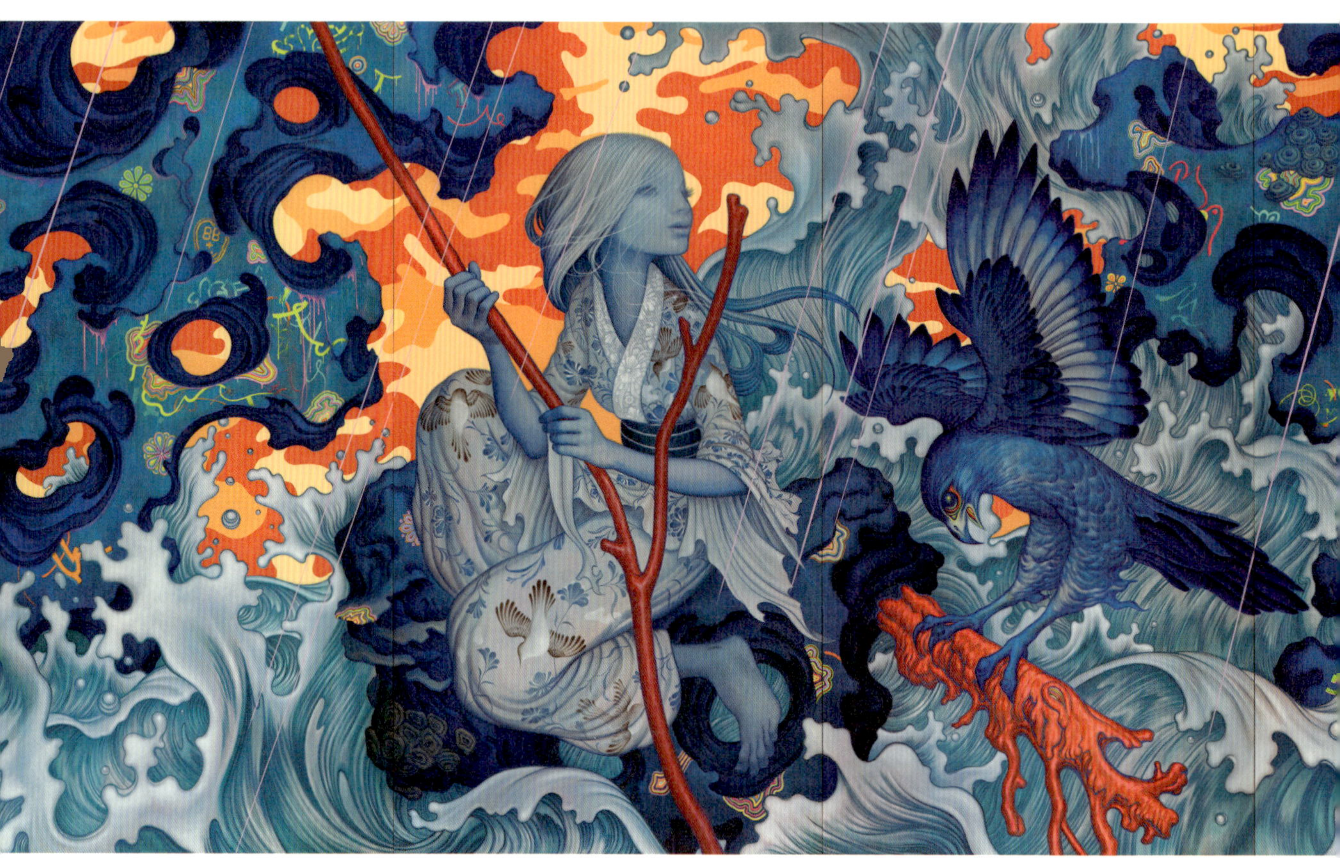

Adrift 漂流
ミクスト・メディア、4 つのカンヴァス / H223.52×W457.2cm / 2015

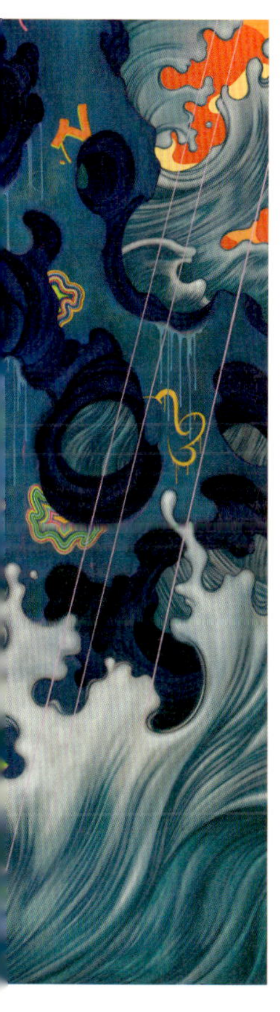

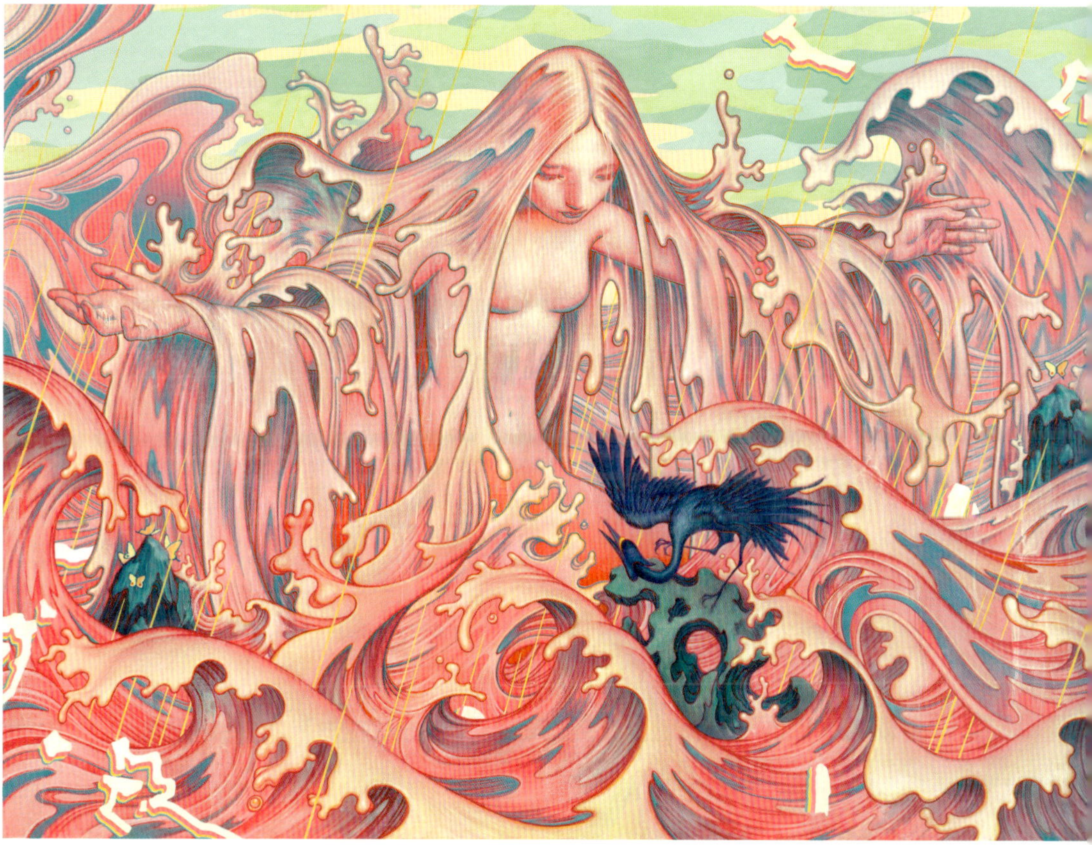

Adrift II 漂流 II
アクリル、カンヴァス / H91.44×W121.92cm / 2016

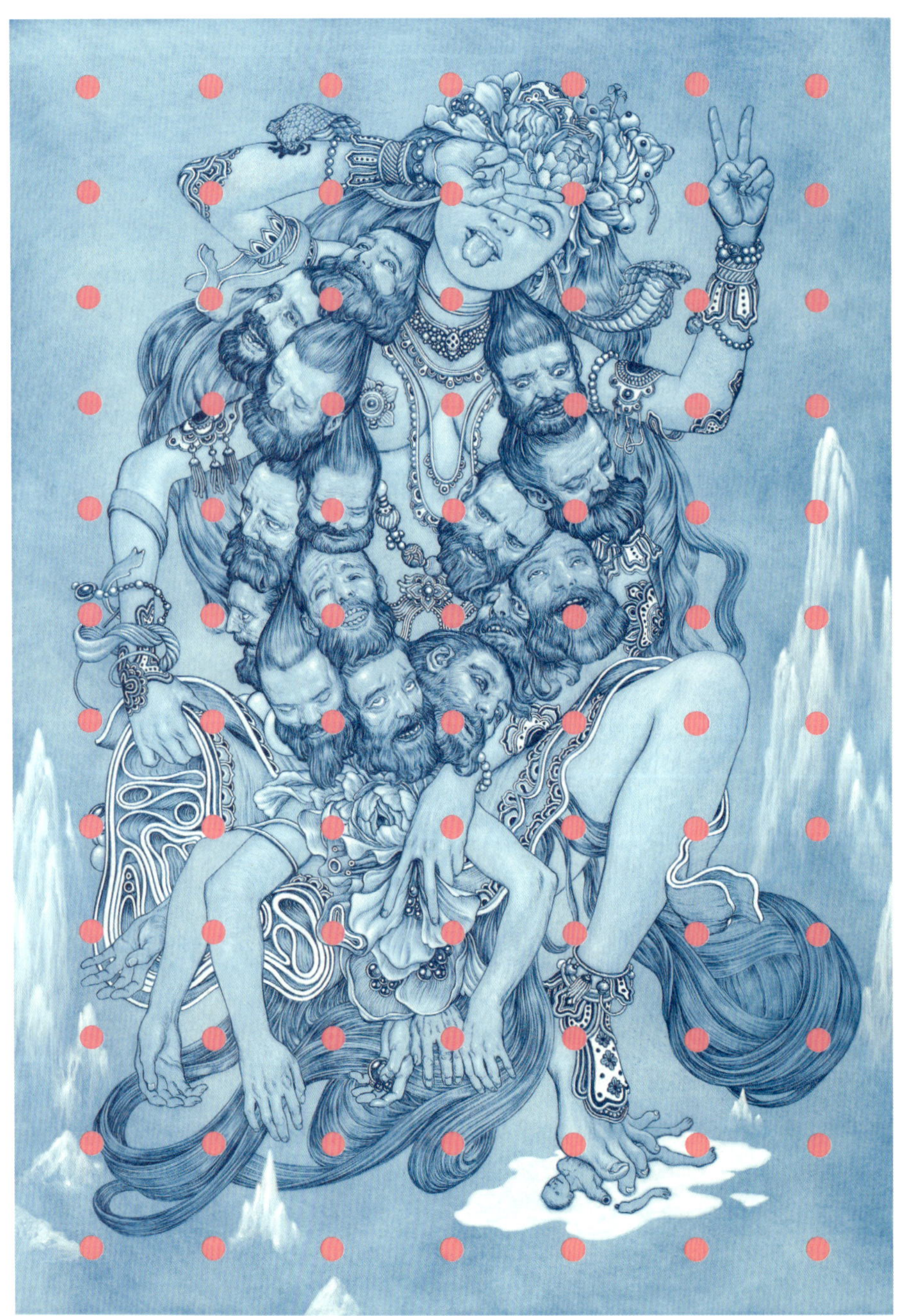

Kali カーリー（ヒンドゥー教の黒女神）
ミクスト・メディア、紙 / H104.14×W76.2cm / 2015

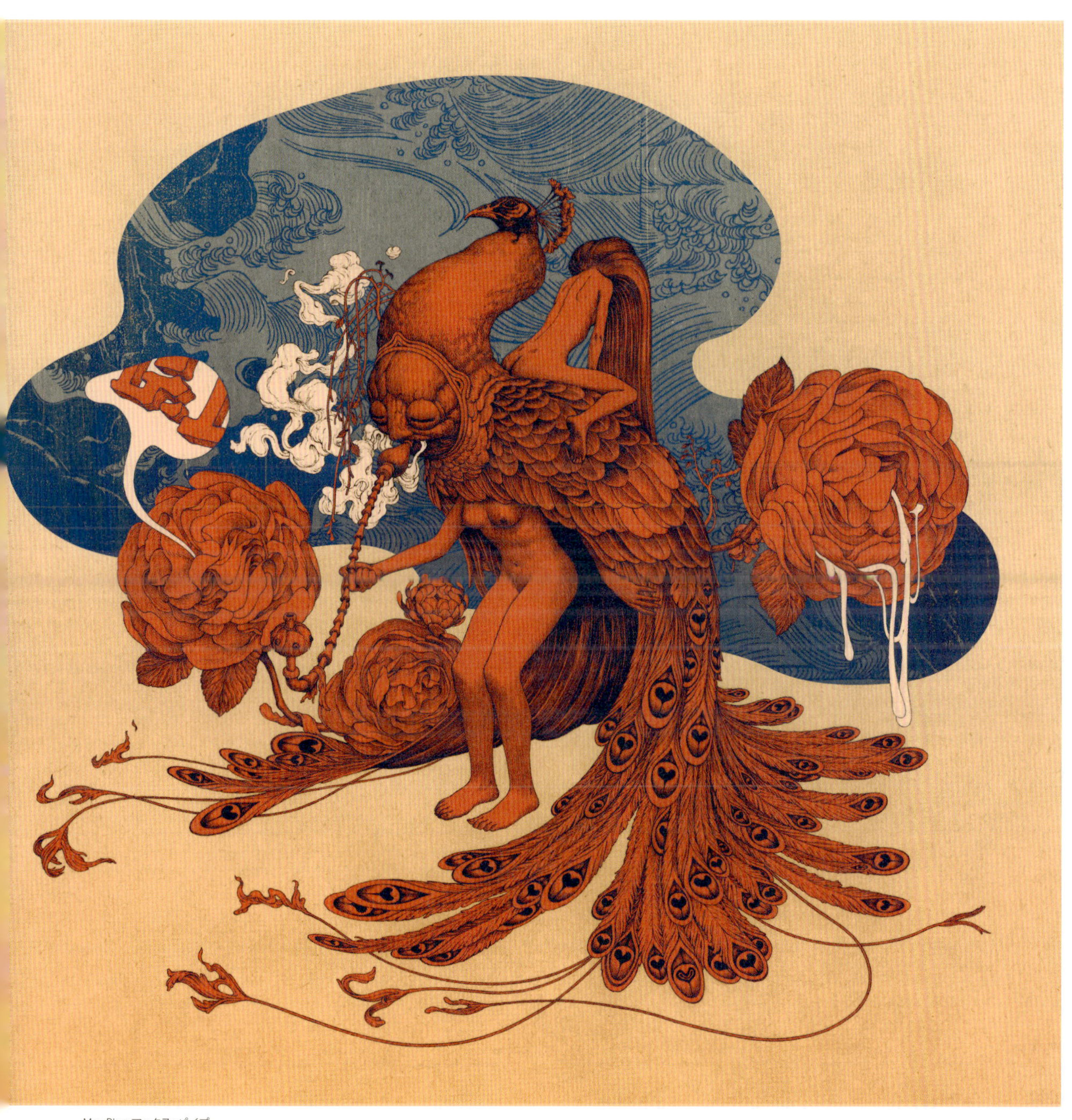

Max Pipe マックス・パイプ
デジタル、インク / H35.56×W36.195cm / 2017

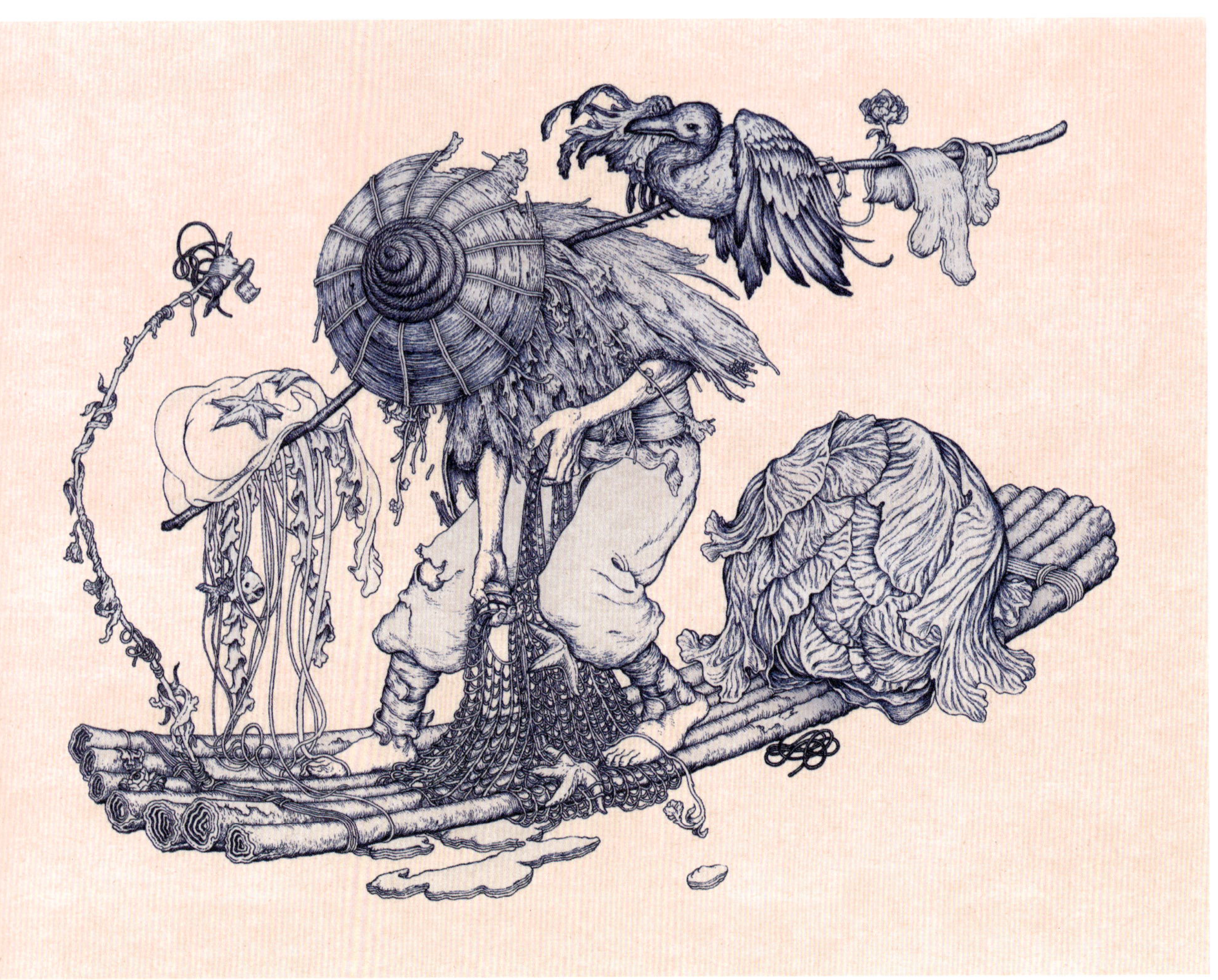

Cormorant ウ飼い
デジタル、インク / H22.225×W29.21cm / 2014

Year of Mokey サル年（部分）
デジタル / H53.34×W40.64cm / 2016

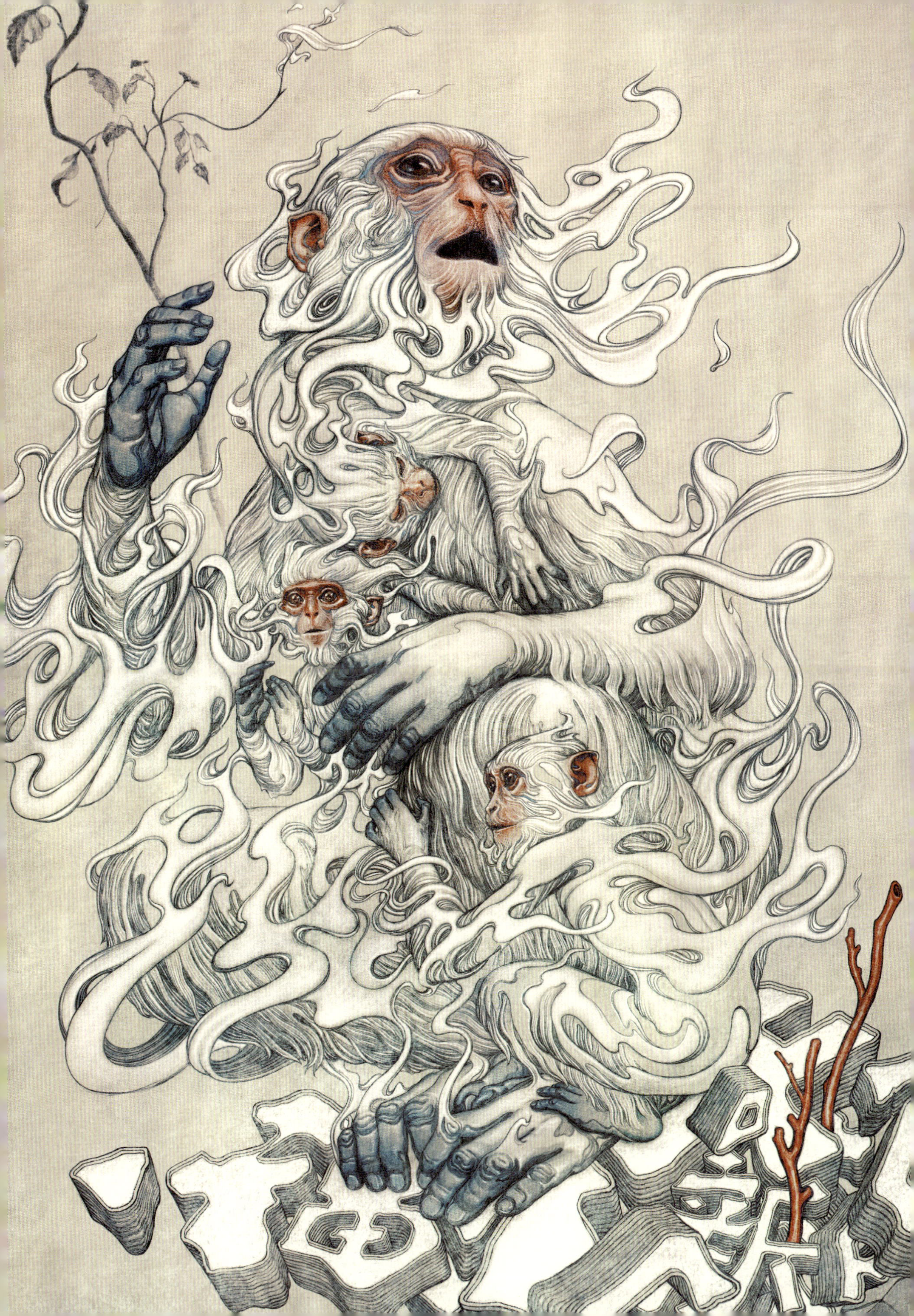

04

Camilla d'Errico

カミラ・デリコ（カナダ　Canada）

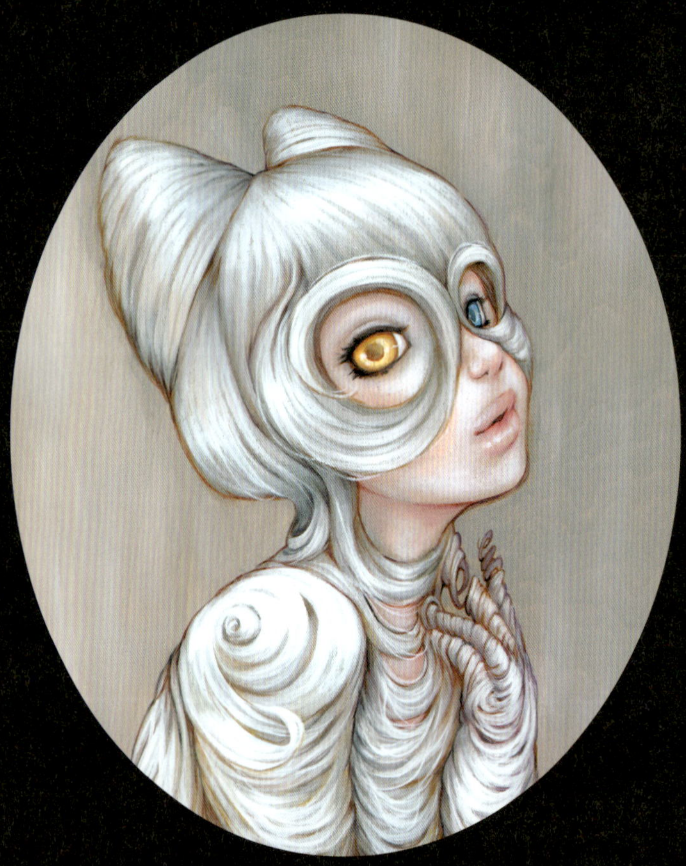

イタリア系カナダ人。マンガの影響を受けたスタイルでファイン・アートとコミックの世界に旋風を巻きこしている。多作なアーティストとして知られ、画家として活動する一方、『BURN（バーン）』『Tanpopo（タンポポ）』『Helmetgirls（ヘルメットガールズ）』といった個性的なキャラクターが主人公のコミック作品を続々と生み出している。キャラクター・デザイン、玩具、ファッション、雑貨も手掛け、ビデオゲーム、映画界にも進出。コミックアートとマンガをシュルレアリスム的手法でみごとに融合させ、情感豊かに表現する卓越した能力を持つ。

Camilla d'Errico is an Italo-Canadian artist who has been making waves in the fine art and comic industries with her manga-influenced style. Ever the prolific artist, Camilla lives the double life of comic artist, character creator and painter. Creator of BURN, Tanpopo and Helmetgirls, she has also expanded her style into designer toys, fashion, merchandise, videogames and even movies. Camilla has distinguished herself through her ability to seamlessly weave comic art and manga with surrealist elements, wrapping it all together with an extensive emotional palette.

www.camilladerrico.com

↑Hairball ヘアボール（部分）
油彩、木製パネル / H35.56×W27.94cm / 2012

→Suckerpunch 殴打（部分）
油彩、木製パネル / H40.64×W30.48cm / 2014

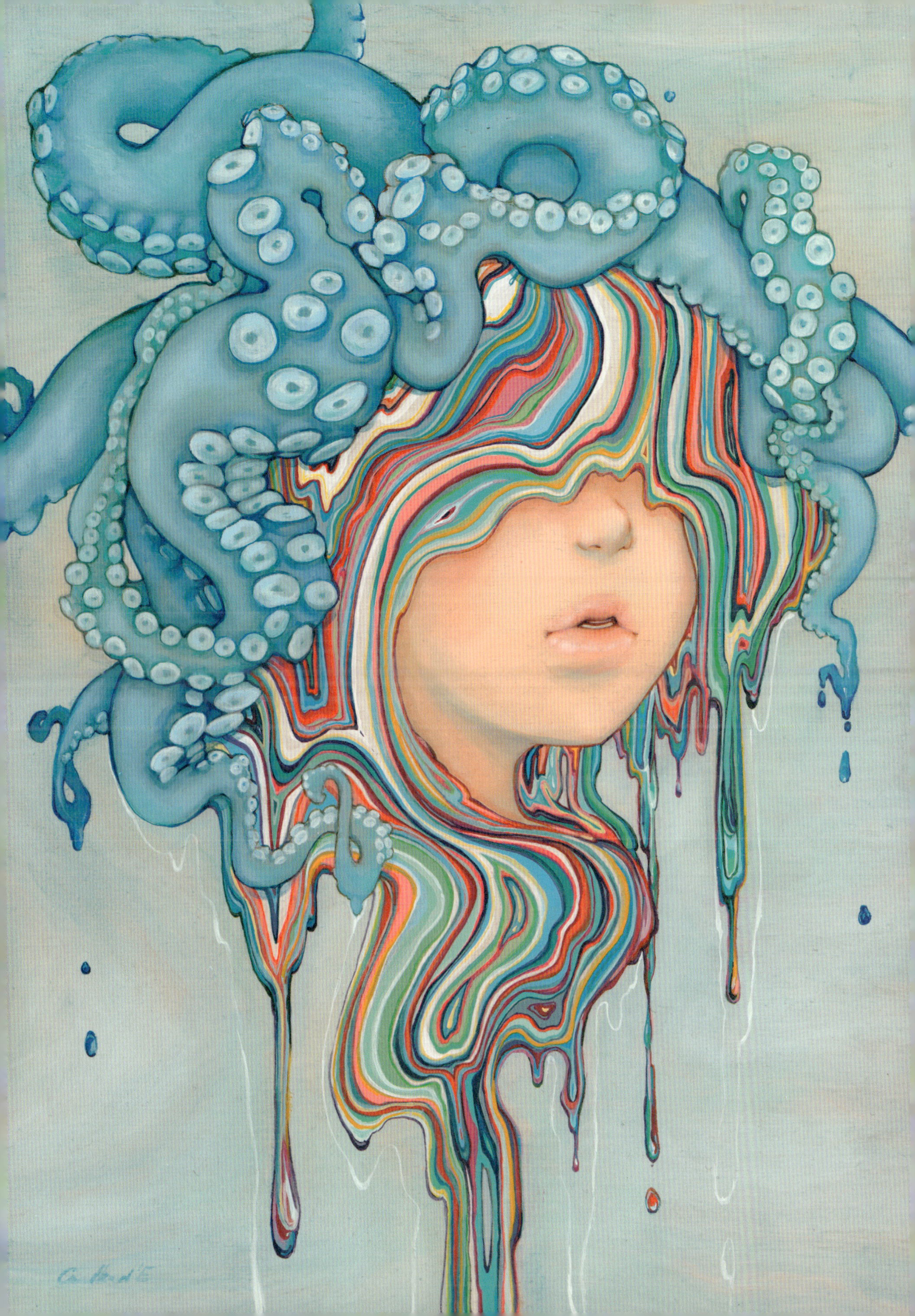

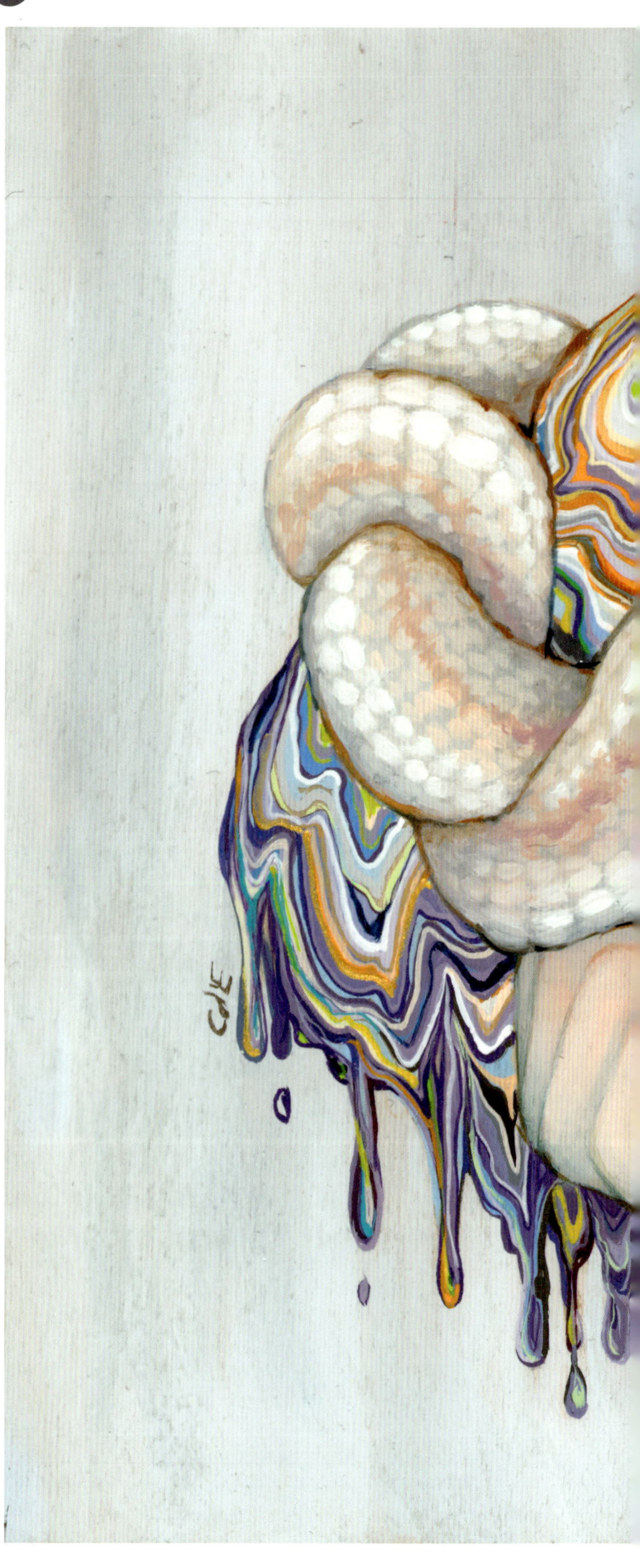

Mamba Mia マンバ・ミーア
油彩、木製パネル / H20.32×W25.4cm / 2016

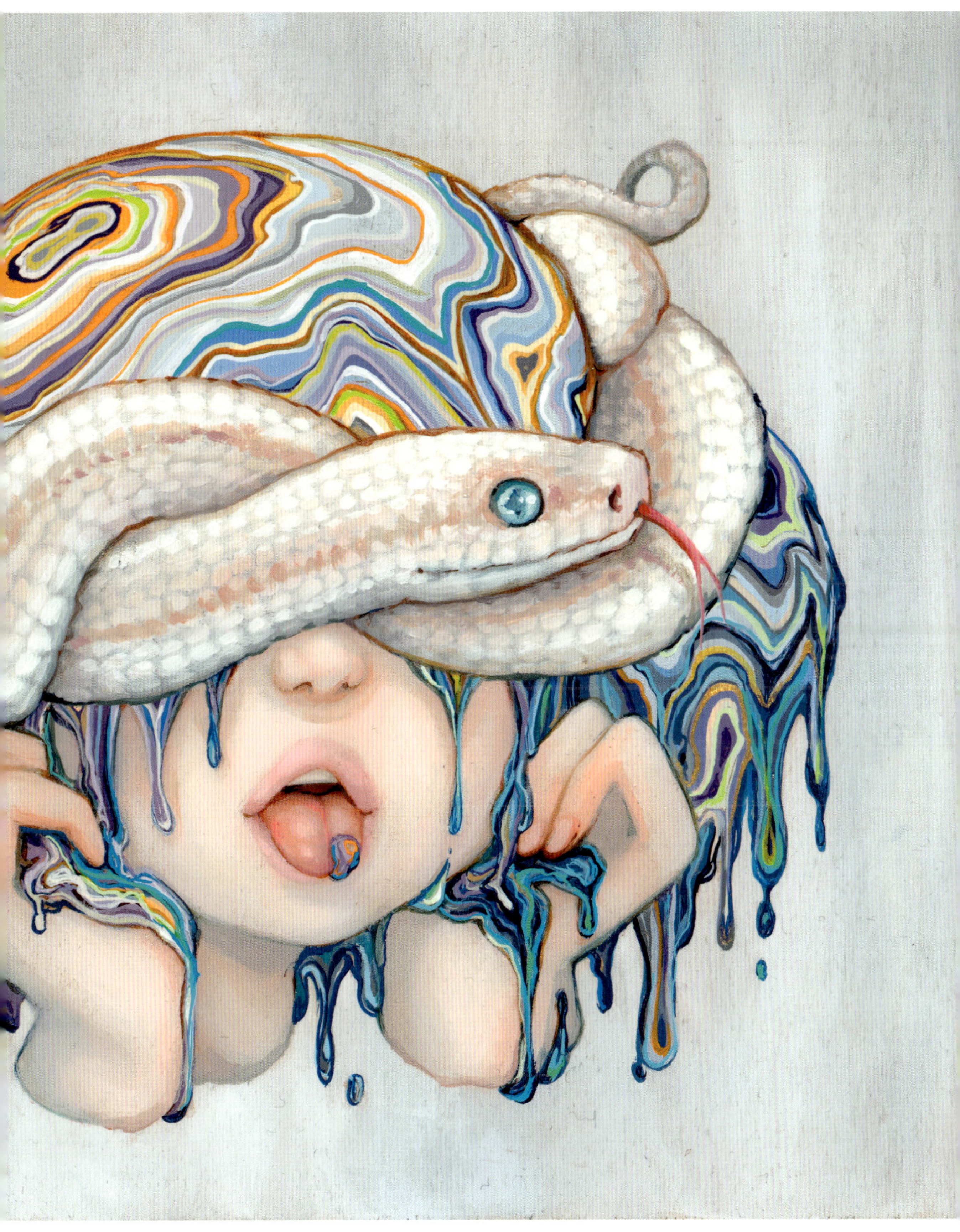

05

Alex Gross

アレックス・グロス（アメリカ USA）

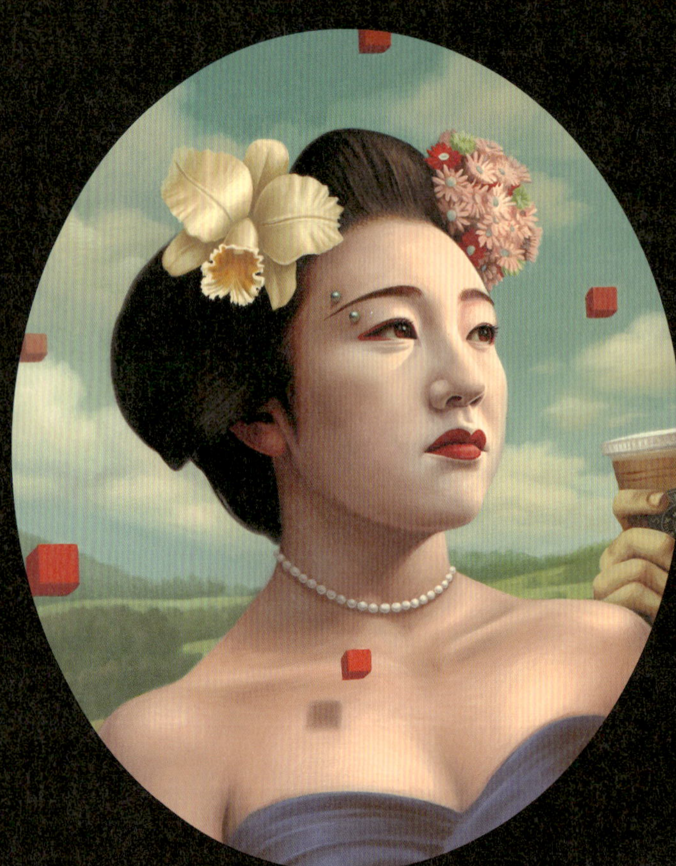

ニューヨーク生まれの画家。1999年以降は主に展覧会に出品する作品を制作。作品はトルコからオーストラリアまで、世界中で重要なコレクションに位置づけられている。2000年国際交流基金の日本研究フェローシップを授与され、日本で2か月間調査研究活動を行った。アートセンター・カレッジ・オブ・デザインで11年間教えていた経験もある。妻と3歳になる息子とロサンゼルスに在住。

Alex Gross is a painter who was born in New York. Since 1999, he has been doing work primarily for gallery exhibition. His work has been placed in important collections across the globe, from Turkey to Australia. Alex was the recipient of the Japan Foundation's Artist's fellowship in the year 2000 and spent two months doing research in Japan. He taught for eleven years at Art Center College of Design. He currently lives in Los Angeles with his wife and three year old son.

www.alexgross.com

↑ Product Placement (detail) プロダクト・プレイスメント（部分）
油彩, カンヴァス／H81.28×W86.36cm／2011
→Mona Lisa モナ・リザ（部分）
油彩, 木製パネル／H121.92×W91.44cm／2018

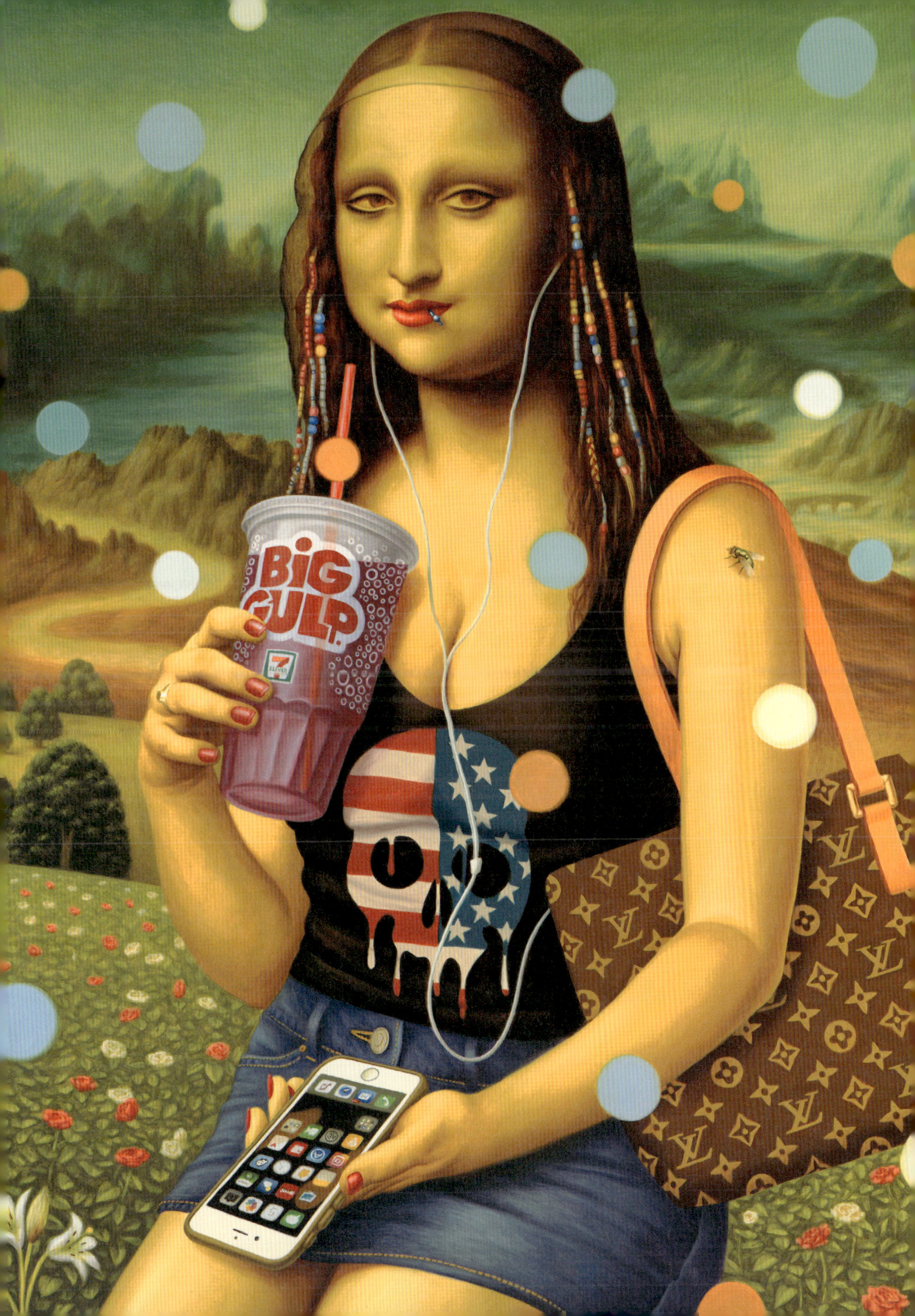

BiG GULP
7-ELEVEN
LV

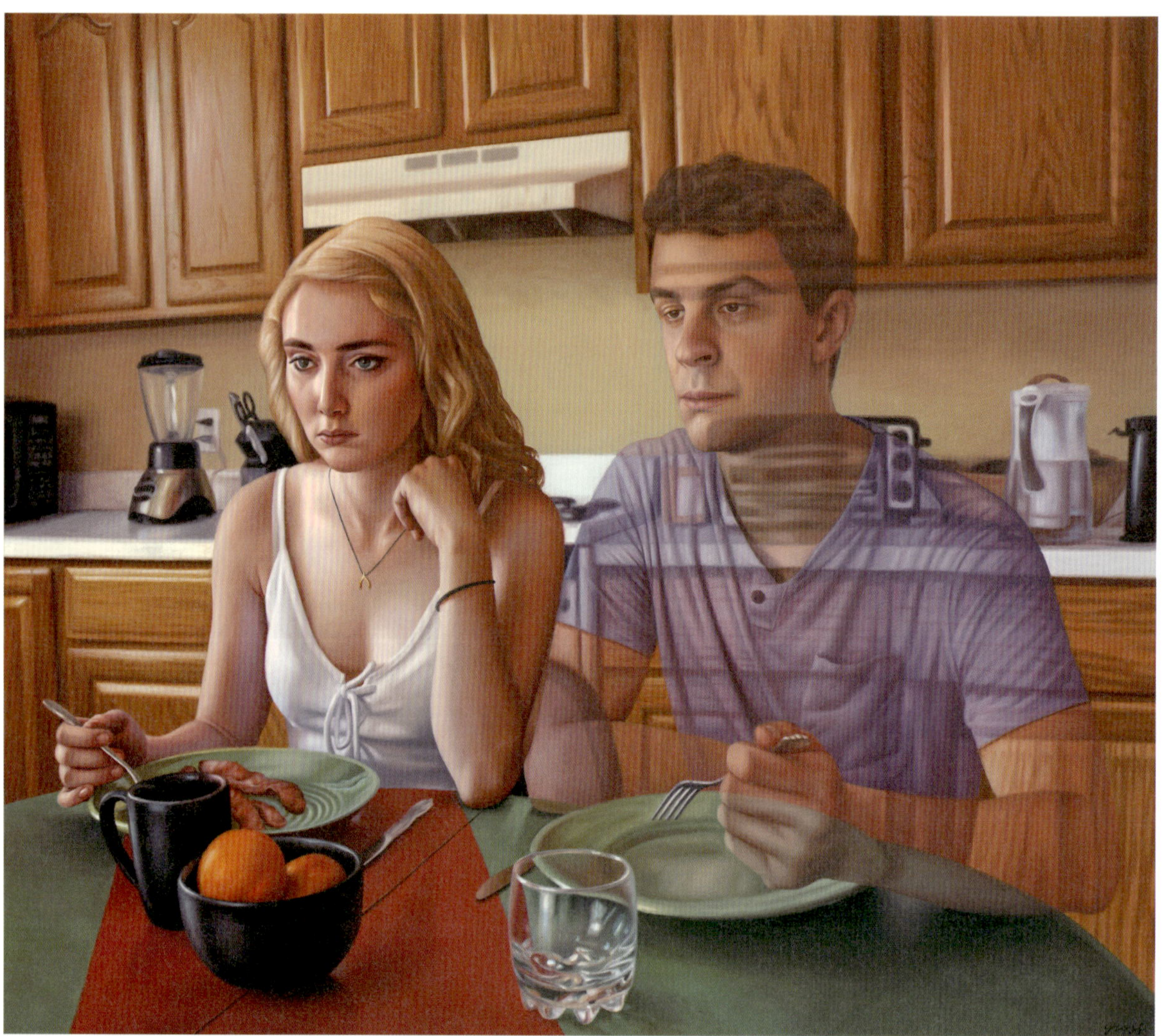

The Meal 食事
油彩、カンヴァス / H73.66×W83.82cm / 2016

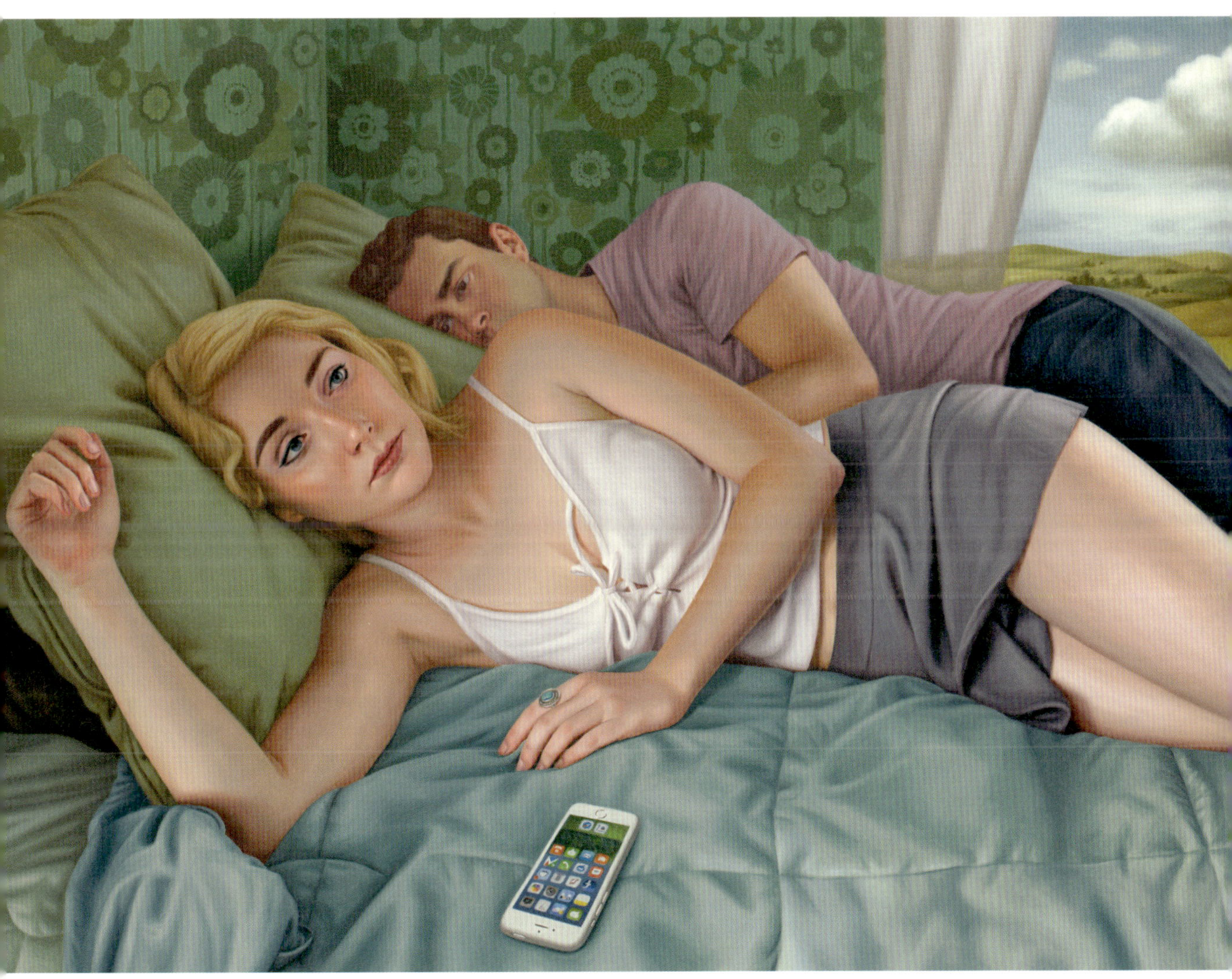

Suspicion 疑い
油彩、カンヴァス / H88.9×W121.92cm / 2016

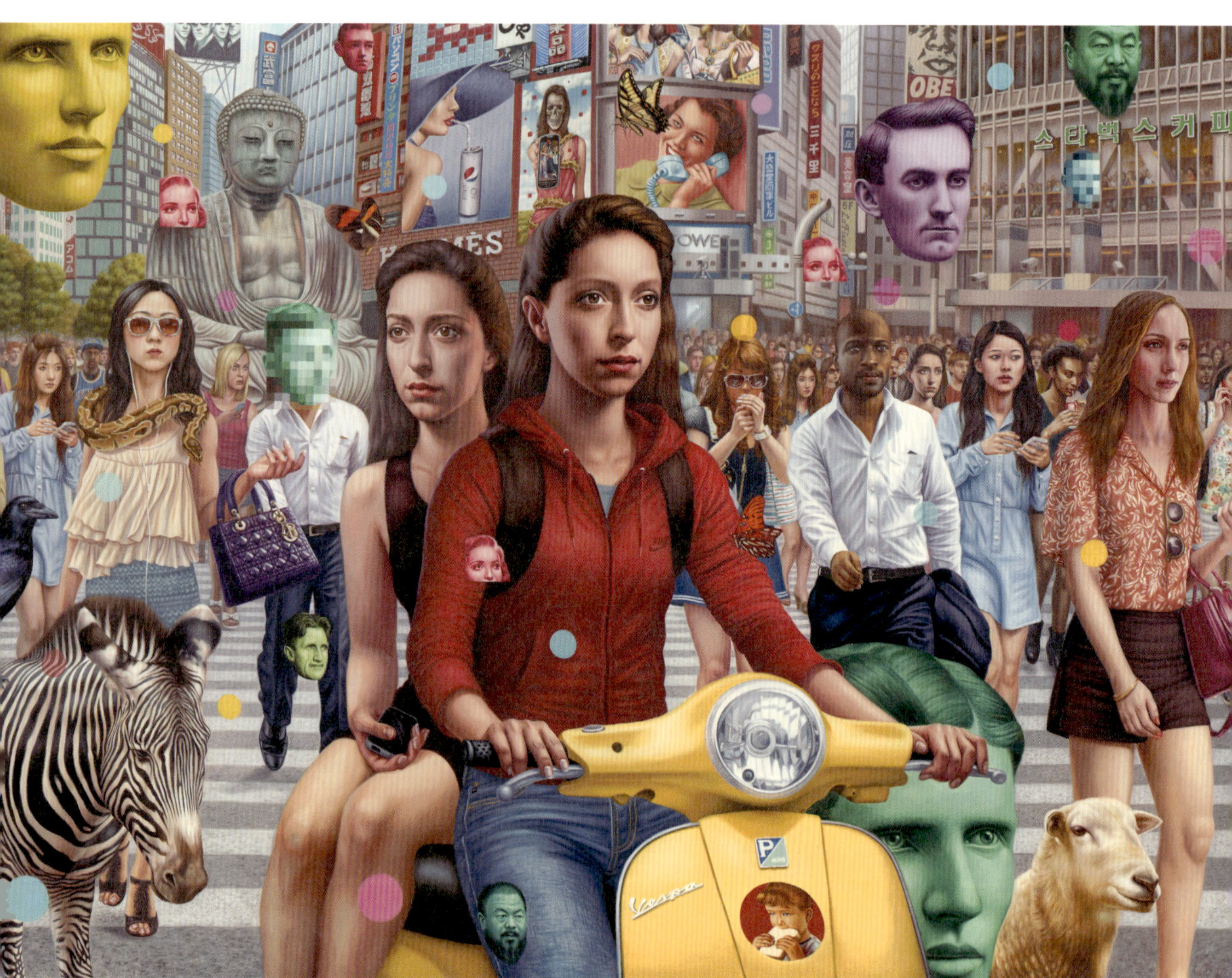

Twins 双子
油彩、カンヴァス / H198.12×W299.72cm / 2013

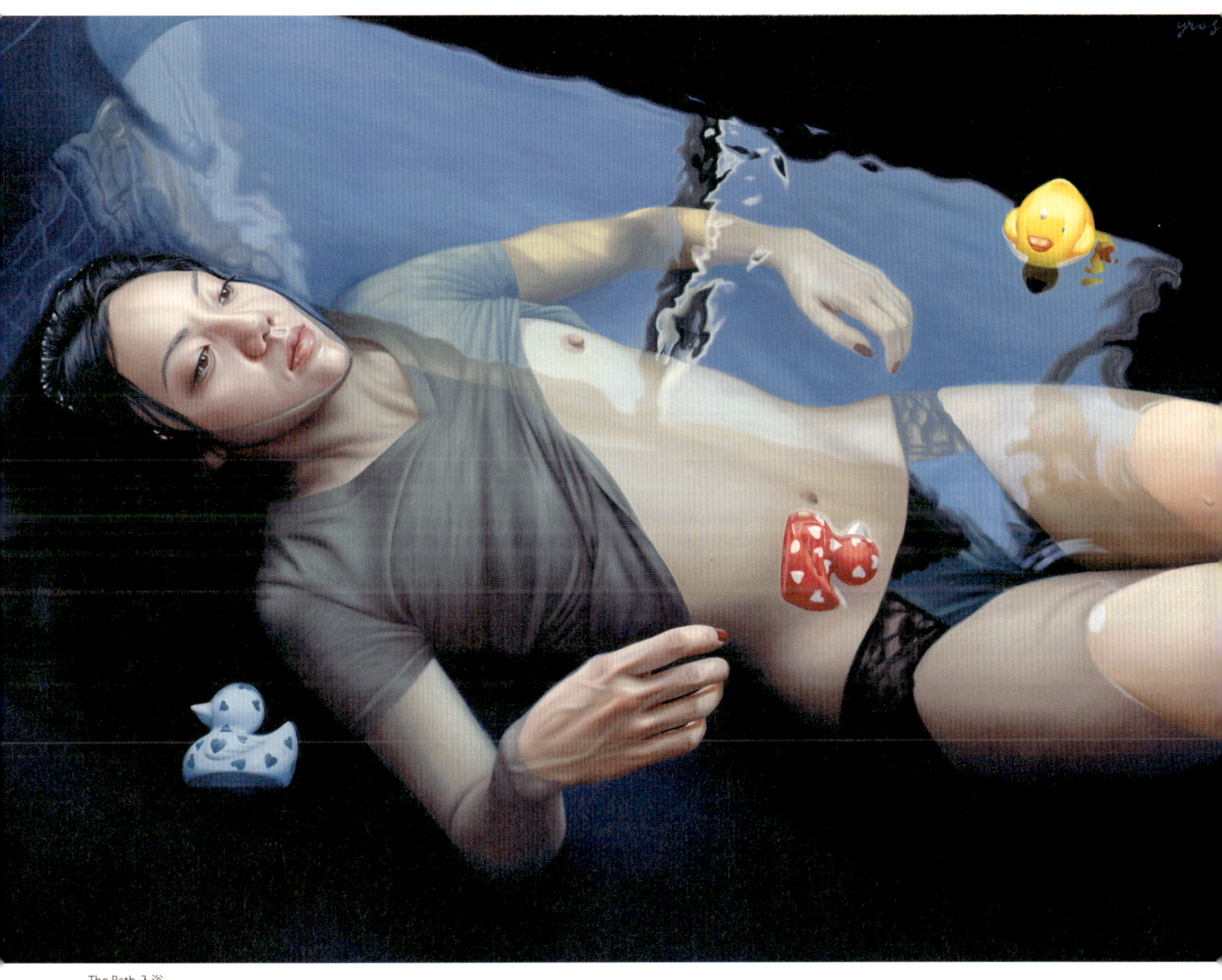

The Bath 入浴
油彩、カンヴァス / H83.82×W114.3cm / 2015

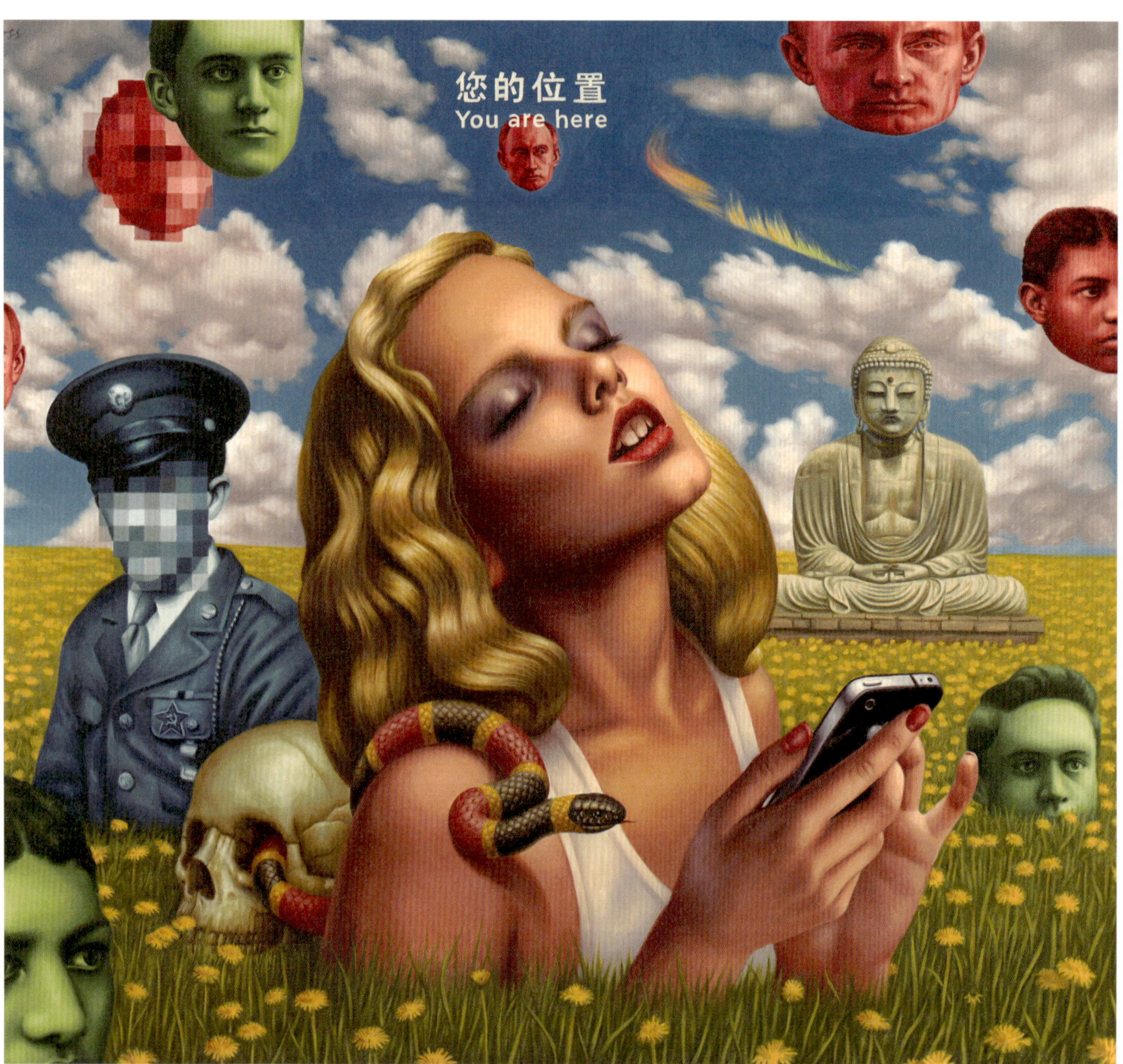

The Devil's Rainbow 悪魔の虹
油彩、カンヴァス / H78.74×W86.36cm / 2012

Contemplation（Slurpee）沈思（スラーピー）
油彩、カンヴァス / H106.68×W81.28cm / 2016

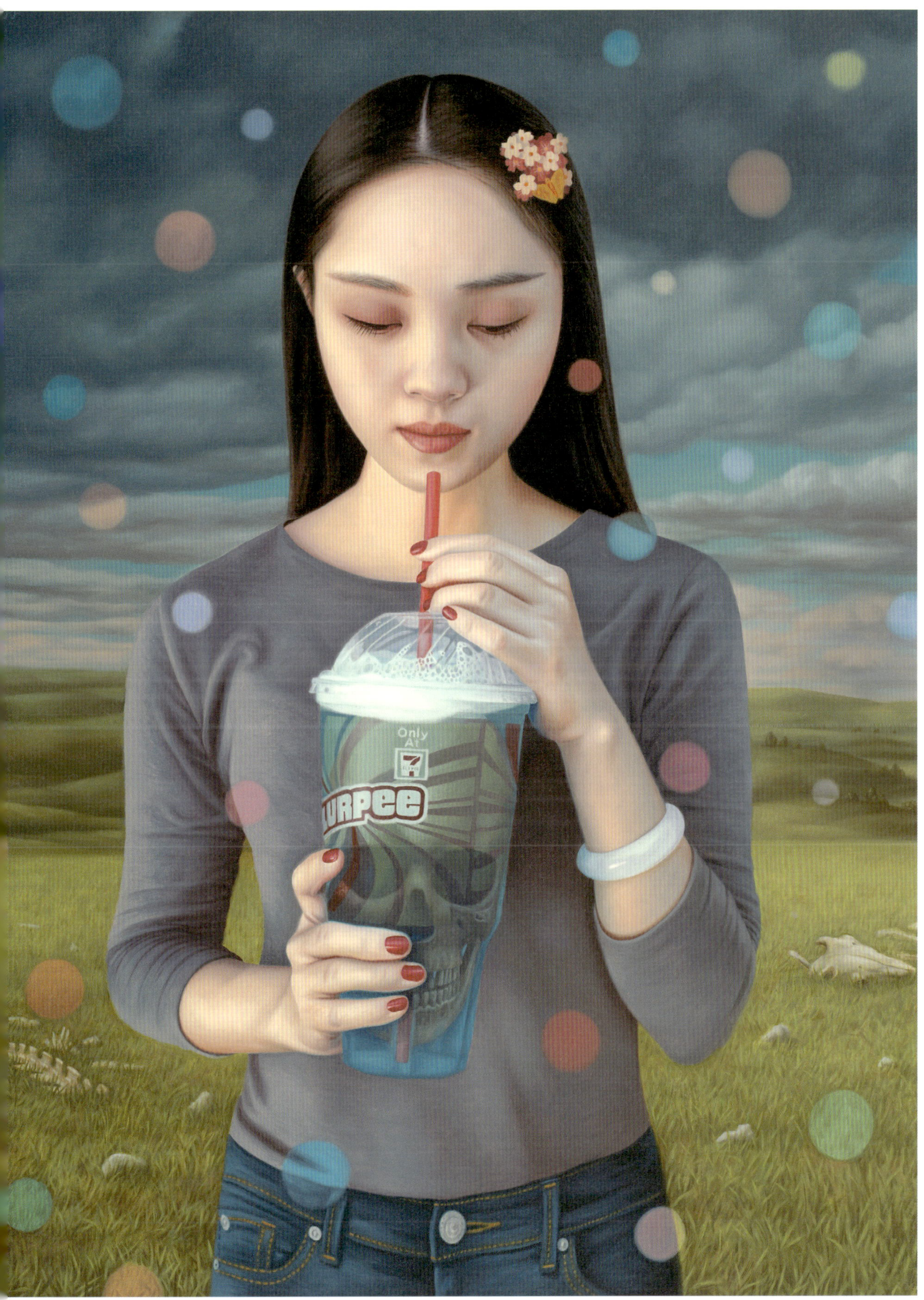
Only At
7-ELEVEN
SLURPEE

06

Dan Quintana

ダン・キンタナ（アメリカ USA）

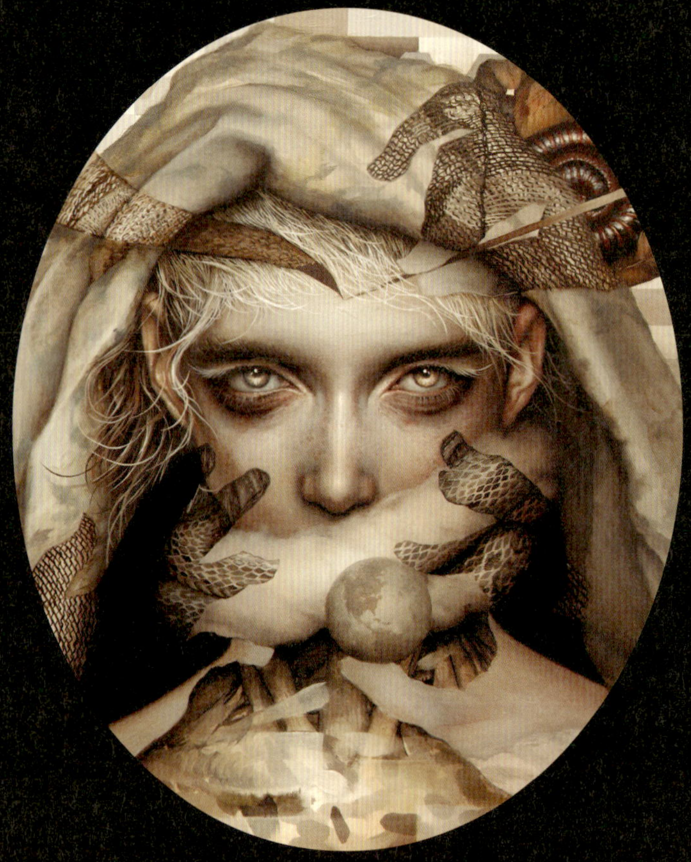

1982年生まれ。ロサンゼルスを拠点に活動。鋭いまなざしを特徴とする美女の幻想的な肖像画を描く。シュルレアリスム的な背景、神秘的なモチーフ、それを最大限に生かす不気味な構図が見る人を惹きつけ、魅了する。ストリート・アート時代の写実的で大胆な表現から、絵画的で抽象的な表現へと変わっていくと同時に作品も進化した。キンタナが表現する女性は小鬼、猛獣、人生に待ち受ける落とし穴や苦難をものともしない人間の勇気の象徴が多数描かれたヒエロニムス・ボス的で幻想的な風景の中に存在する。女性たちの力強い瞳は、置かれた状況にただ耐えているわけではないことを示している。意志が感じられ、敵意に満ちた世界に生きる人間の弱さと強さの両方が映し出している。

Born in 1982, Los Angels CA based painter Dan Quintana paints hazy, ethereal portraits o f beautiful women with piercing eyes. His dreamlike environments and mysterious subjects culminate in erie compositions, intriguing and captivating viewers. His works have evolved as he has evolved as an artist. The graphic in-your-face sensibility from his street art days has moved toward the more ethereal and deeply layered with splashes of painterly abstraction. His female figurative now exist in an abstracted Boschian landscapes rife with leering gremlins and bold fauna, symbols of humanity's courage in the face of the ever-present pitfalls and pains of life. The intensity in the eyes of Quintana's figures makes it known that they are not passively enduring their surroundings. Their will shines through, reflecting both the vulnerability and strength of humanity in the face of a hostile world.

danquintana.com

↑Nova ノヴァ（部分）
油彩、木製パネル／H30.48×W30.48cm／2014

→Polyps ポリープ（部分）
油彩、木製パネル／H121.92×W76.2cm／2017

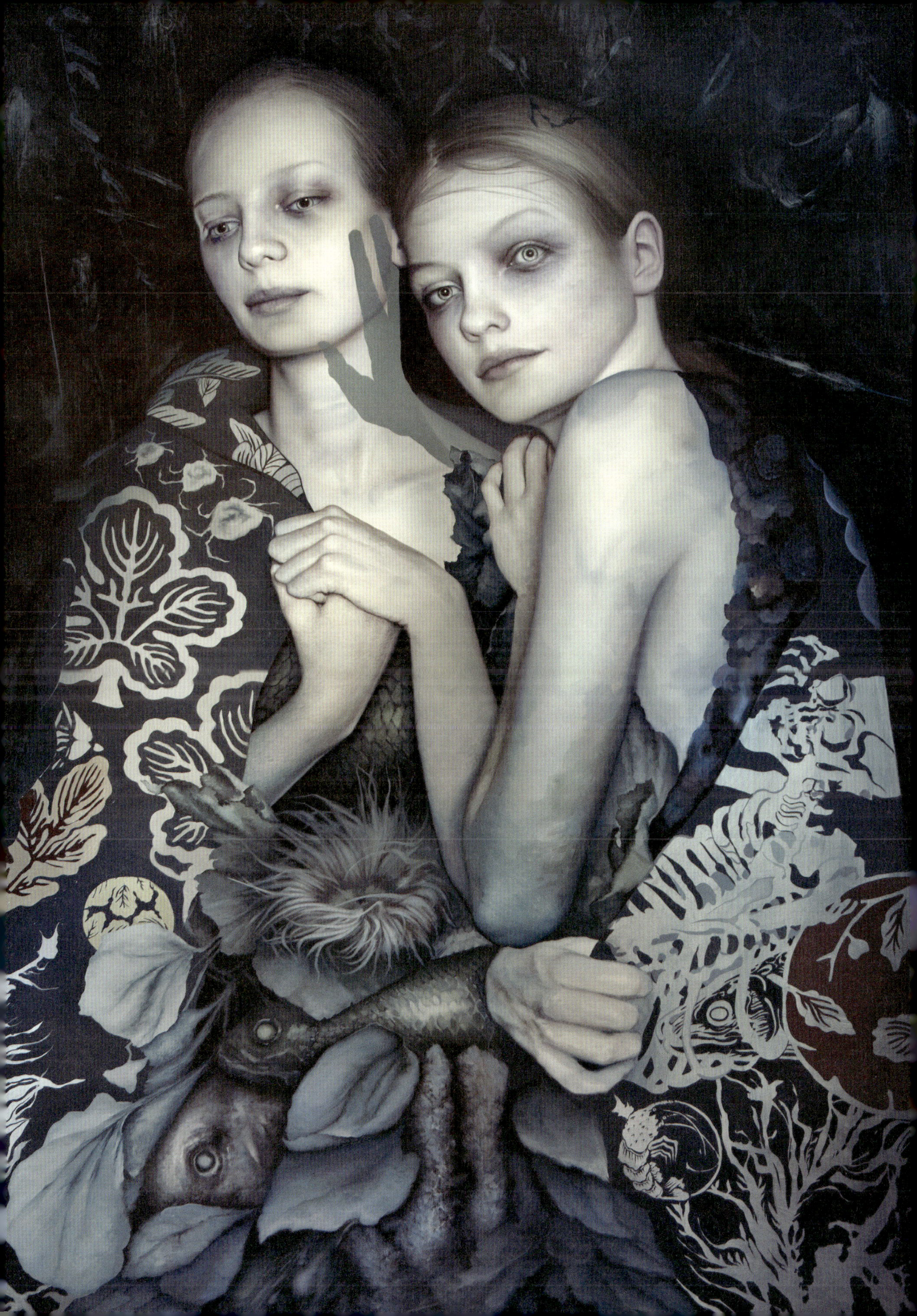

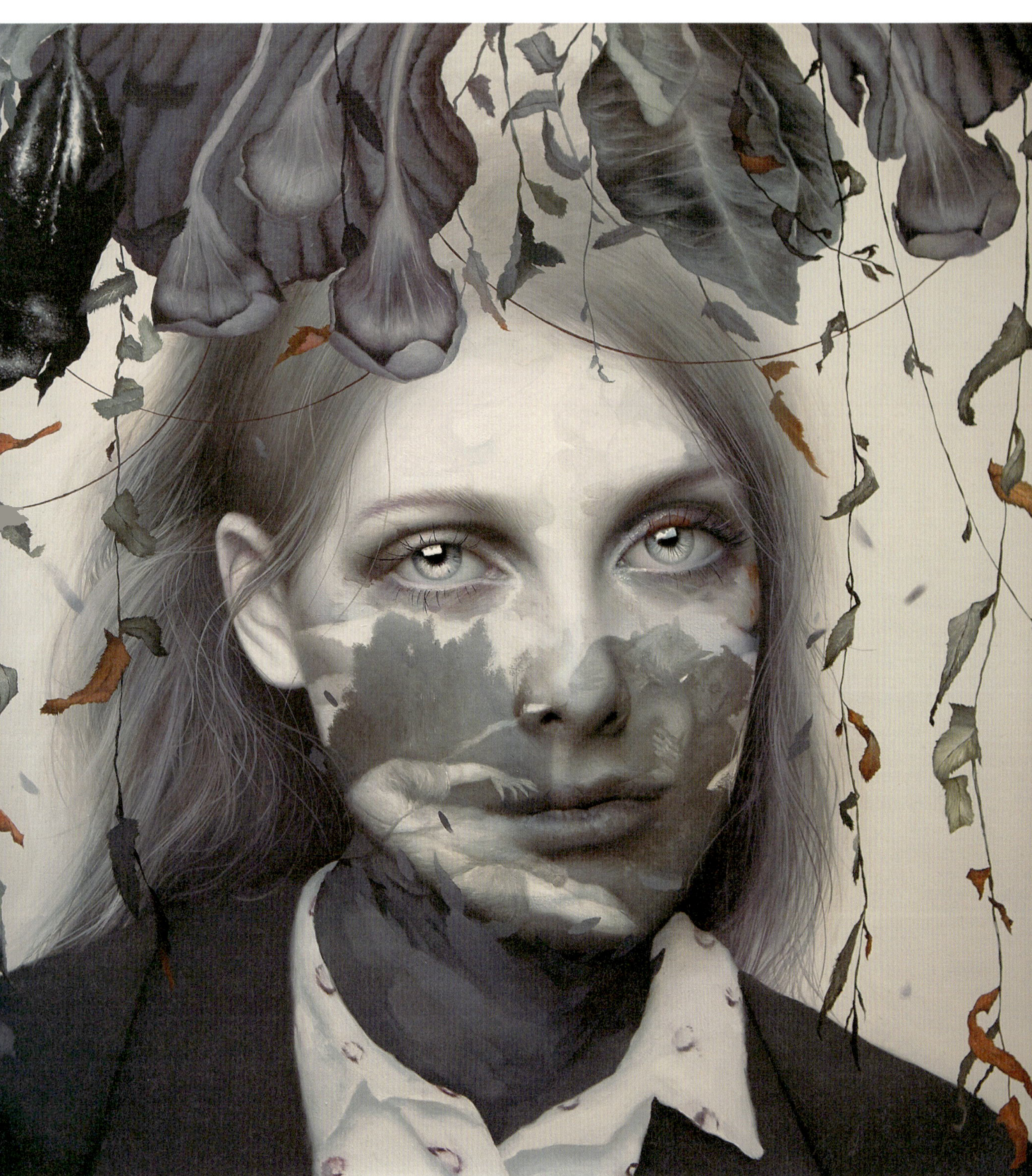

Monstrum 奇形
油彩、木製パネル / H30.48×W30.48cm / 2017

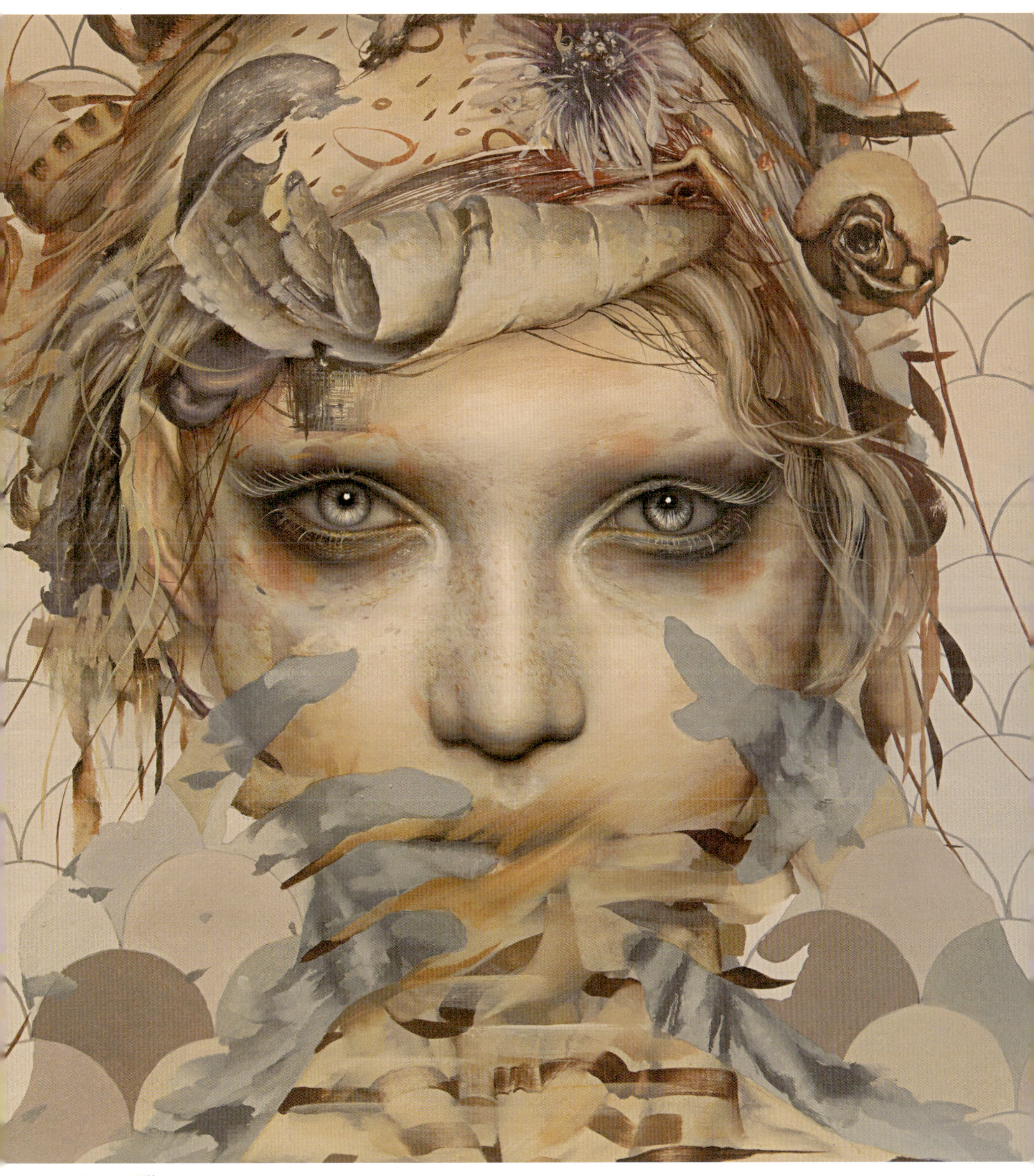

Frequencies 周波
油彩、木製パネル / H30.48×W30.48cm / 2015

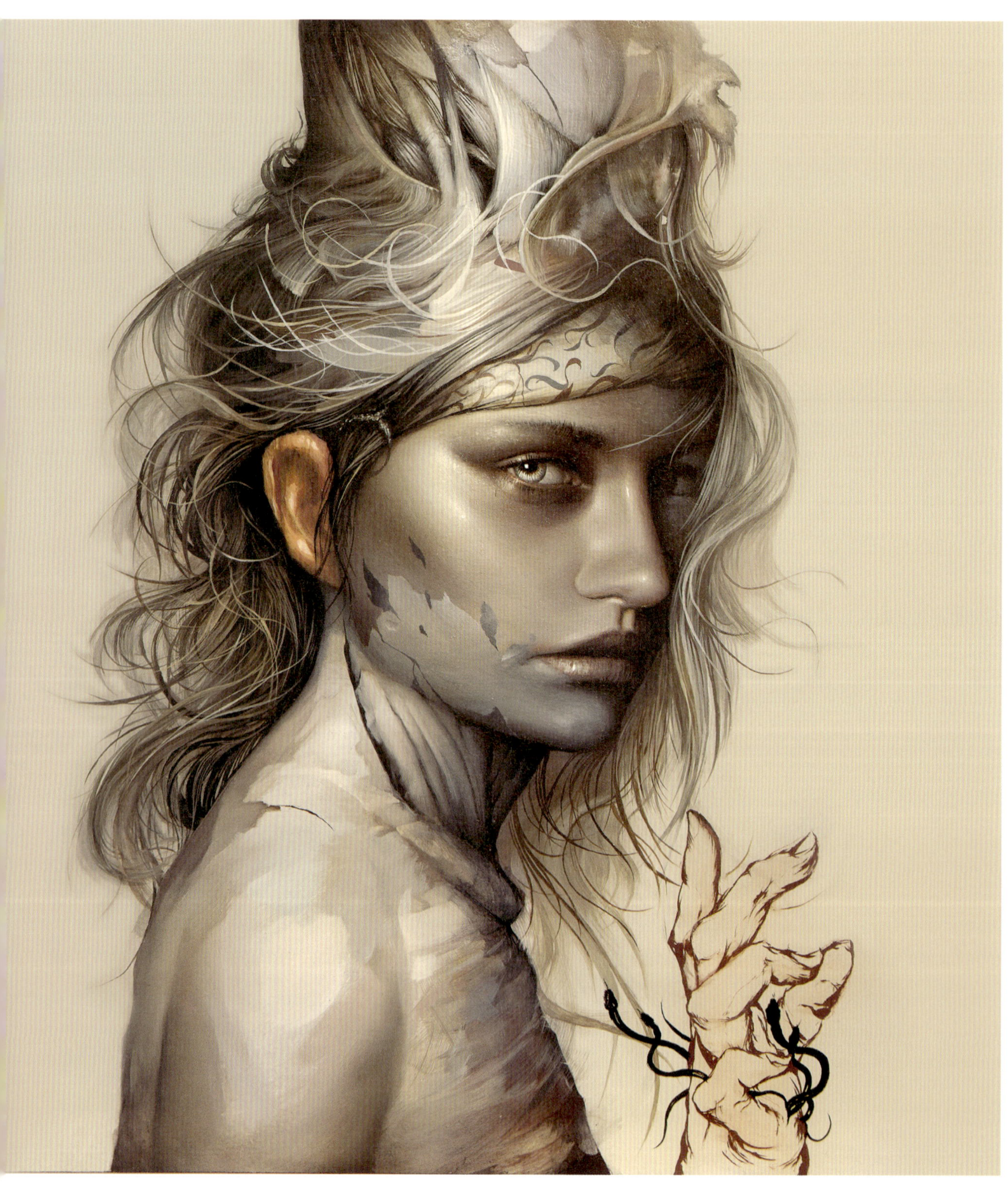

Spectre 3 亡霊3
油彩、木製パネル / H60.96×W45.72cm / 2014

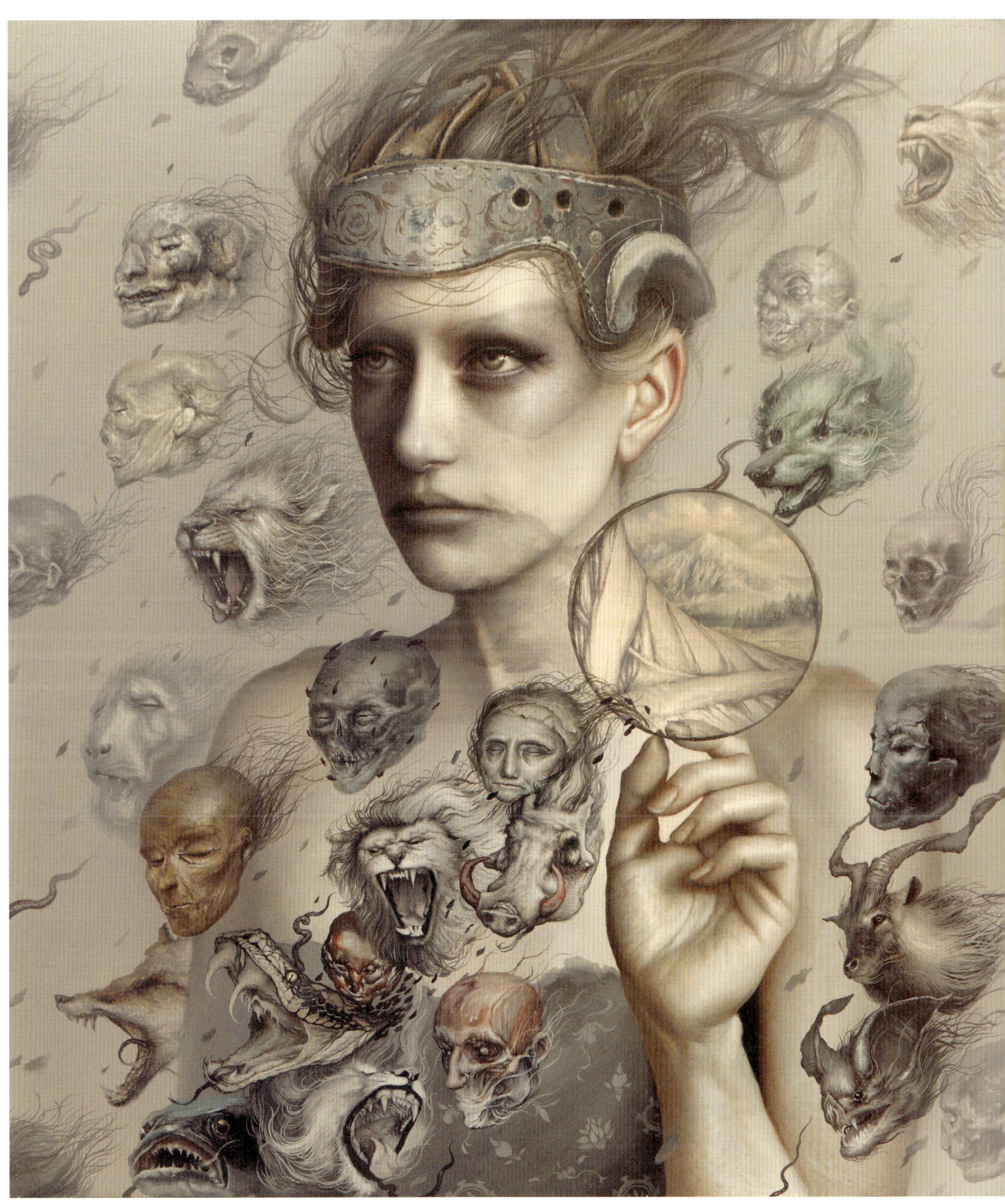

Forward 前へ
油彩、木製パネル / H60.96×W45.72cm / 2015

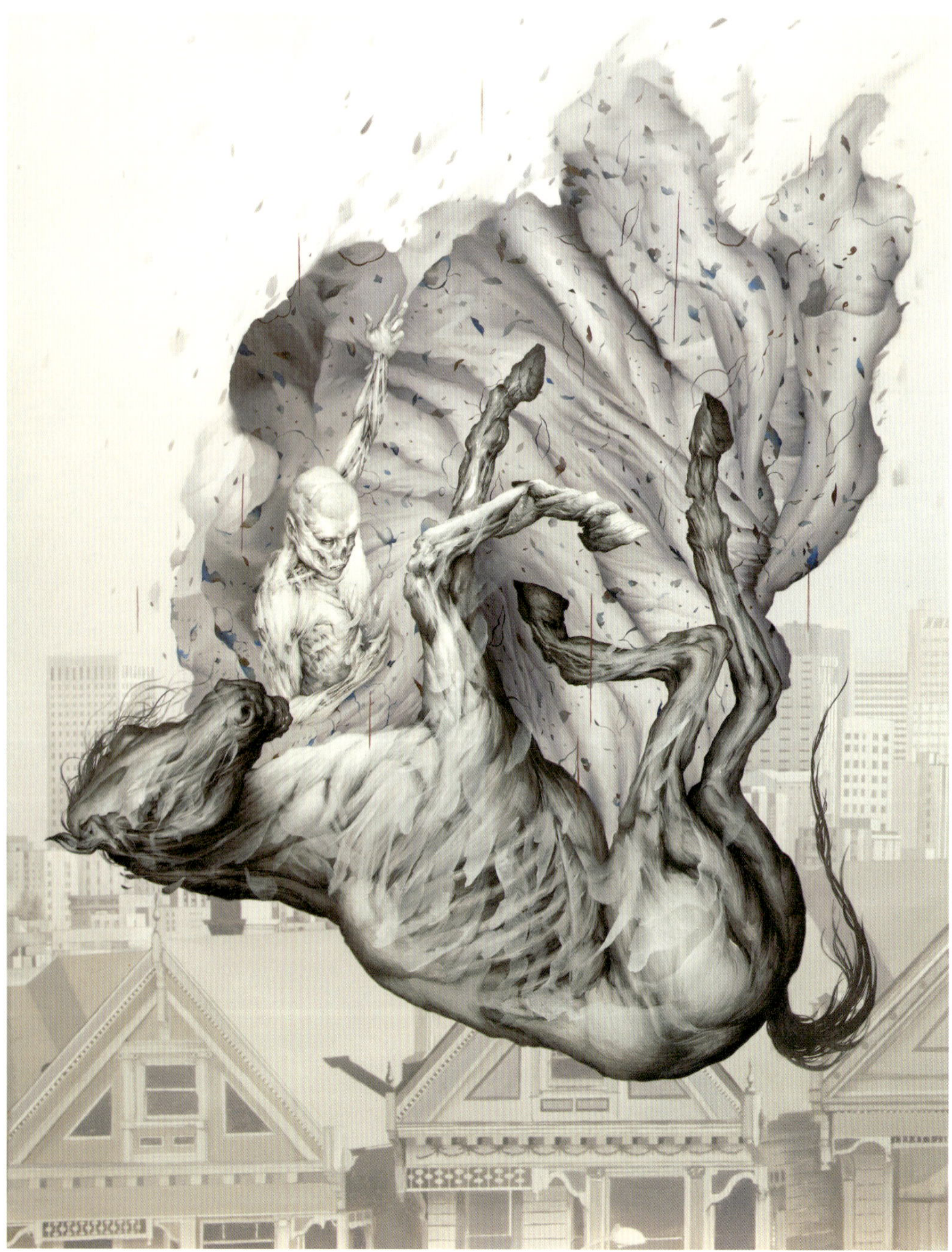

Mayfly かげろう
油彩、木製パネル / H60.96×W45.72cm / 2015

Zero Instruments ゼロ・インストゥルメンツ
油彩、木製パネル / H121.92×W76.2cm / 2013

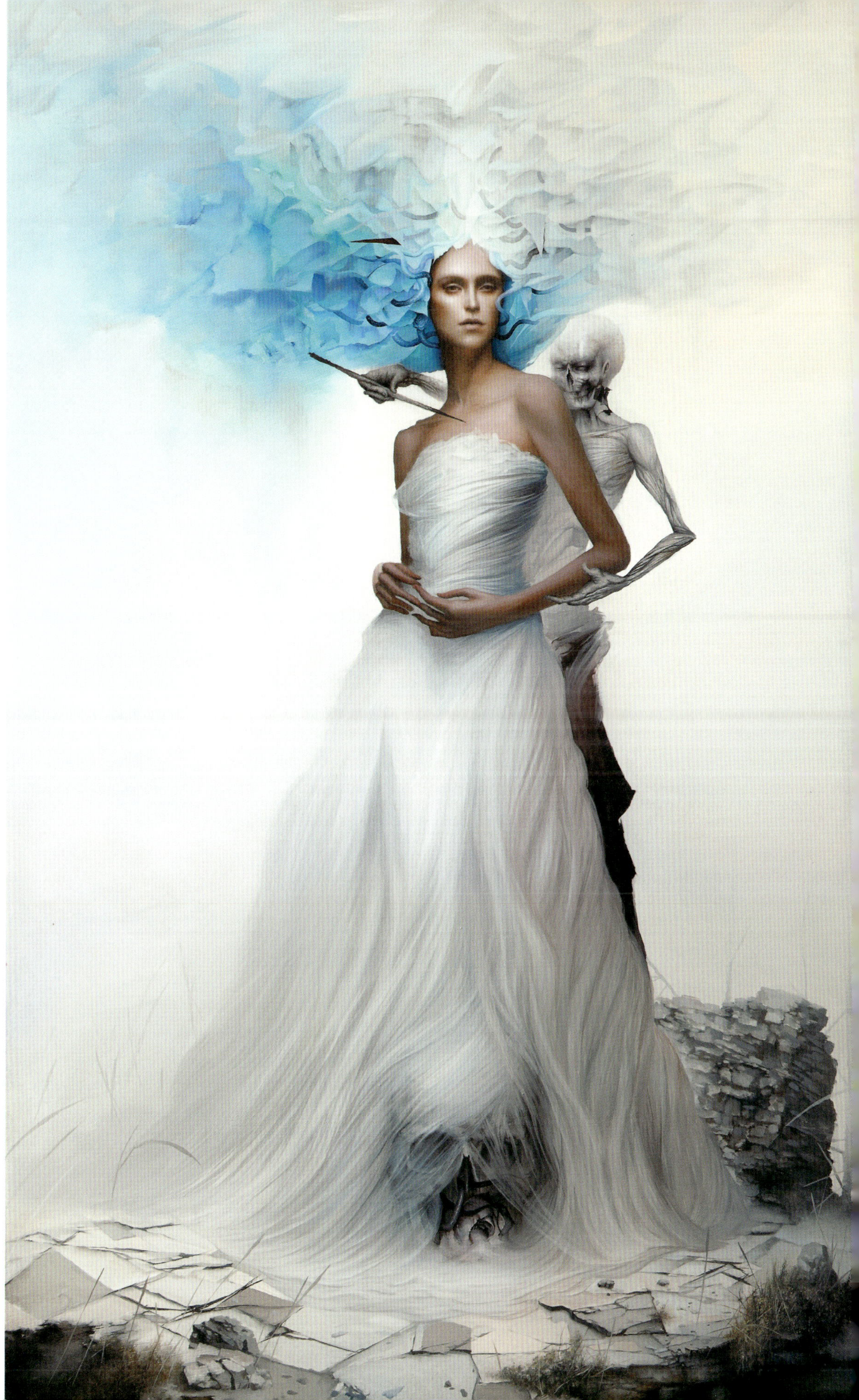

07

Rodrigo Luff

ロドリゴ・ラフ（オーストラリア　Australia）

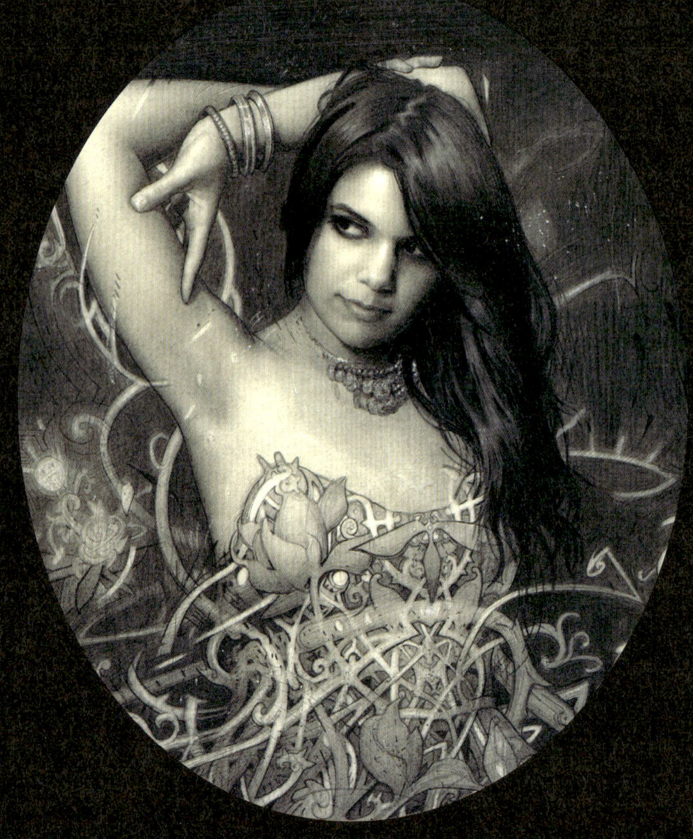

オーストラリアのアーティスト。フクロウ、鳥、自然界の生きものがあふれる幻想的な背景に女性や裸体を描き、耽美で超自然的な世界観の創造を目指す。2006-09年、シドニーのジュリアン・アシュトン・アートスクールに在学。その後、アメリカで4回個展を開催。ロサンゼルス、ニューヨーク、サンフランシスコのギャラリーや美術館のグループ展、ベルリン、メルボルンの国際的な展覧会にも参加している。年に1度、スポーク・アートギャラリーで開催される展覧会、モレスキン・プロジェクトの共同キュレーターも務める。同展は今年7年目を迎え、ニュー・コンテンポラリー・アートを牽引にする有望なアーティストの作品を紹介している。

Rodrigo Luff is an Australian artist who creates ethereal figurative works of women and nudes in beautiful dreamlike settings. His works are ornate and lush, replete with owls, birds and creatures in the natural world. He explores a feeling of the otherworldly by capturing his subjects dwelling in a mysterious, imaginative atmosphere. Luff studied at the Julian Ashton Art School in Sydney from 2006 to 2009. Since then he has had four solo exhibitions, working mostly with Thinkspace and Spoke Art Galleries in the U.S.A. His work has been shown through regular group exhibitions in galleries and museums across the U.S.A in cities such as Los Angeles, New York, San Francisco and international shows in Berlin and Melbourne. He is also the co-curator of the annual Moleskine Project exhibitions at Spoke Art Gallery, now in the seventh year, which features artwork from some of the brightest artists in the new contemporary art movement.

www.rodluff.com

↑Weave 模様（部分）
鉛筆、紙 / H28×W35.5cm / 2013

→Nectar 花蜜
鉛筆、紙 / H53.3×W33cm / 2013

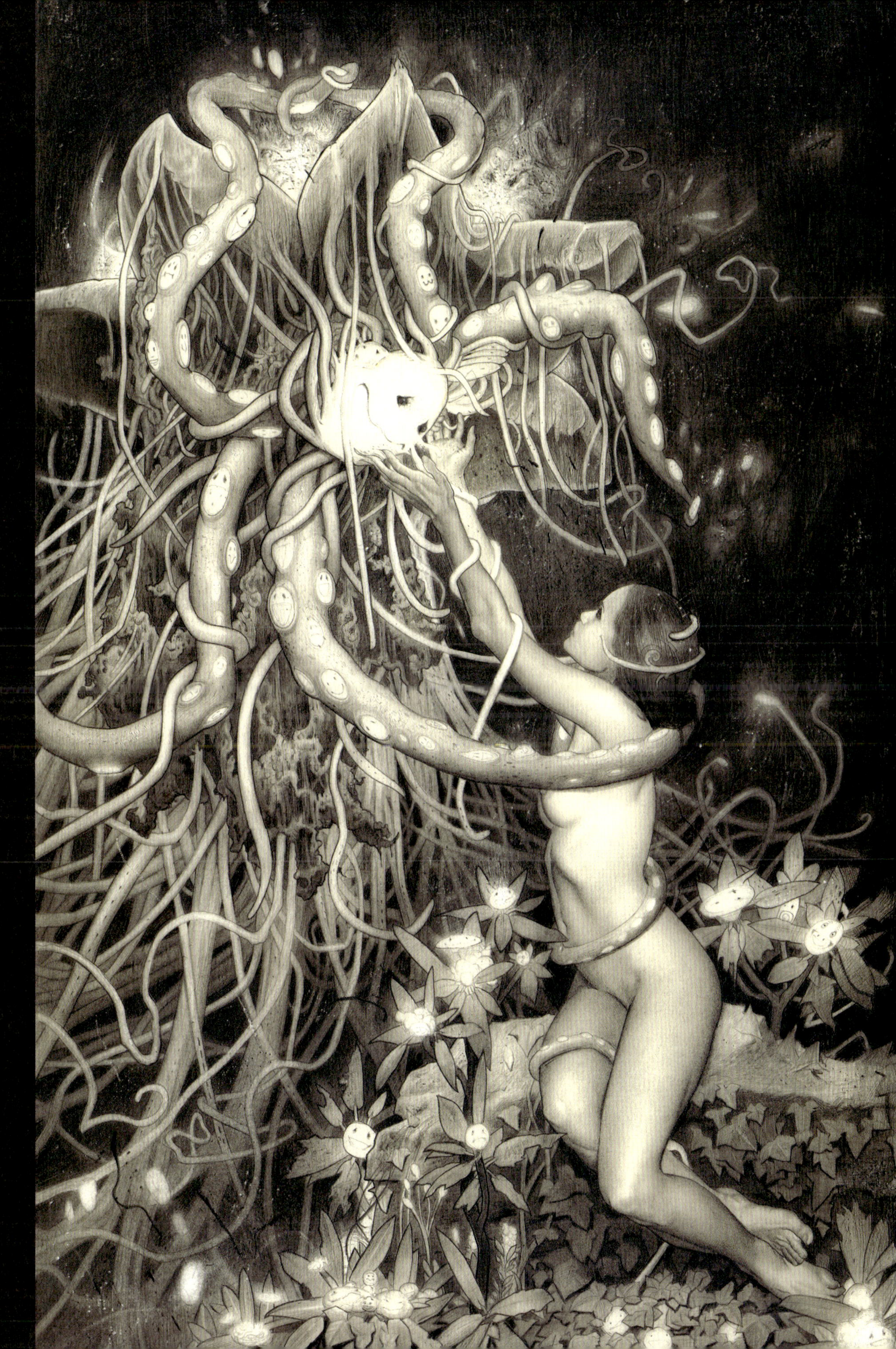

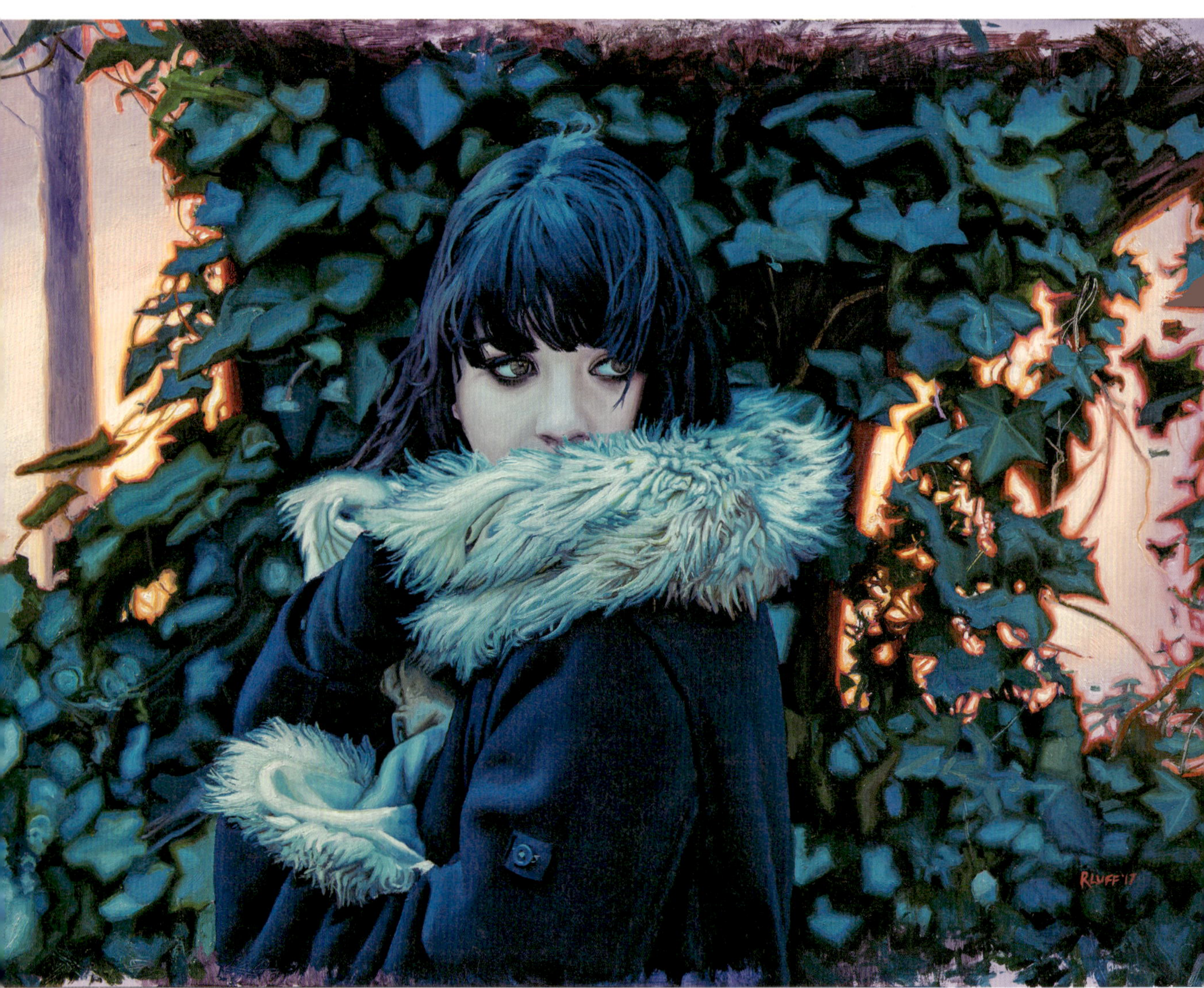

Arboreal Shadow 樹木の影
油彩、パネル / H30.5×W40.6cm / 2017

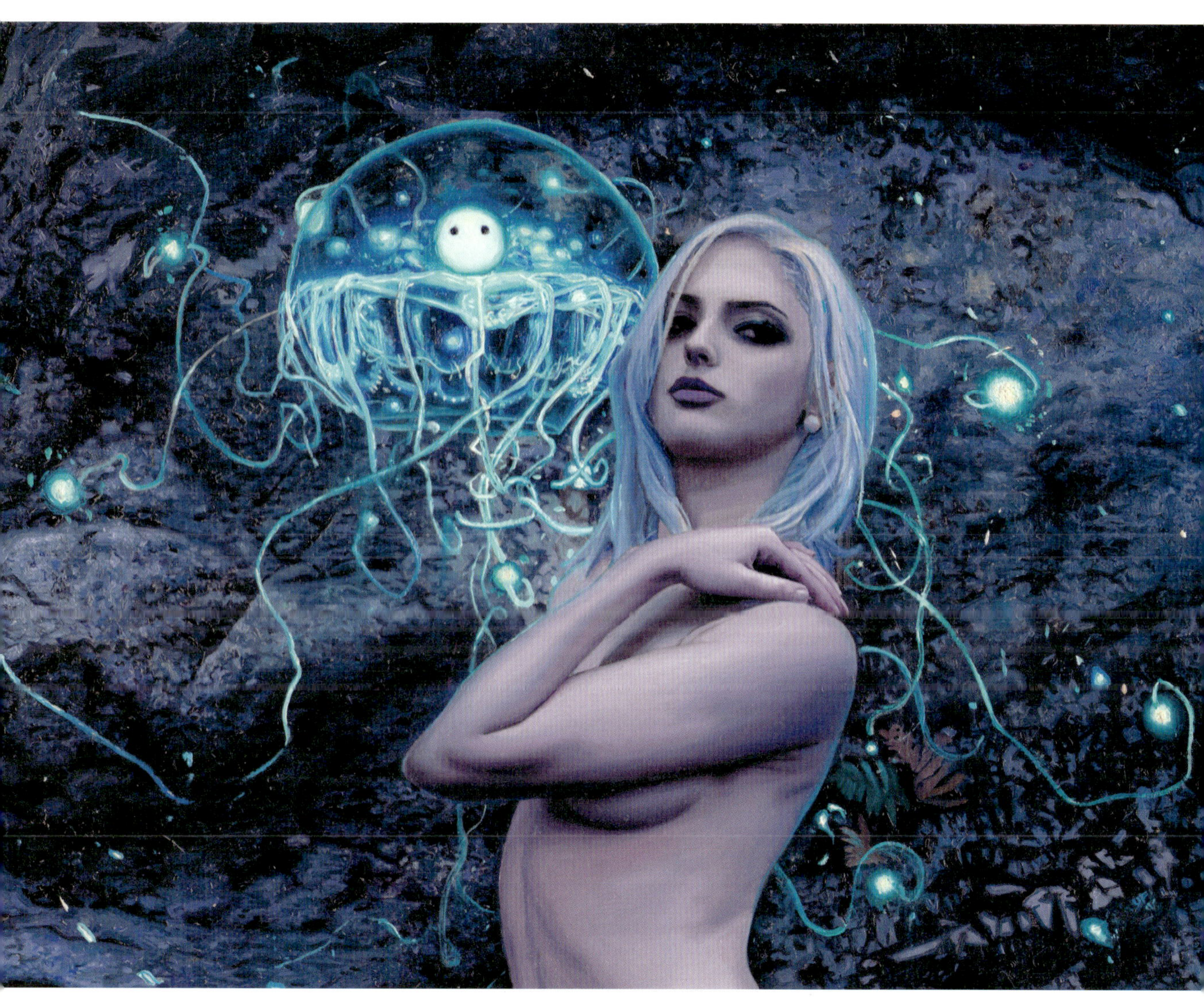

Plasma プラズマ
油彩、パネル / H22.8×W30.4cm / 2016

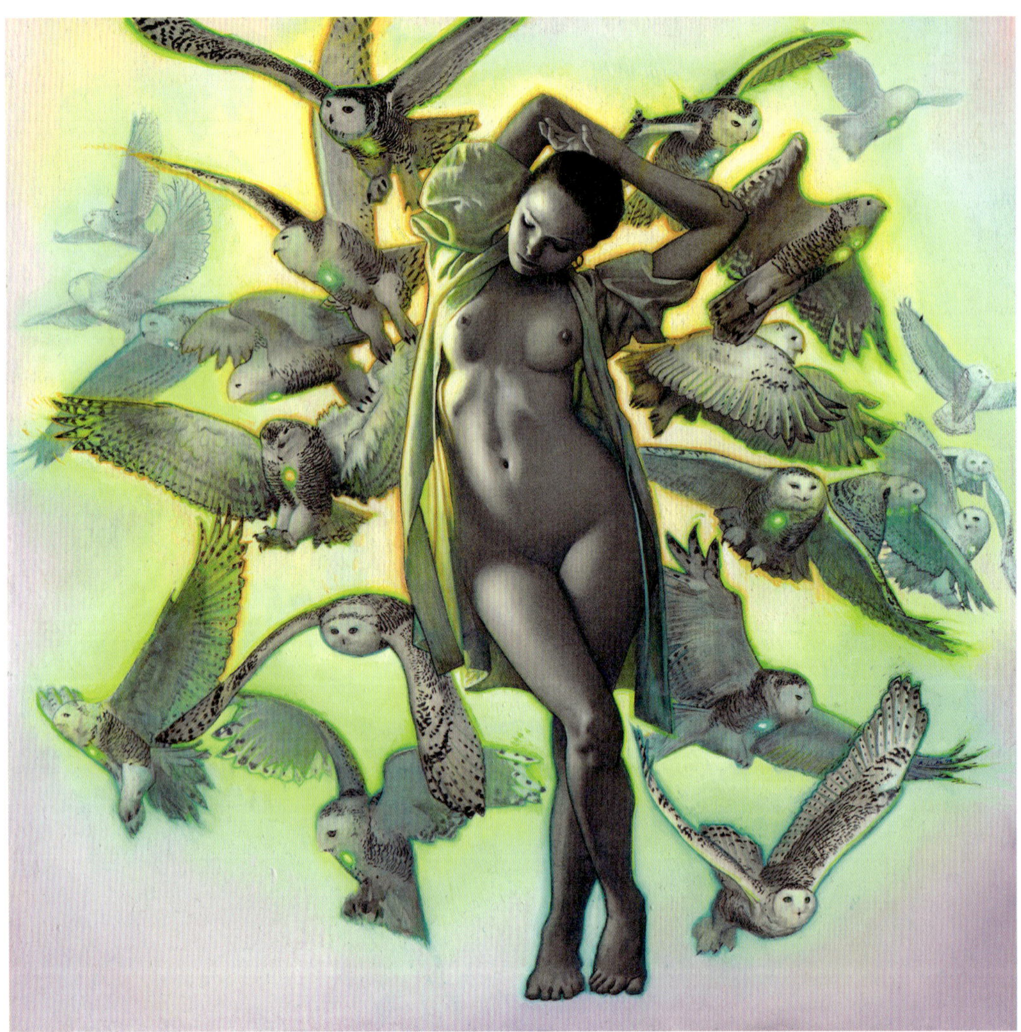

Inward Spin インワード・スピン
鉛筆、水墨、油彩、紙 / H40.6×W40.6cm / 2015

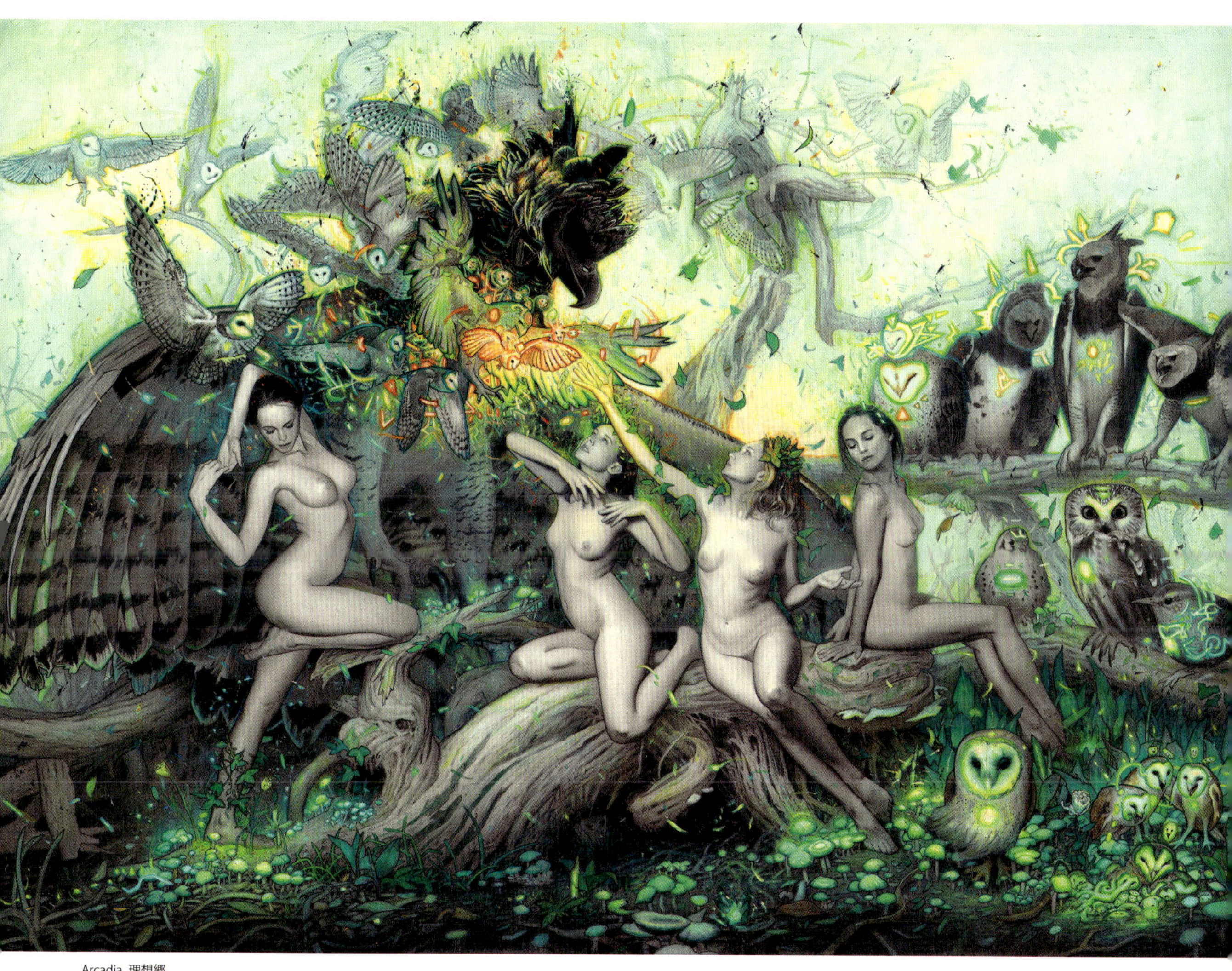

Arcadia 理想郷
鉛筆、水墨、油彩、紙 / H45.7×W75cm / 2016

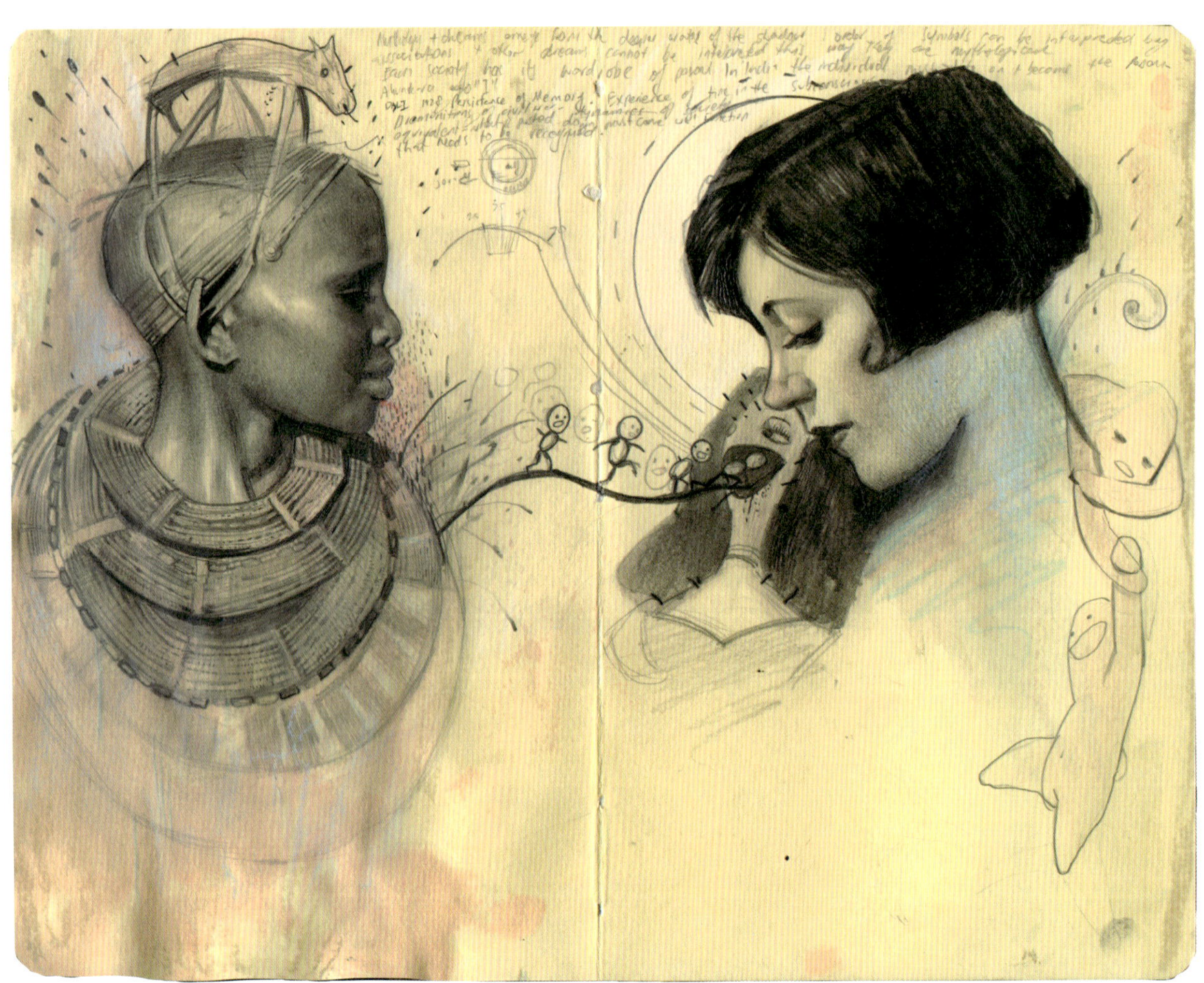

Vintage Sketch ヴィンテージ・スケッチ
鉛筆、アクリル、スケッチブックの紙 / H21×W26cm / 2011

Emergence 羽化
鉛筆、パステル、色鉛筆、アクリル、紙 / H55.8×W35.5cm / 2010

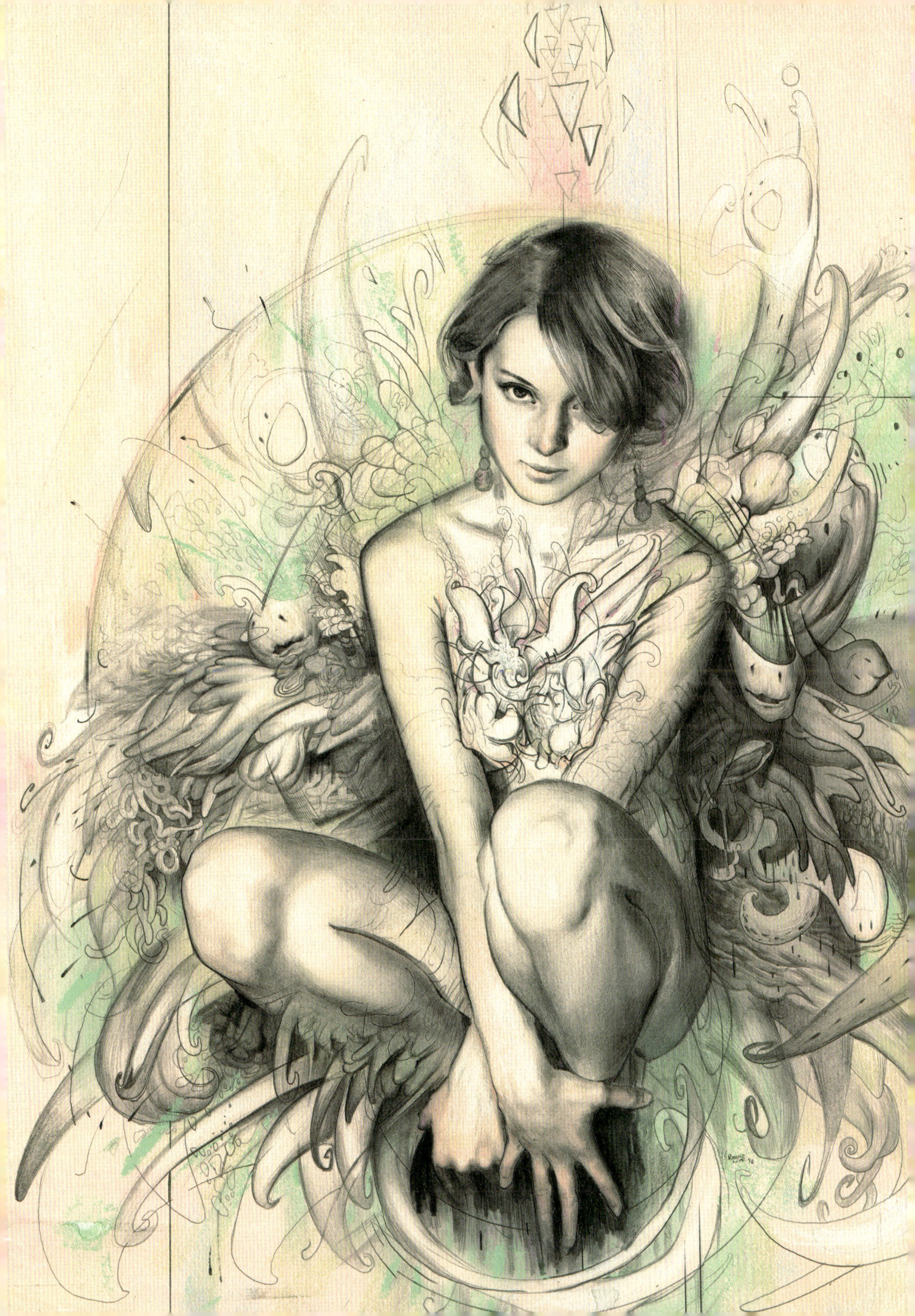

08

KCN

KCN（台湾 Taiwan）

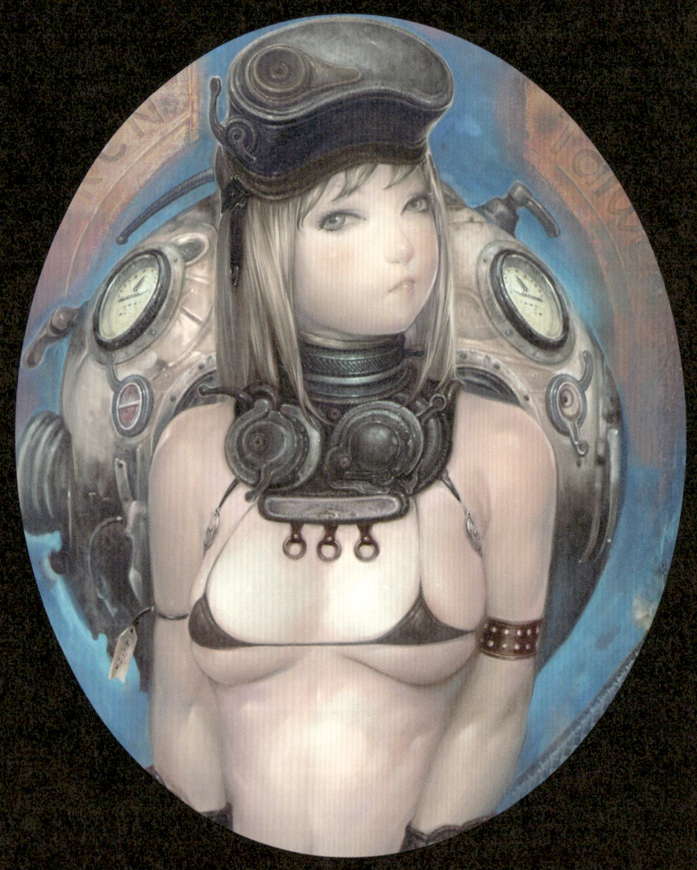

多元文化が織り交じる台湾に生まれ育つ。漫画、イラスト、美術デザインと幅広く手掛け、情熱的に独学で幼少時より制作を行う。KCNは科学元素を引き合いに出しながら、多文化社会の中で受けた直感的なフィーリングとその社会が孕む暗黒面を強調した世界観を創作する。座右の銘は「死ぬまで創作を続ける」である。2007年個展「周期表」、2010年「edge☆アニメとマンガ芸術展@台湾特展」、2011年虎の穴聯展「Taiwan Gallery 2011 in TORANOANA」、2012年個展「Taiwan YoutH」、2013年聯展「霊啓武徳印（れいけいぶとくいん）」、2016年「スチームパンク芸術：過去への未来世界 スペシャル展」、2016年個展「帝国の曙」出展。

Born and raised in the multicultural land of Taiwan, KCN, self-taught from a young age, has been passionately creating in a wide field including comics, illustrations, and art design. Drawing inspiration from scientific elements, KCN makes works reflective of the feeling one gets from a multicultural society and that emphasize the darker side of that society. KCN's motto is "I'll keep creating until I die." KCN's exhibitions include a 2007 solo exhibition "Periodic Table", "Edge: Anime and Manga Art Exhibit @ Taiwan Special Exhibit" in 2010, the group exhibit "Taiwan Gallery 2011 in Toranoana" in 2011, a solo exhibit "Taiwan Potassium Cyanide" in 2012, the group exhibit "Reikeibutokuin" in 2013, and "Steam Punk Art: Future World Heads to the Past - Special Exhibit" in 2016.

twitter @KCN27725878

↑S 硫黄（部分）
CGペインティング、Corel Painter / H7648×W4954pixel / 2015

→Rb ルビジウム
CGペインティング、Corel Painter / H4724×W3072pixel / 2015

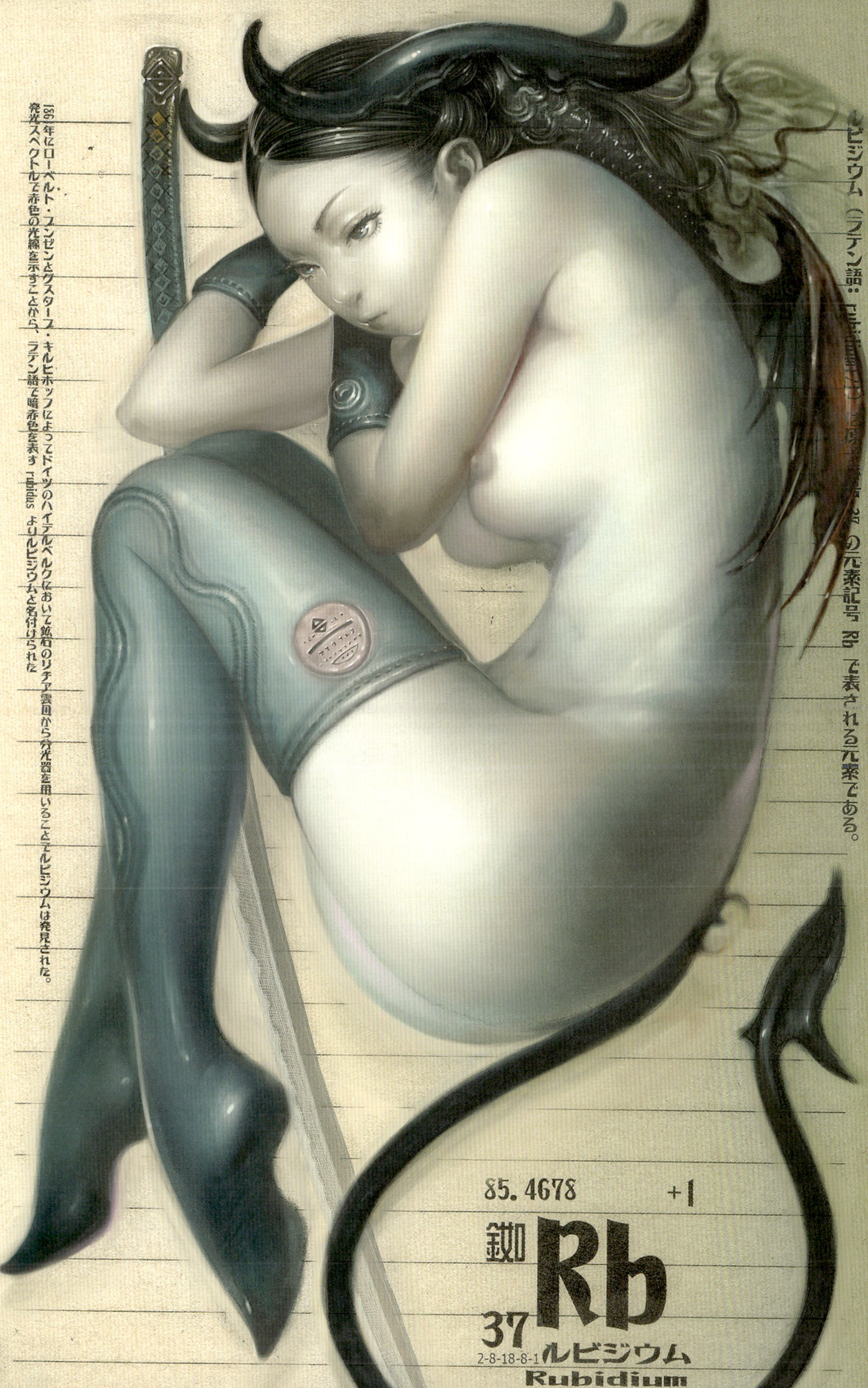

ルビジウム（ラテン語：「深い赤」）は原子番号37の元素記号 Rb で表される元素である。
1861年にローベルト・ブンゼンとグスタフ・キルヒホッフによってドイツのハイデルベルクにおいて鉱石のリチア雲母から分光器を用いることでルビジウムは発見された。発光スペクトルで赤色の光線を示すことから、ラテン語で暗赤色を表す「rubidus」よりルビジウムと名付けられた。
85.4678　　　+1
鉤　Rb
37　ルビジウム
2-8-18-8-1
Rubidium

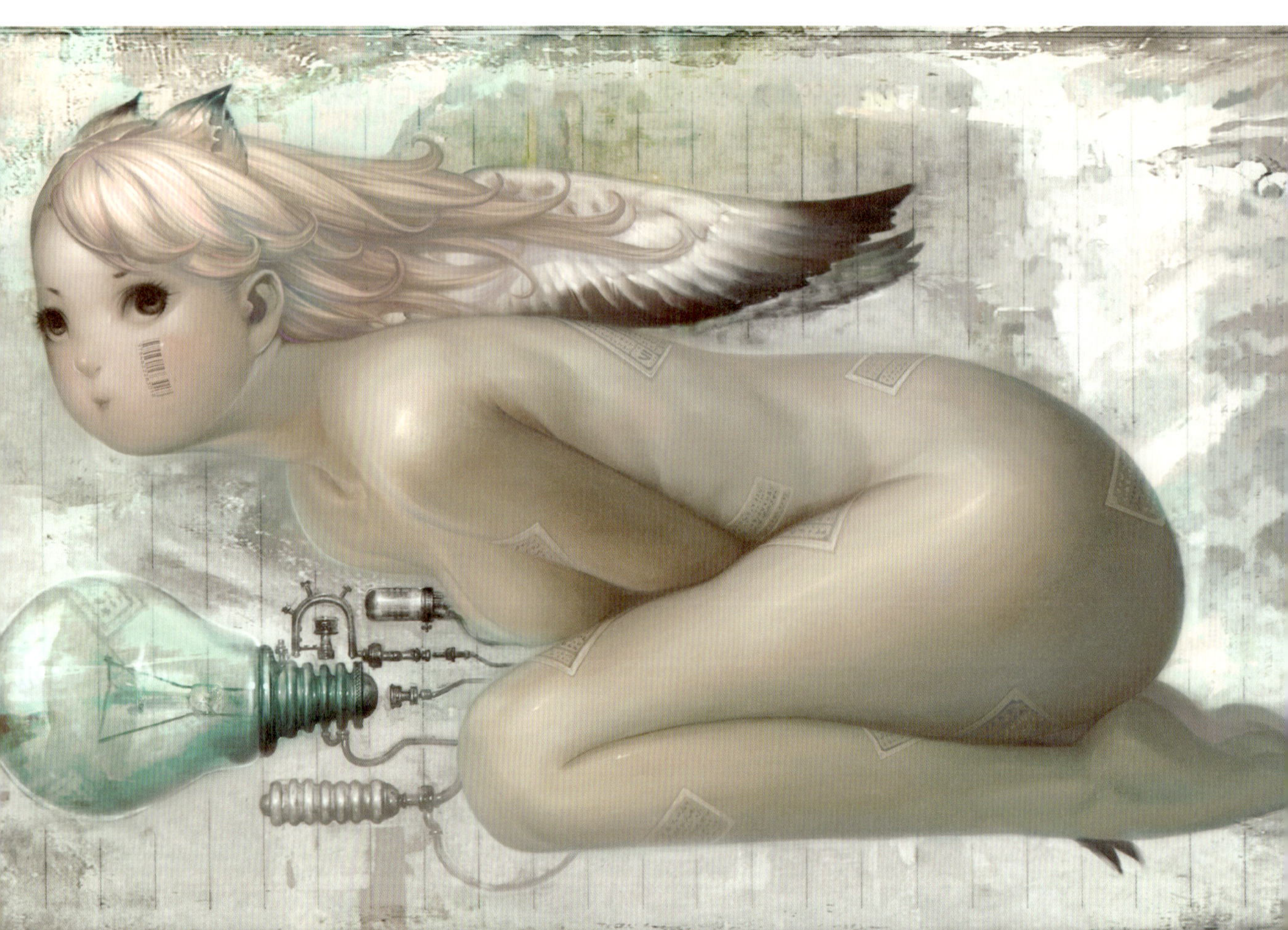

Br 臭素
CGペインティング、Corel Painter / H4719×W7640pixel / 2015

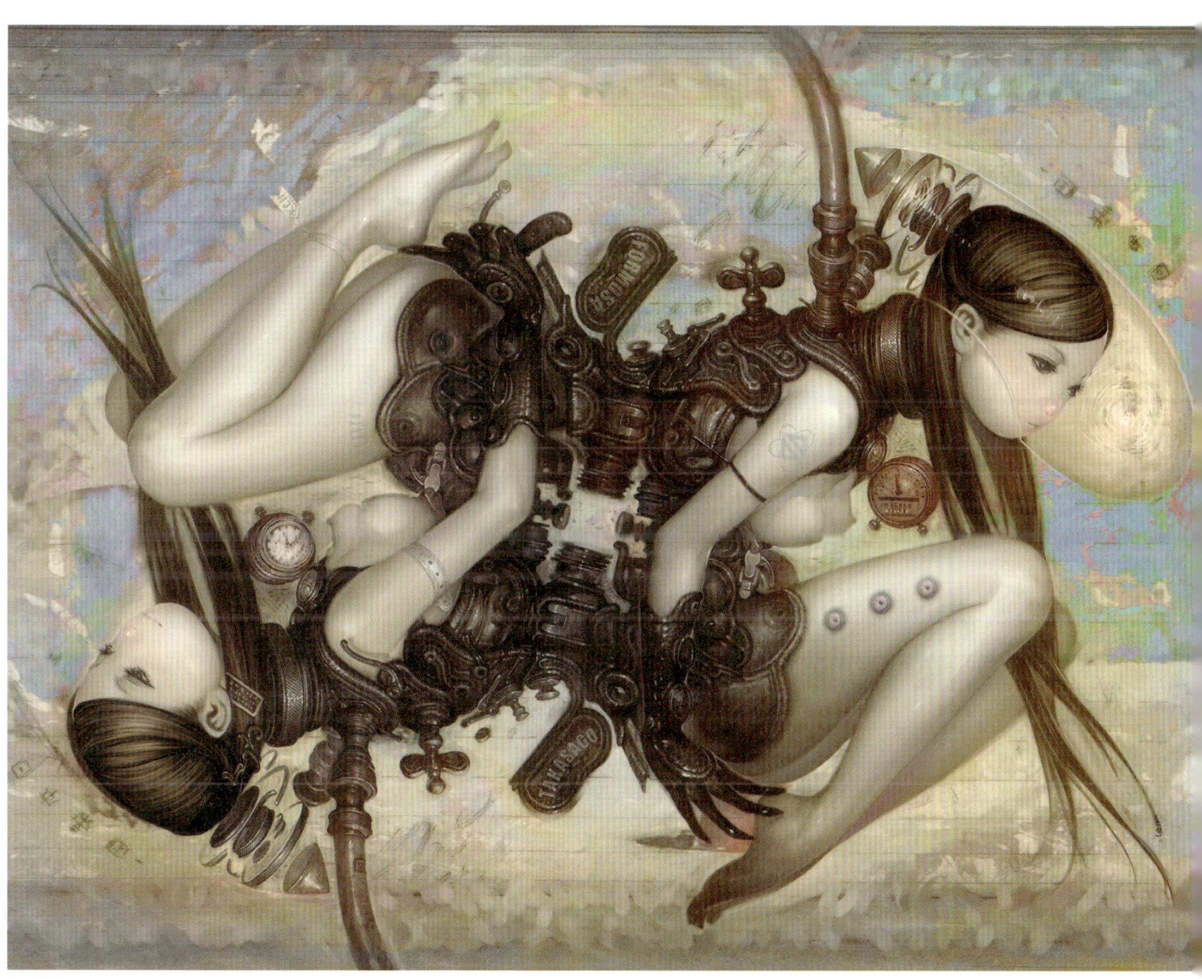

Hg 水銀
CGペインティング、Corel Painter / H5126×W6555pixel / 2015

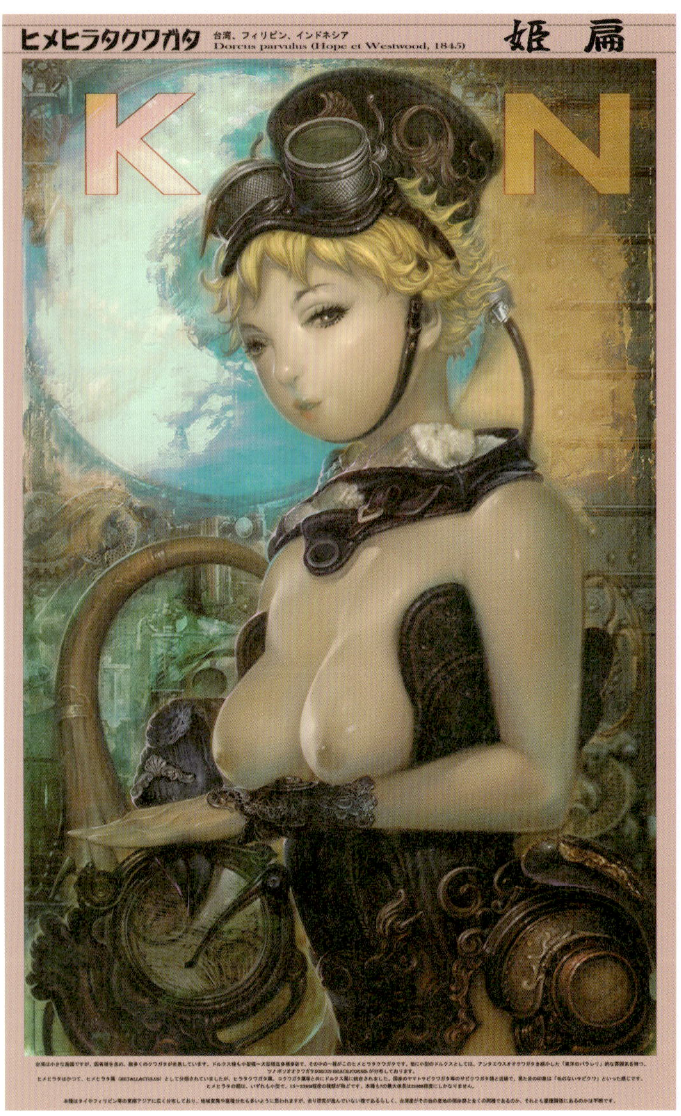

Ne ネオン
CGペインティング、Corel Painter / H6496×W4016pixel / 2008

C 炭素
CGペインティング、Corel Painter / H7648×W5980pixel / 2010

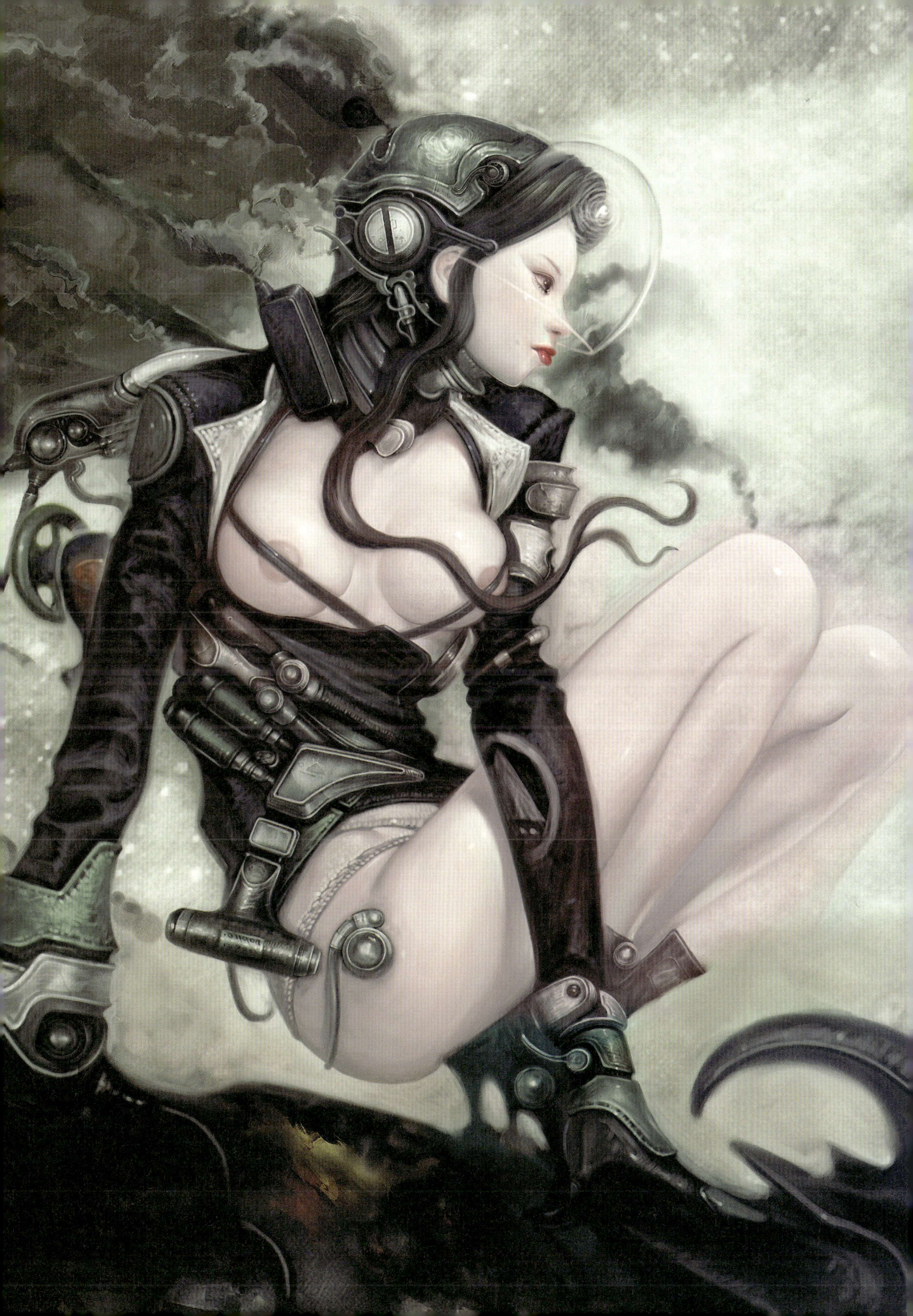

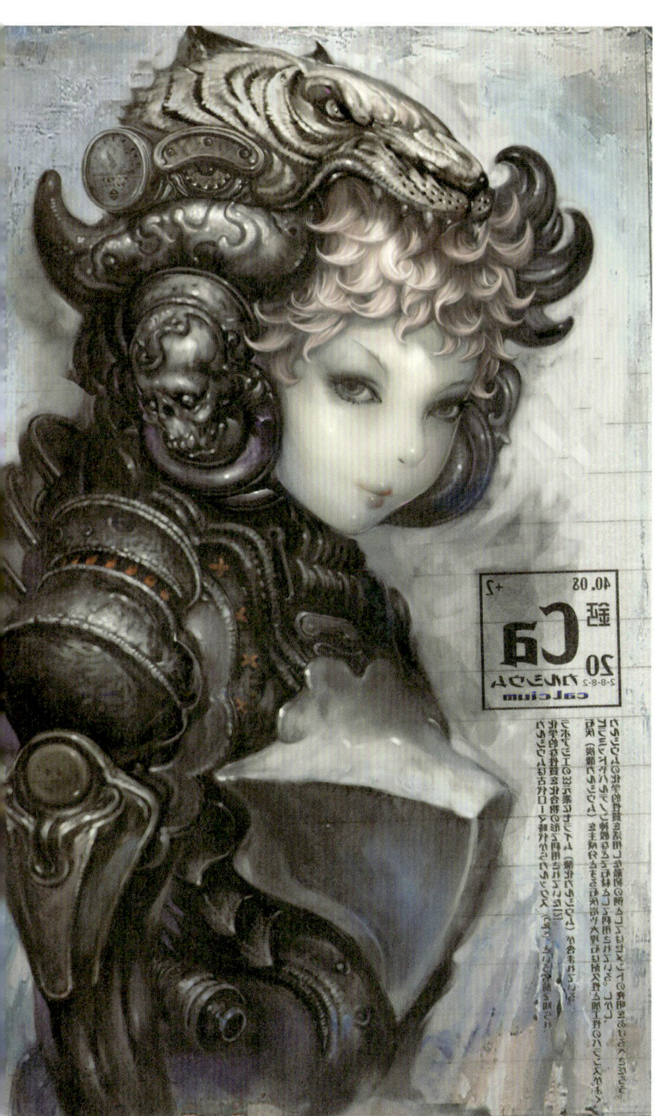

Ca カルシウム
CGペインティング、Corel Painter / H5906×W3740pixel / 2015

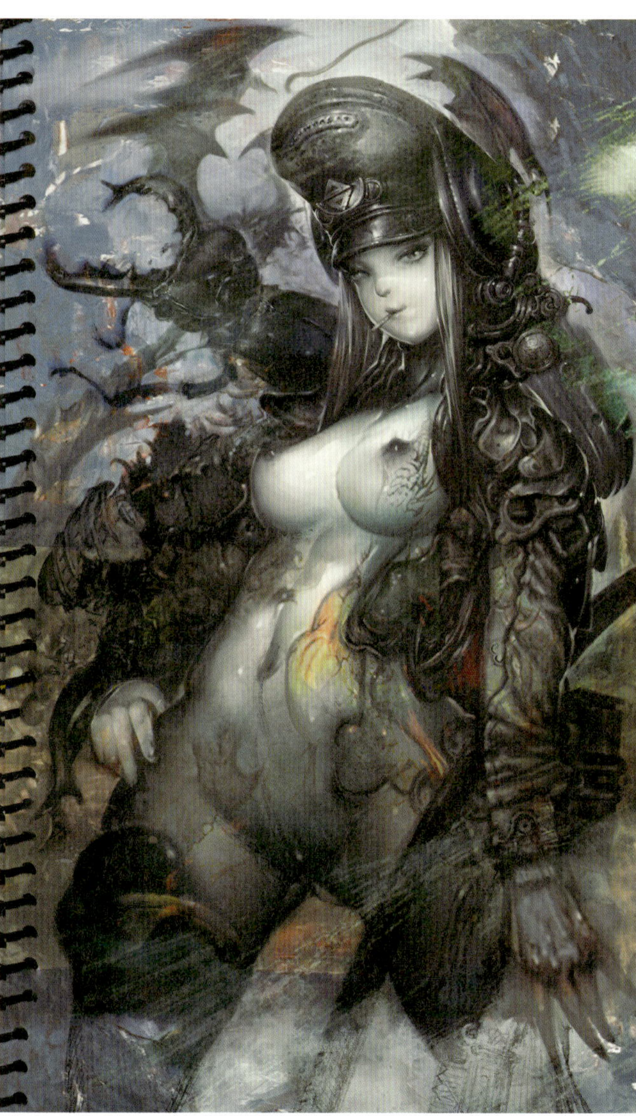

Rg レントゲニウム
CGペインティング、Corel Painter / H7648×W5072pixel / 2015

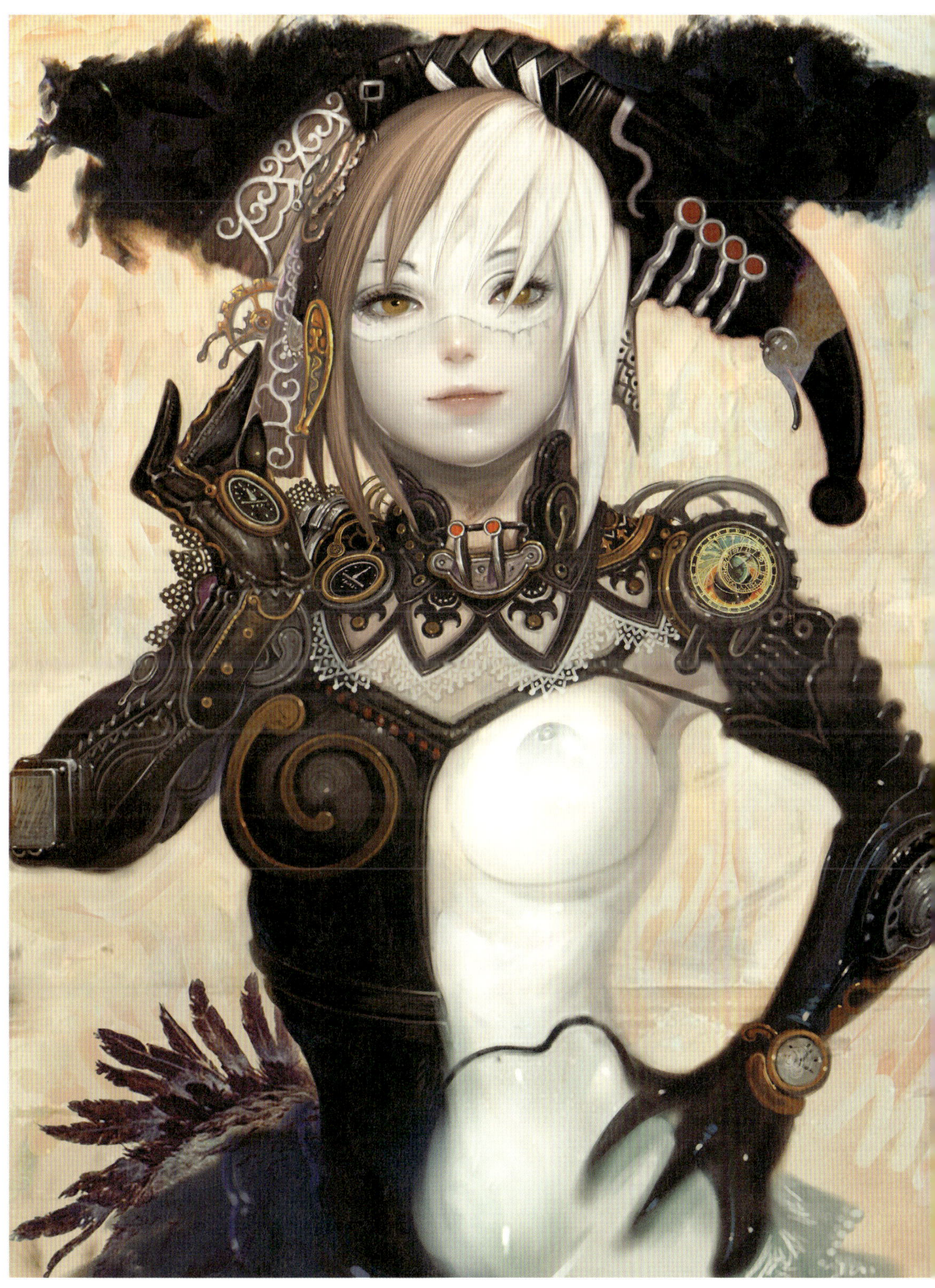

Pb 鉛
CGペインティング、Corel Painter / H7648×W5776pixel / 2008

09

Naoto Hattori

ナオト・ハットリ（日本 Japan）

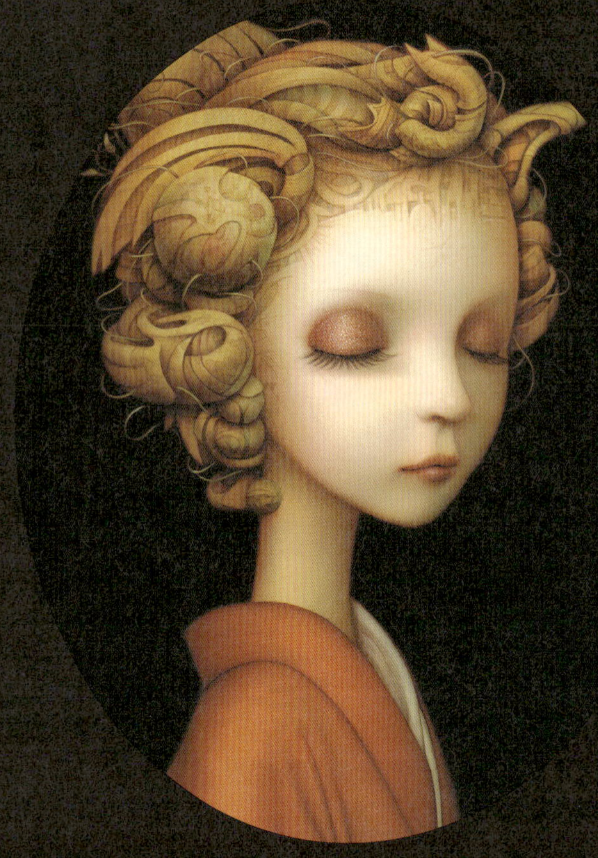

1975年に横浜市で生まれ、東京でグラフィックデザインを学んだ後、ニューヨークに移り、4年制の美術大学スクール・オブ・ビジュアルアーツを2000年に卒業。ソサエティー・オブ・イラストレーターズ、ニューヨーク・ディレクター・クラブ、コミュニケーション・アーツなどのアート協会やアートコンペなどで数々の賞を受賞しており、美術館やギャラリーの展示会を中心に活動。CDジャケットやスノーボードのデザインも手掛け、アパレルやフィギュアのコラボ制作も展開中。

Naoto Hattori was born in 1975 in Yokohama Japan, studied Graphic Design in Tokyo before moving to New York to study in the School of Visual Arts. In the year 2000 he received a BFA in illustration from the School of Visual Arts. He has received Awards from the Society of Illustrators, the New York Directors Club, Communication Arts and also he has won numerous award from many art competitions and has been published in many art magazines. Of his work, He says: "My vision is like a dream, whether it's a sweet dream, a nightmare, or just a weird dream. I try to see what's really going on in my mind, and that's a practice to increase my awareness in stream-of-consciousness creativity. I try not to label or think about what is supposed to be, just take it in as it is and paint whatever I see in my mind with no compromise. That way, I create my own vision."

www.wwwcomcom.com

↑Elegance エレガンス（部分）
アクリル画、ボード / H26.6×W20.3cm / 2014

→Inner Sound 010 インナー・サウンド010（部分）
アクリル画、ボード / H15.2×W10.1cm / 2017

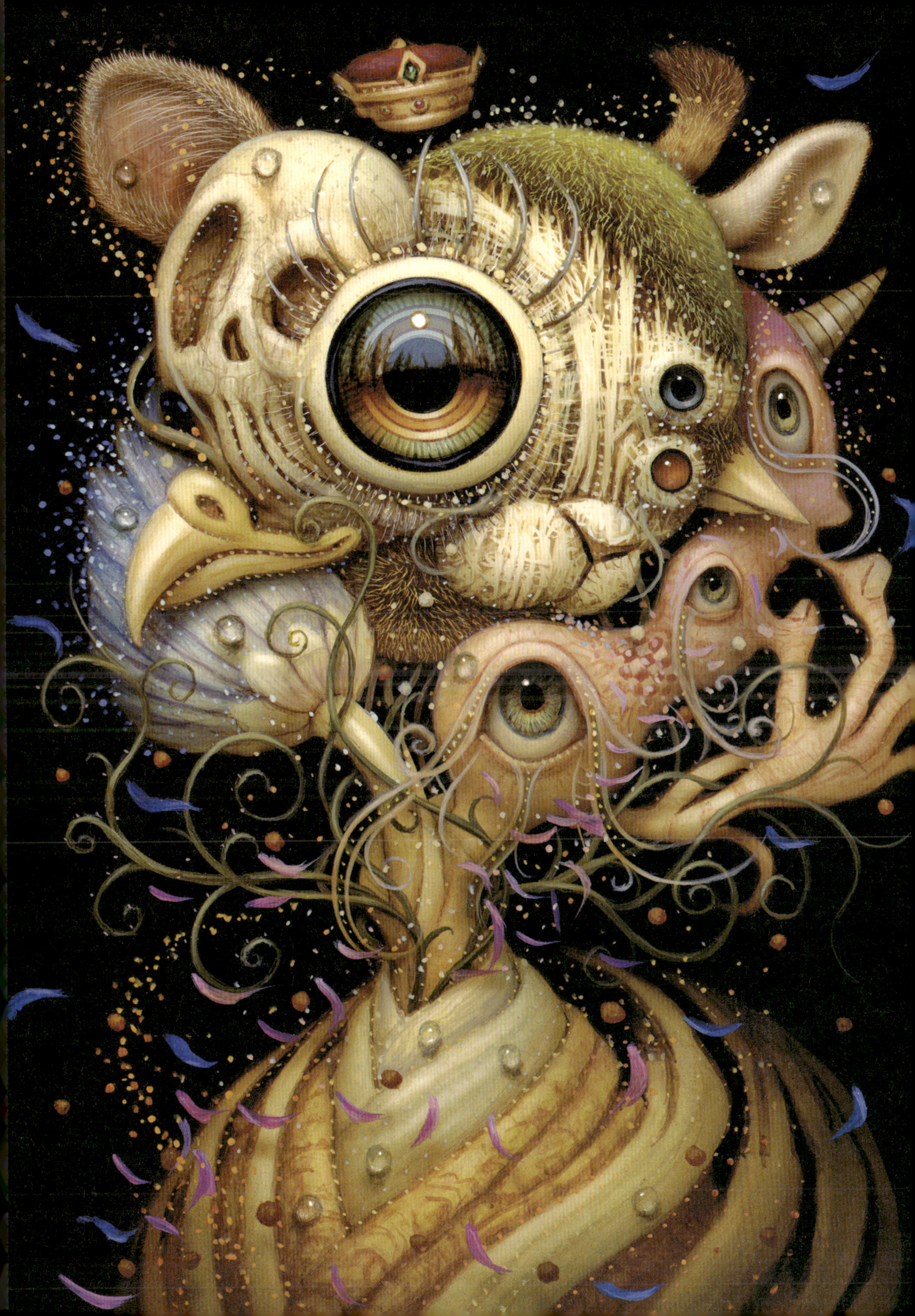

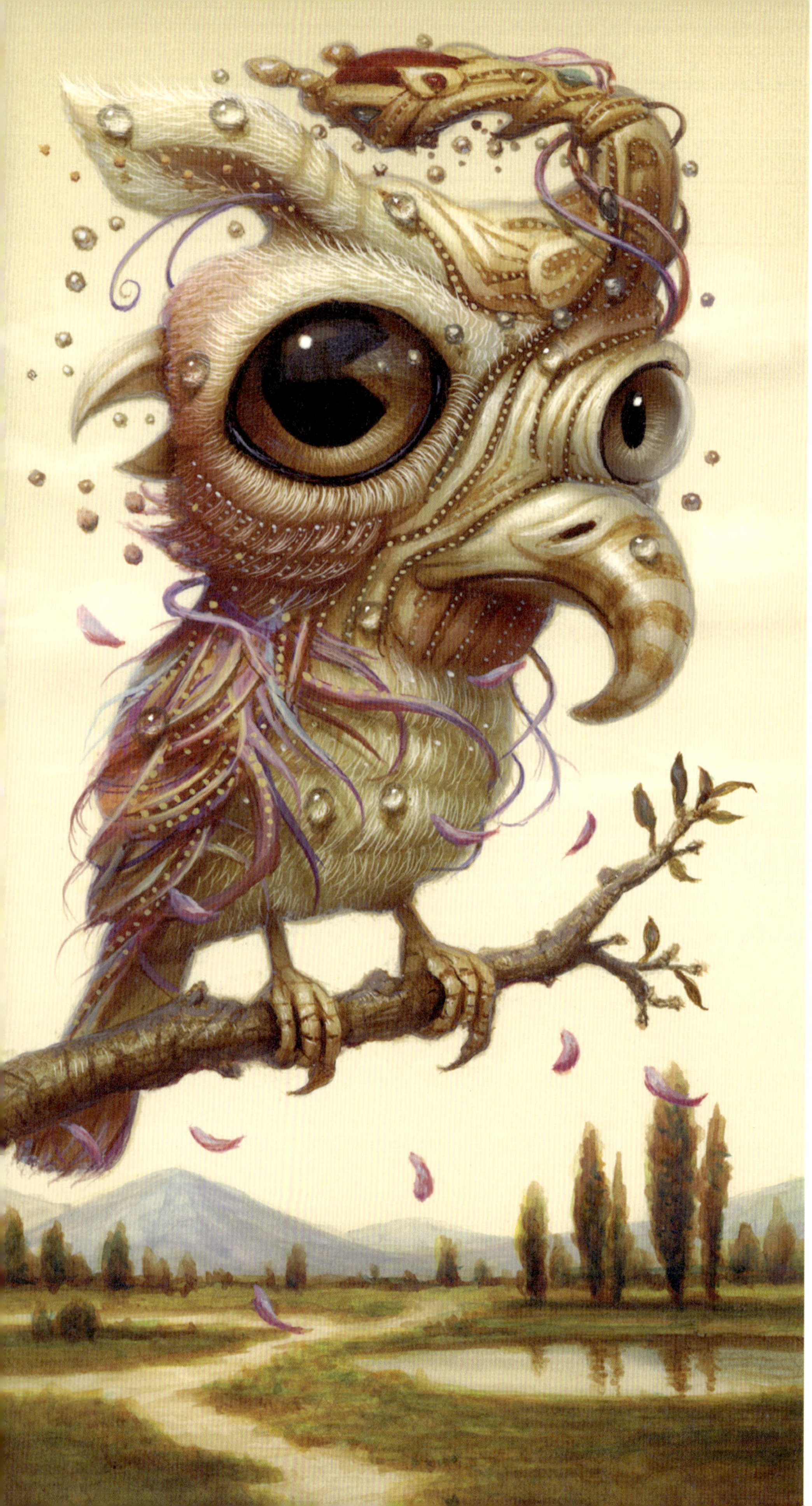

←Lucid Dreamer 023
ルシッド・ドリーマー023
アクリル画、ボード /
H12.7×W6.3cm / 2017

→Mind Emulation
マインド・エミュレーション
アクリル画、ボード /
H22.8×W16cm / 2017

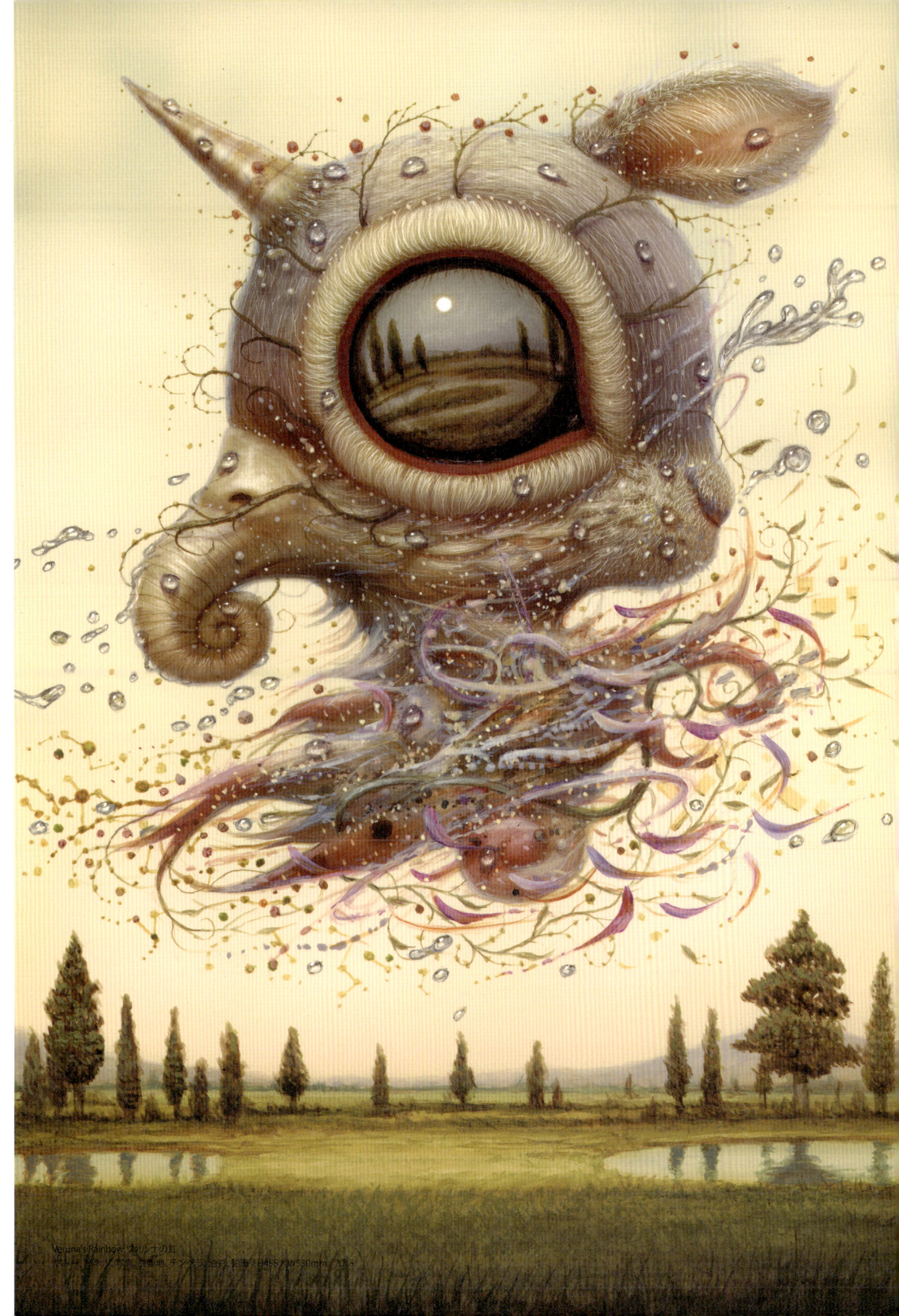

Veruna's Rainbow ヴァルナの虹
たま一、ボード、人写真、白亜地、テンペラと油彩、鉛筆／H455×W530mm／2015

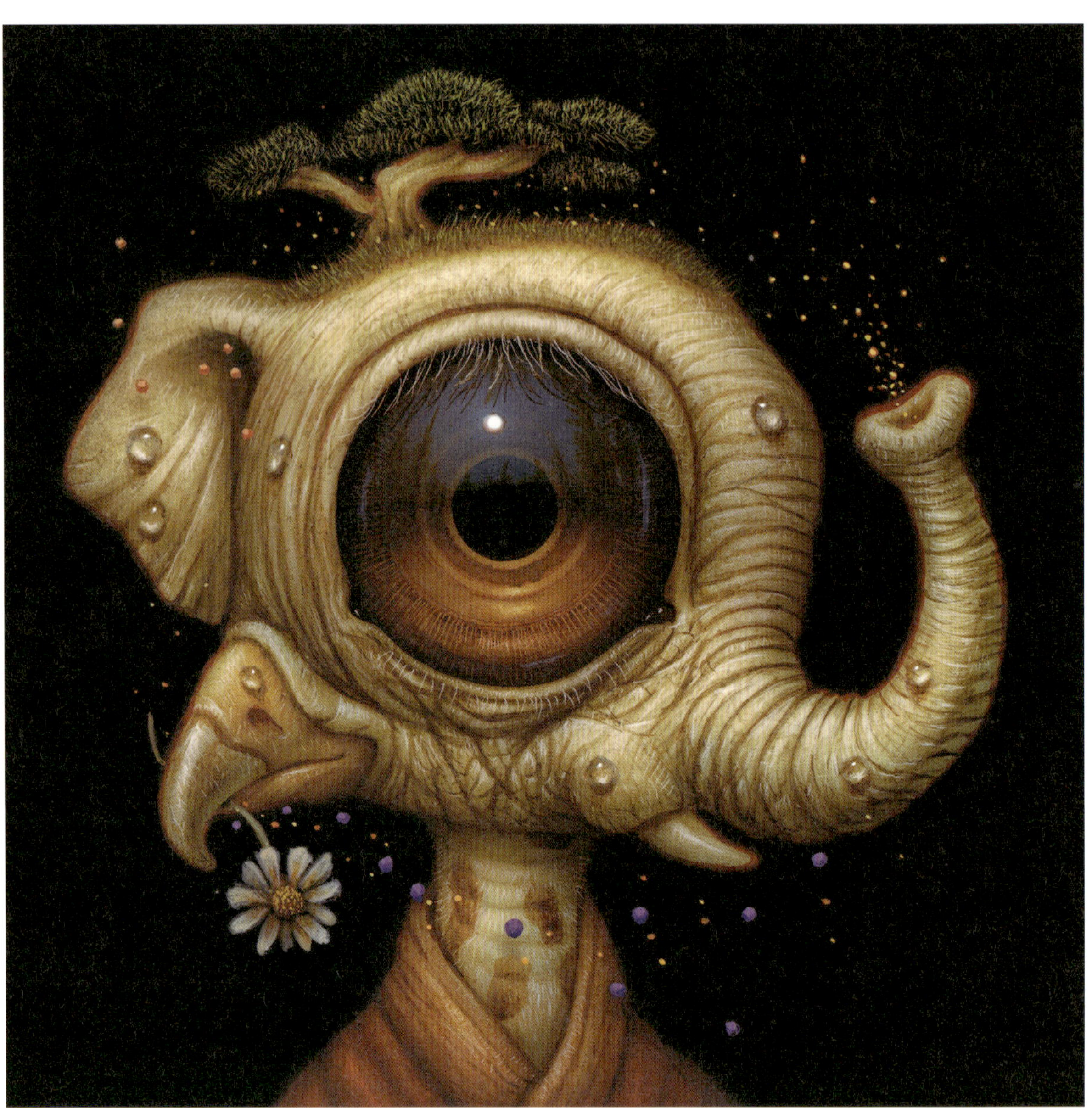

Inner Peace インナー・ピース
アクリル画、ボード / H15.2×W15.2cm / 2017

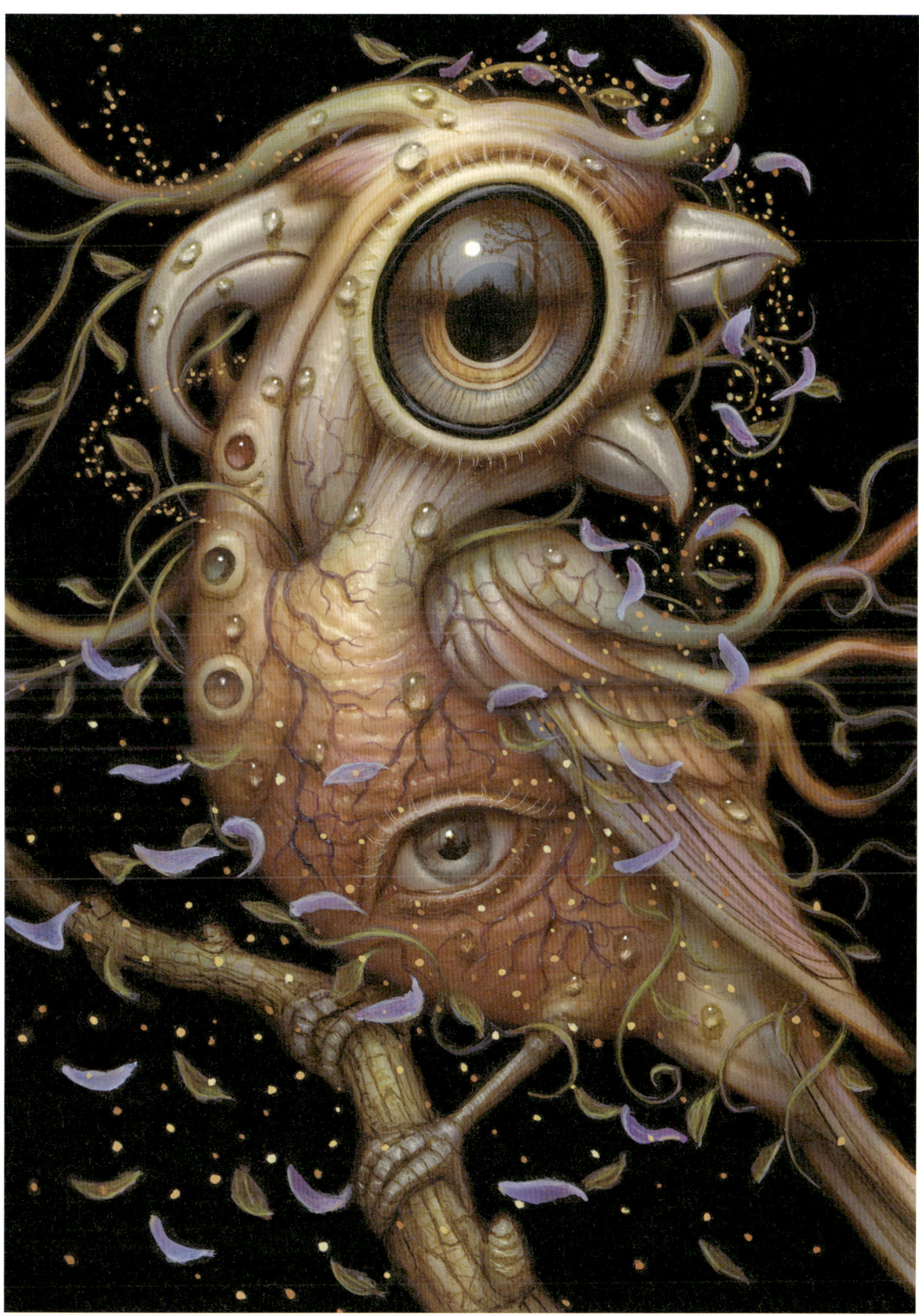

Inner Sound Flow インナー・サウンド・フロー
アクリル画、ボード / H15.2×W10.1cm / 2017

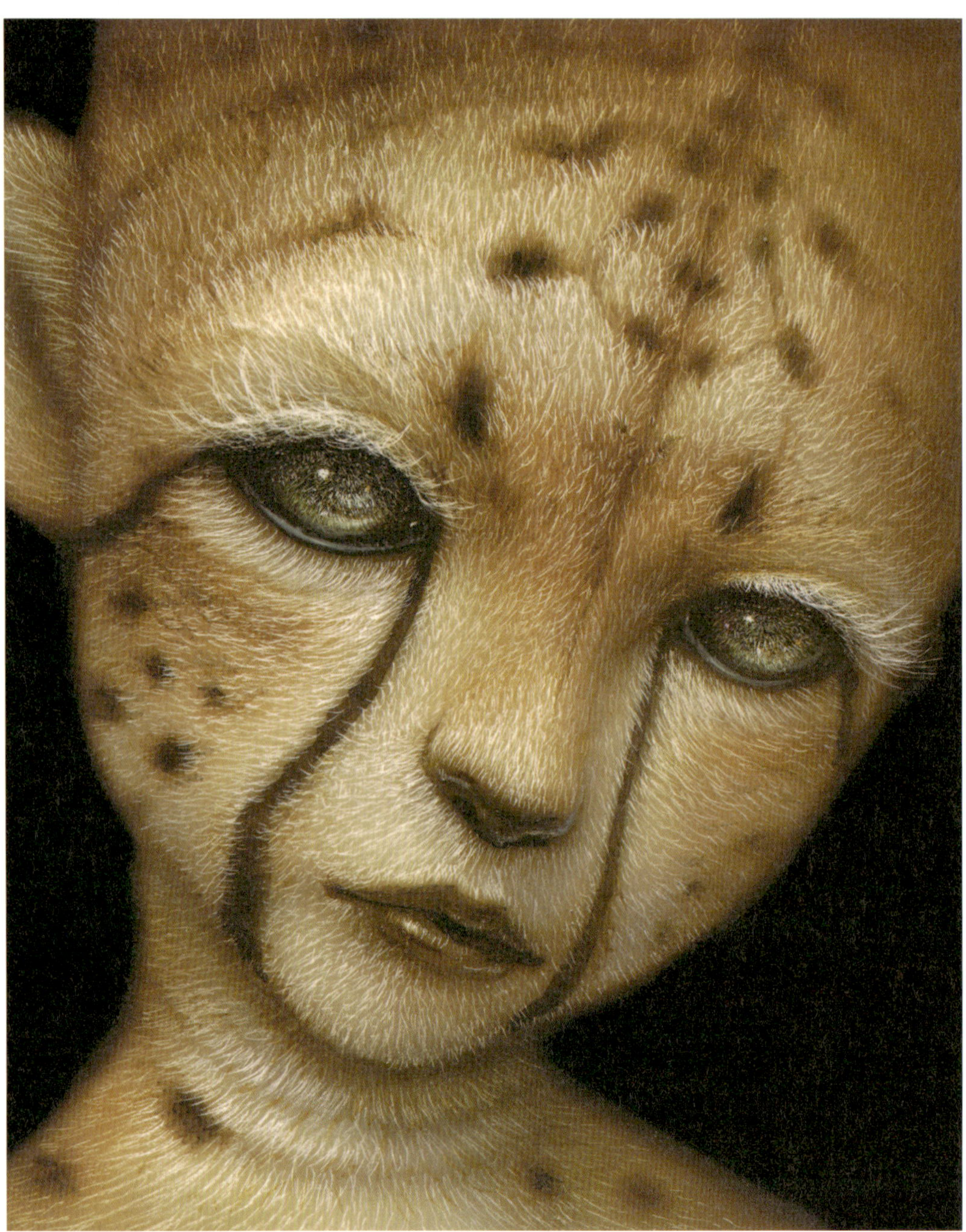

Bewitching ビーウィッチング
アクリル画、ボード / H10.1×W8.1cm / 2017

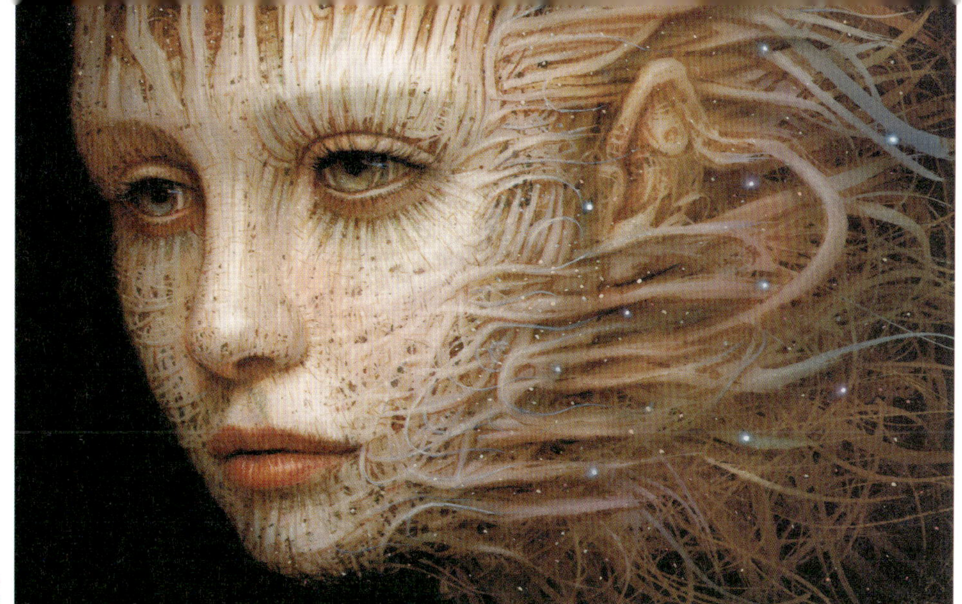

Recollection 054 リコレクション054
アクリル画、ボード / H10.4×W15.2cm / 2016

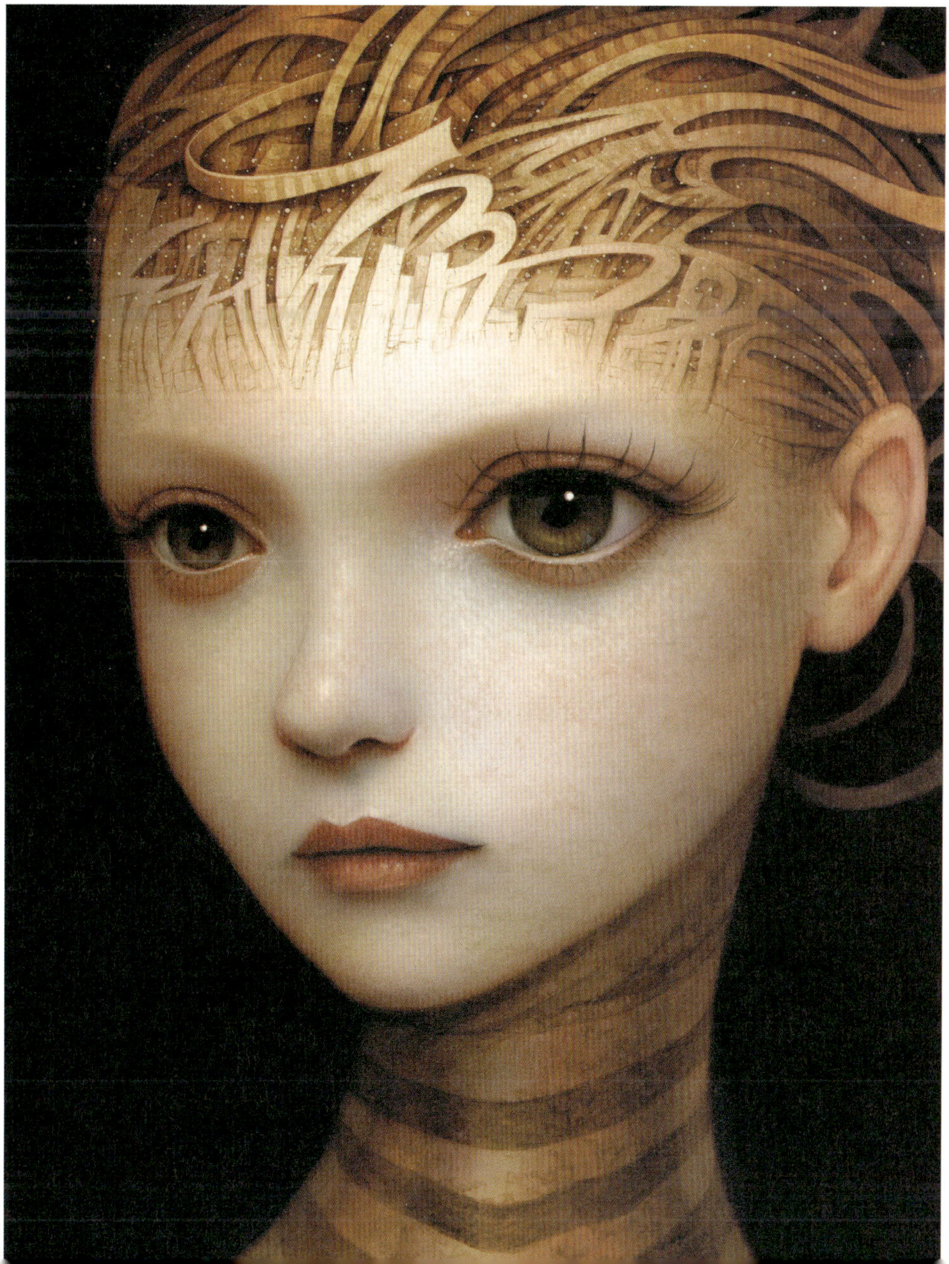

Untamed アンテイムド
アクリル画、ボード / H26.6×W20.3cm / 2014

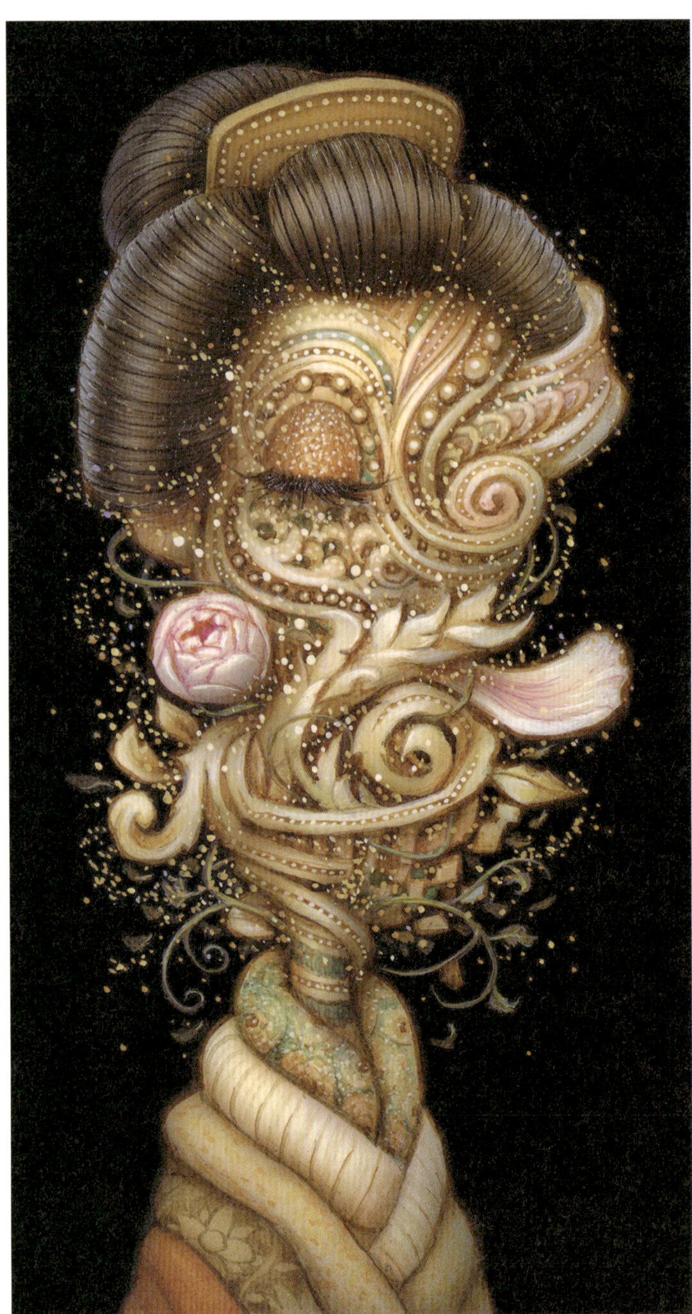

Mind Spark 02 マインド・スパーク02
アクリル画、ボード / H12.7×W7.1cm / 2017

Gathering ギャザリング
アクリル画、ボード / H28.4×W21.5cm / 2007

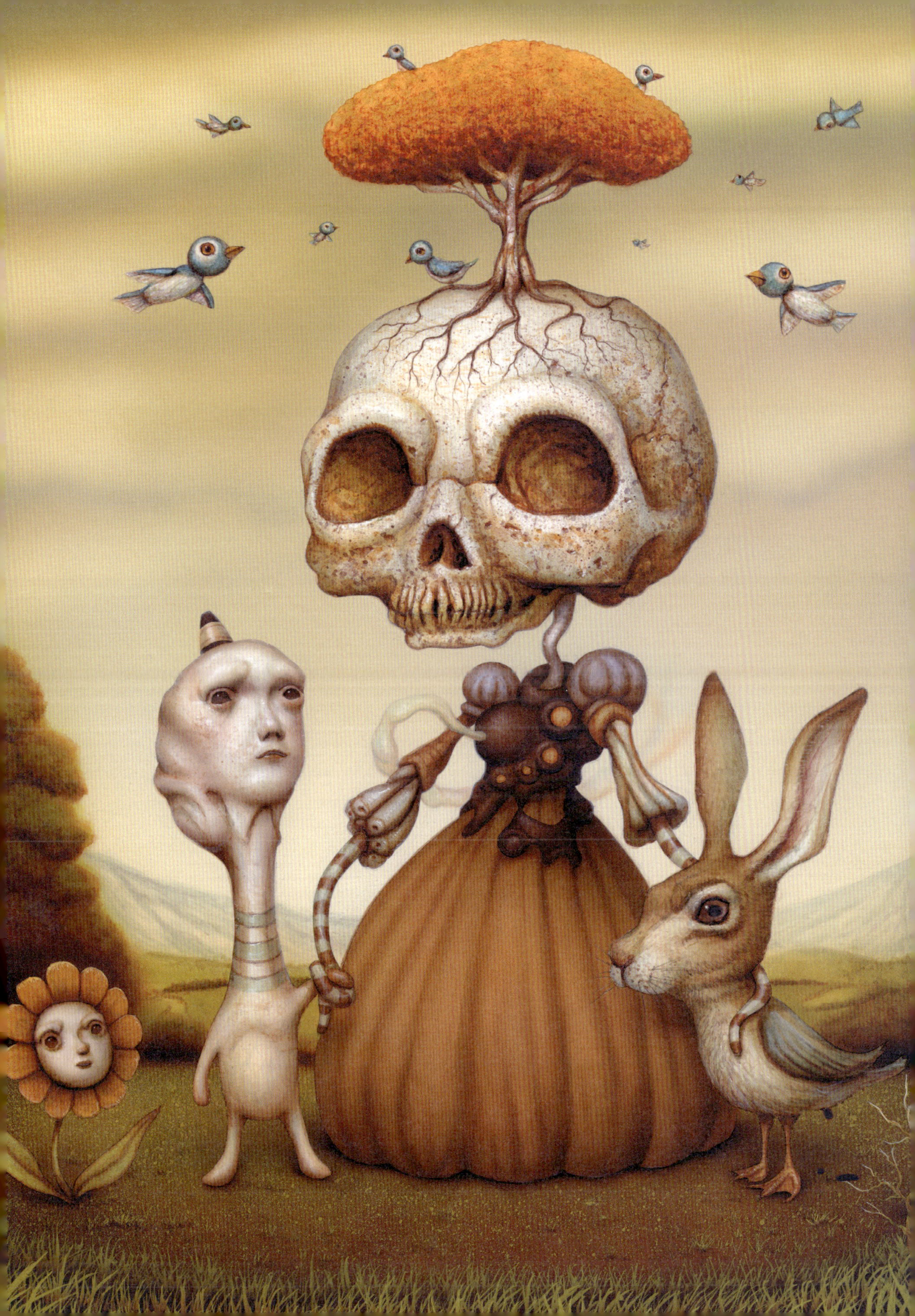

Nicoletta Ceccoli

ニコレッタ・チェッコリ（イタリア　Italy）

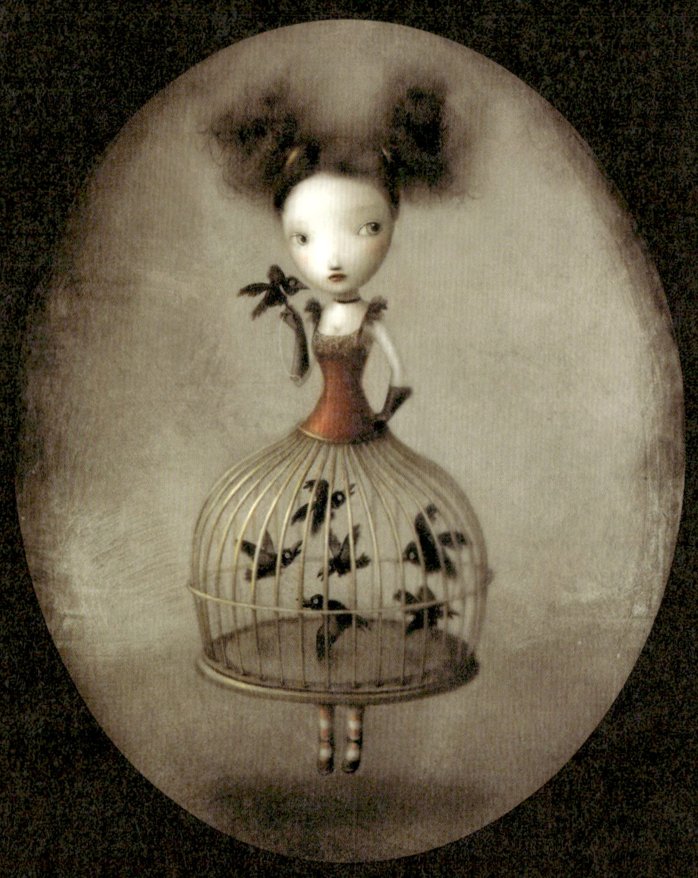

1973年イタリア、サンマリノ共和国生まれ、現在も在住。パステル調の色彩を用い、無垢であどけない美少女の姿をしたファム・ファタール（魔性の女）を描く。欲望、嫌悪、性的倒錯といったダークなシンボリズムが複雑に隠された作品は、蝶の標本のような不気味な美しさをたたえている。ピンで留められた蝶は、抗うことよりも、支配される安楽さを選ぶ人間の不条理な一面を表している。人間の持つ複雑でダークな感情が夢のような幻想的な光景で表現され、見る者を魅了すると同時に、不安や悲しみといった心情を呼び起こす。

Nicoletta Ceccoli was born in Italy in 1973 where she actually still lives . Her "Lovely Lolitas" are femme fatales who seducethrough veils of chastity. The pure and innocent color pallet subtly masks desire, repulsion and perversion. Layers of dark symbolism and complexity are presented like a magnificent butterfly collection; exquisite subjects on display to the world, complacently pinned in place by life's cold truths. Hopes of being saved are overwhelmed by the ease of being controlled. Beneath the alluring imagery, disturbing feelings are intricately examined with a tenderness and beauty that both entices and saddens the viewer.

www.nicolettaceccoli.com

↑Sheryl シェリル
アクリル、紙、Photoshop / 2006
→Just dessert ジャスト・デザート
アクリル、紙 / 2011

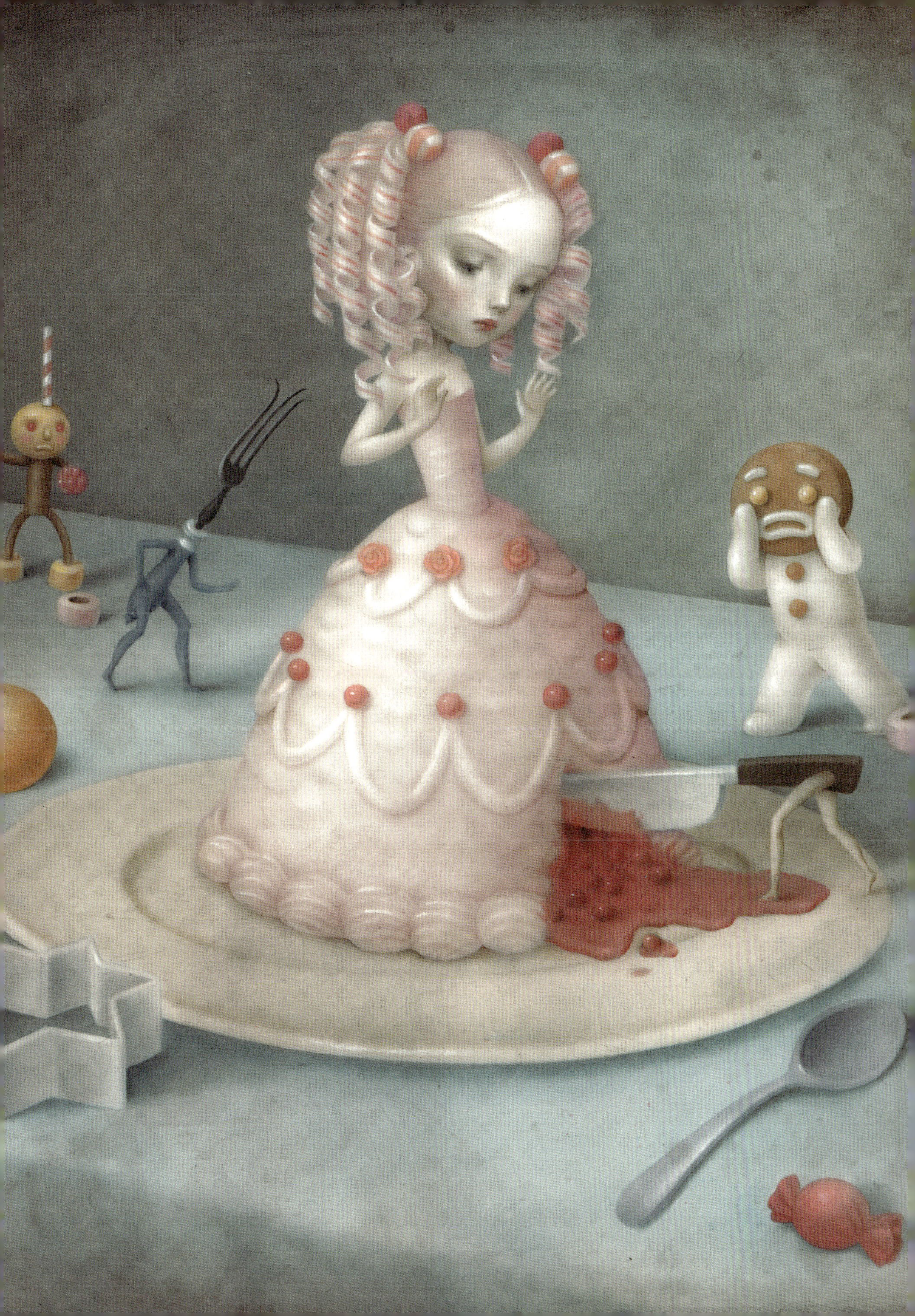

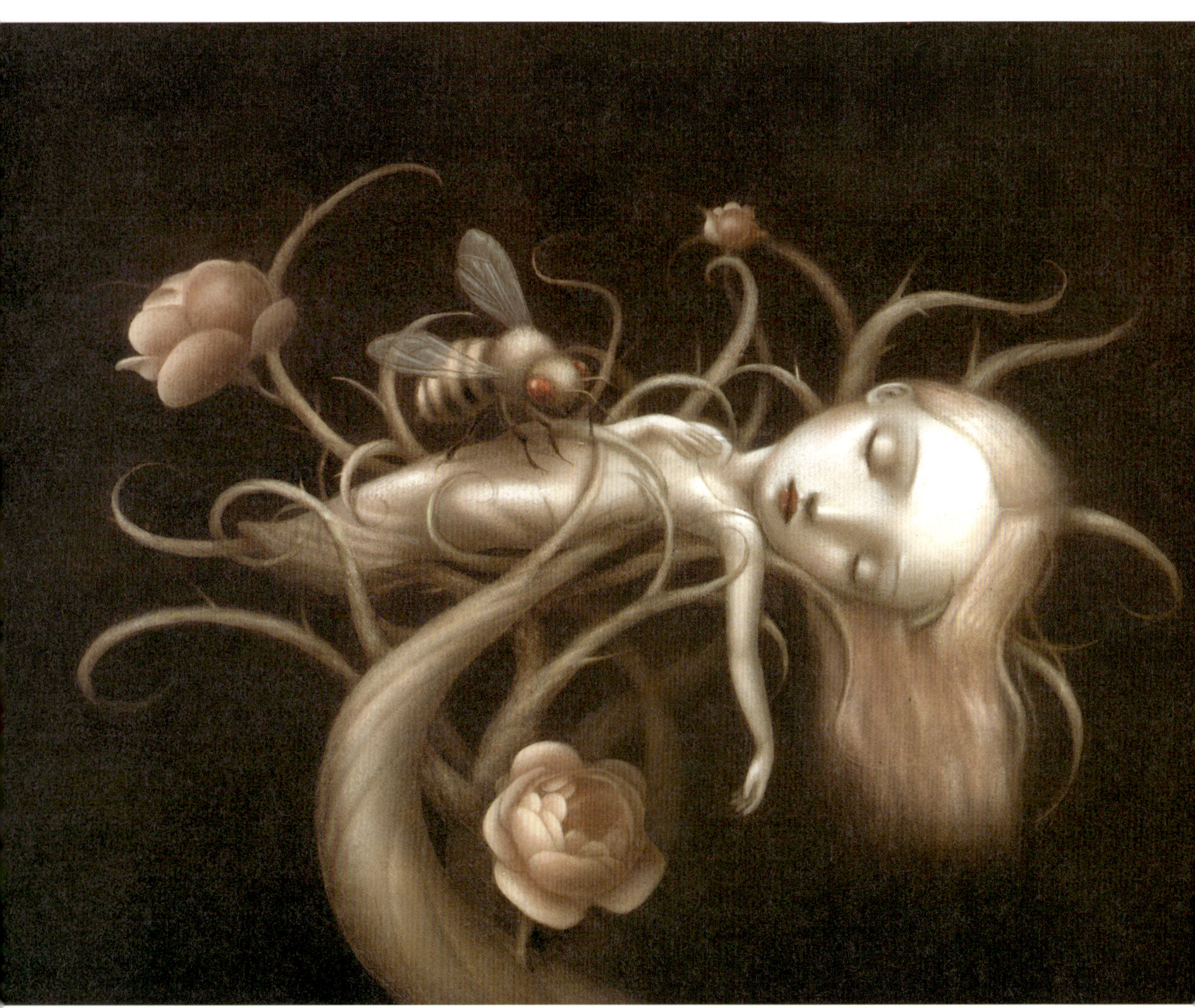

Aurora オーロラ
アクリル、紙 / 2007

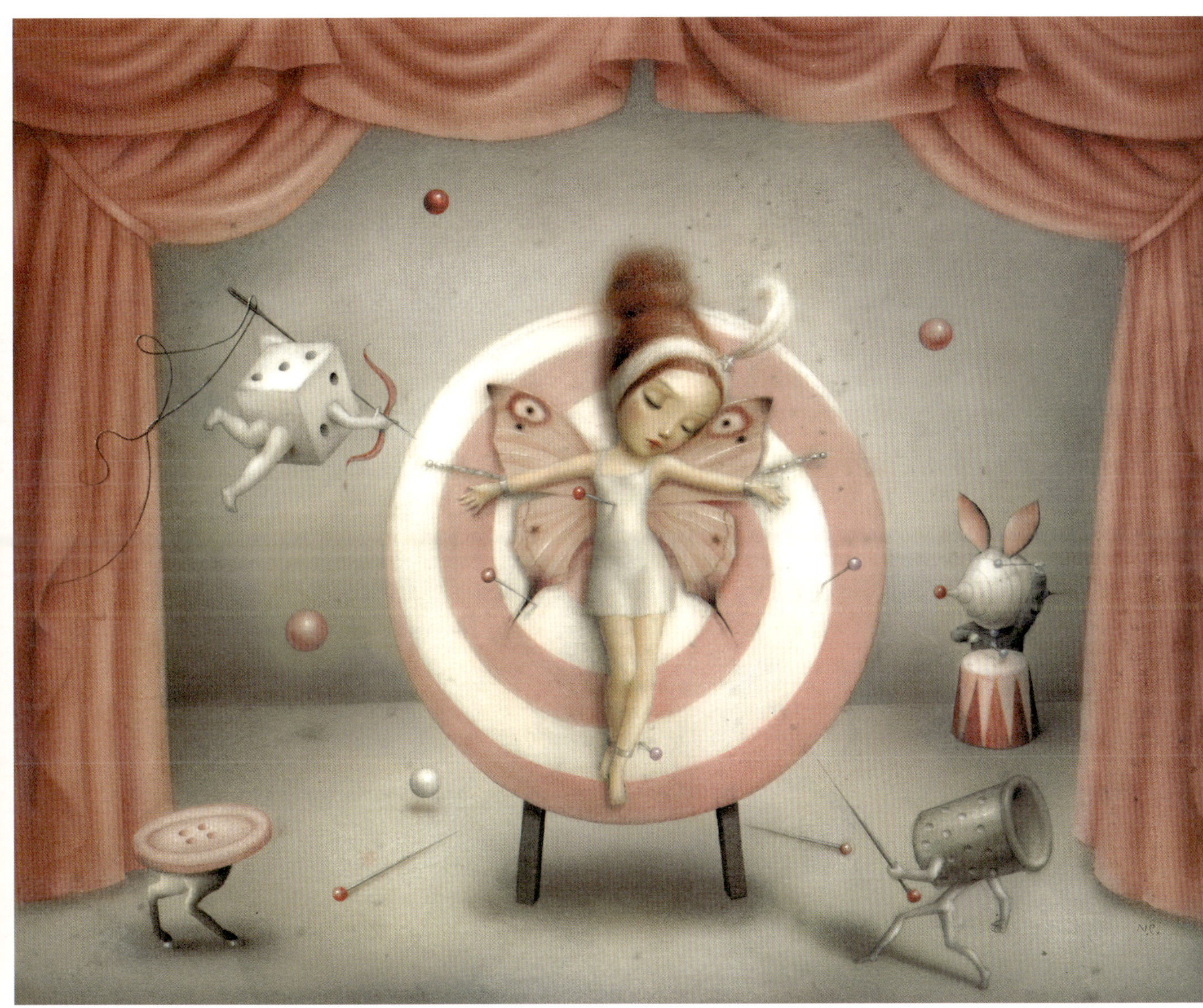

The Magician's Assistant 魔法使いの助手
アクリル、紙 / 2011

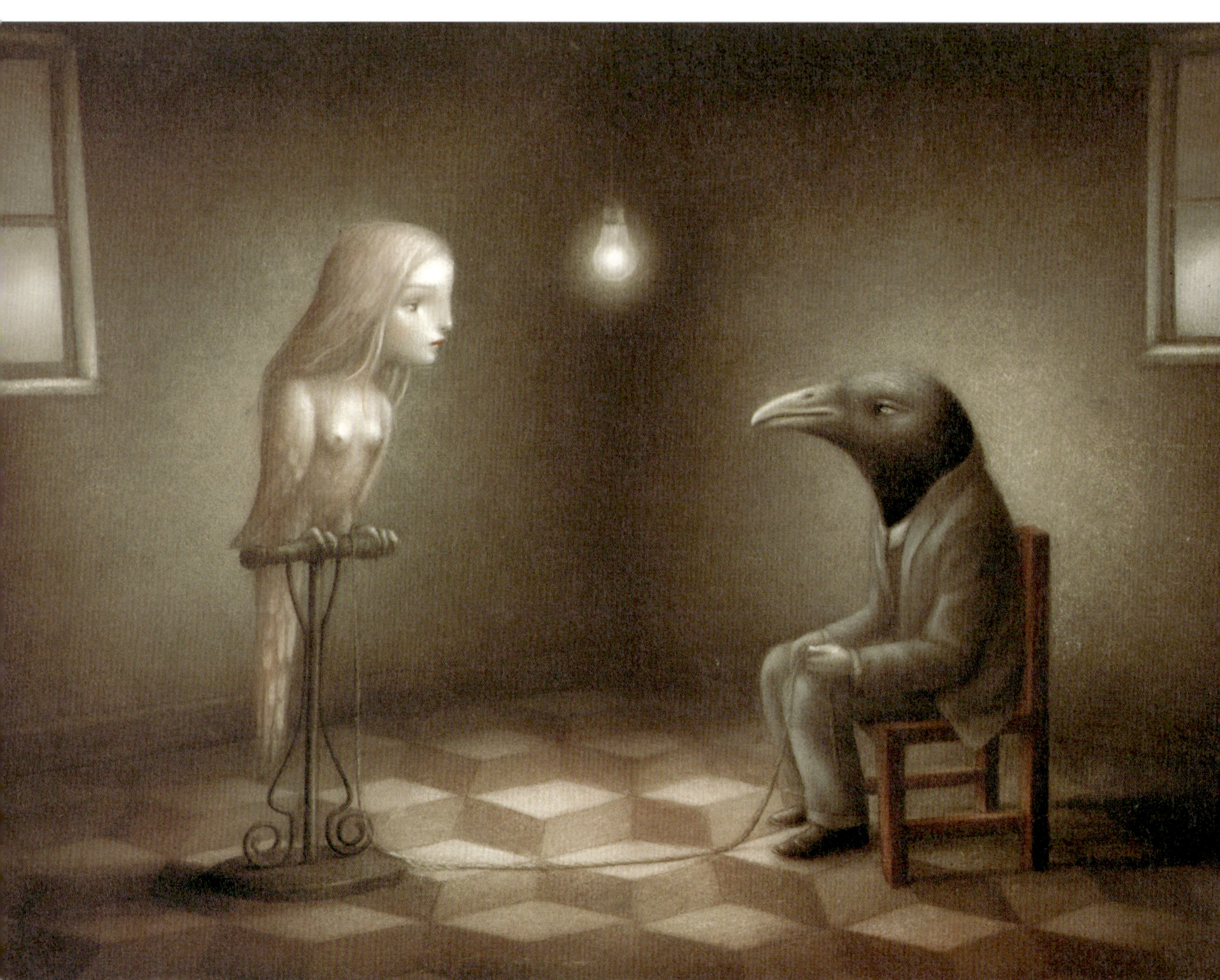

Arpya アルピヤ
アクリル、紙 / 2008

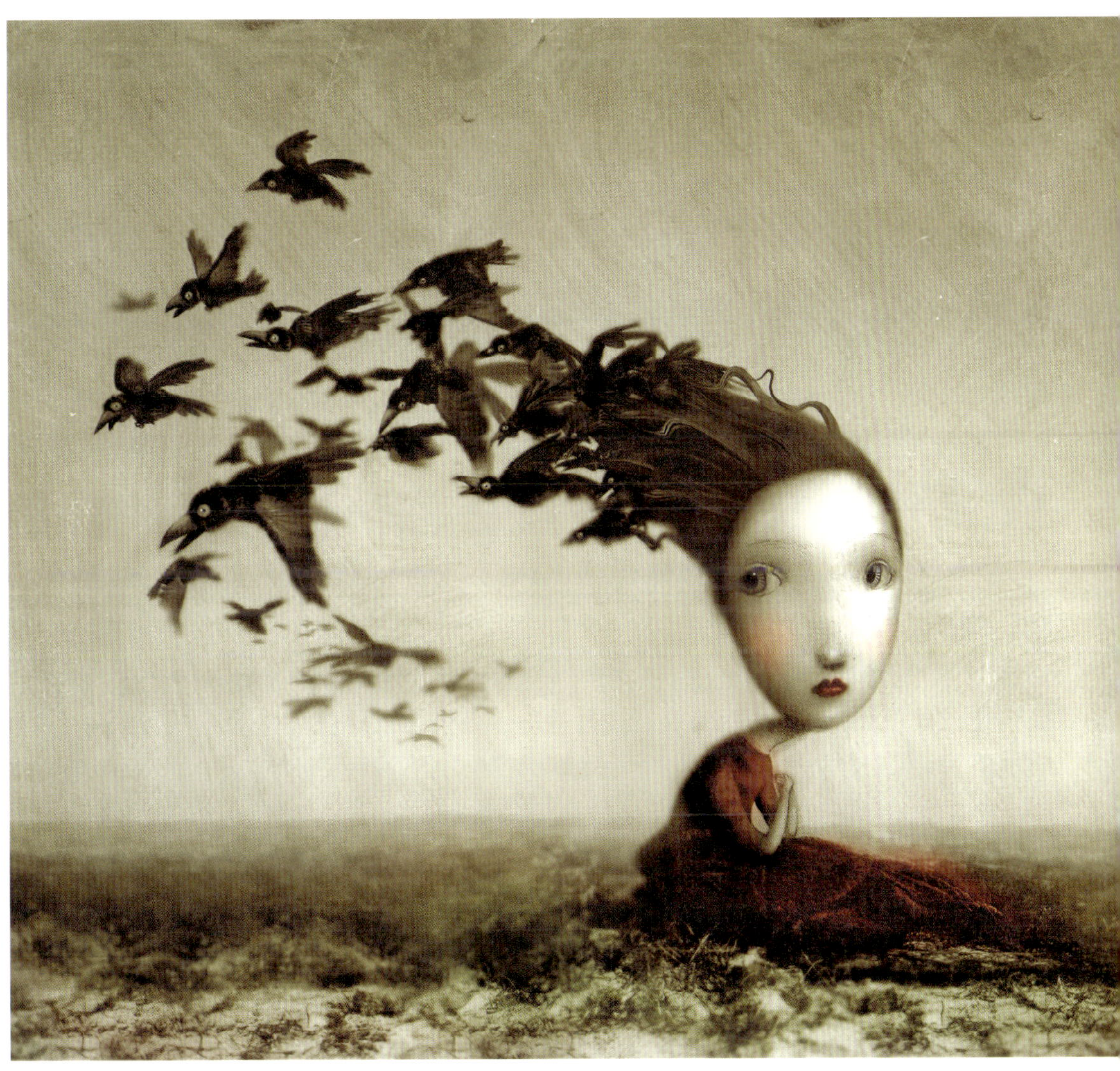

Crows カラス
アクリル、紙、Photoshop / 2006

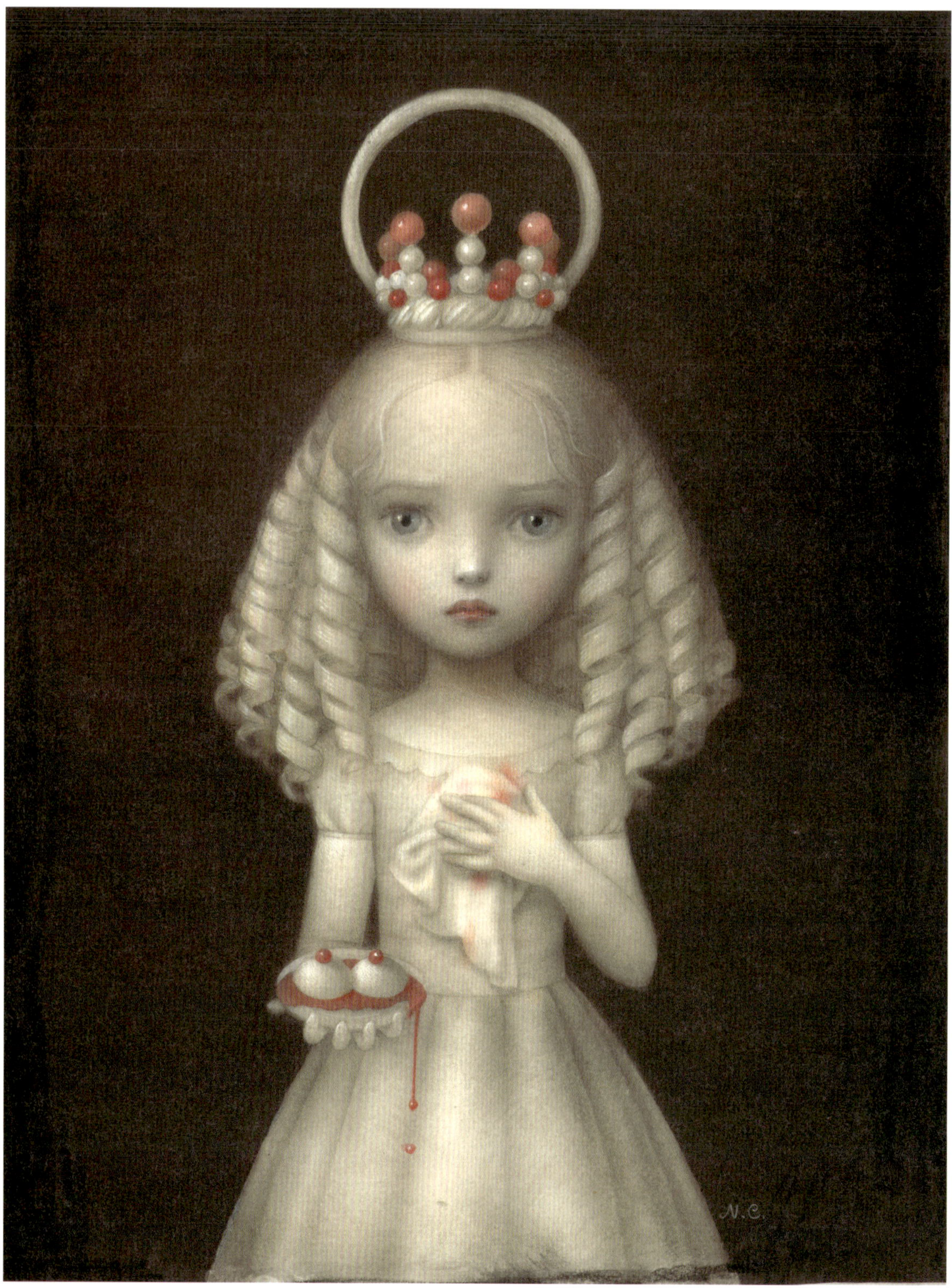

Dulcis Agatha ダルシス・アガサ
アクリル、紙 / 2014

Katherine キャサリン
アクリル、紙、Photoshop / 2006

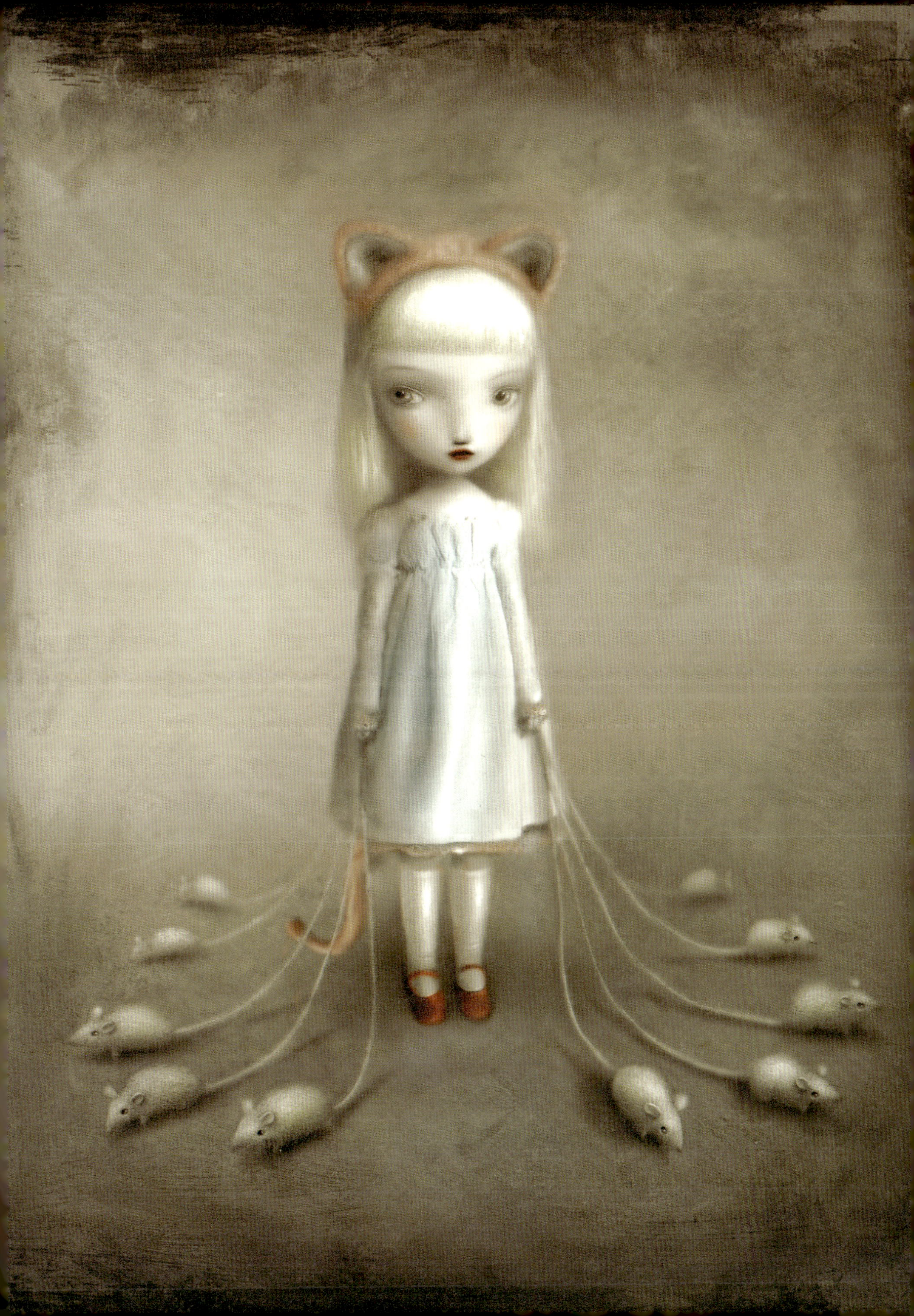

Miss Van

ミス・ヴァン（フランス France）

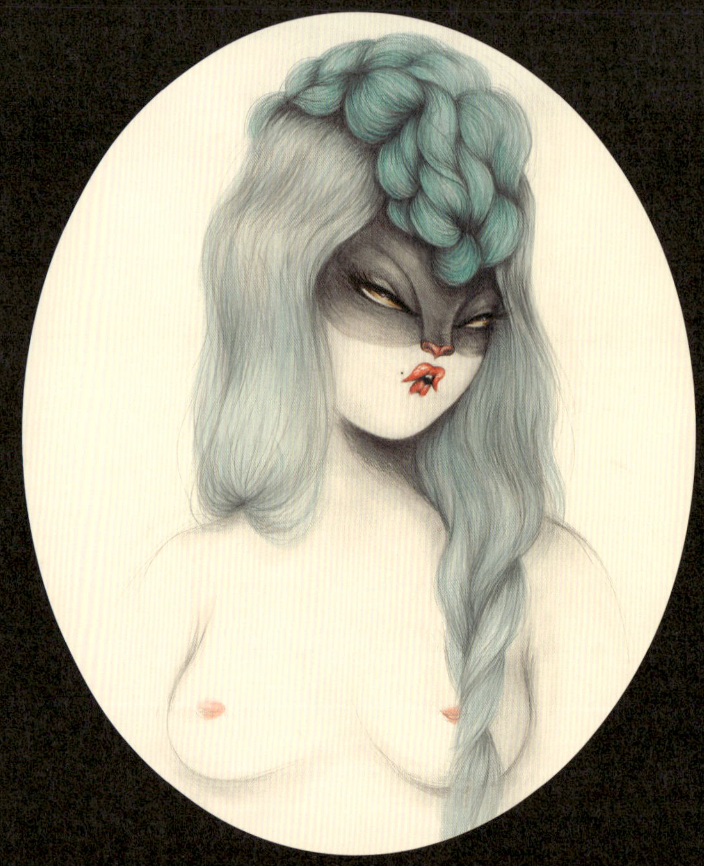

1973年フランス、トゥールーズ生まれ。グラフィティ、ストリート・アーティスト。ヴァネッサ・アリス・ベンシモン、ヴァネッサ・カステックスとしても知られている。18歳のときに、マドモワゼル・キャットとともにトゥールーズの街の壁に絵を描き始める。プペ（フランス語で人形の意味）と呼ばれる女性のキャラクターがトレードマーク。世界各国で壁画を描き、フランス、ヨーロッパ、アメリカのギャラリーで、キャンバス作品の展示も行っている。ストリート・アートと見なされていた彼女の作品は、現在ではファイン・アートとして認められるようになり、両者の境界線はますます曖昧になっている。現在はスペインのバルセロナ在住。

Born in 1973 in Toulouse, France, as Vanessa Alice Bensimon and also known as Vanessa Castex, is a graffiti and street artist. She started painting on the street of Toulouse alongside Mademoiselle Kat at the age of 18. Primarily, her work is marked by the use of unique characters, called poupées, or dolls. Her work has appeared on streets internationally, although she also exhibits canvases in galleries across France, Europe and the United States. Today, her work is characterized by both street art and fine art, blurring the lines between both worlds. She currently resides in Barcelona, Spain.master multiple artistic disciplines; he has been a ceramist, sculptor, painter, and

missvan.com

↑Green Grappe Hair 青いブドウの髪（部分）
アクリル、黒鉛、紙 / 2012

→Gorditas De Chicharron Ⅳ ゴルディタス・デ・チチャロンⅣ
アクリル、カンヴァス / 2014

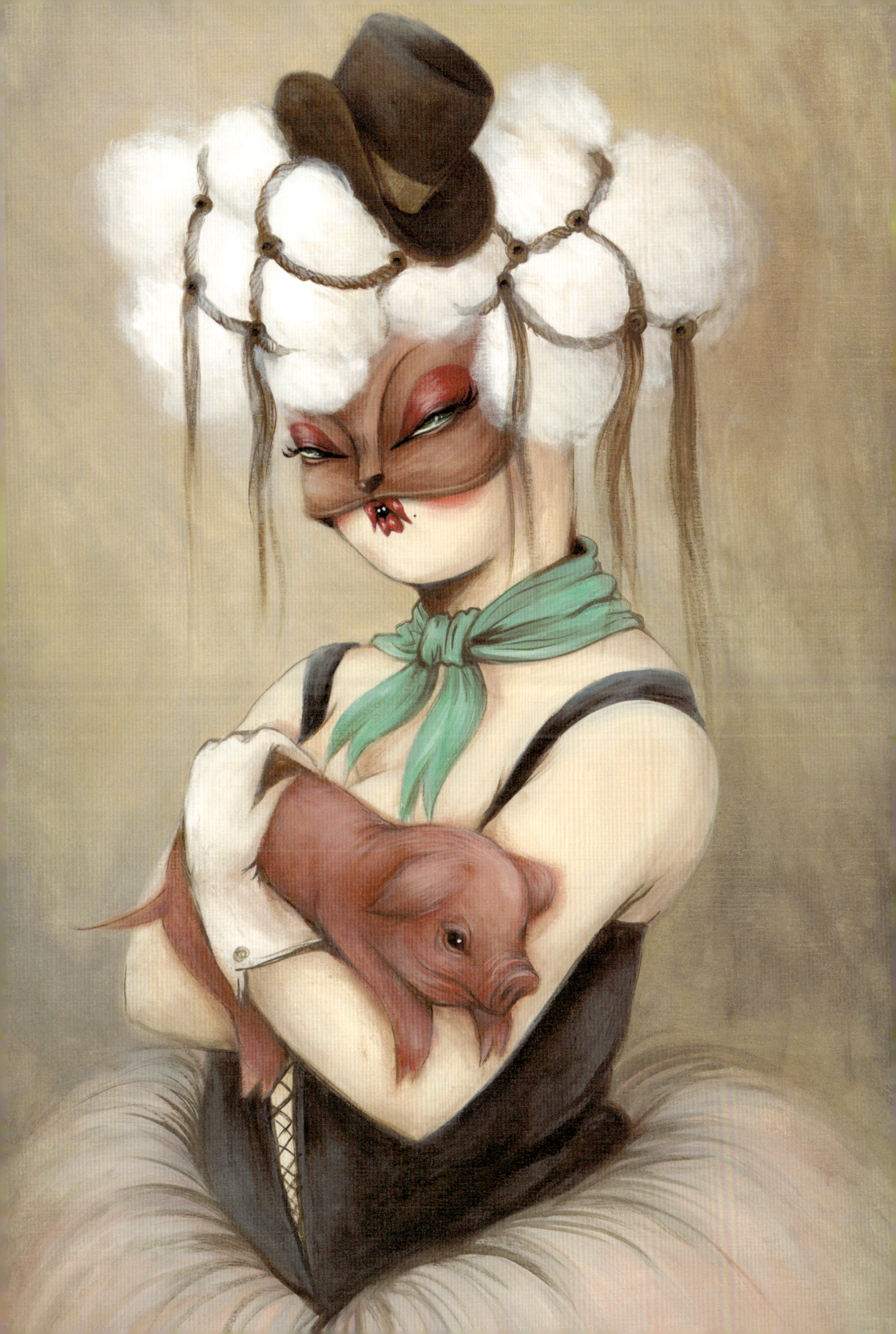

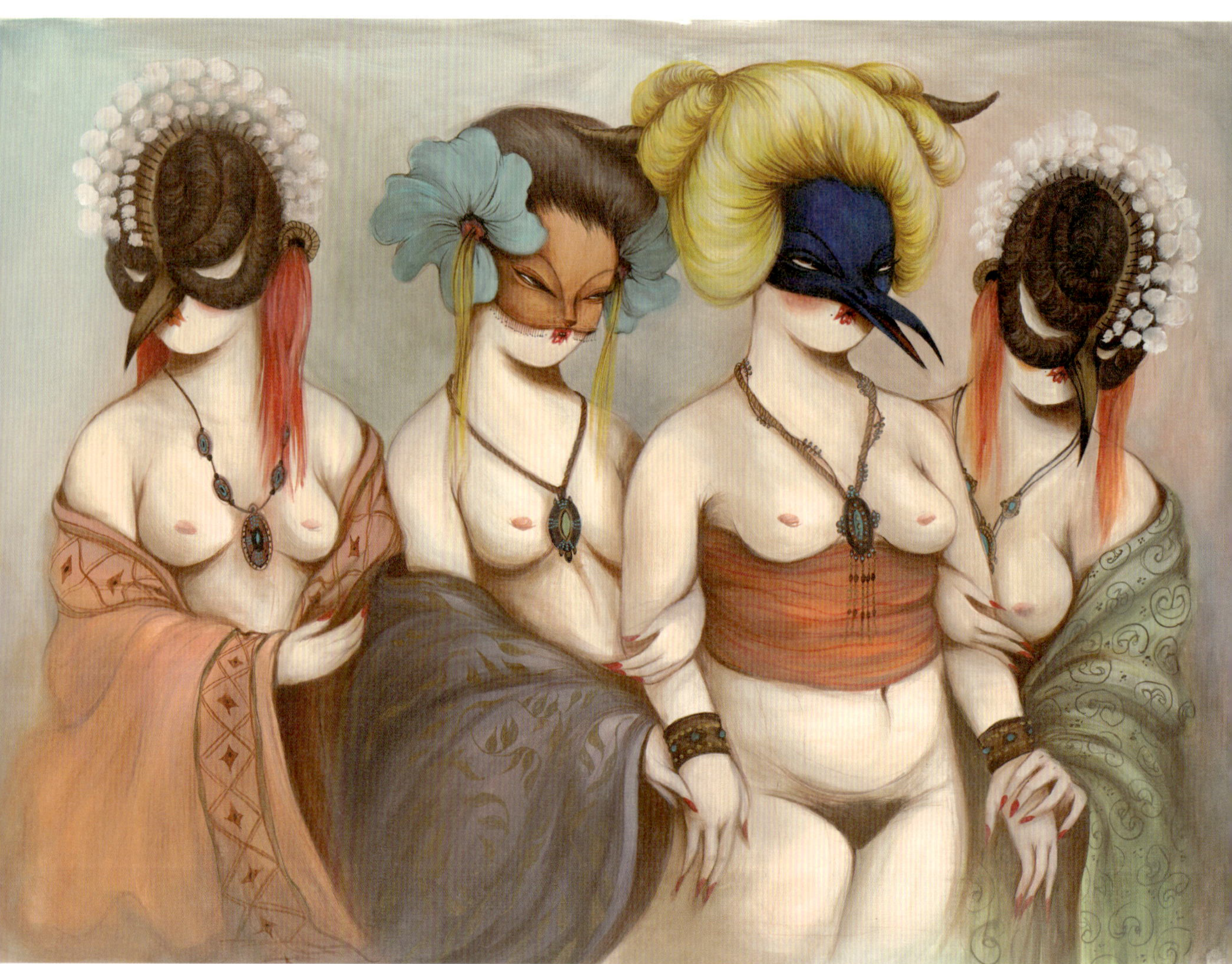

Gorditas De Chicharron II ゴルディタス・デ・チチャロンII
アクリル、カンヴァス / 2014

Coiled (collaboration with Dan Quintana) ぐるぐる巻き（ダン・キンタナとの共同作品）
アクリル、油彩、木製パネル / 2012

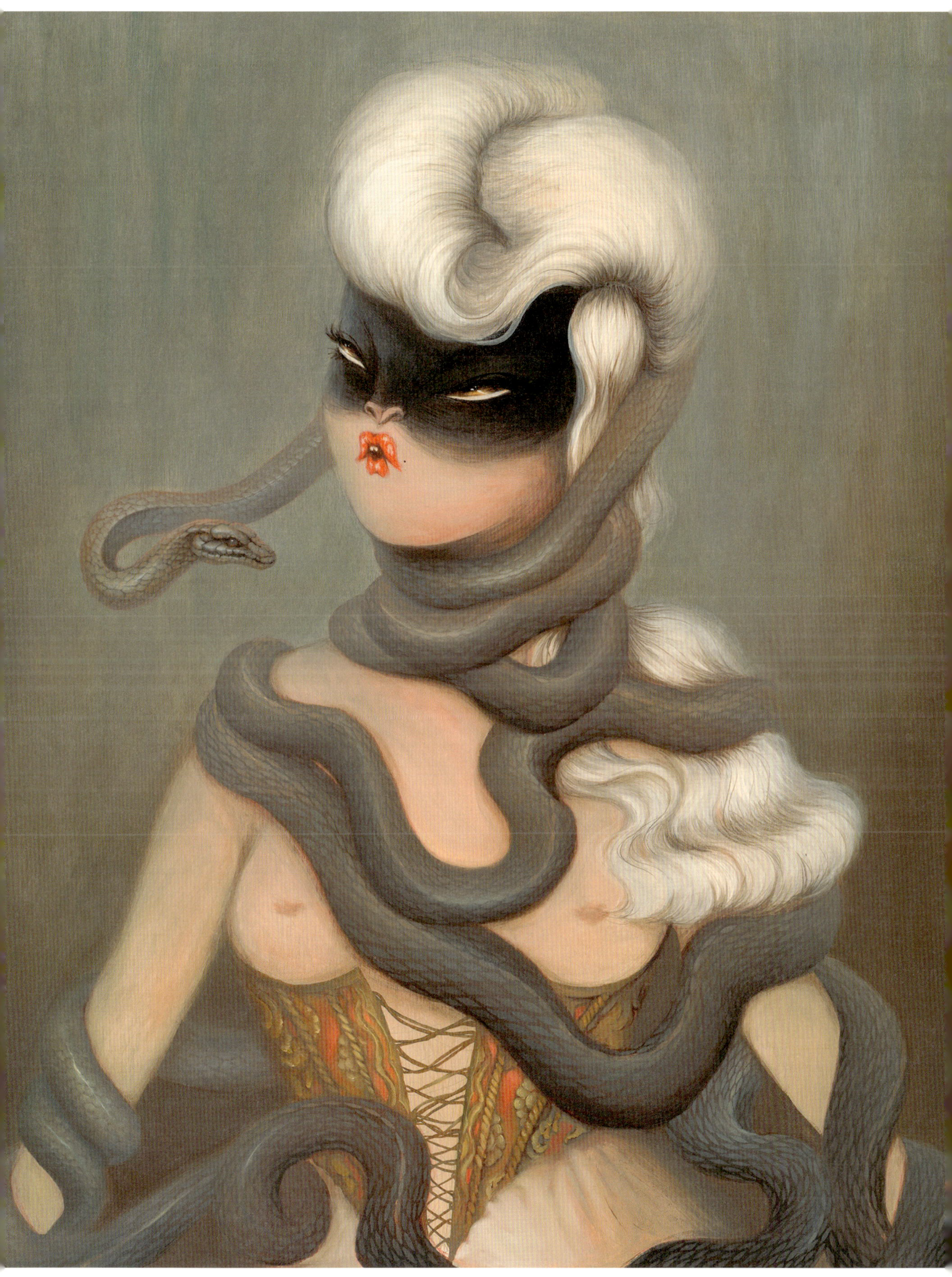

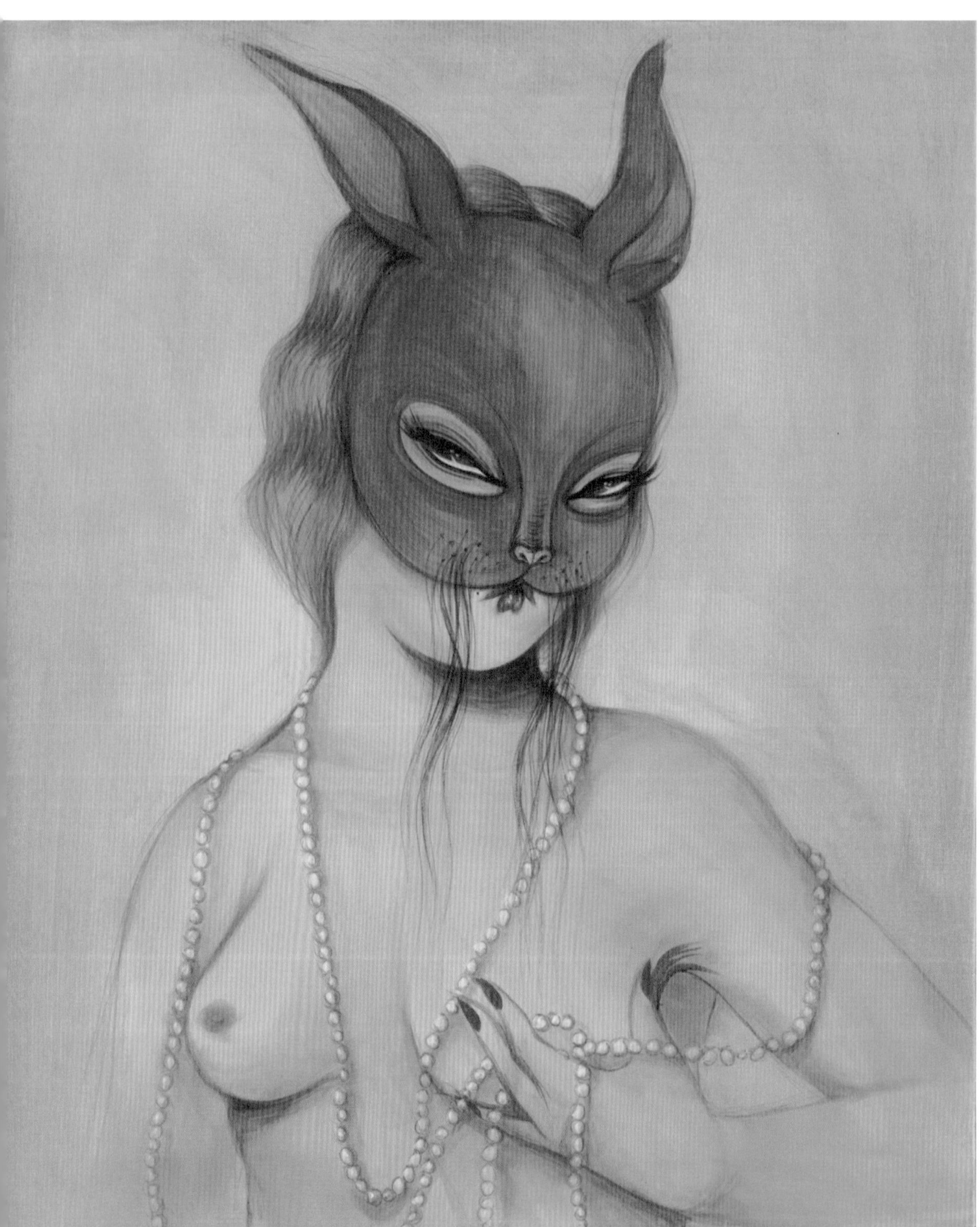

Red Bunny Lover レッド・バニー・ラヴァー
アクリル、カンヴァス / 2013

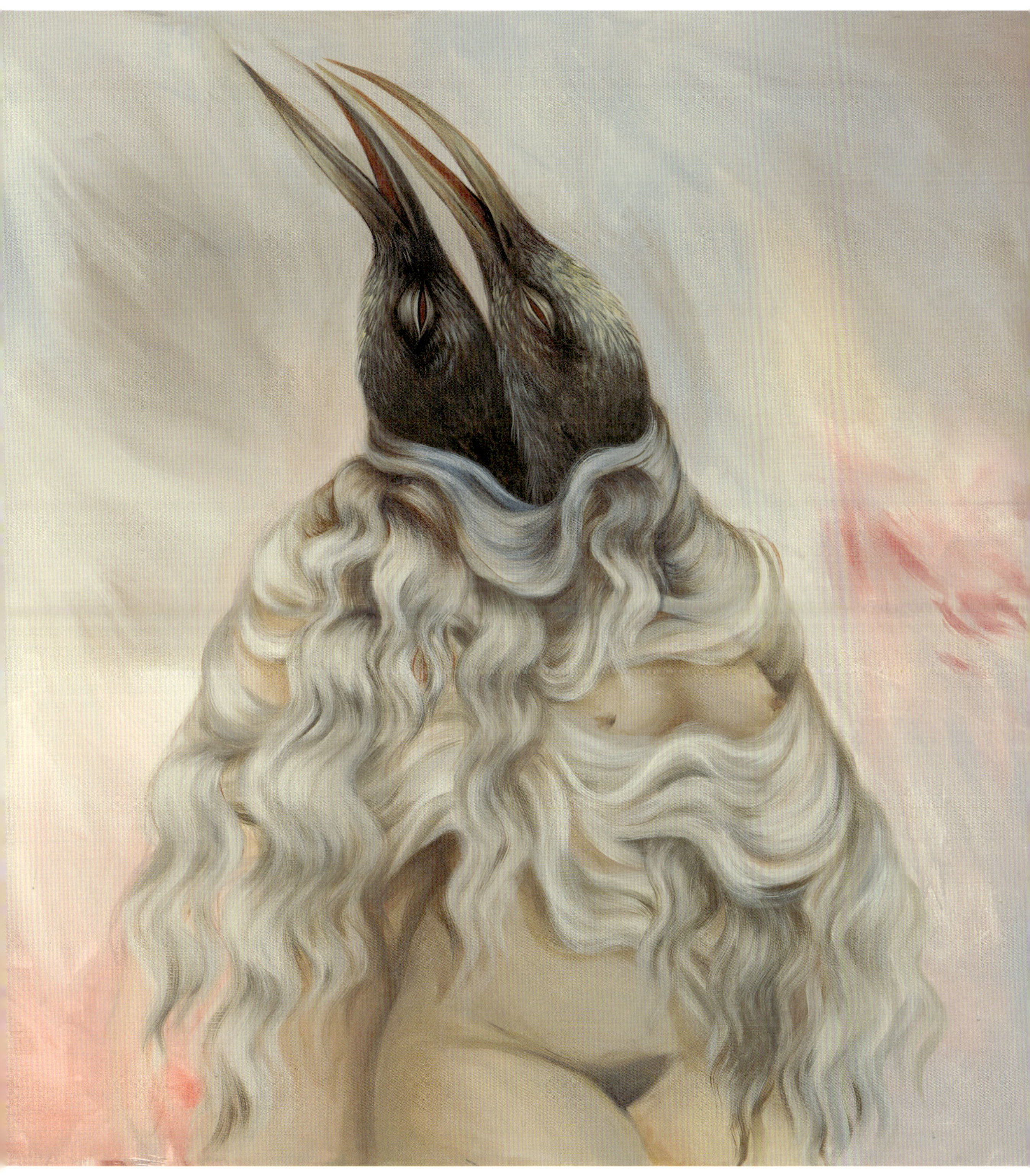

Mujeres Pájaros II 鳥女 II
アクリル、カンヴァス / 2016

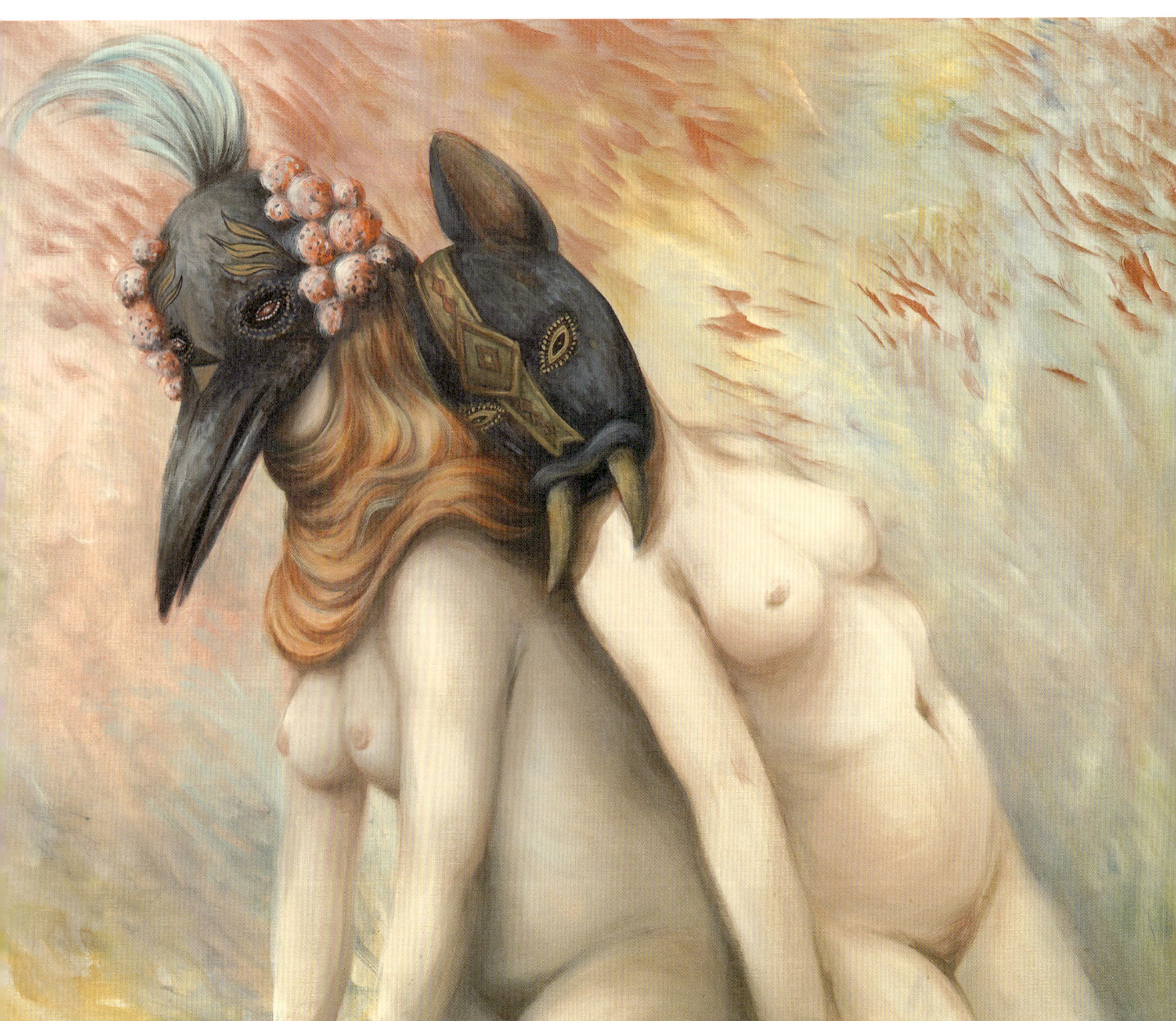

I Feel Safer Here ここだと安全な気がする
アクリル、カンヴァス / 2016

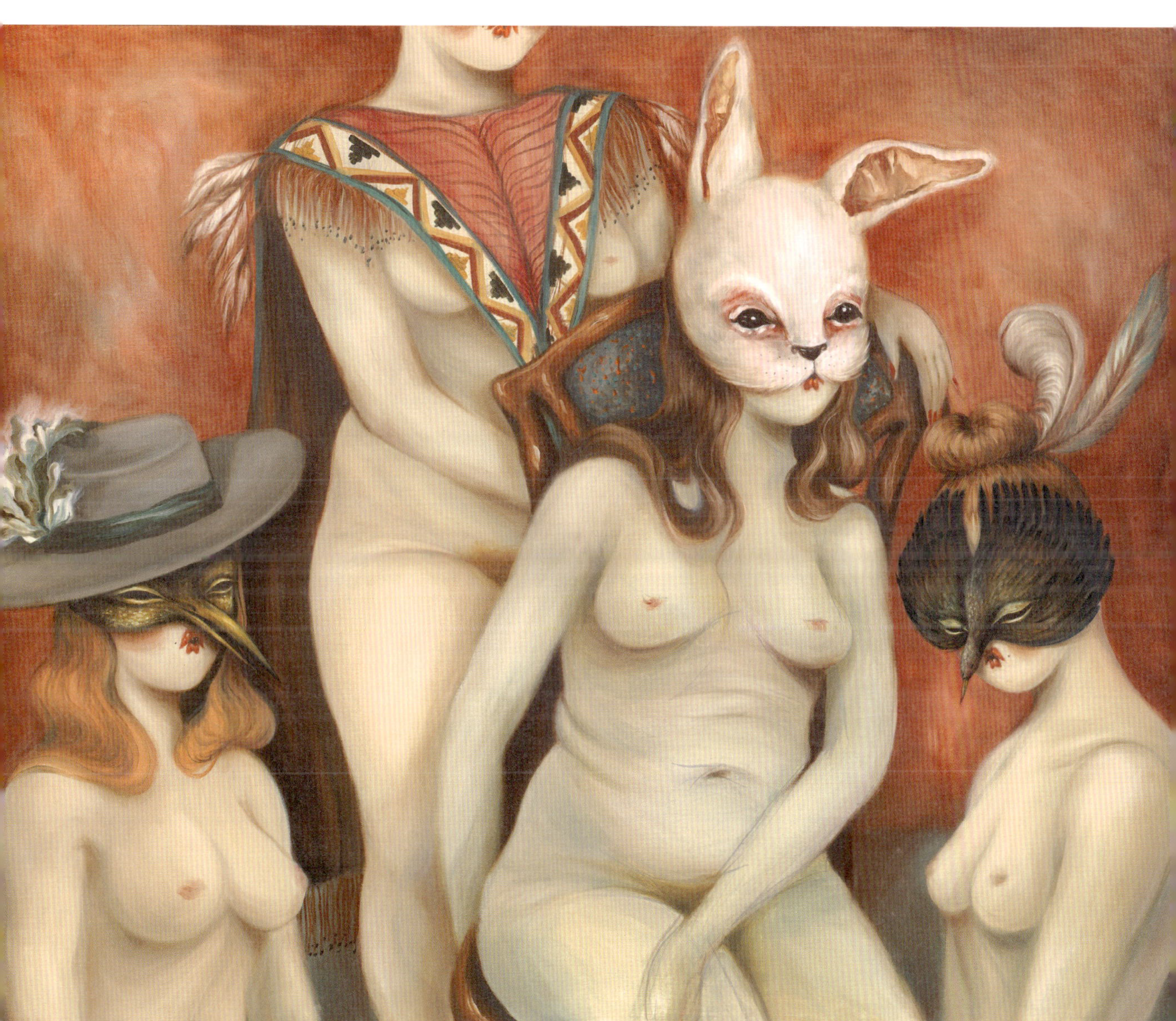

While She was Waiting for You 彼女があなたを待つ間
油彩、カンヴァス / 2017

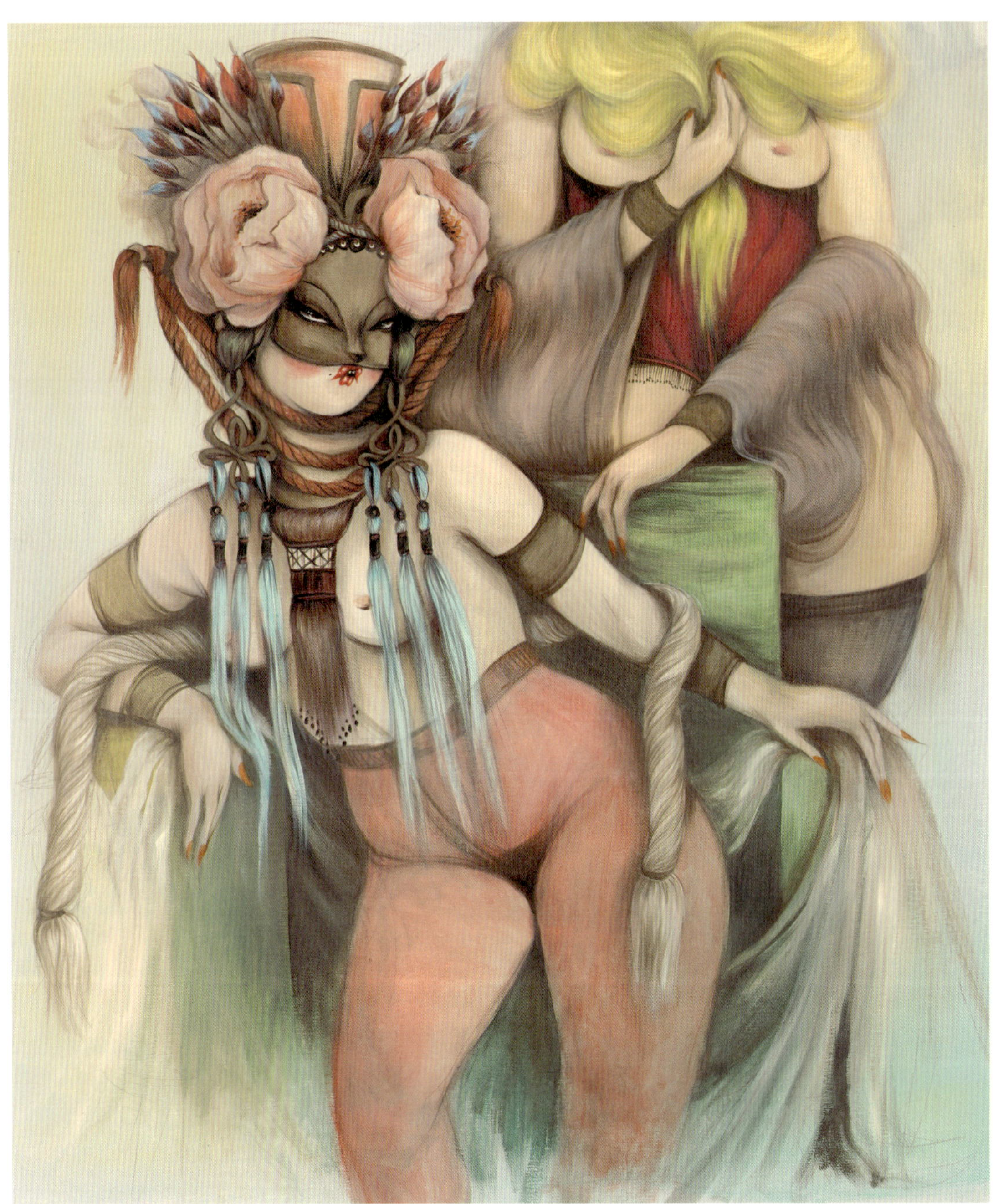

Gorditas De Chicharron Ⅴ ゴルディタス・デ・チチャロンⅤ
アクリル、カンヴァス / 2014

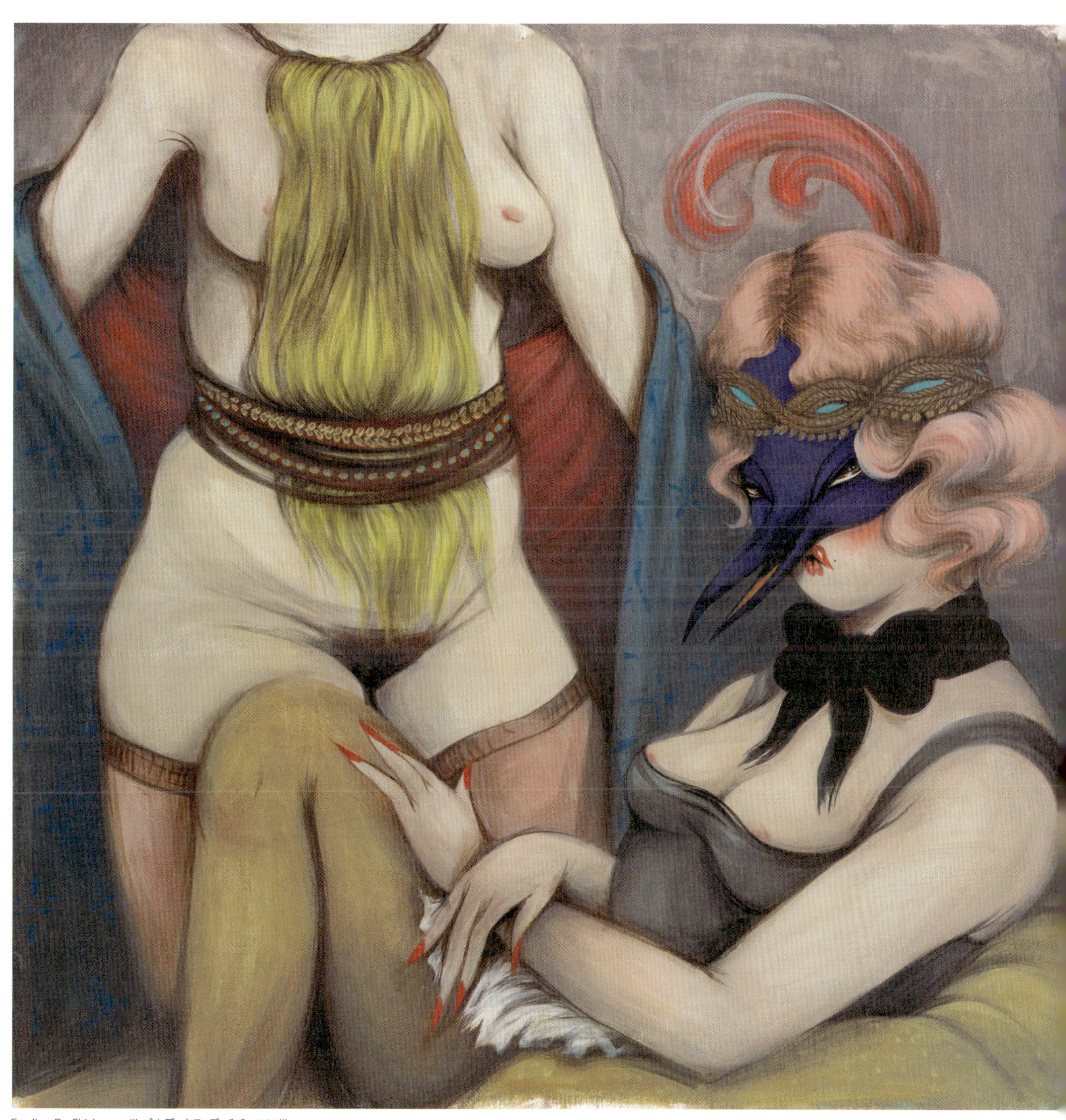

Gorditas De Chicharron III　ゴルディタス・デ・チチャロンIII
アクリル、カンヴァス / 2014

David Bray

デヴィッド・ブレイ（イギリス UK）

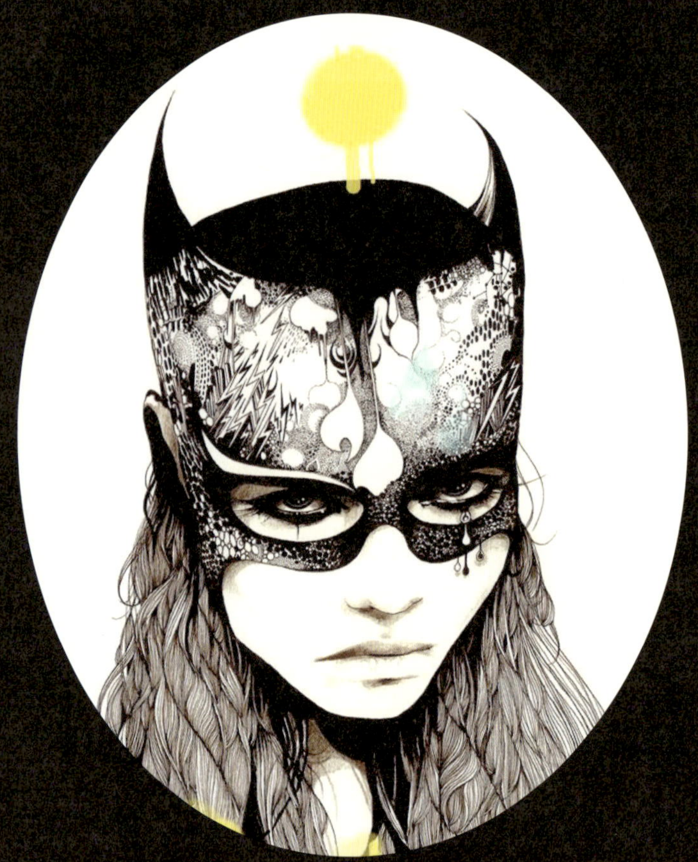

サウス・ロンドンを拠点に活動するイラストレーター、アーティスト。1992年ロンドン芸術大学セントラル・セント・マーティンズ・カレッジ・オブ・アート・アンド・デザイン卒業。商業イラストレーターとして、アブソルート・ウオッカ、プーマ、フォルクスワーゲン、ボーダフォン、BBCなど数多くの企業をクライアントに持つ一方、アーティストとして、ロンドン、東京、ニューヨーク、香港、アムステルダム、ポートランド、ロサンゼルス、パースなど世界中で個展を開催している。ハーヴェイ・ニコルズの広告キャンペーンで、ファッション・フォトグラファーのティム・ブレット・デイとコラボレーションした「HN on Earth」のポスターは、現在ルーブル美術館で常設展示されている。

David Bray is an illustrator/artist based in South London. He has been working as a freelance illustrator since his graduation from Central St. Martins in 1992 with clients such as Absolut, Puma, Volkswagen, Vodafone, BBC to name but a few. As an artist David has exhibited in London, Tokyo, New York, Hong Kong, Amsterdam, Portland, Los Angeles and Perth. His collaboration with photographer Tim Bret Day on the Harvey Nichols advertising campaign 'HN on Earth' is now in the permanent poster collection at the Louvre.

www.davidbray.eu

↑By Night 夜までに（部分）
ペン、鉛筆、紙 / H29×W21cm / 2008

→Bad Wisdom 2 悪知恵2
ペン、鉛筆、紙 / H40×W28cm / 2009

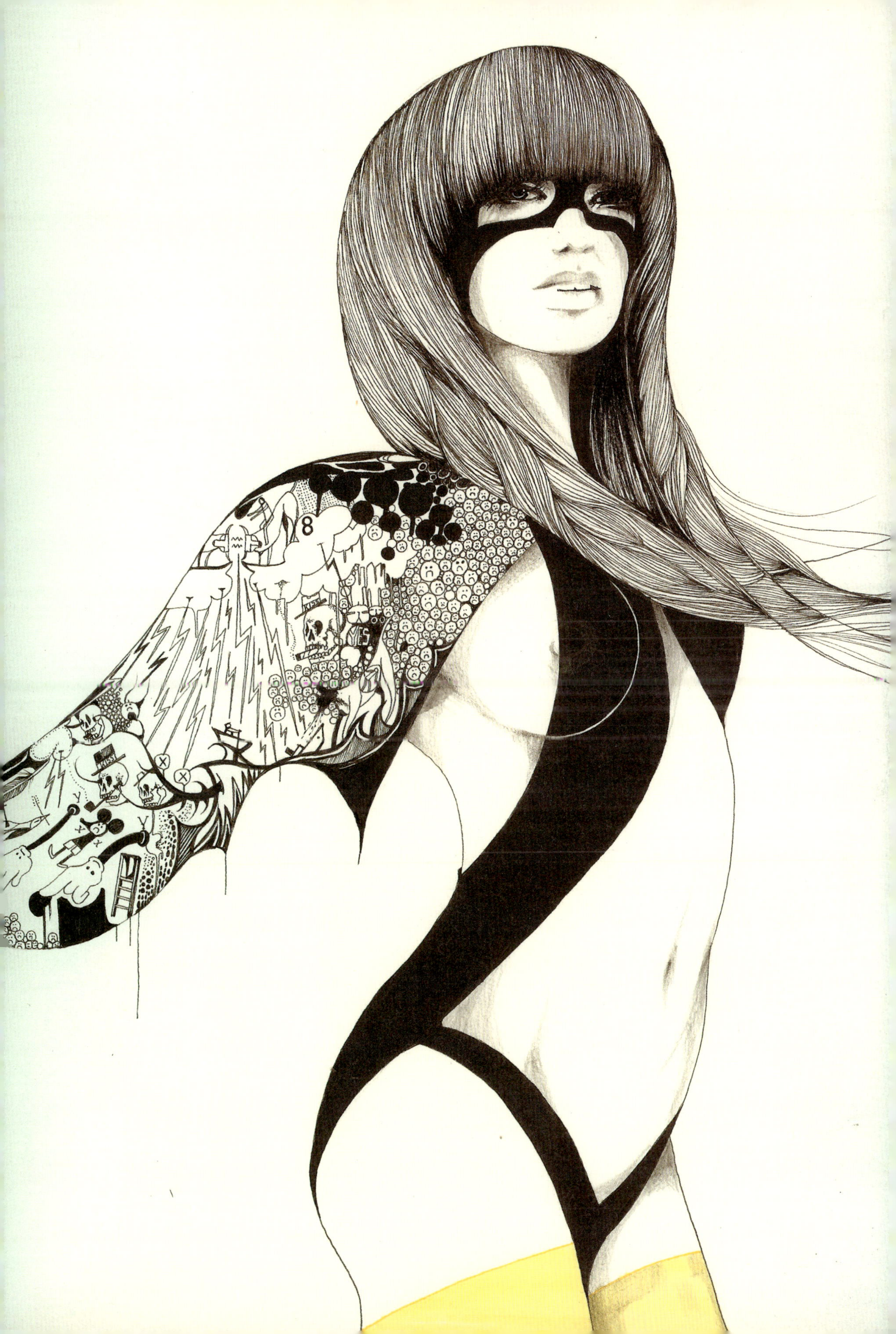

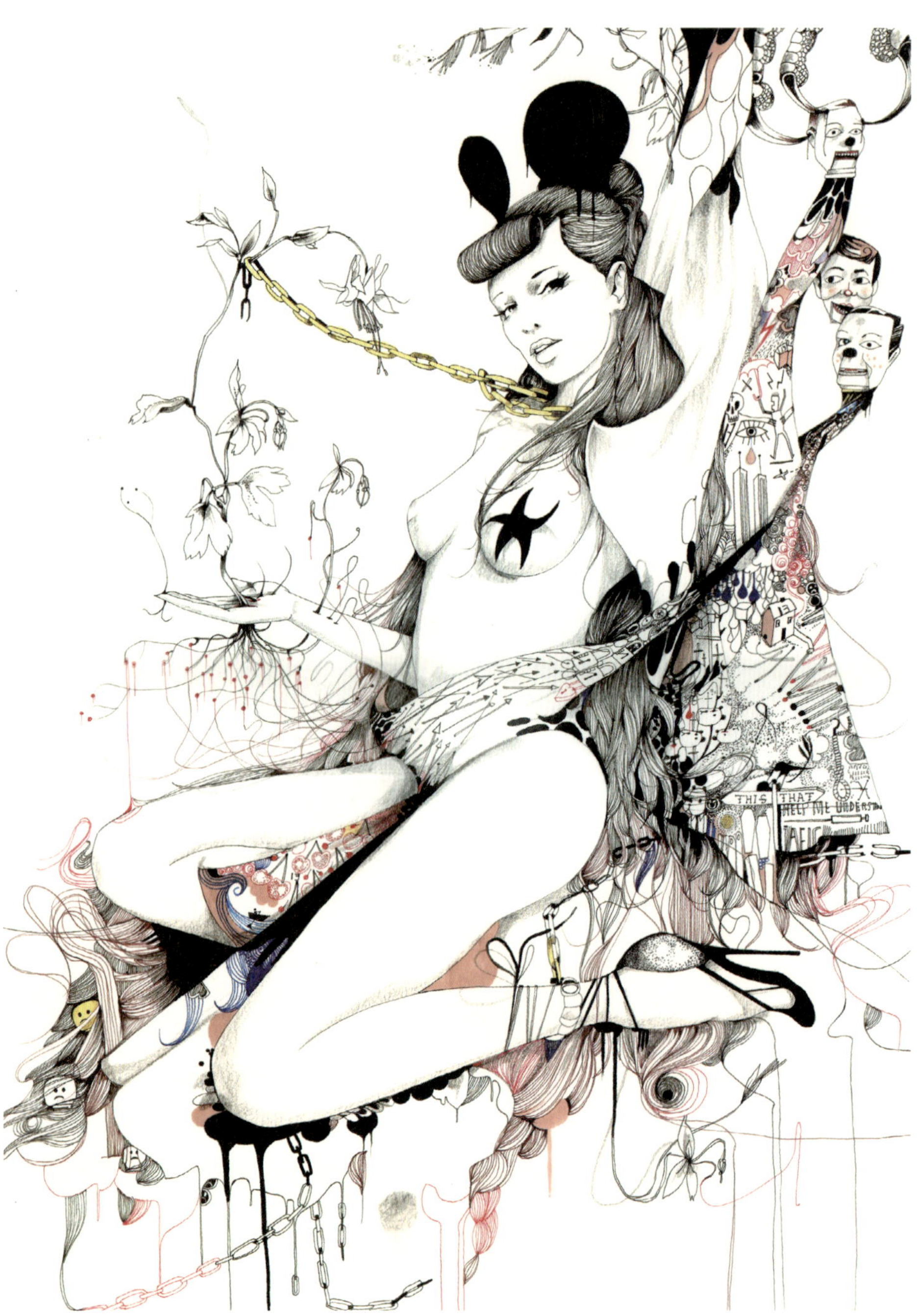

River Becomes a Stream 川が一筋の流れになる
ペン、鉛筆、紙 / H42×W29cm / 2009

Perseid ペルセウス座
ペン、鉛筆、紙 / H57×W38cm / 2010

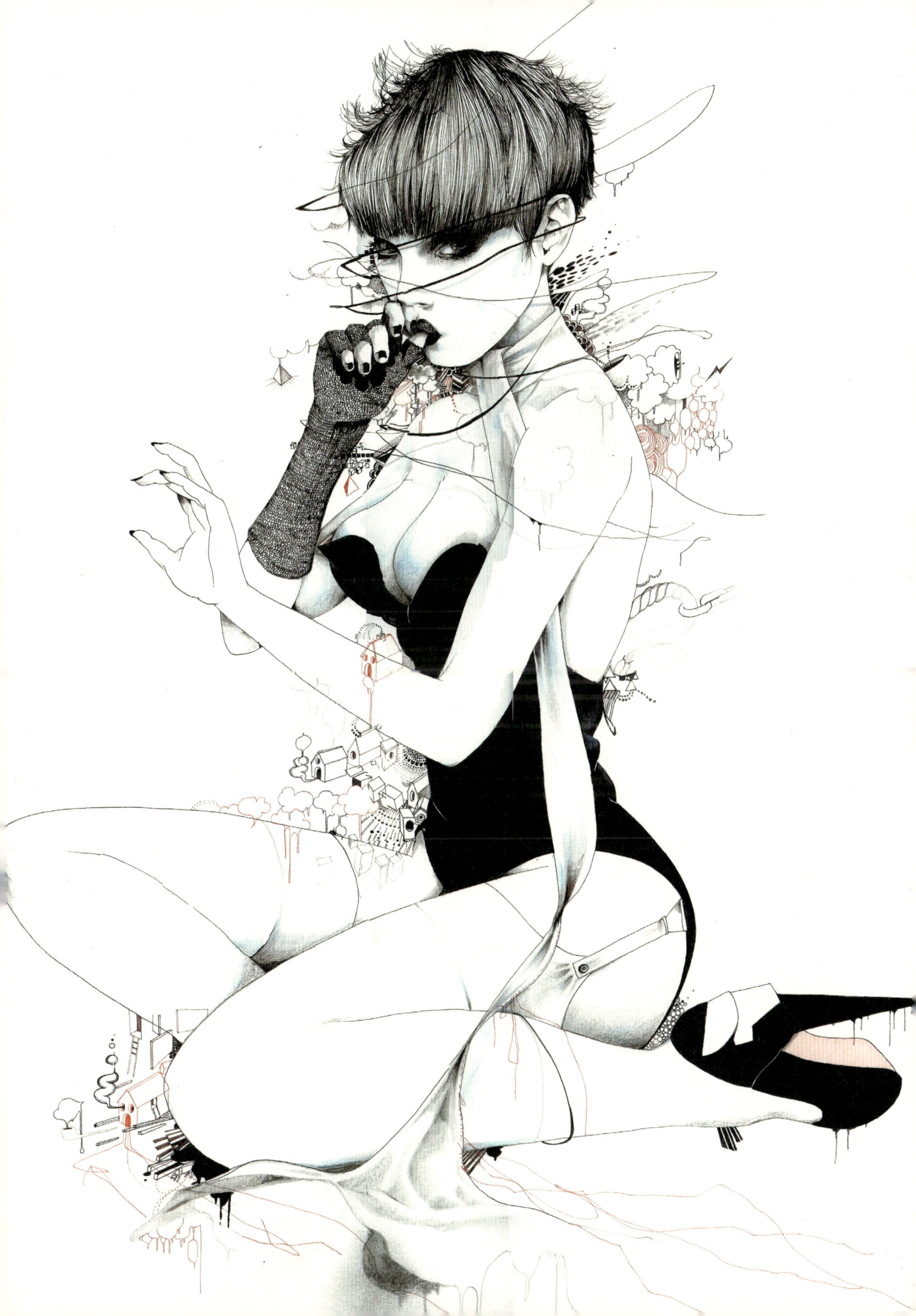

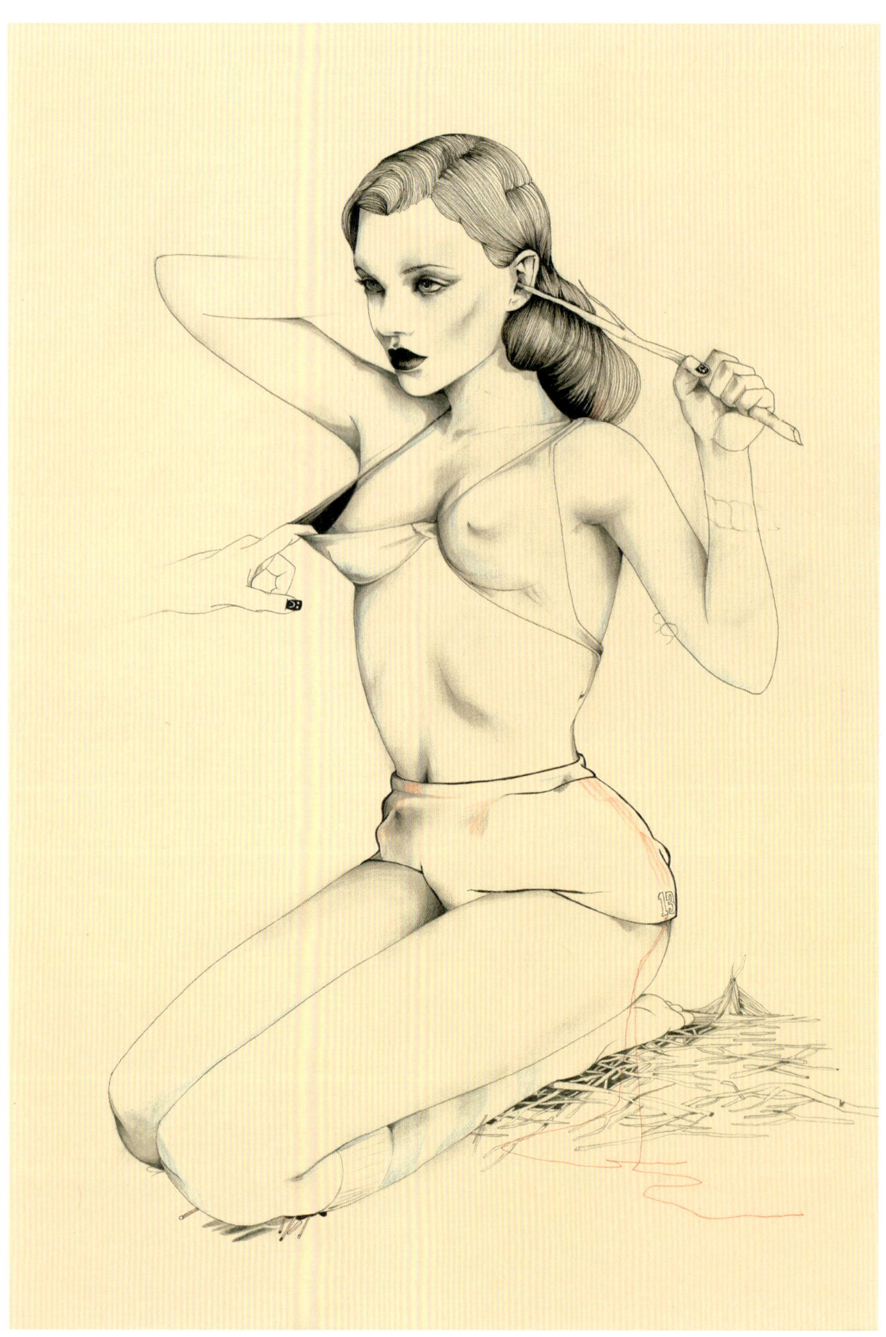

A Letter to Three Wives 3人の妻への手紙
ペン、鉛筆、紙 / H57×W38cm / 2011

Modern Rural Sports モダン・ルーラル・スポーツ
ペン、鉛筆、紙 / H57×W38cm / 2011

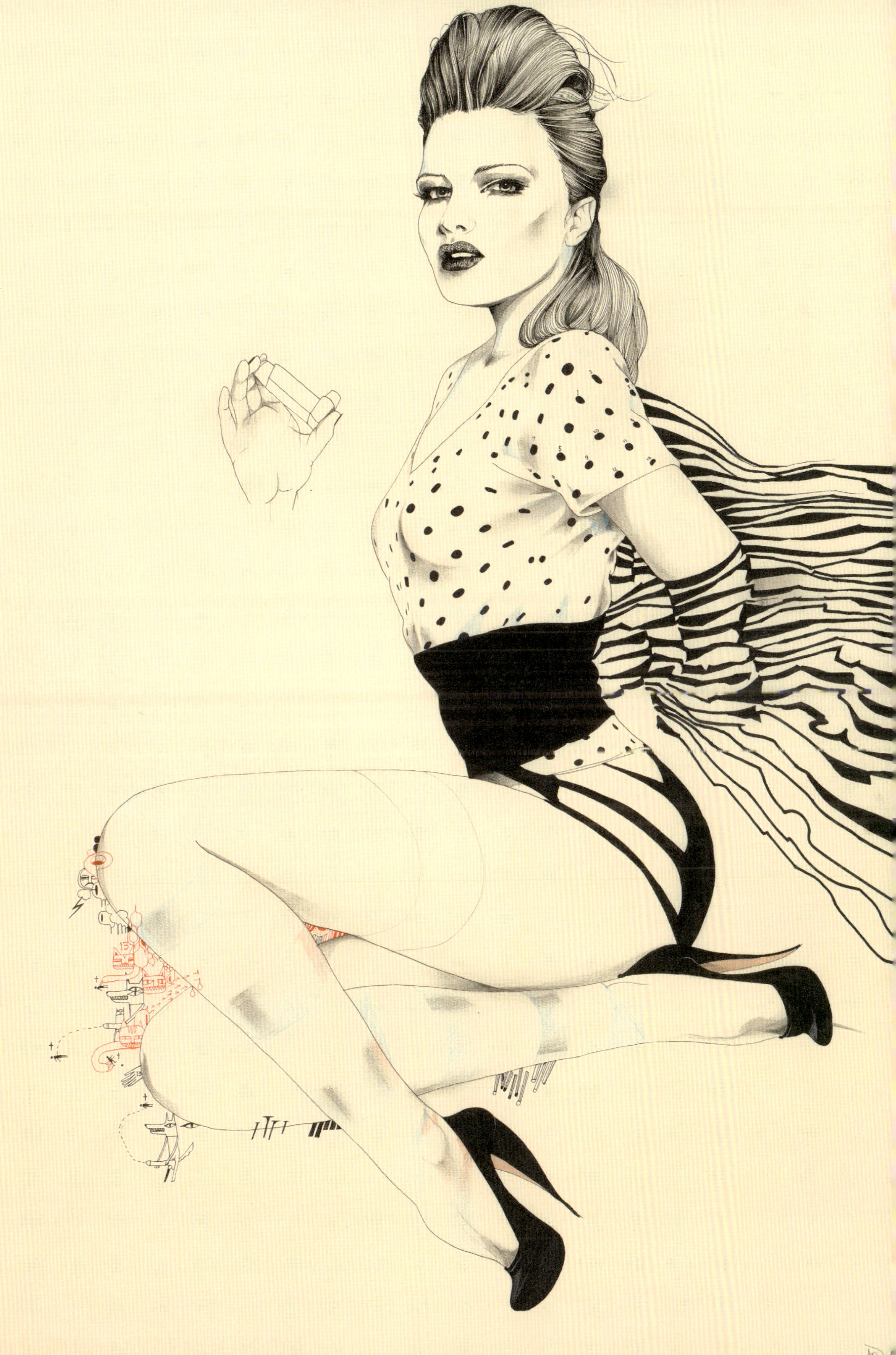

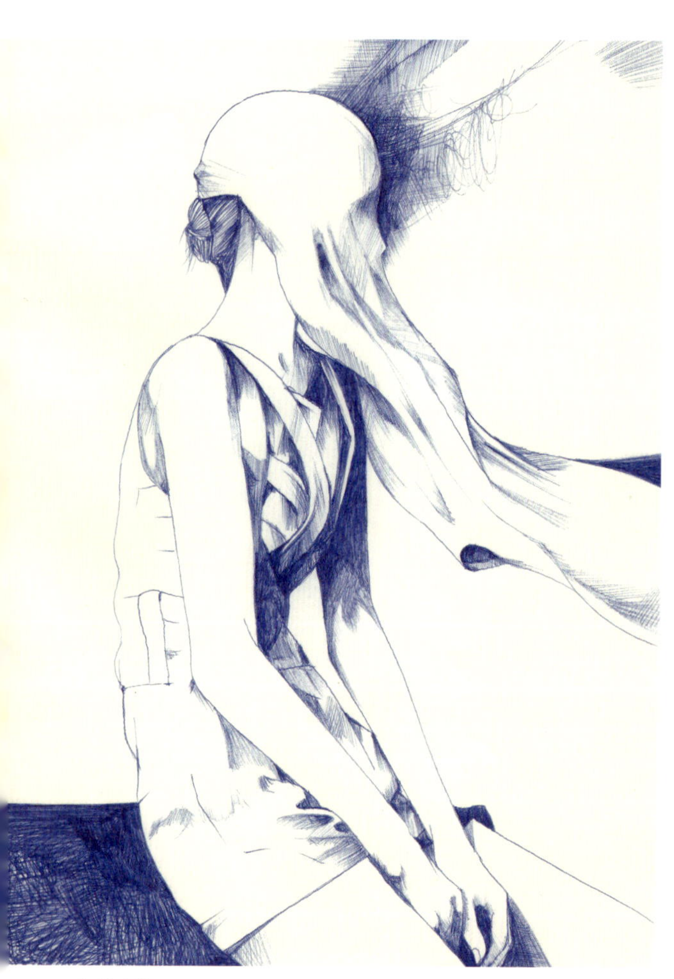

No title 無題
ペン、紙 / H36×W24cm / 2013

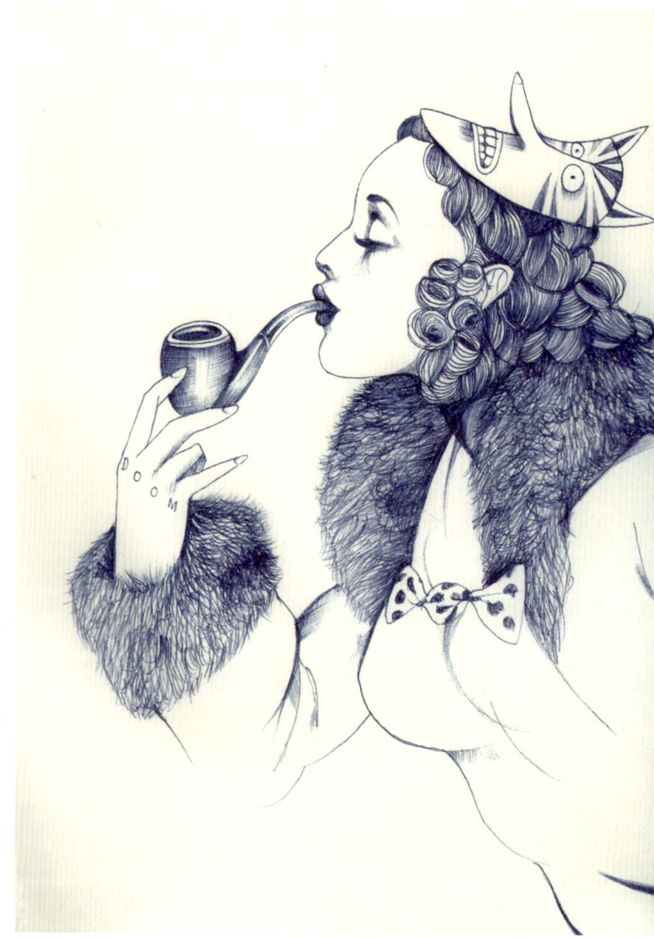

No title 無題
ペン、紙 / H36×W24cm / 2013

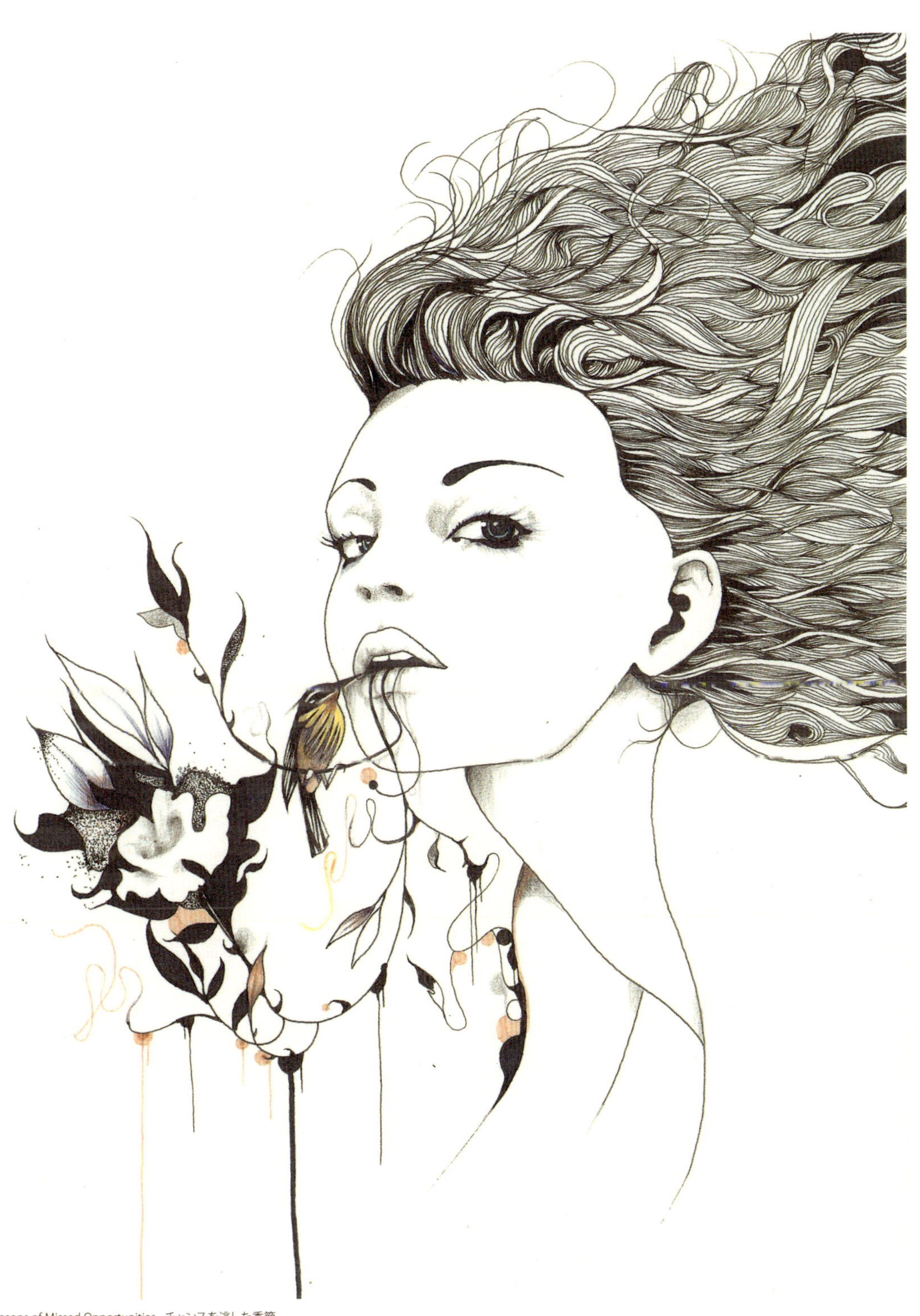

Seasons of Missed Opportunities　チャンスを逃した季節
ペン、鉛筆、紙 / H87×W61cm / 2008

Guido Crepax

ガイド・クレパックス（イタリア Italy）

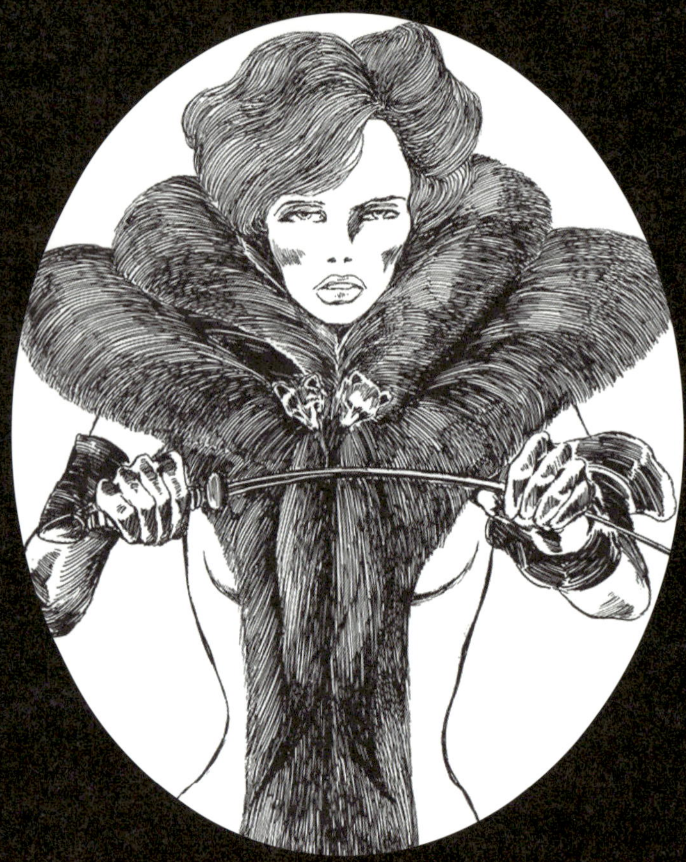

1933年、ミラノ生まれ。成人向け漫画家として世界的に知られた巨匠。12歳にしてはじめてコミック・ストリップ（つづき漫画）を描く。大学の建築学科を卒業後、絵を職業にすることを決意、グラフィック・デザイナーとして「シェル」、「カンパリ」、「エッソ」、「ダンロップ」、「富士フイルム」、「ホンダ」などの企業広告を手がけた。1965年に漫画界へ復帰し、彼を一躍有名にしたキャラクター、ヴァレンティーナを生み出した。『ドラキュラ』、『フランケンシュタイン』など古典文学の漫画化にも取り組んだ。5000を超えるコミック・ストリップをのうち約200版が主要言語に翻訳される。アクセサリー、インテリア・デザイン、劇場、映画、テレビの分野でも活躍。2003年7月31日逝去。

Born in Milan in 1933, Guido Crepax is viewed as one of the foremost comic book authors, probably the best known internationally in the field of comics fir adults. He created his first comic strip when he was 12 years old. After graduating in architecture, he decided to devote himself to drawing — creating advertising campaigns for Shell, Campari, Esso, Dunlop, Fuji and Honda. He returned to the world of comics in 1965, creating the character that made him famous all over the world: Valentina. His retellings in comic form of literary classics are meticulous and polished works, as are the more recent movie versions. Altogether, he drew over 5,000 comic-strip plates, and about 200 editions of his books have been published in all the major languages. He also designed accessories and home décor. He also worked in theater, cinema and television. He passed away on July 31st, 2003.

www.raimondicampbell.com

↑"Venus in fur" page 11 漫画『毛皮のヴィーナス』11ページ（部分）
インク、厚紙／H51×W36.5cm／1983

→"Anthropology" page 55 漫画『ヴァレンティーナ ── アンスロポロジー』55ページ
インク、厚紙／H51×W36.5cm／1977

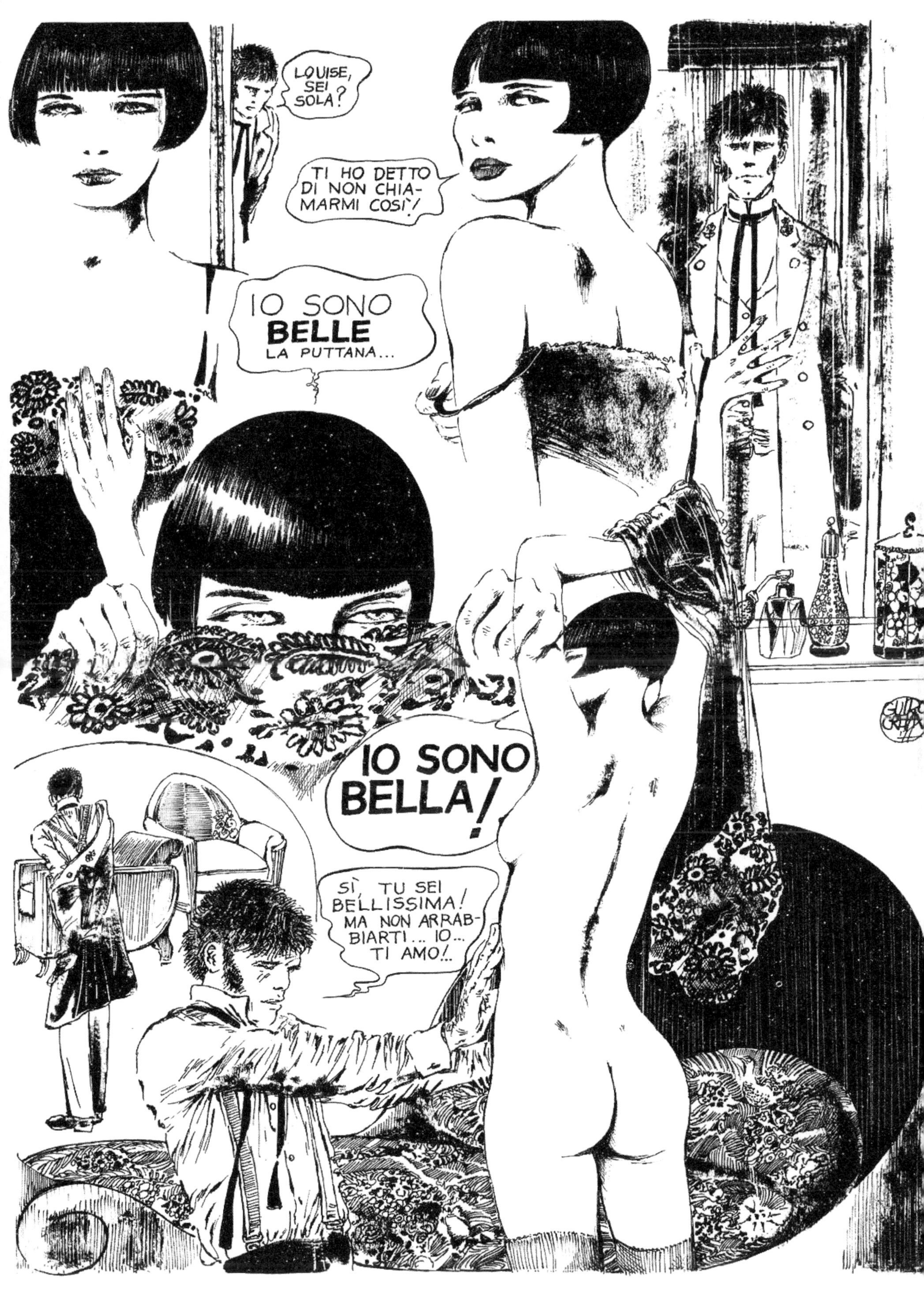
LOUISE, SEI SOLA?
TI HO DETTO DI NON CHIAMARMI COSÌ!
IO SONO BELLE LA PUTTANA...
IO SONO BELLA!
SÌ, TU SEI BELLISSIMA! MA NON ARRABBIARTI... IO... TI AMO!..

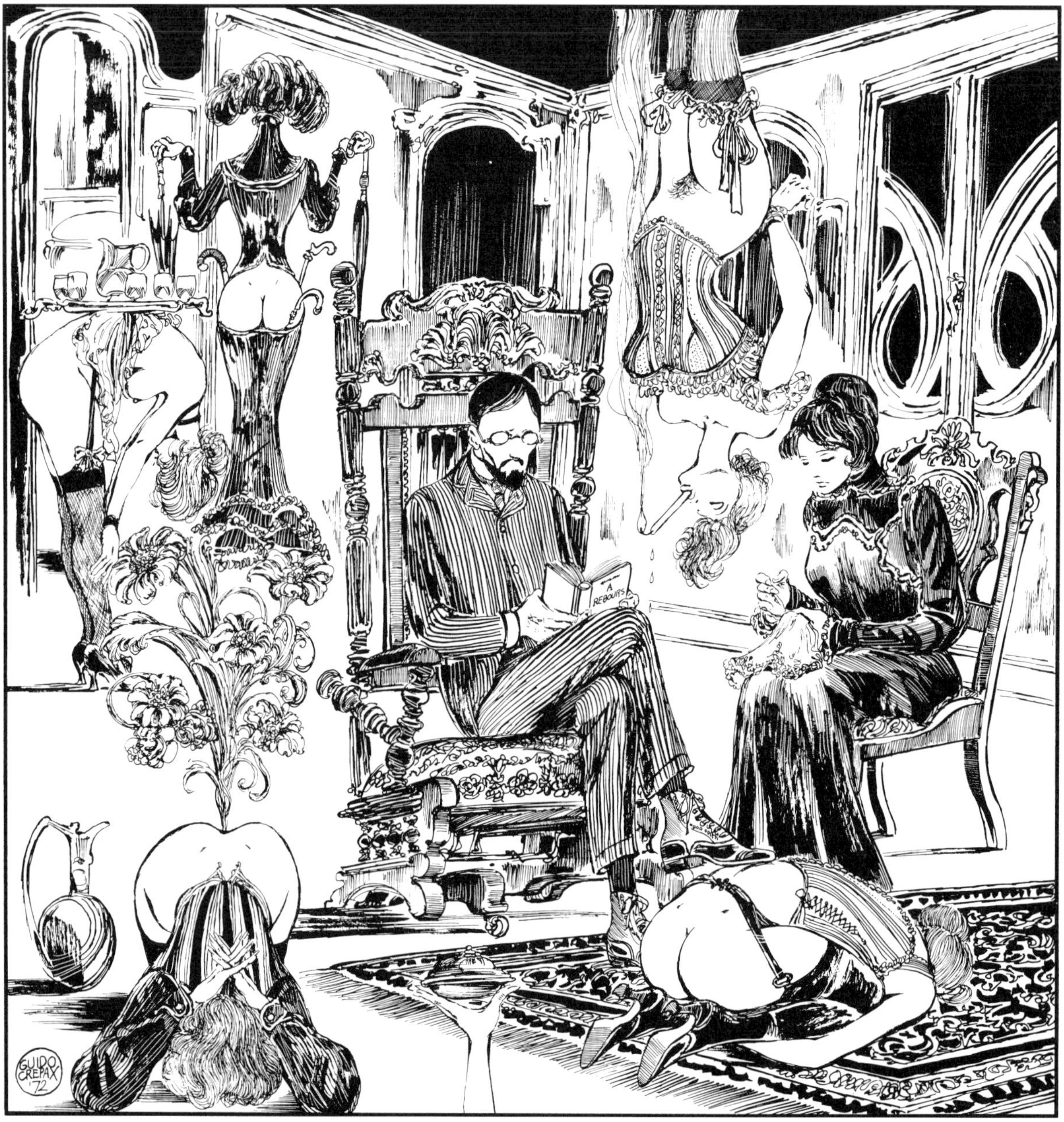

"Bluebeard" page 1 漫画『ヴァレンティーナ ── 青ひげ』1ページ
インク、厚紙 / H51×W36.5cm / 1972

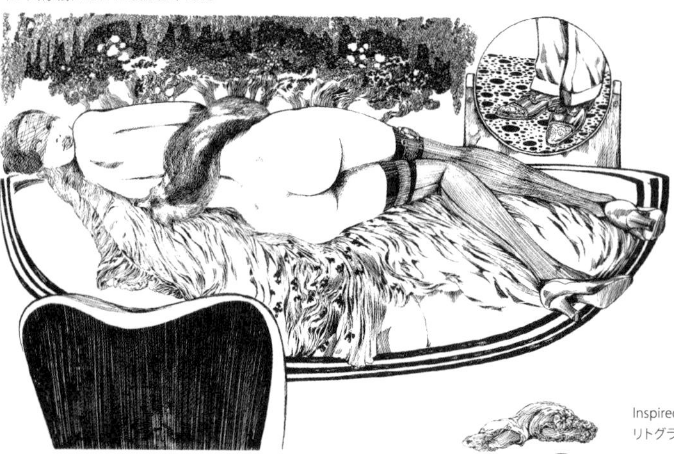

Inspired by "Histoire d'O" 『O嬢の物語』から着想を得た作品
リトグラフ / H50×W70cm / 1976

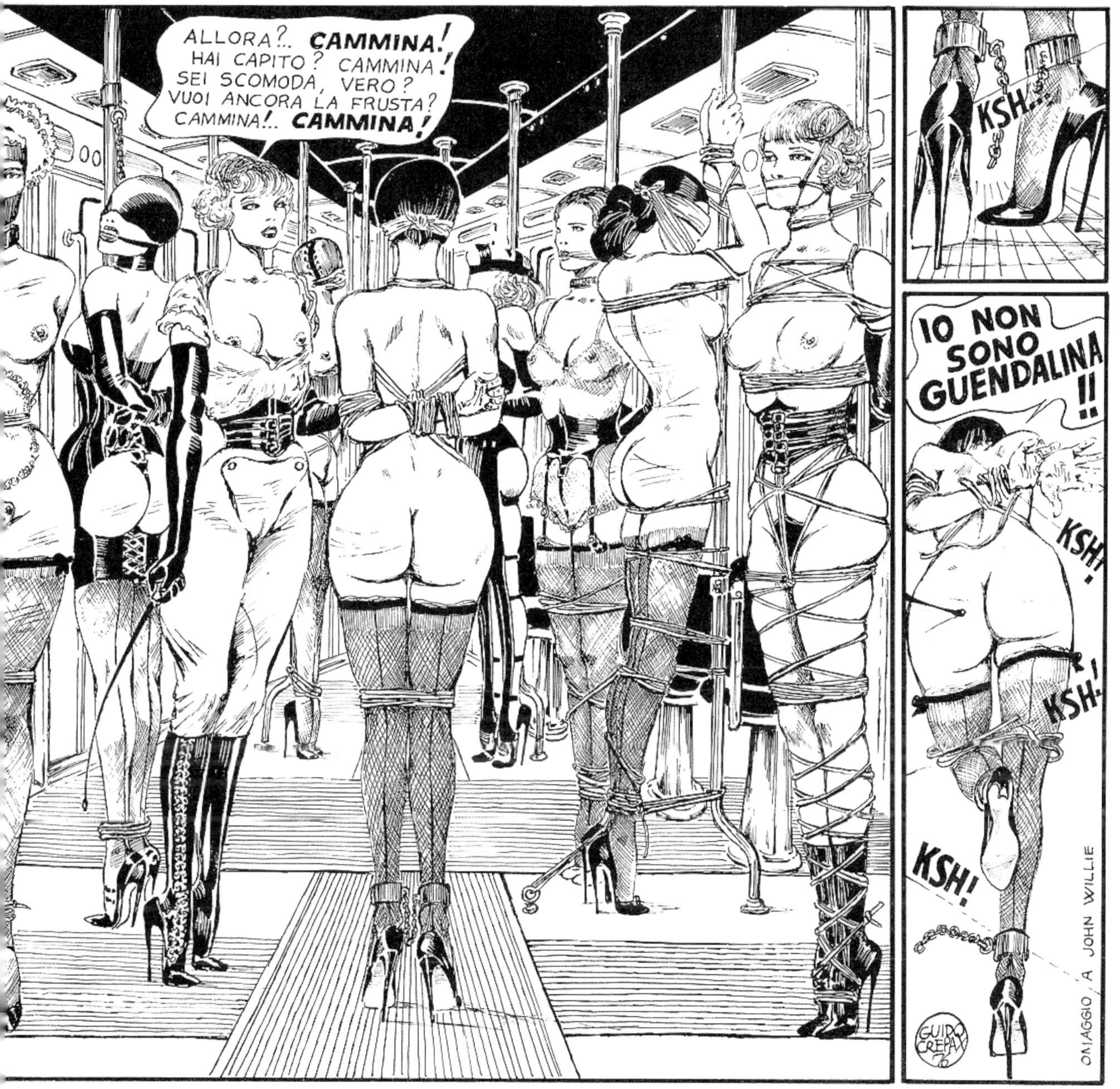

Valentina in the Subway (tribute to John Willie, Gwendolyn) 漫画『地下鉄のヴァレンティーナ』(ジョン・ウィリーのグウェンドリンへの賛辞)
インク、厚紙 / H51×W36.5cm / 1976

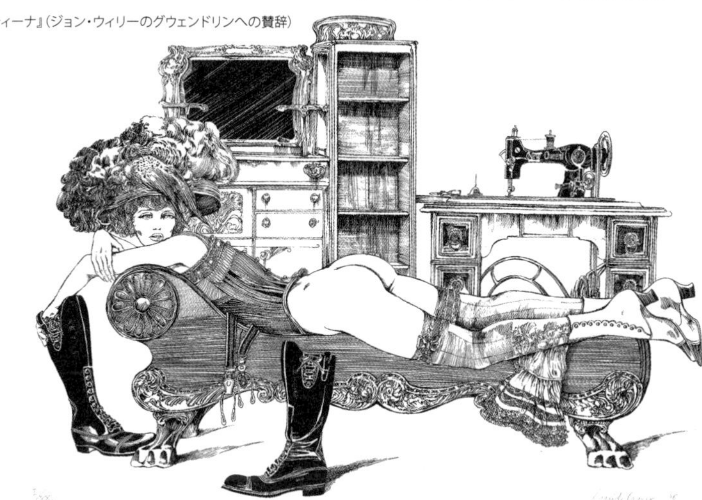

Boots ブーツ
リトグラフ / H50×W70cm / 1977

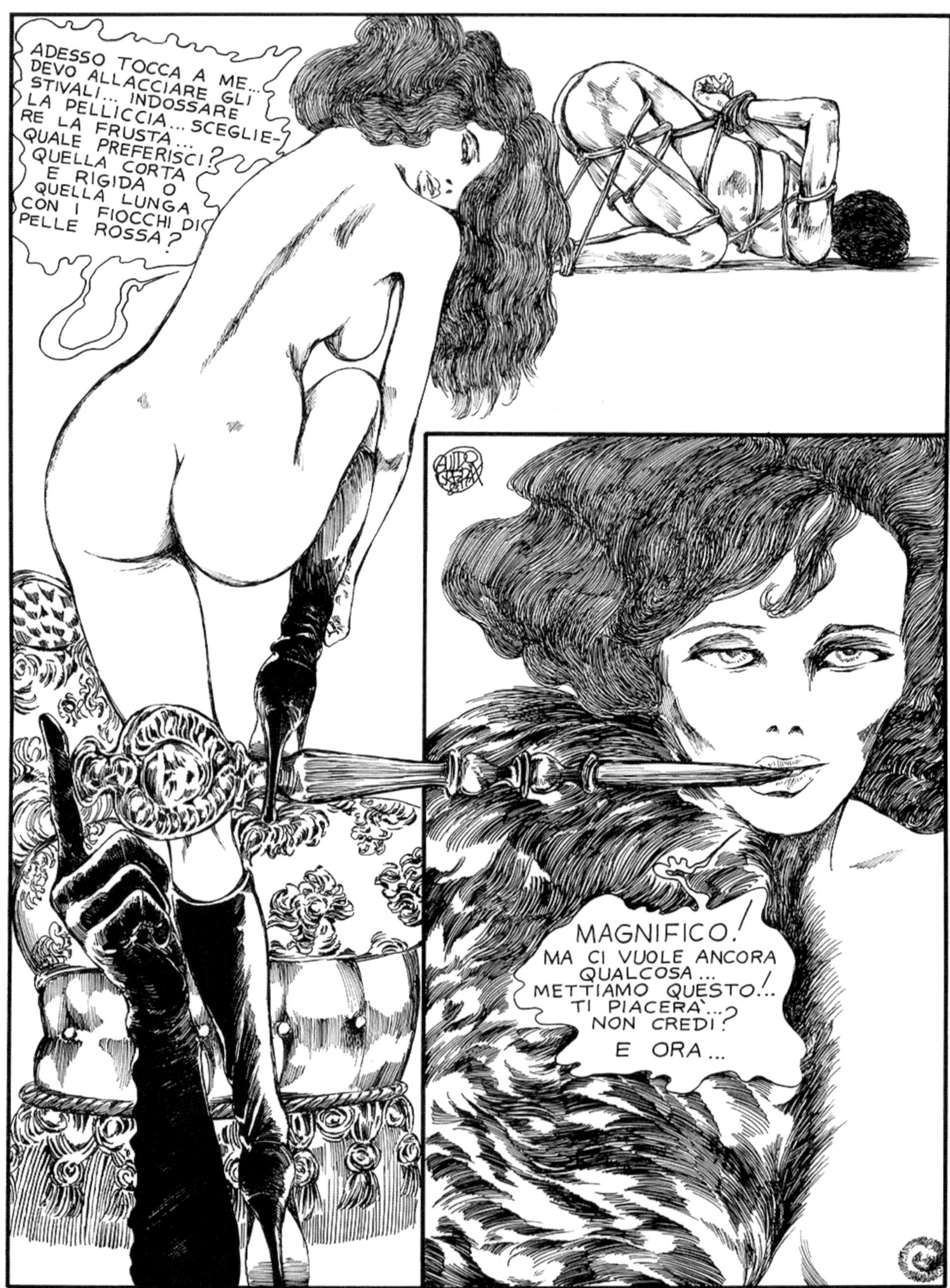

"Venus in fur" page 52 漫画『毛皮のヴィーナス』52ページ
インク、厚紙 / H51×W36.5cm / 1983

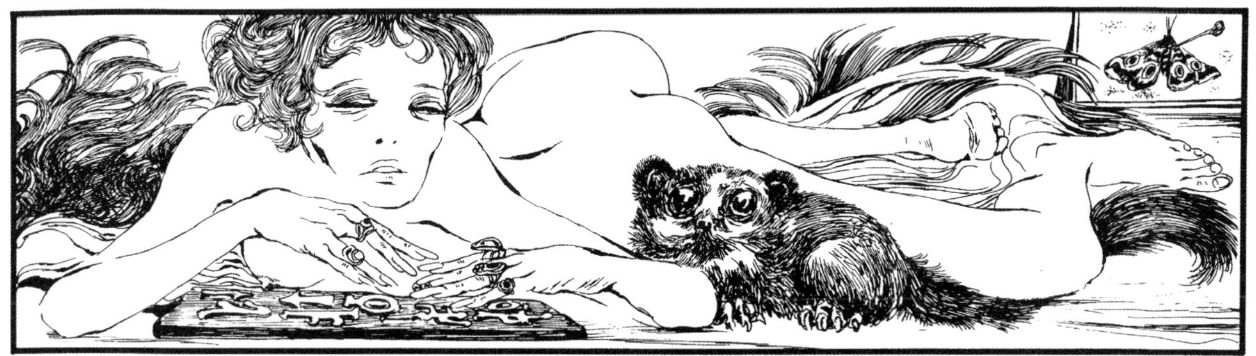

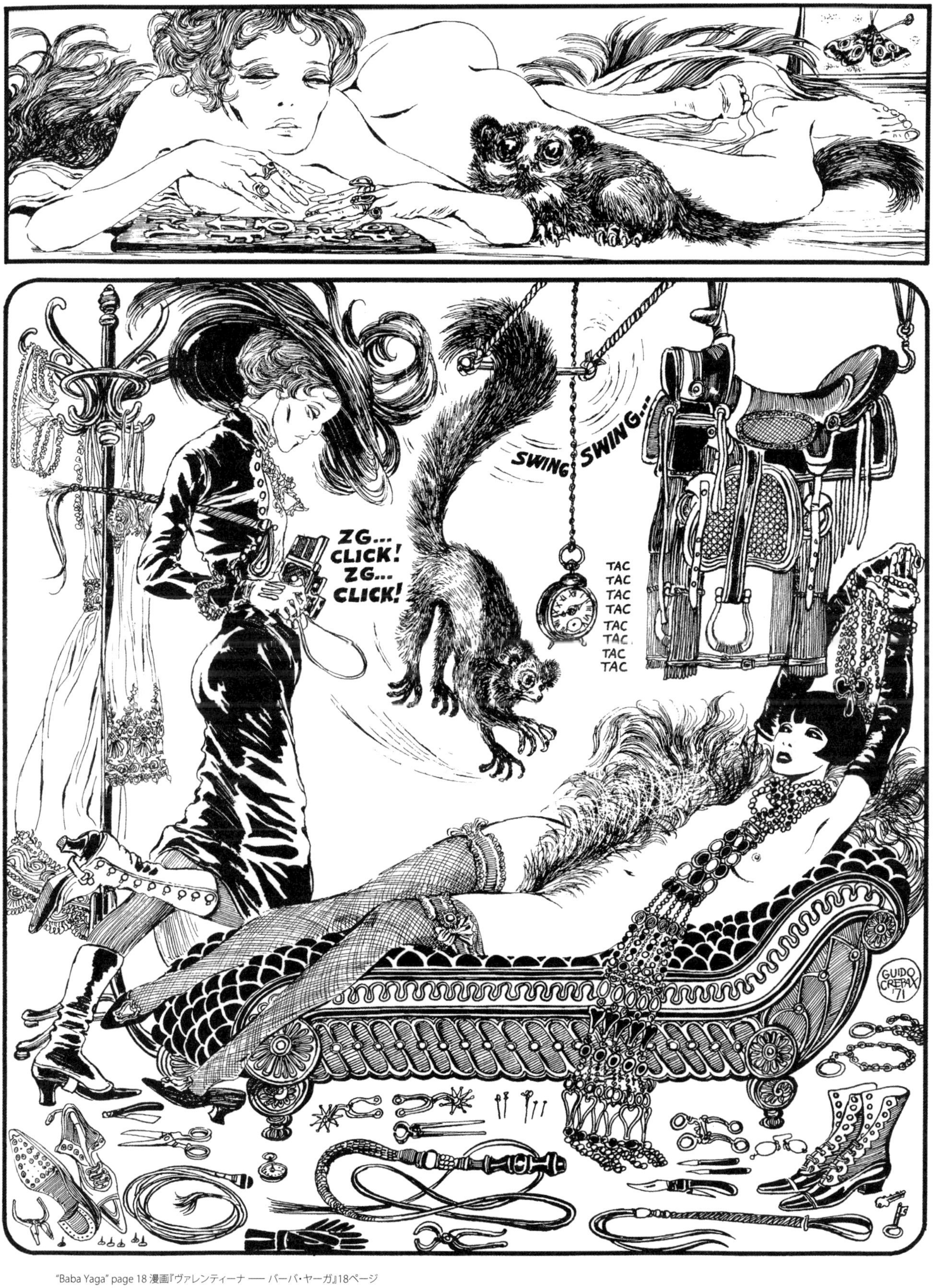

"Baba Yaga" page 18 漫画『ヴァレンティーナ ── バーバ・ヤーガ』18ページ
インク、厚紙 / H51×W36.5cm / 1971

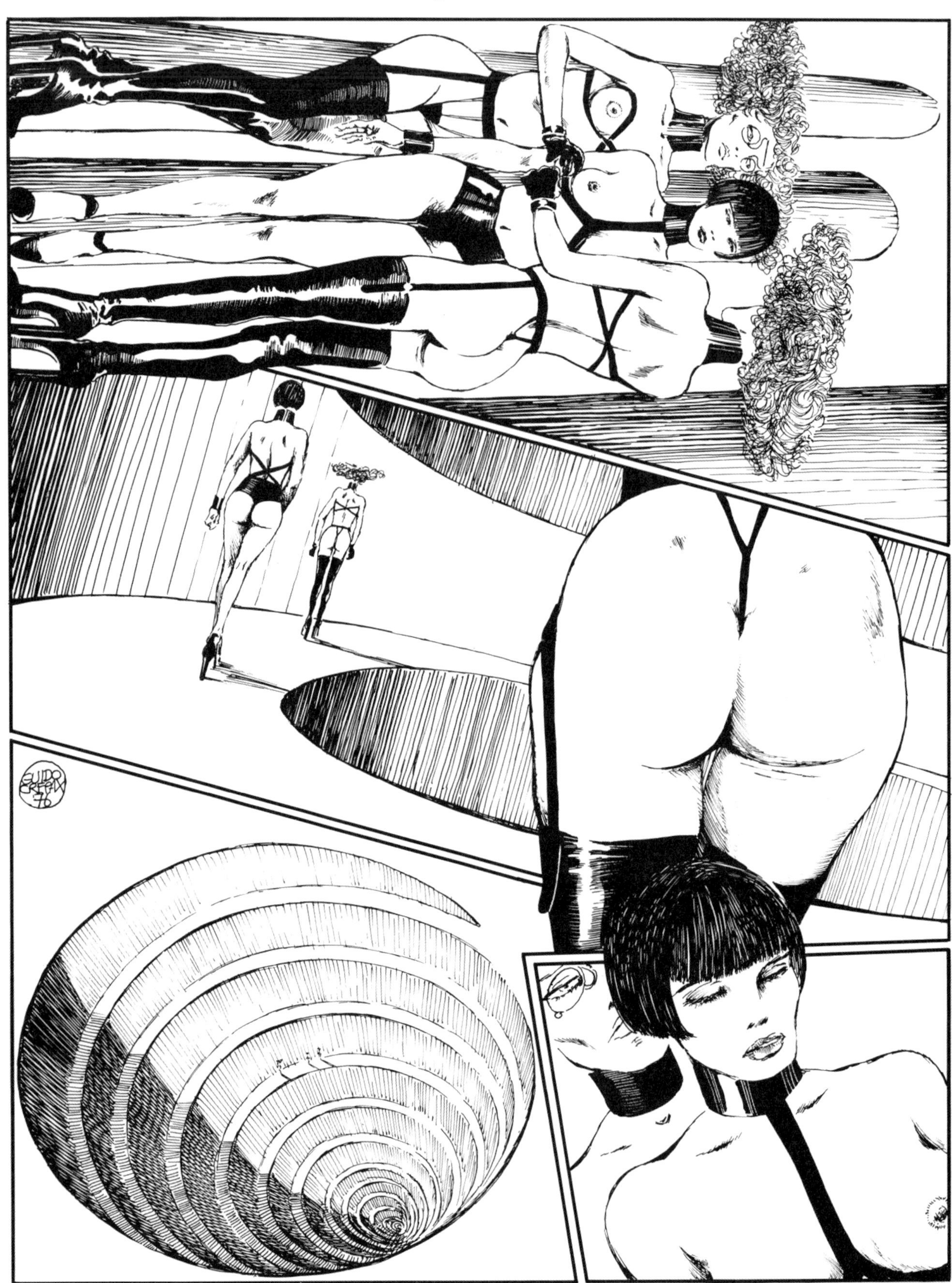

"Magic Lantern" page 13 漫画『ヴァレンティーナ──マジック・ランタン』13ページ
インク、厚紙 / H51×W36.5cm / 1976

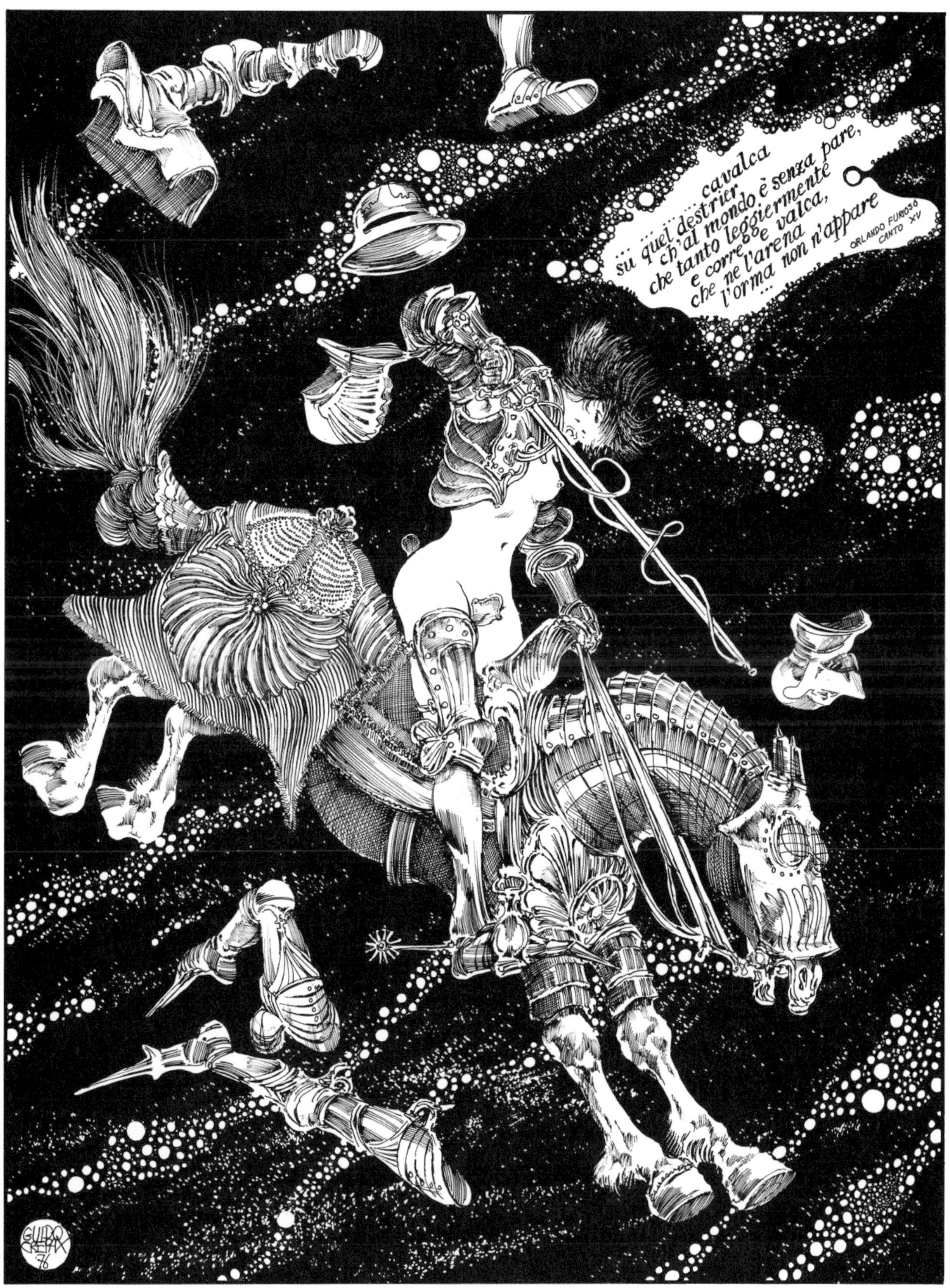

"Valentina the Pirate" page 17 漫画『ヴァレンティーナ──海賊』17ページ
インク、厚紙 / H51×W36.5cm / 1976

14

Soey Milk

ソイ・ミルク（韓国 Korea）

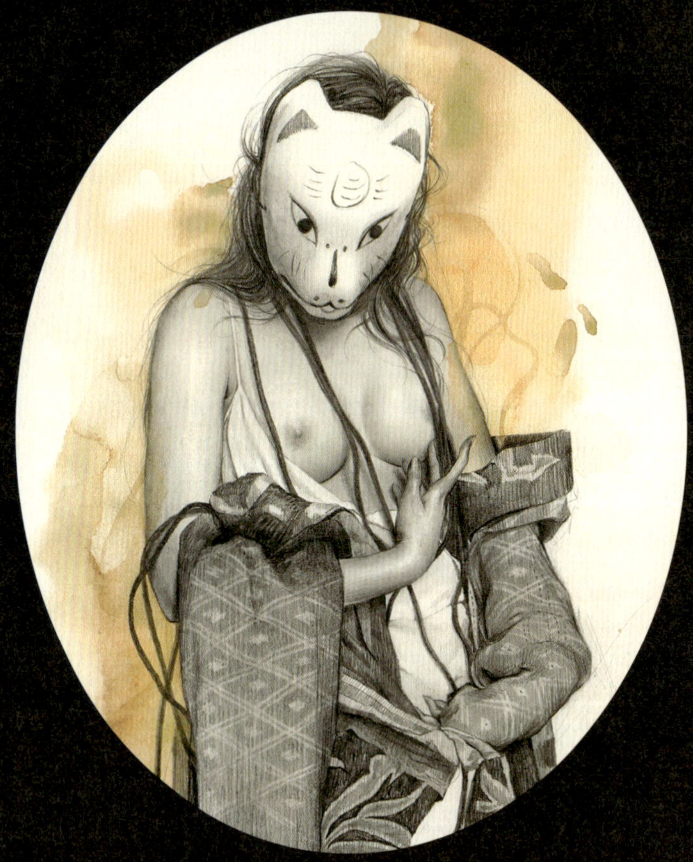

1989年韓国ソウル生まれ。11歳のときにアメリカに移住。パサデナのアート・センター・カレッジ・オブ・デザイン
卒業。現在はロサンゼルスに在住。さまざまな素材、花びらなどの自然の植物を組み合わせて魅惑的な女性を
大胆に描く。

Soey Milk is a Seoul born artist living and working in Los Angeles. Drawn to the female figure, she often
incorporates various mediums and objects from nature into her bold and seductive paintings. Milk studied
at the Art Center College of Design in Pasadena, CA.

Soeymilk.com

↑Propinquity 類似（部分）
グラファイト鉛筆、水彩、紙 / H36.83×W27.94cm / 2014

→Oulida (Study) オウリダ（習作）
油彩、ハイビスカスのドライフラワー、パネル / H22.86×W7.62cm / 2015

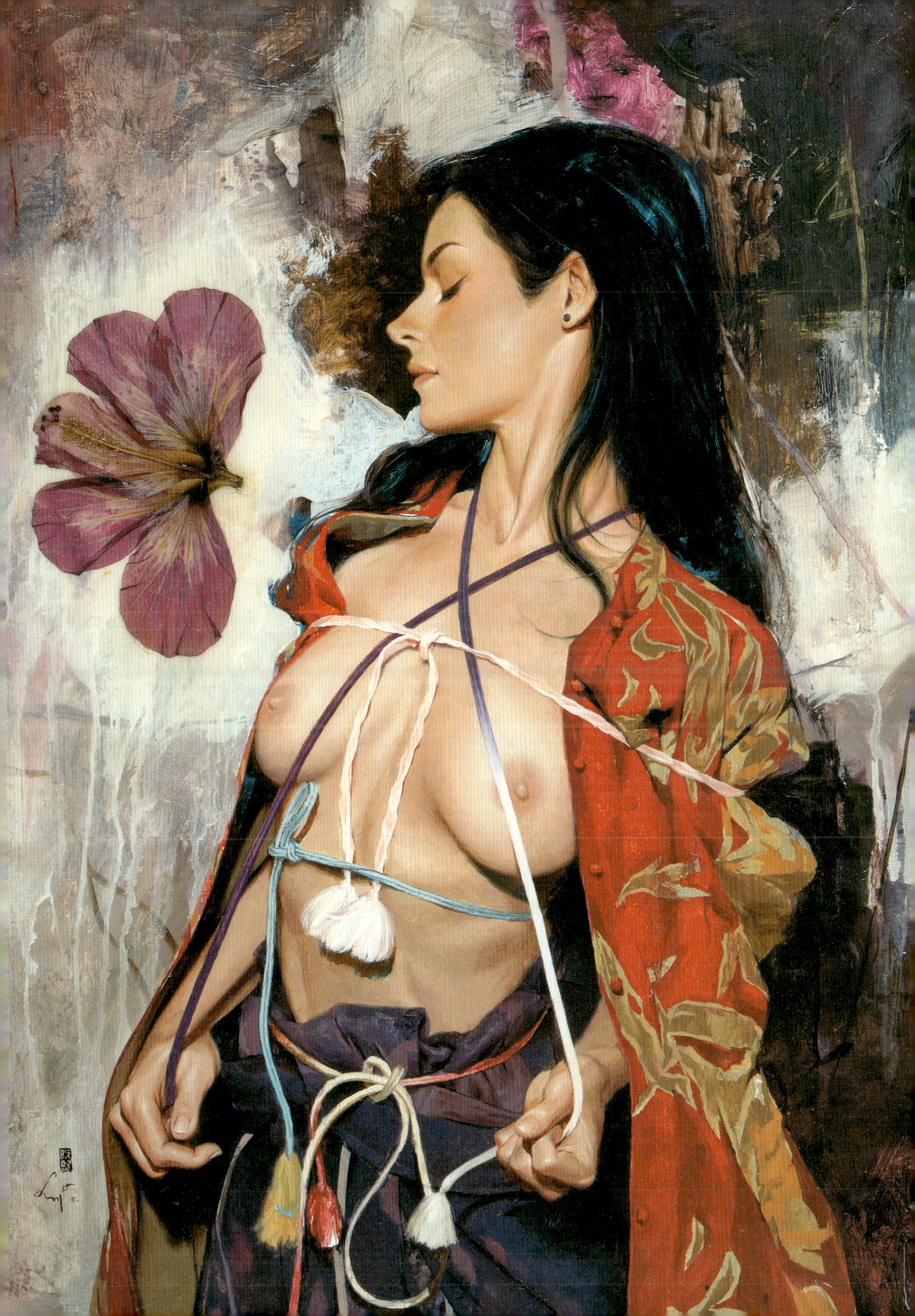

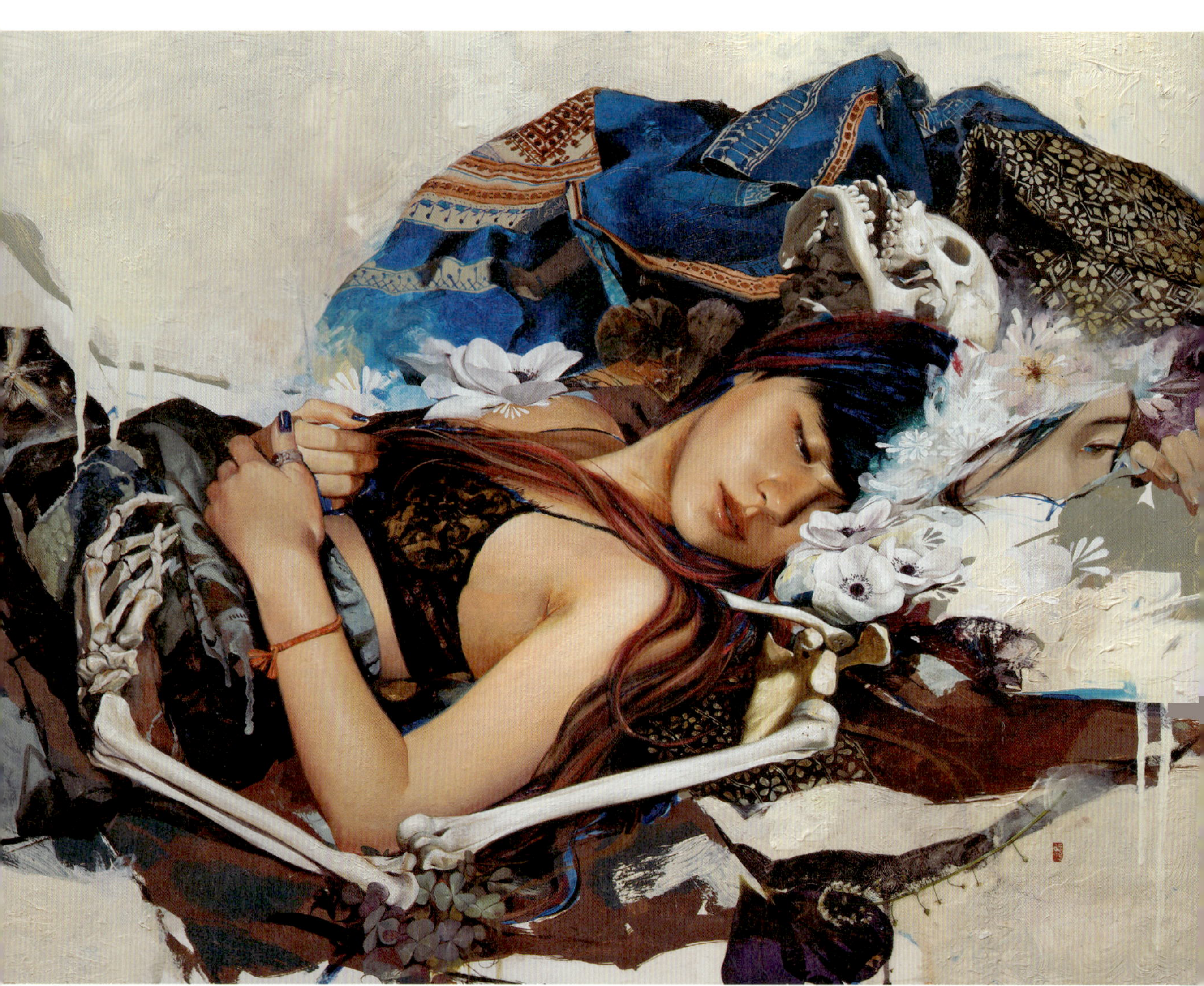

Love Will Linger Like Poison in the Veins 静脈に残る毒のように愛は長引く
油彩、ドライフラワー、パネル / H45.72×W60.96cm / 2016

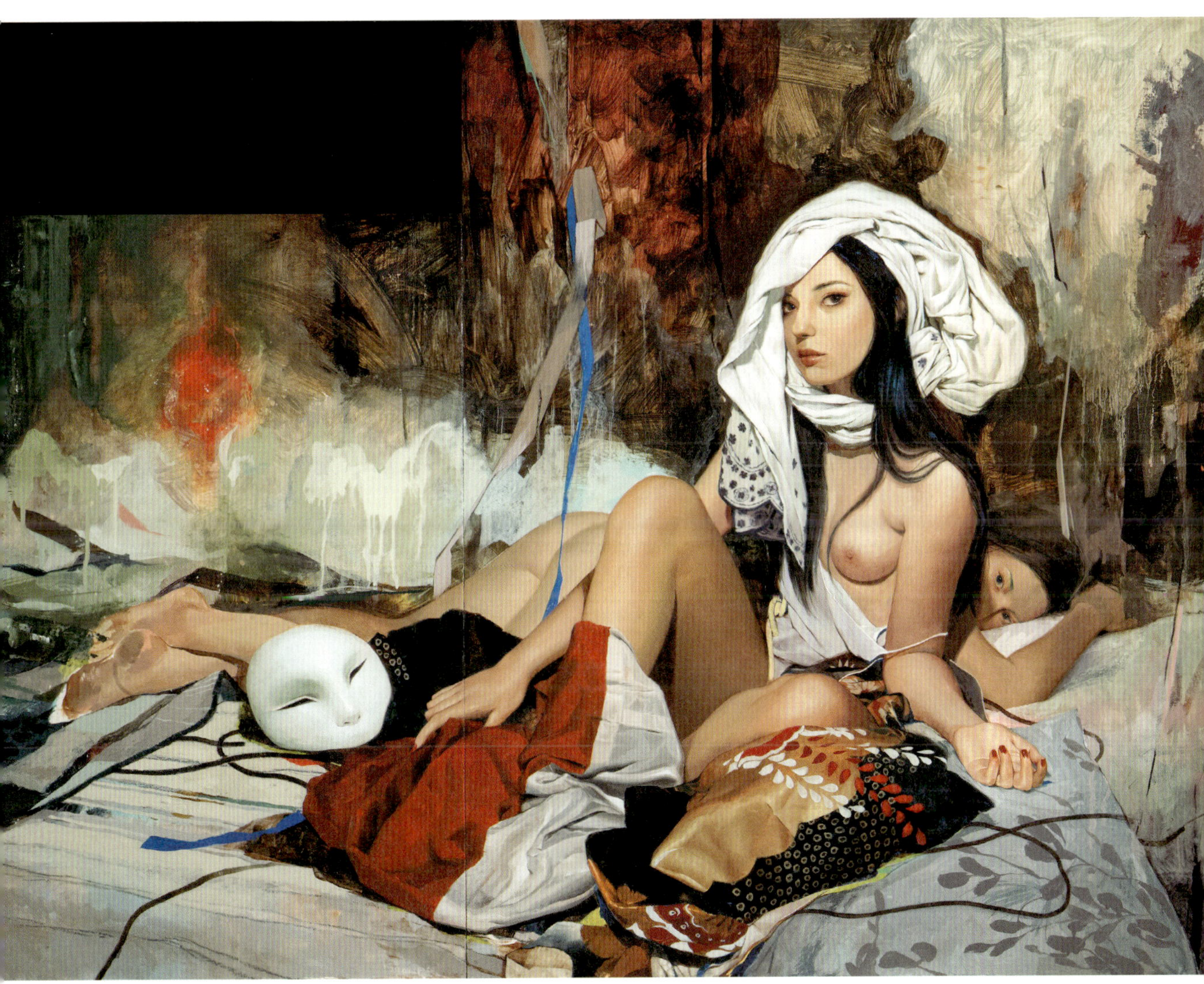

Dokebi Light Study: Inconnu ドケビ・ライト・スタディ——見知らぬ人
油彩、ドライフラワー、虹色細工、パネル / H76.2×W106.68cm / 2015

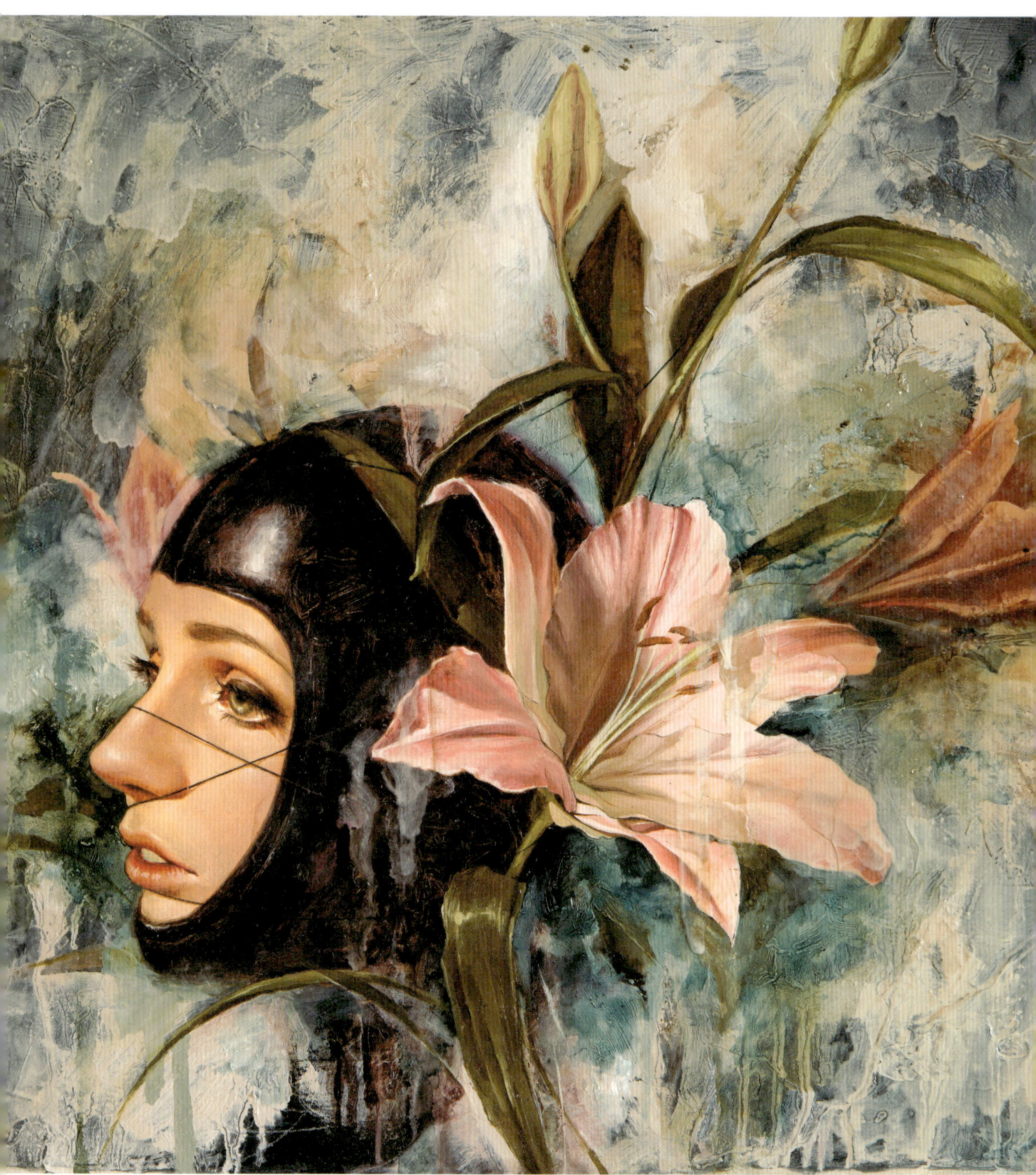

Hyang (perfume) 香り
油彩、パネル / H30.48×W30.48cm / 2013

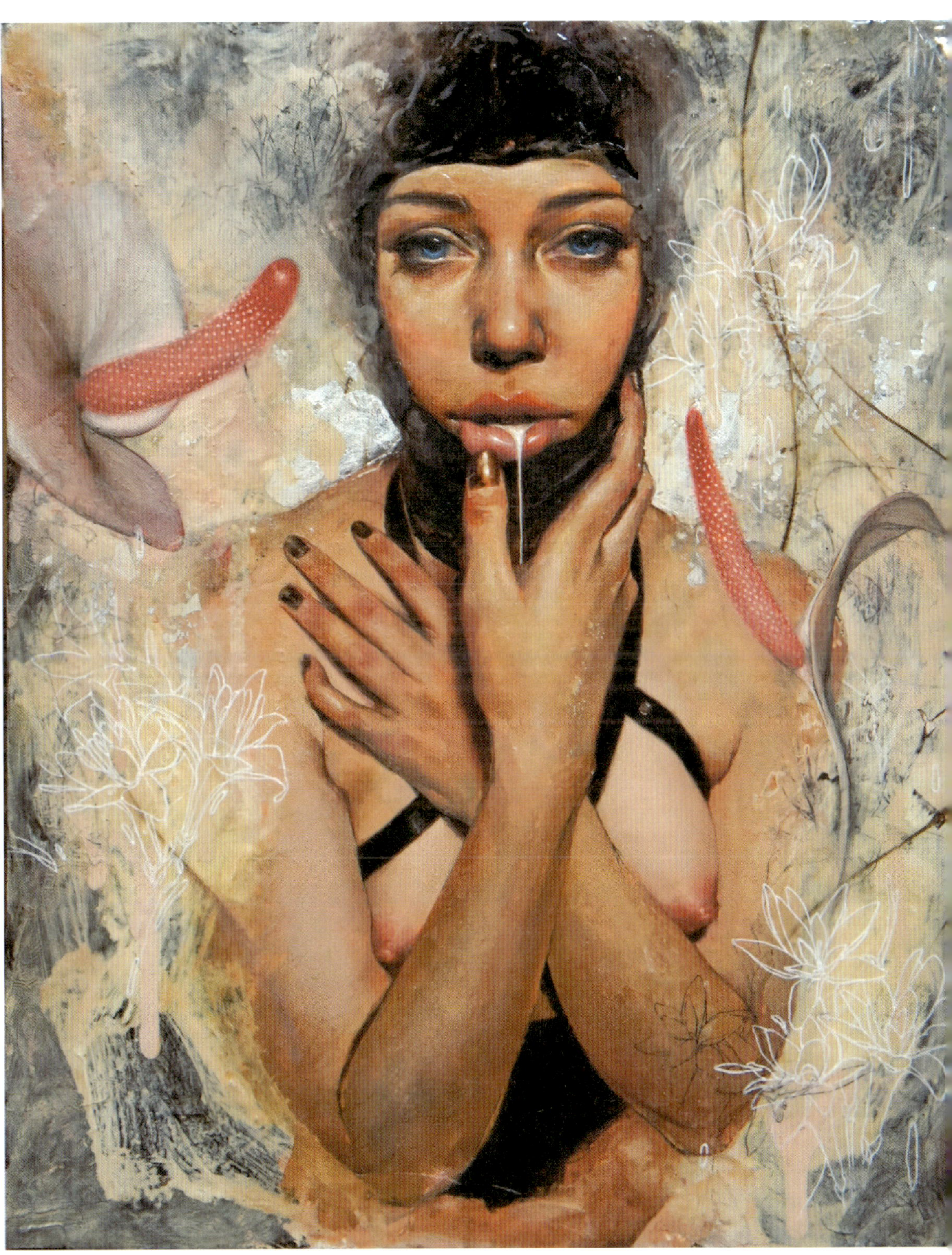

White Anthurium 白い秋
油彩、銀箔、パネル / H25.4×W20.32cm / 2013

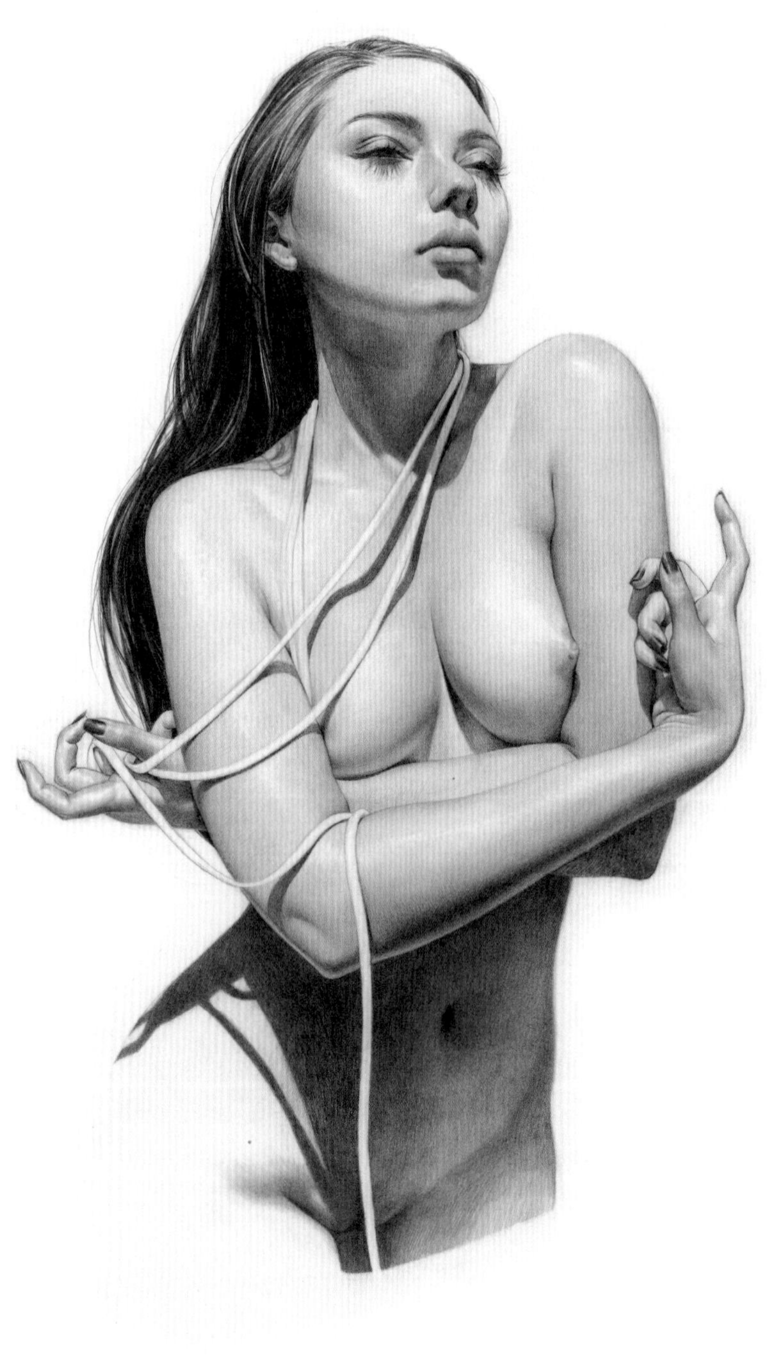

Sunlit 日に当たって
グラファイト鉛筆、紙 / H40.64×W29.21cm / 2015

The Quiet One 静かなるもの
グラファイト鉛筆、紙 / H58.42×W40.64cm / 2014

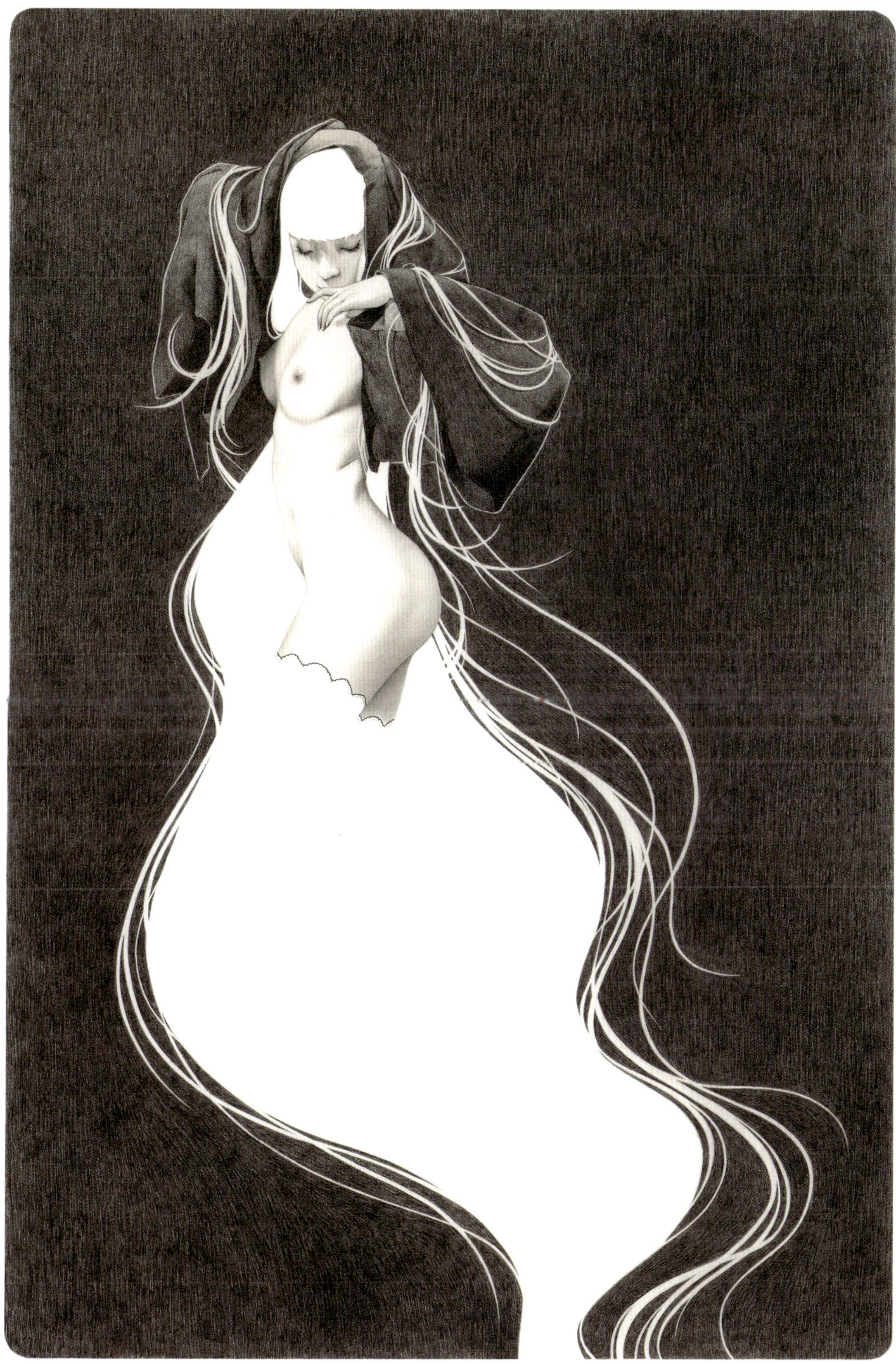

15

Elisa Ancori

エリサ・アンコリ（スペイン Spain）

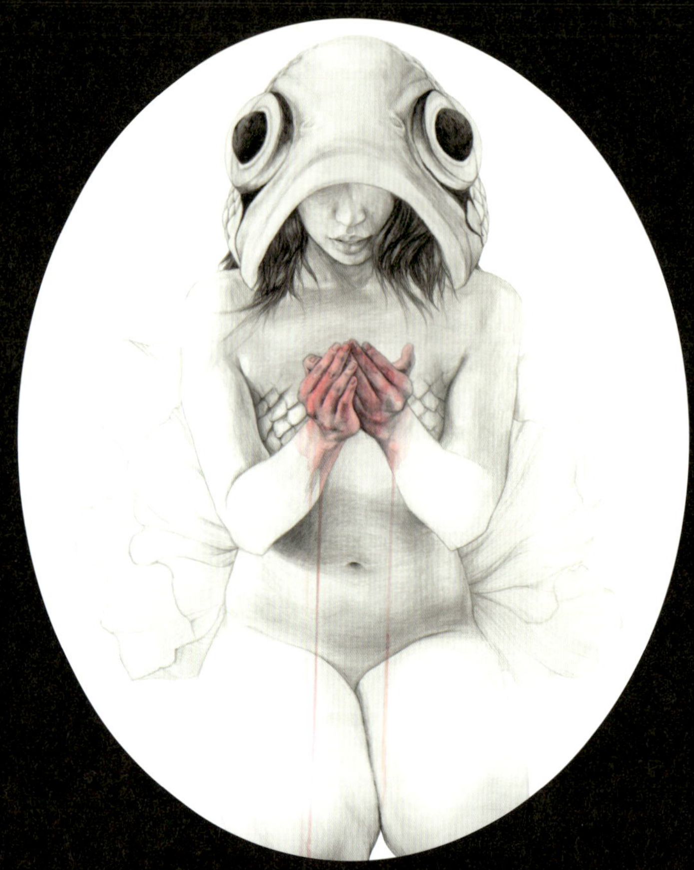

1990年生まれ。バルセロナ大学美術学部・ドローイング（線画）・ペインティング（油画）科卒業。2012年、Bau
大学大学院イラストレーション研究科修了。現在はアート作品の制作をしながら、フリーランスで広告、ファッ
ション、出版関係のイラストを手掛けている。自然と人間の結びつきをテーマにし、肉体と魂の融合を力強い
線で描く。それらの調和や、自然界のあらゆる場所で日々生み出されるものを模索し続けている。作品「メタモ
ルフィッシュ」シリーズは人間と水中生物が共存する世界に棲む寓話上の生きもの。浮遊感と繊細さをあわせ
持つ作品は感覚的な世界に深くアプローチしている。その世界に浸ると、魅惑的な深海の夢を追い求めること
ができるだろう。

Born in 1990. Graduated in Fine Arts at the University of Barcelona, specialized in drawing and painting. In
2012 makes a Illustration Graduate in Bau University. Today is dedicated to artistic production and freelance
illustration work in advertising, fashion and publishing. His works revolve around the connection of nature
with man. A fusion of body and soul which is scanned by a strong line in all his work. A continuous search for
that balance, that unceasingly gives rise in every corner of nature. "Metamorfish" is a bestiary of creatures
belonging to a world that represents the synergy between humans and aquatic nature. A weightless and
nuanced work that delves into the cosmos of perception, and in which we must seek the captivating and
deep sea dream.

elisaancori.com

↑ Metamorfish: Aphrodite メタモルフィッシュ──アフロディーテ（部分）
鉛筆、水彩、画用紙 / H100×W70cm / 2014

→Metamorfish: Jellyfish VII メタモルフィッシュ──海月VII
鉛筆、水彩、画用紙 / H100×W70cm / 2016

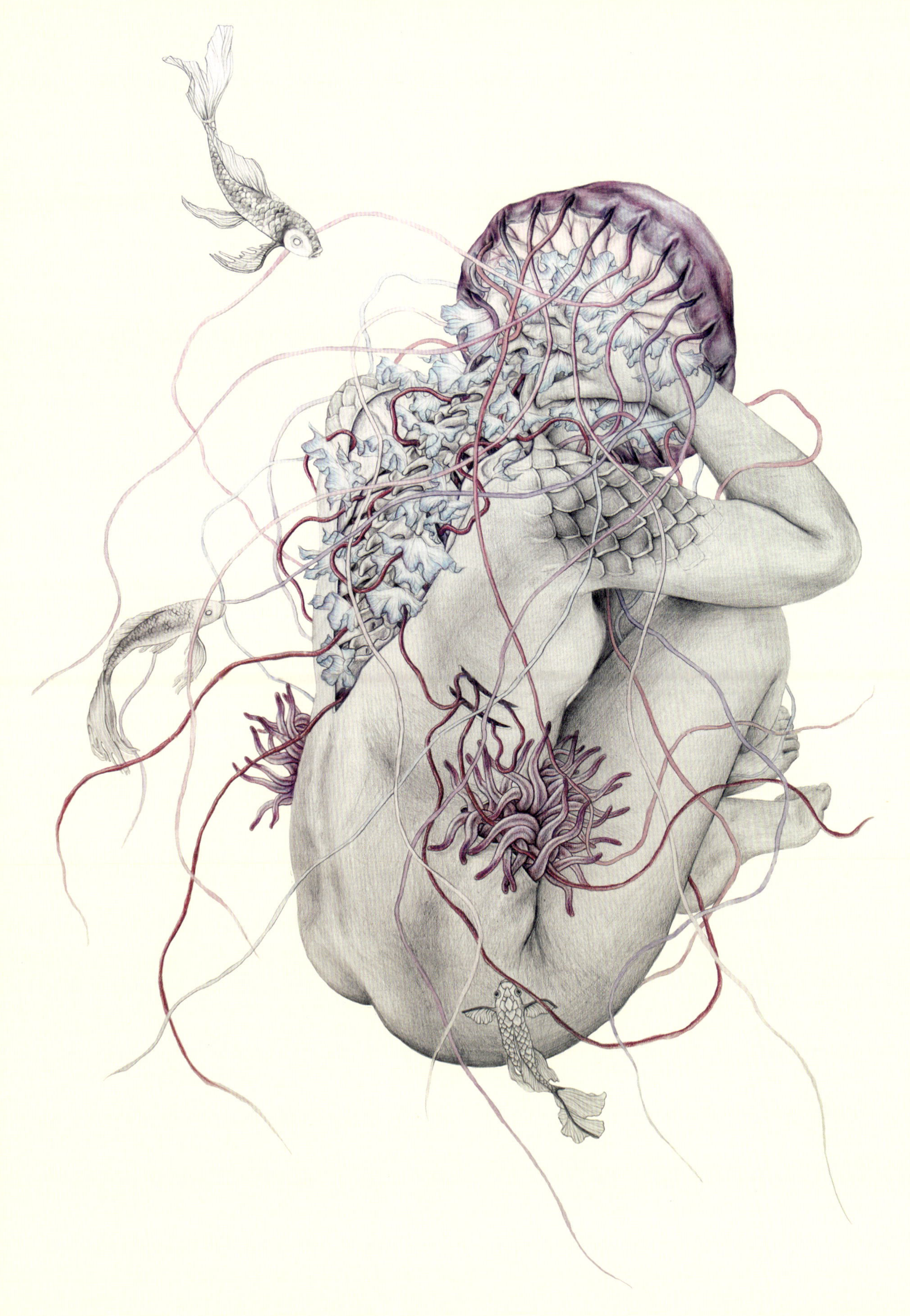

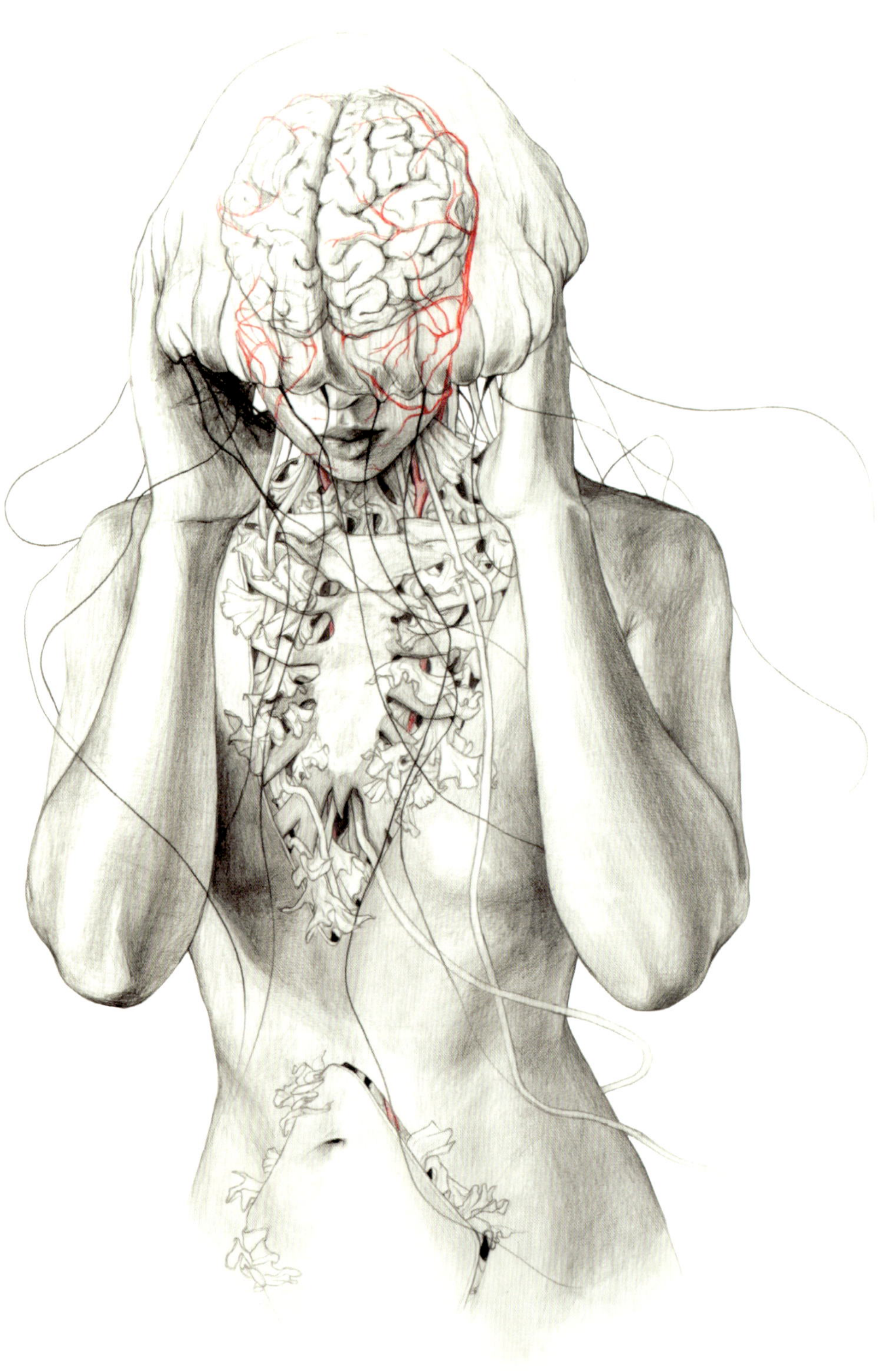

Metamorfish: Jellyfish II　メタモルフィッシュ――海月 II
鉛筆、水彩、画用紙 / H70×W50cm / 2014

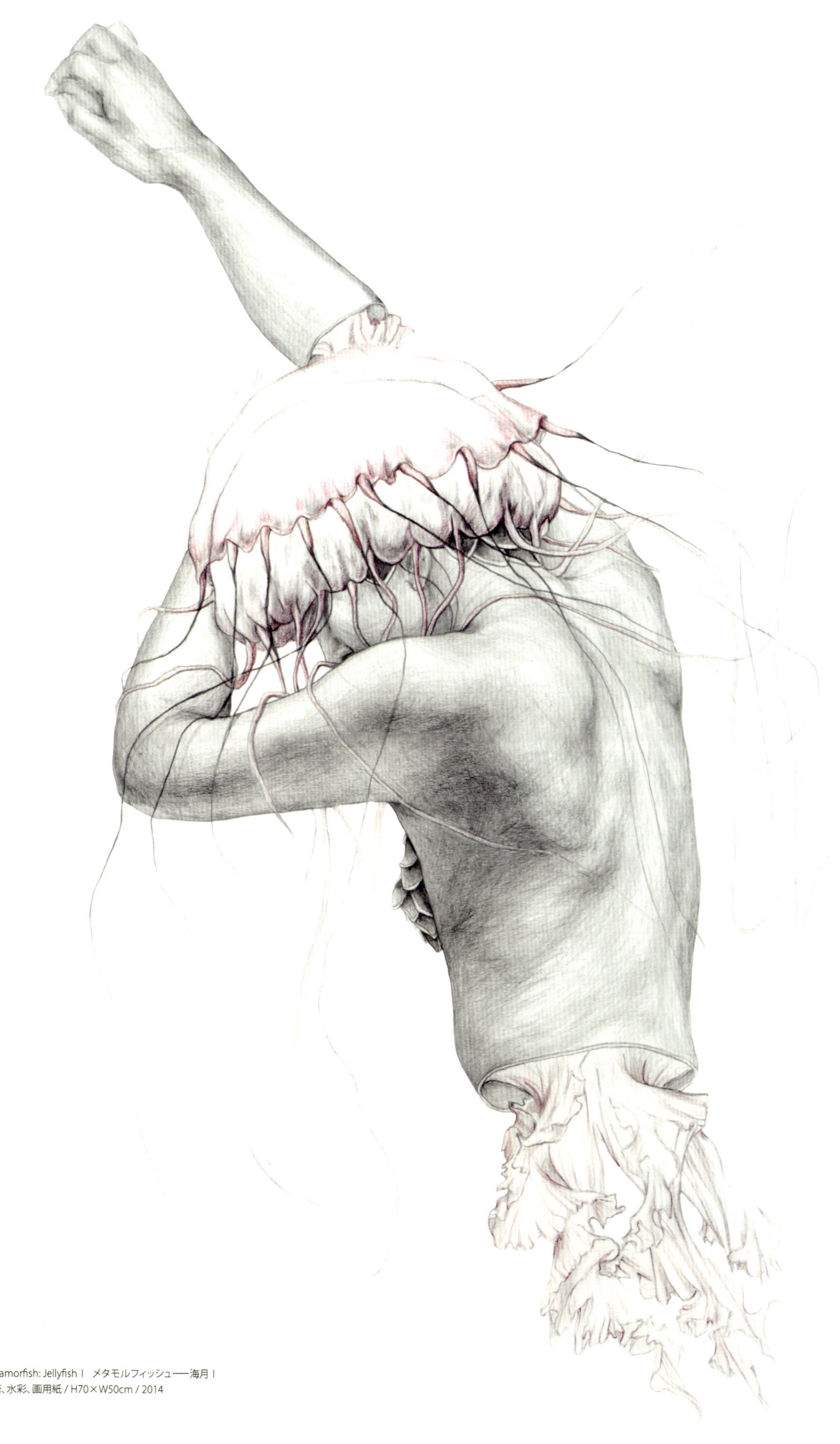

Metamorfish: Jellyfish I　メタモルフィッシュ——海月 I
鉛筆、水彩、画用紙 / H70×W50cm / 2014

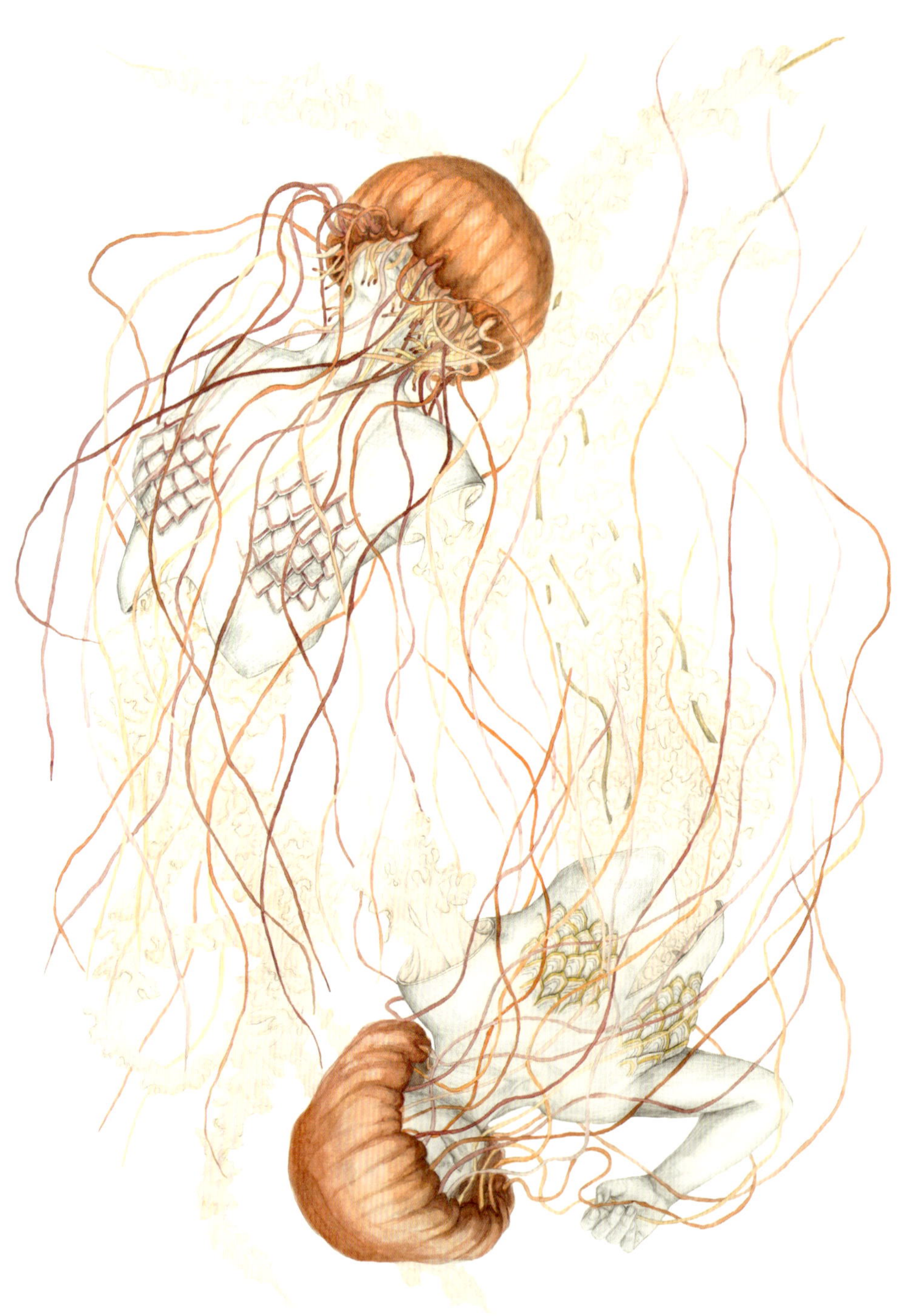

Metamorfish: Jellyfish V　メタモルフィッシュ──海月 V
鉛筆、水彩、画用紙 / H100×W70cm / 2015

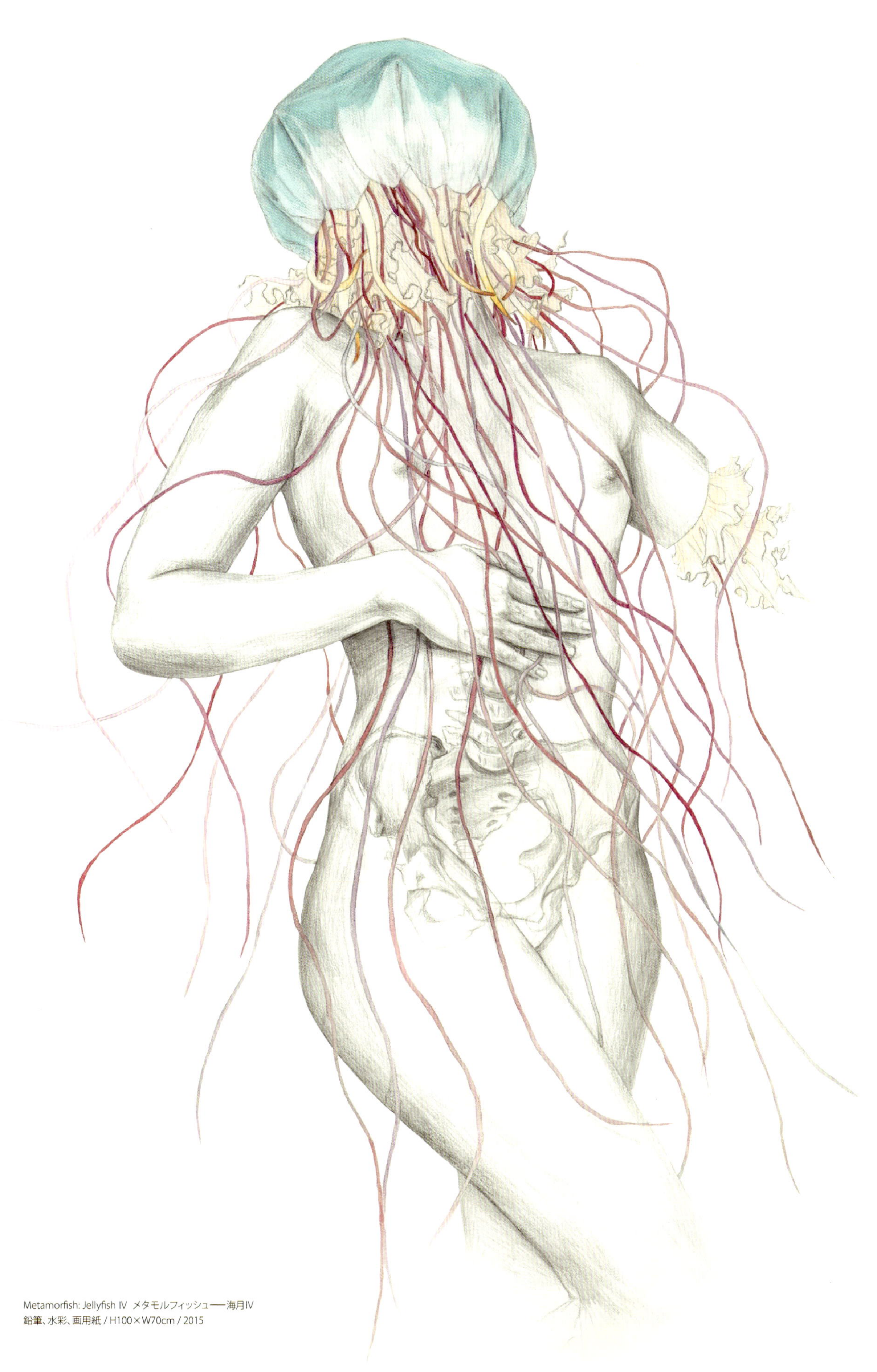

Metamorfish: Jellyfish IV　メタモルフィッシュ——海月IV
鉛筆、水彩、画用紙 / H100×W70cm / 2015

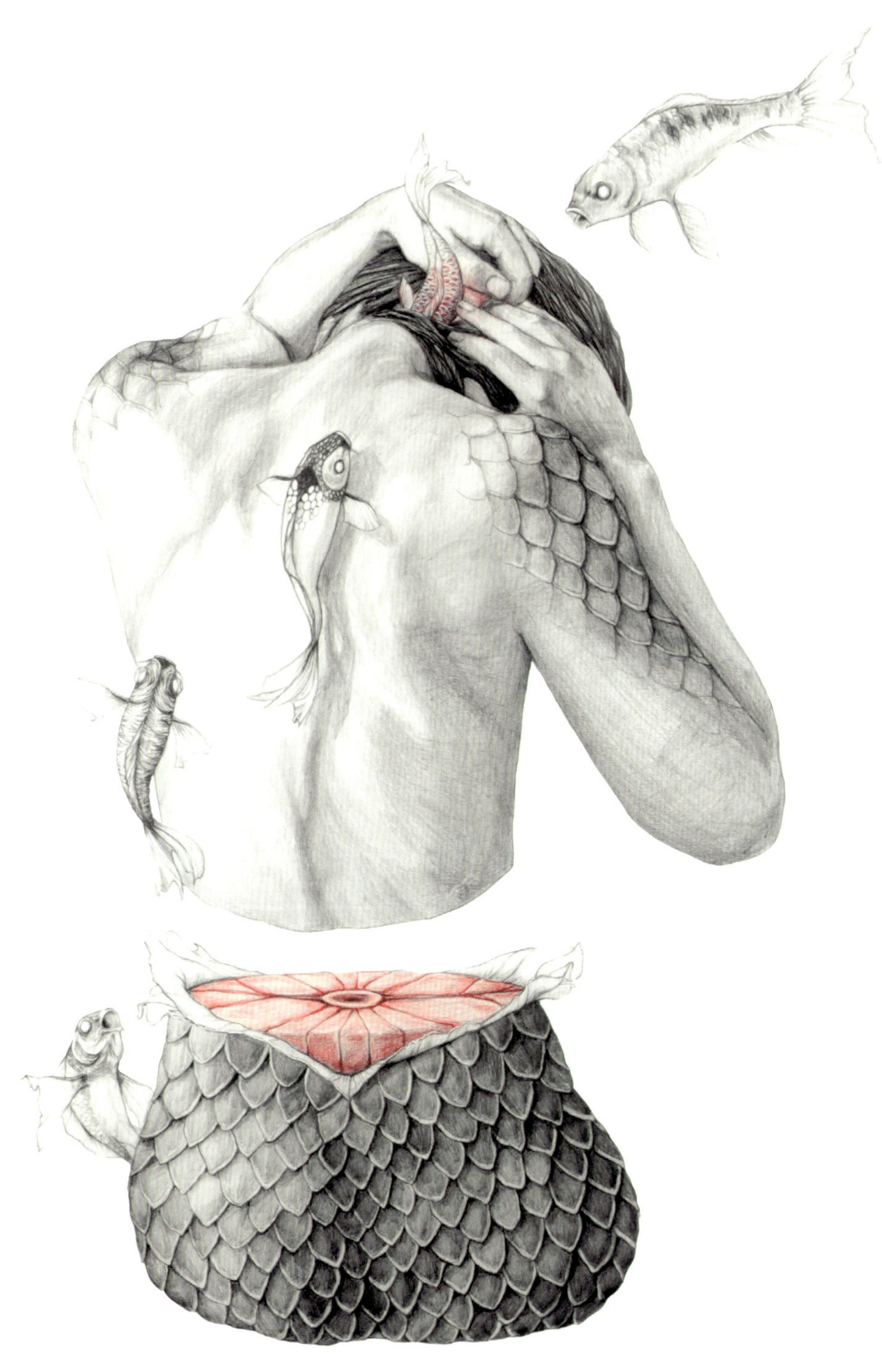

Metamorfish: Koi I メタモルフィッシュ——鯉 I
鉛筆、水彩、画用紙 / H70×W50cm / 2014

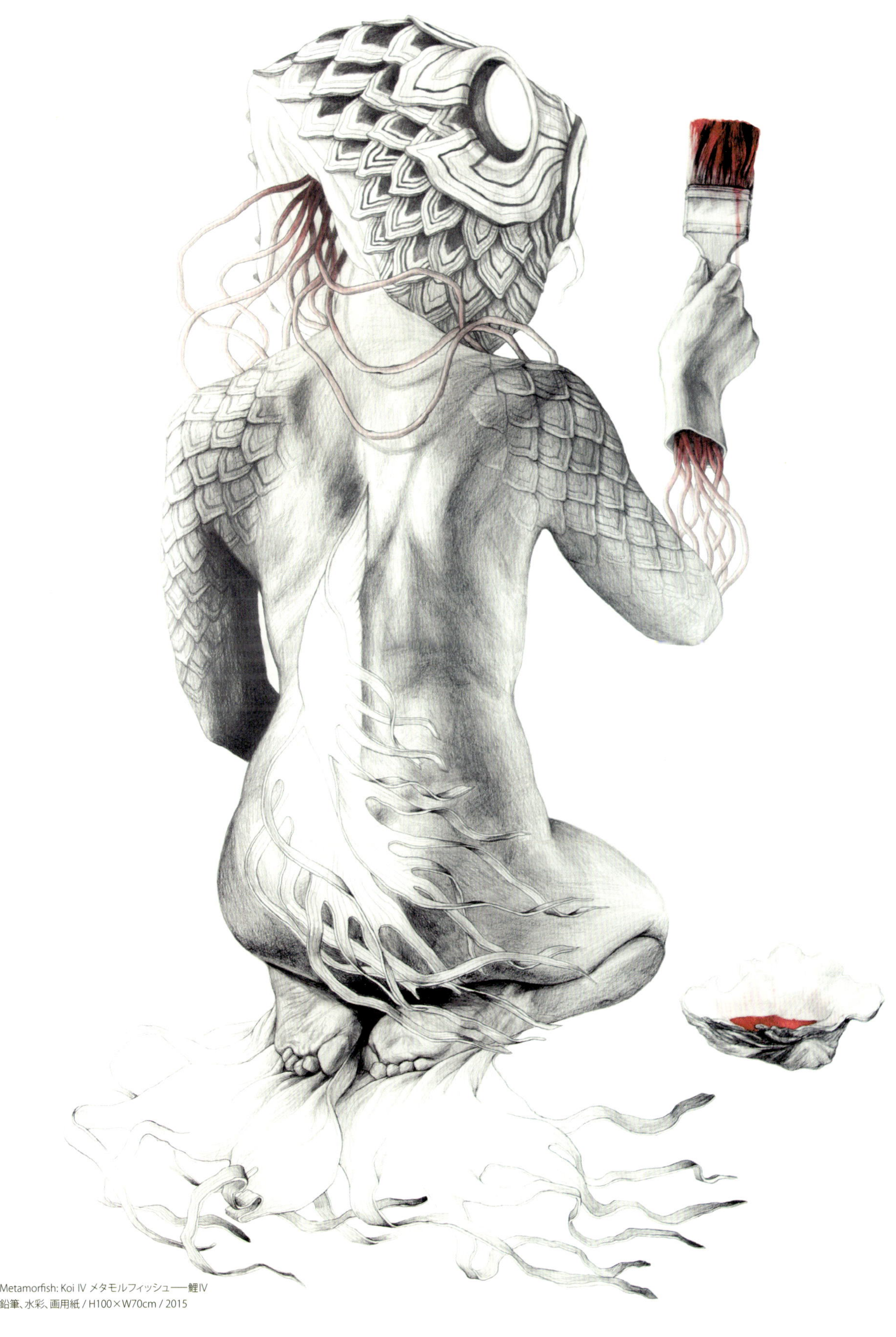

Metamorfish: Koi IV メタモルフィッシュ──鯉IV
鉛筆、水彩、画用紙 / H100×W70cm / 2015

16

Zoe Lacchei

ゾーイ・ラケイ（イタリア　Italy）

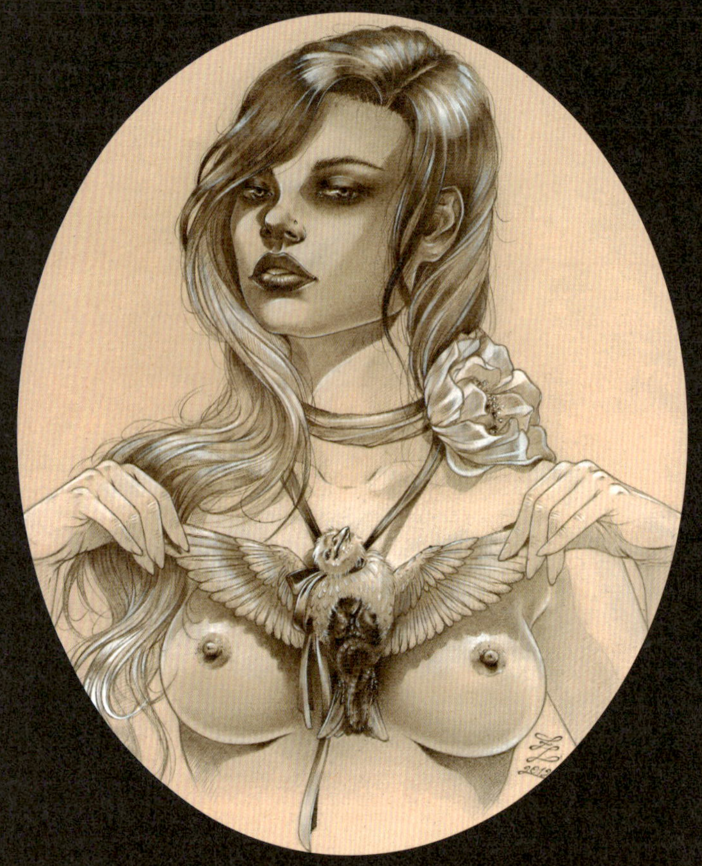

ゾーイ・ラケイはローマの近くの小さな町で育った。高校卒業後、大好きな人体解剖学と日本文化を題材にした作品を制作している。日本文化はゾーイに多大な影響を与えた。ゾーイは奇異で相反する魅力を持つ日本に魅了されている。日本は古いものだけではなく、マンガ、アニメ、ビデオゲームに代表される新しいものも芸術的センスにあふれている。折衷主義で情熱的なゾーイは作品集を出版し、多くの展覧会に参加している。伝統的な技法と画材を融合させたスタイルは彼女独特のものだ。

Zoe Lacchei grew up in a small town near Rome. After high school she focused on the subjects she loved the most, such as human anatomy and Japanese culture. This last one has affected her enormously: she simply adores Japan, with its contradictions and oddities, with its great sense for the art of image, in a traditional and at the same time modern way, given by Manga, Anime and Videogames. Eclectic, passionate, Zoe Lacchei has published several works and has taken part to many exhibitions. Her unmistakable style is a fusion of several traditional techniques and materials.

www.zoelacchei.com

↑Eros and Thanatos エロスとタナトス（部分）
墨、ホワイト・テンペラ、再生紙 / H28×W28cm / 2012

→Madame La Guillotine ギロチン刑の婦人
墨、ホワイト・テンペラ、再生紙 / H50×W35cm / 2012

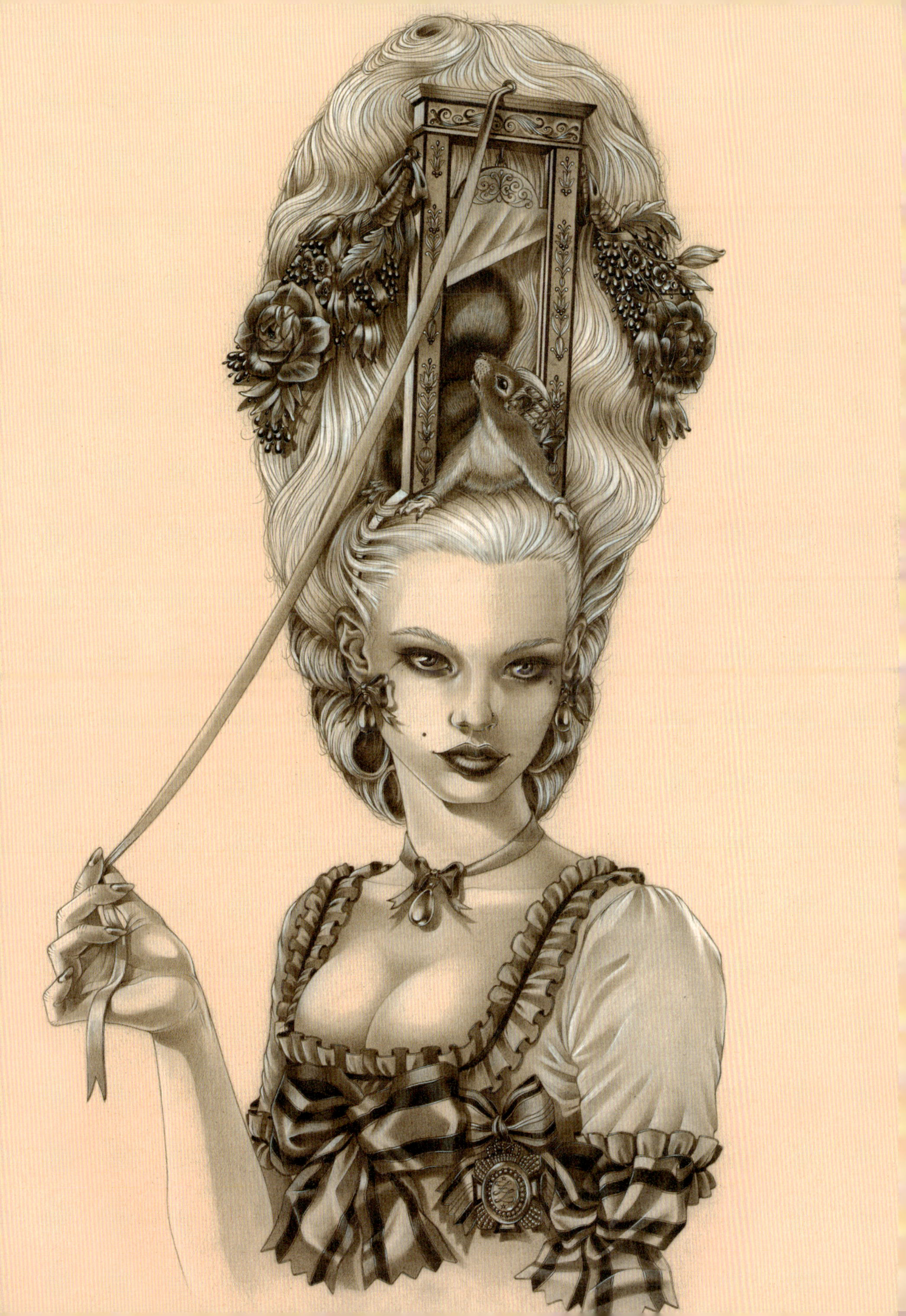

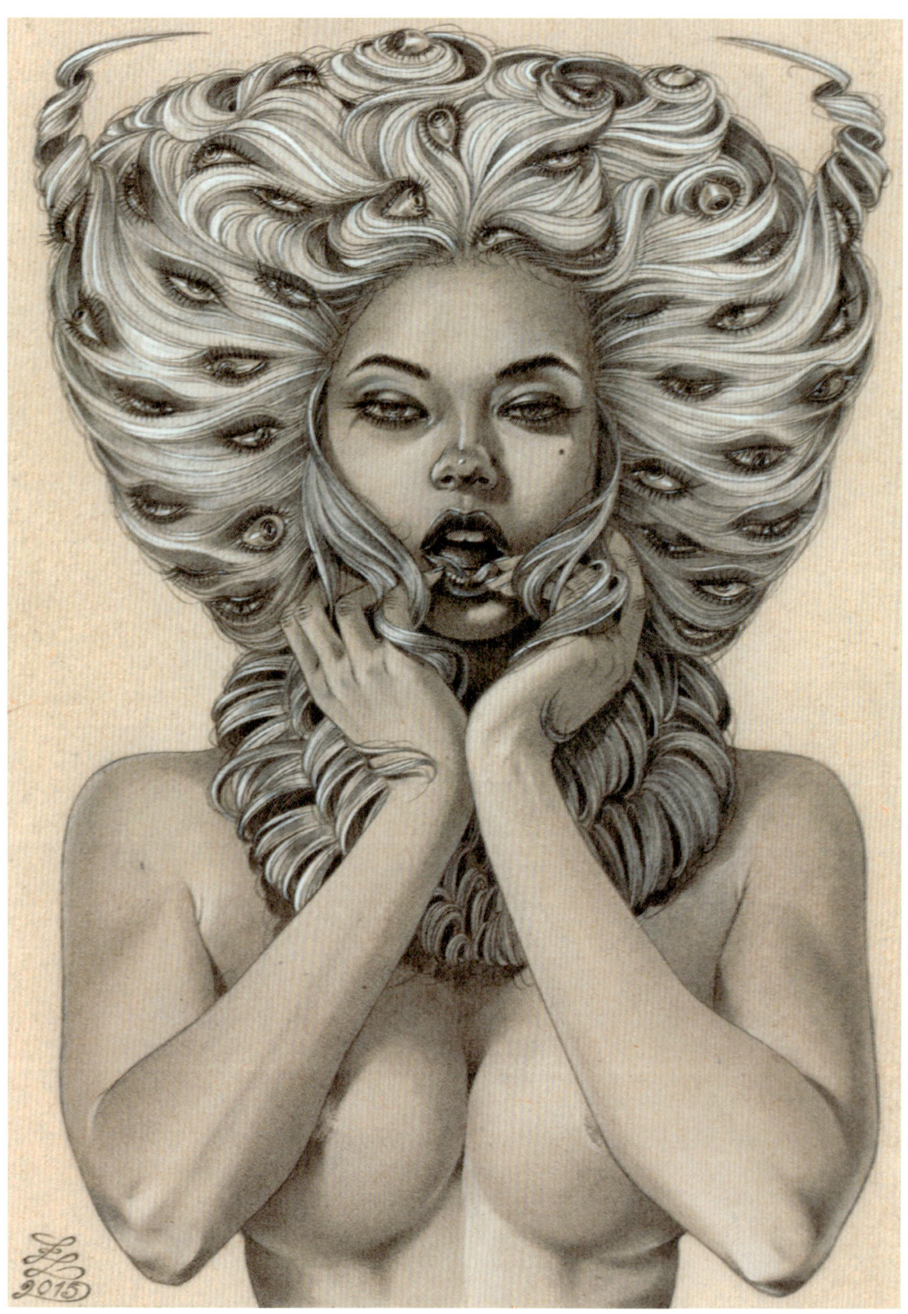

The Demon of Lust 欲望の悪魔
墨、ホワイト・テンペラ、金箔、再生紙 / H20×W15cm / 2015

Dagiraz Girl ダギラズ・ガール
ミクスト・メディア、再生紙 / H30×W20cm / 2016

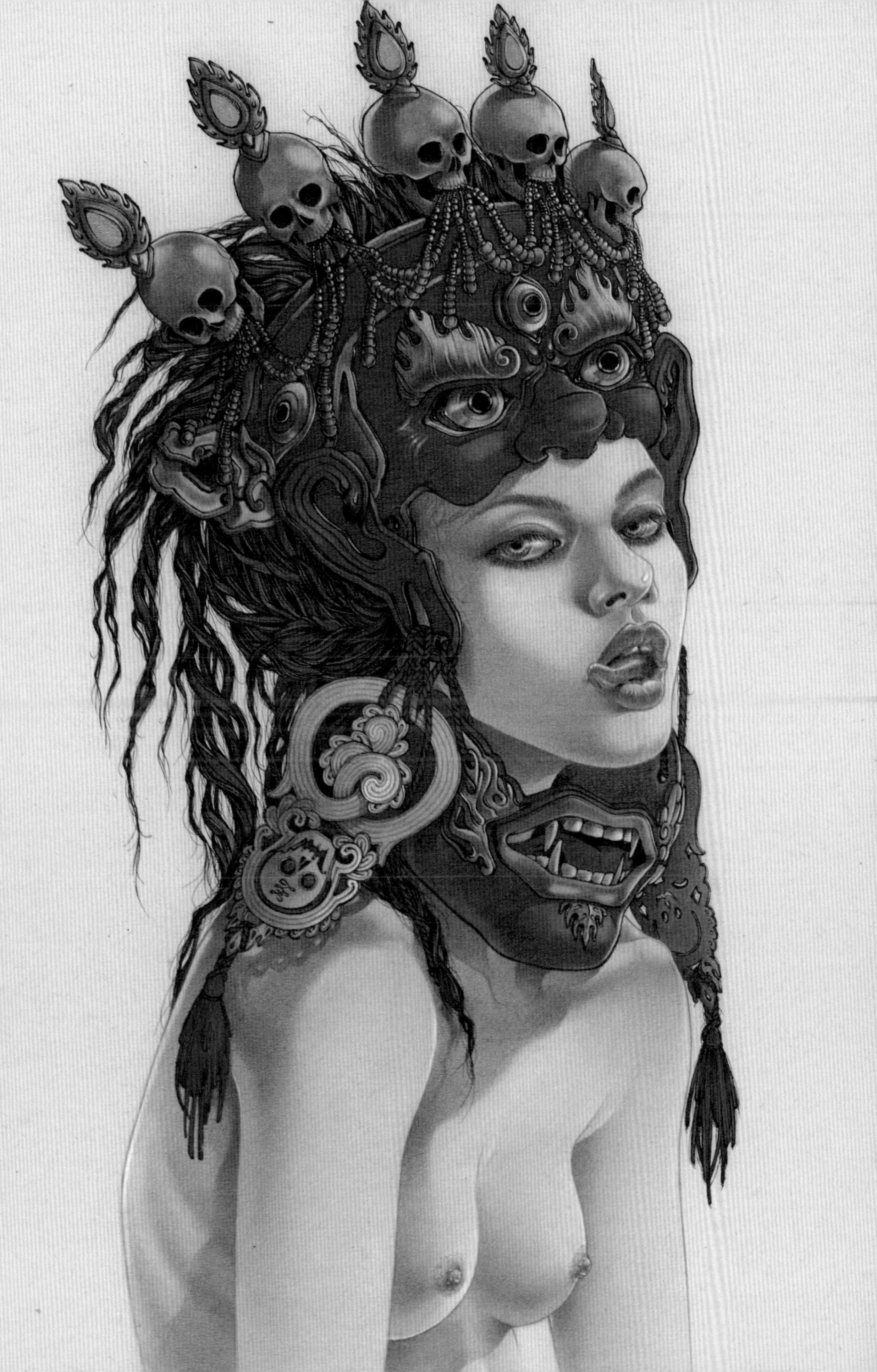

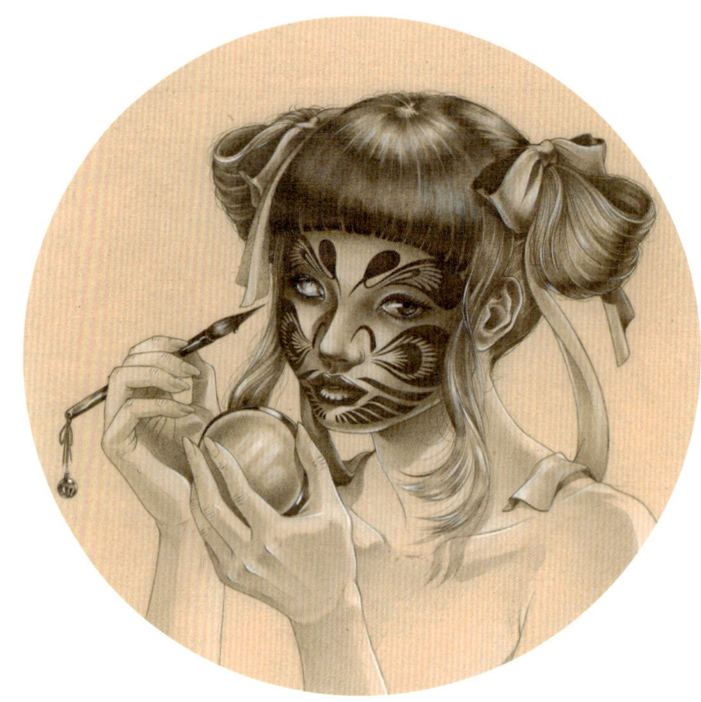

Daruma Girl ダルマ・ガール
墨、ホワイト・テンペラ、再生紙 / H28×W28cm / 2012

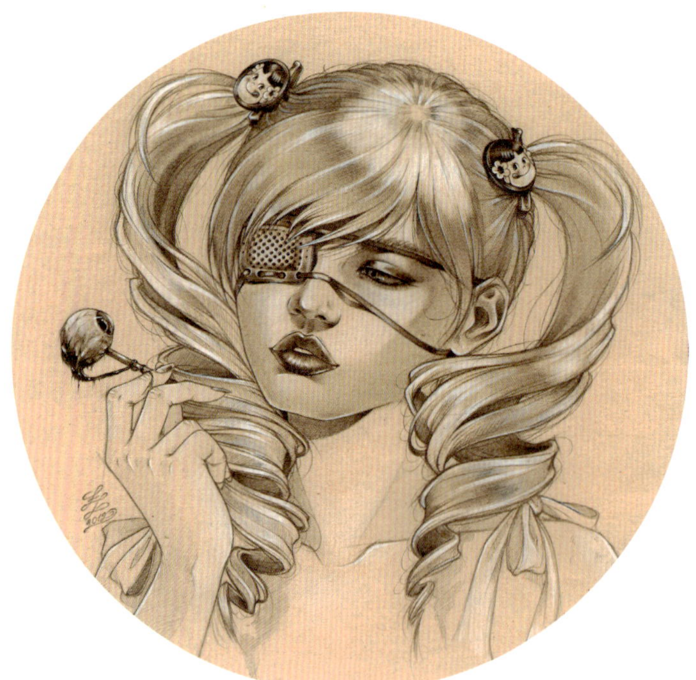

Eyeball Lollipop アイボール・ロリポップ
墨、ホワイト・テンペラ、再生紙 / H28×W28cm / 2012

Benisato 紅里
墨、ホワイト・テンペラ、金箔、再生紙 / H20×W15cm / 2015

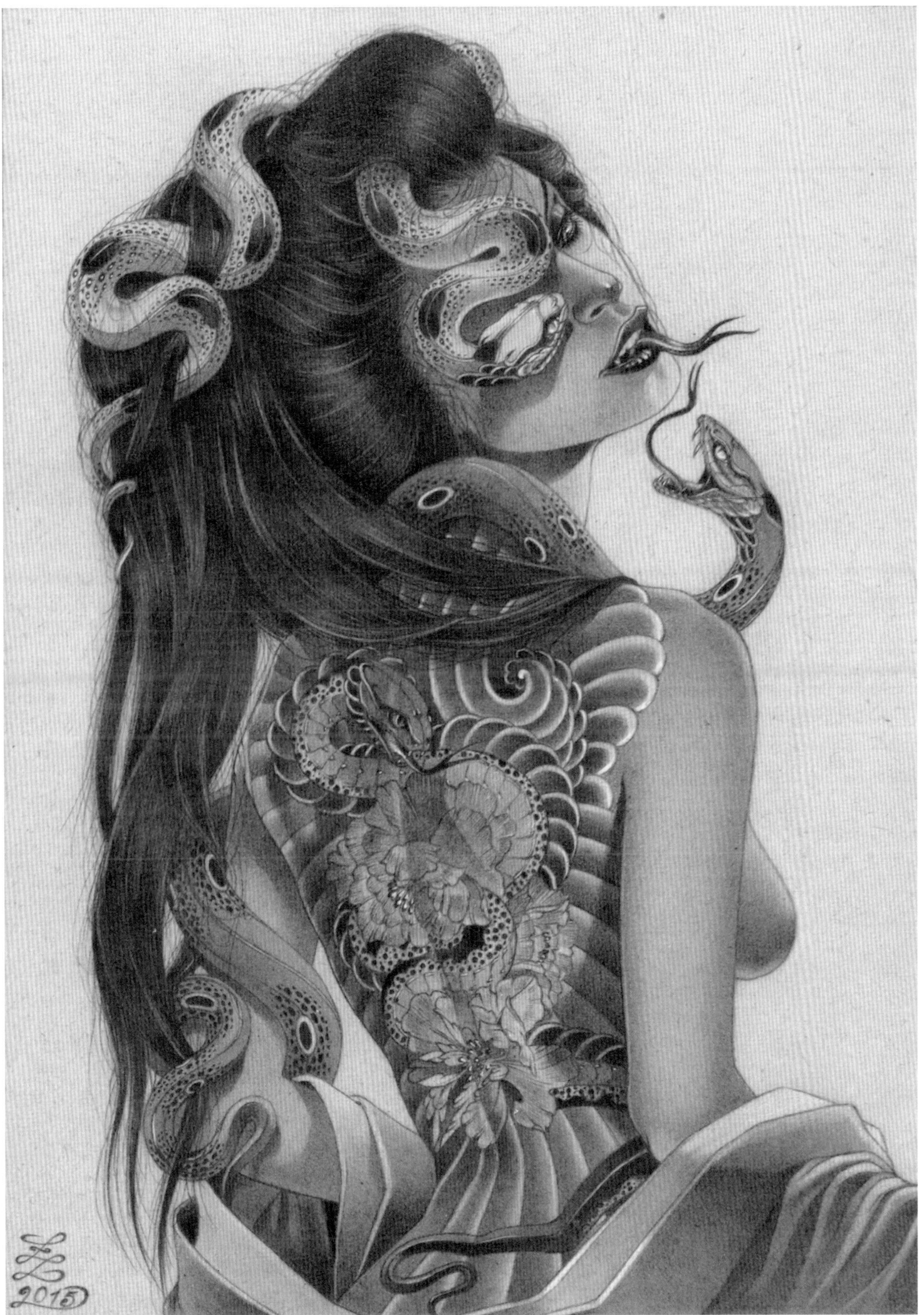

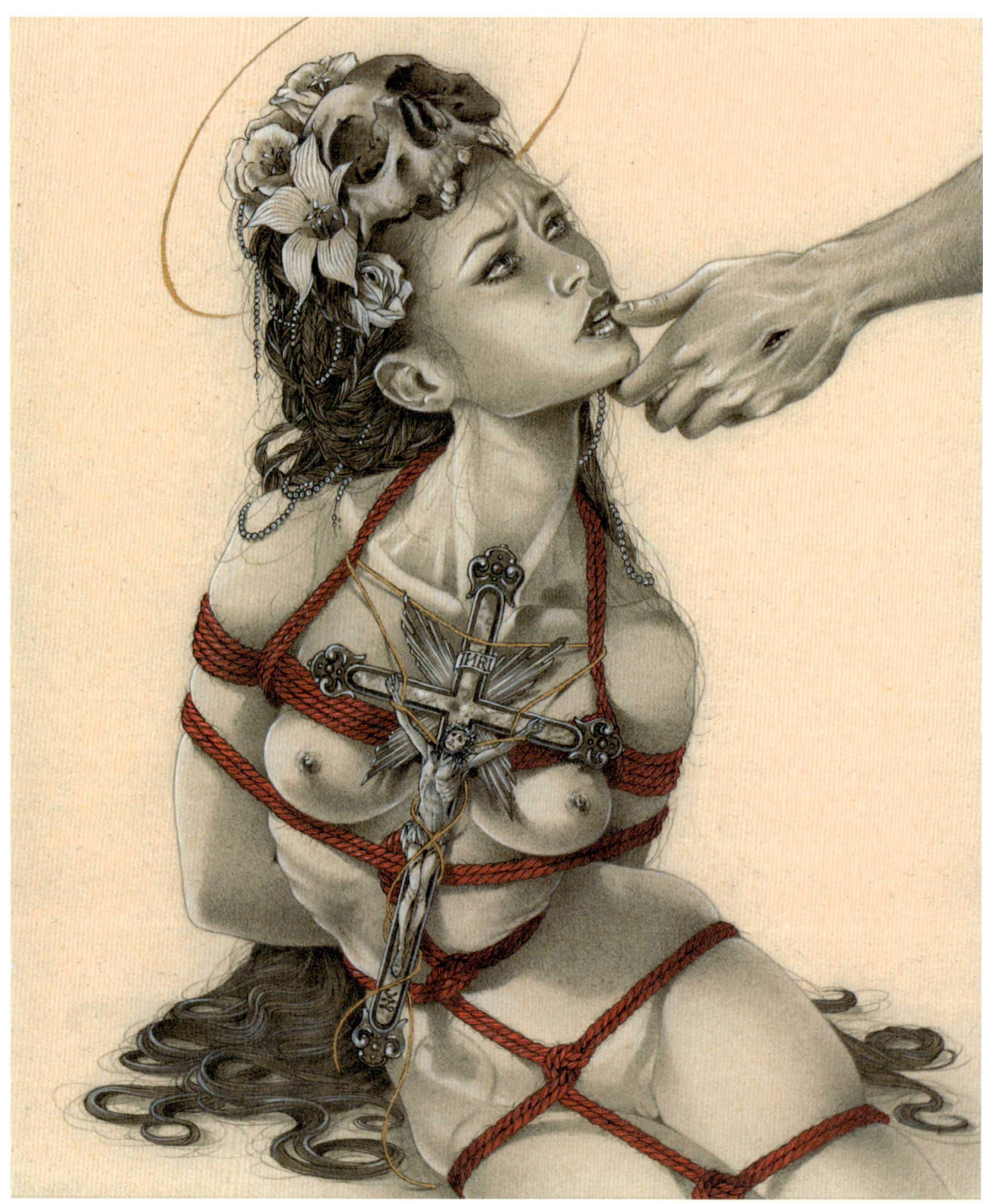

The Penitent Magdalene 悔悟のマグダラ
墨、ホワイト・テンペラ、再生紙 / H18×W15cm / 2015

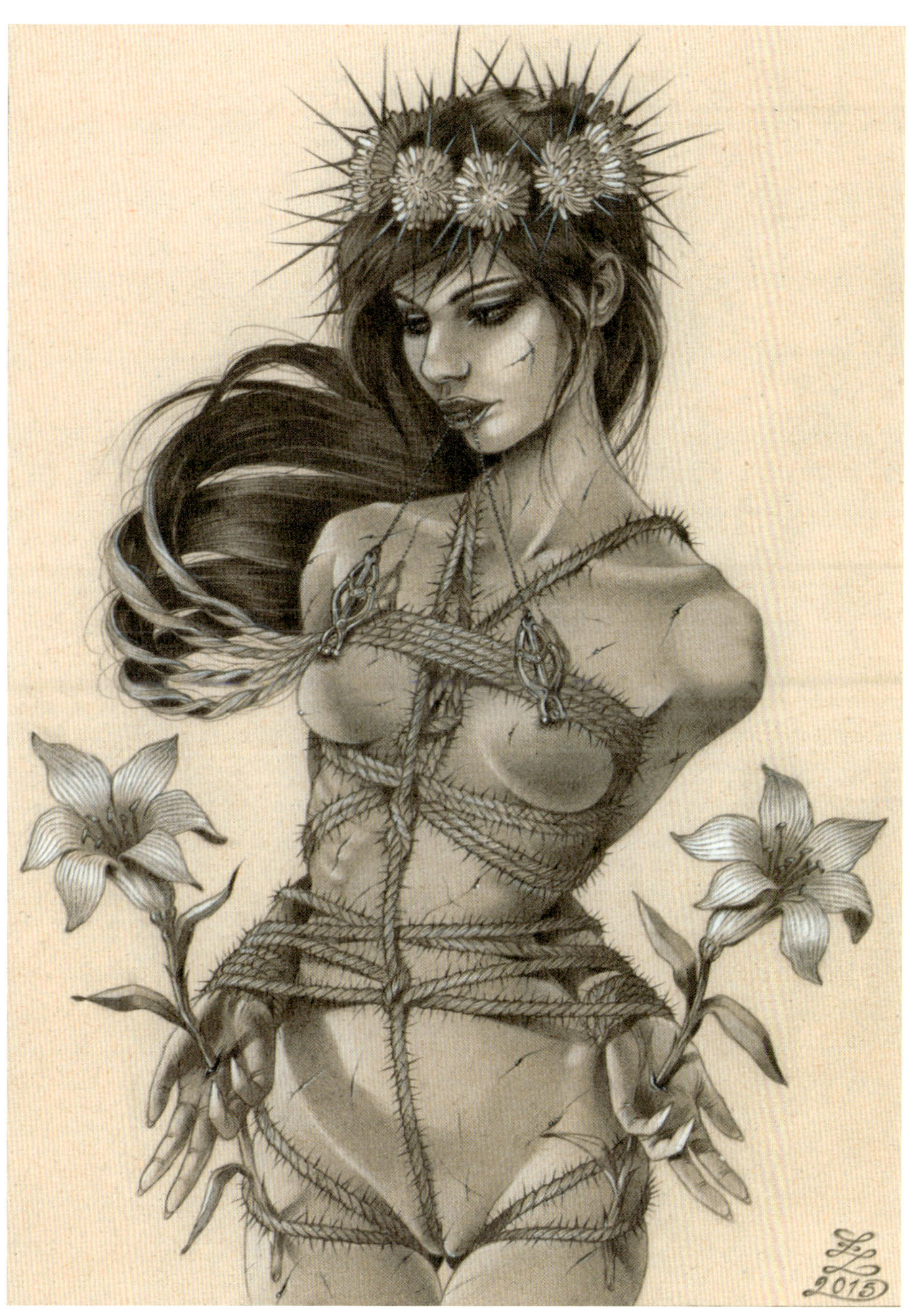

Martyr of Love 愛の殉教者
墨、ホワイト・テンペラ、金箔、再生紙 / H20×W15cm / 2015

Kristin Shiraef

クリスティン・シラーフ（アメリカ USA）

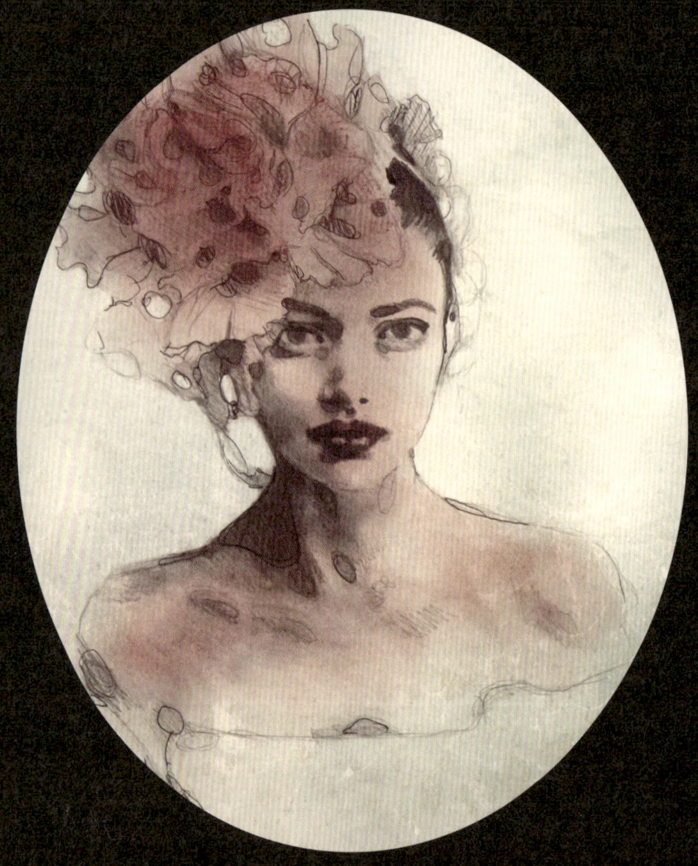

私の心をのぞいてみてください。そこには果てしなく広がる世界があります。さあ、イマジネーションを解き放ちましょう。私の作品は独自の感性や特徴があり、みなさんをちがう場所や時代へと誘います。子ども時代、夢からインスピレーションを得てできた作品、感情をぶつけた作品、どの作品にも私の情熱が込められています。どの作品からも私の空想世界、私と一緒に旅してほしい場所の一部を見ることができます。現在、私は実生活を完璧なものにするという難題と格闘中ですが、今の私をつくり上げた過去の作品も楽しんでいただけると幸いです。

Peek inside my mind into a world with no boundaries. Let your imagination ravel around the unique emotions and personalities within each of my creations as they take you on a journey to another place and time. Within each creation lies a passion from inside me, whether it be derived from my childhood, from within my dreams or merely an expression of a personal emotion. They all possess a small piece of my imaginary world and the place I want others to journey with me. As I attempt to master this ongoing task of perfecting my reality, I hope you enjoy the process of my past creations that guide me there.

www.kristinfineart.com

↑Fae フェイ（部分）
コンテ、インク、テクスチャ素材紙 / H20.32×W12.7cm / 2014

→Feral 野生の女
木炭、インク、テクスチャ素材紙 / H20.32×W12.7cm / 2013

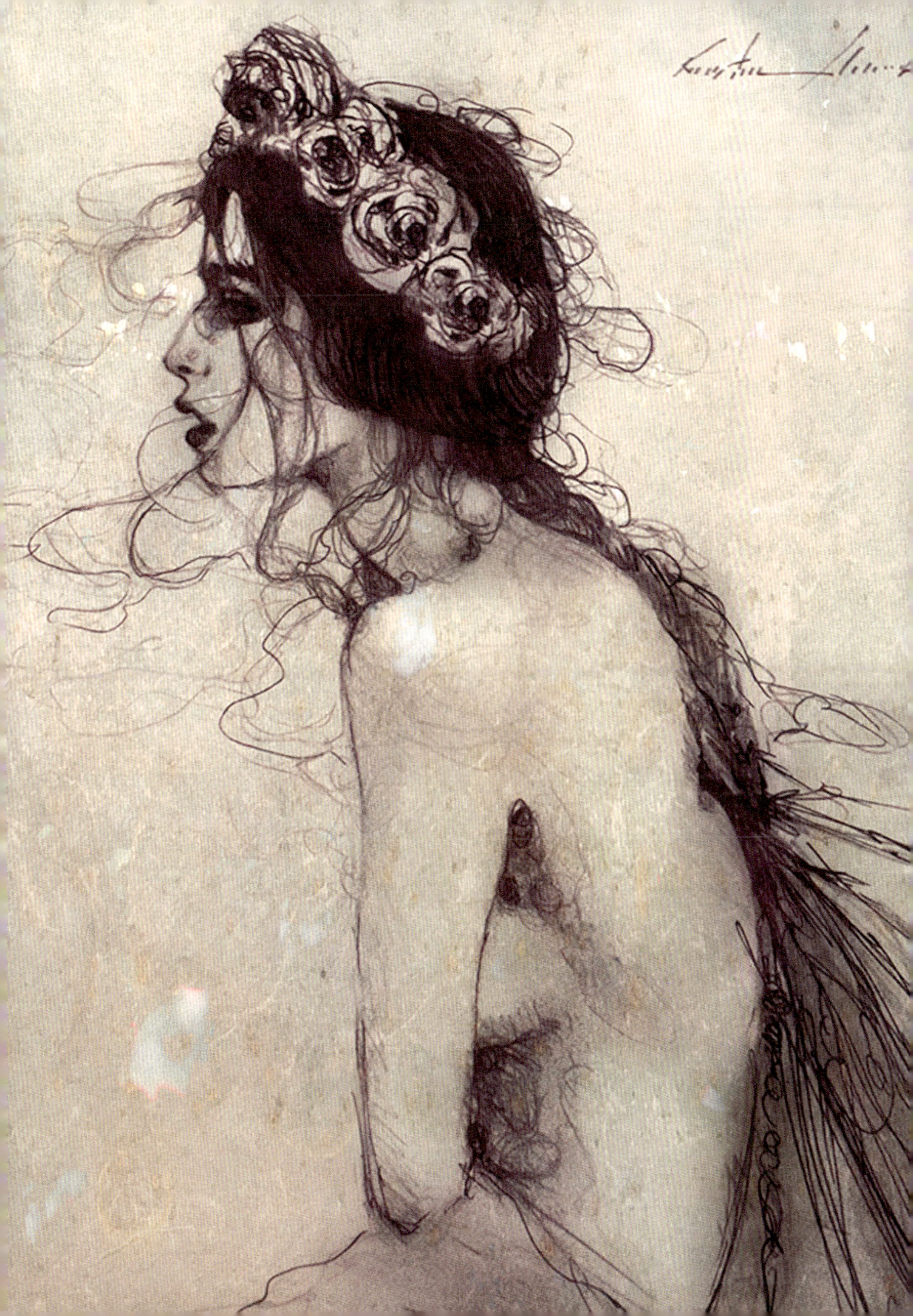

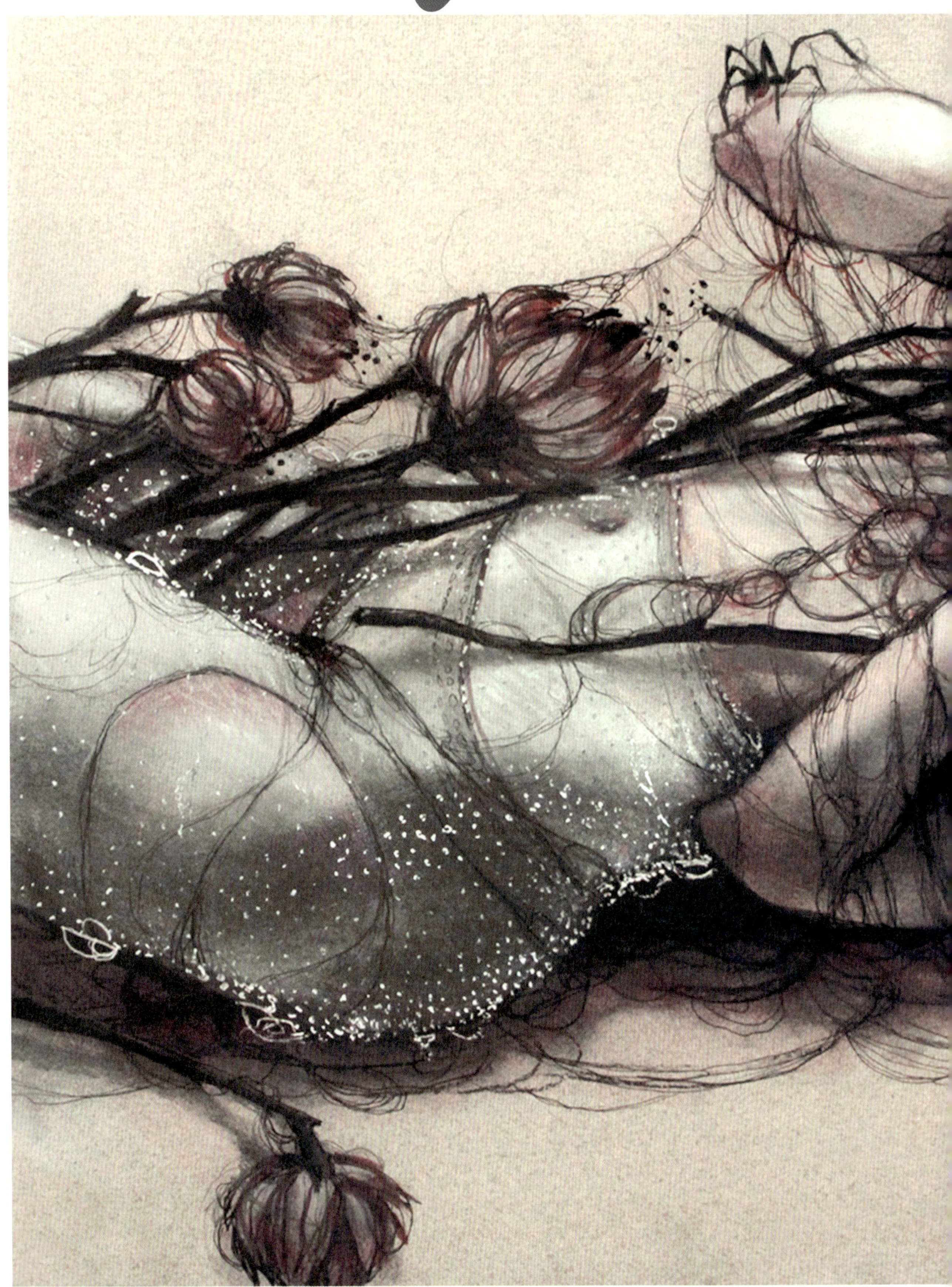

Black Silk Enchanter 黒シルクの魅惑者
ミクスト・メディア、色板紙 / H35.56×W48.26cm / 2014

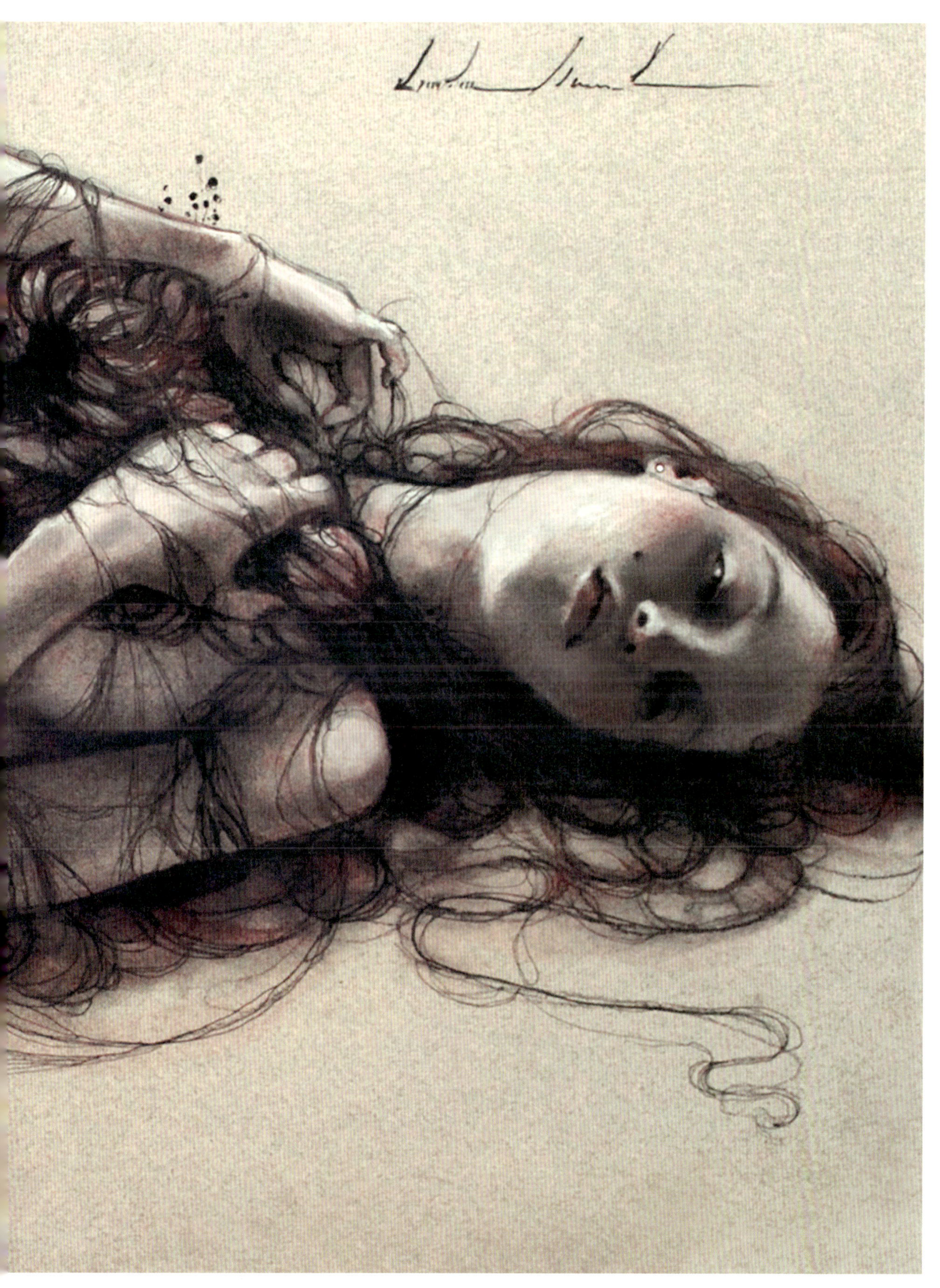

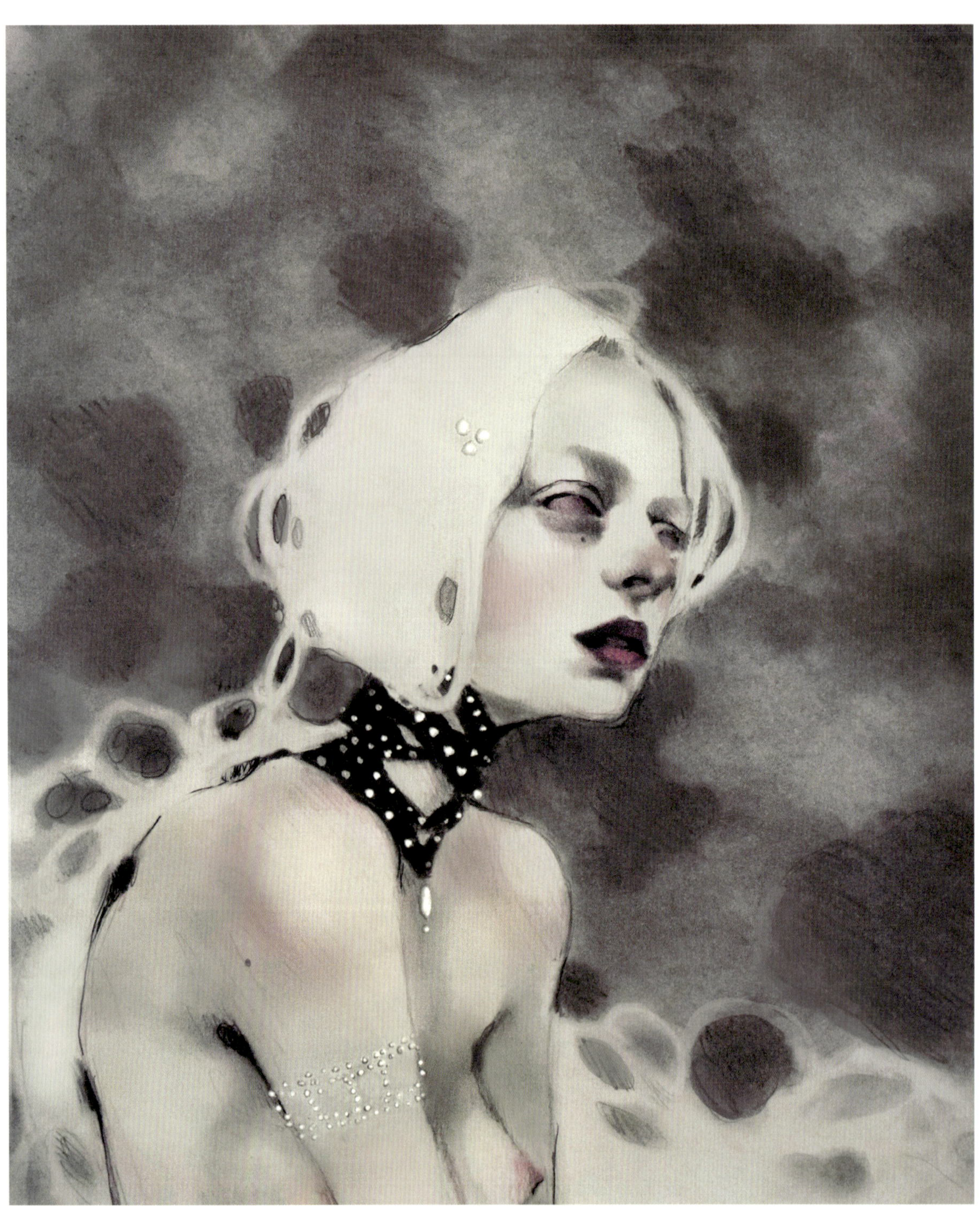

The Oracle 預言者
木炭、インク、メタリック・シルバー・アクリル、色鉛筆、紙 / H25.4×W20.32cm / 2014

Mirror of Vainglory 虚栄の鏡
ミクスト・メディア、紙 / H25.4×W20.32cm / 2014

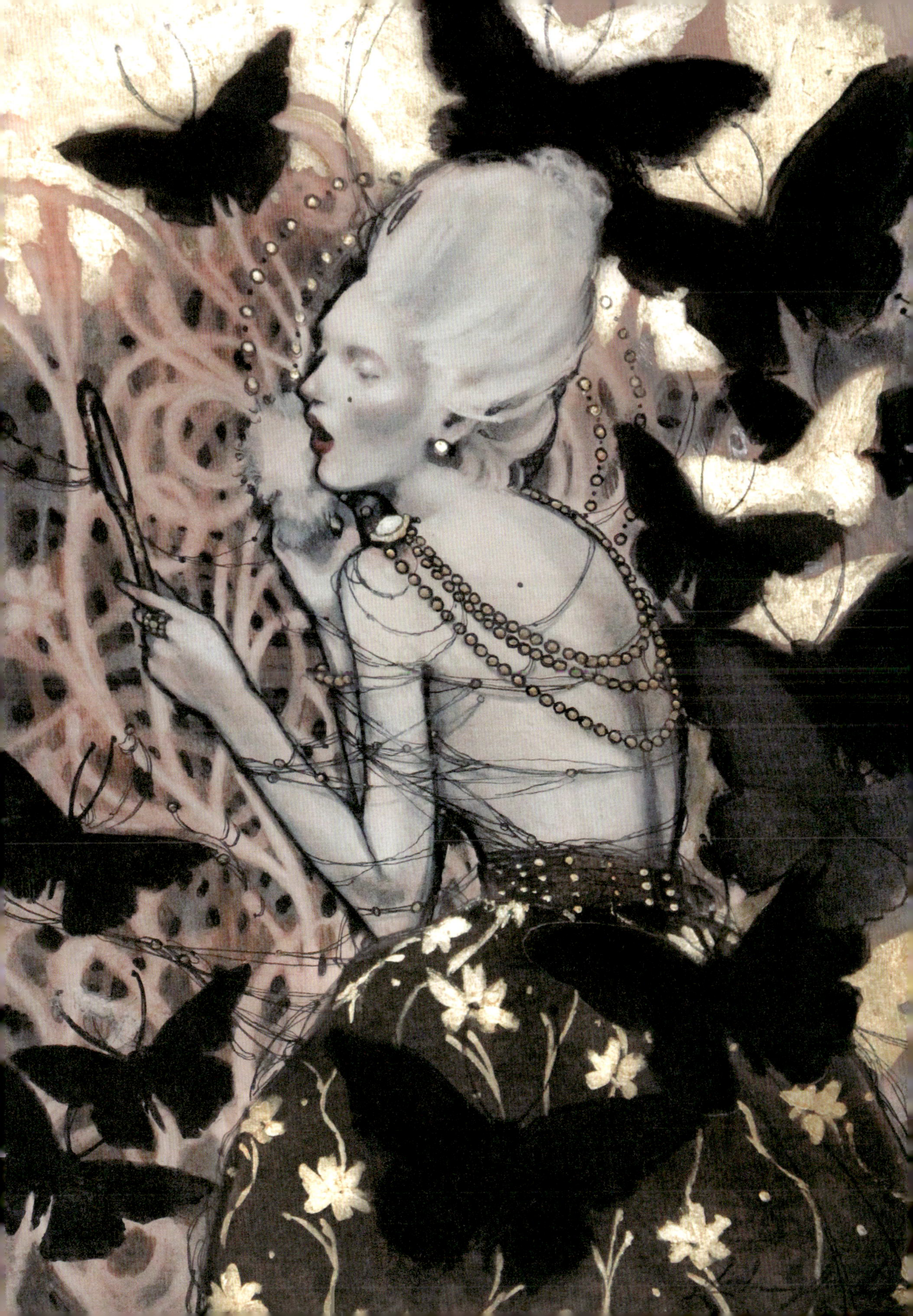

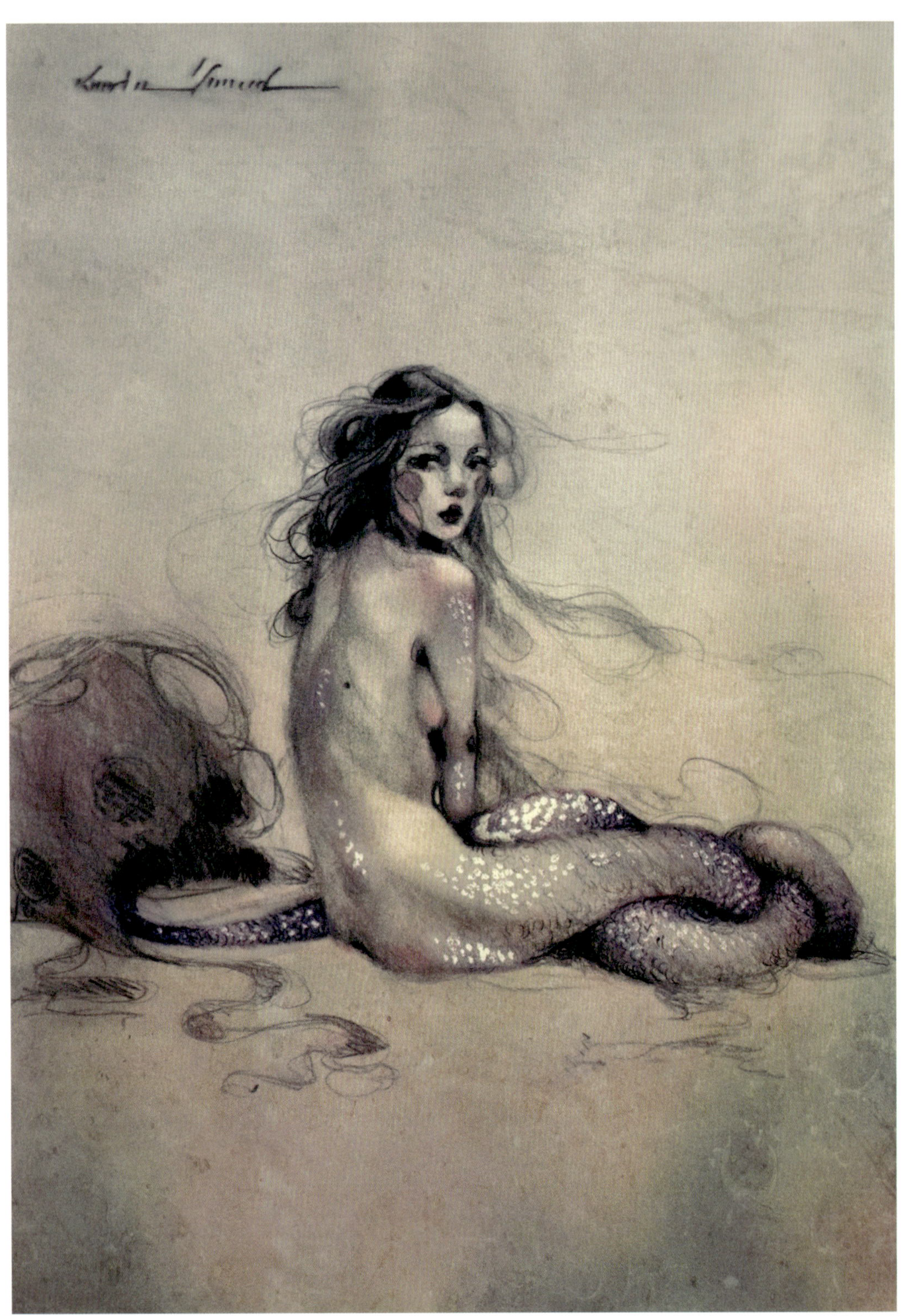

Last of Us ラスト・オブ・アス
墨、メタリック・シルバー・インク、黒インク、テクスチャ素材紙 / H25.4×W20.32cm / 2015

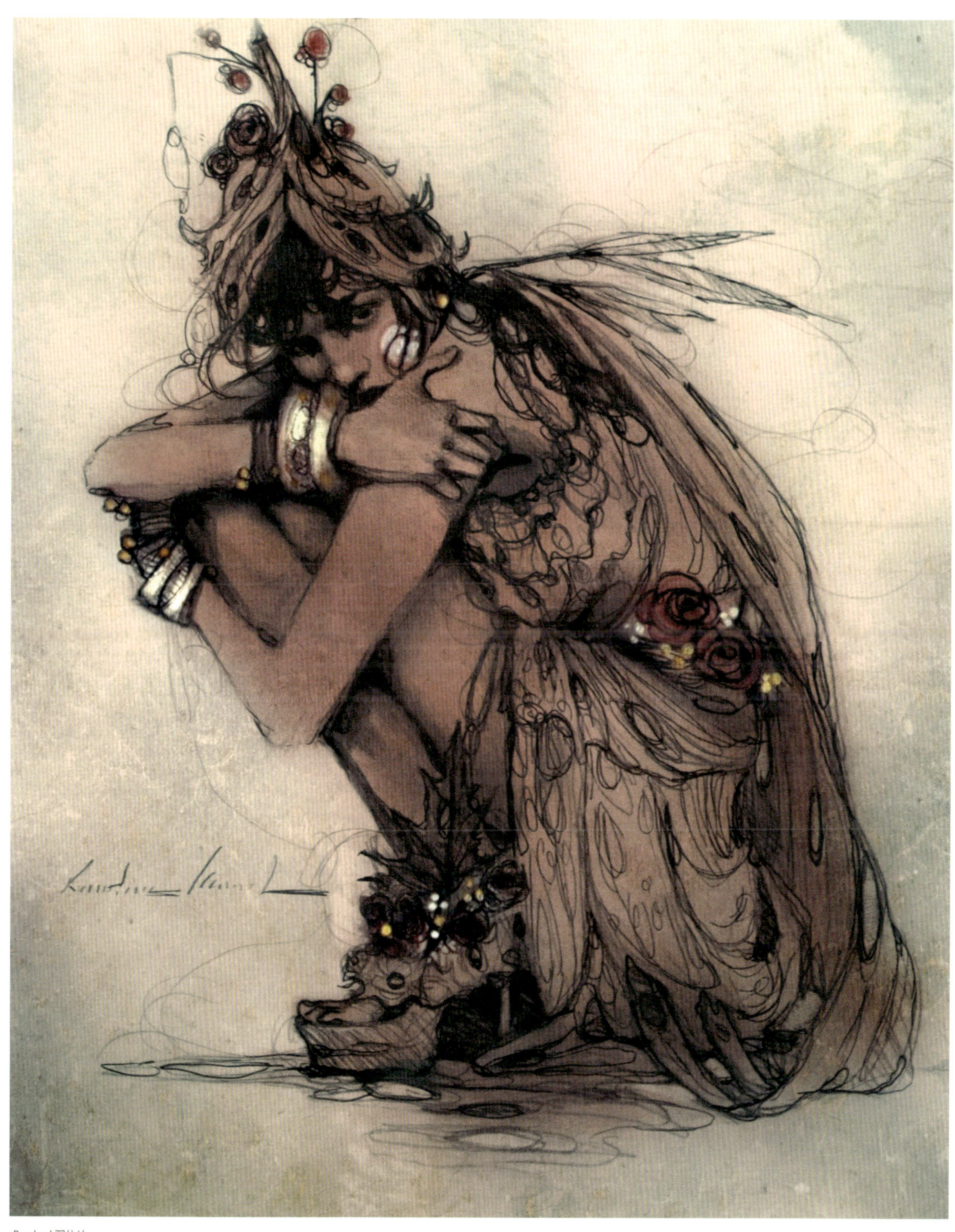

Perched 羽休め
コンテ、墨、インク、メタリック・ゴールド・インク、色鉛筆、テクスチャ素材紙 / H20.32×W12.7cm / 2014

18

Jel Ena

ジェル・イーナ（セルビア Serbia）

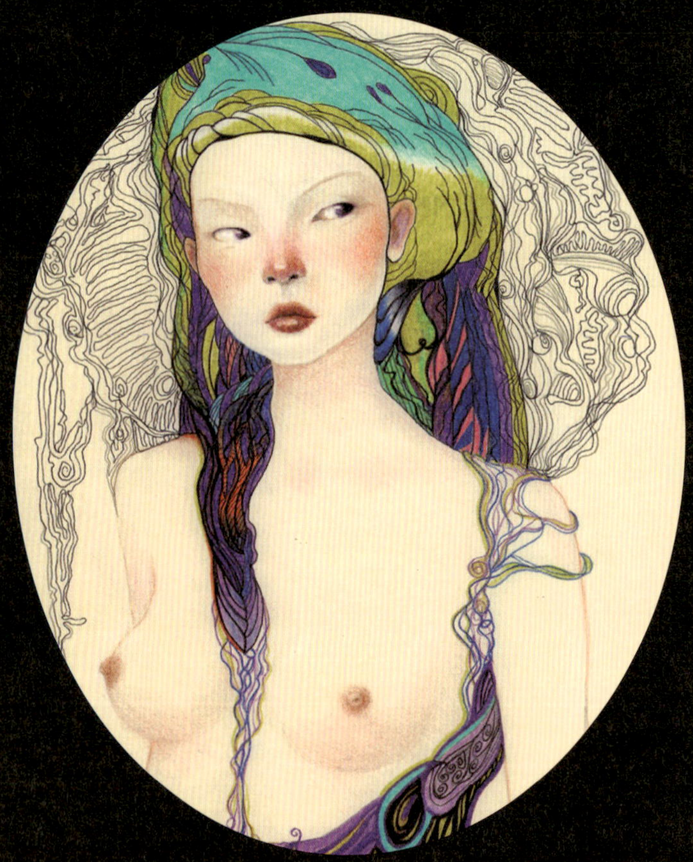

セルビア生まれのマルチメディア・アーティスト。現在は第二の故郷ロサンゼルス在住。芸術家一家に育ち、家族の全面的な支援を受けて美術の道に進む。ベオグラード大学美術学部に入学、絵画で美術学修士号を取得。作品は世界中のギャラリーで展示され、コレクターも多い。フリーランスのデザイナーとして映画、テレビ、ビデオゲームの制作にも携わる。圧倒的な描写力と巧みな色使いで、独自のスタイルを確立。アクリル絵具、油絵具、パステル、グラファイト鉛筆、色鉛筆を用い、叙情的な世界を創り出している。シュルレアリスムに徹した作品は見る者を魅了し、暗く官能的な世界に誘う。

Jel Ena is a Serbian born multi-media artist living in her adopted home of Los Angeles. She comes from a family of professional artists in every field who supported her pursuit of the fine arts. Jel Ena attended the Academy of Fine Art, Univesity of Belgrade, where she received her MFA in painting. She has been showing in galleries around the world where her work is widely collected, as well as freelancing in the movie, tv, video game industry as a designer. Her work displays a mastery of the figure and color. Her style is instantly recognizable and extraordinarily matchless in its visualization. Utilizing her mastery of acrylic/oil paints, pastels, graphite and colored pencils; intricate emotions and hyper surreal visions are born and enchant every viewer into her dark sensual dreamscape.

www.jel-ena.com

↑ Izanami イザナミ（部分）
インク、色鉛筆、紙 / H27.94×W21.59cm / 2012

→Charging 充電
デジタル・プリント / H60.96×W40.64cm / 2011

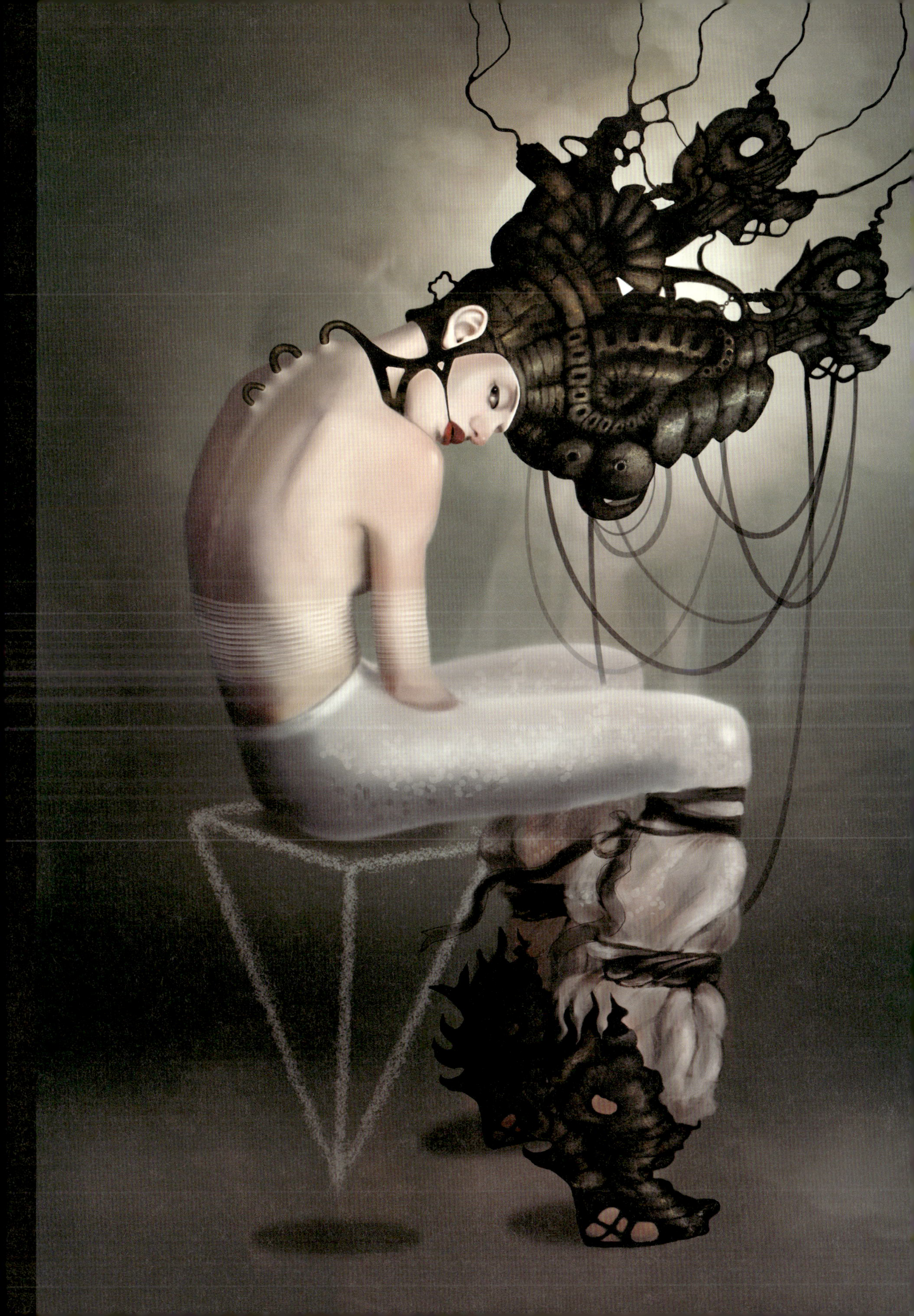

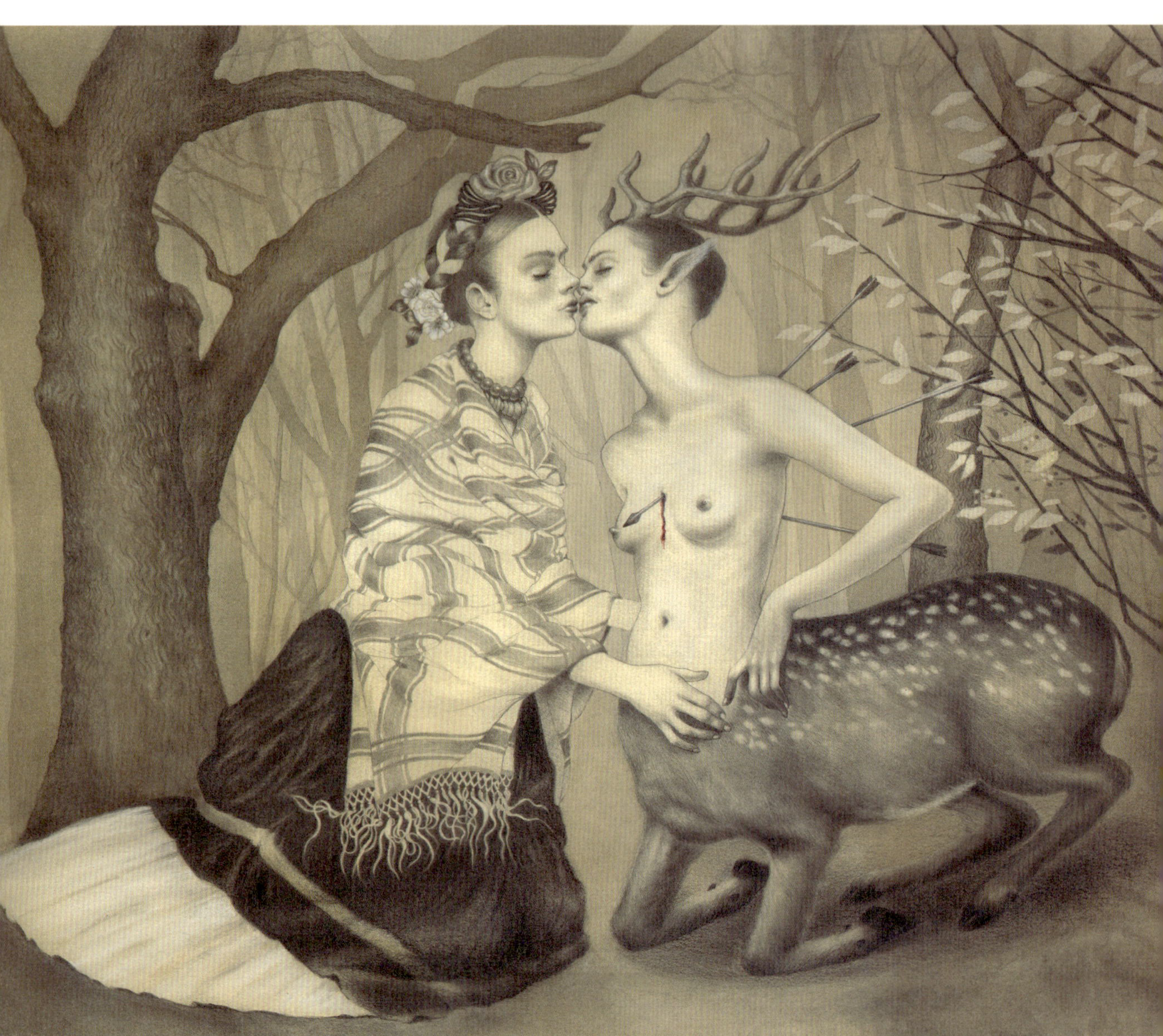

Lacrimosa: tribute to Frida Kahlo ラクリモーサ──フリーダ・カーロに捧ぐ
墨、手彩色の紙 / H40.64×W50.8cm / 2015

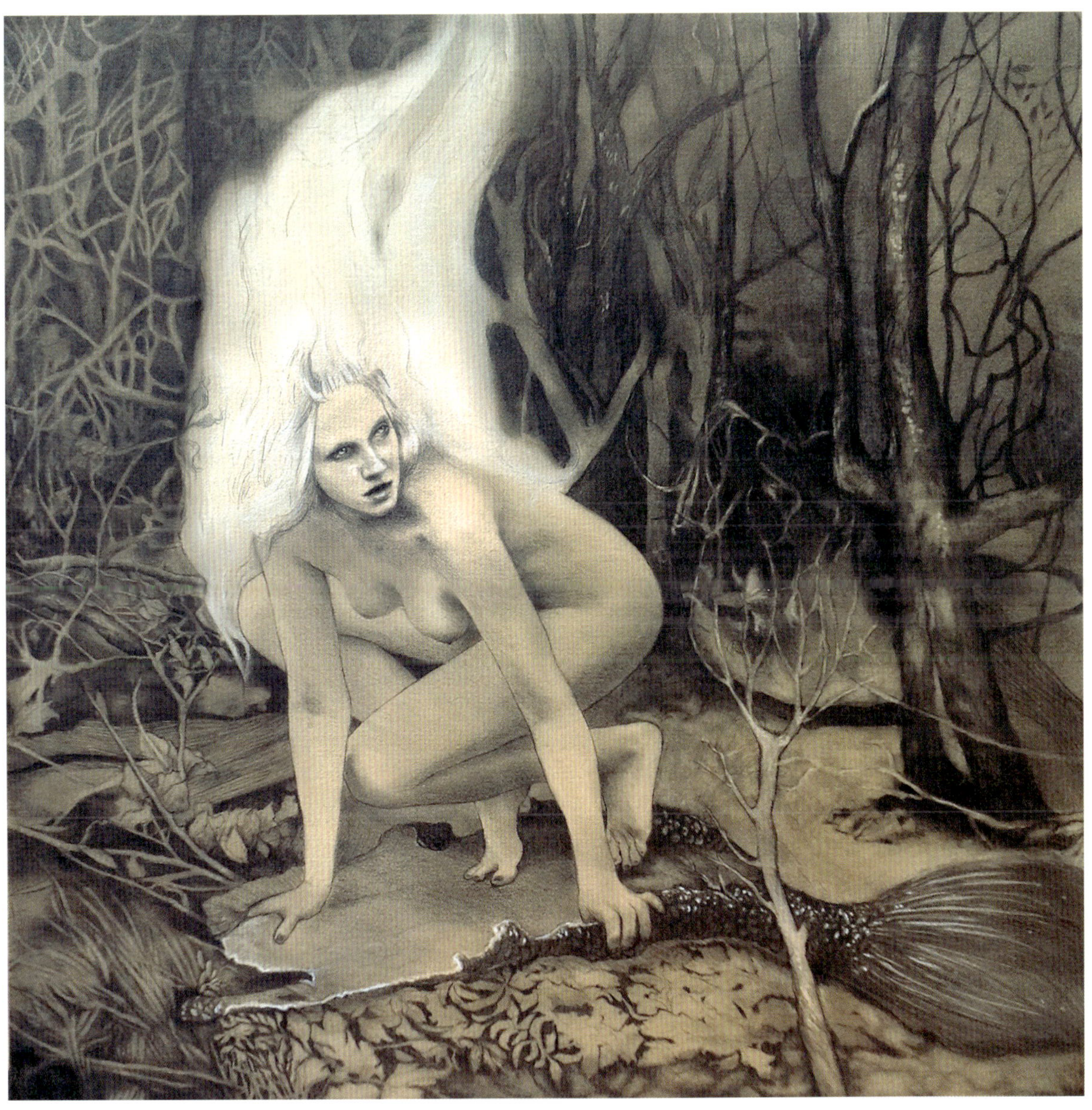

Little Mermaid 人魚姫
墨、パステル、手彩色の紙 / H50.8×W50.8cm / 2015

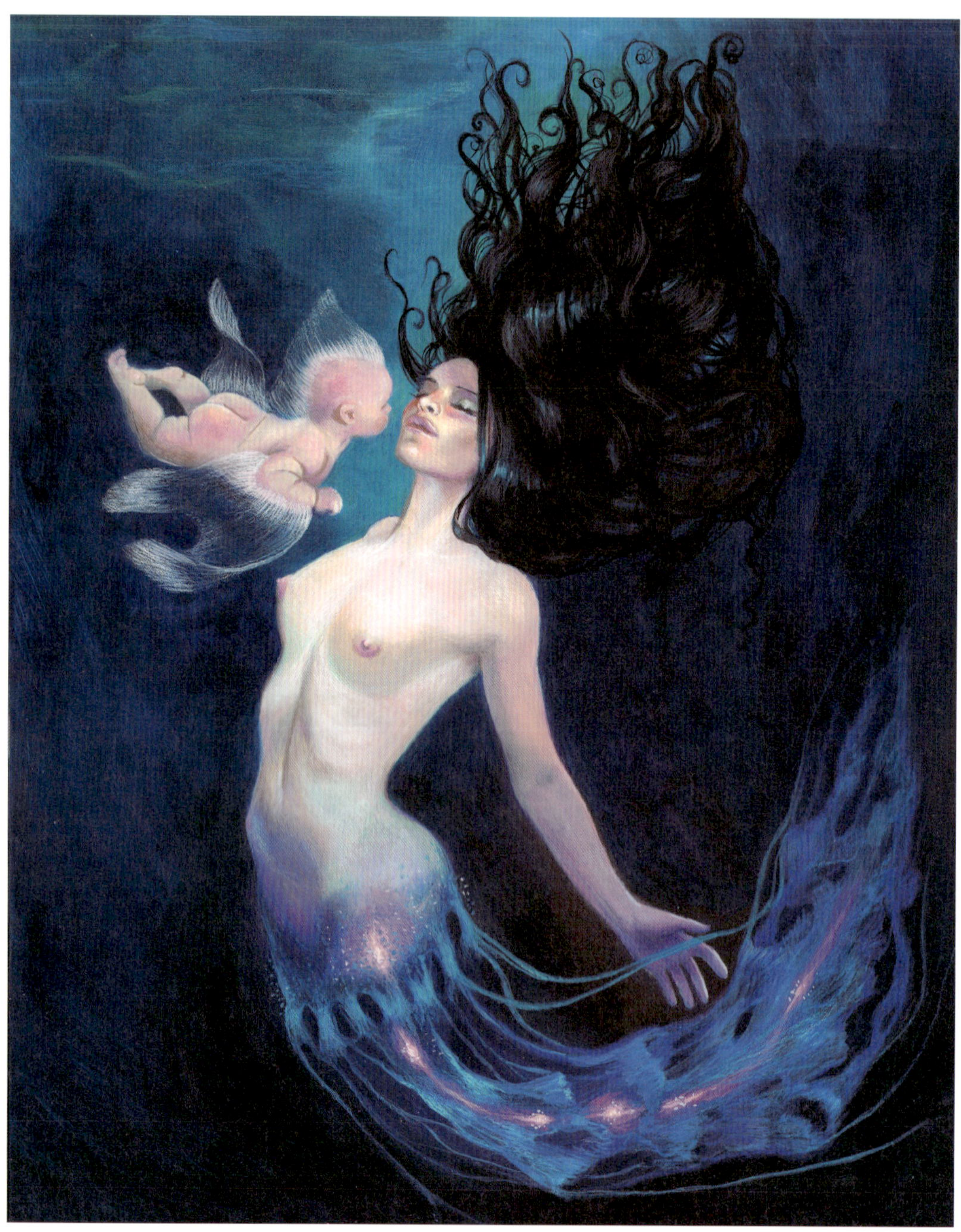

Medusa's Dream メドゥーサの夢
アクリル、ワックス・パステル、パネル / H35.56×W27.94cm / 2013

Sanctum Infernum 聖なる地獄
墨、木炭、パステル、紙、バーチ材パネル / H60.96×W45.72cm / 2015

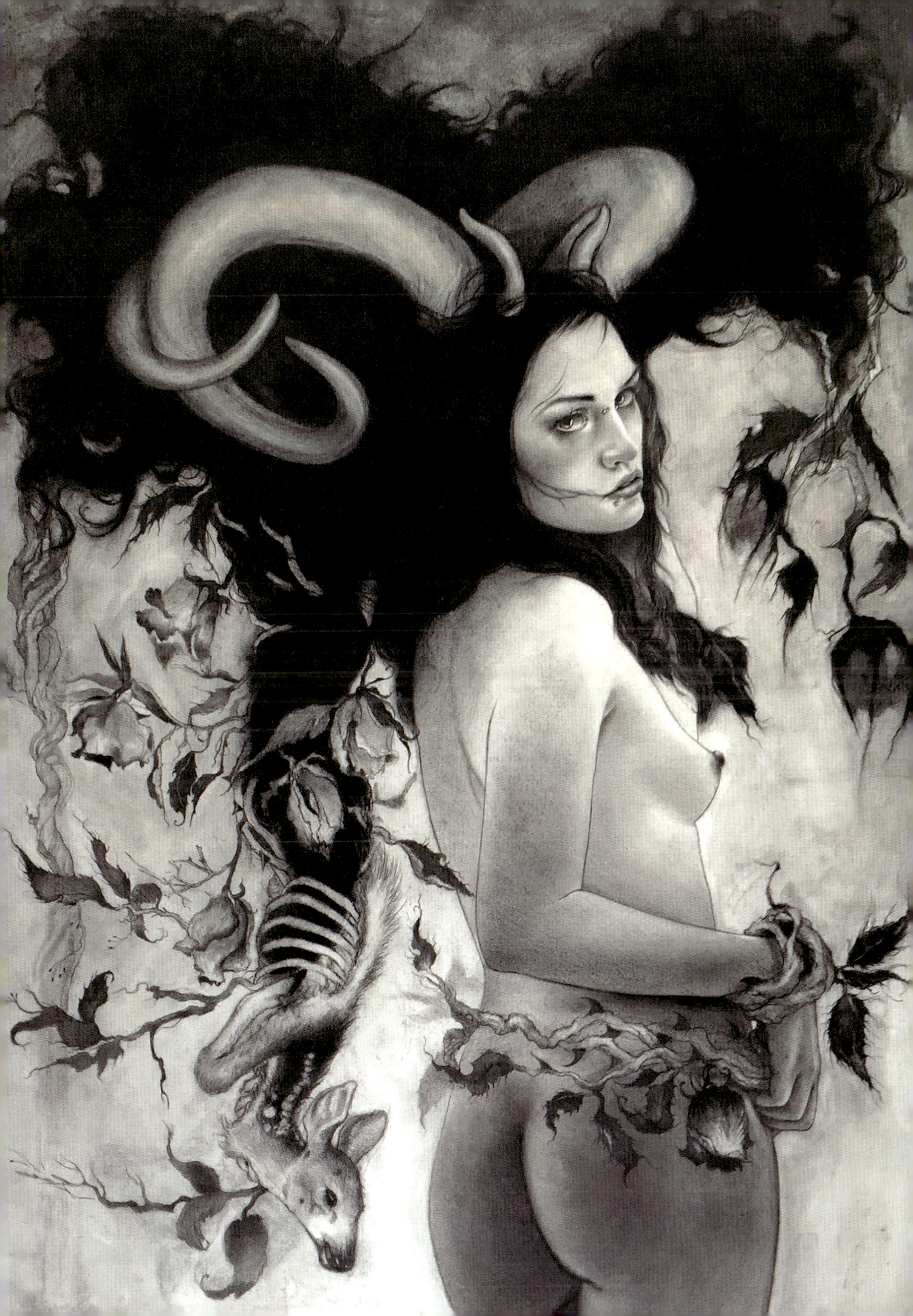

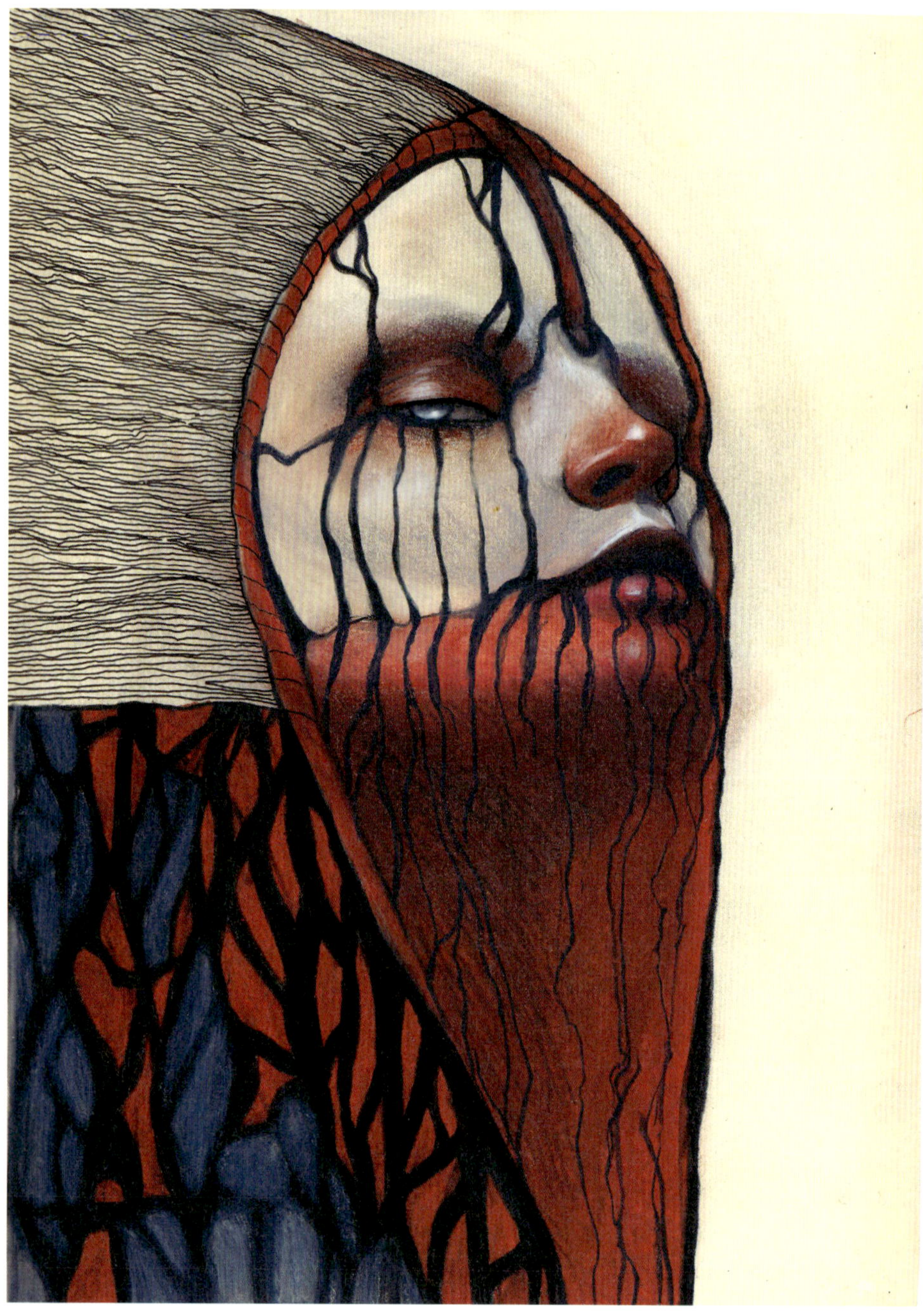

Bleeder 血友病者
色鉛筆、ワックス・パステル、紙 / H27.94×W21.59cm / 2011

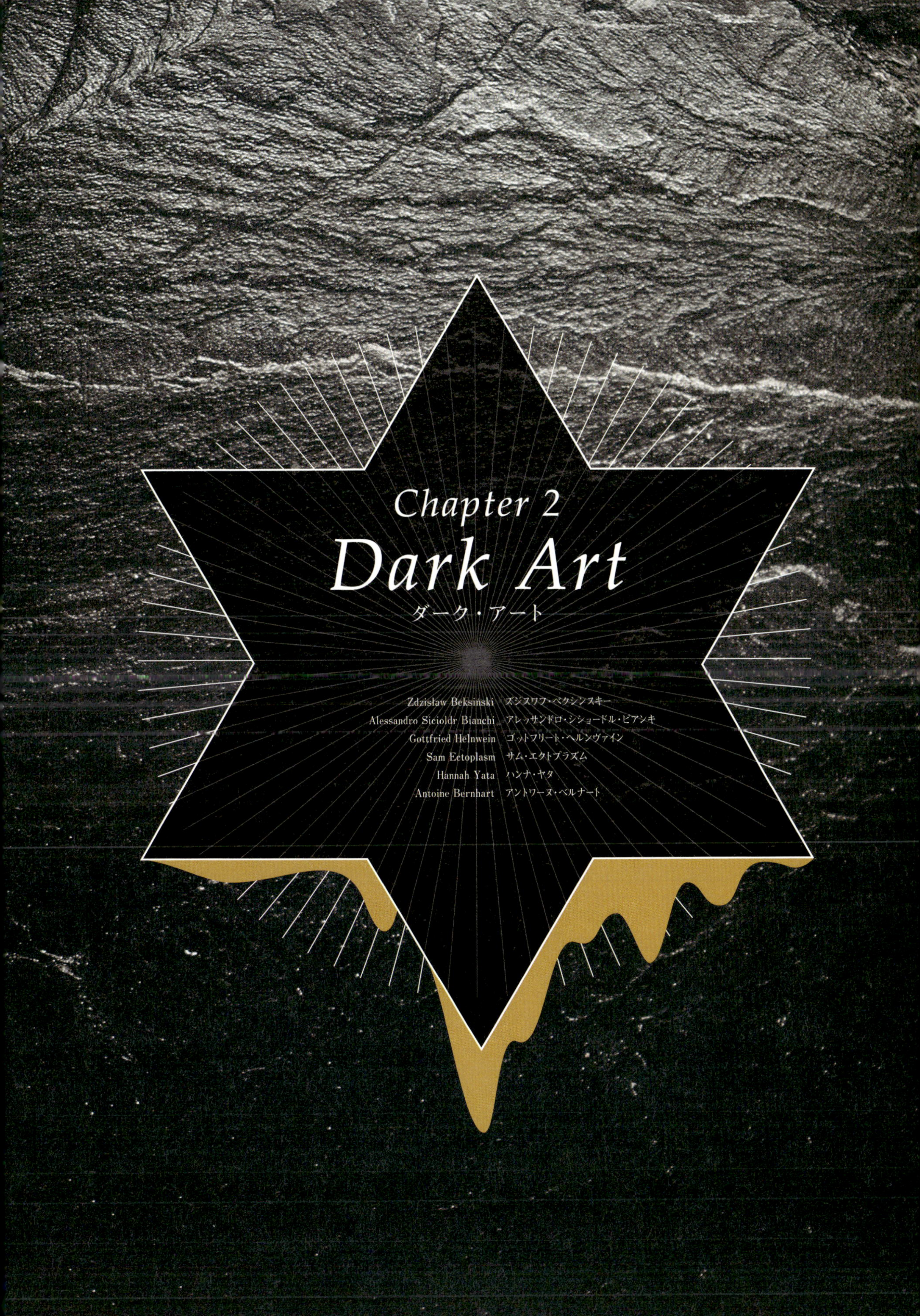
Chapter 2
Dark Art
ダーク・アート

Zdzisław Beksinski　ズジスワフ・ベクシンスキー
Alessandro Sicioldr Bianchi　アレッサンドロ・シショードル・ビアンキ
Gottfried Helnwein　ゴットフリート・ヘルンヴァイン
Sam Ectoplasm　サム・エクトプラズム
Hannah Yata　ハンナ・ヤタ
Antoine Bernhart　アントワーヌ・ベルナート

19

Zdzisław Beksiński

ズジスワフ・ベクシンスキー（ポーランド Poland）

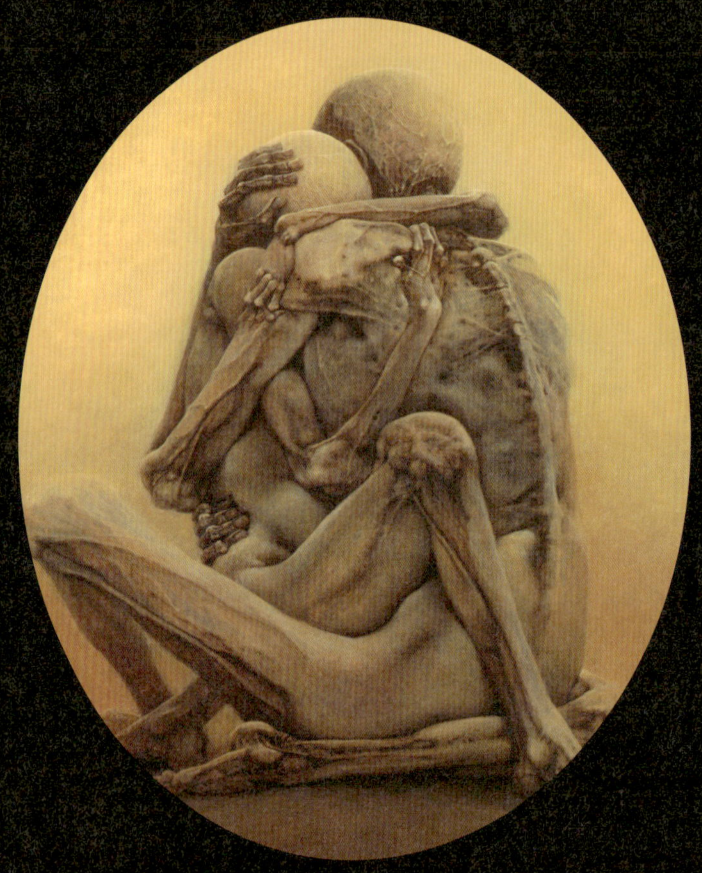

1929年2月24日〜2005年2月21日。ポーランドの画家、写真家、彫刻家。「ディストピアン・シュルレアリスム（暗黒郷の超現実主義）」のジャンルで活躍した。自身が「バロック」または「ゴシック」と呼ぶ技法で描かれた作品は、主に第1期と第2期に分けられる。1期は「ユートピアン・リアリズム（桃源郷の現実主義）」の力強いスタイル、強烈な色彩を用いてシュルレアリスム的な建造物を描き、独自の終焉の光景を創り出した。第2期はより抽象的で、形式主義を重んじる画風に移行した。

Zdzisław Beksiński (February 1929 – 21 February 2005) was a Polish painter, photographer and sculptor, specializing in the field of dystopian surrealism. Beksiński did his paintings and drawings in what he called either a 'Baroque' or a 'Gothic' manner. His creations were made mainly in two periods. The first period of work is generally considered to contain expressionistic color, with a strong style of "utopian realism" and surreal architecture, like a doomsday scenario. The second period contained more abstract style, with the main features of formalism.

↑No title 無題（部分）
油彩、ハードボード / 1984
→No title 無題
油彩、ハードボード / 1984

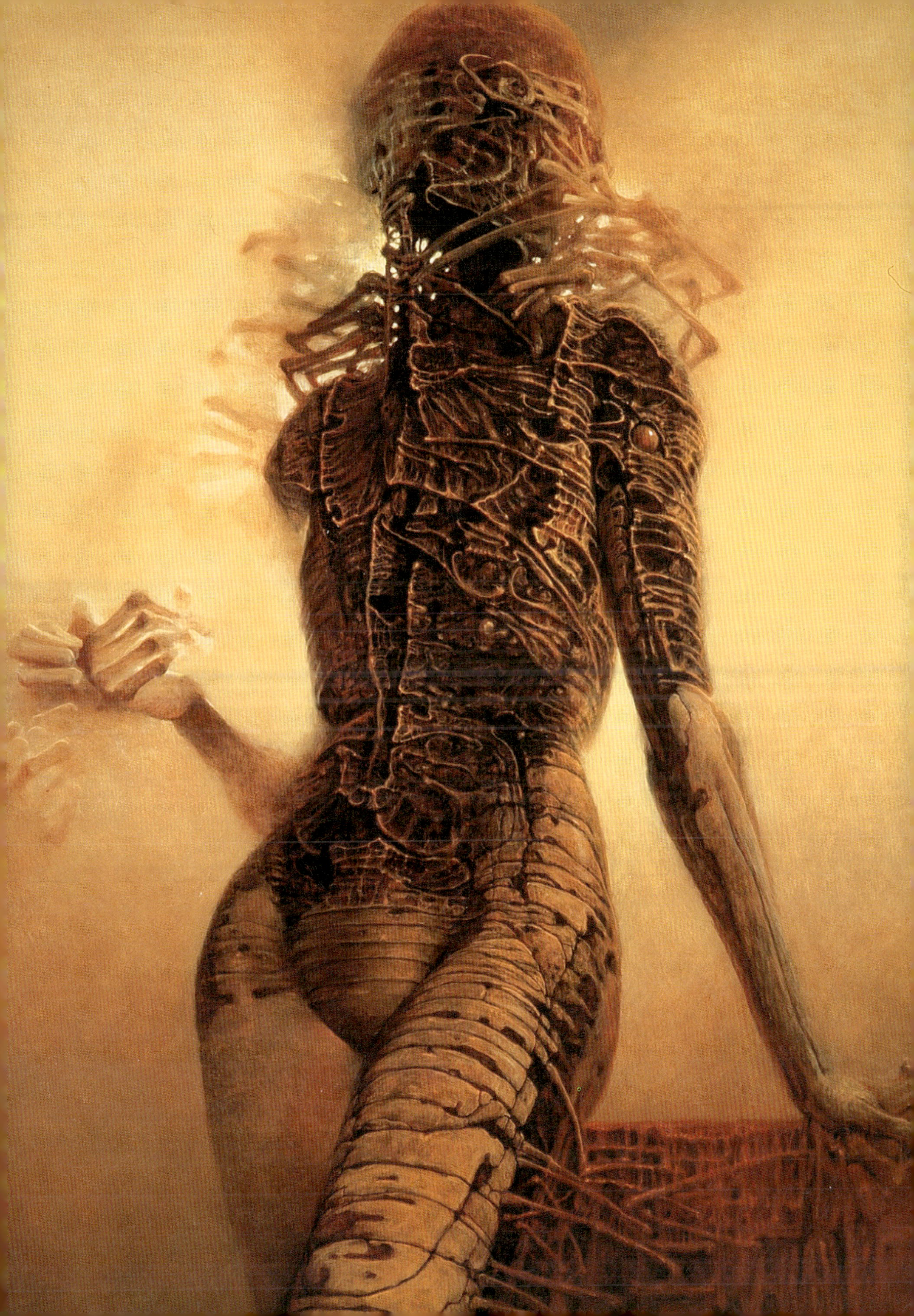

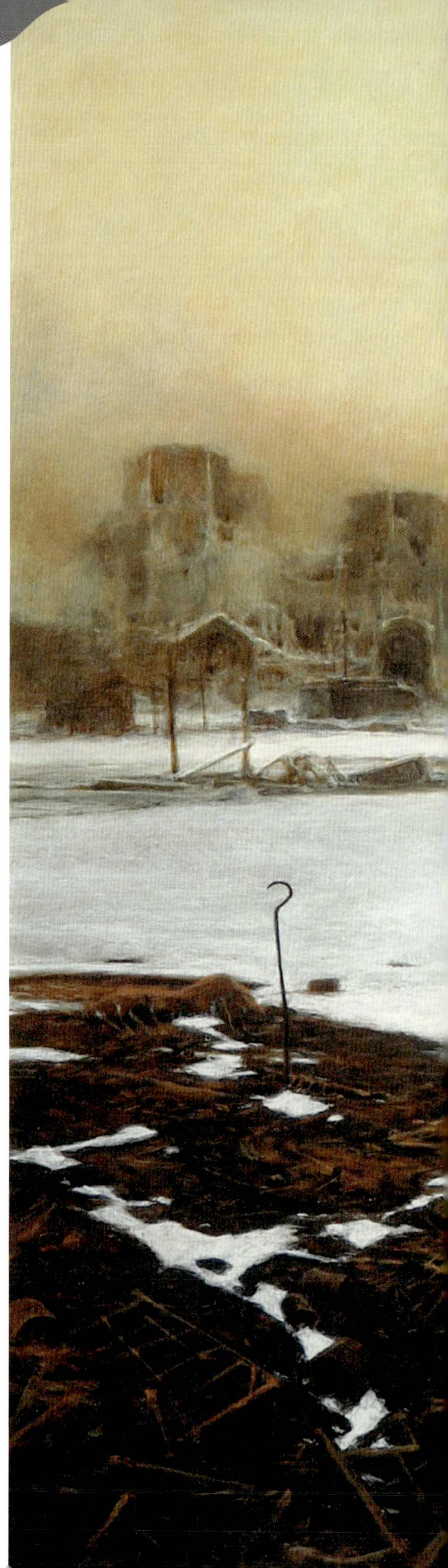

No title 無題
油彩、ハードボード / 1984

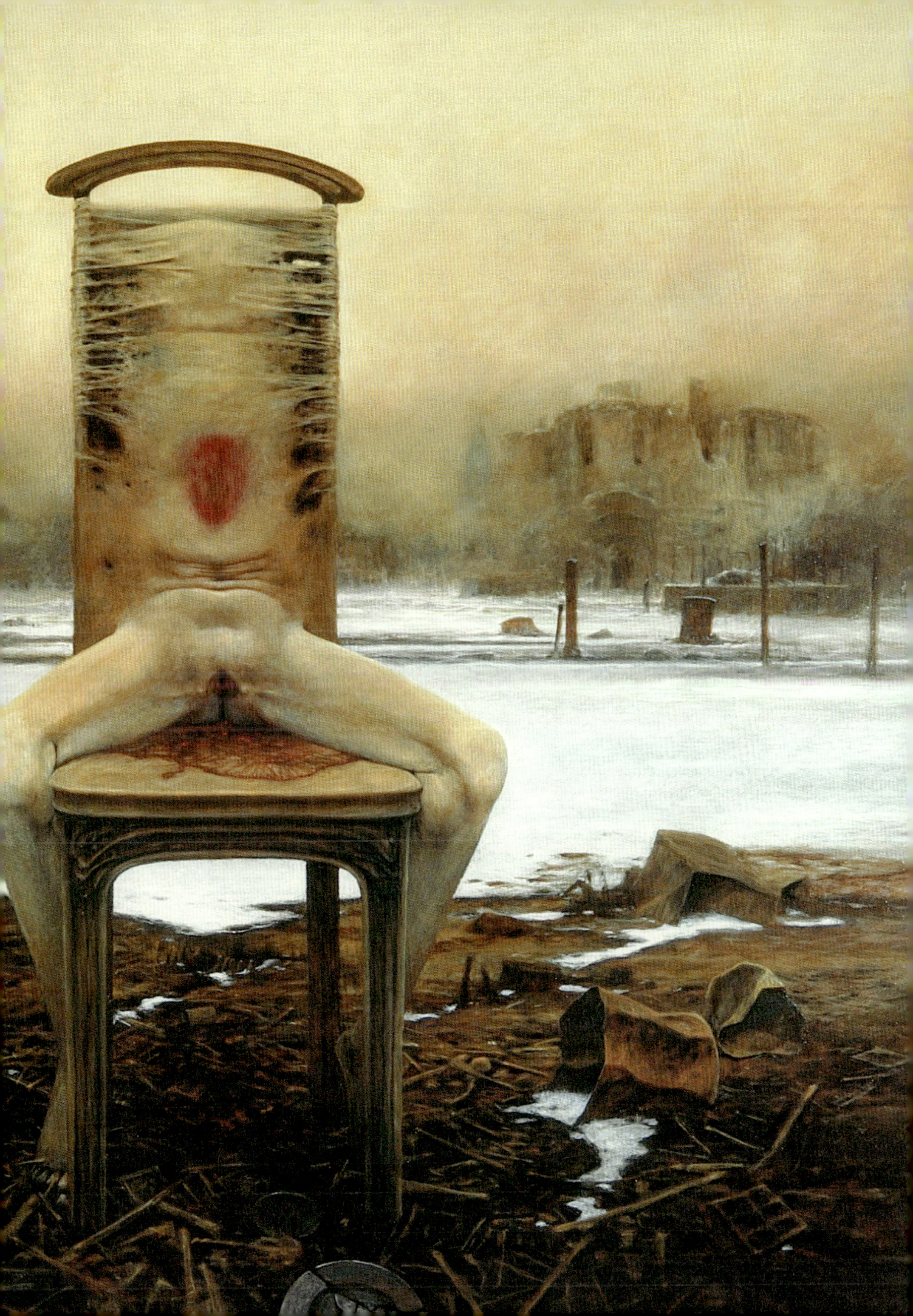

20

Alessandro Sicioldr Bianchi

アレッサンドロ・シショードル・ビアンキ（イタリア　Italy）

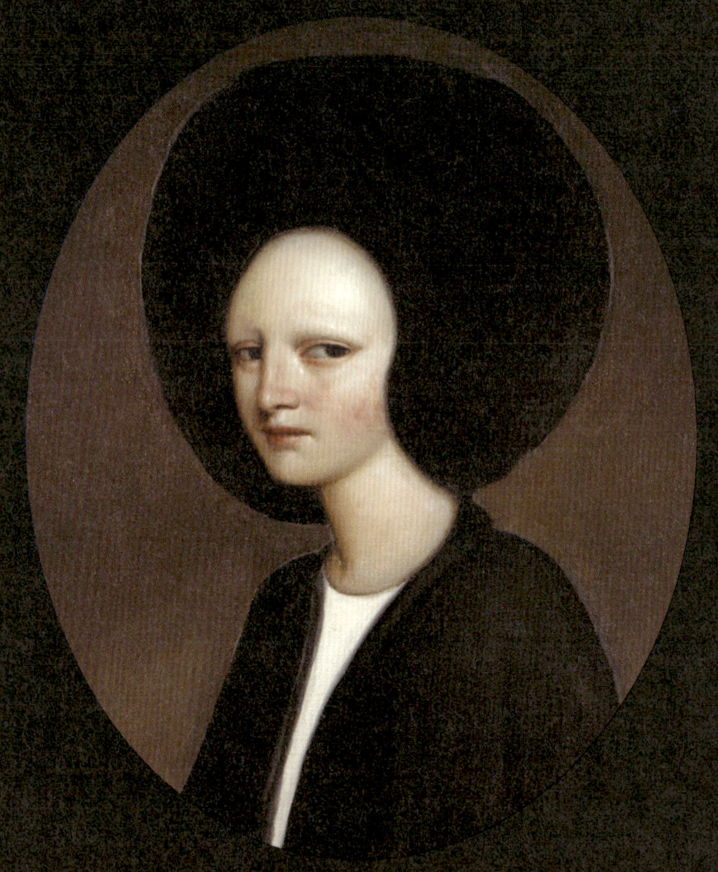

1990年生まれのイタリアの画家。エトルリア文明が栄えたトスカーナ地方の古都に暮らし、創作活動に励んでいる。無意識の幻視を題材とし、それを伝統的な絵画と線画の技法を用いて表現している。同じく画家である父の手ほどきを受け、昔ながらのアトリエでイタリアの伝統的な絵画の基礎をみっちり叩き込まれた。恐ろしい幻想を写実的に描くことで、普段あまり目を向けられることのない無意識が生み出す世界が現実であるかのように見せている。

Sicioldr is an italian painter born in 1990, living and working in Tuscania, an ancient etruscan town. His subjects are visions coming from the unconscious mind that he represents using traditional painting and drawing techniques. He studied under the guidance of his father, also a painter, in his classical atelier, where he learned all the basic principles of painting in the italian tradition. The use of a detailed and accurate painting style to represent a morbid and dreamy imagery gives the possibility to the author to make real and tangible the world of unconscious visions, which otherwise could be lost in the stream of daily life.

www.sicioldrart.com

↑Enigma Dell'Infanta 王女の謎（部分）
油彩、リネン / H50×W35cm / 2017

→La Sibilla シビラ
油彩、木製パネル / H30×W40cm / 2016

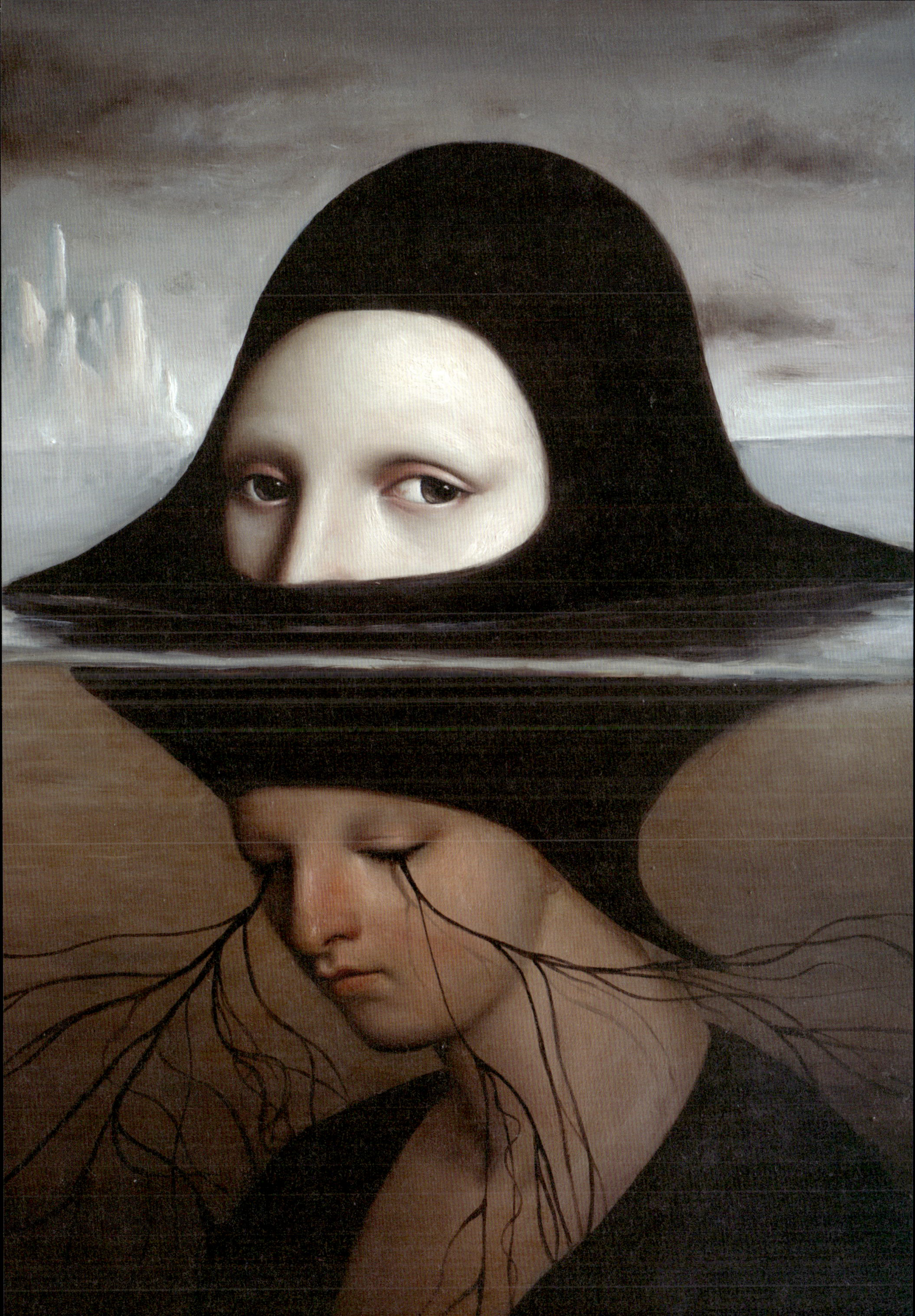

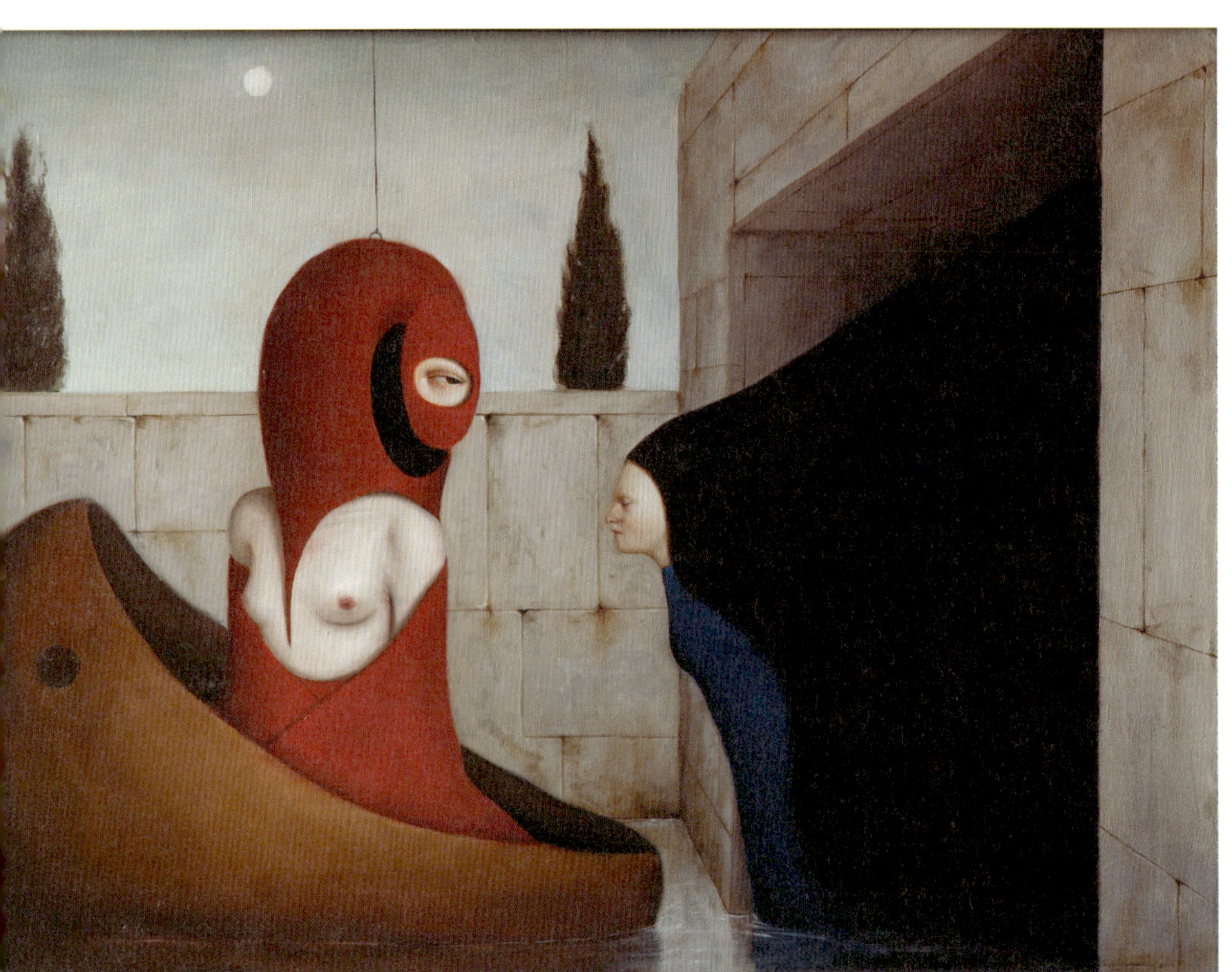

Embryo's dream 胎芽の夢
油彩、リネン / H65×W85cm / 2017

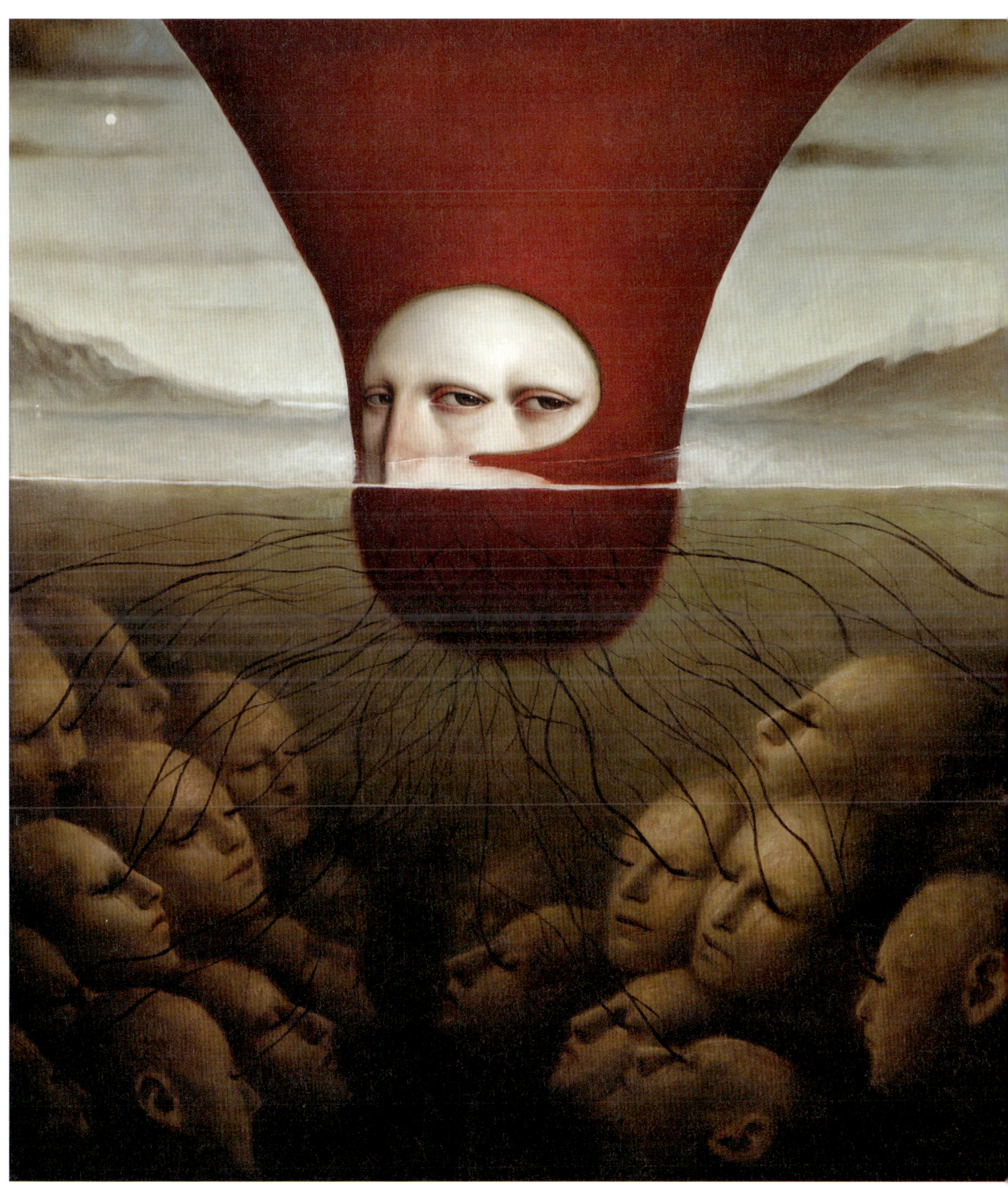

The Goddess 女神
油彩、リネン / H100×W90cm / 2017

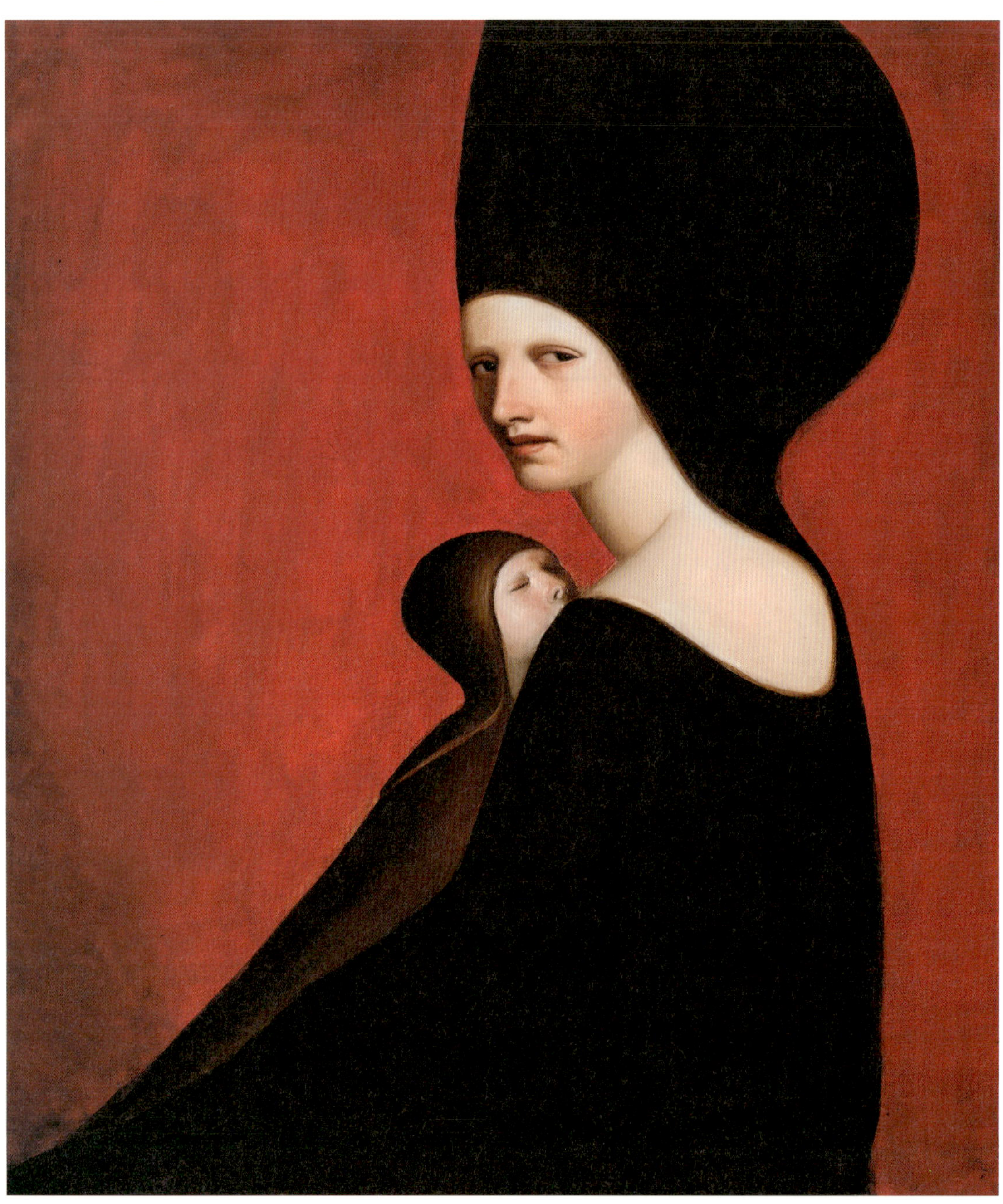

Silence or the Prayer 静寂または祈り
油彩、リネン / H70×W60cm / 2017

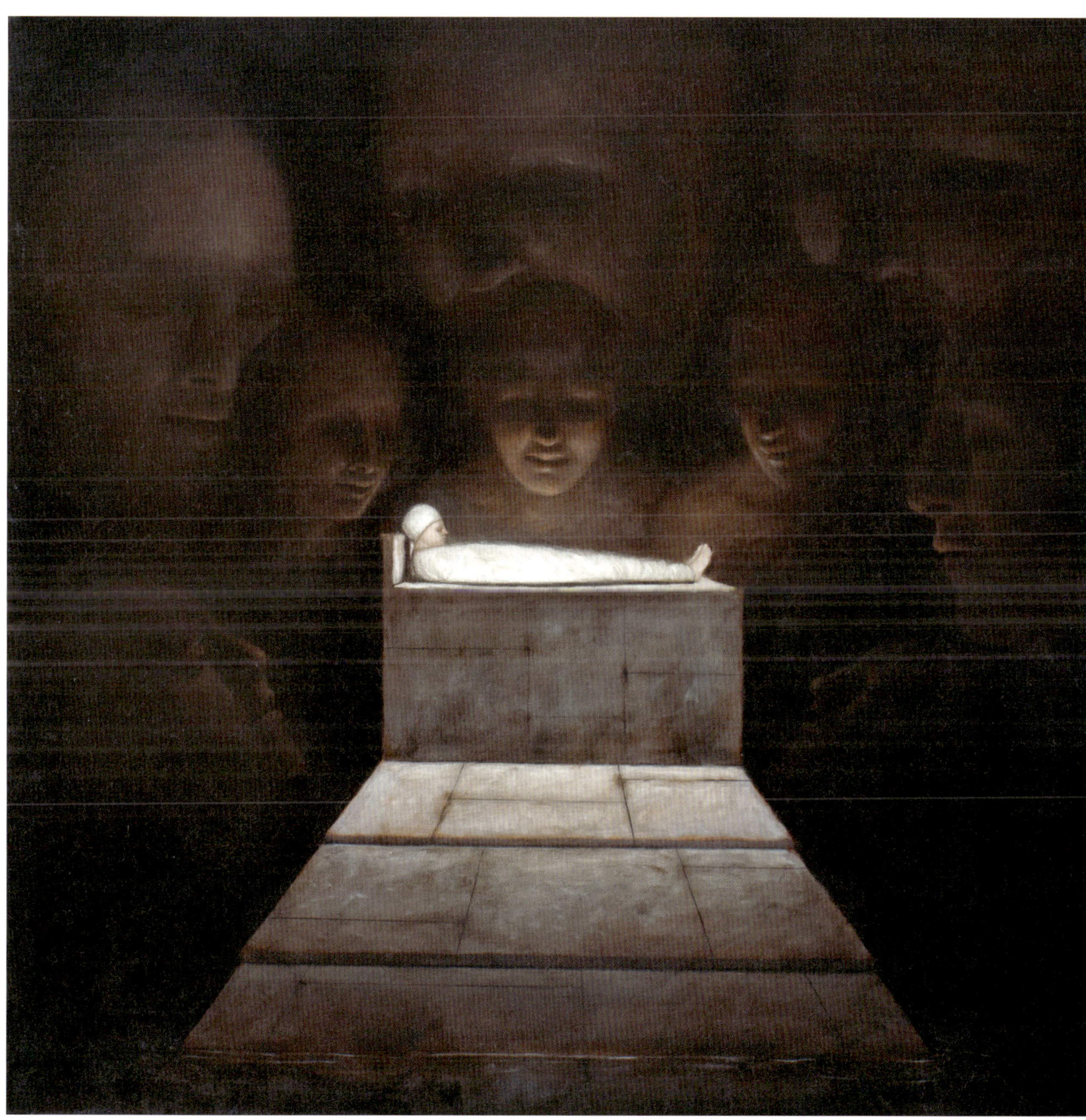

Enigma del Sogno o il Risveglio 夢または覚醒の謎
油彩、リネン / H100×W100cm / 2016

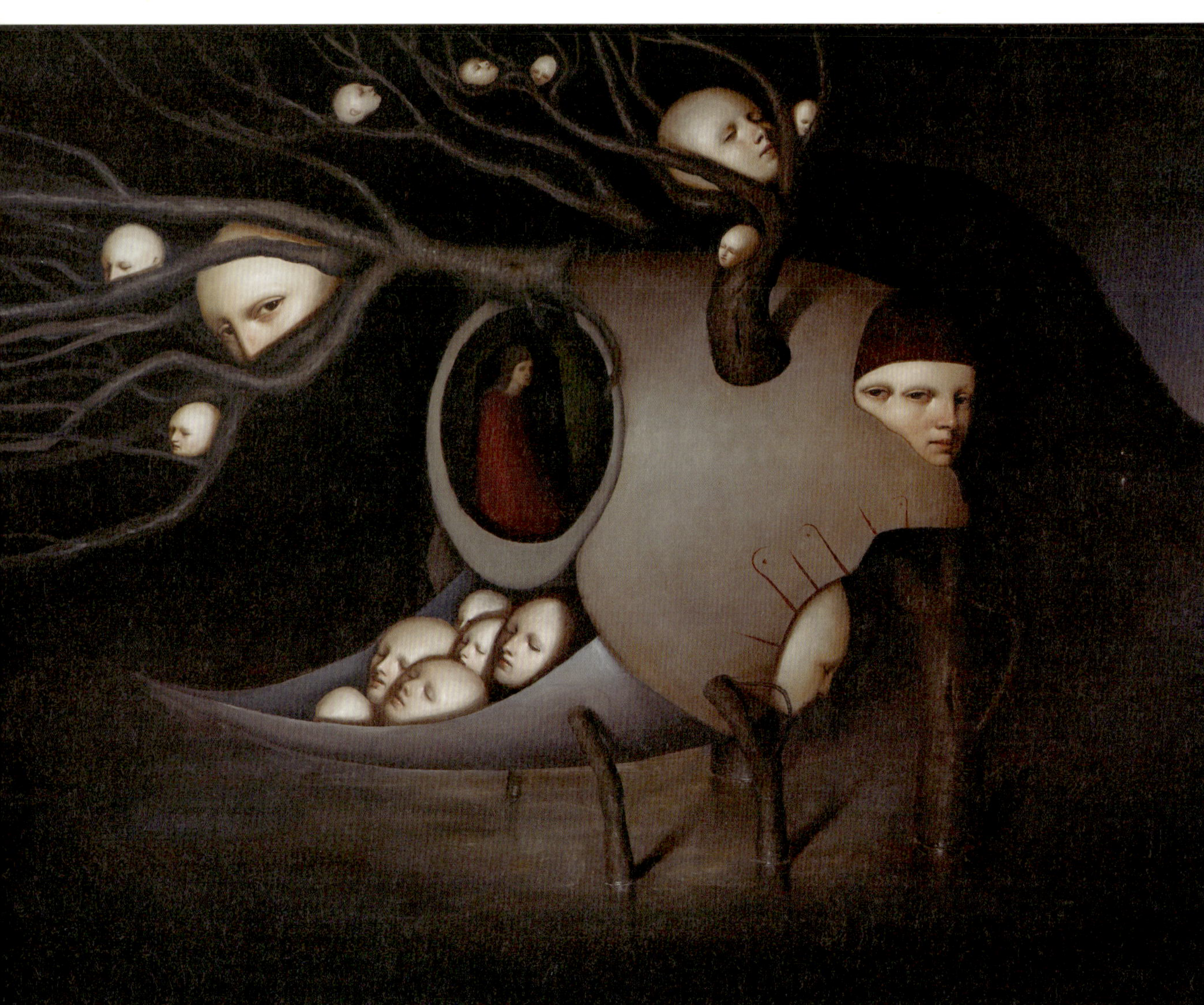

Persephone's Dream ペルセポネの夢
油彩、木製パネル / H85×W115cm / 2017

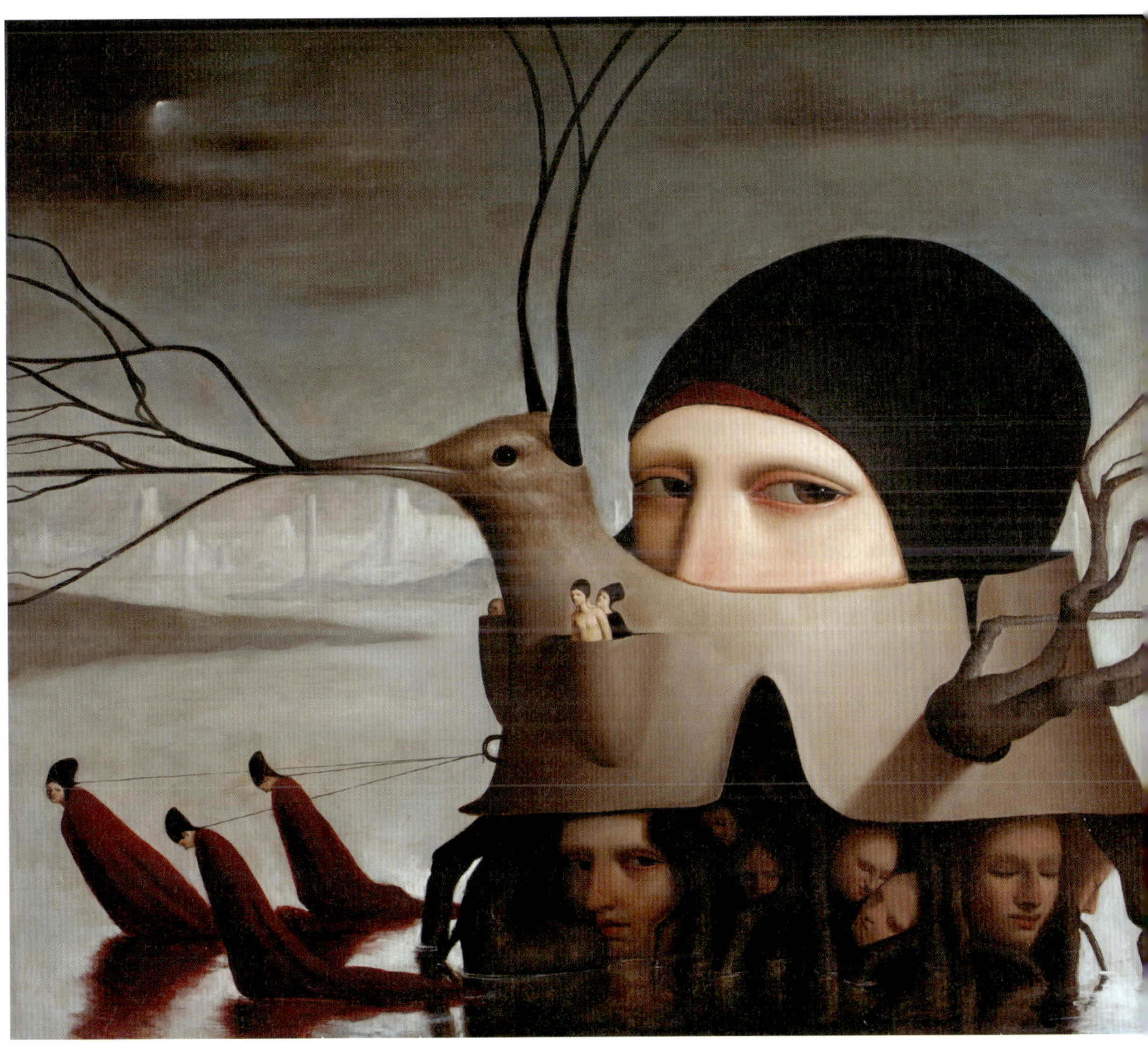

Visione del Grande Carro 巨大荷車の光景
油彩、木製パネル / H87×W100cm / 2017

21

Gottfried Helnwein

ゴットフリート・ヘルンヴァイン（オーストリア　Austria）

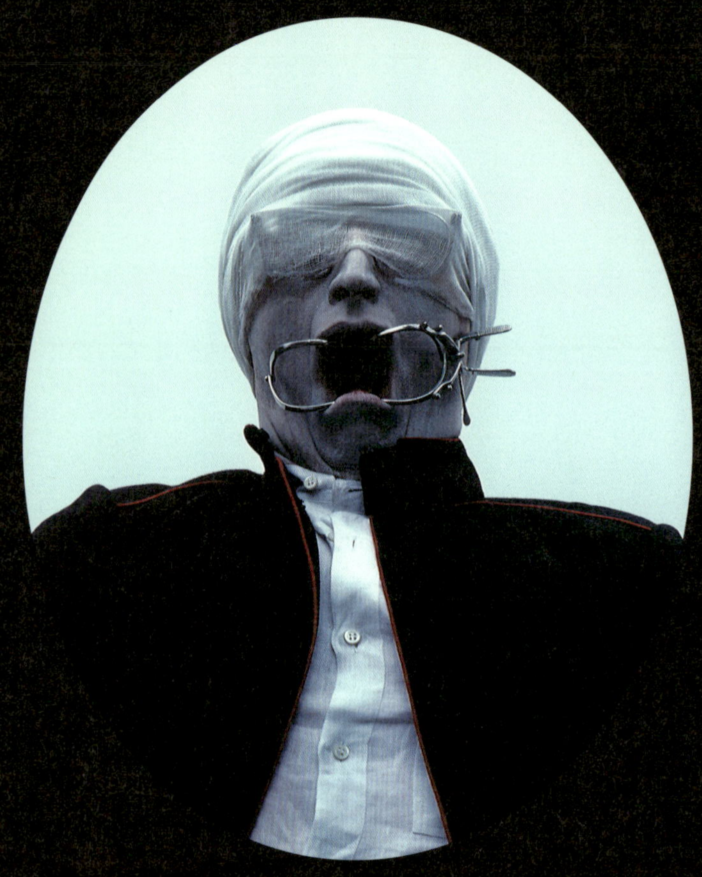

1948年10月8日生まれ。オーストリア系アイルランド人のヴィジュアル・アーティスト。絵画、デッサン、壁画、写真、彫刻、インスタレーション、さらにはパフォーマンスと、様々な手法、媒体を用いて幅広い分野で活躍。主に心理学的・社会学的不安感や、歴史・政治問題を取り上げ、人間をテーマにした作品を創り上げている。肉体的、心理的に傷ついた子供たちを数多く描いている。ウィーン美術アカデミーで視覚芸術を学ぶ。アイルランドとロサンゼルスを拠点に活躍。

Gottfried Helnwein (born 8 October 1948) is an Austrian-Irish visual artist. He has worked as a painter, draftsman, photographer, muralist, sculptor, installation and performance artist, using a wide variety of techniques and media. His work is concerned primarily with psychological and sociological anxiety, historical issues and political topics. His subject matter is the human condition. The metaphor for his art is dominated by the image of the child, particularly the wounded child, scarred physically and emotionally from within. Helnwein studied at the University of Visual Art in Vienna (Akademie der Bildenden Künste, Wien). He lives and works in Ireland and Los Angeles.

www.helnwein.com

↑Song of the Deputies 副官の歌（セルフ・ポートレート、部分）
写真、ミクスト・メディア / 1986

→The last Days of Pompeii II ポンペイ最後の日 II（セルフ・ポートレート）
写真、ミクスト・メディア / 1987

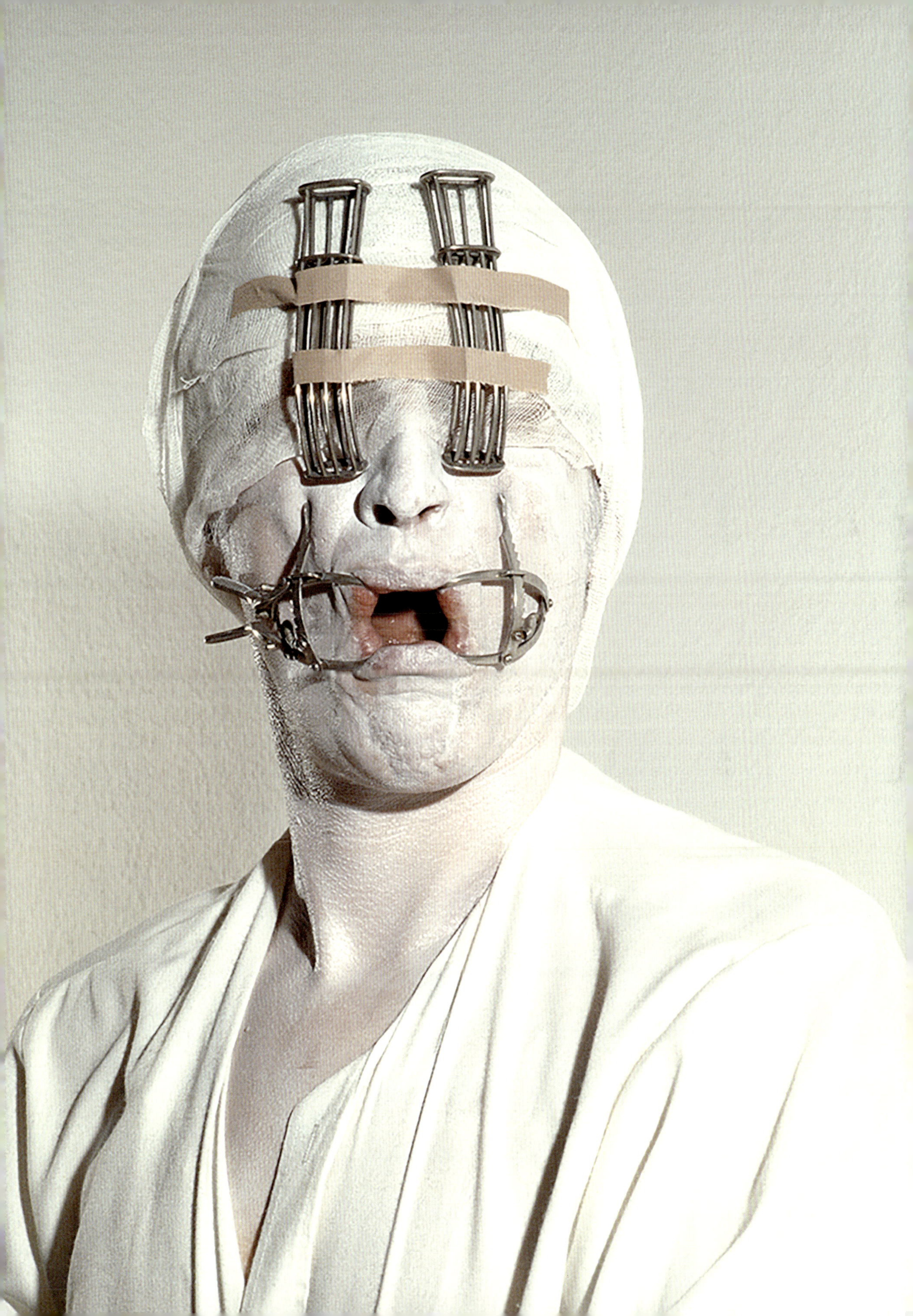

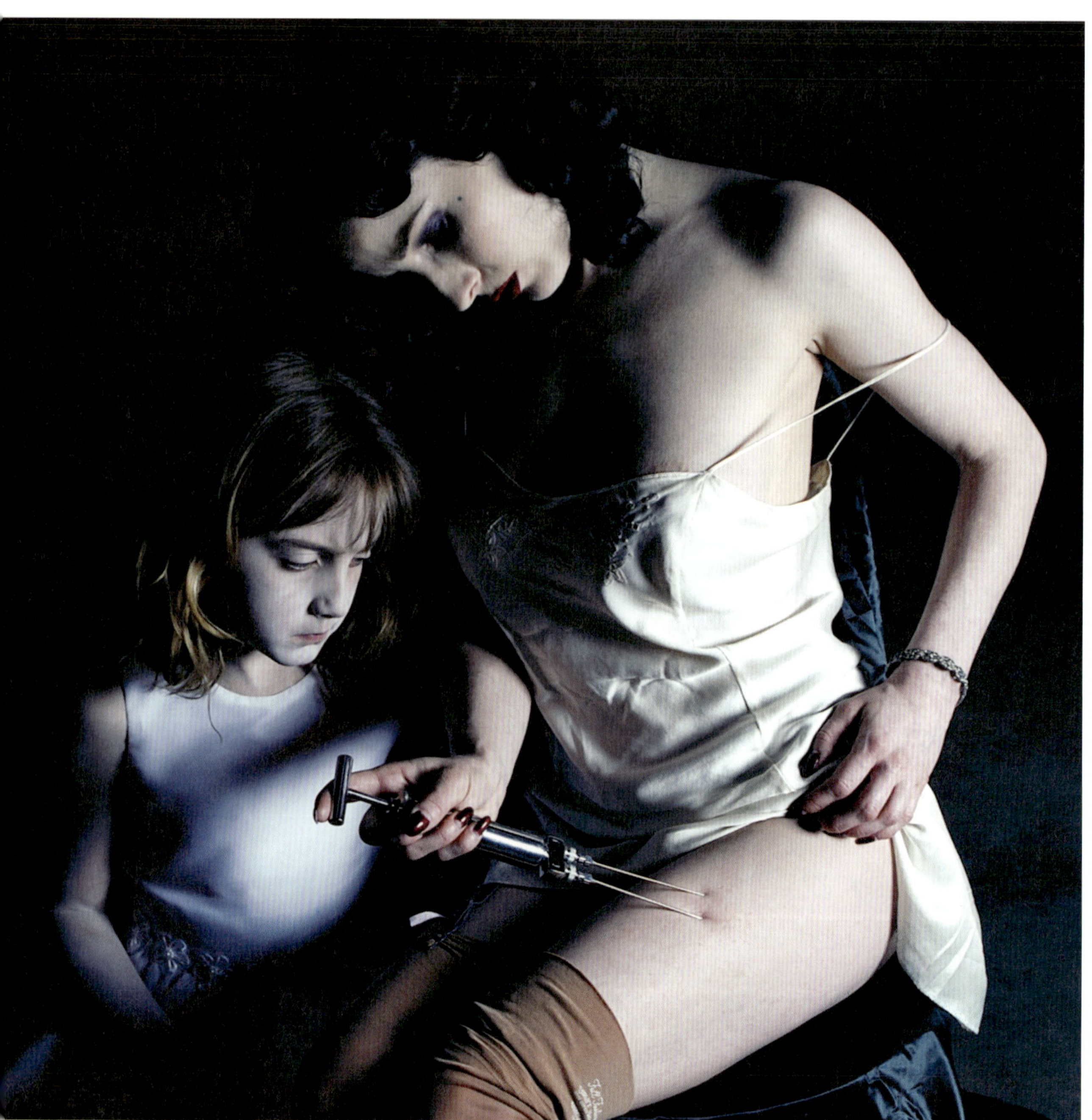

The Golden Age (Mother 1) 黄金時代（母1）
写真、ミクスト・メディア / 2003

The Disasters of War 16 戦争の惨禍16
ミクスト・メディア（油彩、アクリル、カンヴァス） / 2007

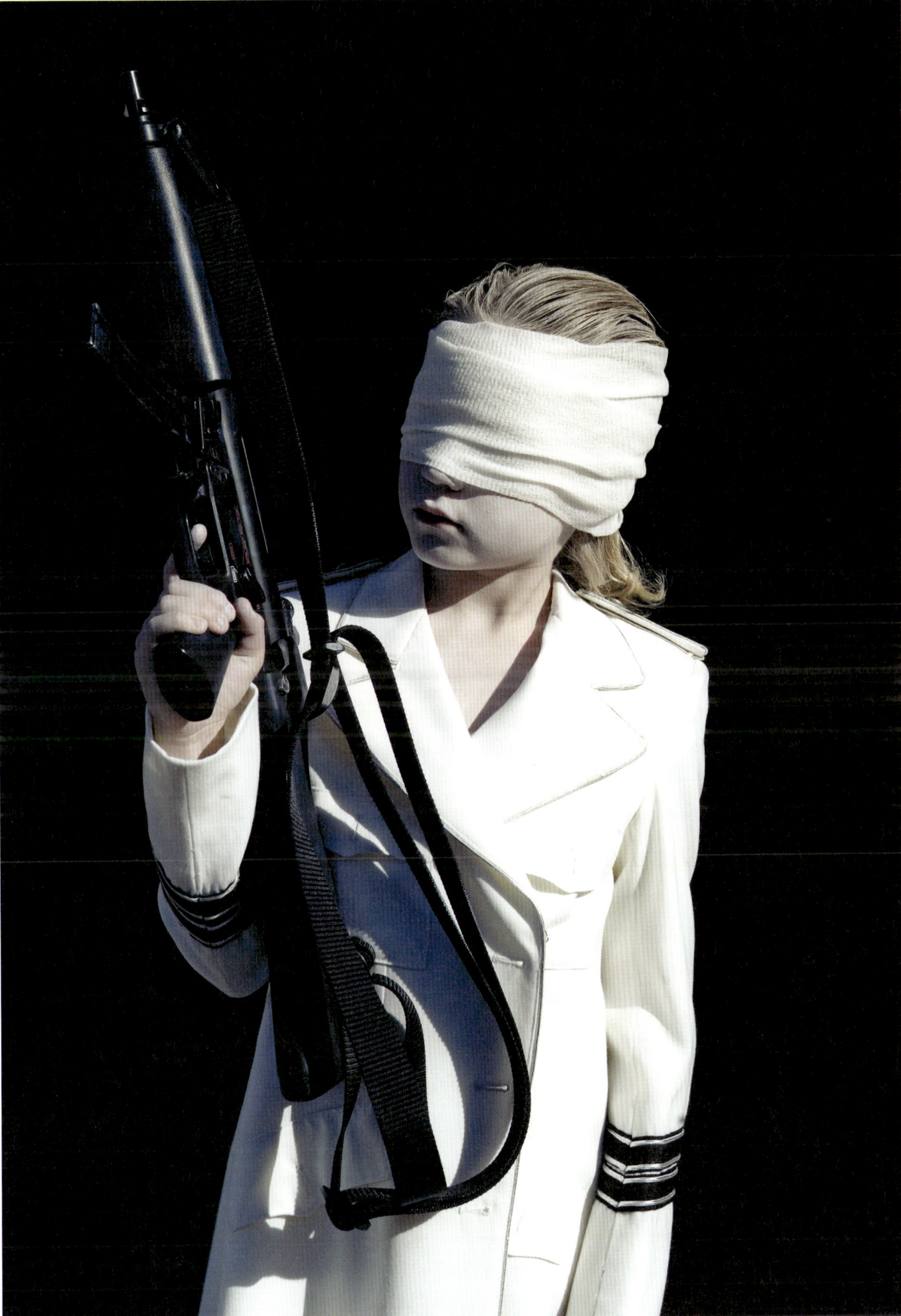

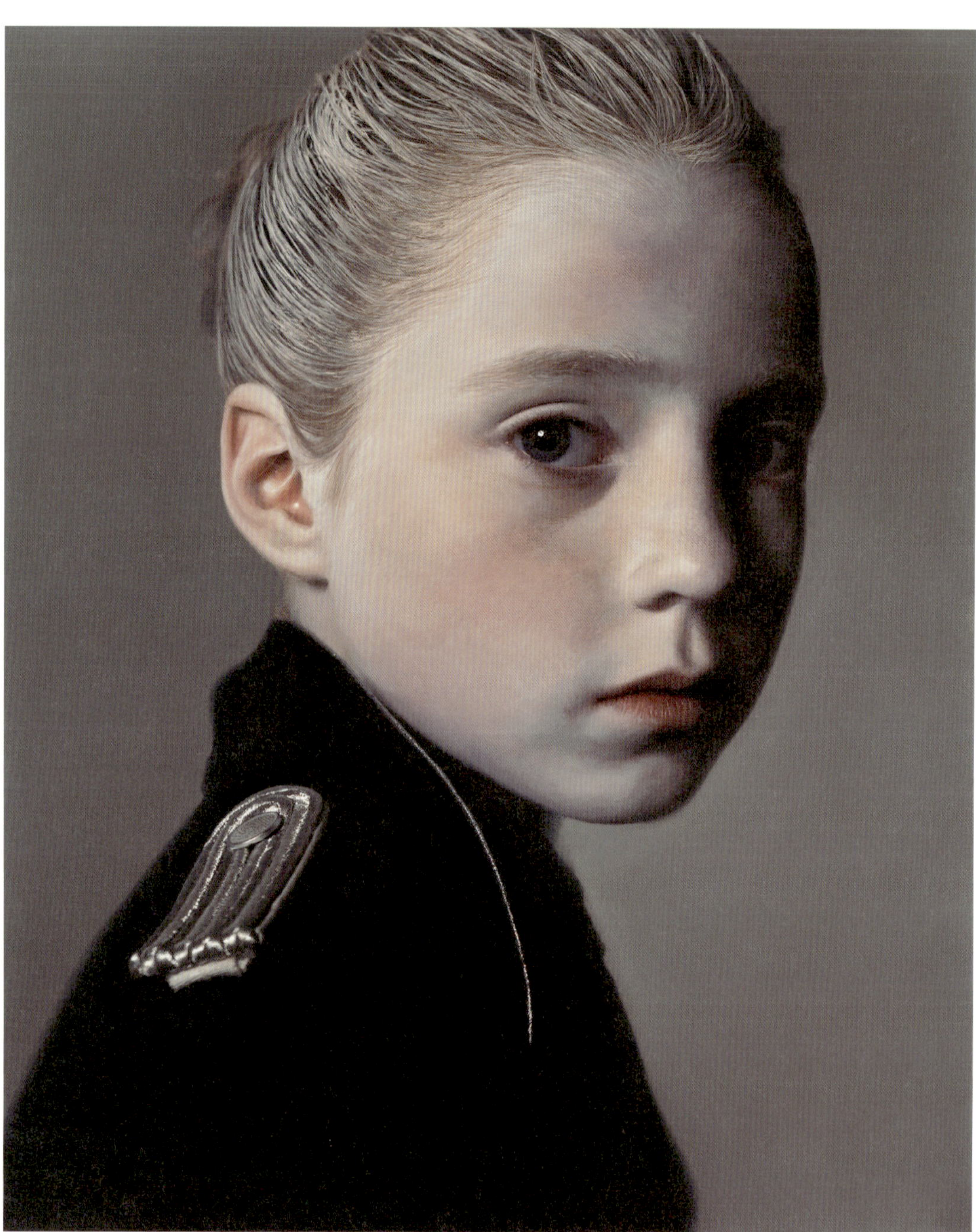

The Disasters of War 47 戦争の惨禍47
ミクスト・メディア（油彩、アクリル、カンヴァス）/ H150×W122cm / 2015

Head of a Child 17 子どもの頭17
ミクスト・メディア（油彩、アクリル、カンヴァス）/ H180×W120cm / 2014

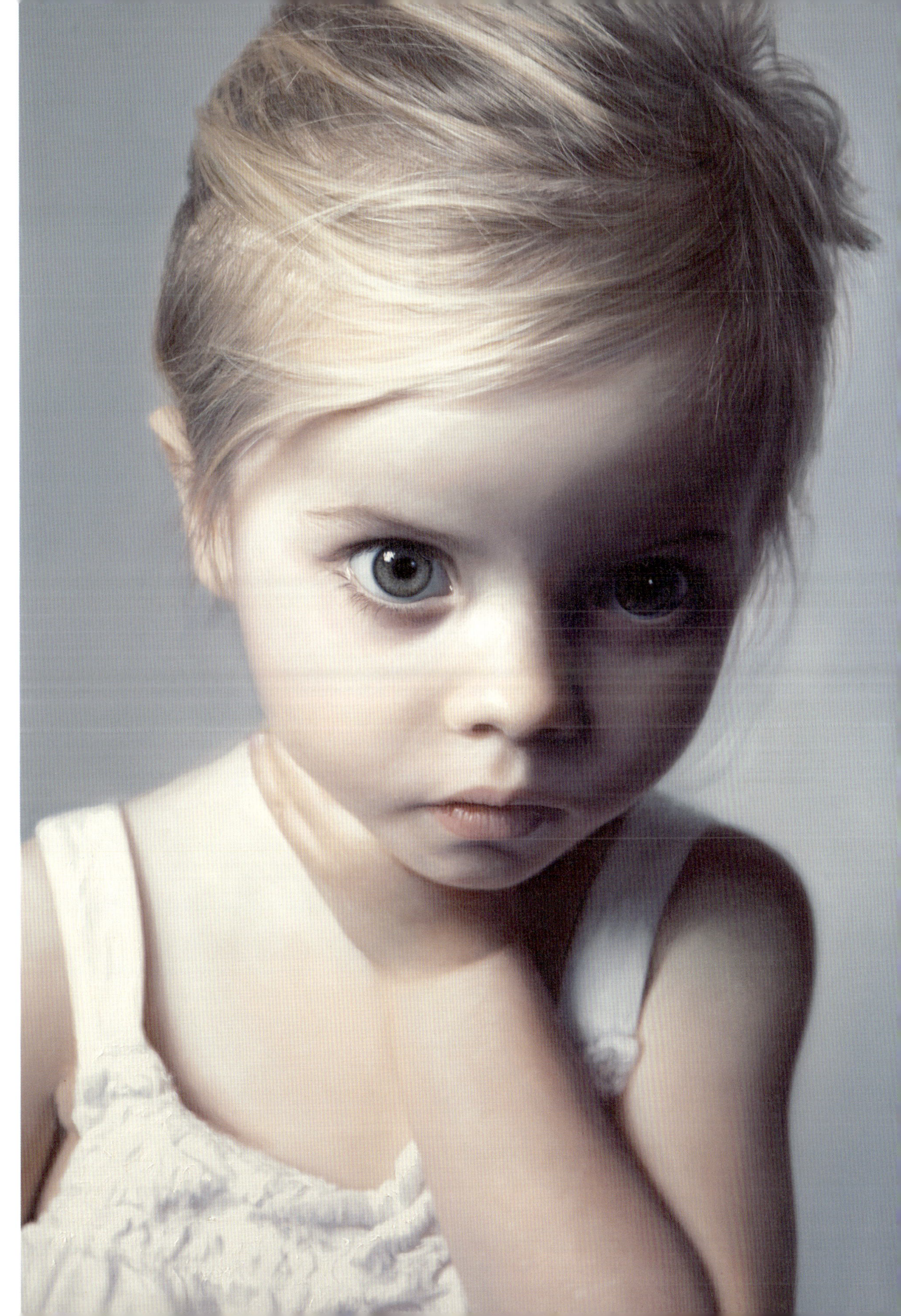

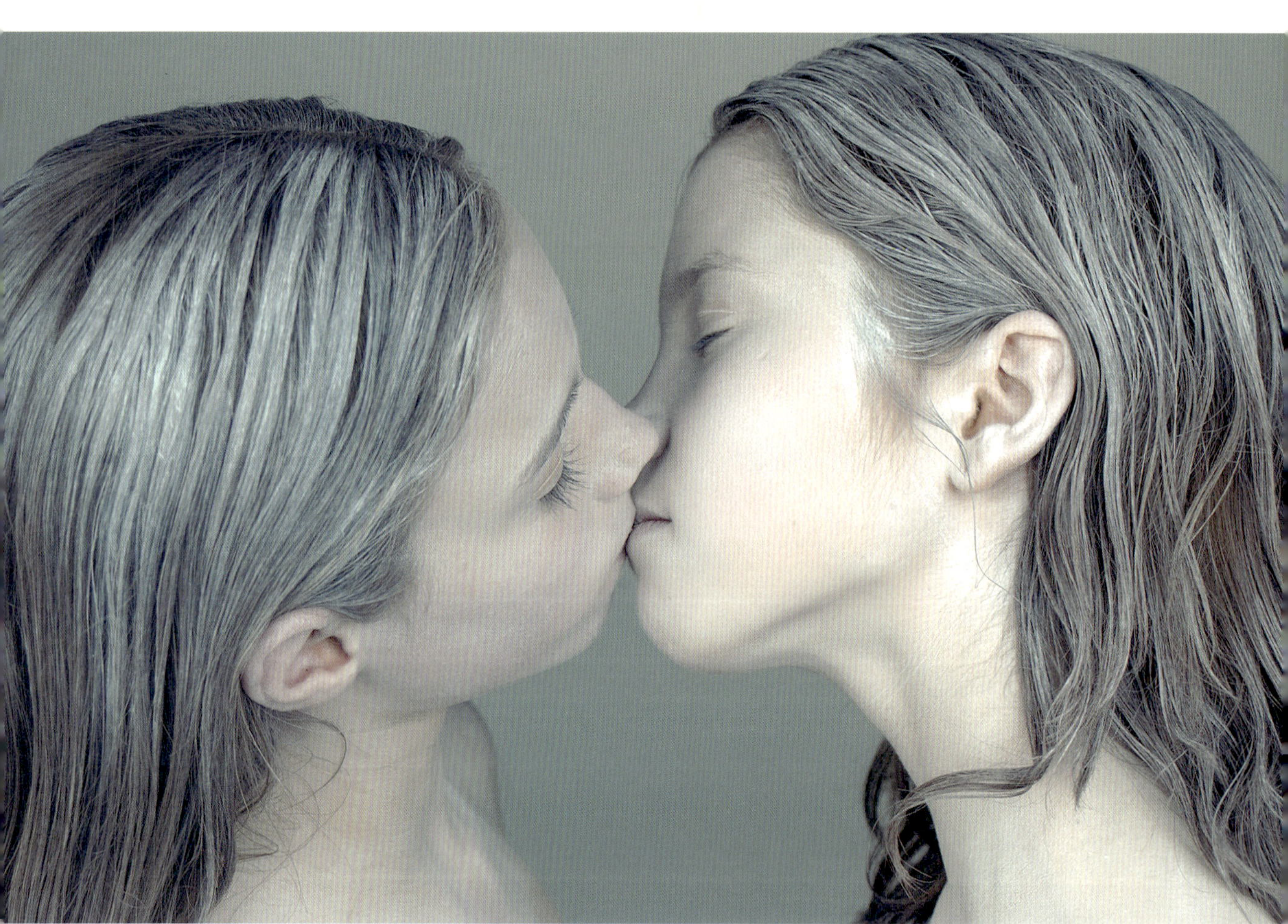

Das Paradies und die Peri 楽園とペリ
インスタレーション / 2004

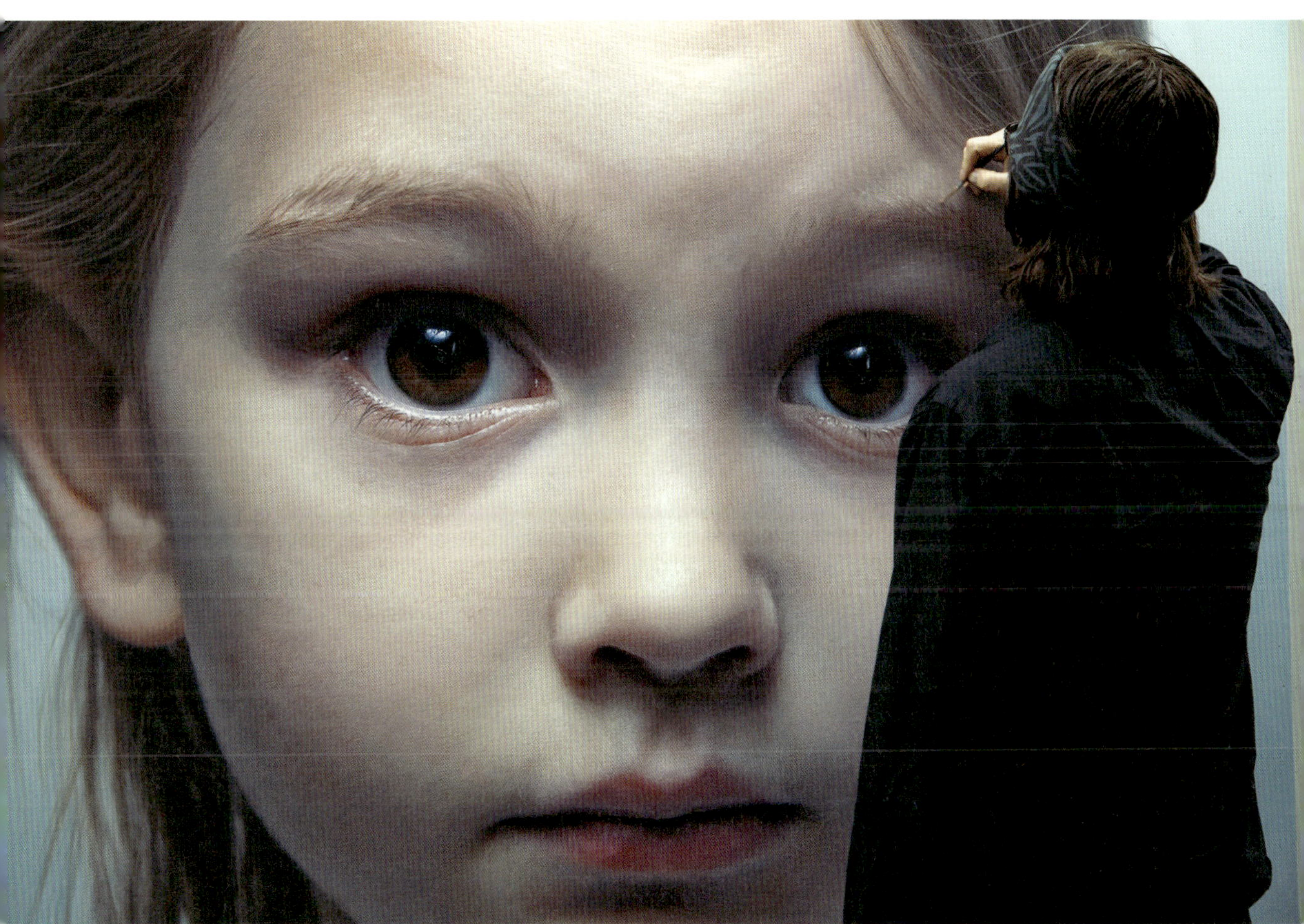

Gottfried Helnwein working on "Head of a Child 12 [Croʃ]"「子供の頭12 "クロイ"」を描くゴットフリート・ヘルヴァイン

22

Sam Ectoplasm

サム・エクトプラズム（フランス France）

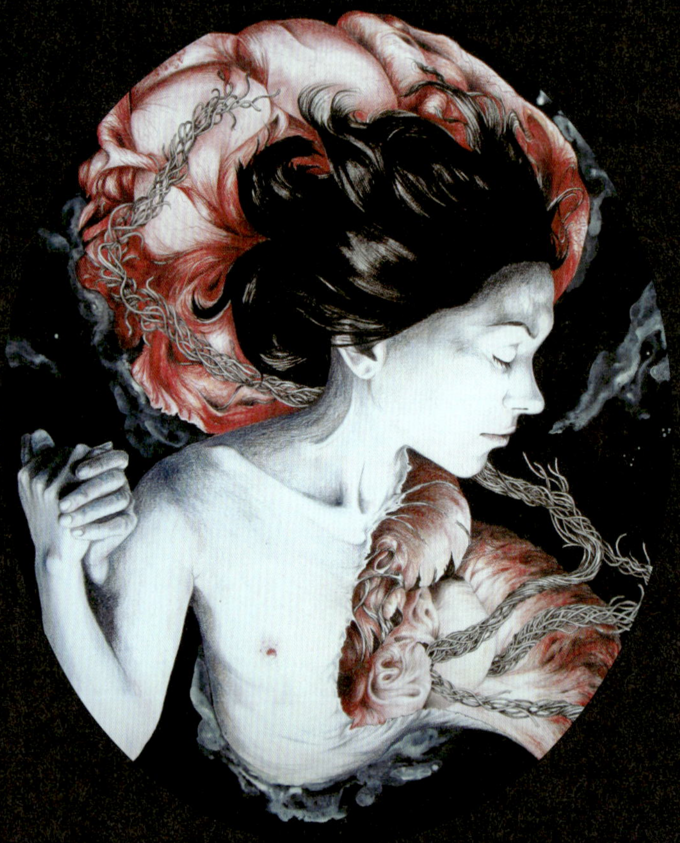

1986年フランス、マルセイユ生まれの線画家。現在はカナダのモントリオール在住。女性の肉体が変異する美しさを表現している。水彩画、鉛筆画、インク画など、独学で学んだ伝統的なイラストレーショの技法を駆使して描かれた作品は、繊細で様々な要素が含まれている。絡み合う人体と植物が、朽ちていくことを免れない自然のリズムに合わせ、成長し、浸食し合い、退化する過程を精巧に描いている。日本、カナダ、アメリカ、アイルランドの展覧会に出品。

Sam Ectoplasm is a drawing artist born in 1986 in Marseille, France, currently living and working in Montréal Canada. Her drawing on paper develops an aesthetic of the mutation, centered on the feminine figure. The blend of traditionnal illustration techniques (watercolor, pencils, inkpen) she has learnt on her own allows her to create a hybrid and delicate imagery. Anatomy and botanical references are transformed into a detailed and complex structure that grows, interpenetrates and deteriorates according to a natural entropic rhythm. She has been part of exhibitions in Japan, Canada, USA and Ireland.

samectoplasm.wordpress.com

↑Protection（保護）（部分）
インク、ペン、鉛筆、紙 / H76.2×W55.88cm / 2014

→Dans les bois（In the wood）森の中で
ミクスト・メディア、紙 / H60.96×W45.72cm / 2017

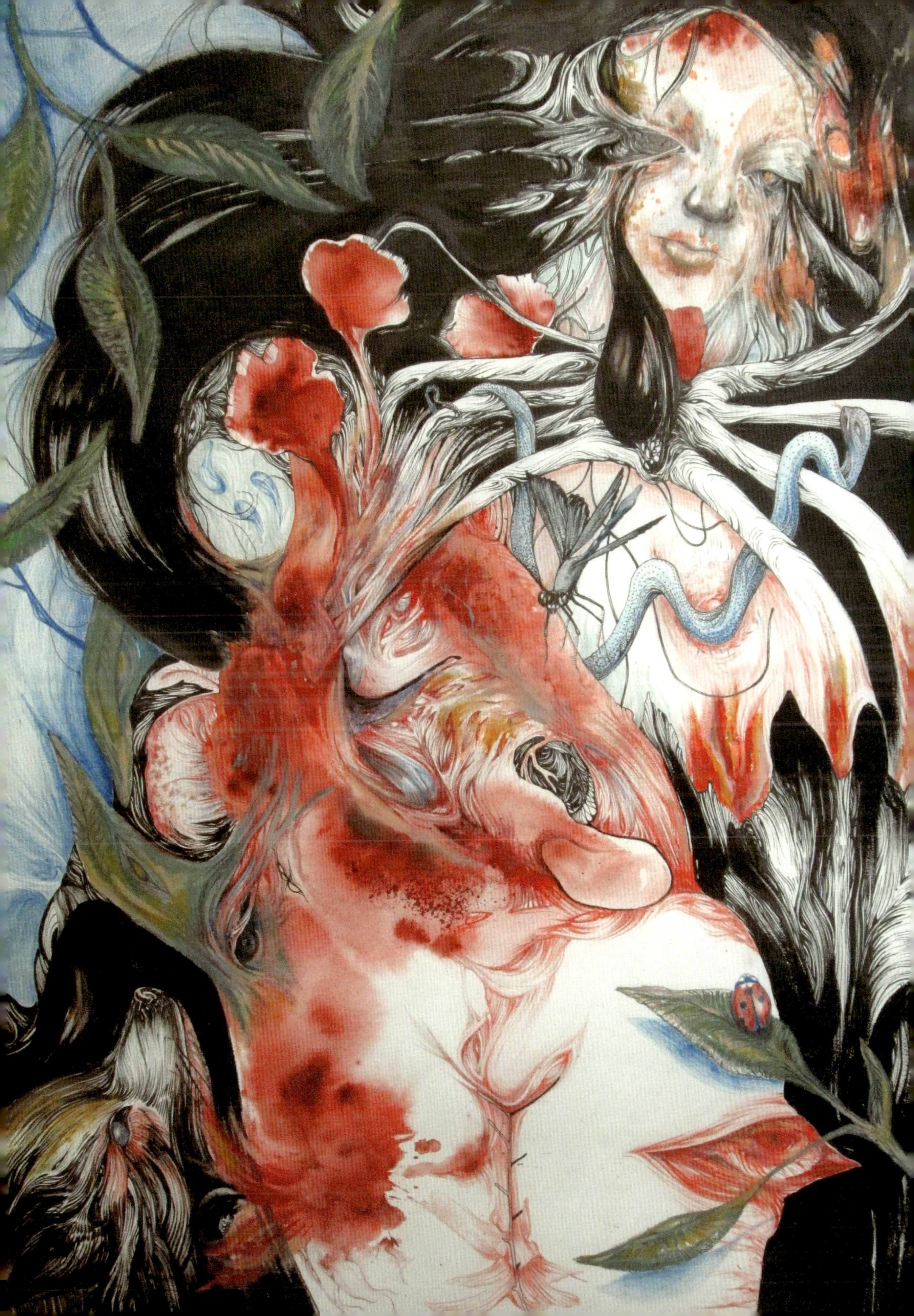

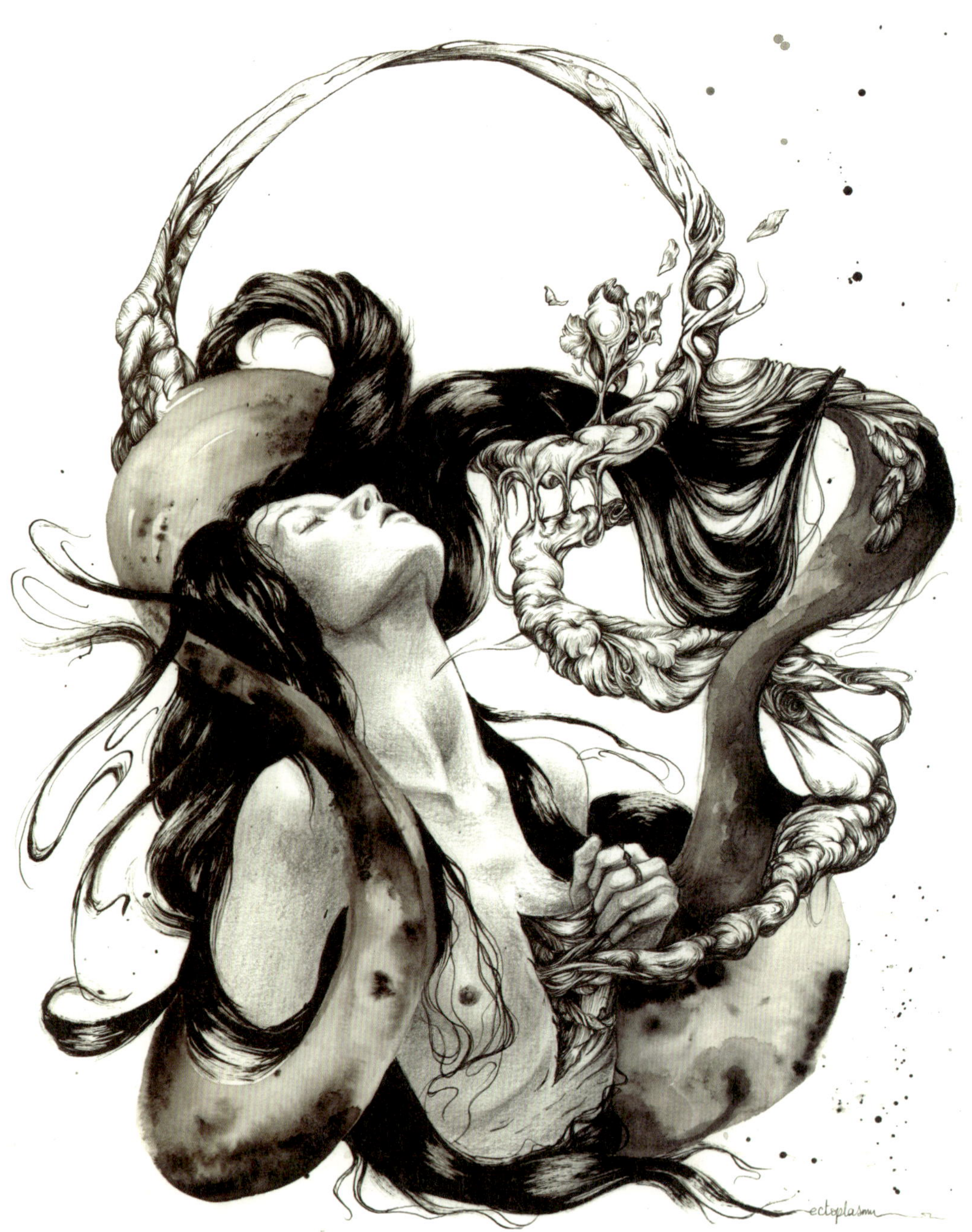

Under your spell | あなたの虜になって |
インク、ペン、鉛筆、紙 / H35.56×W27.94cm / 2015

Justine ジャスティン
インク、ペン、鉛筆、紙 / H43.18×W35.56cm / 2016

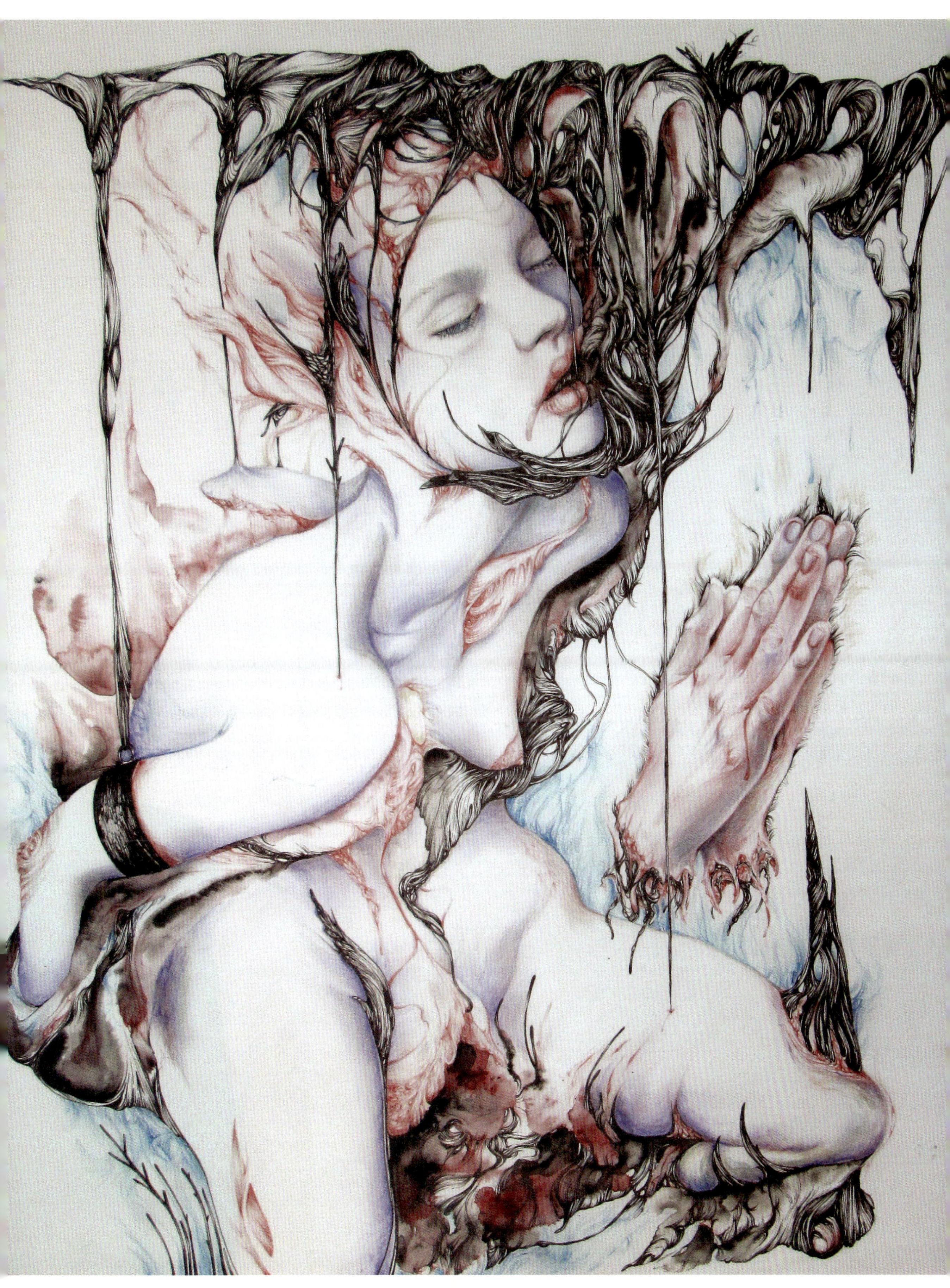

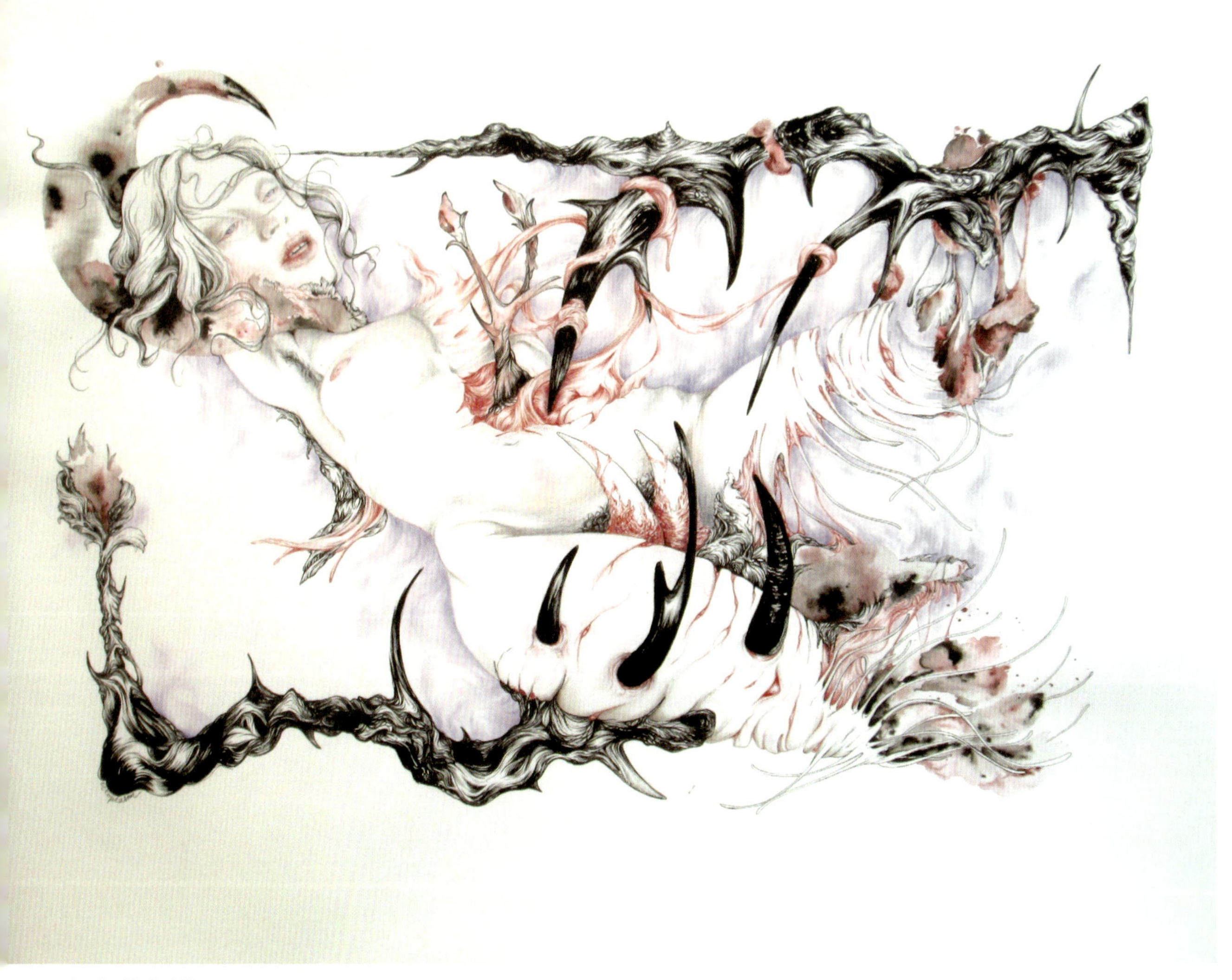

Le piège（The Trap）罠
インク、ペン、鉛筆、紙 / H55.88×W71.12cm / 2016

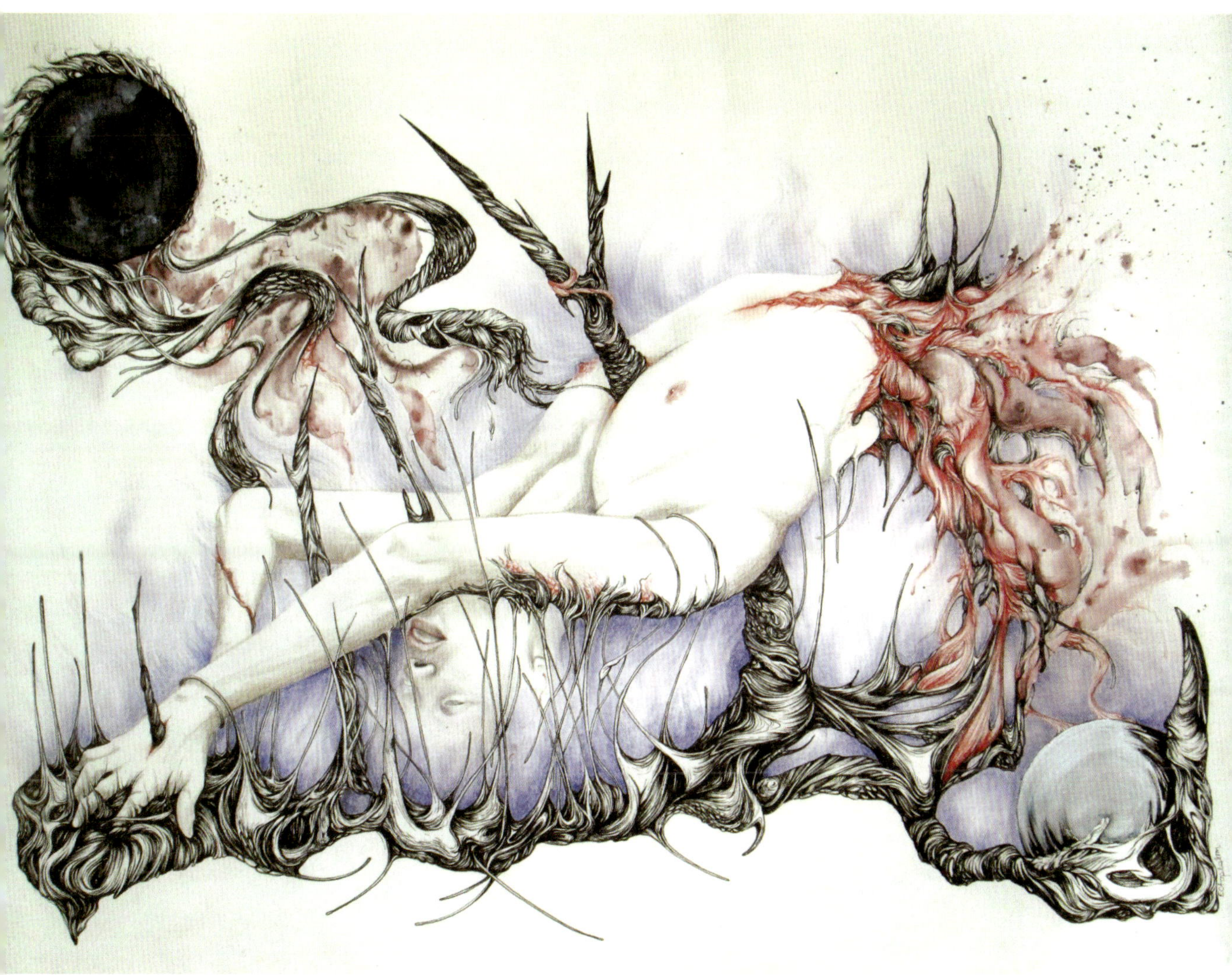

Le piège chapitre Ⅱ（The Trap chapter Ⅱ）罠——第 2 章
インク、ペン、鉛筆、紙 / H35.56×W43.18cm / 2016

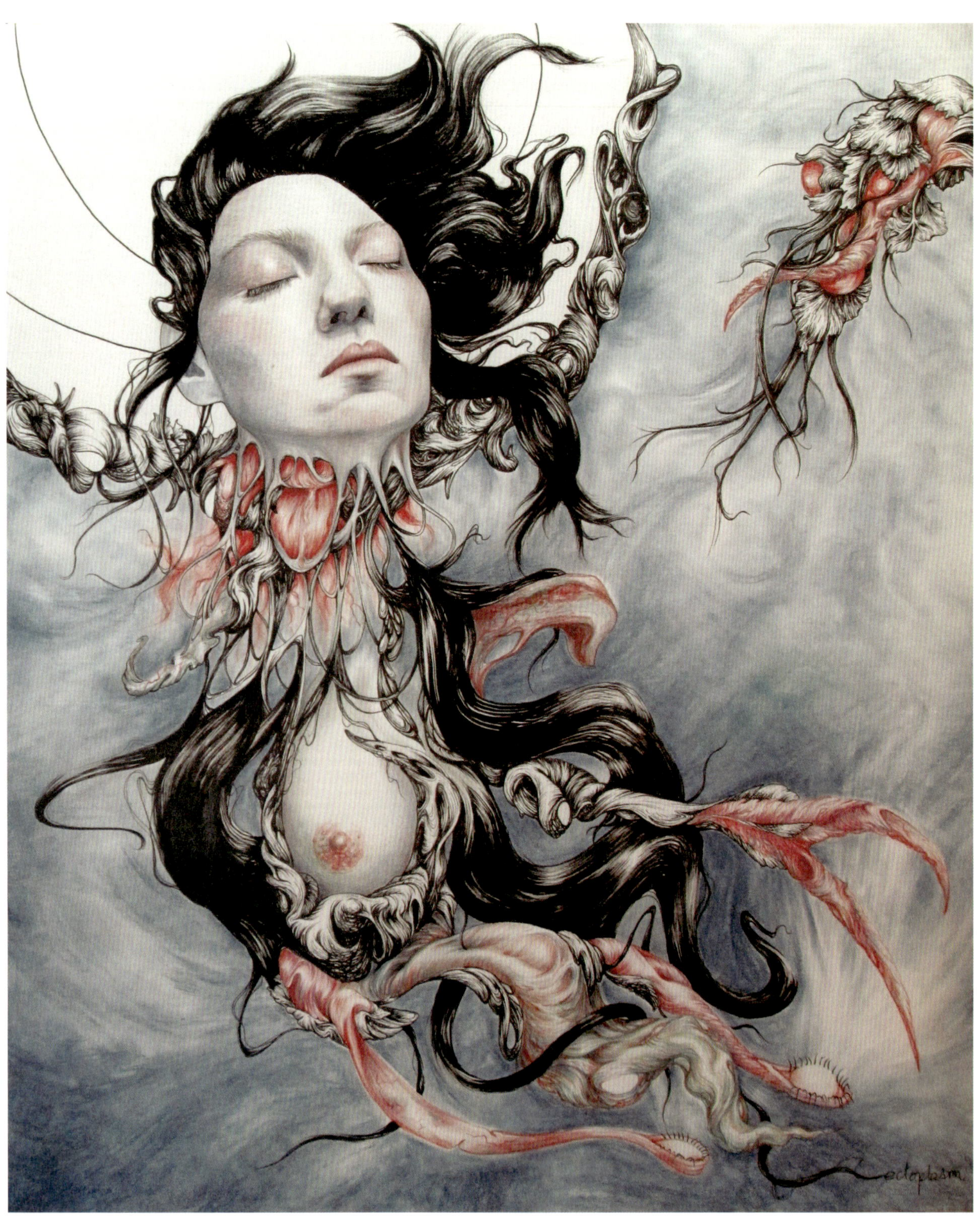

Metamorphosis I 変態 I
ミクスト・メディア、紙 / H43.18×W35.56cm / 2016

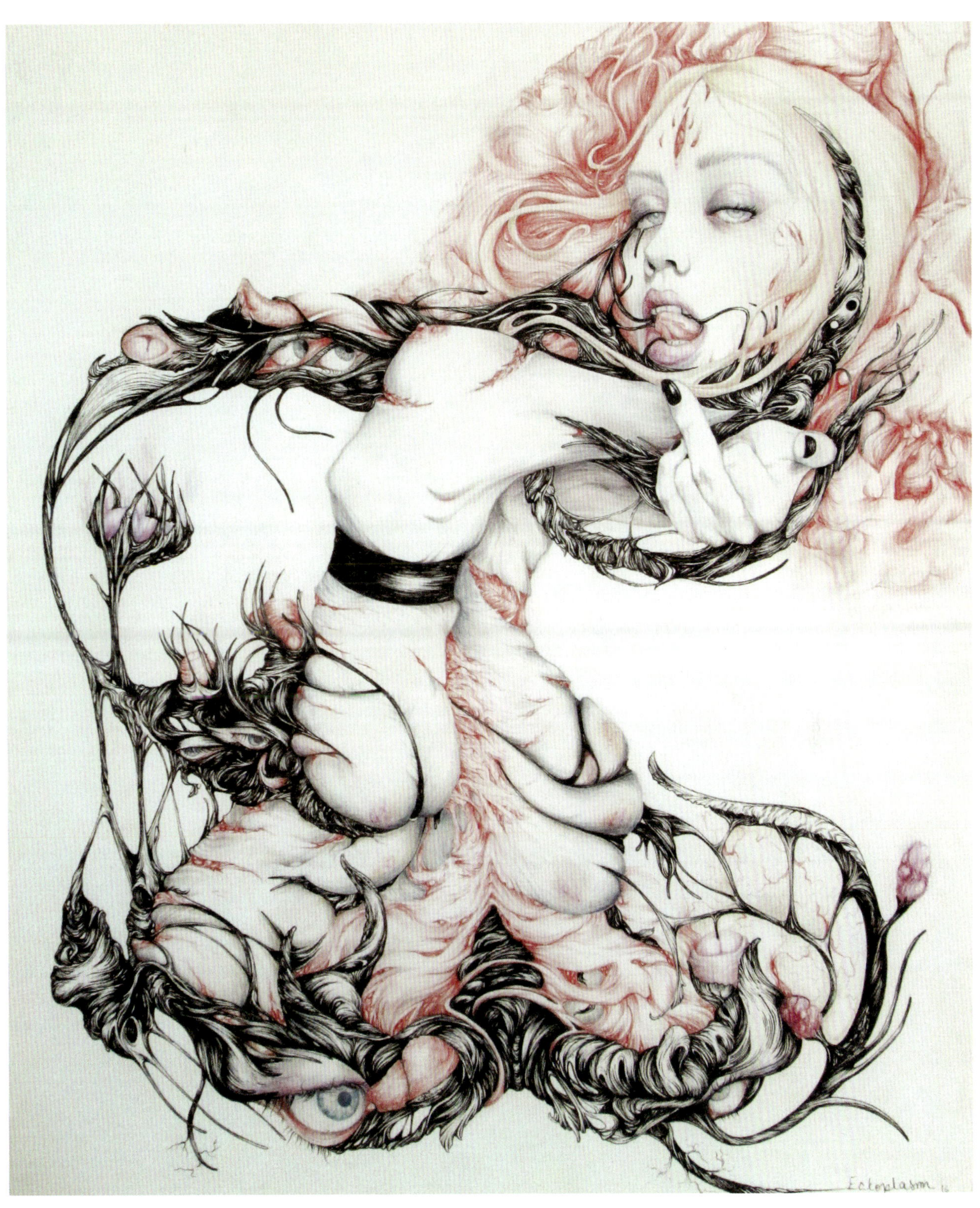

Juliette ジュリエット
インク、ペン、鉛筆、紙 / H43.18×W35.56cm / 2016

23

Hannah Yata

ハンナ・ヤタ（アメリカ USA）

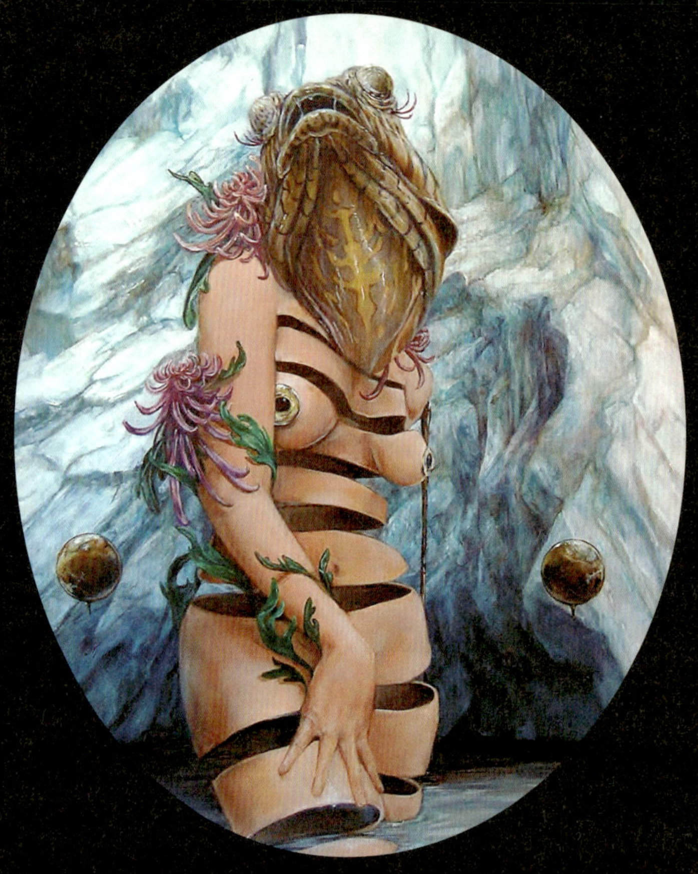

マジカル・シュルレアリスト・ペインターのハンナ・ヤタは、1989年、ジョージア州ダグラスヴィルで、日本人とアメリカ人の両親のもとに生まれる。ジョージア州で育ち、2012年ジョージア大学を卒業、美術学士号を取得。同年ニューヨークに移り、翌年には国際的な展覧会に出品するようになる。有名なラッパー、B.o.Bのオリジナルアルバム「Psycadelik Thoughtz」やリミックスを手がけた作品を集めたアルバム「Elements」のジャケットでも知られる。現在は夫でアーティストのジャン・ピエール・アルボレダとともにペンシルベニア州ローズ・バレーを拠点に活動。2016年にコーリー・ヘルフォード・ギャラリーにて個展を開催。

Hannah Faith Yata is a half Japanese half American magical surrealist painter. She currently lives and works with her husband and fellow artist, Jean Pierre Arboleda, in Lords Valley, Pennsylvania. Yata was born in 1989 in Douglasville, Georgia. She grew up in Georgia and graduated from the University of Georgia in 2012 with a BFA in Fine Art. She moved the same year to New York City and began to exhibit internationally within the following years. Yata's work was commissioned by renown rapper/musician B.o.B for album covers including "Psycadelik Thoughtz" and the series of mixtapes entitled the "Elements." Her most recent solo exhibition was in 2016 at Corey Helford Gallery.

hannahyata.com

↑Leak 漏出（部分）
油彩、カンヴァス / H50.8×W40.64cm / 2013

→Lilith リリス（部分）
油彩、カンヴァス / H91.44×W60.96cm / 2016

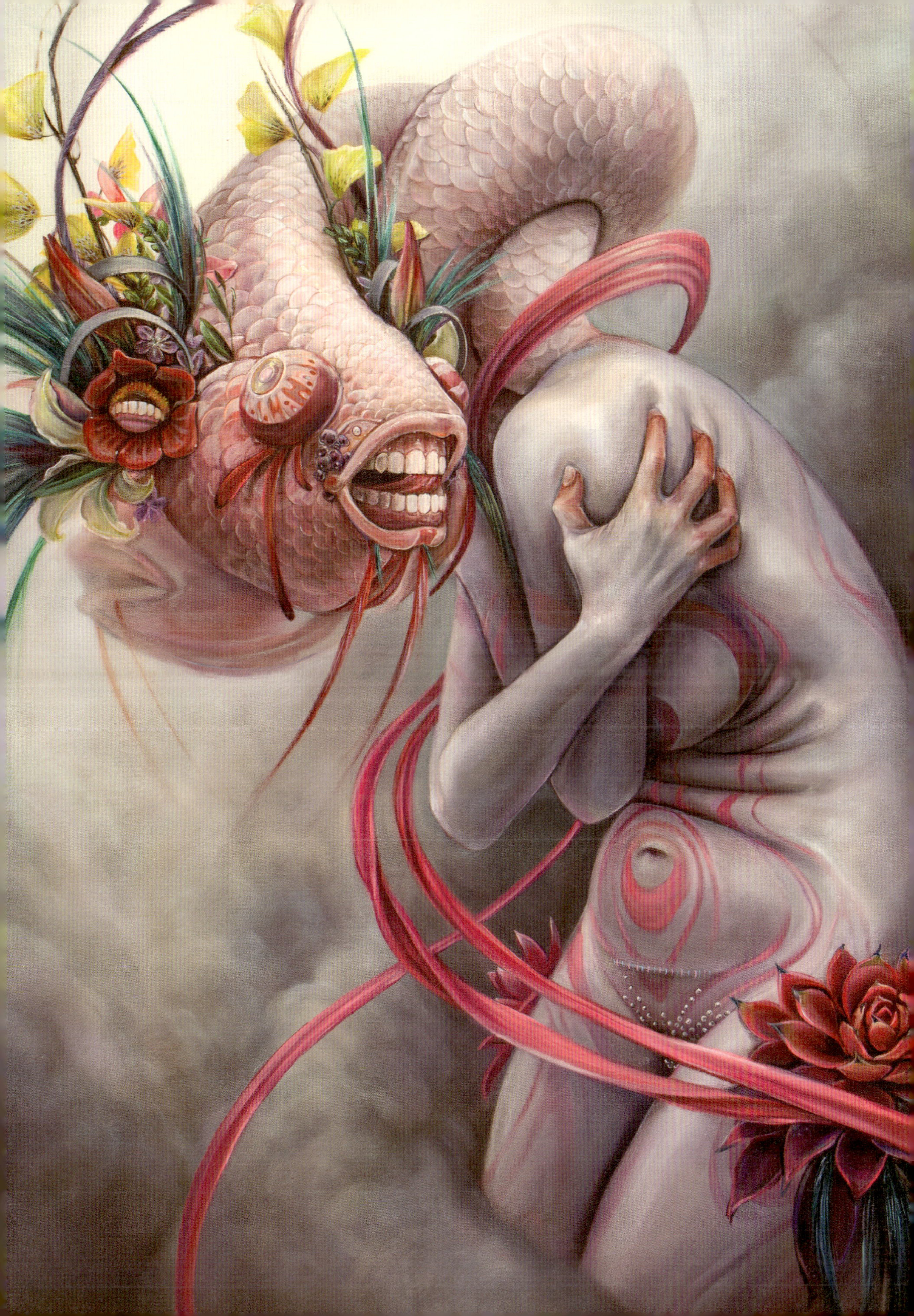

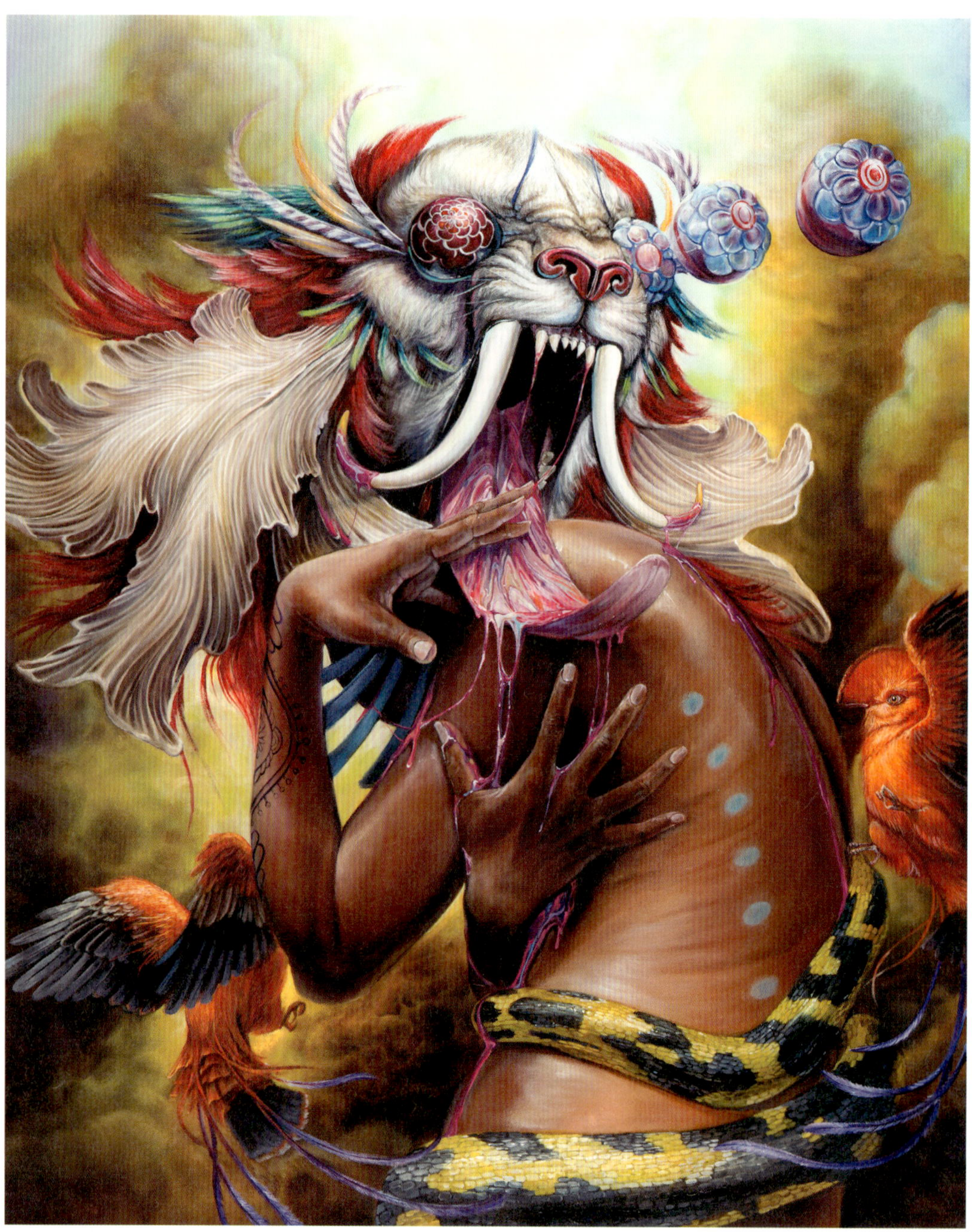

Unrepentant Susanna 悔悟することのないスザンナ
油彩、カンヴァス / H76.2×W60.96cm / 2015

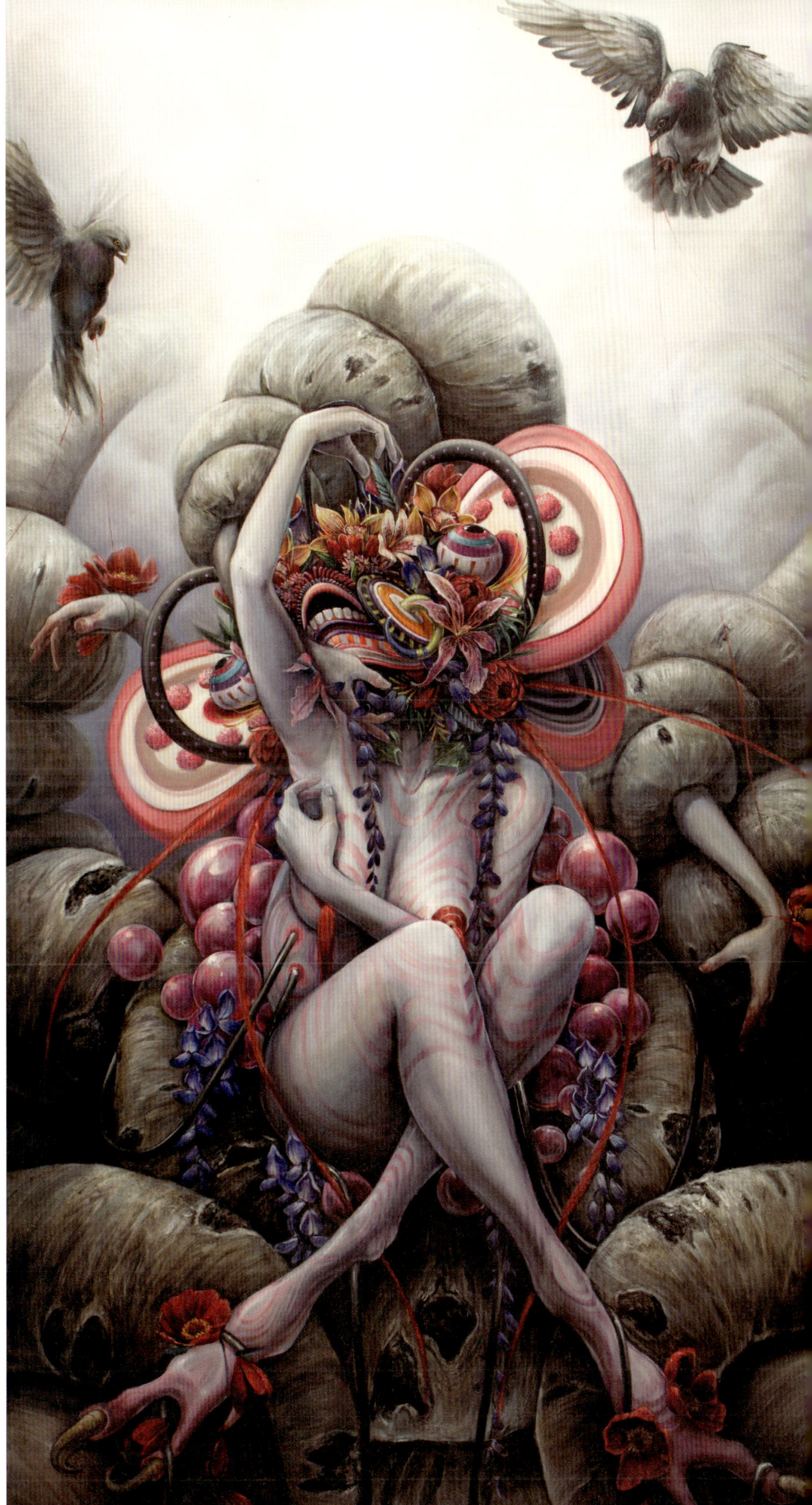

Diaphonia 不協和音
油彩、カンヴァス /
H172.72×W91.44cm / 2016

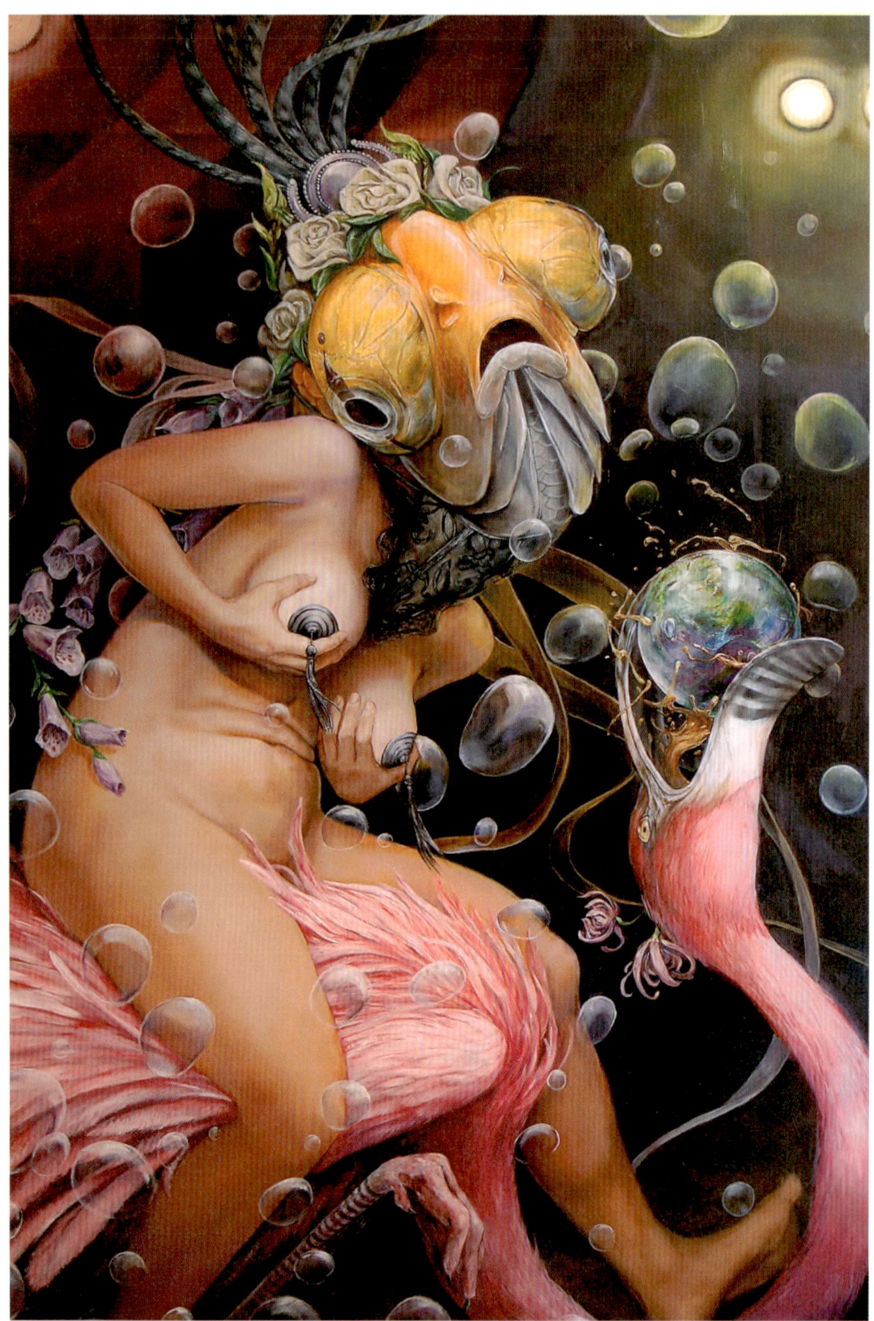

Take Me Seriously 真面目に私をつかまえて
油彩、カンヴァス / H121.92×W76.2cm / 2013

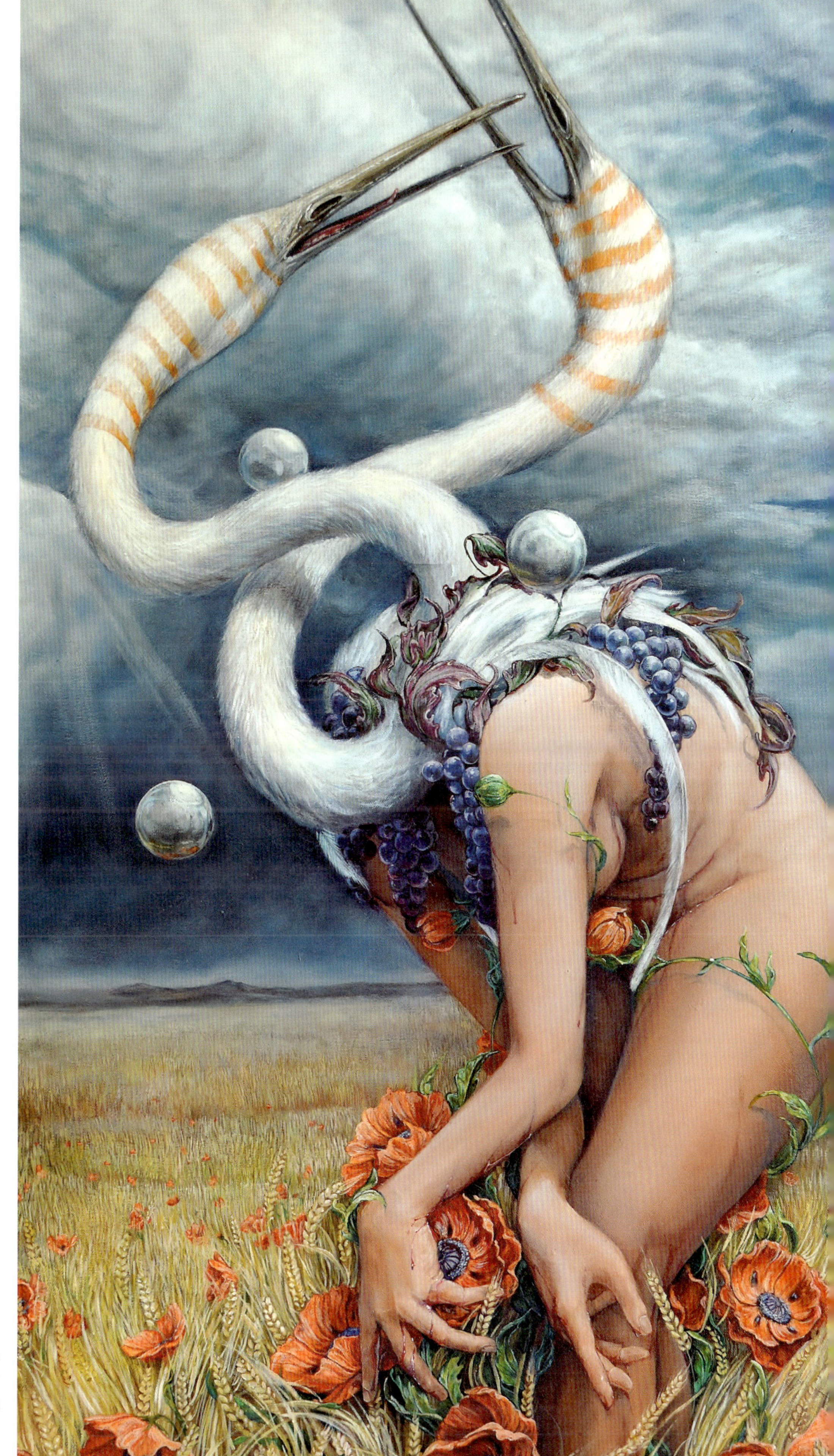

Demeter デメテル
（ギリシア神話の豊穣の女神）
油彩、カンヴァス /
H91.44×W50.8cm / 2014

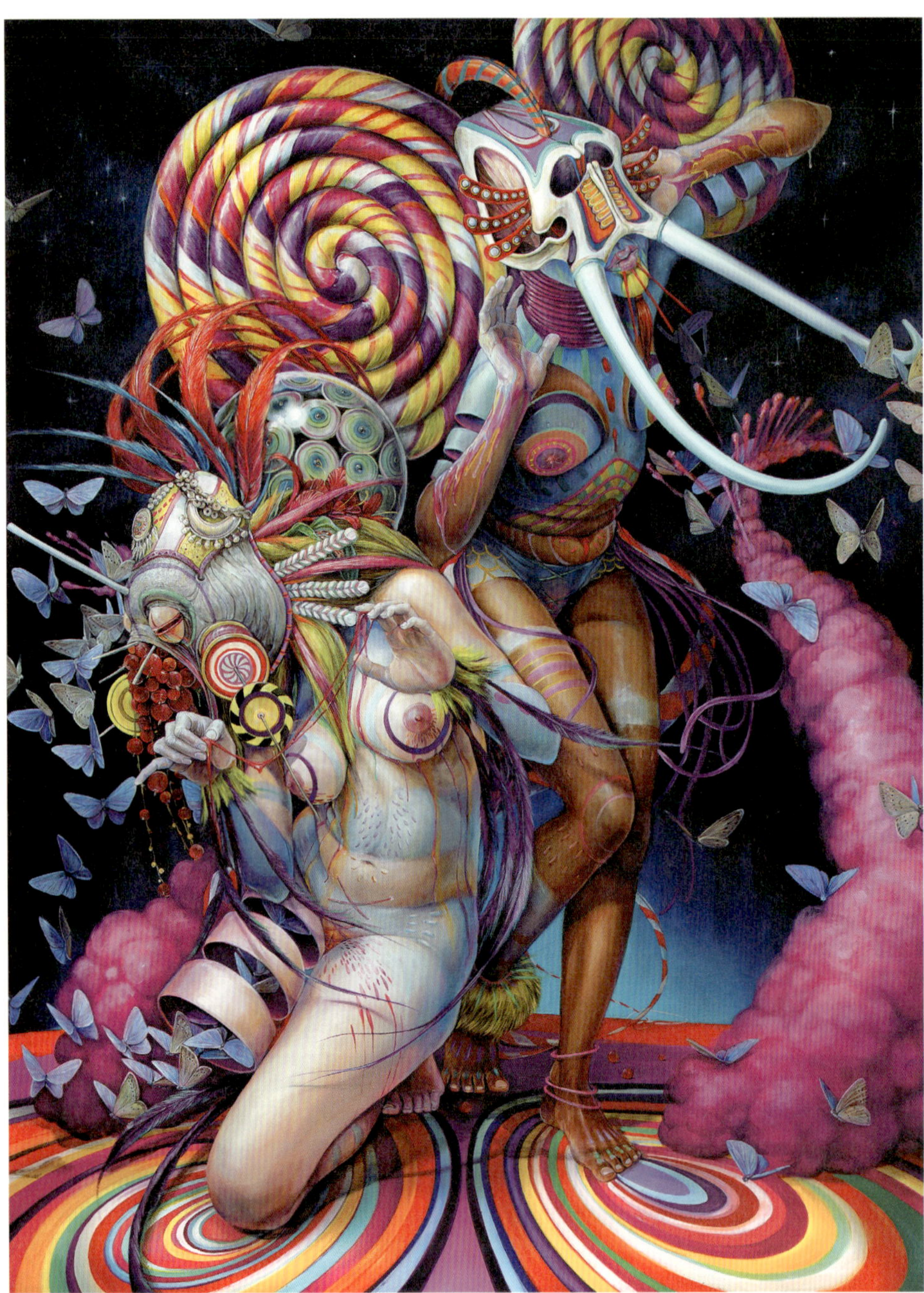

Daughters 娘たち
油彩、カンヴァス / H167.64×W121.92cm / 2015

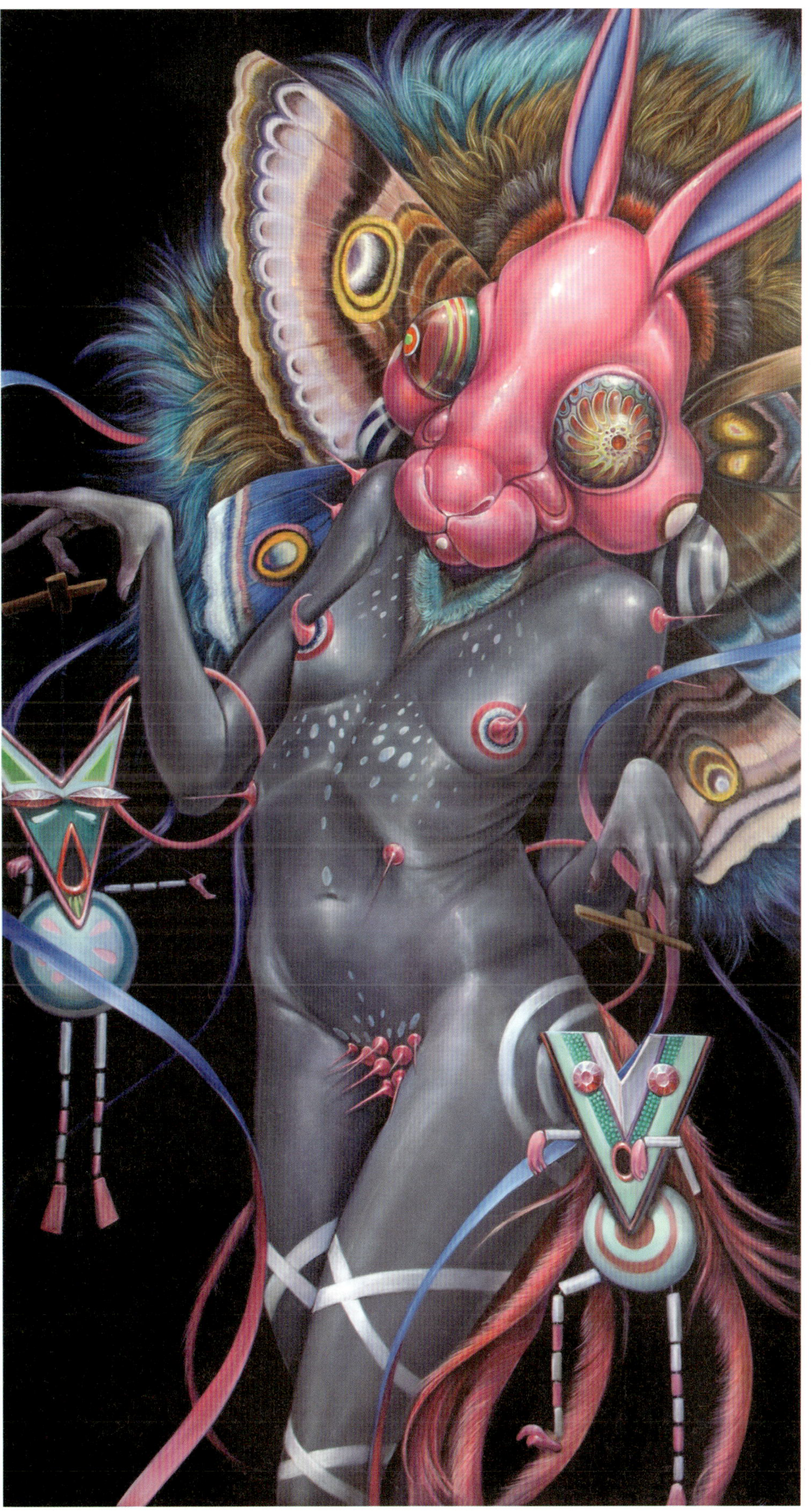

Toys and Reasons 玩具と理性
油彩、カンヴァス /
H121.92×W60.96cm / 2017

Antoine Bernhart

アントワーヌ・ベルナール（フランス France）

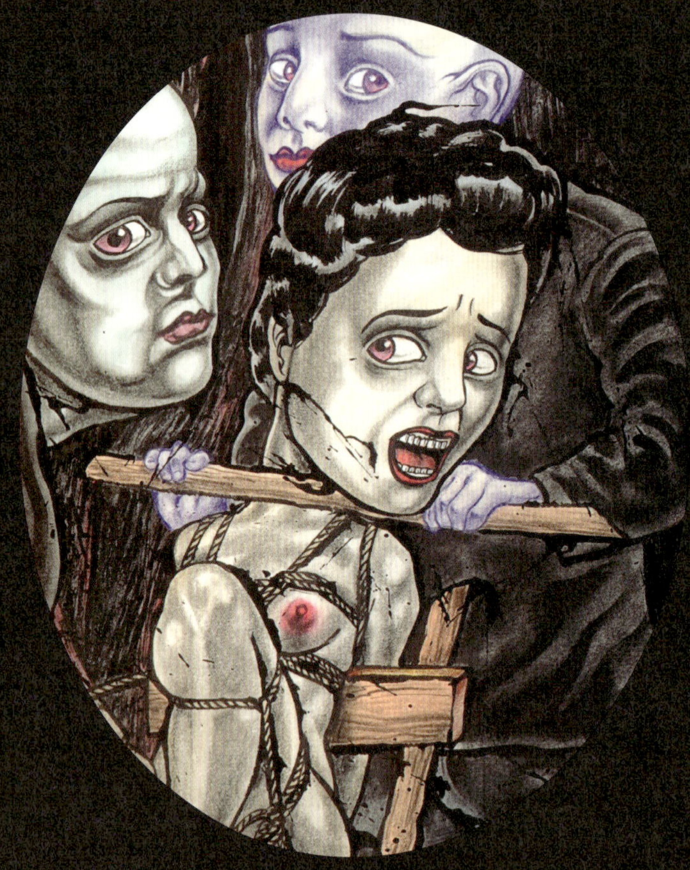

過激な表現で知られる画家。1968年、クリスチャン・ベルナールとの共著、画集『H』を出版したあと、1968年にネオ・シュルレアリスム運動「Phases」に参加、のちに「ポルノの乱用」により追放される。エロティックな作品に加えて、「ザ・メトロス」、「クランプス」、「ミルクシェイクス」、「トールボーイズ」、「ヴァイプス」、「ナイン・インチ・ネイルズ」、「アンセイン」、「メルヴィンズ」、「ファズトーンズ」など、多くのロックバンドのポスターを手掛ける。画集『トパーズ』、『SMスナイパー』、『Kinshoku Club』、『Igyou no soiree』を通じて、悪名は日本にまでとどろいた。ジュネーブ近現代美術館において、2008年「L'infini chez soi」、2015年に「Jouer avec le feu」と題した個展を開催。2009年には、パリのミュージアム・オブ・エロティシズムで「l'Enfer des Enfers」が開催された。ベルナートがドローイングとペインティングをミックスした技法に興味を持っているのは作品に顕著に表れている。それが物議をかもす作品に芸術的なクオリティを与えている。

Antoine BERNHART has made a name for himself through his work representing the extreme. He entered the neo-surrealist group Phases in 1968 after the publication of his book "H" done in collaboration with Christian BERNARD. He was later expelled from the group because of his "pornographic delirium". In addition to his erotic production he has also done many posters for rock groups such as "The Meteors," "The Cramps," "Milkshakes," "Tall Boys," "Vibes," "Nine Inch Nails," "Unsane," "Melvins," "Fuzztones," etc. His notoriety spread all the way to Japan through his pictures published in "Topaz" and "SM Sniper" as well as his books Kinshoku Club and Igyou no soirée. The Museum of Modern and Contemporary Art (MAMCO) in Geneva organized two exhibits of his work, "L'infini chez soi" in 2008 and "Jouer avec le feu" in 2015. The Museum of Eroticism in Paris also hosted his work in the 2009 exhibit "l'Enfer des Enfers". Throughout his work his curiosity for the use of techniques which mix both drawing and painting is manifest. This brings an undeniable artistic quality to his controversial subjects.

www.antoine-b.com

↑No title 無題（部分）
日本製カラー・スティック、インク、水彩、色鉛筆、グワッシュ、紙 / H40.3×W28.5cm / 2015-17

→No title 無題
日本製カラー・スティック、インク、水彩、色鉛筆、グワッシュ、紙 / H40.3×W28.5cm / 2015-17

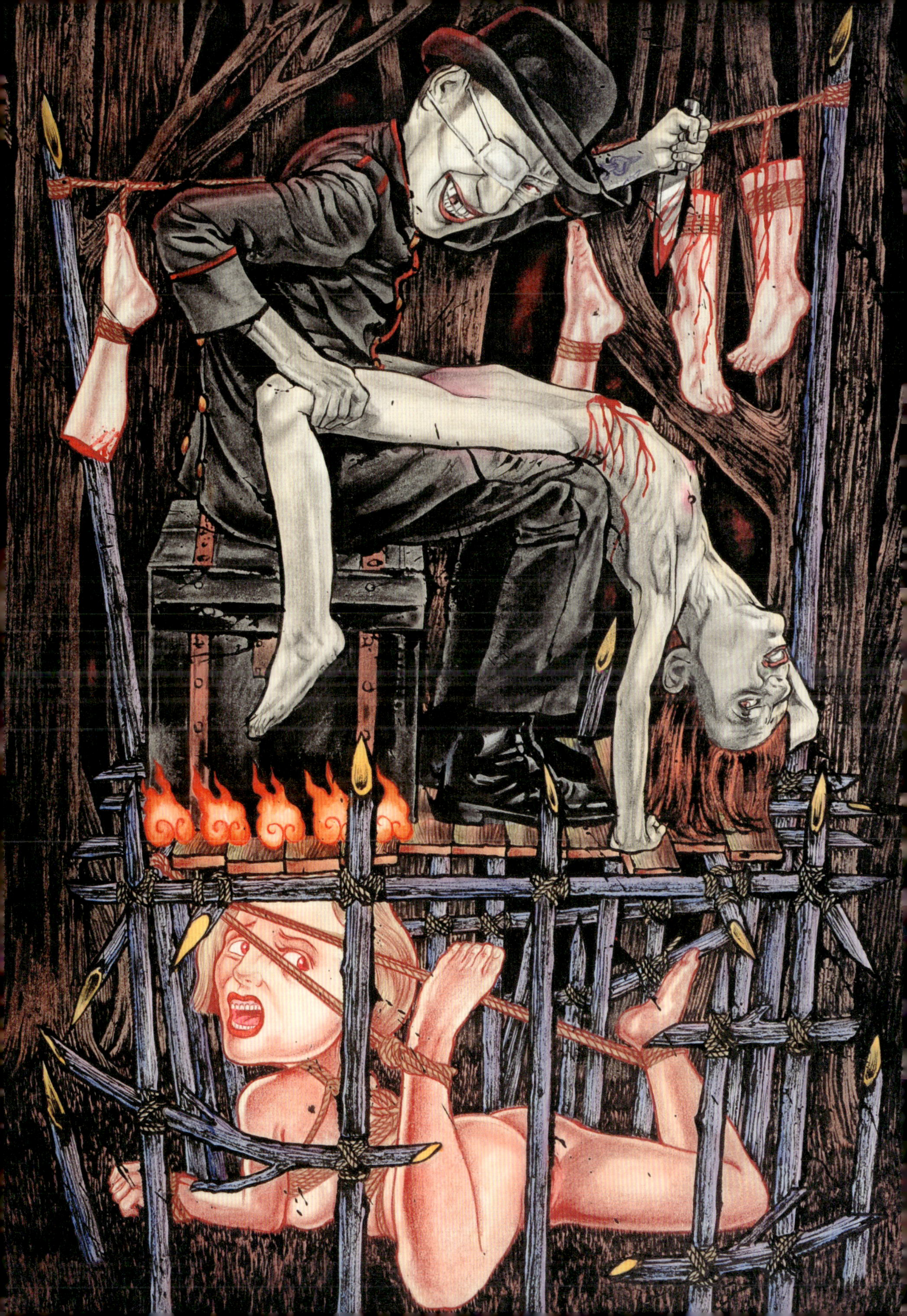

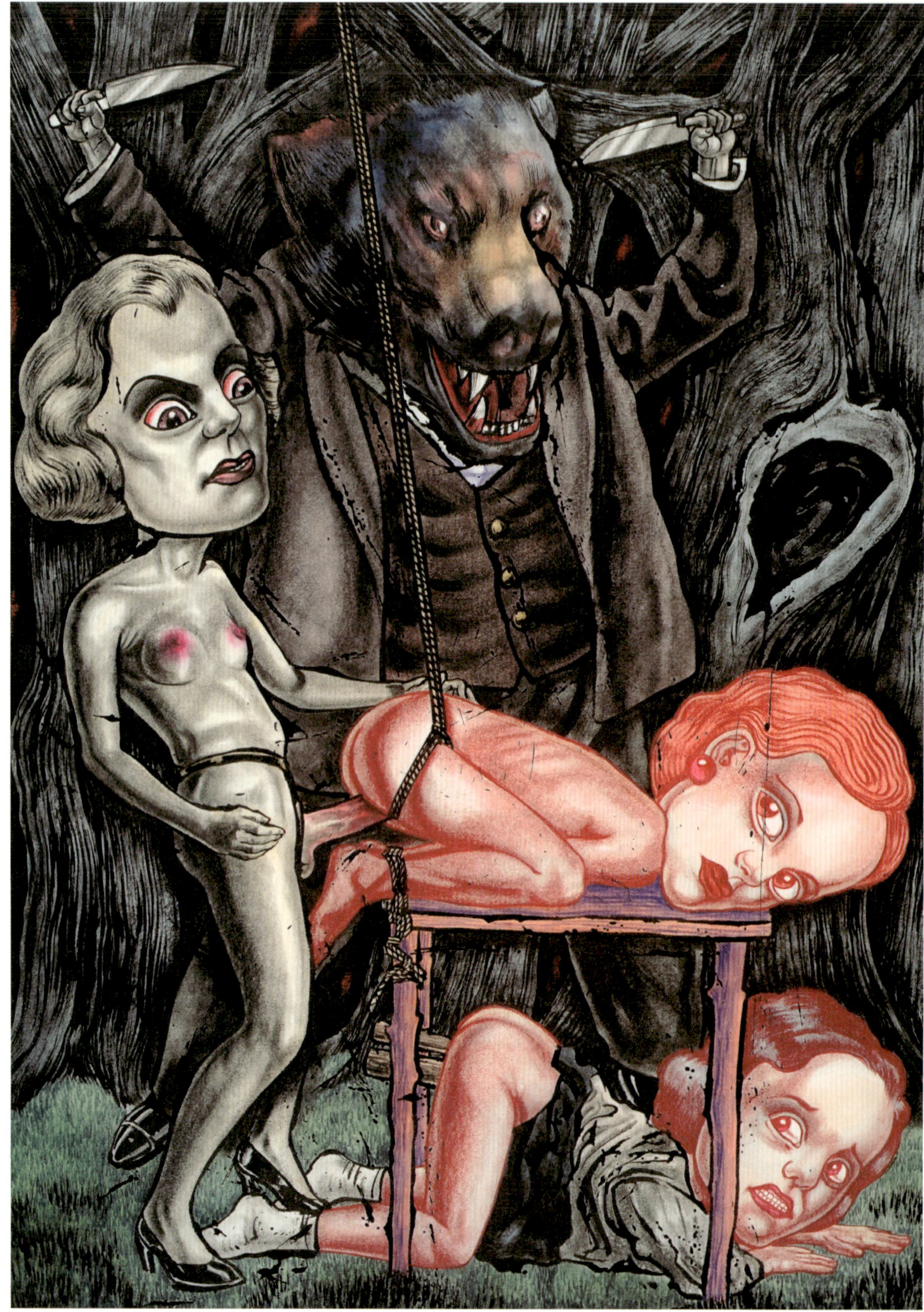

No title 無題
日本製カラー・スティック、インク、水彩、色鉛筆、グワッシュ、紙 / H40.3×W28.5cm / 2015-17

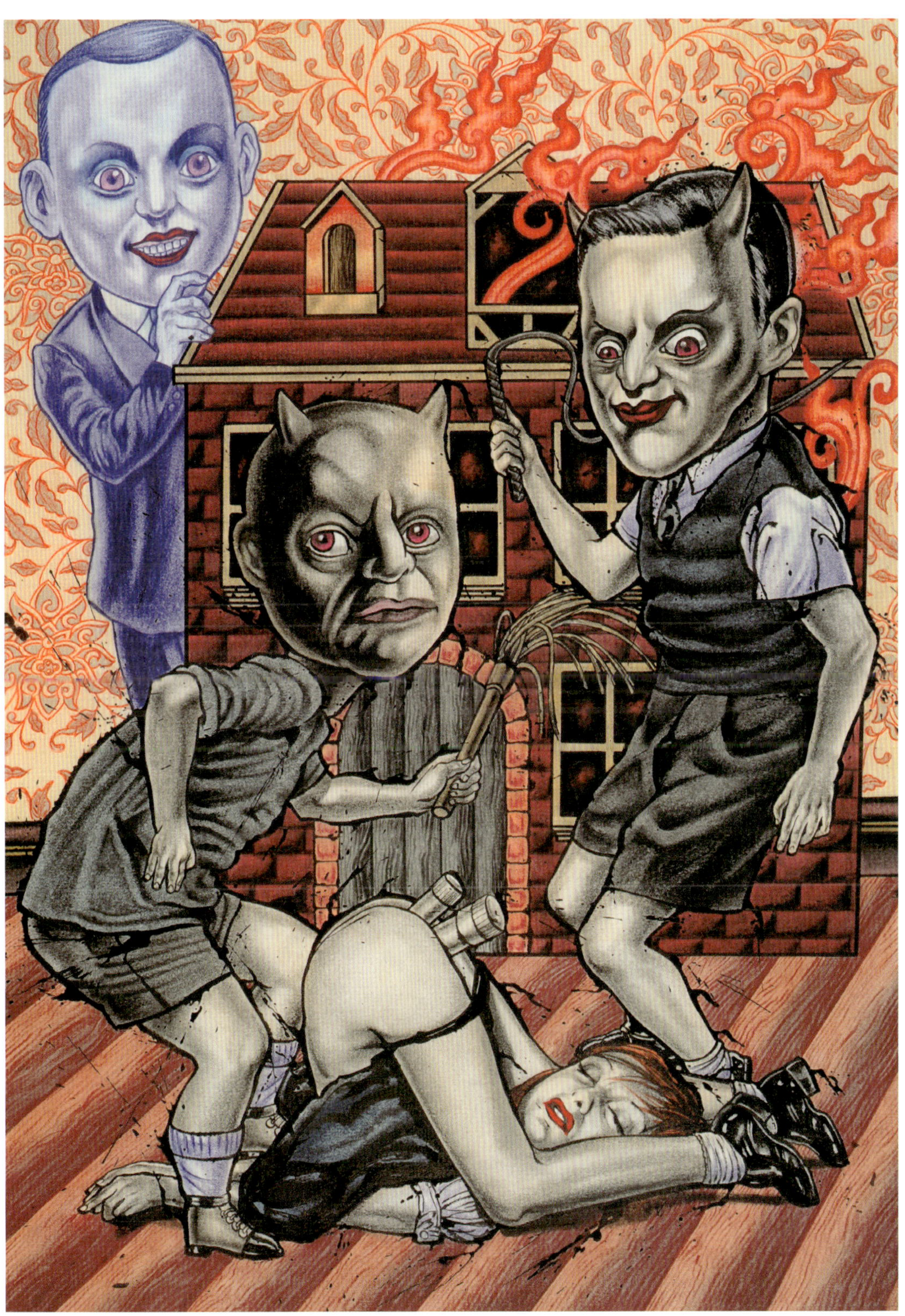

No title 無題
日本製カラー・スティック、インク、水彩、色鉛筆、グワッシュ、紙 / H40.3×W28.5cm / 2015-17

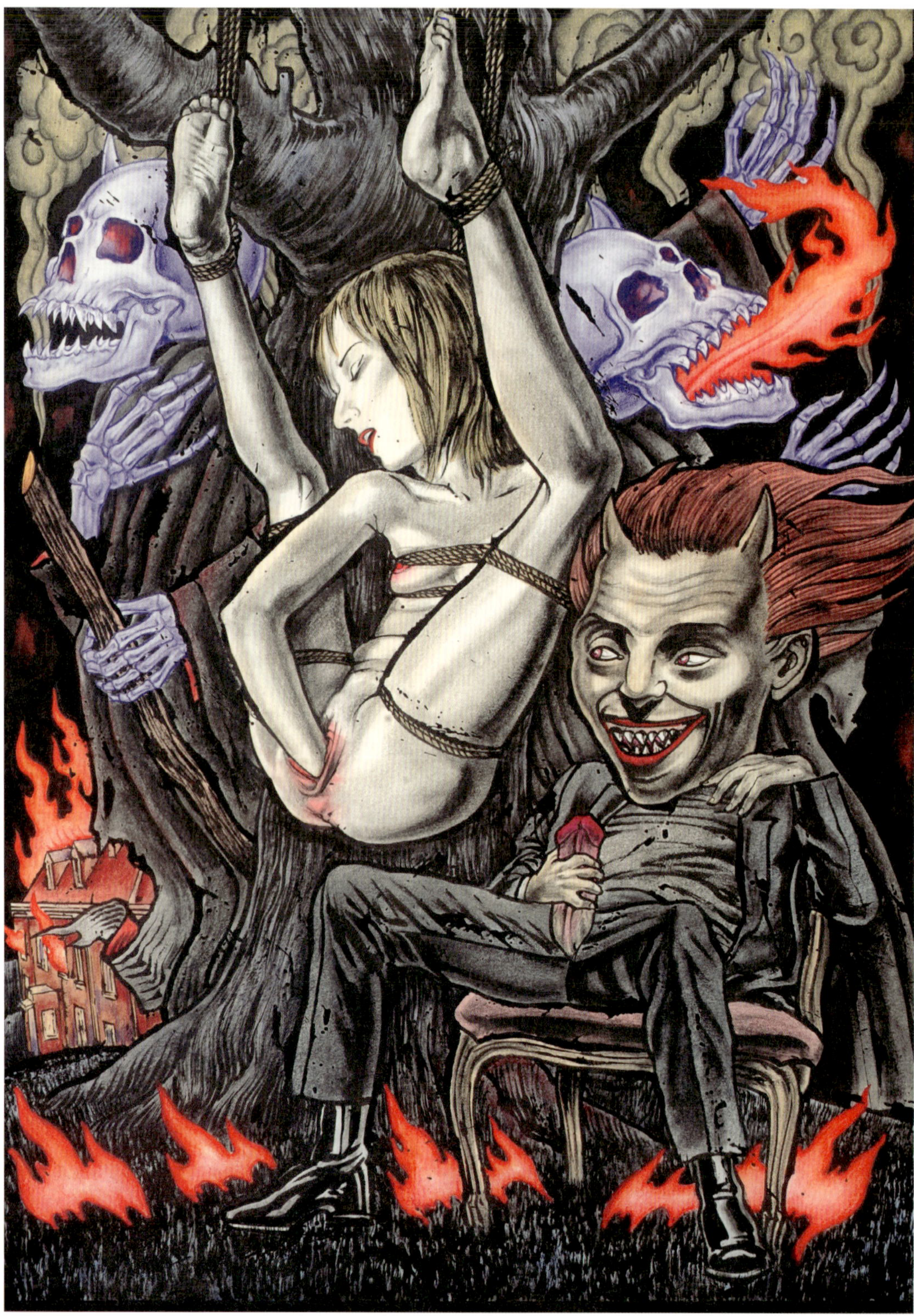

No title 無題
日本製カラー・スティック、インク、水彩、色鉛筆、グワッシュ、紙 / H40.3×W28.5cm / 2015-17

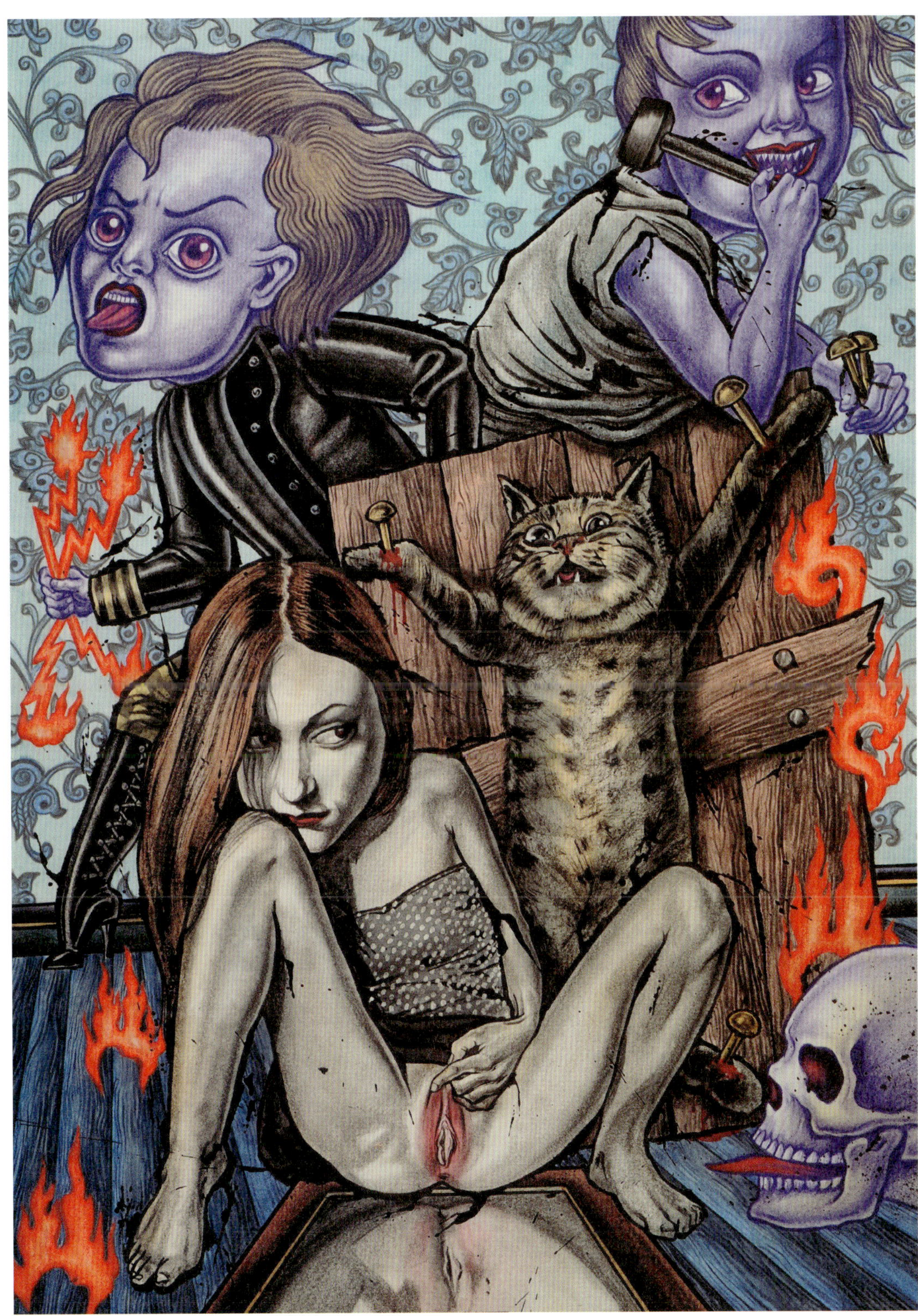

No title 無題
日本製カラー・スティック、インク、水彩、色鉛筆、グワッシュ、紙 / H40.3×W28.5cm / 2015-17

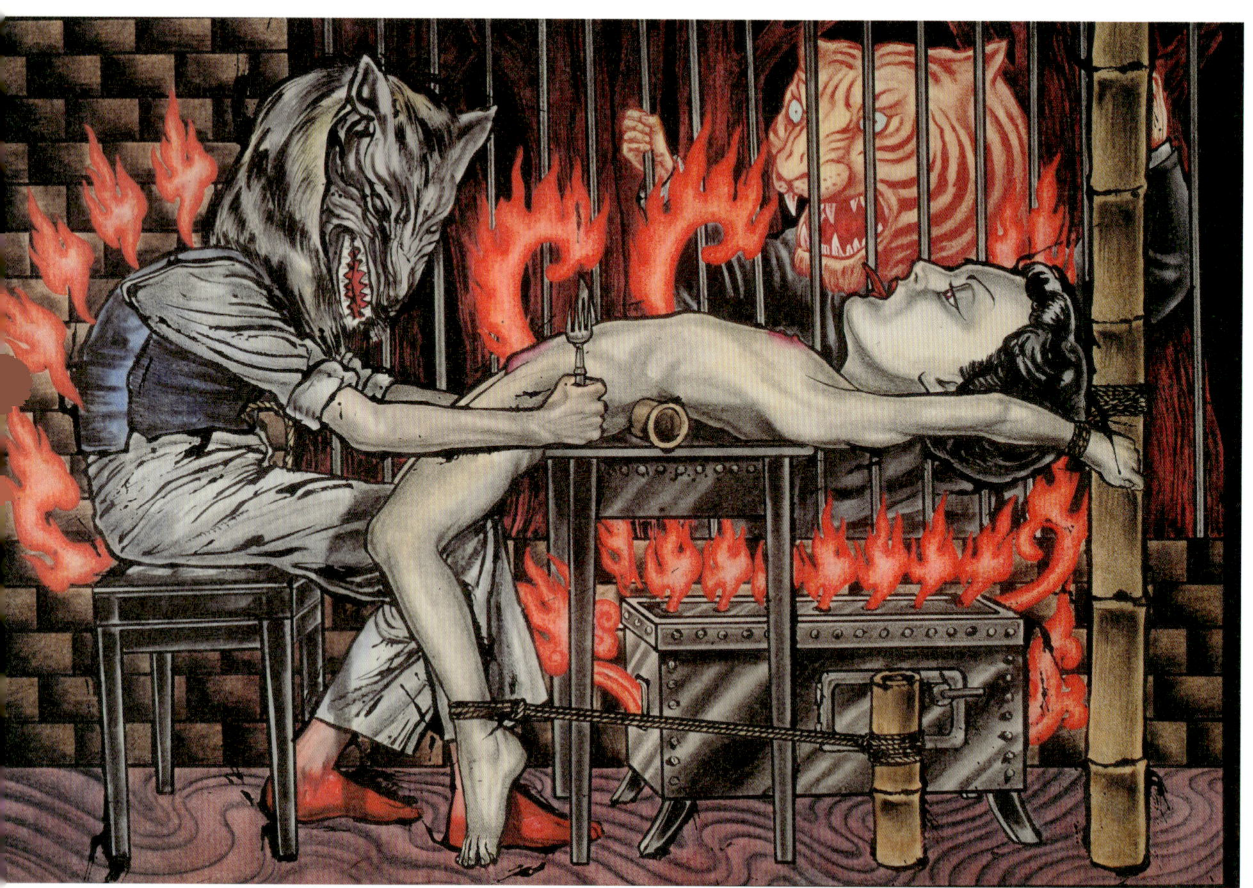

No title 無題
日本製カラー・スティック、インク、水彩、色鉛筆、グワッシュ、紙 / H28.5×W40.3cm / 2015-17

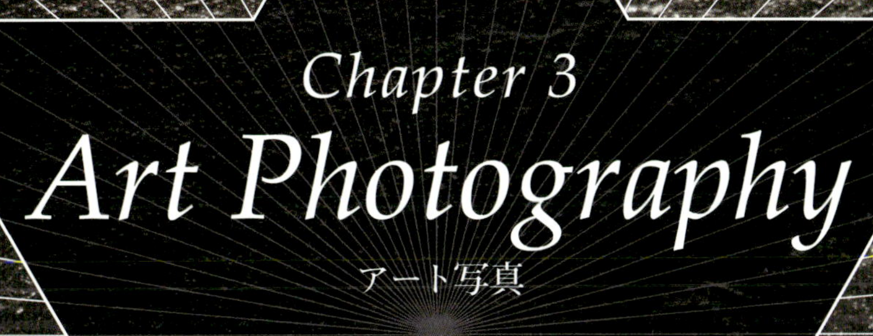

Chapter 3
Art Photography

アート写真

John Santerineross

ジョン・サンテリネロス（アメリカ USA）

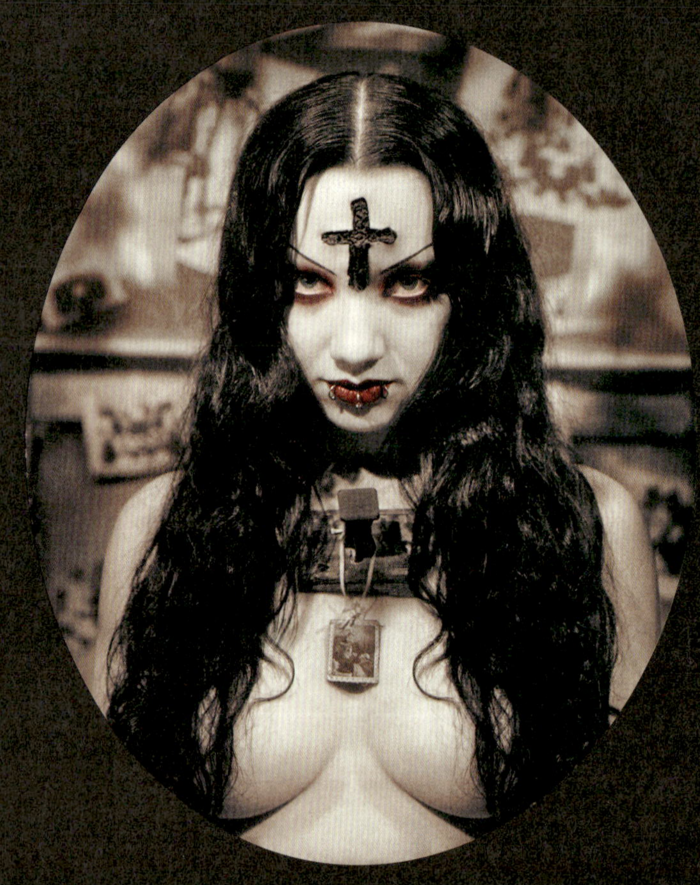

ジョン・サンテリネロスはアメリカの写真家で、19世紀象徴主義を汲み取り、新たな解釈を加える「新象徴主義者」または「黒の象徴主義者」として知られる。独自の複雑な美学はカトリック、サンテリアへの接触、並びにギリシア神話、世界の宗教、聖像学への情熱から生まれたものである。1955年にニューヨークに生まれ、現在はアメリカ南部、ジョージア州に拠点を置く。彼の作品は暗くエロティックな雰囲気を湛えることで名を馳せ、アメリカ11都市、欧州とアジアの12の国々で公開された。その他、陶芸家、彫刻家、画家、ミックス・メディア・アーティストとしても活躍。アート・フィルムにも取り組み、現在はアヴァンギャルド短編作品 "Ningyoushi" の試作段階にある。

John Santerineross is an American photographer and considered to be a "neo-symbolist", or a Black symbolist as he refers to himself, an artist that continues or reinterprets the 19th century art movement Symbolism. His complex aesthetic is derived from a combination of his exposure to Catholicism and Santeria and by his fascination with Greek mythology, world religions and iconography. Born in 1955 in New York City, he lived most of his life in the NYC area and now works and lives in the southern part of the USA in Athens, Georgia. He is known for his dark, erotic images and has been shown both nationally and internationally in over 11 American cities and 12 European and Asian countries. Throughout John's artistic career, he has been a ceramist, sculptor, painter, and mixed media artist. He has recently delved into the world of moving images. Currently, he is in the preproduction phase of an adaptation of an avante-garde short story entitled "Ningyoushi."

www.santerineross.com

↑Veruna's Rainbow ヴァルナの虹（部分）
印画紙にプリント／H71×W55cm

→Dream 夢（部分）
印画紙にプリント／H71×W55cm

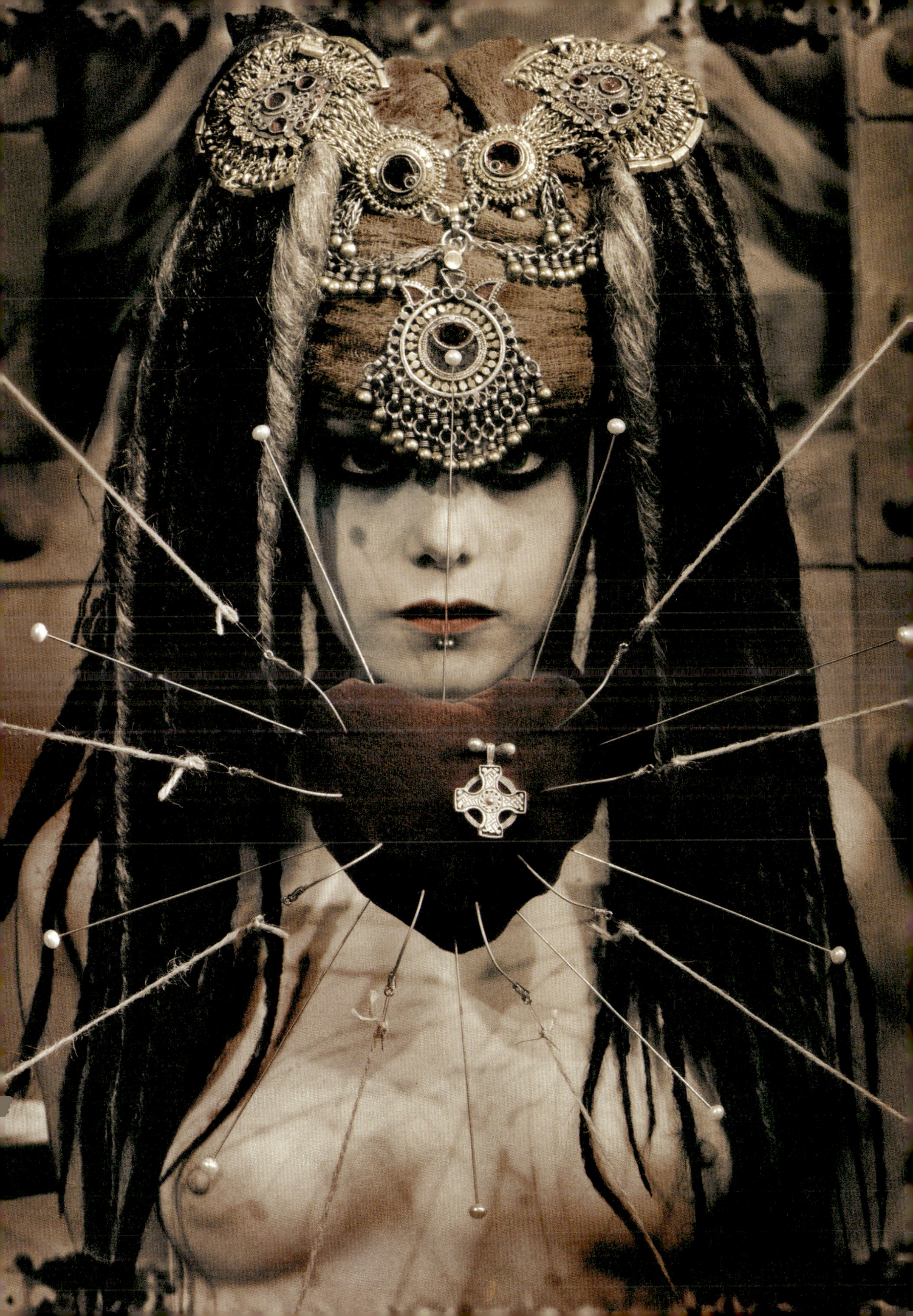

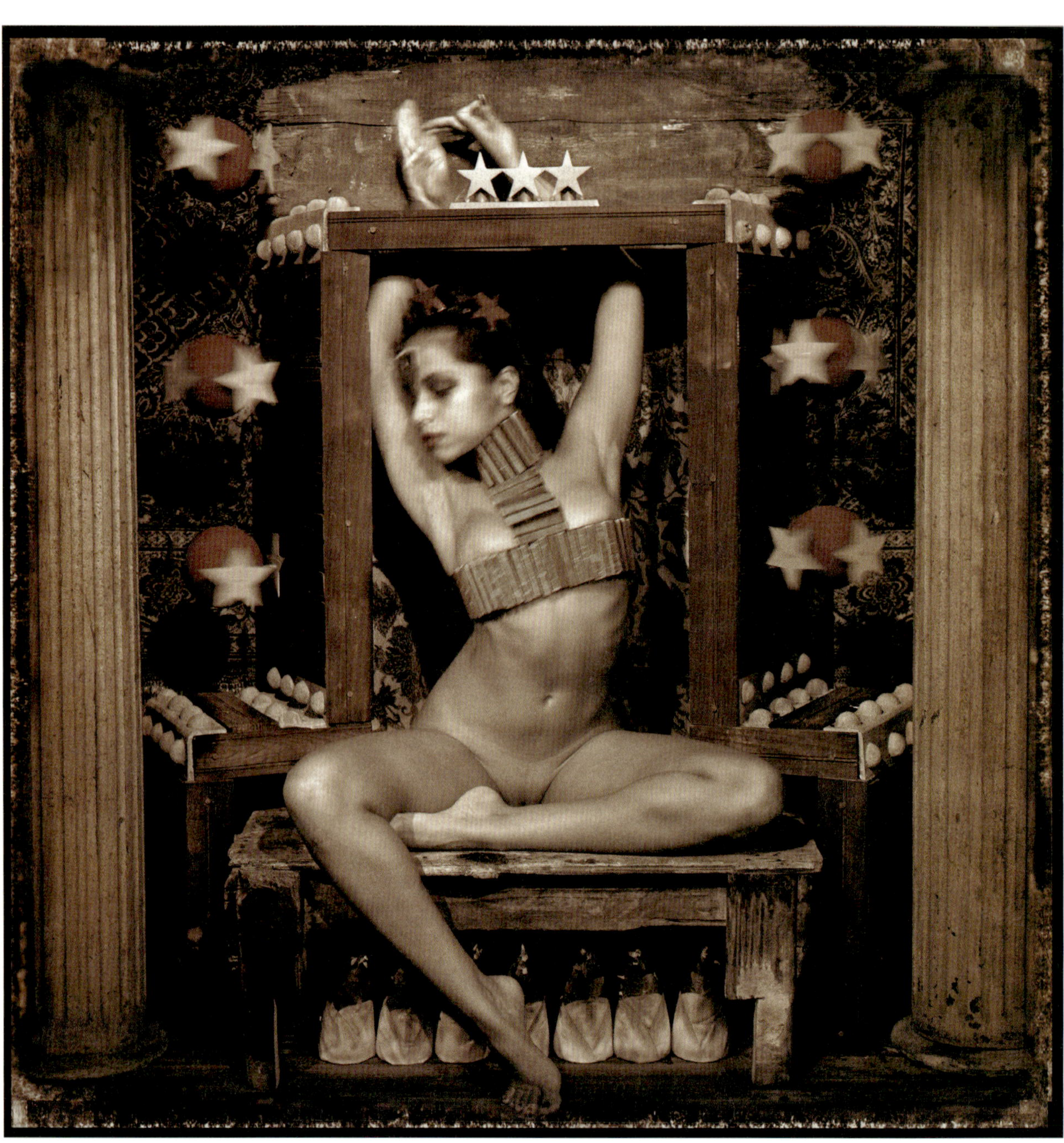

Karma 業
印画紙にプリント / H71×W55cm

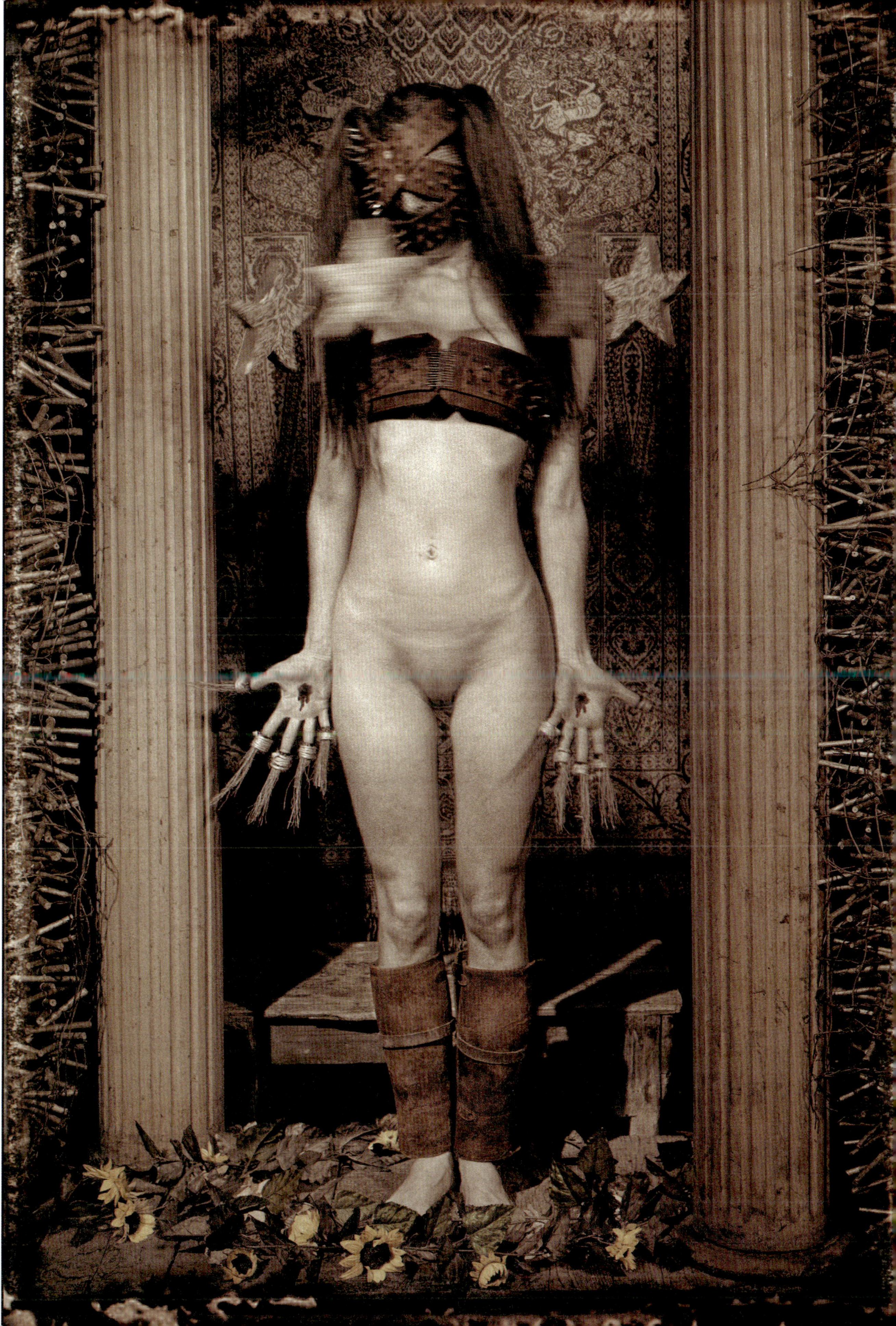

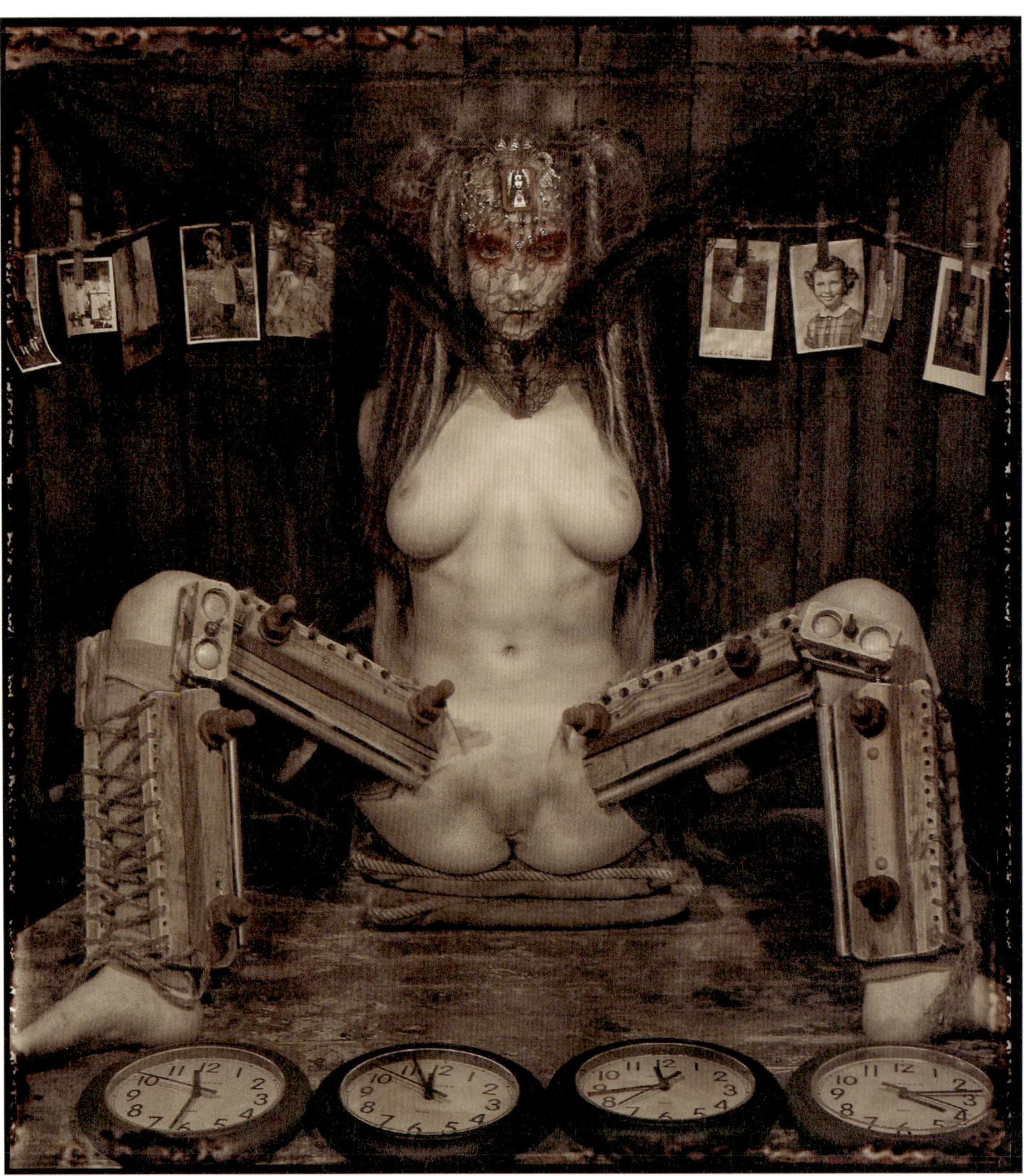

One's Time ある物の時
印画紙にプリント / H71×W55cm

Chapter 3 Art Photography   John Santerineross

Embrace of Solitude 孤独の抱擁
印画紙にプリント / H71×W55cm

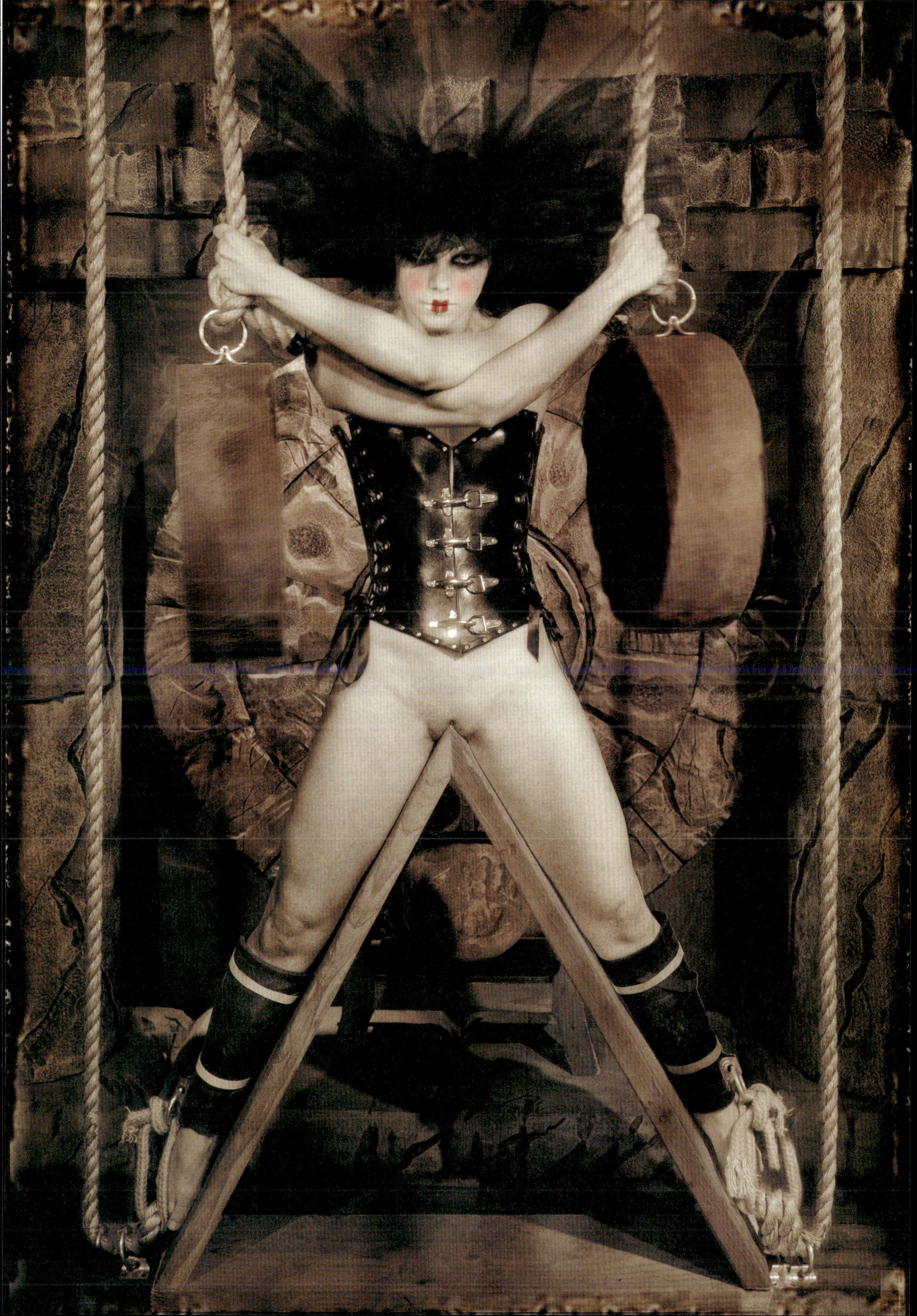

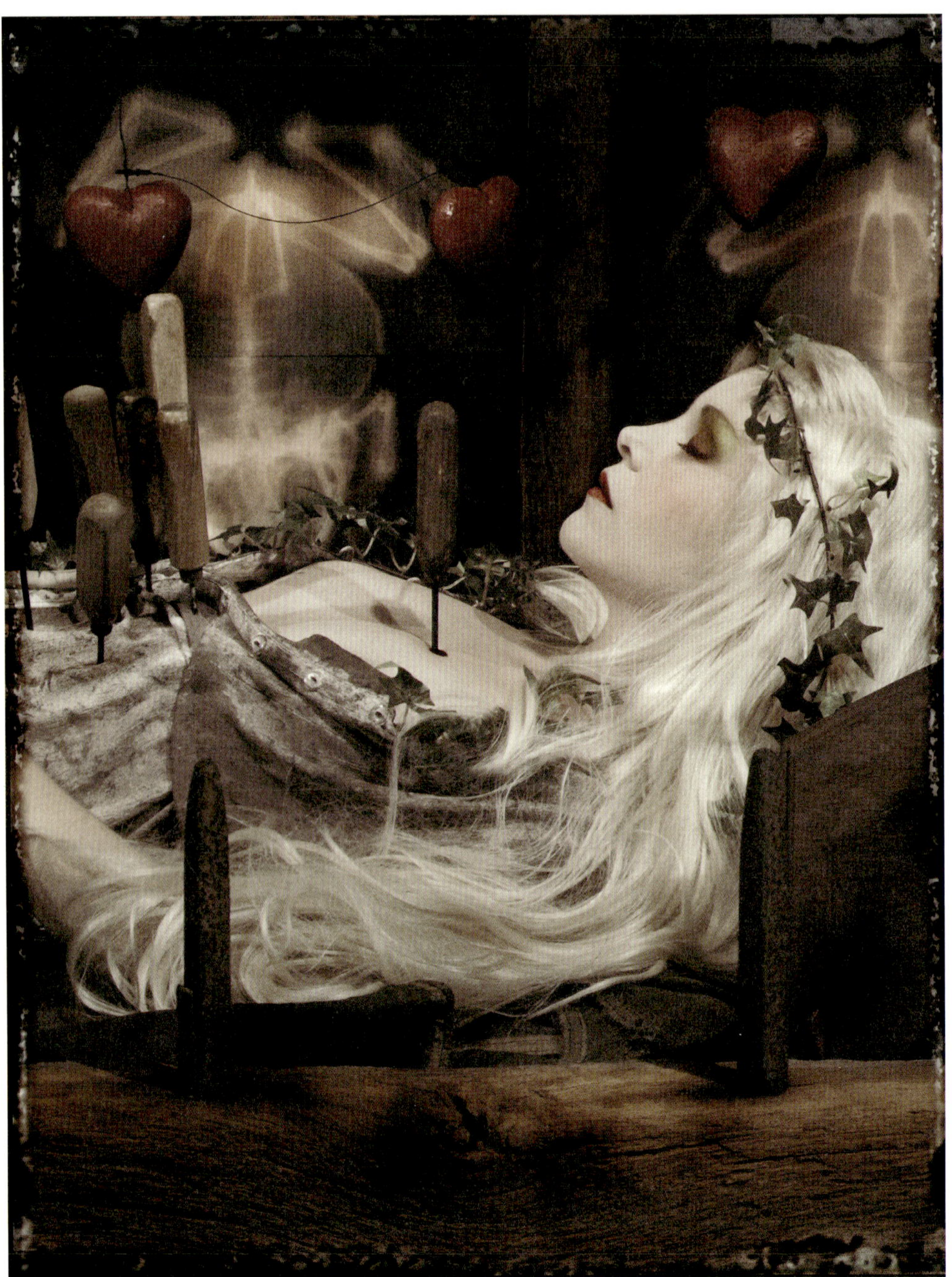

In a Dream 夢の中
印画紙にプリント / H71×W55cm

Unleashing the Deep 深淵の解放
印画紙にプリント / H71×W55cm

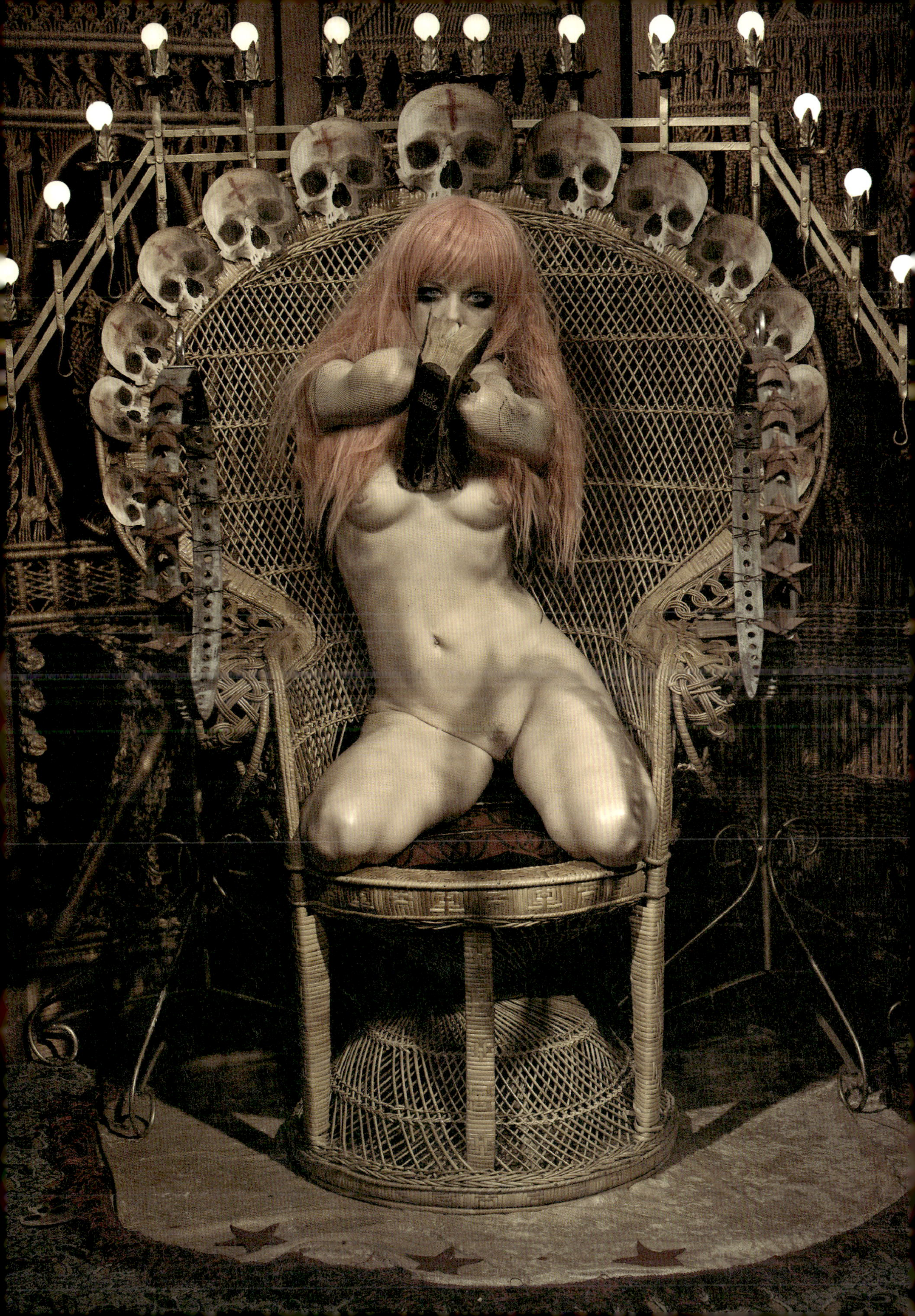

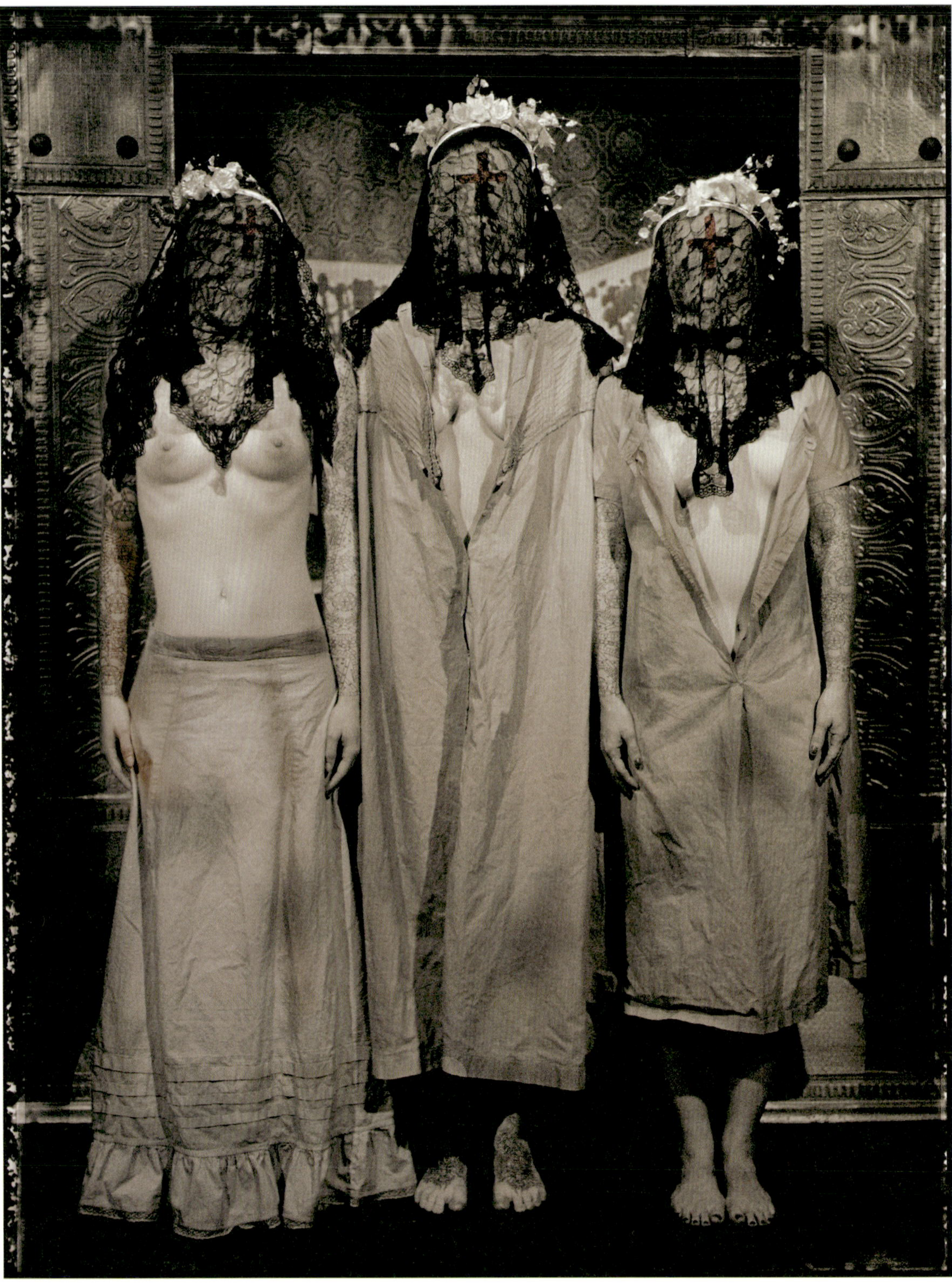

Assembly of the Kindred 一族の集い
印画紙にプリント / H71×W55cm

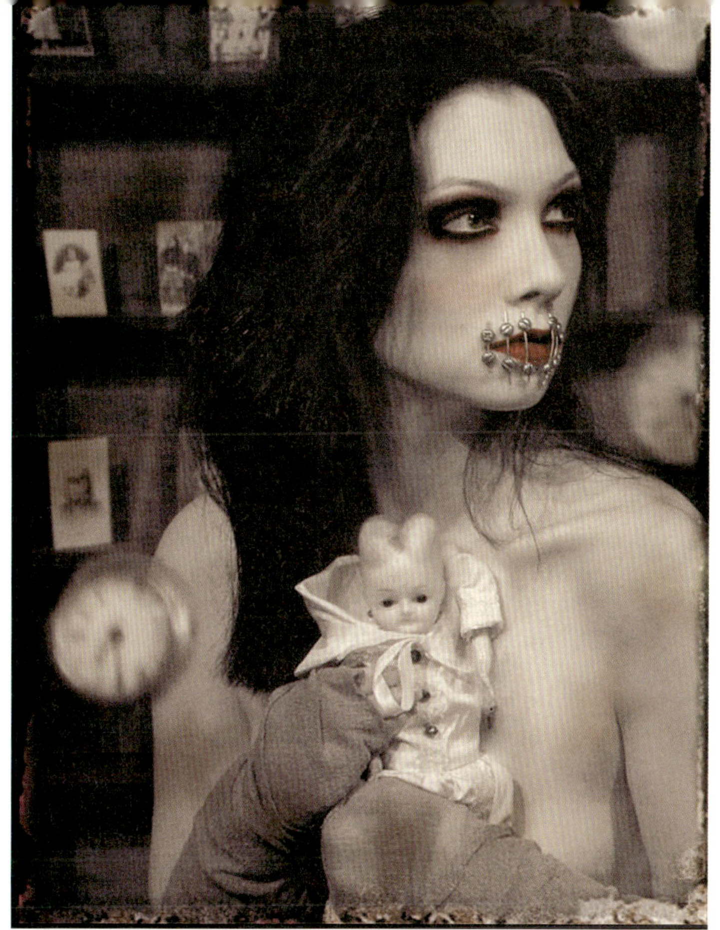

The Beauty of Silence 沈黙に宿る美
印画紙にプリント / H71×W55cm

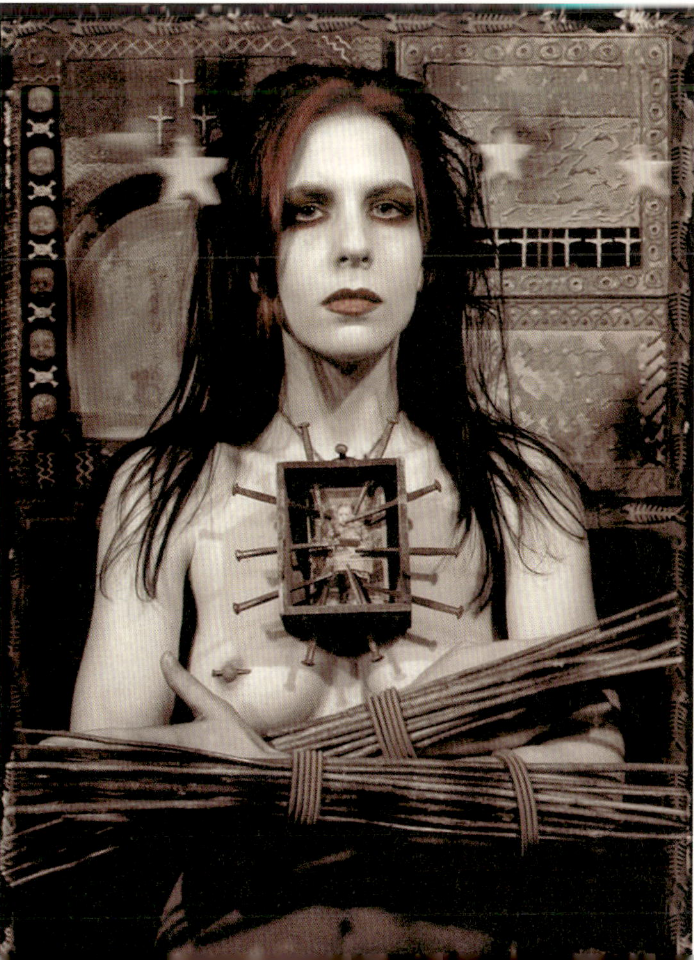

Cradled Me 抱かれて
印画紙にプリント / H71×W55cm

26

Daria Endresen

ダリア・アンドレセン（ノルウェー　Norway）

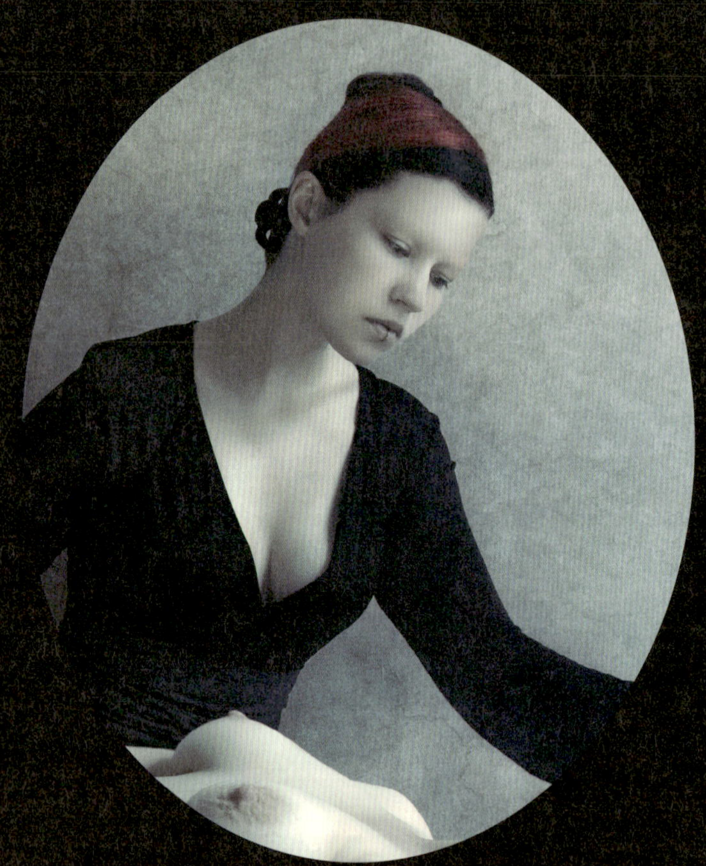

写真家、デジタル・アーティスト。ノルウェーのオスロを拠点に、自身の経験からインスパイアされた作品を制作。鋭い観察力と感性で非日常的な幻想の世界を創り出す。冷たい雰囲気の作品は物悲しく、不吉でさえある。作品はヨーロッパ、海外の数多くの出版物、美術書に取り上げられ、ノルウェー、スウェーデン、フランス、ドイツ、ベルギー、イタリア、イギリス、ポーランド、トルコ、アメリカなど世界中の展覧会に参加している。

Photographer and digital artist, based in Oslo, Norway, Daria Endresen draws her inspiration from her most intimate, personal stories. Observant and sensitive, Daria creates surreal dream scapes, drowned in icy atmosphere and laden with pain and mystery. Her works have been featured in numerous publications and artbooks in Europe and overseas, and she took part in many shows across the world, among others in Norway, Sweden, France, Germany, Belgium, Italy, the UK, Poland, Turkey and the United States.

dariaendresen.com

↑ Untitled VII 無題VII（部分）
モデル：ダリア・アンドレセン / フォト・マニピュレーション / 2012

→Distant Shore 遠くの岸（部分）
モデル：イングヴィルド・エイリン / フォト・マニピュレーション / 2015

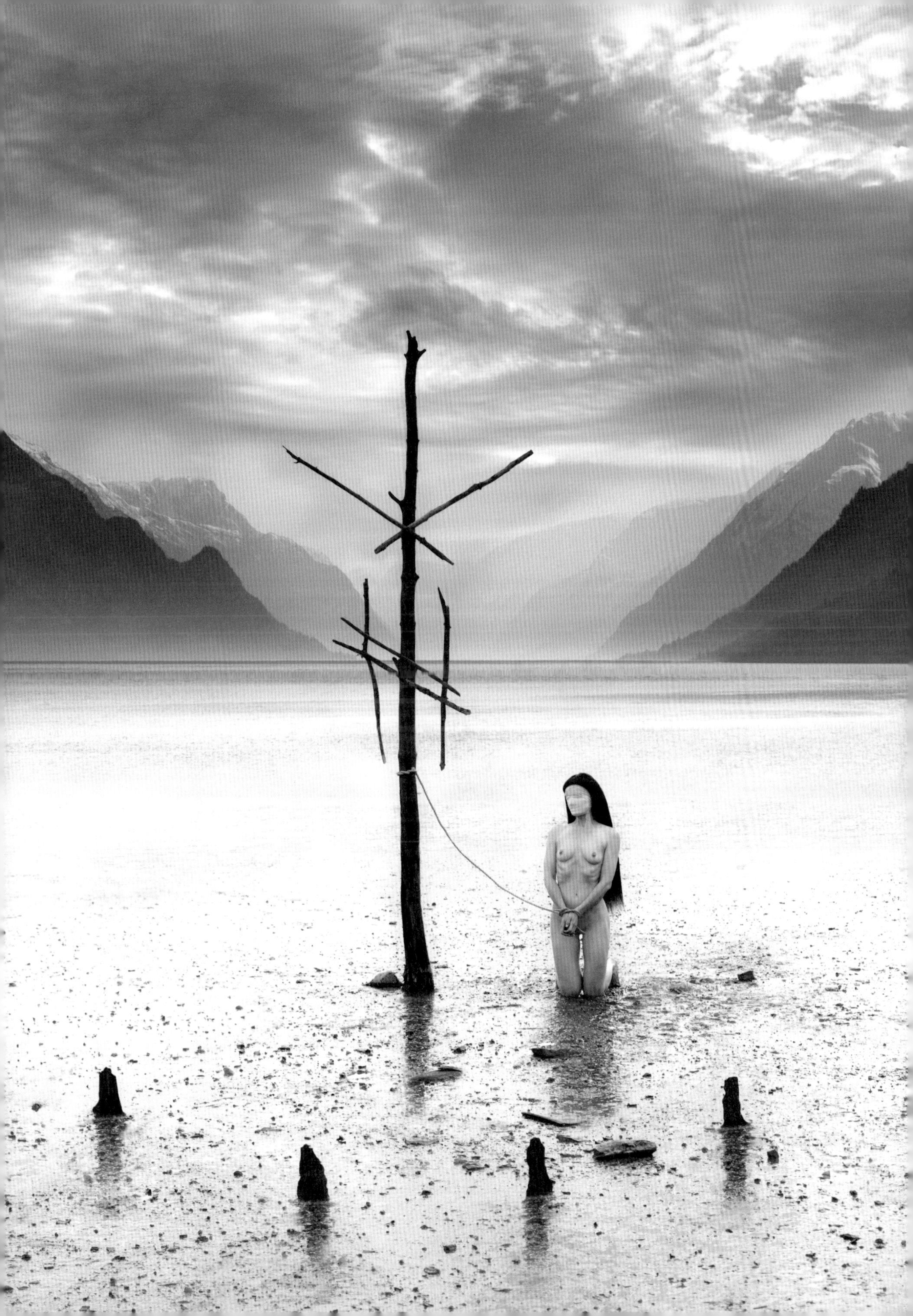

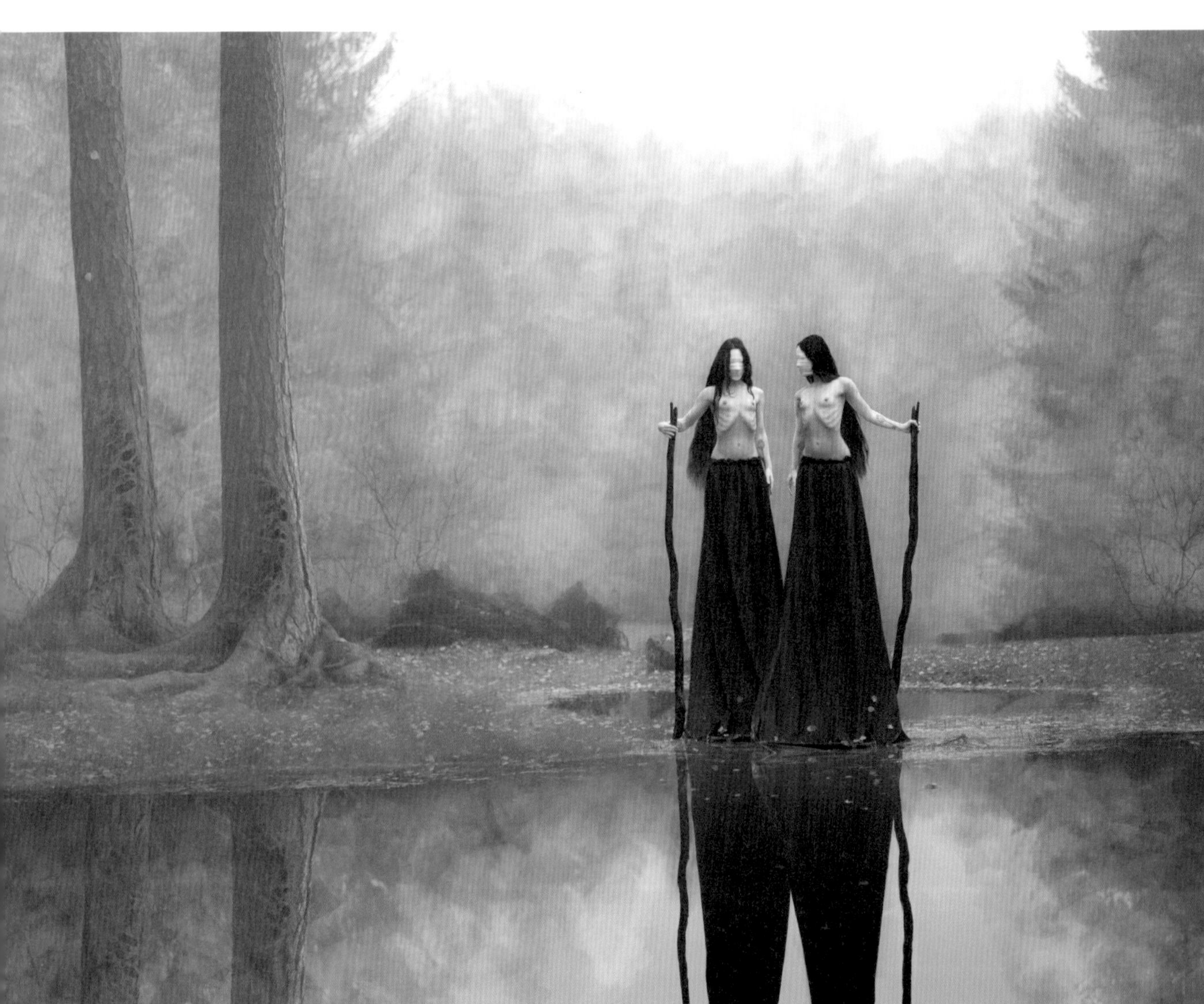

Darkwood ダークウッド
モデル：エルベレス・ラソンブラ / フォト・マニピュレーション / 2014

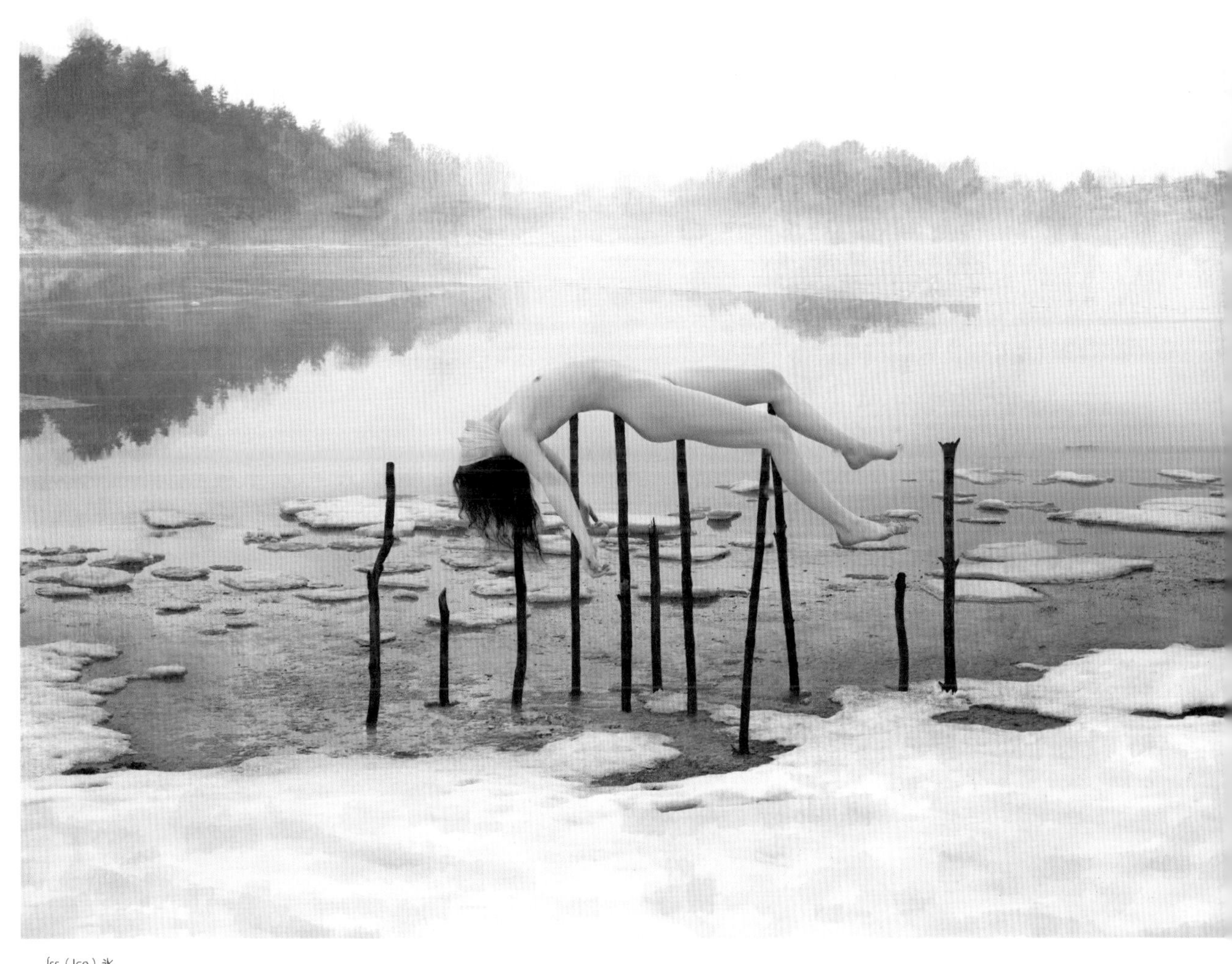

Íss（Ice）氷
モデル：イングヴィルド・エイリン / フォト・マニピュレーション / 2016

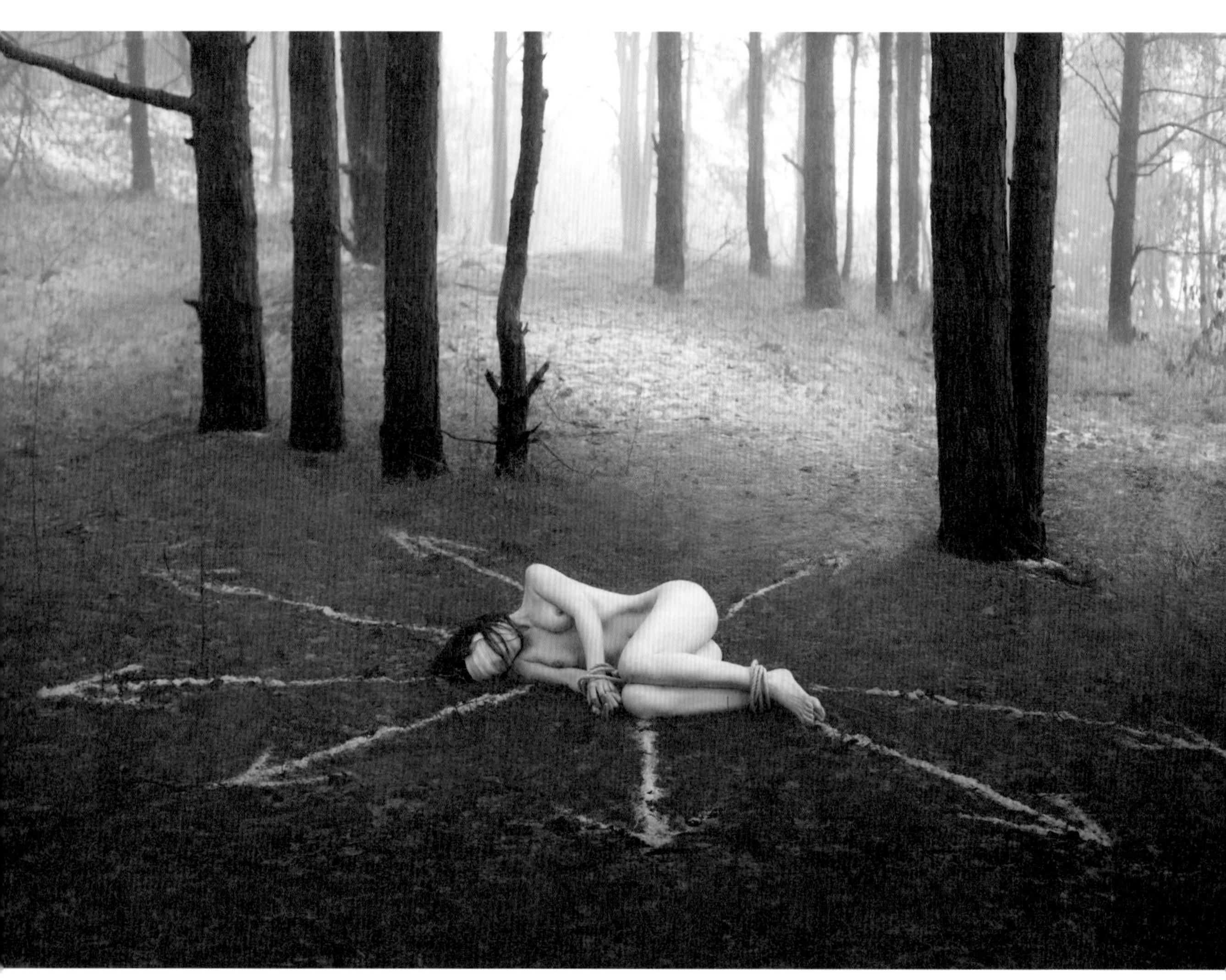

The Rite 儀式
モデル：イングヴィルド・エイリン / フォト・マニピュレーション / 2016

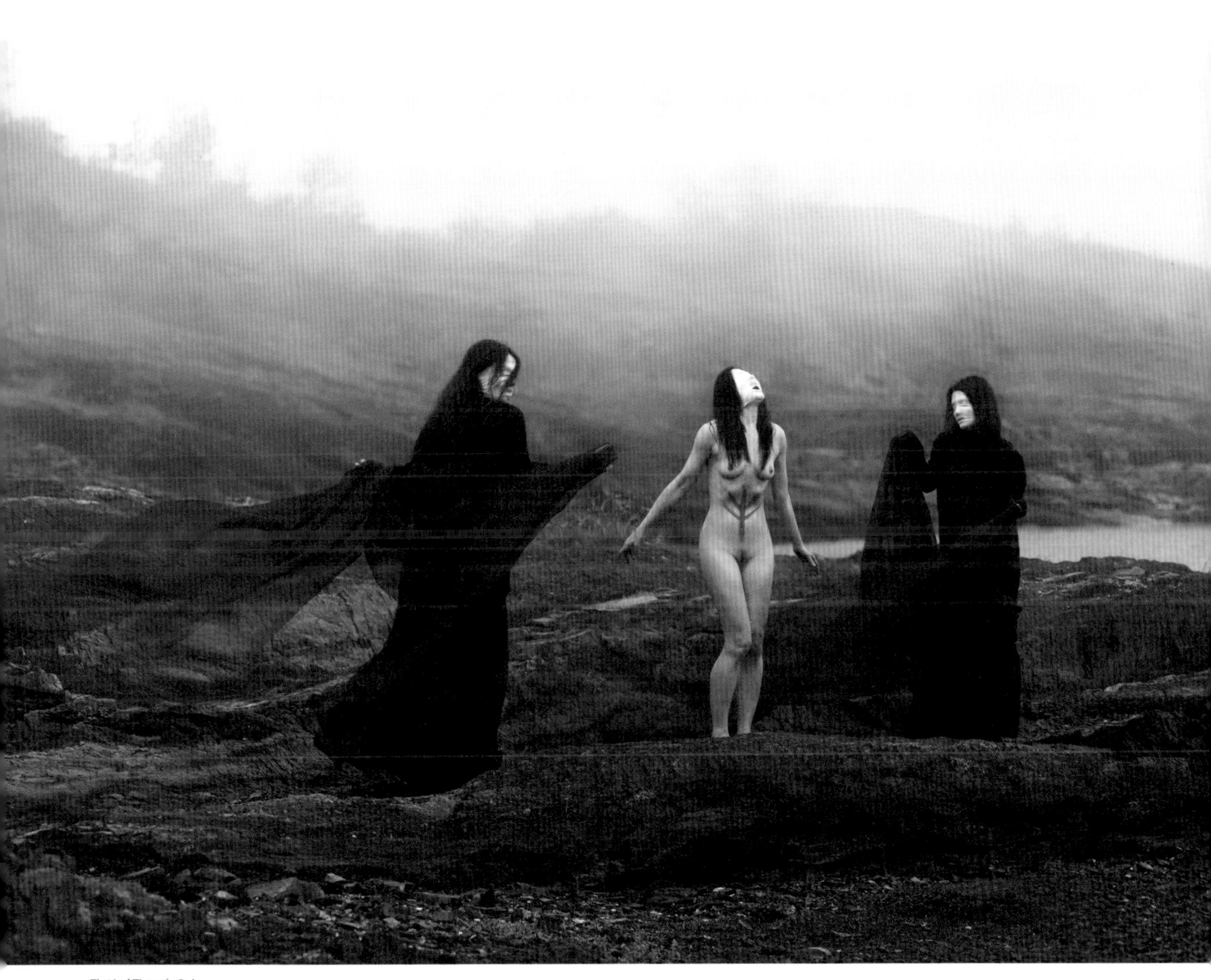

Thrjár（Three）3人
モデル：イングヴィルド・エイリン / フォト・マニピュレーション / 2015

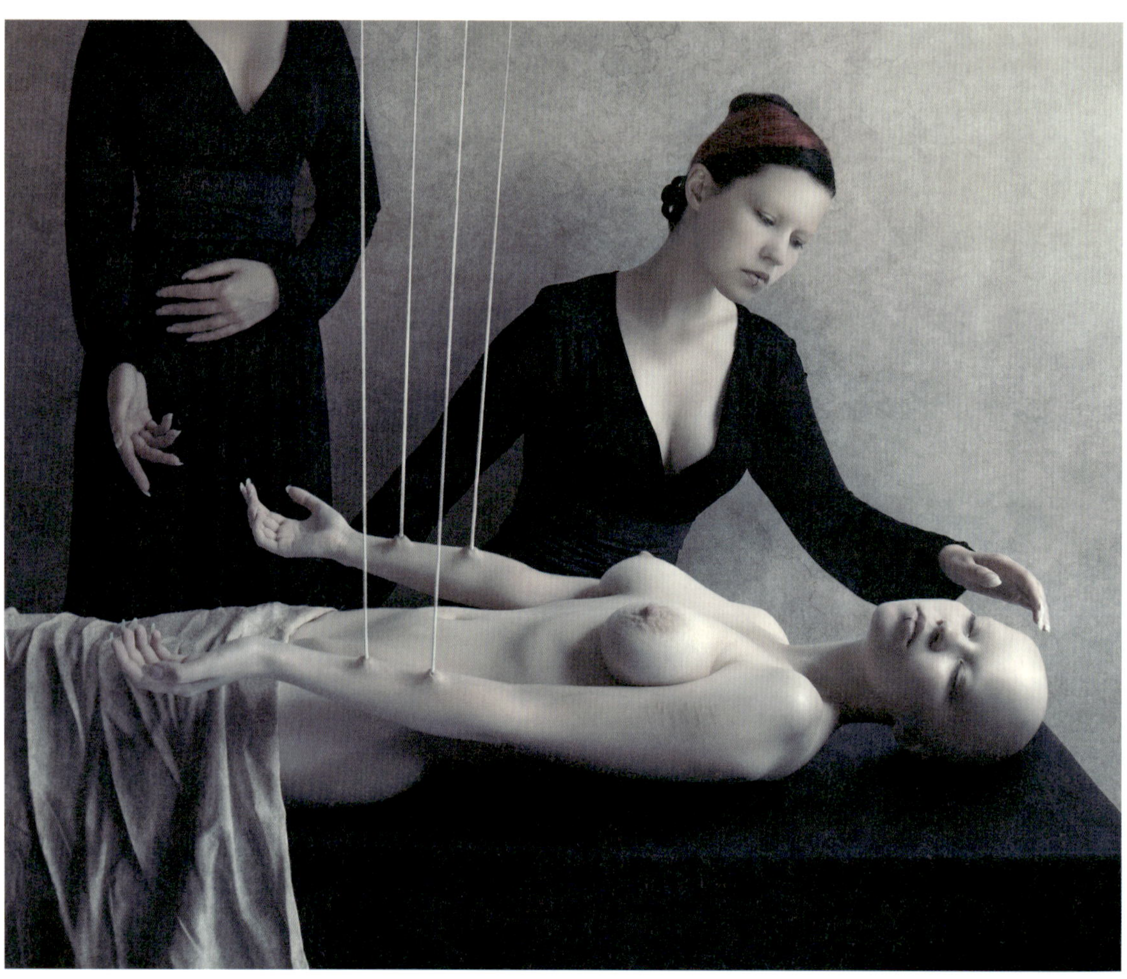

Untitled VII 無題VII
モデル:ダリア・アンドレセン / フォト・マニピュレーション / 2012

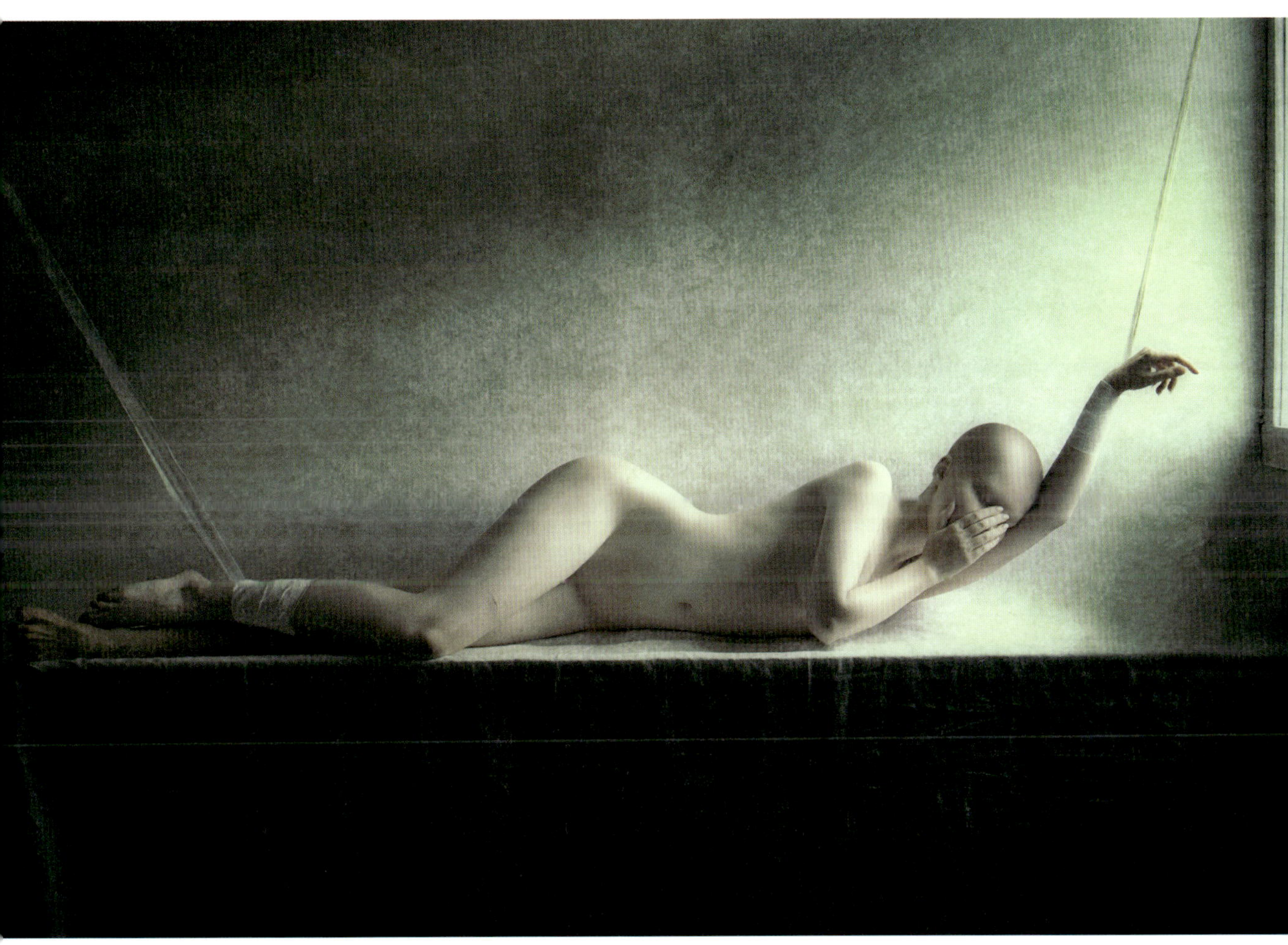

Zu Warten（To Wait）待機
モデル：ダリア・アンドレセン / フォト・マニピュレーション / 2009

27

Mira Nedyalkova

ミラ・ネディヤルコーヴァ（ブルガリア　Bulgaria）

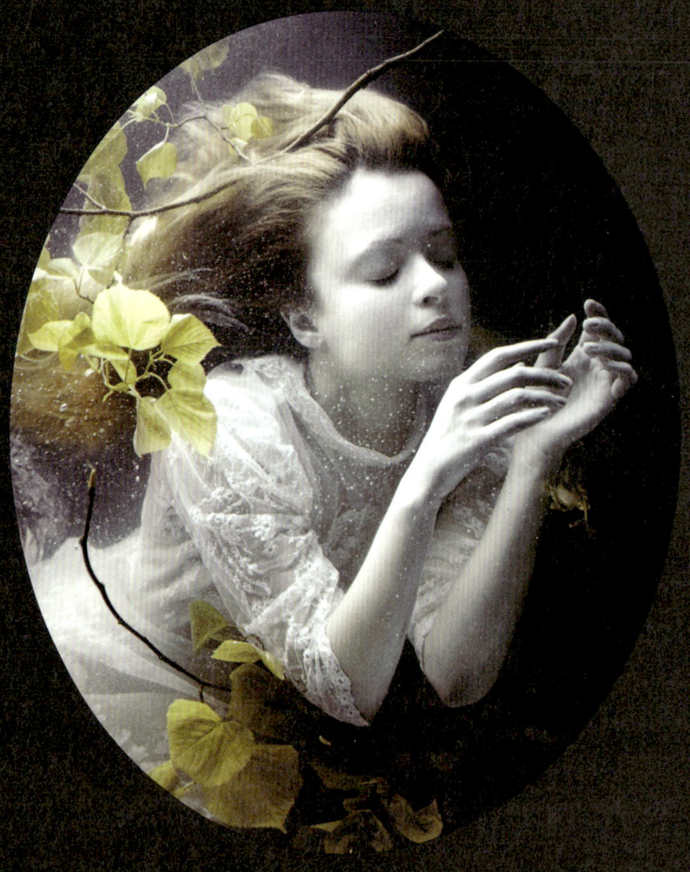

18歳でモデルとしてはじめて写真の世界に入る。最初はスケッチを学んだが、2007年に写真こそ自分を表現する手段だと気づき、絵をやめる。心の奥で感じたものをひたすら表現する。ミラにとって苦しみは美であり、エロティシズムは心の有り様に影響を及ぼすもので、自分自身や心の内を表現している。彼女の作品からは、美、人生に対する強い意志、悲しみ、苦しみ、愛、エロティシズムを感じることができる。生きていく上で欠かせないこれらのものを織り交ぜ、ひとつのイメージをつくり上げることに喜びを感じる。作品を見る人が人生を知り（たとえ理想とはちがっていても）あるがままを受け入れ、愛するきっかけになることを望んでいる。

First of all she came into the world of photography as a model when she was 18 years old. She has always loved photography as art, but i started with drawing. Later in 2007 she discovered photography as a means to express herself and completely replaced painting. She just try to expresses what she feel, in the deepest sense. In her images she uses pain as a beauty, erotic as a psychological way of life. She expresses herself and her intimate inner life. In her works you would find beauty and strong will for life, sorrow and pain, love and eroticism as constant part of our life⋯She likes to fuse all this into a single image, because she believes this is the way to start knowing life, to accept it and perhaps love it for what it is (or it is not).

www.miranedyalkova.com

↑ Revival 再生（部分）
デジタル写真 / 2015

→Reminiscence 回想
デジタル写真 / 2015

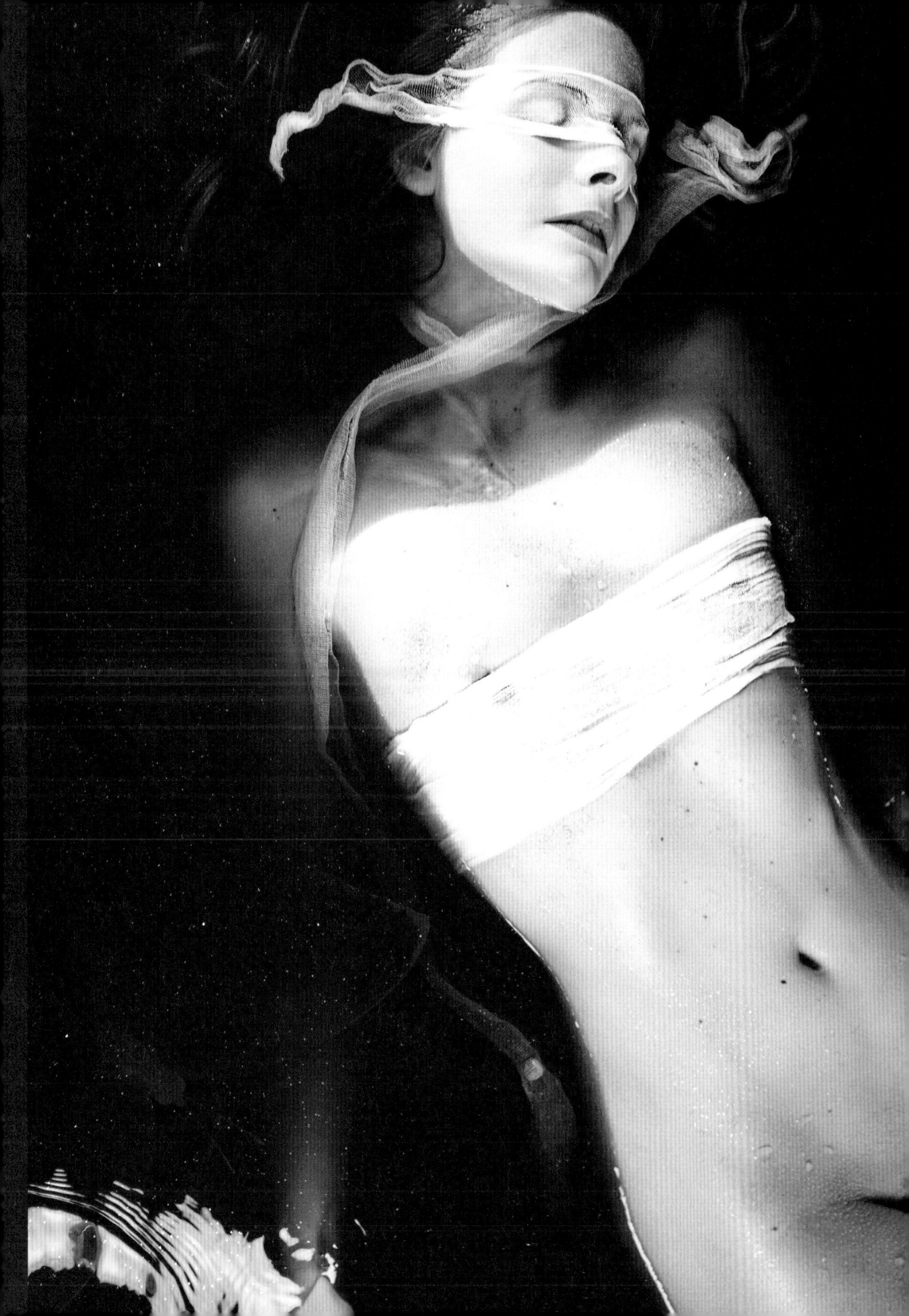

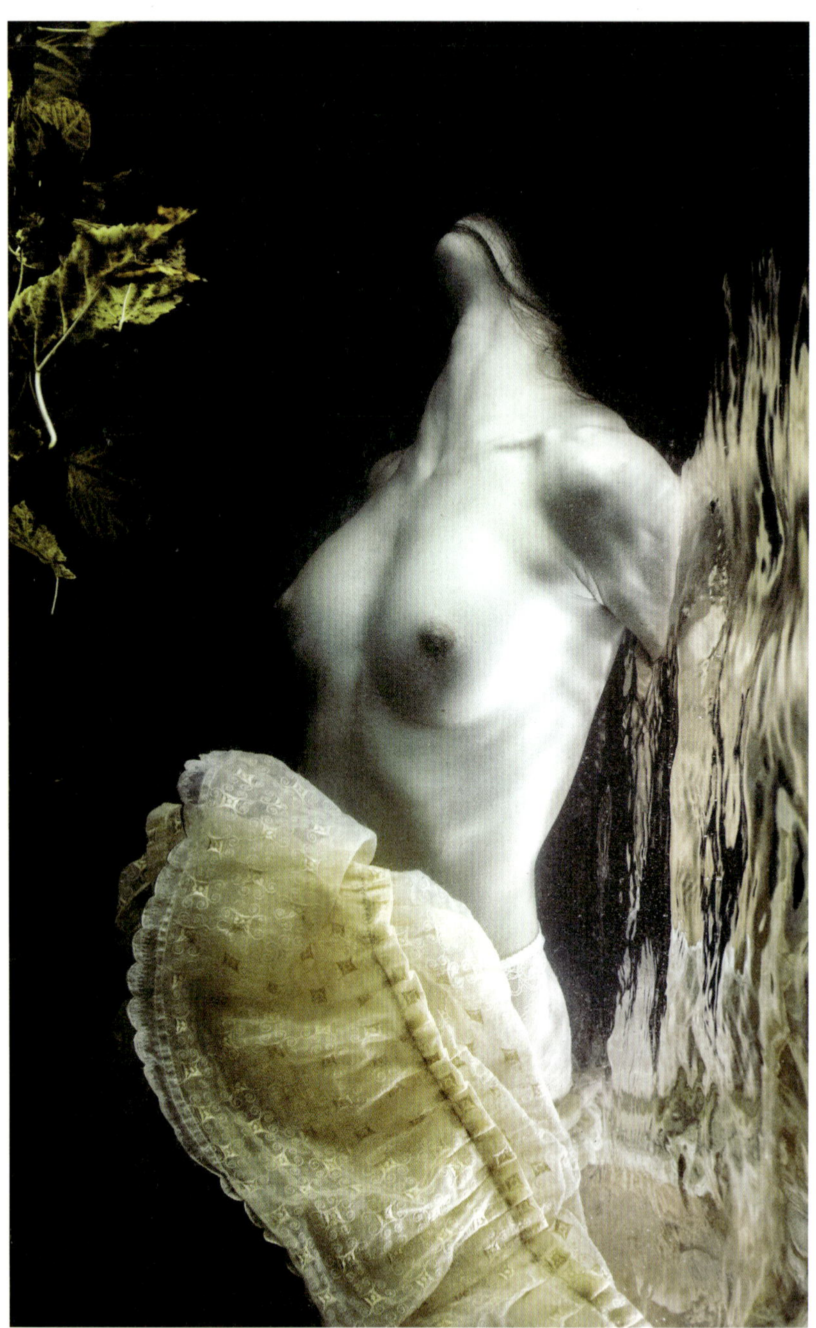

Moons of Neptune 海王星の衛星
デジタル写真 / 2015

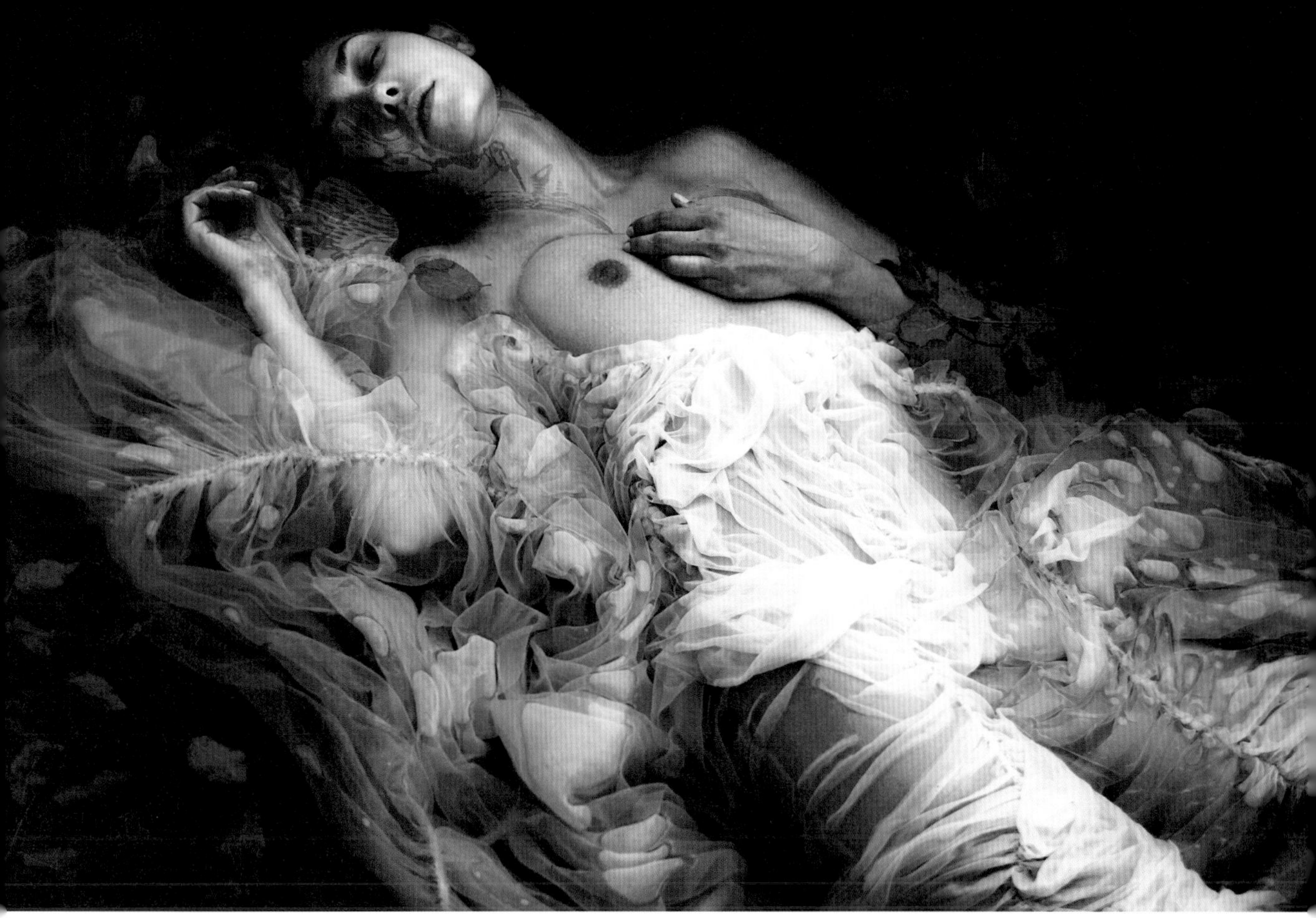

↑ Sin 罪
デジタル写真 / 2014

| Planet Vega 琴座のヴェガ
デジタル写真 / 2014

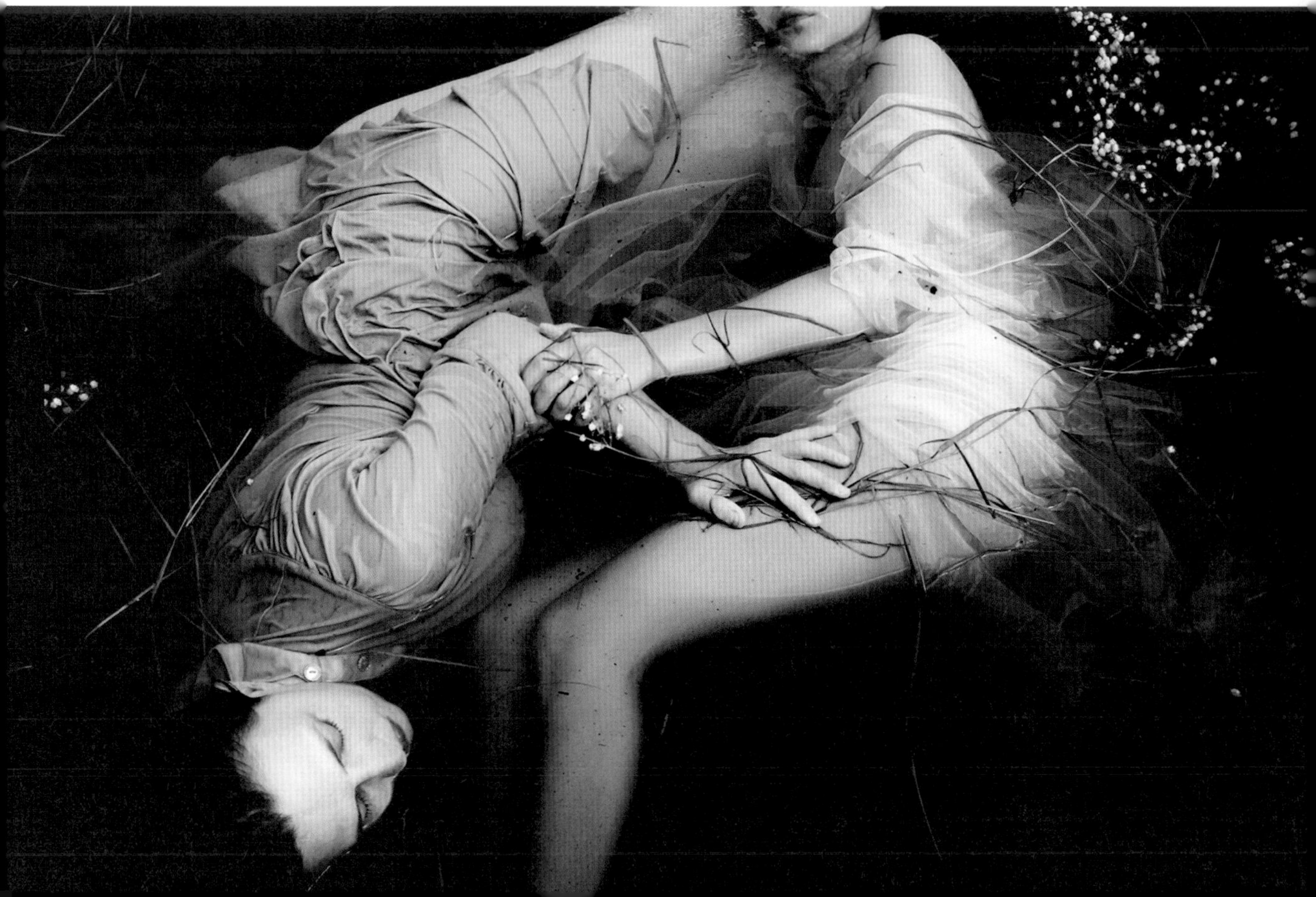

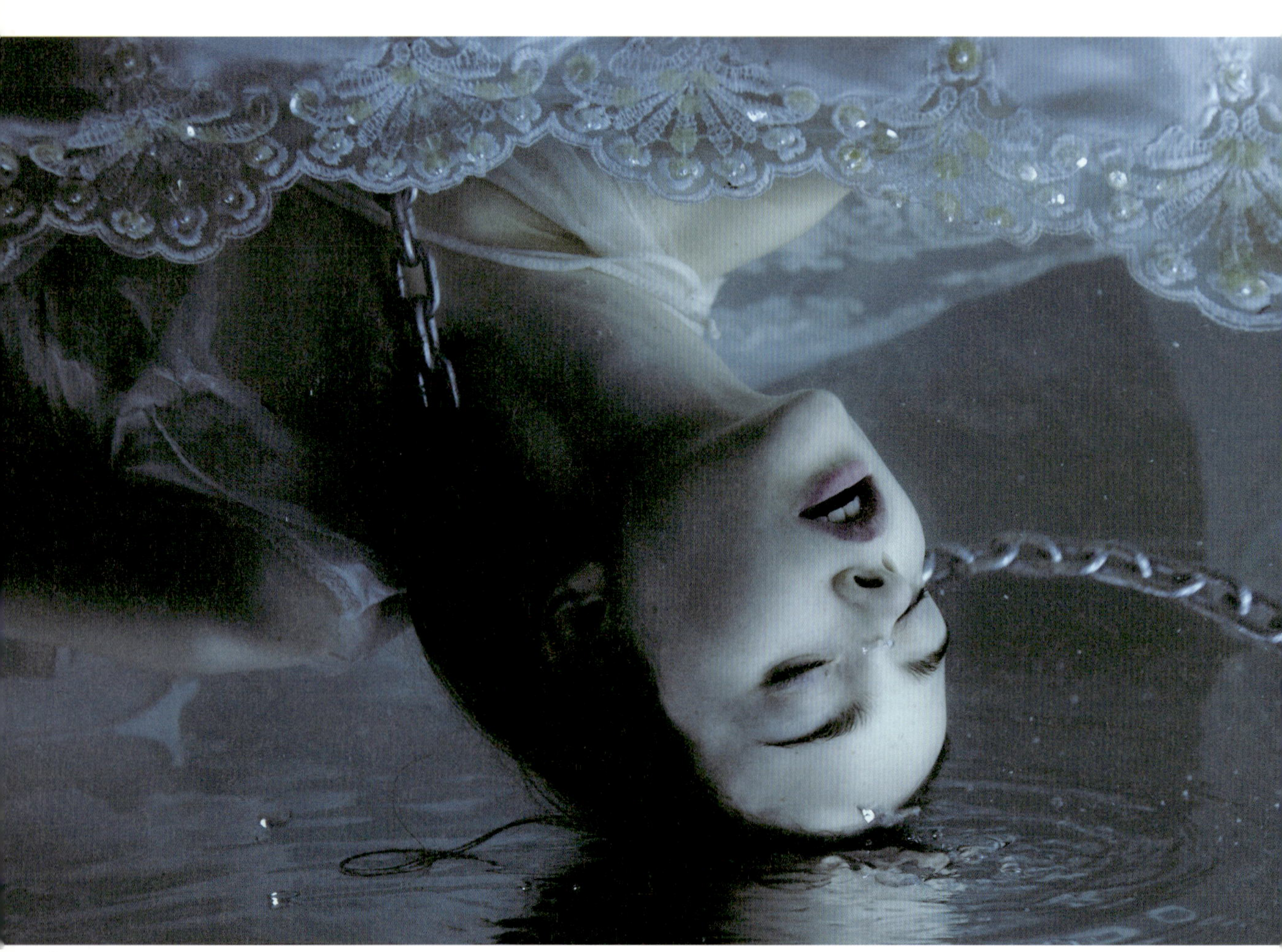

Toxic 中毒
デジタル写真 / 2016

Adoration 崇敬
デジタル写真 / 2017

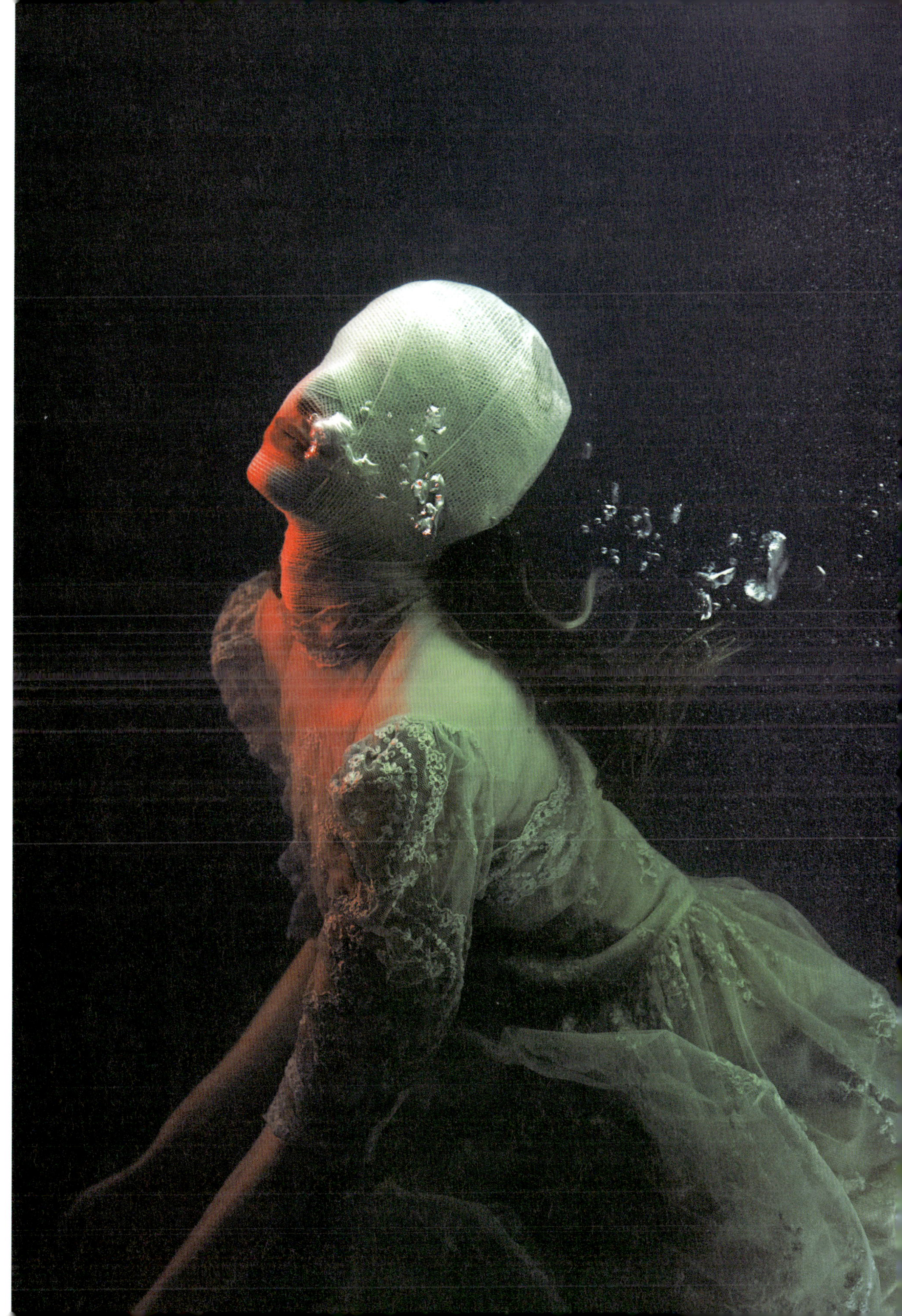

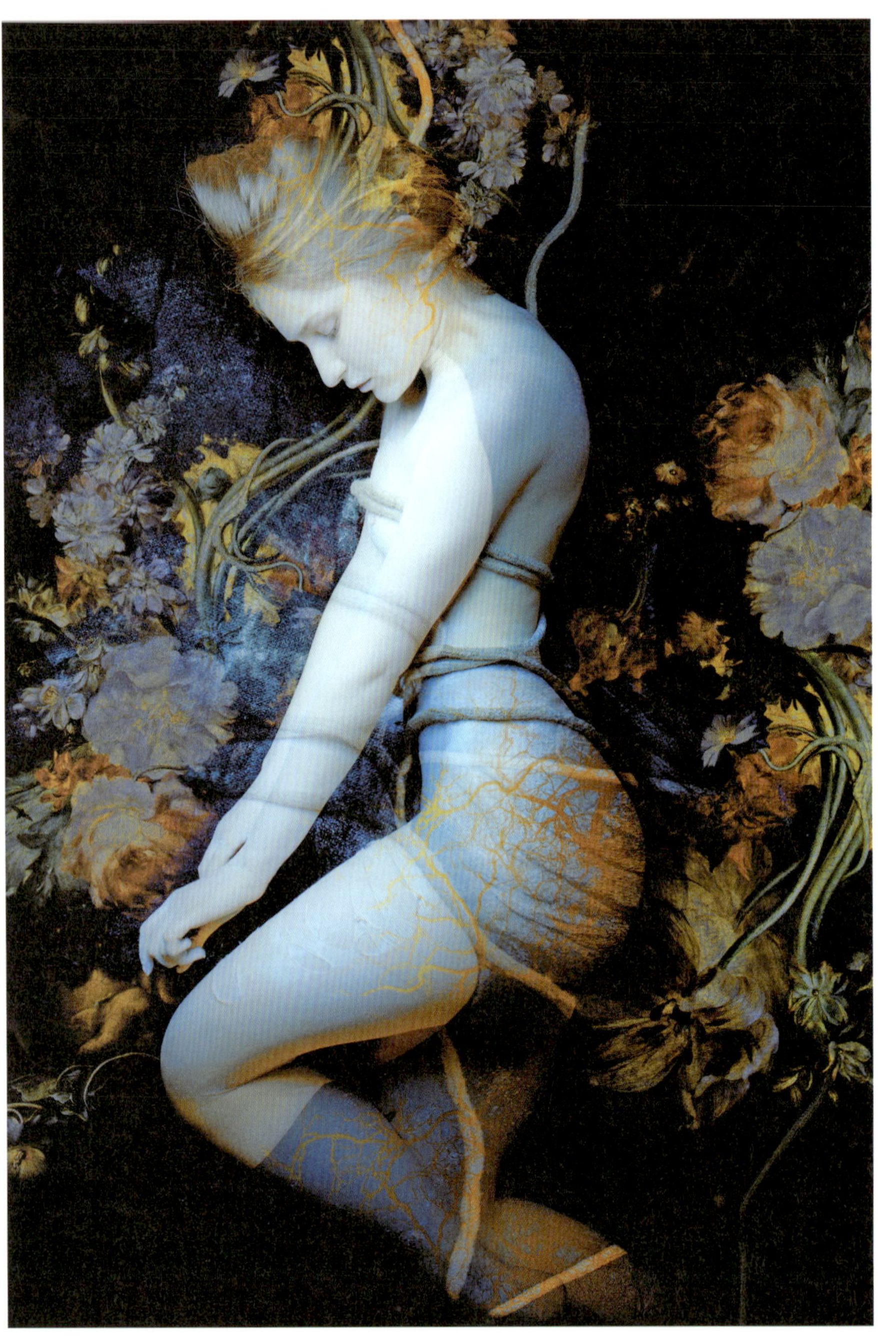

Indigo Poetry インディゴ・ポエトリー
デジタル写真 / 2017

Oceania オセアニア
デジタル写真 / 2016

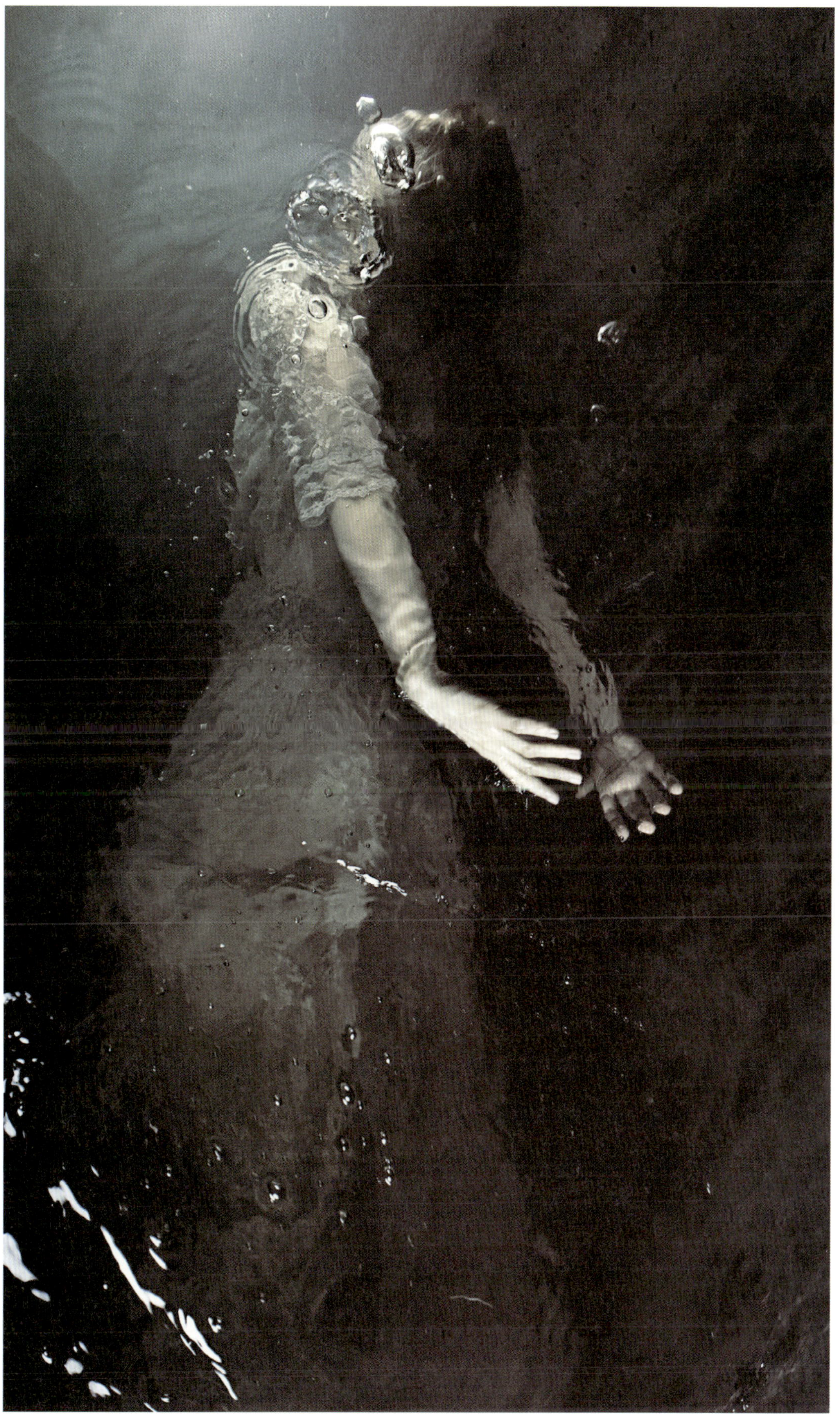

Garth Knight

ガース・ナイト（オーストラリア　Australia）

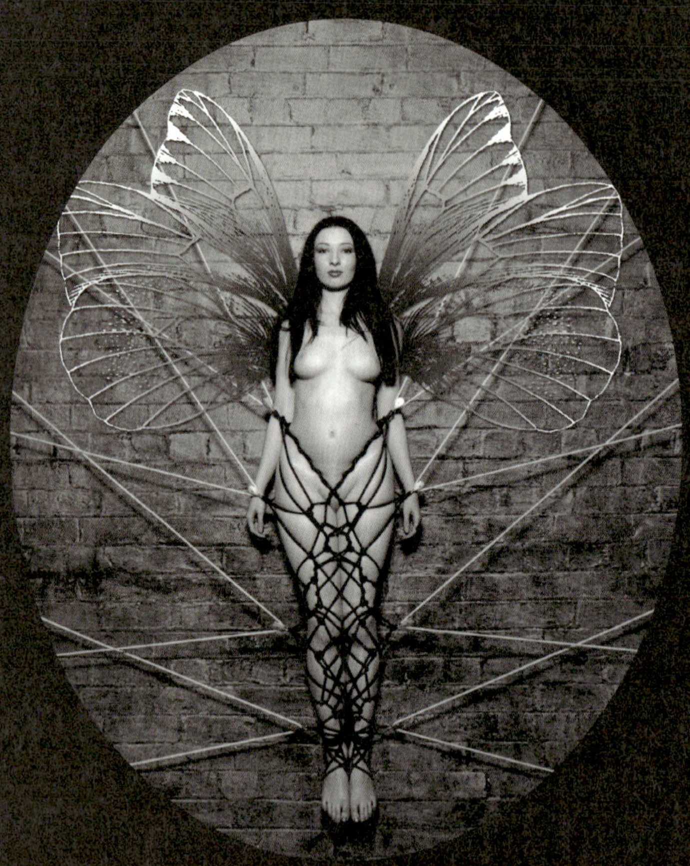

岩や縄、人間の体を素材に、伝統的な緊縛と禅の思想、多神教の神話を組み合わせた寓話的なインスタレーションを制作。縄が描く複雑で装飾的な模様は、力とその力に屈し、身をゆだねる歓びを表現している。ガースにとって作品を作ることは儀式であり、啓示を受けるための瞑想の実践にほかならない。複雑なインスタレーションの制作には何日もかかり、極限まで感覚を研ぎ澄ませ、人間の体を断続的に縛りながらイメージを形にする工程は、すべてを超越した異次元の世界への旅である。オーストラリア国内のみならず、世界中で展覧会を開催。自費出版した著書もある。シドニー在住。

Garth Knight works with rocks, rope and bodies as sculptural forms, creating allegorical installations that combine Zen concepts and pagan mythology with the traditions of kinbaku and rope bondage. His tableau of intricate, decorative networks connect ideas of strength and pleasure with those of surrender and abandonment. His installations and performance focus on the ritual of making, becoming an act of meditation and a process leading to illumination. Complex installations are created over many days, with bodies being intermittently bound into the sculpture - a journey into another world using extreme sensations as pathways to transcendence and awe. His works have been exhibited widely in Australia and internationally and he has self published several books. He lives and works in Sydney.

www.garthknight.com

↑ Priscilla with Butterfly Wings 蝶の羽をつけたプリシラ（部分）
さまざまな素材、デジタル・プリント / 2004

→The Blue Tree 2 (Sam)　青い木 2（サム）
さまざまな素材、デジタル・プリント / 2011

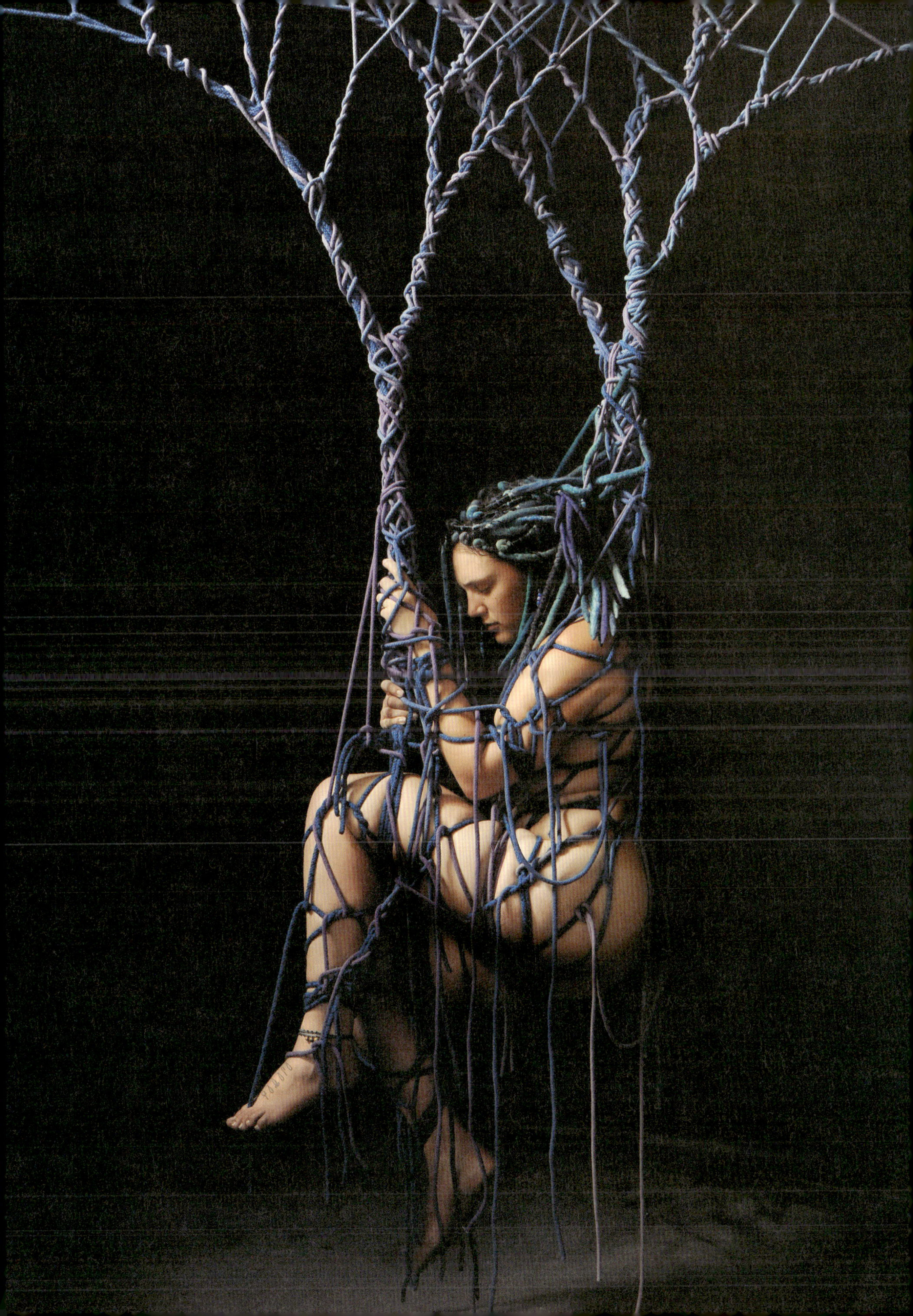

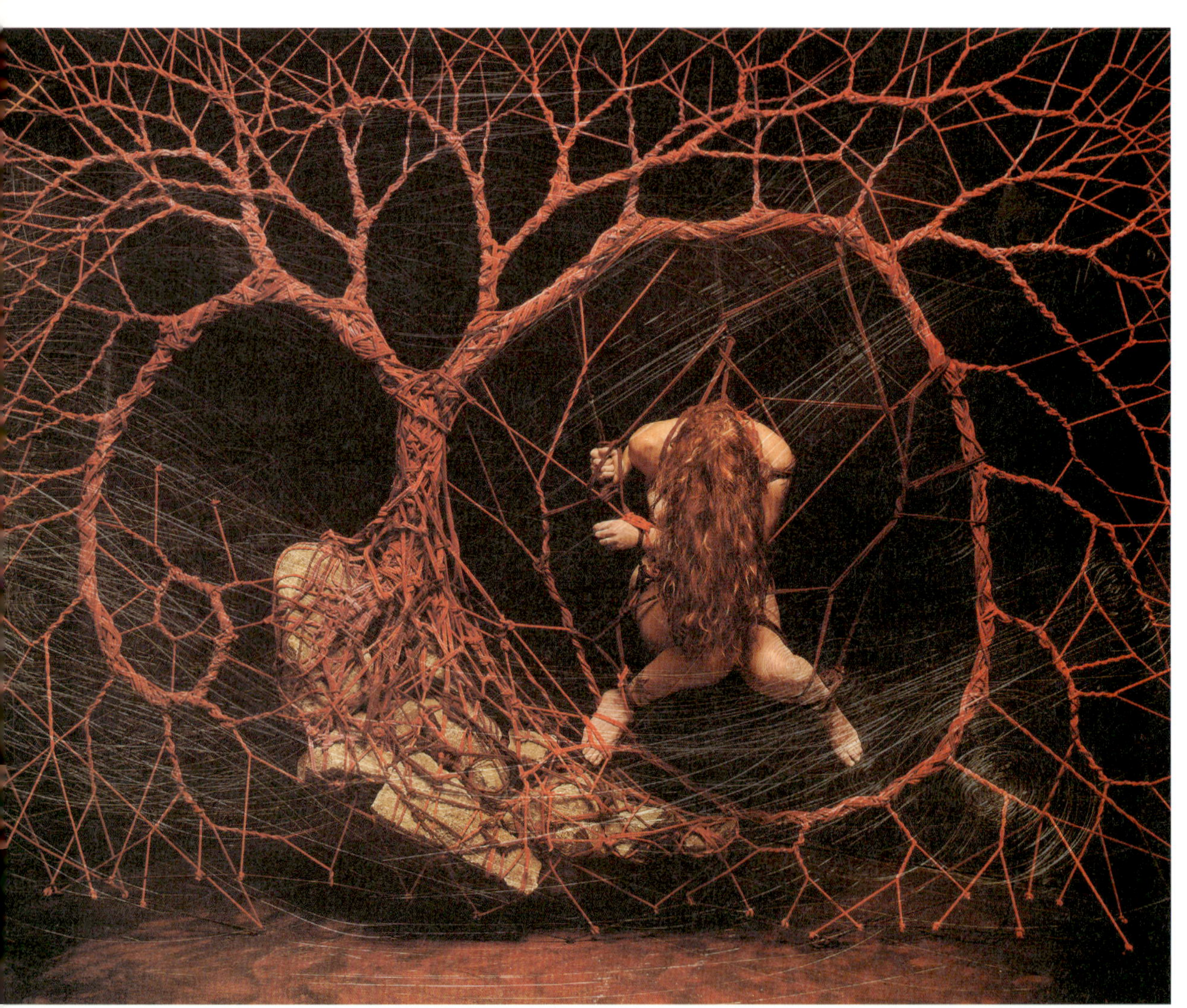

The Red Tree 9（Rachael）　赤い木 9（レイチェル）
さまざまな素材、デジタル・プリント / 2011

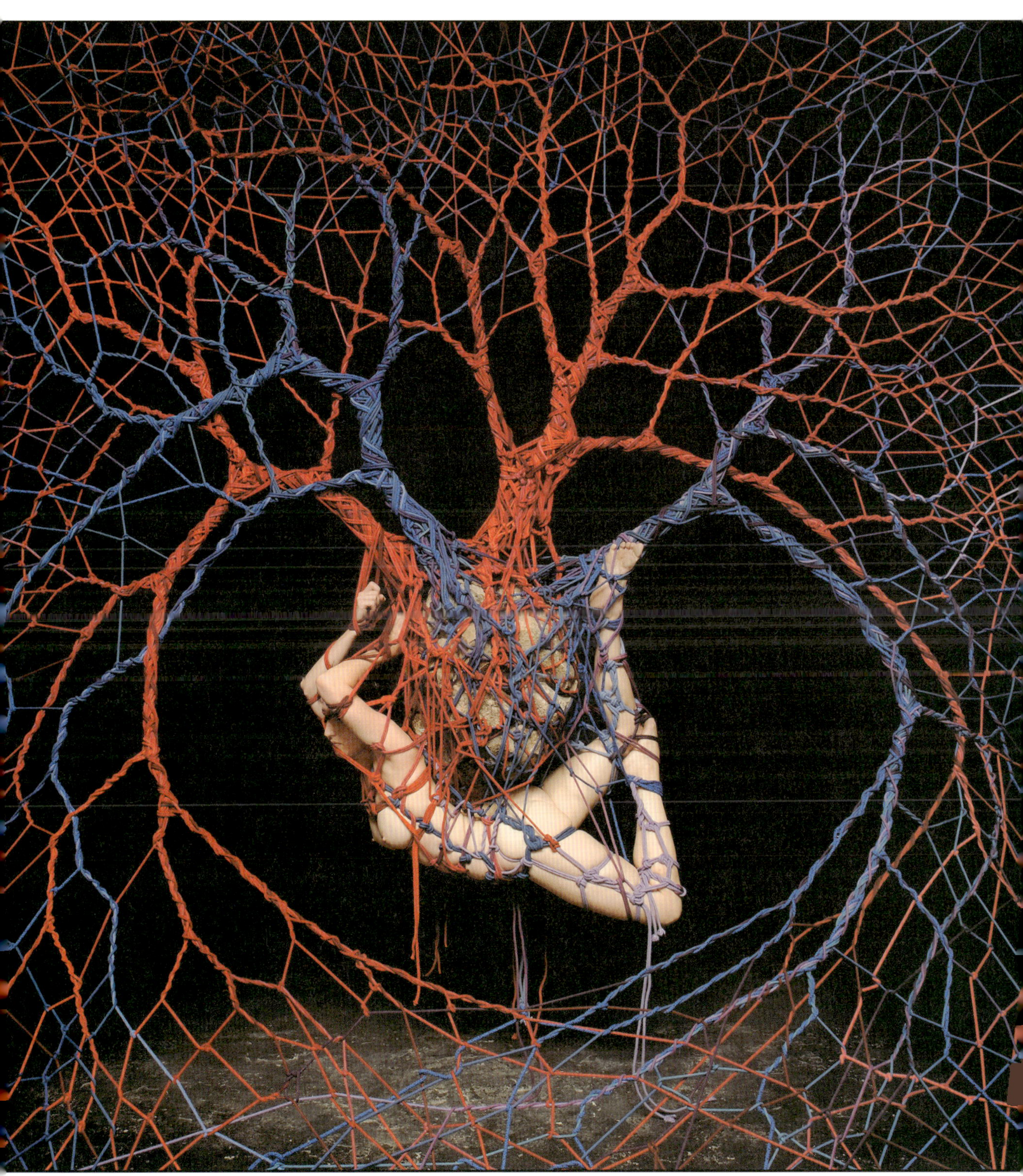

Blood Consciousness 6 (Pieta)　血の意識 6（ピエタ）
さまざまな素材、デジタル・プリント / 2013

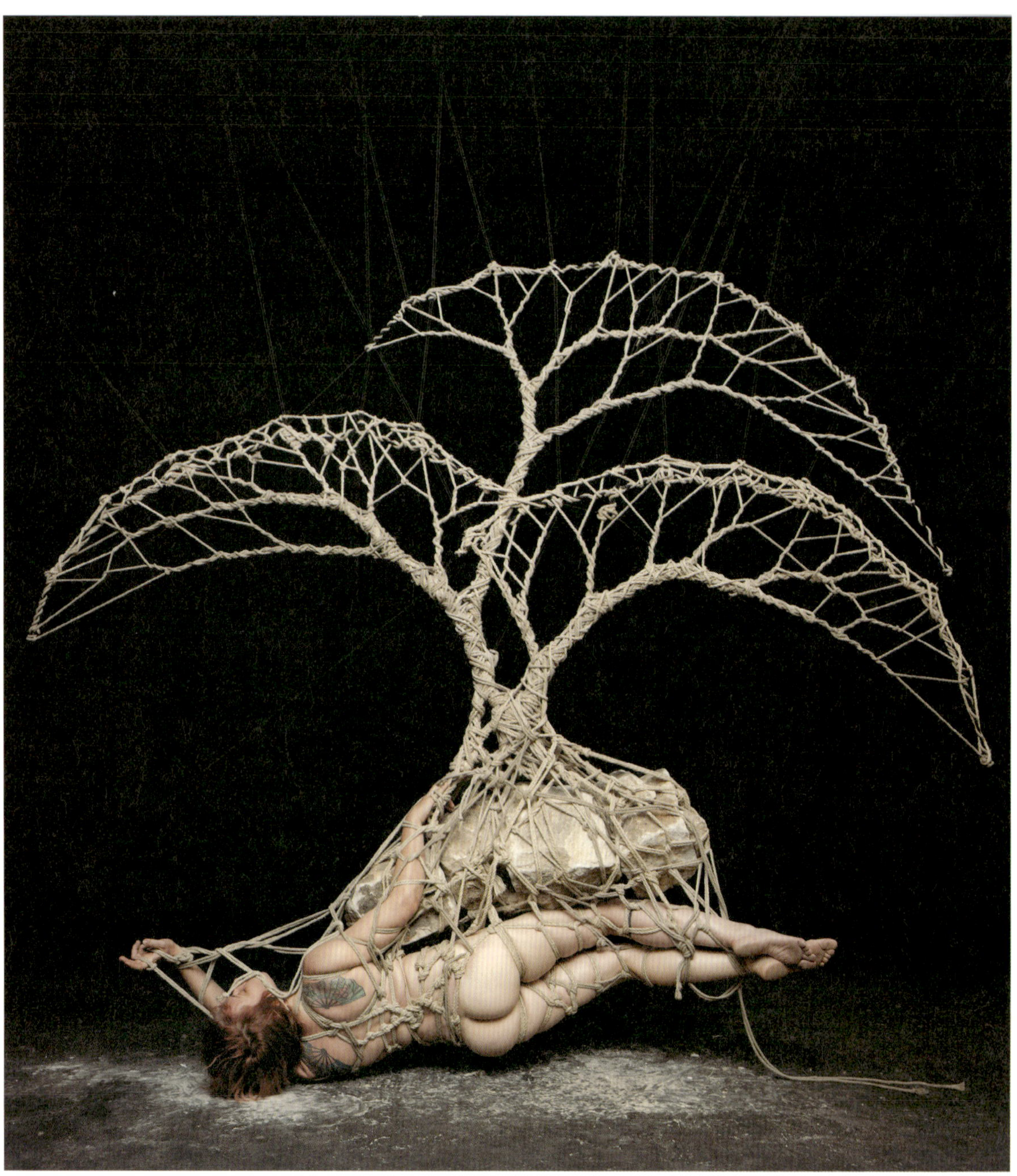

Chthonic 2（Vix）地中 2（ヴィクス）
さまざまな素材、デジタル・プリント / 2015

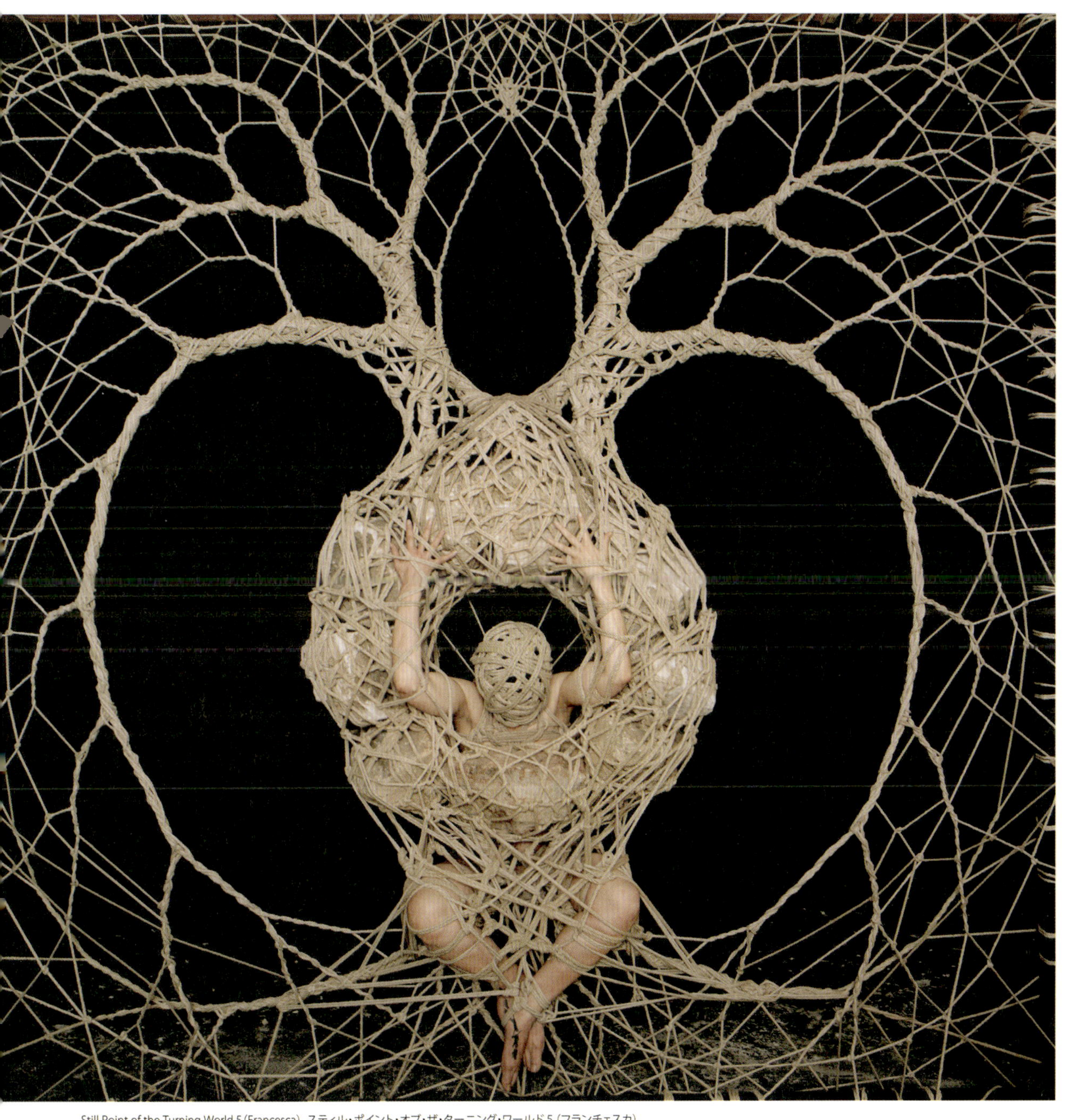

Still Point of the Turning World 5 (Francesca)　スティル・ポイント・オブ・ザ・ターニング・ワールド 5 (フランチェスカ)
さまざまな素材、デジタル・プリント / 2014

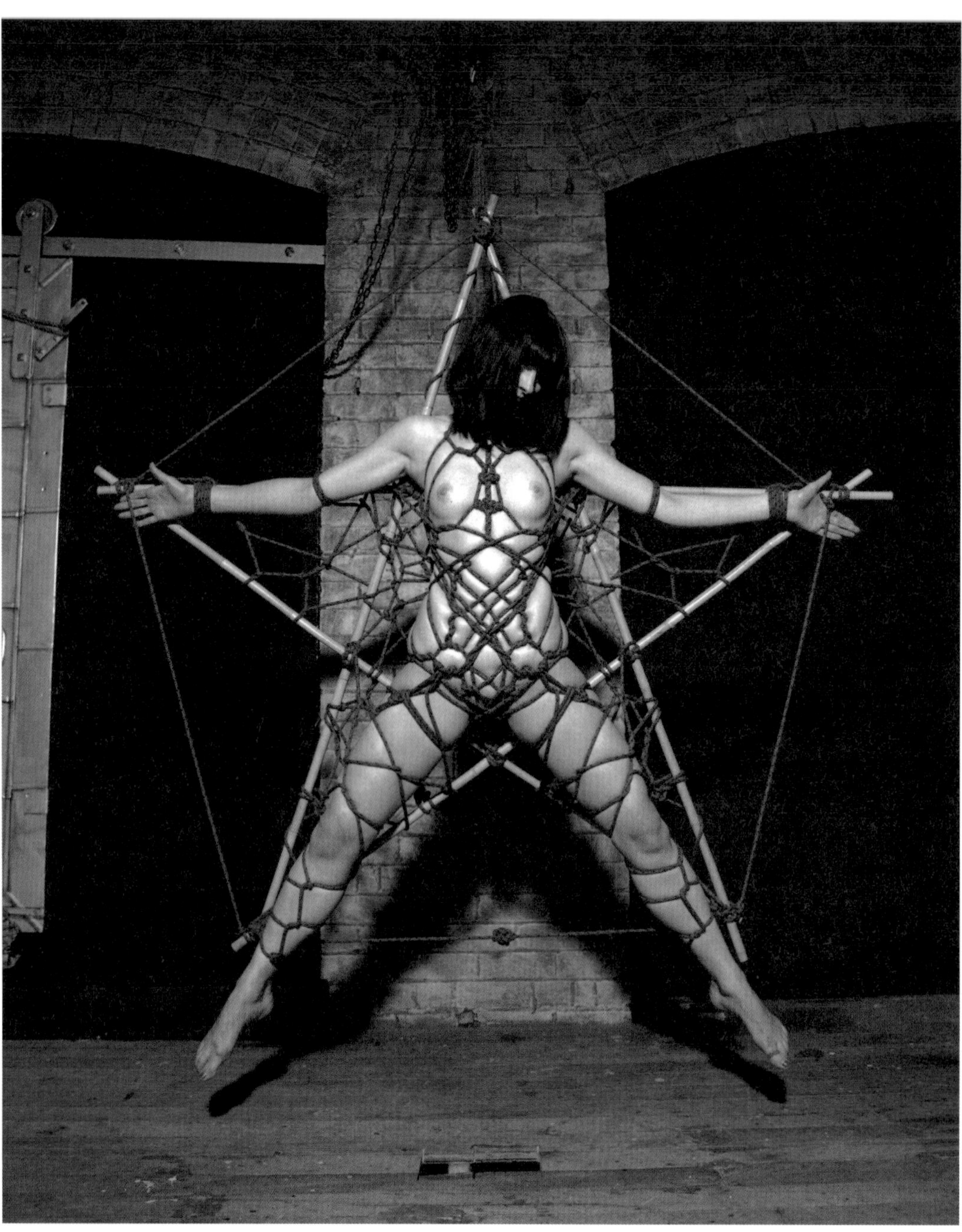

Leap of Faith 9（Kate）　盲信 9（ケイト）
さまざまな素材、デジタル・プリント / 2005

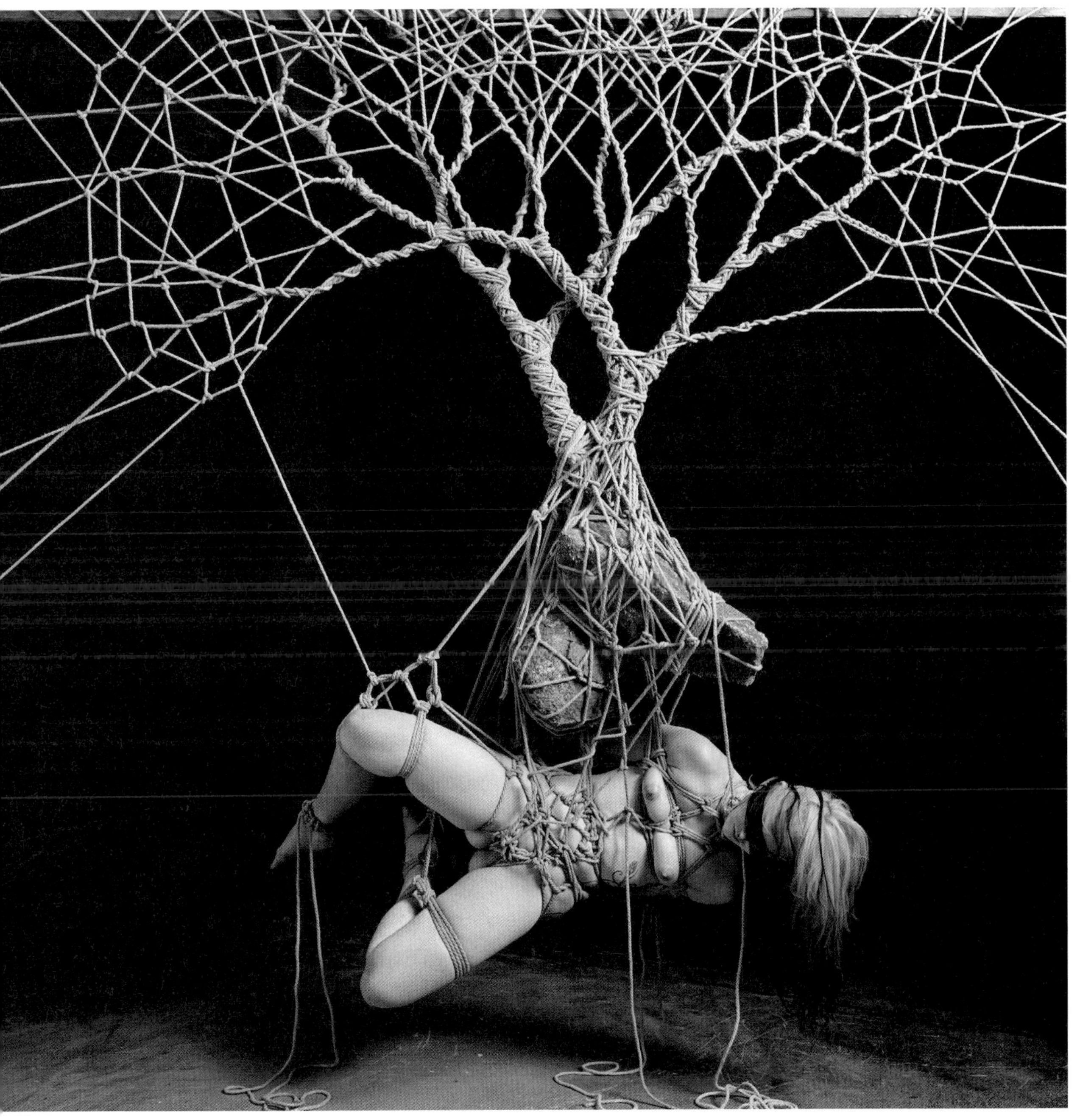

The Heart Tree 4 (Sam) ハート・ツリー 4 (サム)
さまざまな素材、デジタル・プリント / 2011

Katarzyna Widmańska

カタジーナ・ウィドマンスカ（ポーランド Poland）

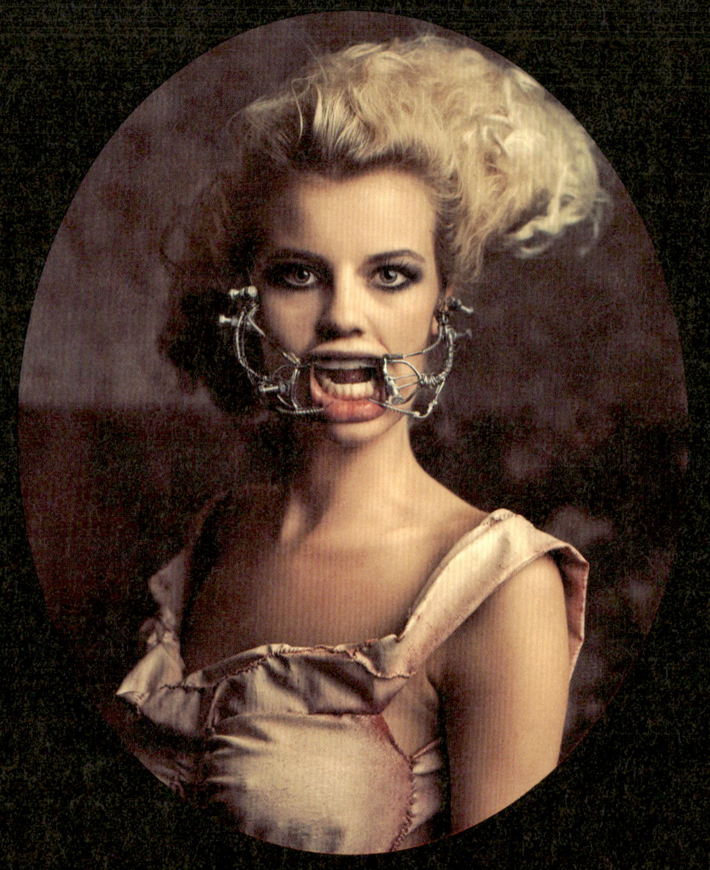

ポーランド、クラクフ生まれの写真家。レッドラム・イメージ・カンパニーで映画の監督、撮影もこなす。主に女性を被写体に、ポートレートからファッション、ビューティー、さらにはテーマ性の高いアートまで幅広いジャンルの写真を手掛ける。様式美を感じさせる小道具、光と影のコントラストを用い、さまざまなテーマやモチーフを表現し、独特の雰囲気を醸し出す。クラクフ教育大学芸術学部卒業。ポーランド文化の発展と推進に貢献した若い芸術家に授与されるアルス・クエレンディ賞を受賞。長年、ワルシャワ写真学校、クラクフ映画学校で写真を教えている。作品は国内外の数多くの出版物に掲載され、国内外の一流のギャラリー、美術館で展示されている。

Katarzyna Widmanska, born in Krakow, Poland. Fine art, fashion, portrait and beauty photographer. Filmmaker and cinematographer in Redrum Image company. Main art's subject are women - both in traditional portrait and fashion photography, as well as series of thematic pictures. In these cycles, depicting various themes and motifs, the artist creates an atmosphere with stylized props and a game of light. Graduated artistic education in fine arts at the Art Institute of the Pedagogical University in Cracow. Winner of the Ars Quaerendi Prize for outstanding activities for the development and promotion of polish culture. Long-term lecturer of photography (Warsaw School of Photography, Krakow Film School). Numerous publications in the national and foreign press. Her work has been presented in many prestigious galleries and museums in the country and abroad.

www.widmanska.com

↑ "Necromantic" Series 「黒魔術」シリーズ（部分）
デジタル写真 / 2011

→ "Brothell" Series 「売春宿」シリーズ
デジタル写真 / 20115

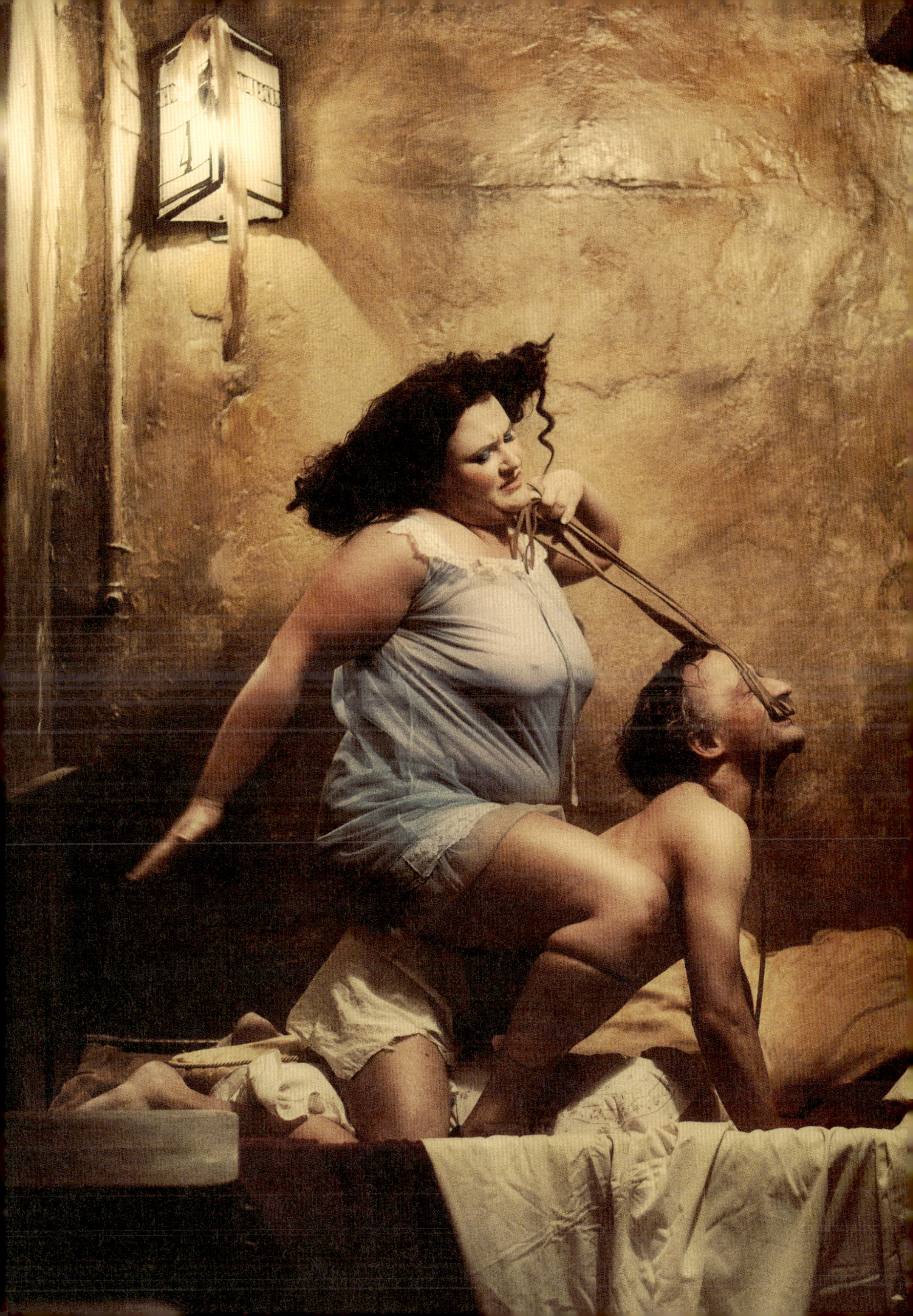

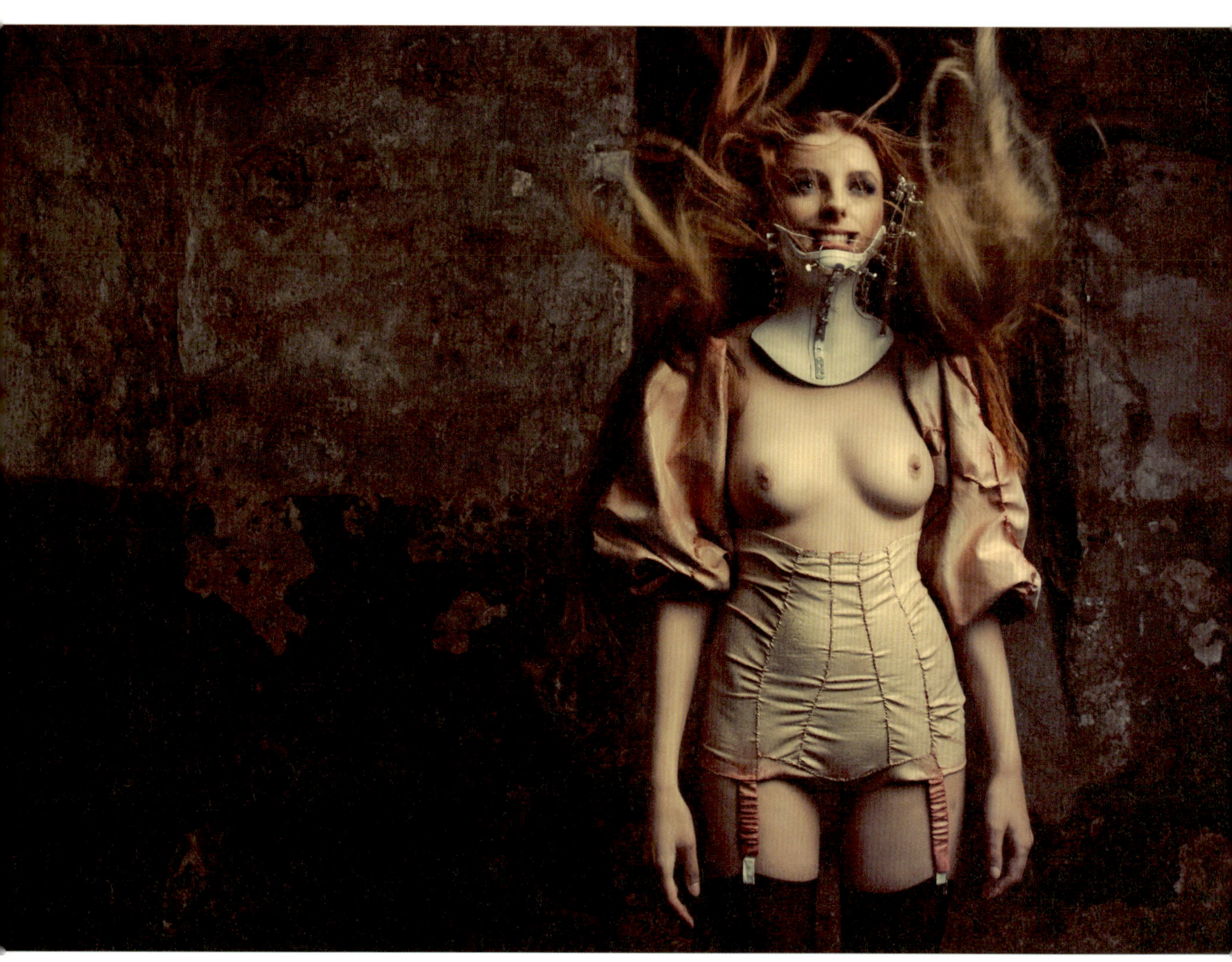

"Necromantic" Series 「黒魔術」シリーズ
デジタル写真 / 2011

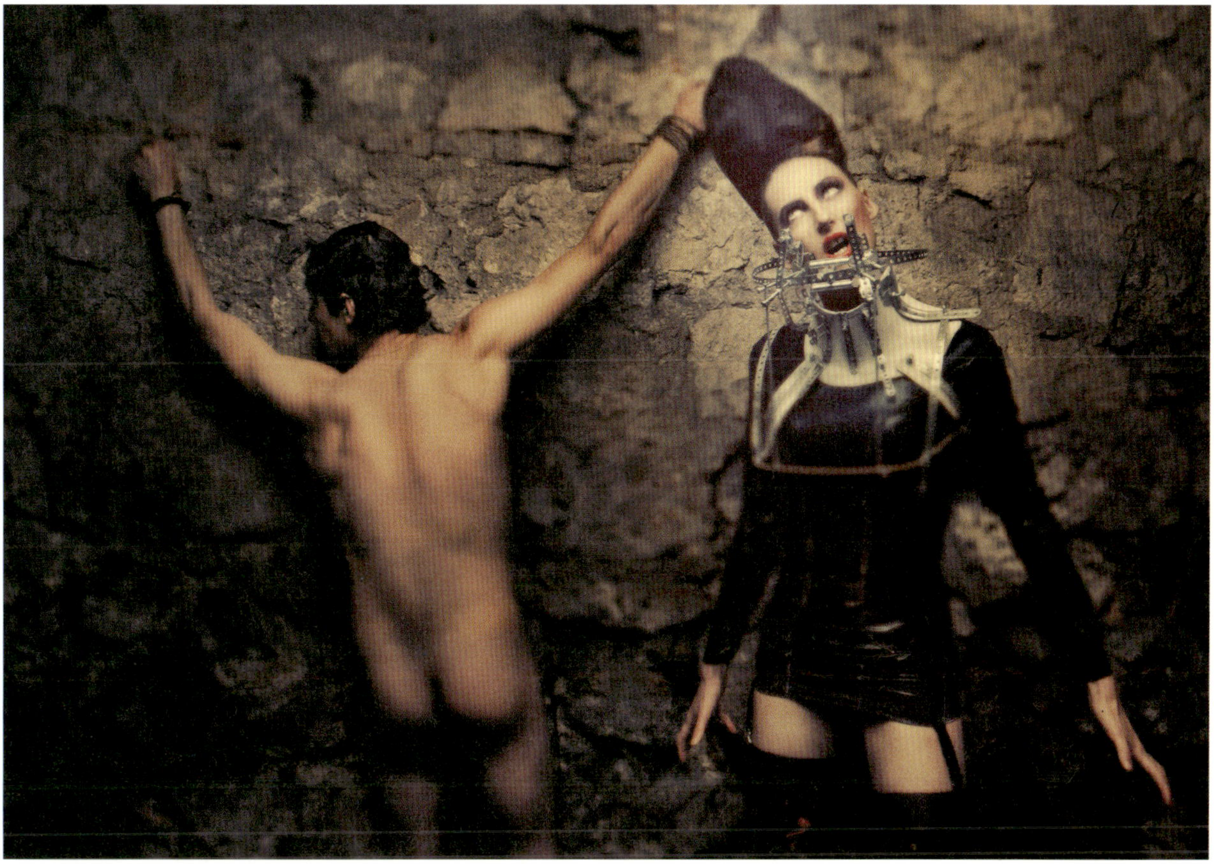

↑ "Necromantic" Series 「黒魔術」シリーズ
デジタル写真 / 2011

→ "Necromantic" Series 「黒魔術」シリーズ
デジタル写真 / 2011

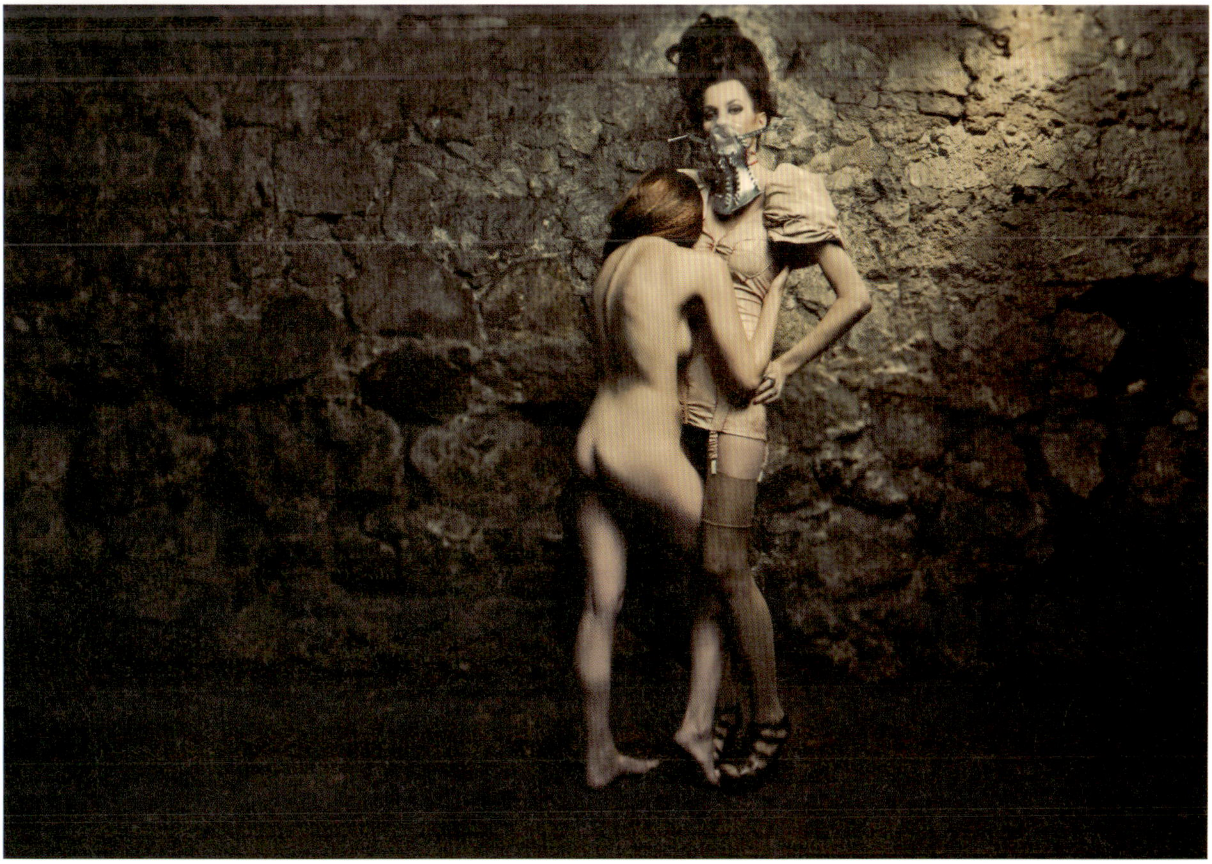

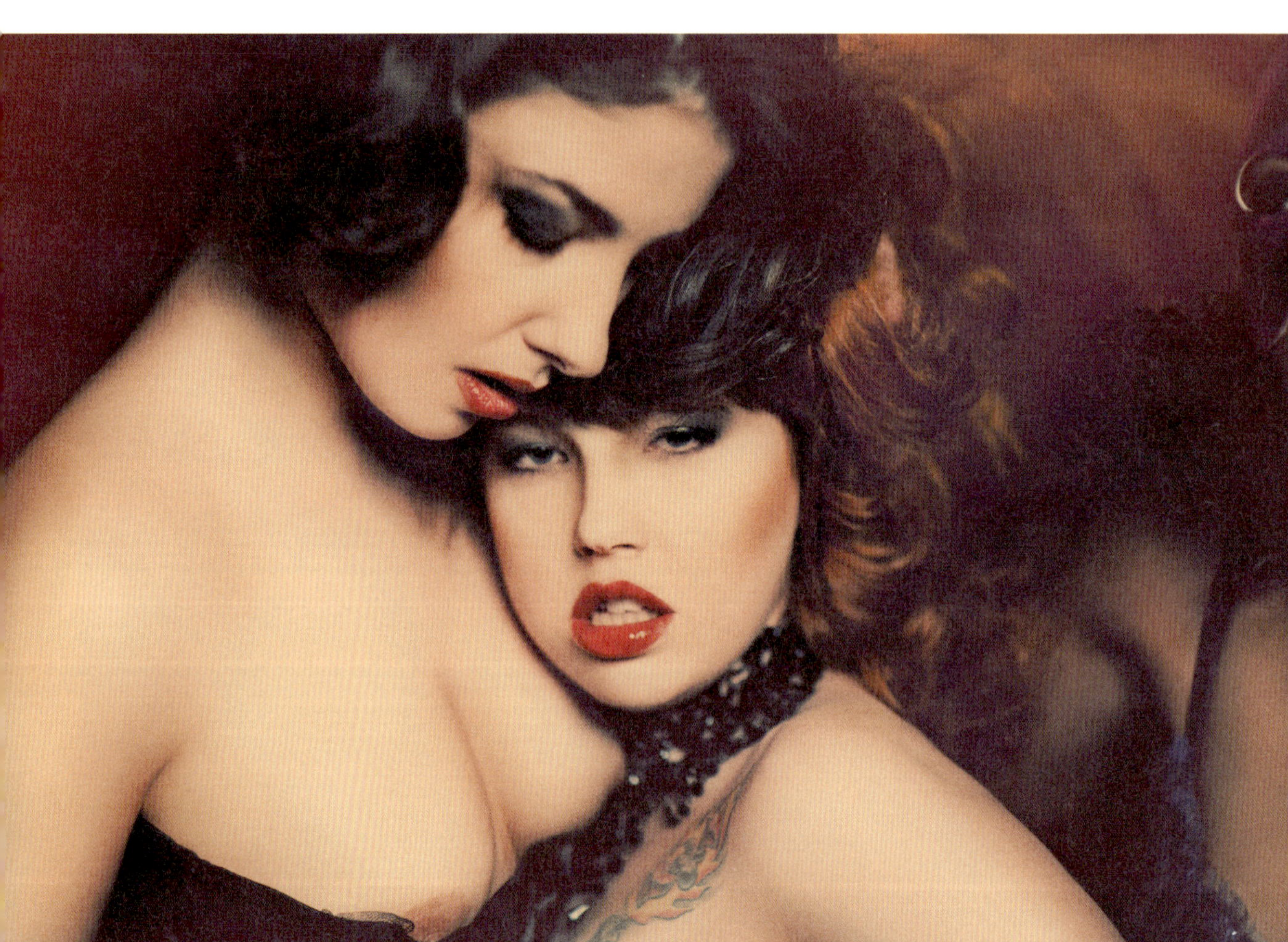

"Moulin Rouge" Series 「ムーラン・ルージュ」シリーズ
デジタル写真 / 2010

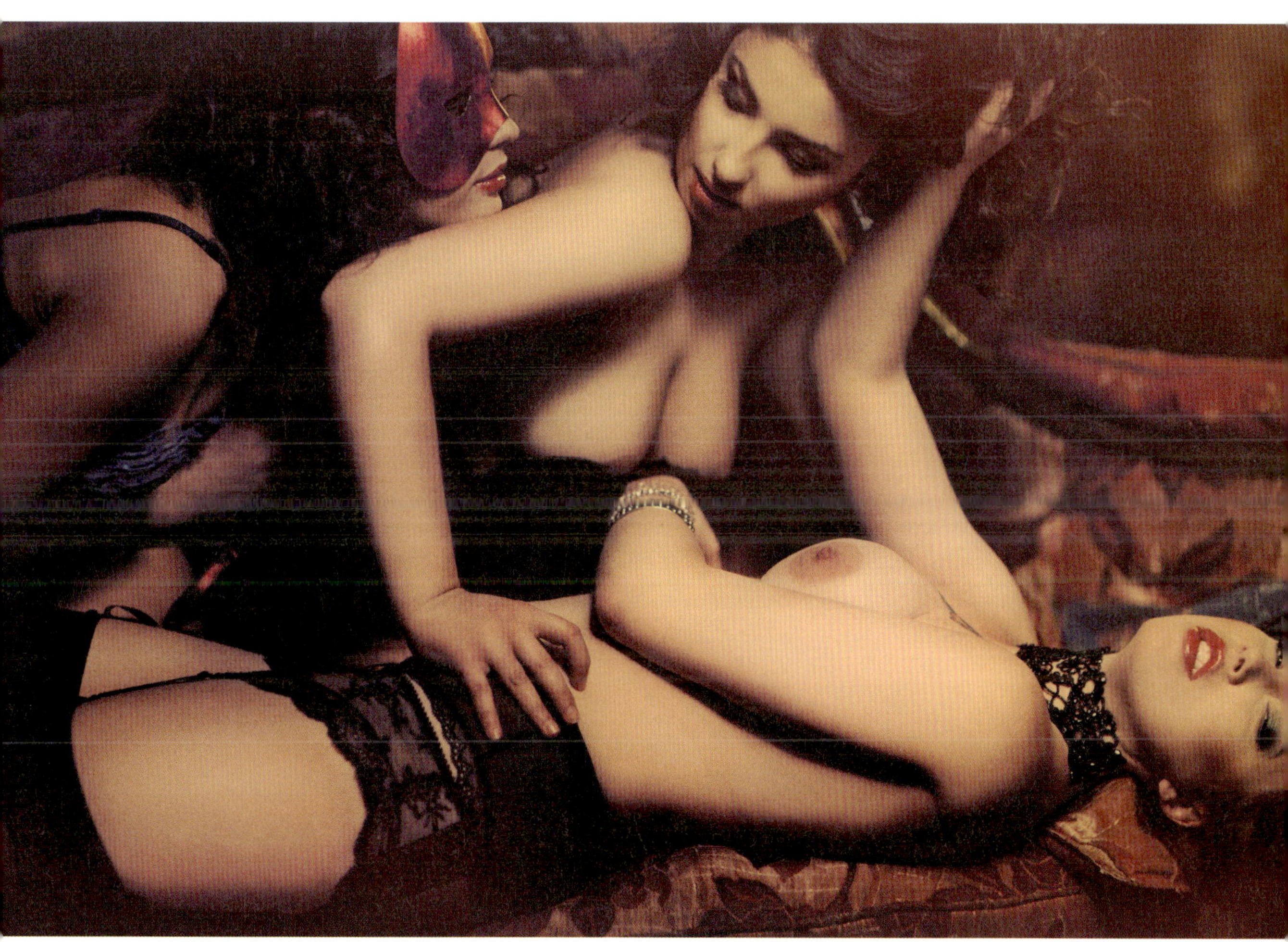

"Moulin Rouge" Series 「ムーラン・ルージュ」シリーズ
デジタル写真 / 2011

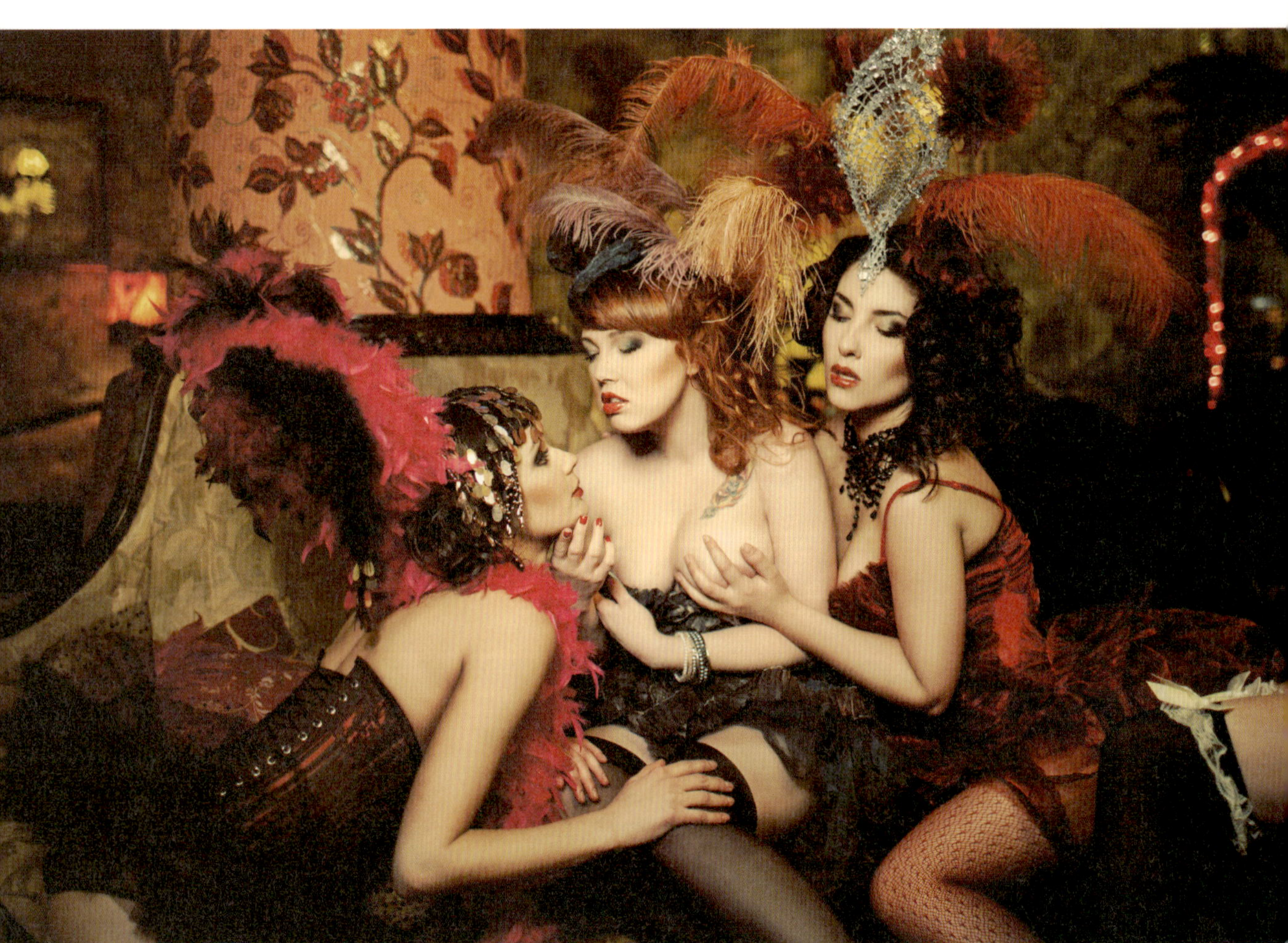

"Moulin Rouge" Series 「ムーラン・ルージュ」シリーズ
デジタル写真 / 2011

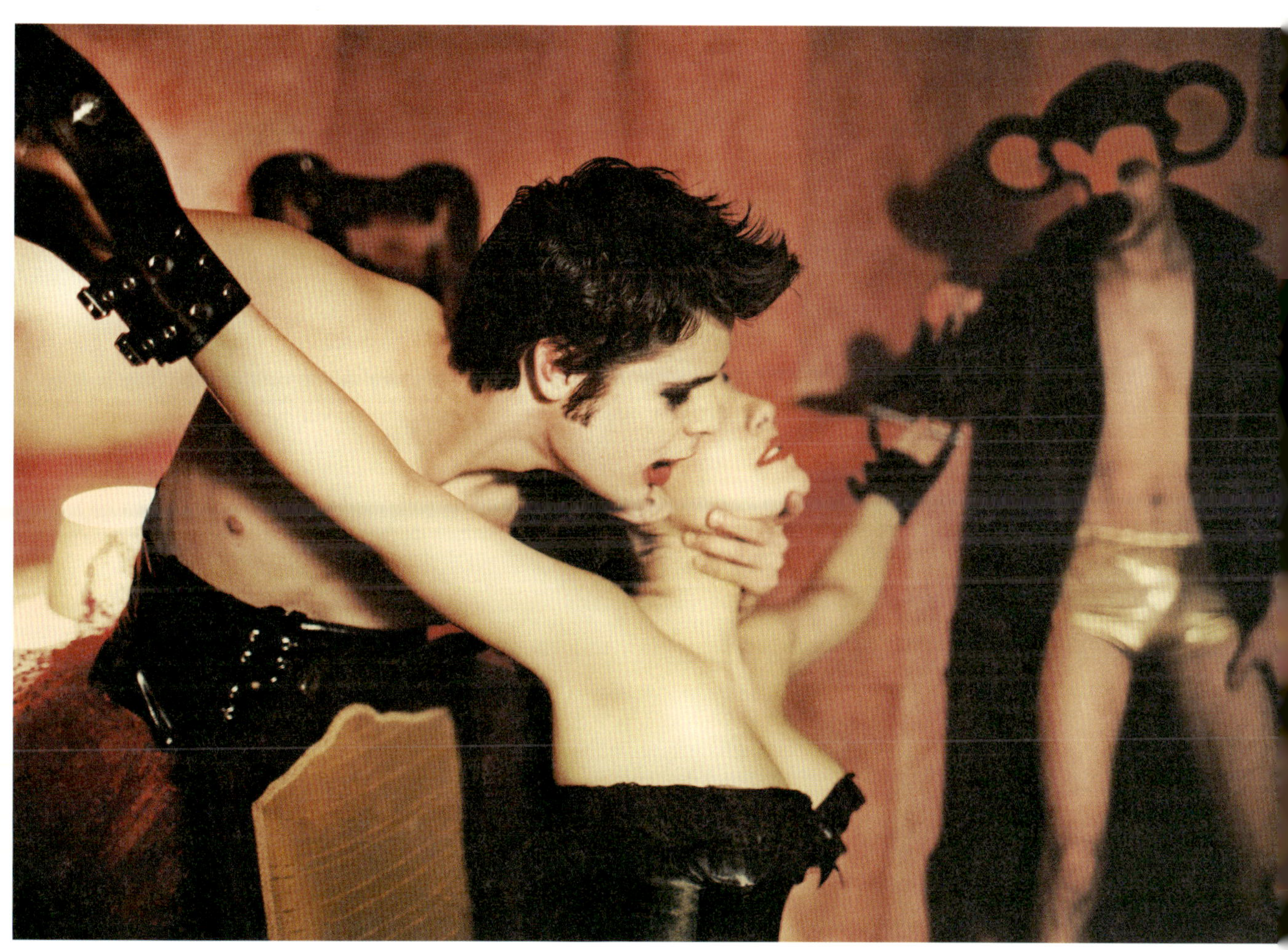

"Entertain Me" Series 「私を慰めて」シリーズ
デジタル写真 / 2010

Schilte & Portielje

シルテ＆ポーティーリャ（オランダ Netherlands）

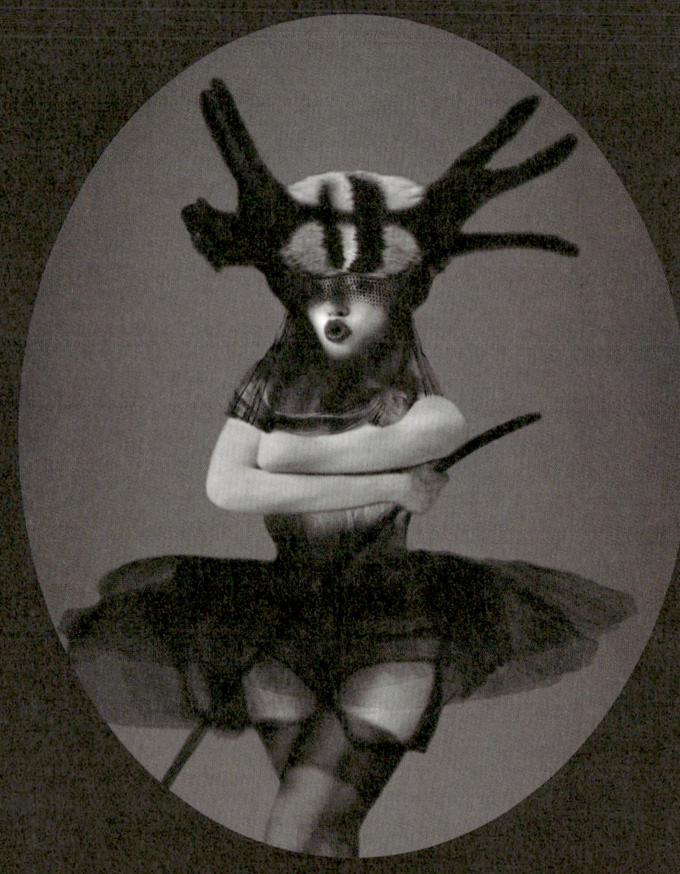

オランダ、ロッテルダムを拠点に活動するアーティスト・デュオ。人間をデフォルメしたユニークな写真で知られる。その詩的で幻想的な人物の姿は、見る人を驚きと奇跡の世界に引き込む。彼らの作品はモデルの顔が見えないのが特徴だ。黒と白のコントラストが際立つ背景で不自然なポーズをとるモデルからはエロティシズムが漂い、静かなる欲望の詩を奏でているようだ。モノクロ写真を使いスタイルやデザインは古典的だが、最先端のデジタル・コラージュ技術を用いてトレードマークのデフォルメされた人物をつくり出している。いたって現代的だ。現在、世界中で展覧会を開催し、作品は多くの個人や団体が収蔵してる。

The couple, who live and work in Rotterdam, are primarily known for their photography of series of unusual and very recognizable figurines. They display an intricate way of playing with and relating to each other: fantastic poetic, dreamlike figures who abduct the spectator into the artists world of wonders and miracles. During recent years, the artists perfected their mise en scene. Subtle eroticism, demanding poses or the quiet poetry of desire are the elements used in this dark world rich in contrast. The subjects of Schilte & Portielje are extremely timely. Their forms and design with historical patterns - like the consistent use of black-and-white photography reference analog role models. But the photographers use a well developed digital collage technique to achieve their trademark figurine, very much anchored in the present. Their work has been featured in numerous exhibitions worldwide and has been included in numerous international private and corporate collections.

schilteportielje.com 　※All the works are courtesy Kahmann Gallery Amsterdam.

↑No title 09/A18 無題（部分）
デジタル・アートワーク、プレキシガラスを使ったラムダプリント／
H195×W120cm／2009

→No title 11/A3 無題（部分）
デジタル・アートワーク、プレキシガラスを使ったラムダプリント／
H195×W120cm／2011

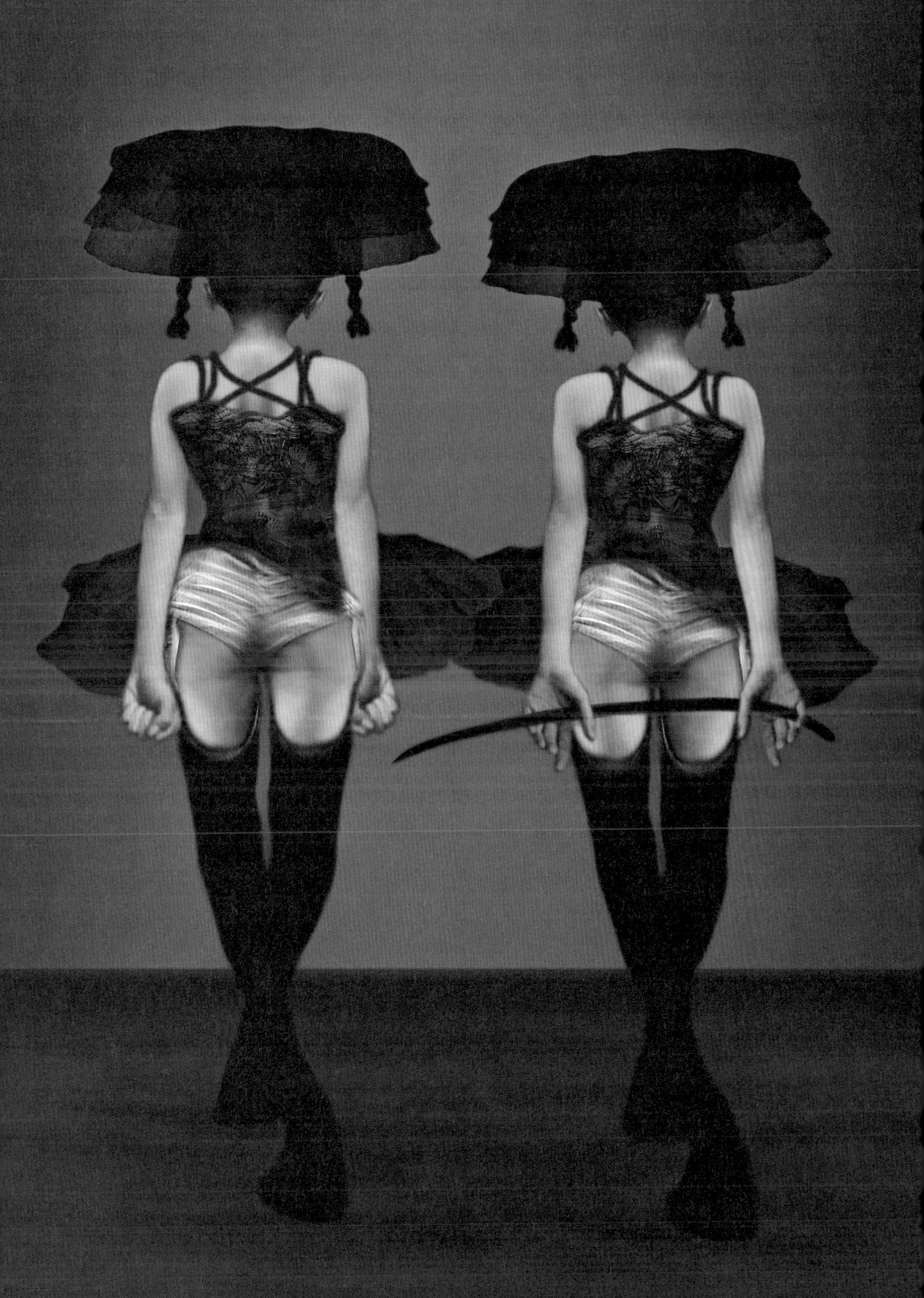

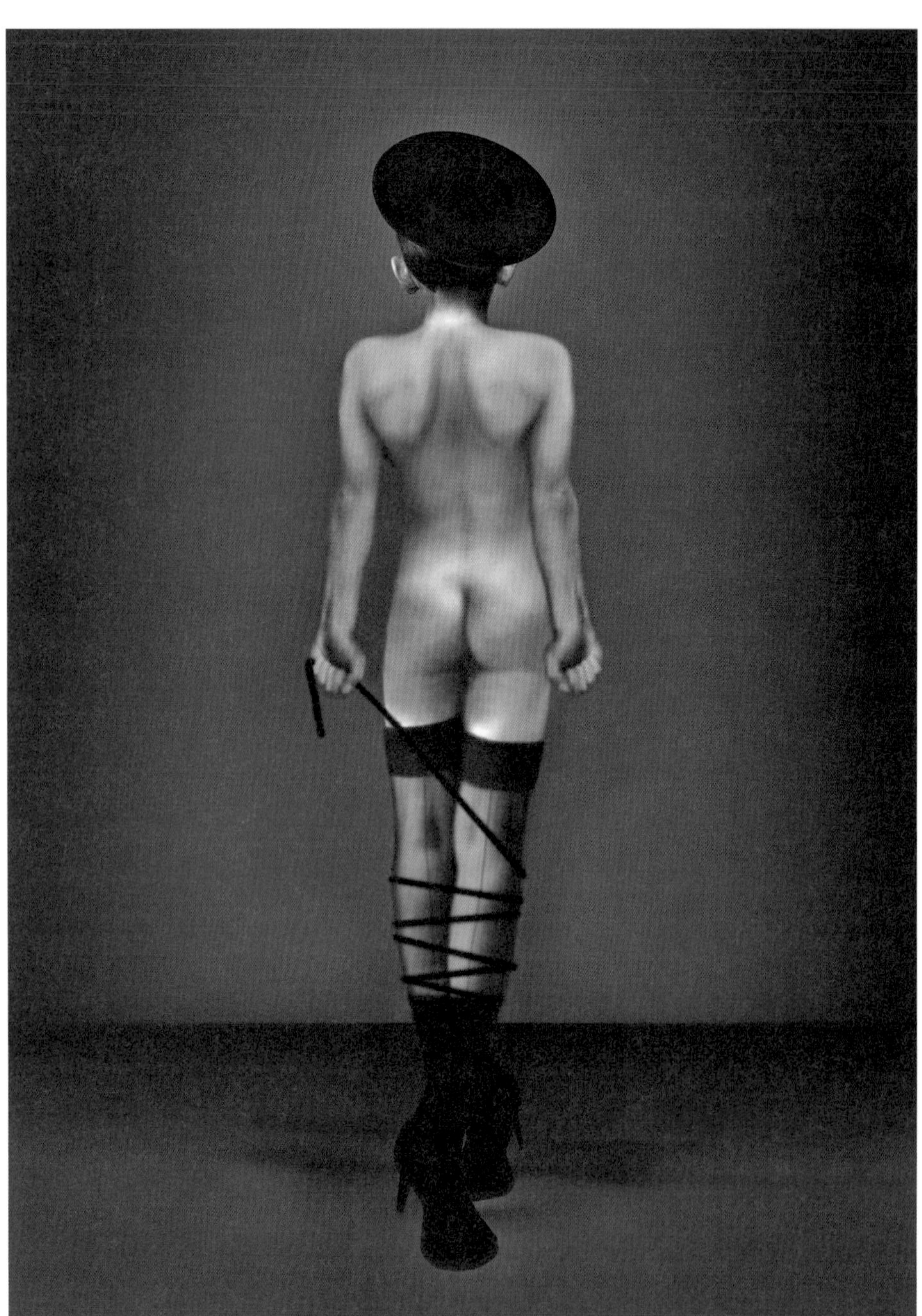

No title 17/A3 無題
デジタル・アートワーク、プレキシガラスを使ったラムダプリント / H195×W120cm / 2017

No title 10/A6 無題
デジタル・アートワーク、プレキシガラスを使ったラムダプリント / H195×W120cm / 2006

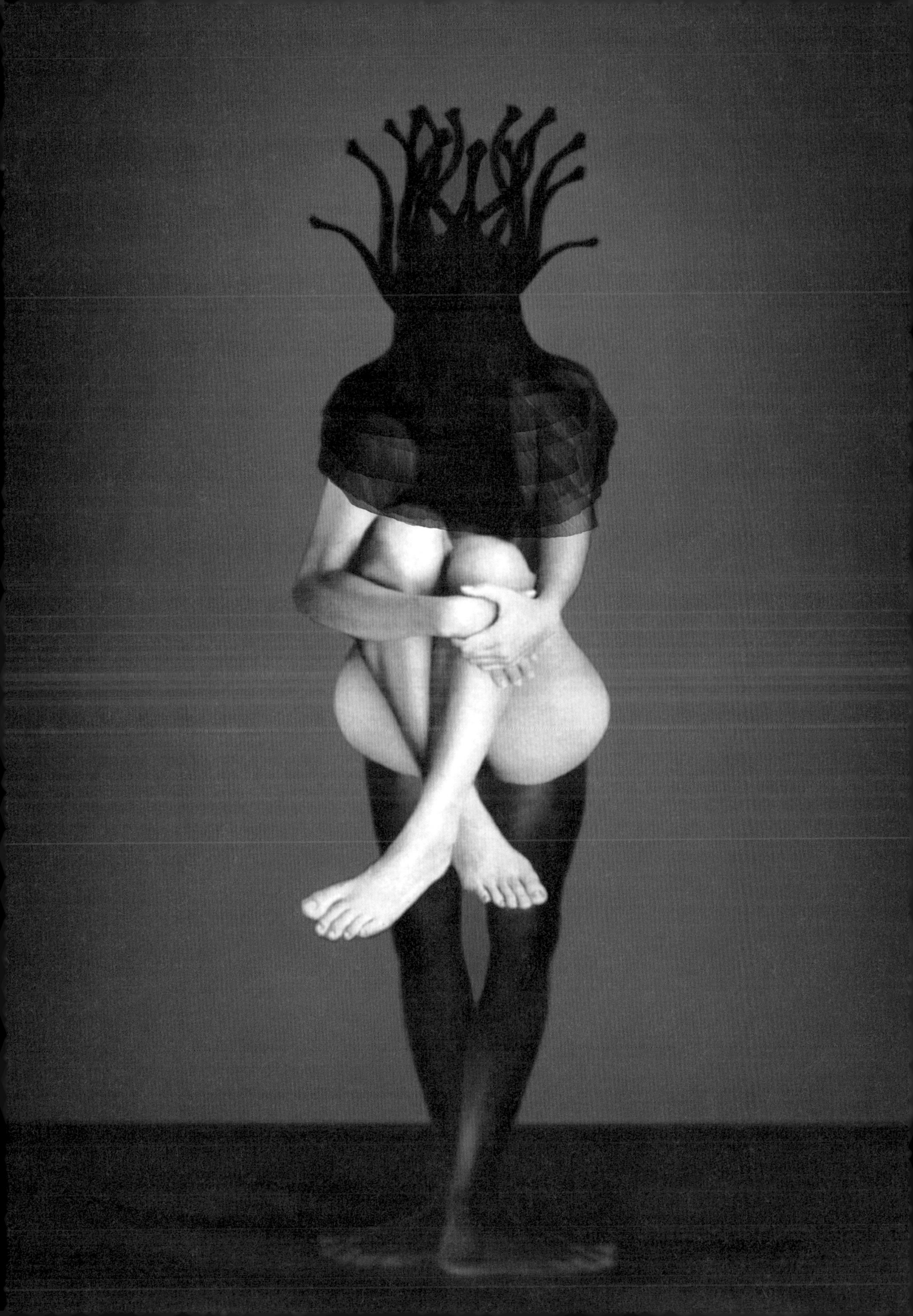

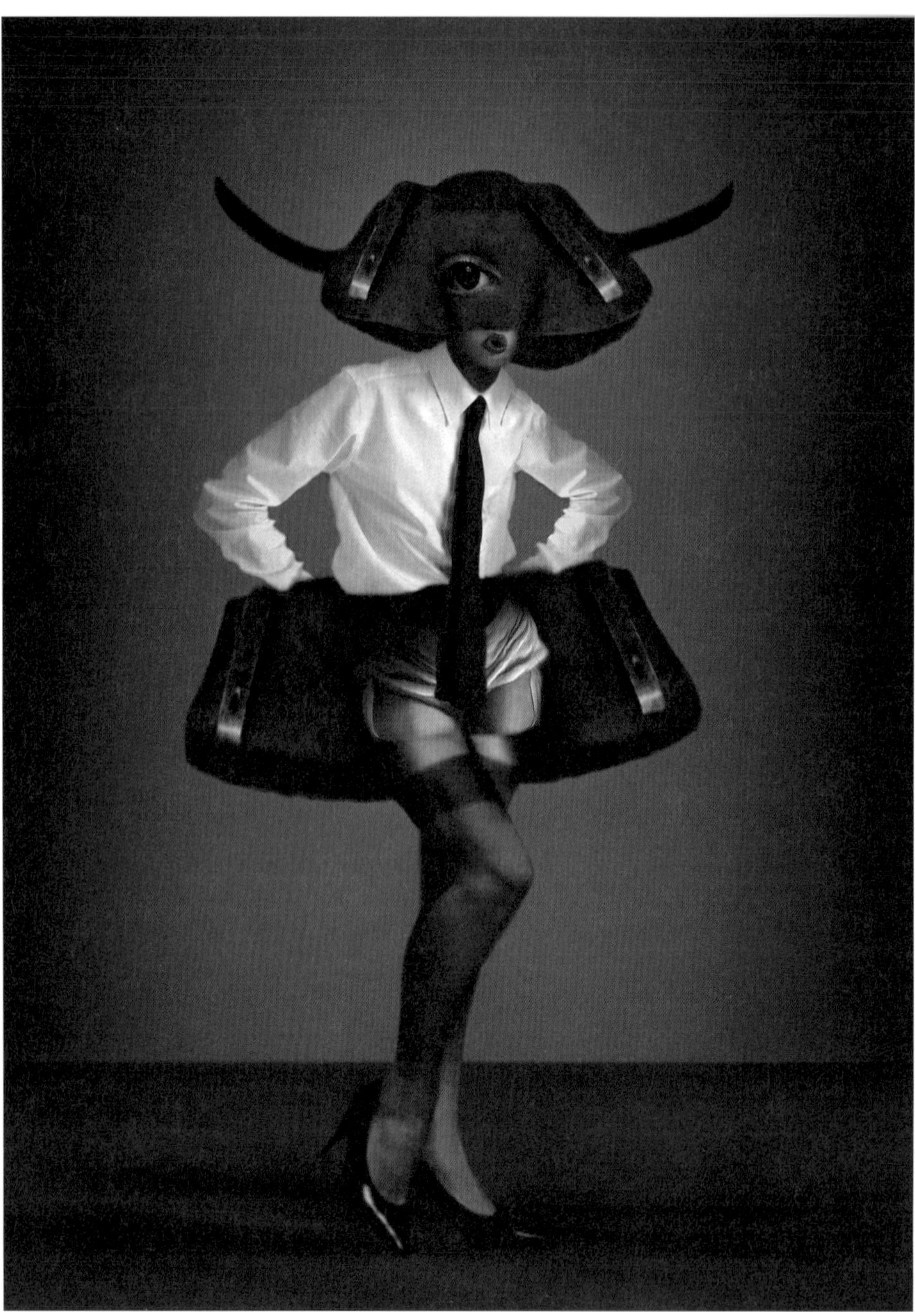

No title 12/A15 無題
デジタル・アートワーク、プレキシガラスを使ったラムダプリント / H195×W120cm / 2015

No title 10/A17 無題
デジタル・アートワーク、プレキシガラスを使ったラムダプリント / H195×W120cm / 2010

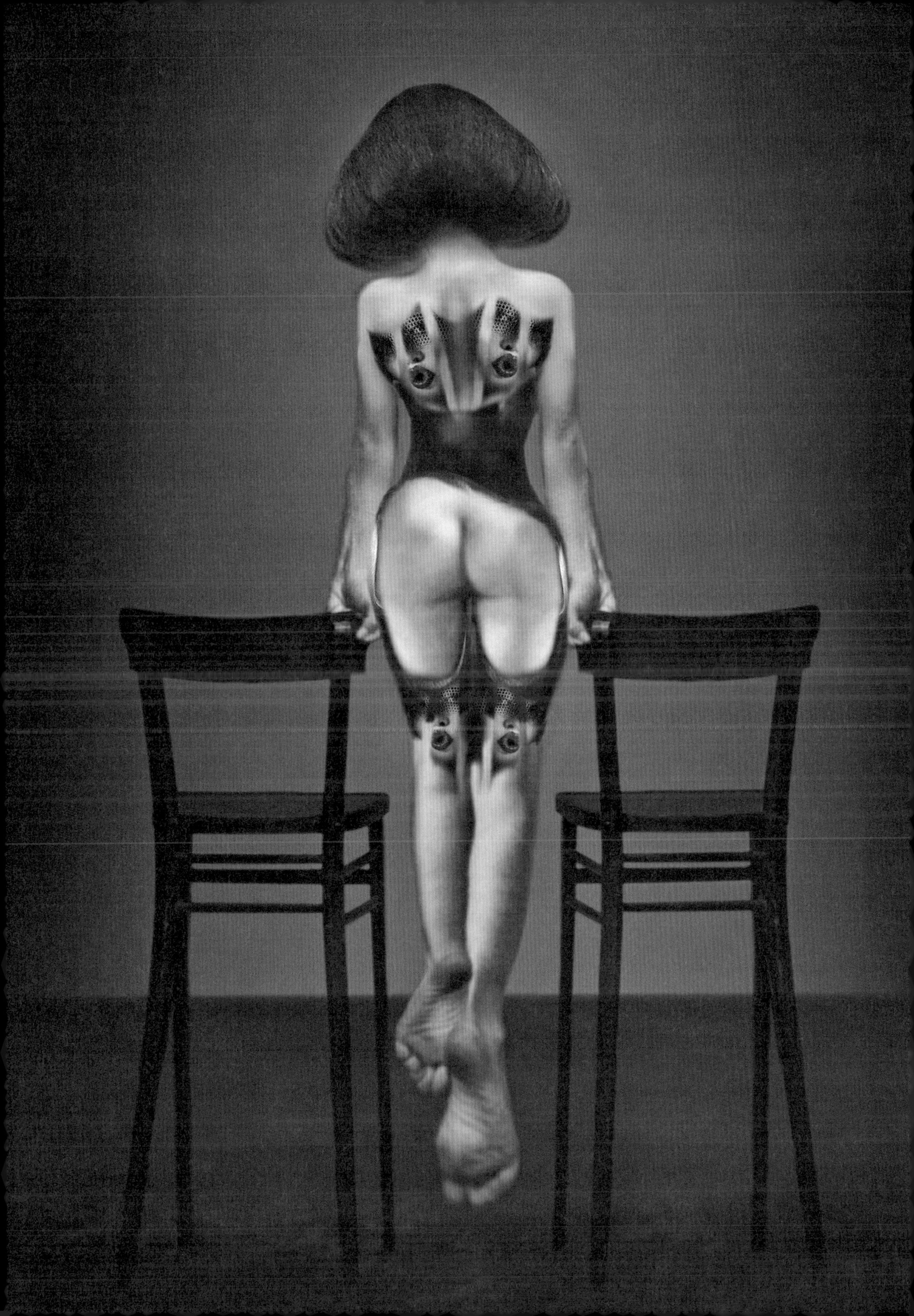

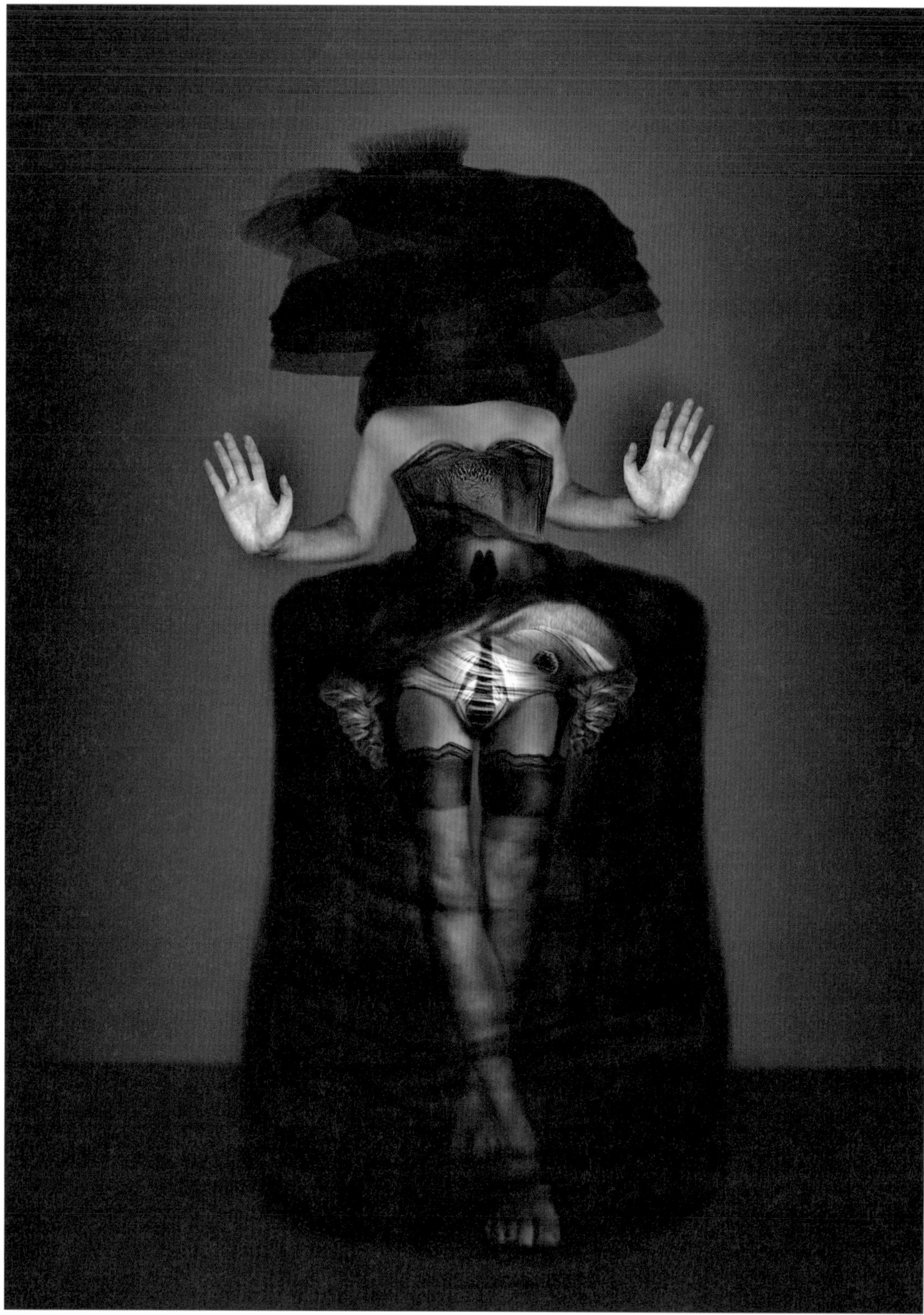

No title 09/A3 無題
デジタル・アートワーク、プレキシガラスを使ったラムダプリント / H195×W120cm / 2009

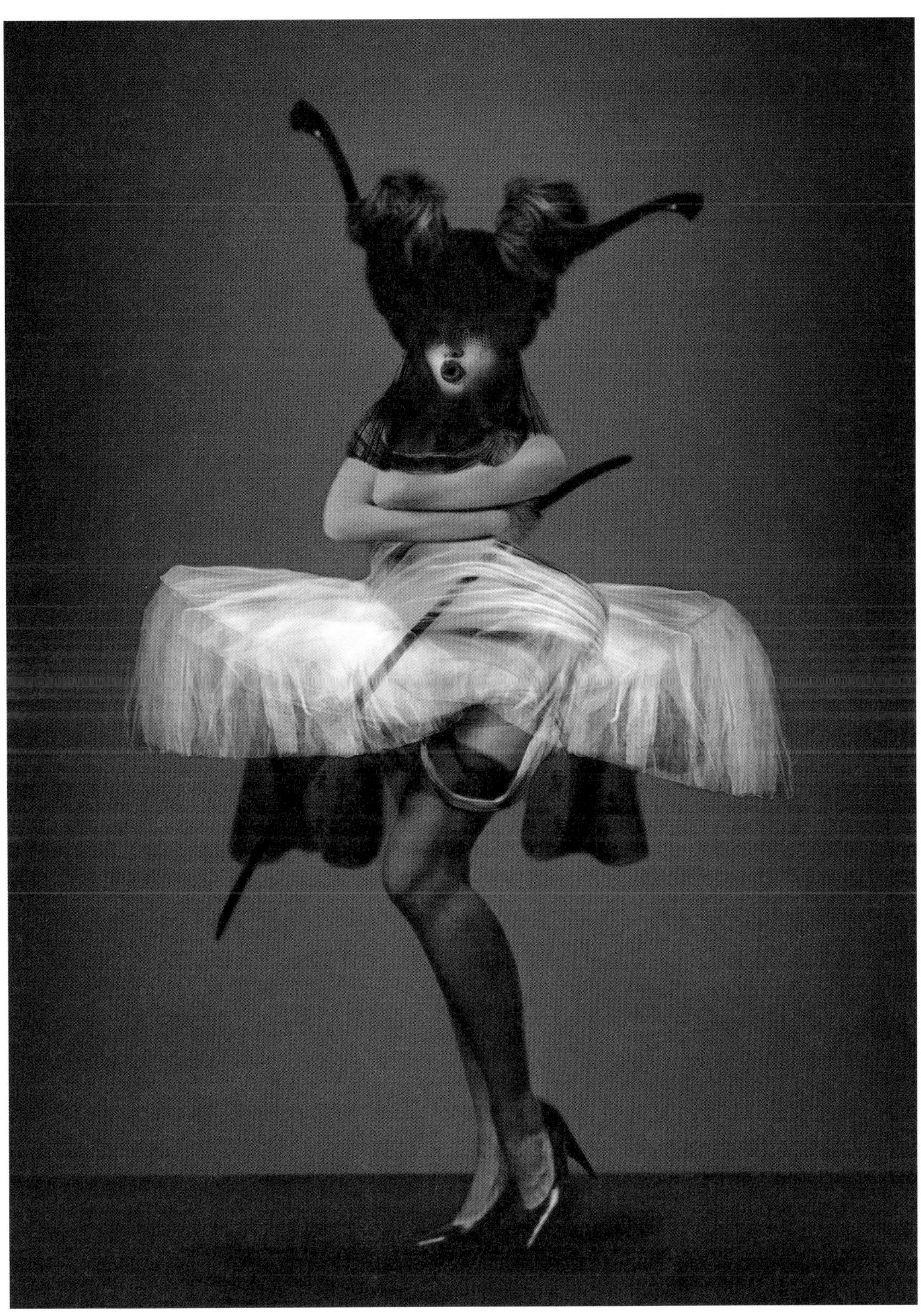

No title 09/B10 無題
デジタル・アートワーク、プレキシガラスを使ったラムダプリント / H195×W120cm / 2009

31

Federico Bebber

フェデリコ・ベーベル（イタリア Italy）

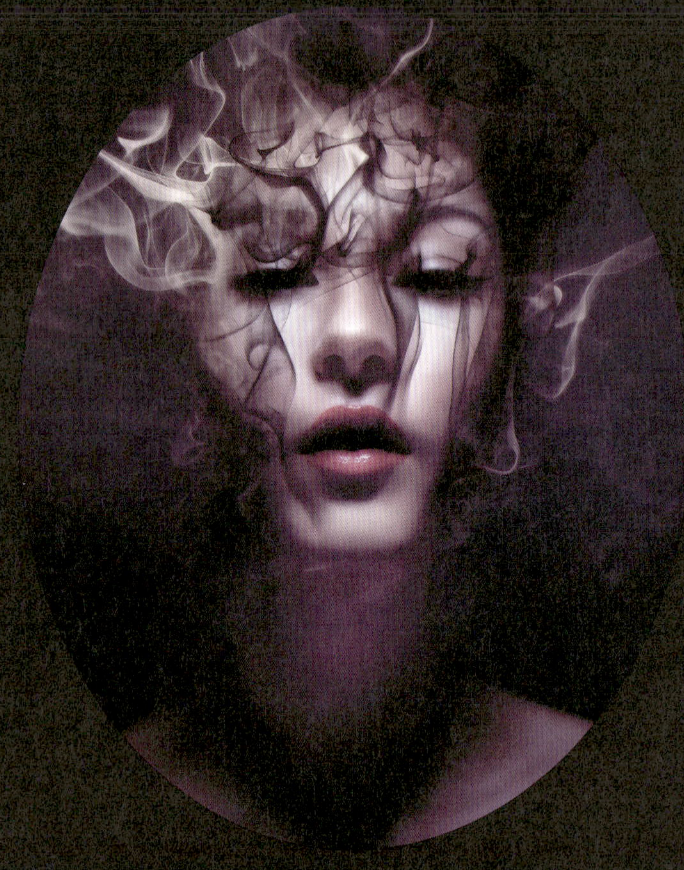

1974年、イタリア、ウーディネ生まれ。1988年から写真関連のデジタル技術を用い、デジタル・アートの制作を開始する。創作活動は夜に行い、作品の制作には多大な時間を要する。モチーフである女性のポートレート写真を加工し、幻想的でシュールな夢の世界を創り出す。写真は原形をとどめず、見る者に現実の意義を問いかける。

Federico Bebber was born in 1974 in Udine, Italy. Since 1998 he deals with digital art. He uses digital tools based on photography. His creative process usually takes place slowly and at night. Federico Bebber's subjects undergo a fantastical metamorphosis, as he warps portraits into a dreamlike, surreal environment. Starting with a photograph as a base, Federico digitally twists and distorts the image until it is unrecognizable, and the final result questions reality.

www.eiko.biz

↑You Hate Yourself あなたは自分自身を憎んでる（部分）
デジタル編集写真、紙 / H100×W70cm / 2013

→Sleeping Beauties (Stephen King's book cover) 眠れる美女たち（ステファン・キングによる小説の表紙）
デジタル編集写真、紙 / H100×W70cm / 2013

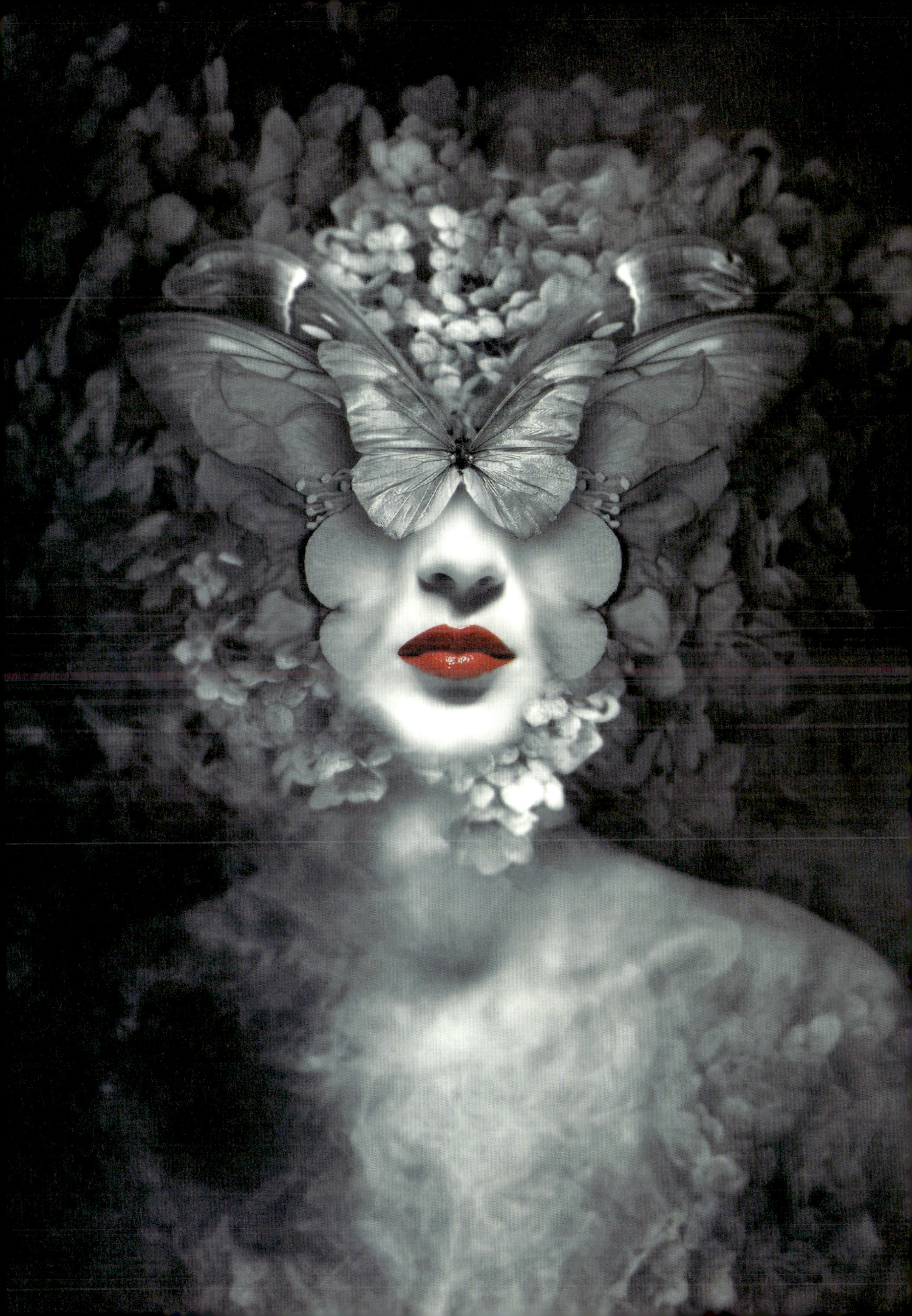

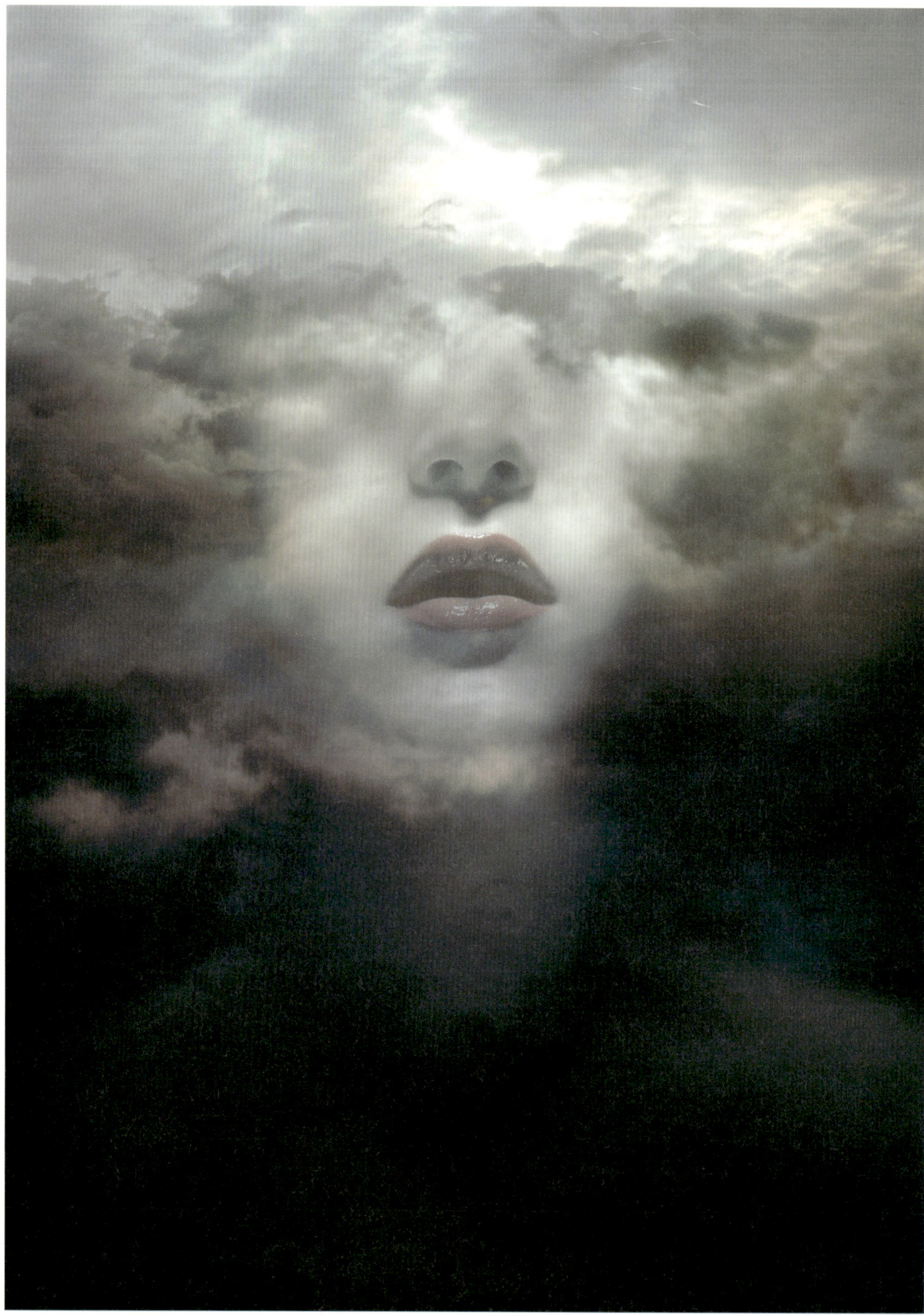

360 Seconds After Dawn 夜明け後の360秒
デジタル編集写真、紙 ／ H100×W70cm / 2014

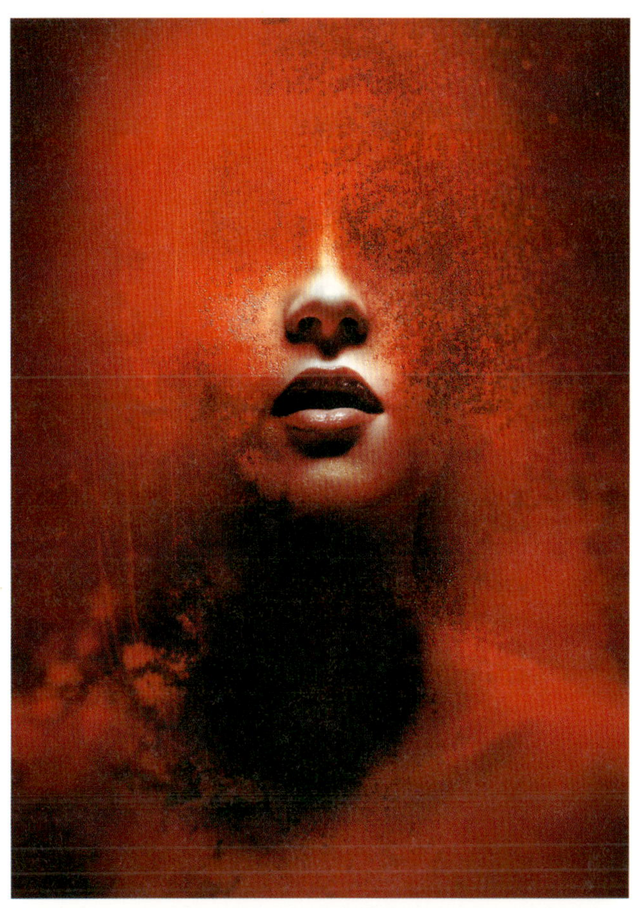

Fear Of The Dark 暗闇への恐怖
デジタル編集写真、紙 / H100×W70cm / 2014

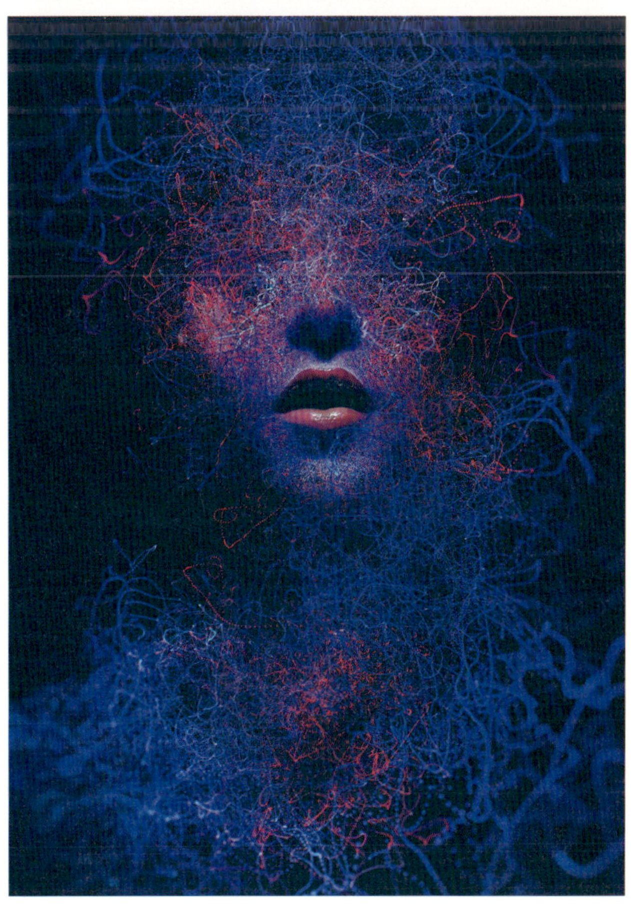

I Know I Have To Go 行かなければならないことは分かってる
デジタル編集写真、紙 / H100×W70cm / 2014

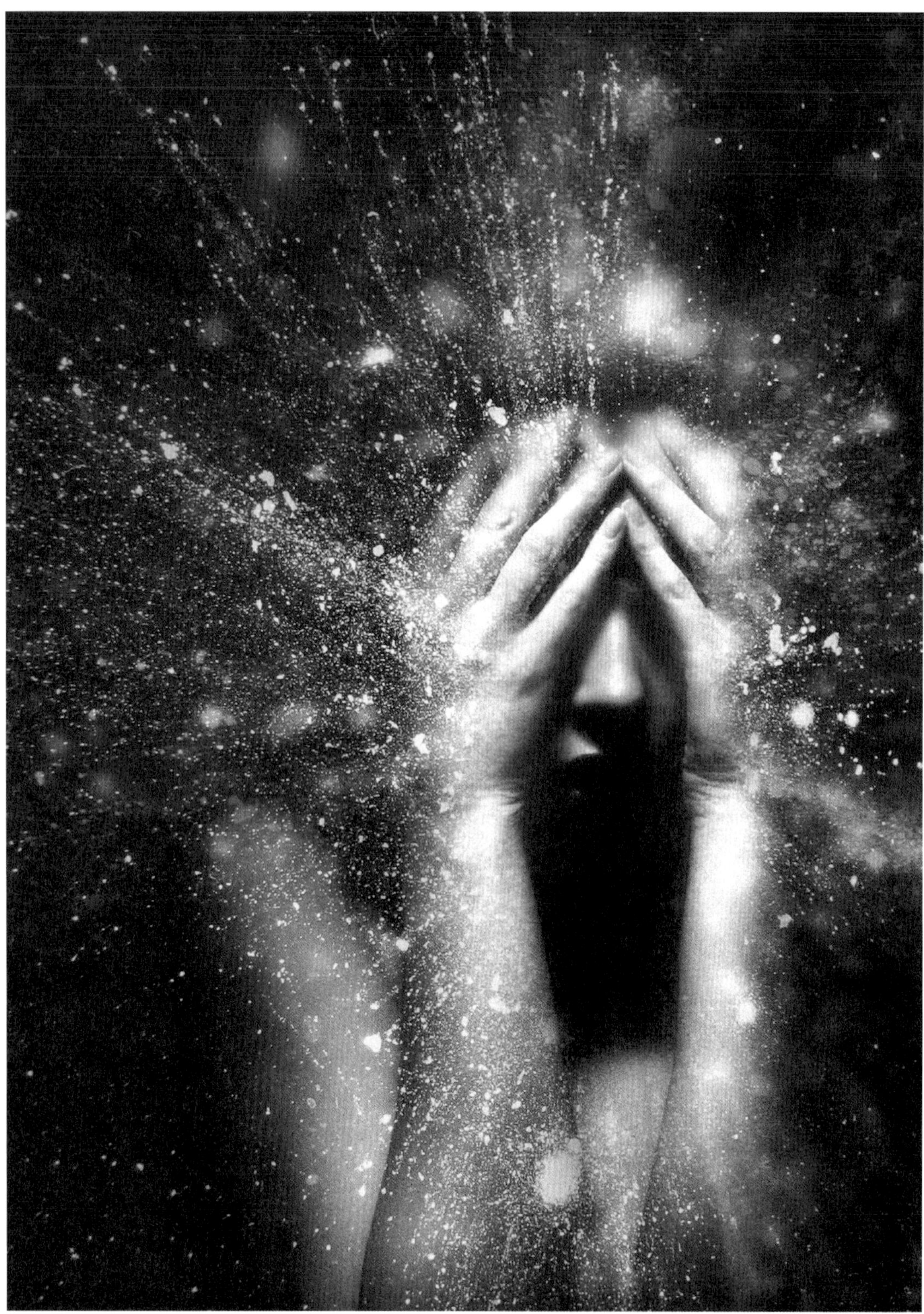

Bipolar Day 二極化した日
デジタル編集写真、紙 / H100×W70cm / 2011

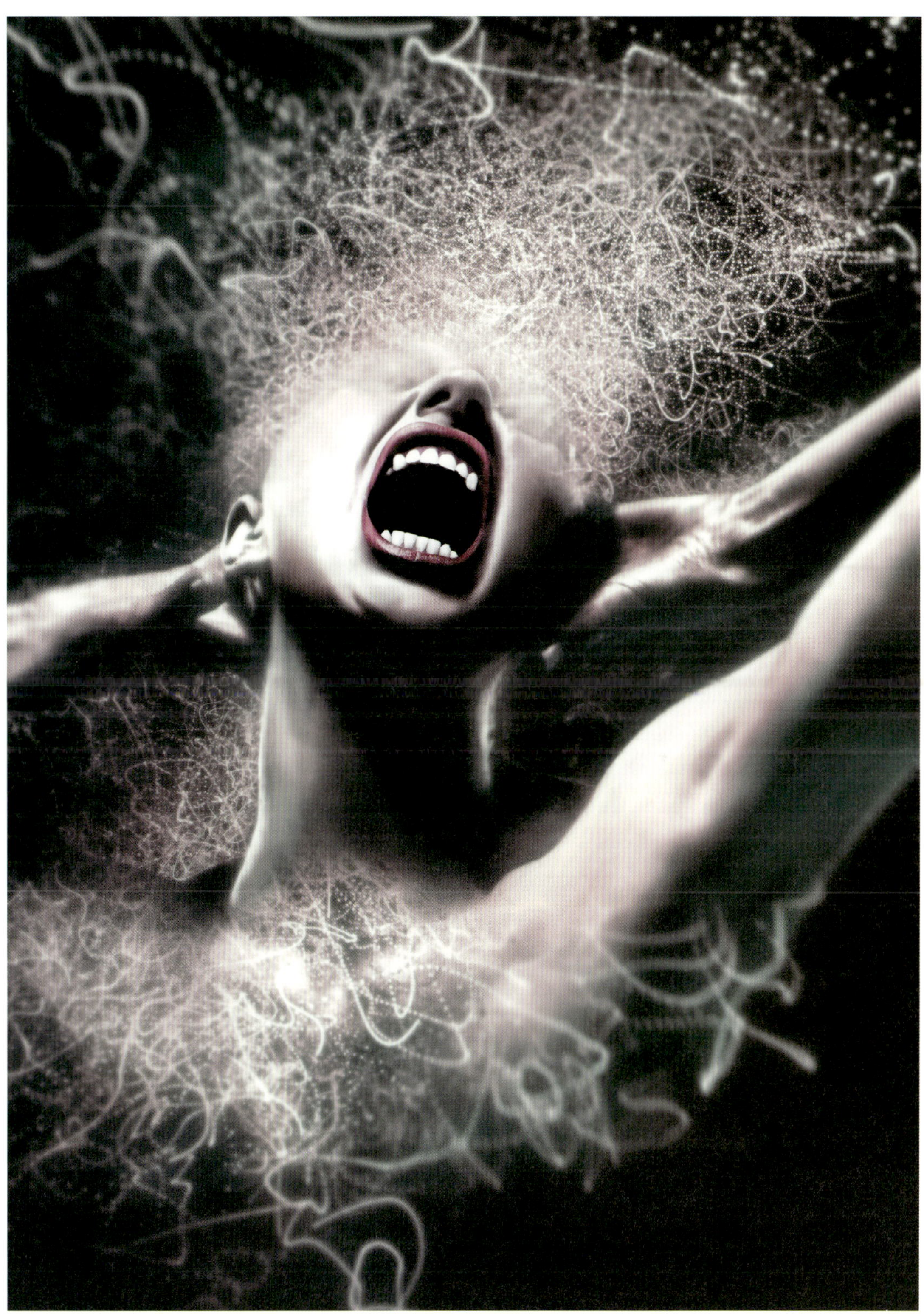

Demons 悪魔たち
デジタル編集写真、紙 / H100×W70cm / 2016

Insect Queen 昆虫の女王
デジタル編集写真、紙 / H100×W70cm / 2012

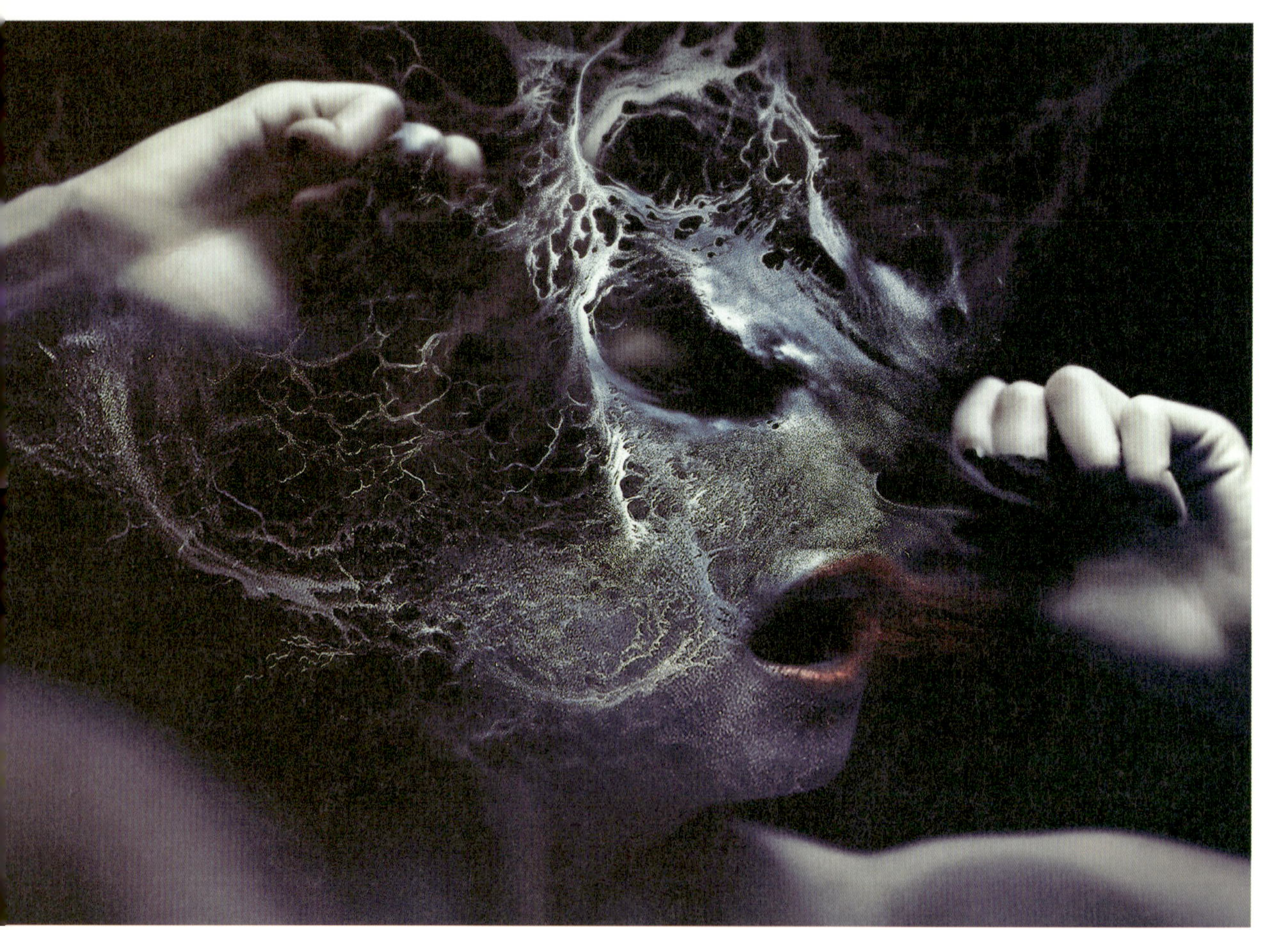

You'll Rebel To Anything あなたは何事にも反発するでしょ
デジタル編集写真、紙 / H70×W100cm / 2017

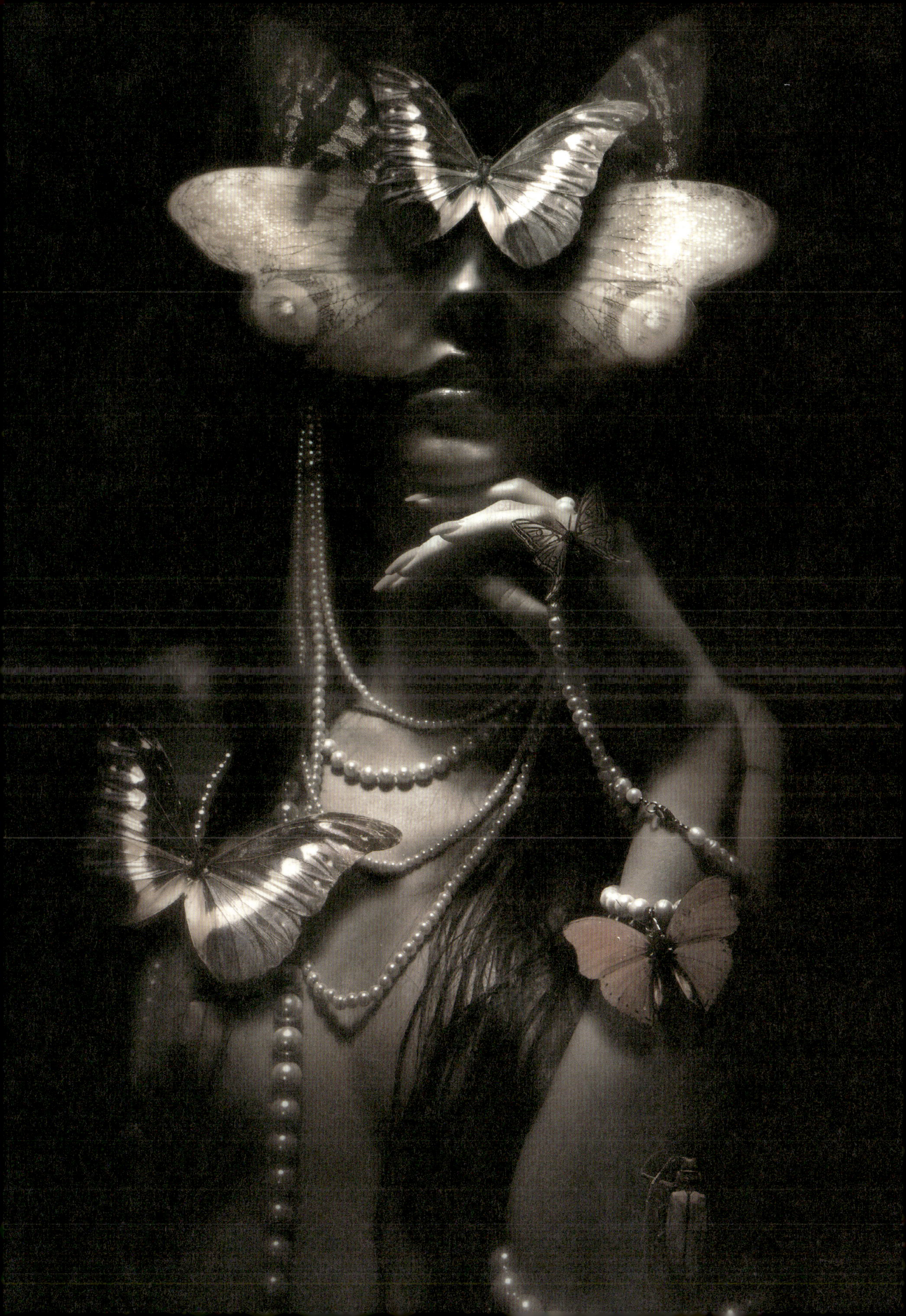

32

Neil Craver

ニール・クレイヴァー（アメリカ USA）

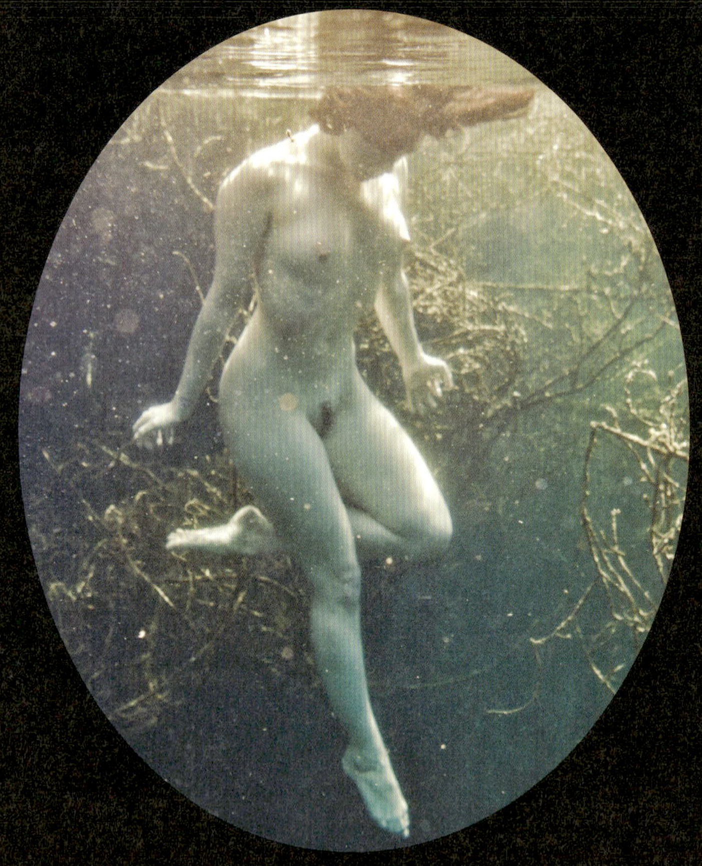

アメリカ、ノース・カロライナ出身。もともとは抽象画と具象彫刻を制作していたが、彩度が心身に与える影響に興味を持ち、写真に転向。写真にはあらゆるジャンルの芸術の本質的な価値が備わっているが、存在の基盤であるという点が異なっている。ニール・クレイヴァーにとって写真を撮ることは、精神の探求であり、「独創的なアイデア」を表現する現代の知を追求すること。
「フォトン（光子）なしには何も存在しない。あらゆることがフォトンの使い方でコントロールされている。」

As a youth in North Carolina; he begun his path as an abstract painter and figurative sculptor; motivations grew from his interest of the psychophysical effects of chroma. Photography holds all the intrinsic values of all the other arts; but differers in the fact the it's the foundation of existence. His creations are the exploration of his inner facilities; in the pursuit of contemporary knowledge expressing "original thoughts".
"Nothing can exist without the photon, and every aspect is controlled by it's usage"

www.neilcraver.com

↑ Brilliantly Despairing 鮮やかな絶望（部分）
写真 / 2011

→Into Everything すべてに（部分）
写真 / 2011

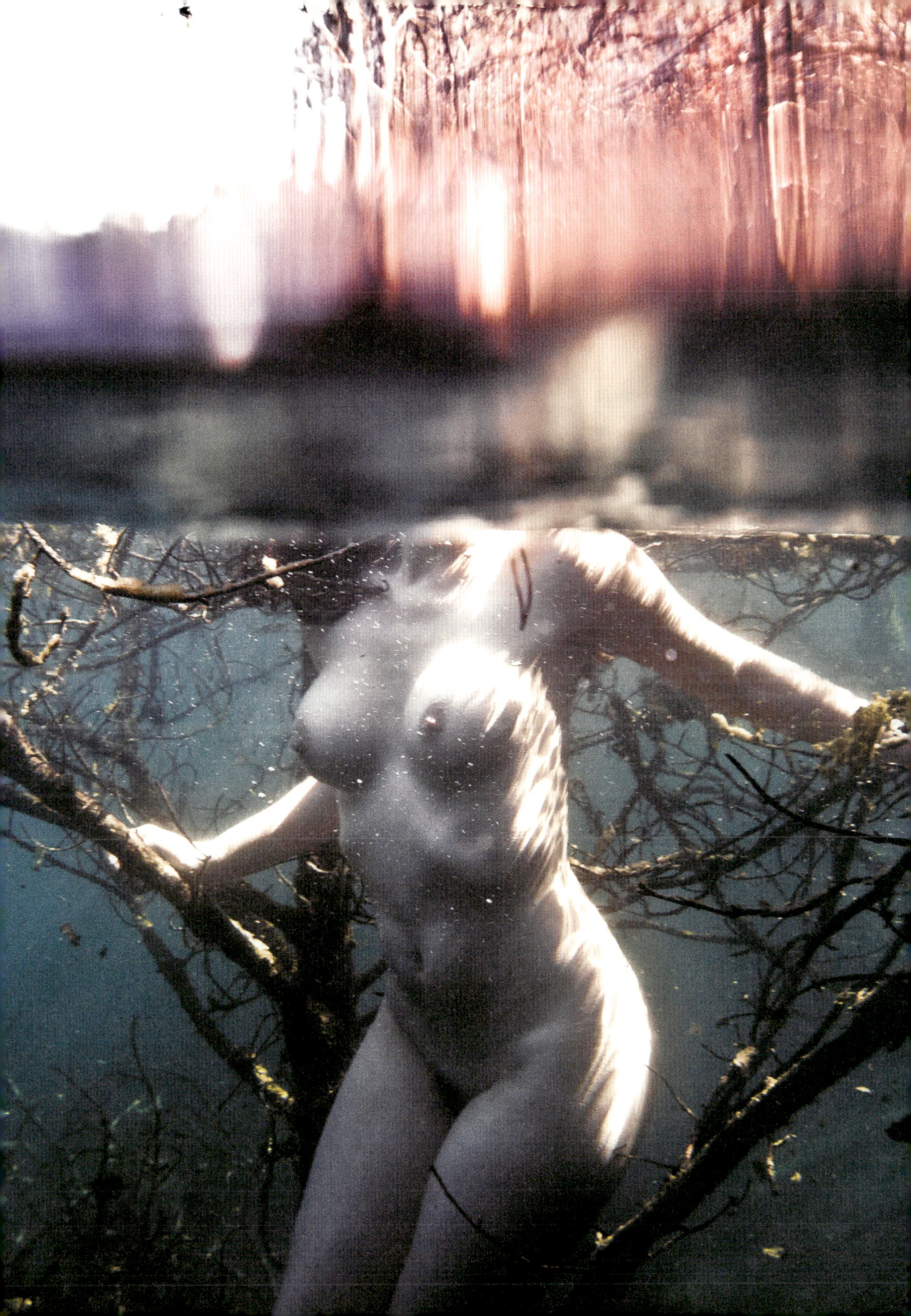

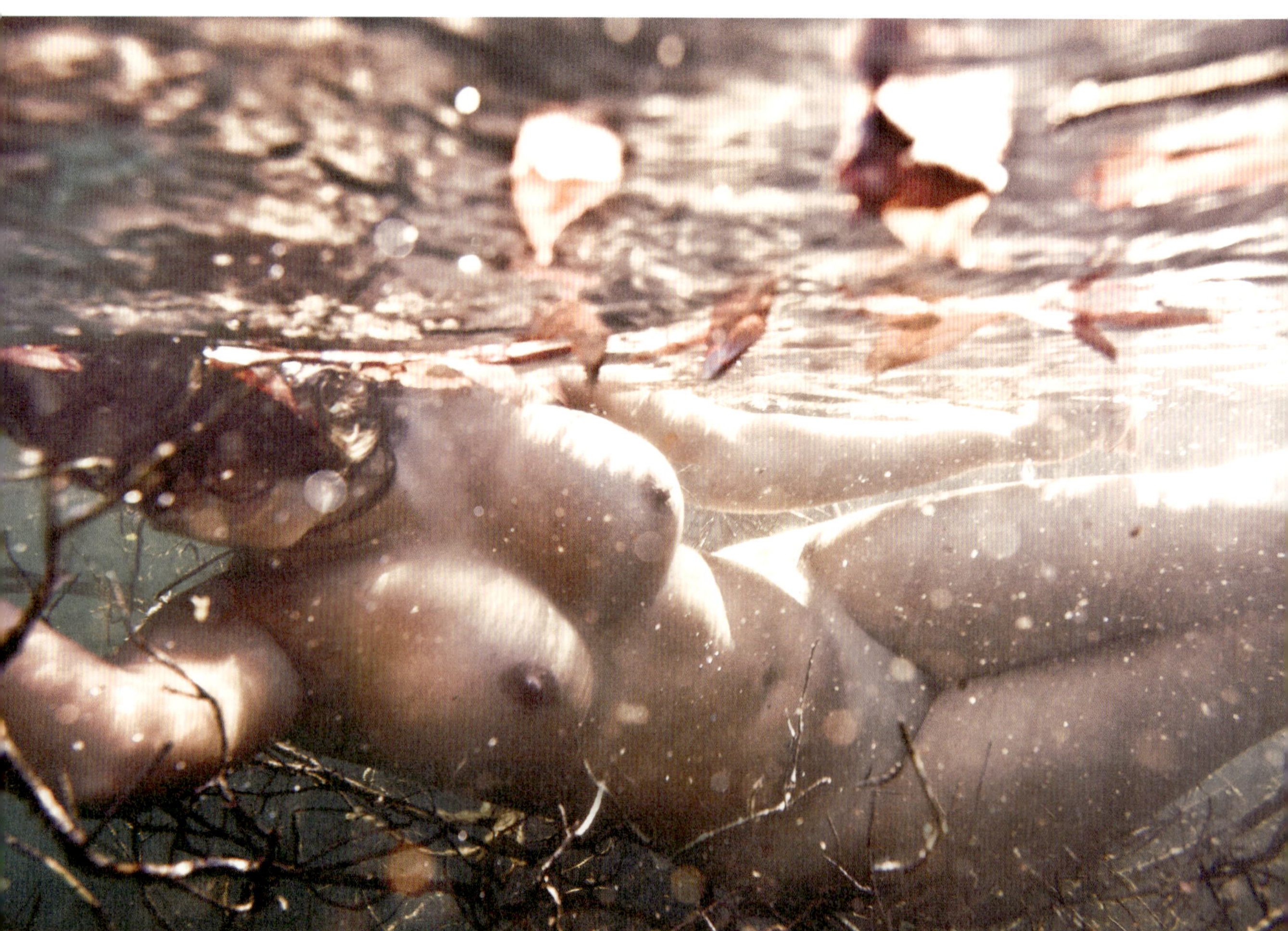

When the Light Came 光が差した時
写真 / 2011

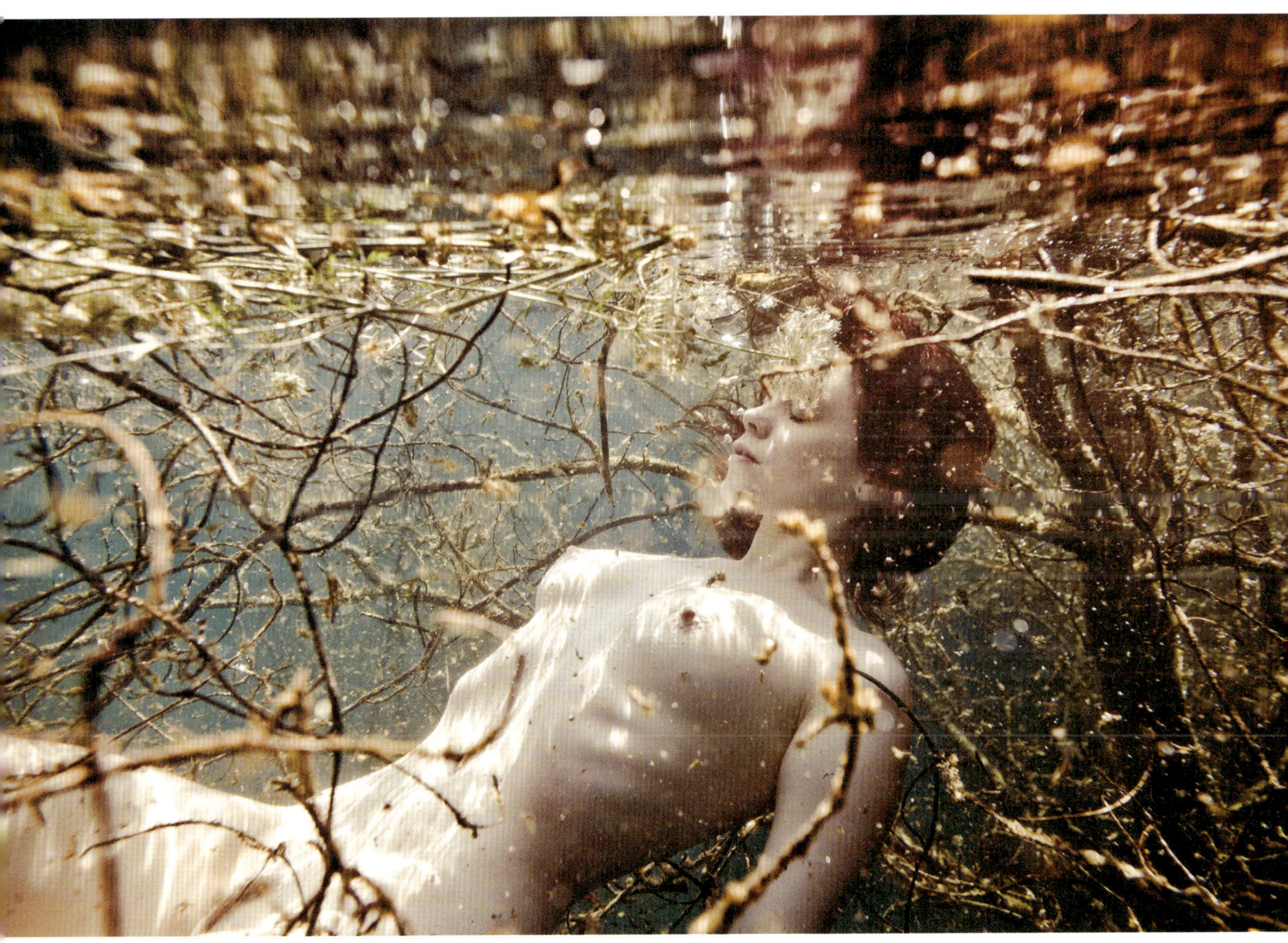

Dreaming of a Dream 夢を夢見る
写真 / 2011

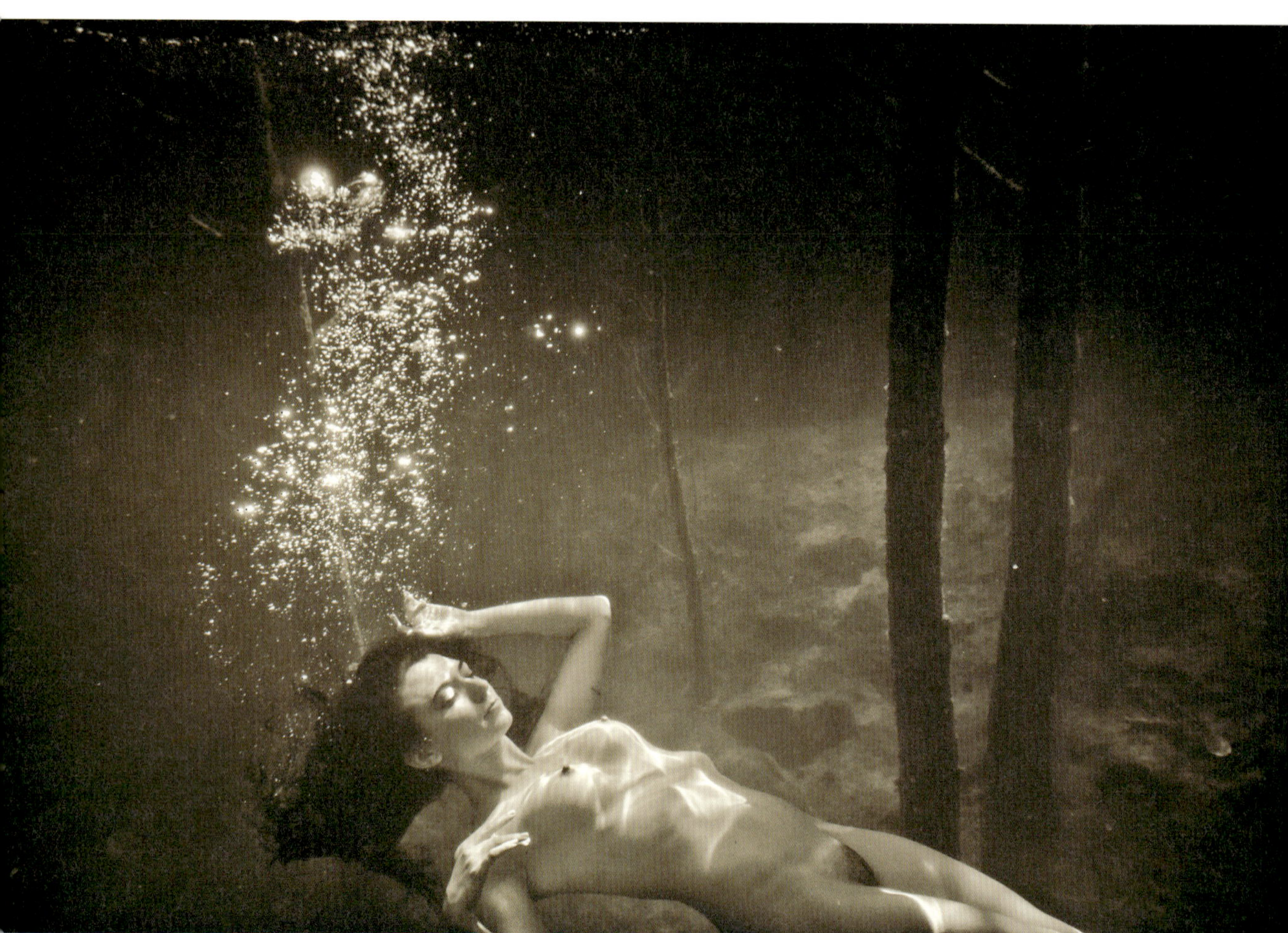

Intrinsic Inundation 内因性浸水
写真 / 2011

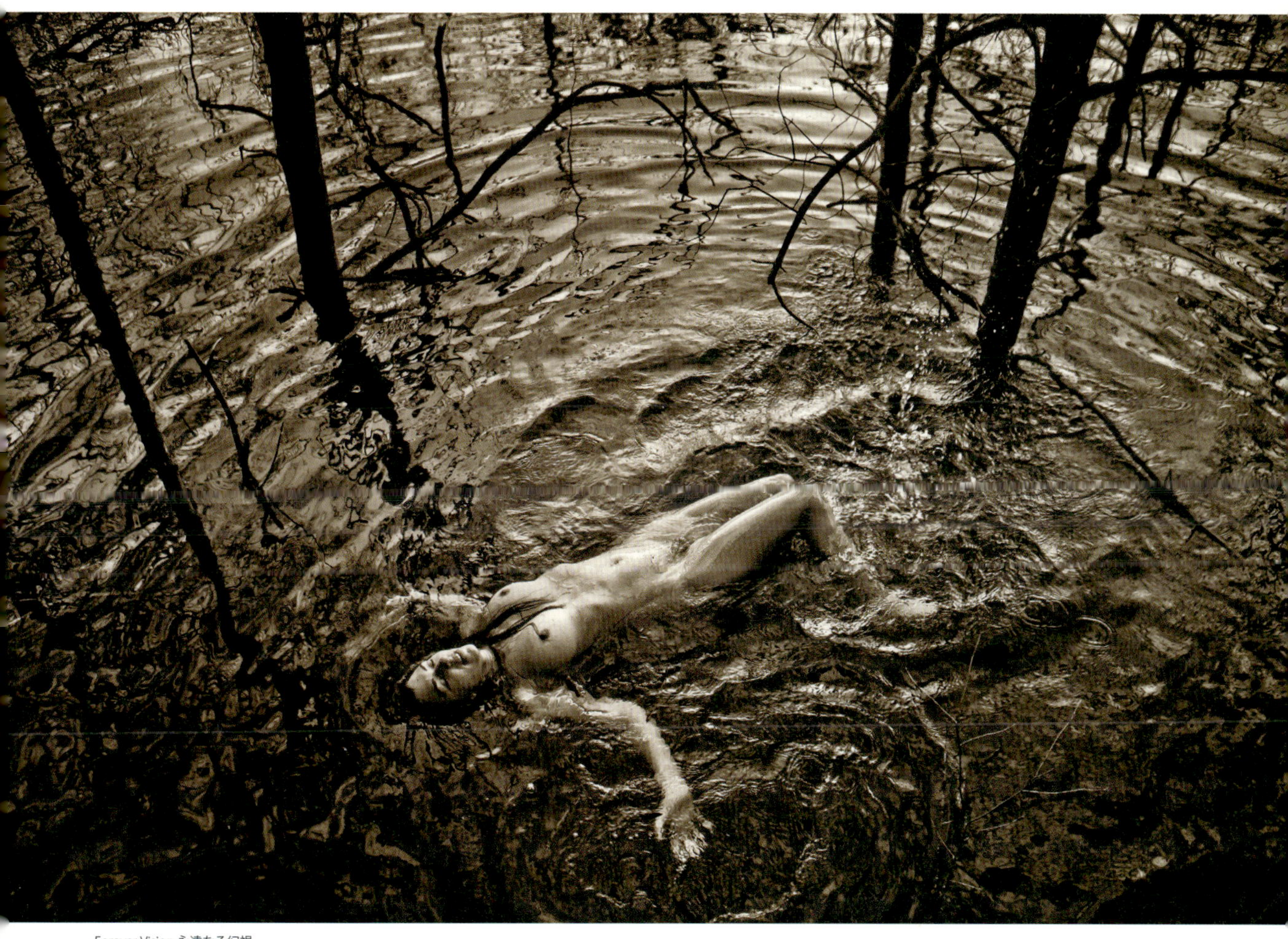

Forever Vision 永遠なる幻視
写真 / 2011

33

Diana Dihaze

ディアナ・ディハーゼ（ウクライナ　Ukraine）

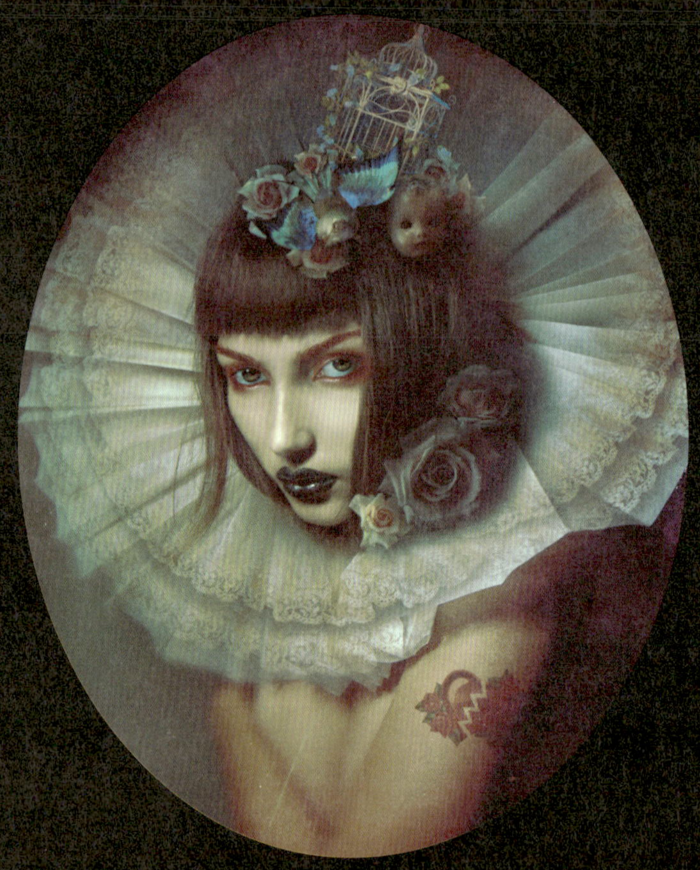

ウクライナ出身。写真家、デジタル・アーティスト。目に見えない曖昧な世界、女性の心に潜む闇や幻想、官能、忘却の美しさ、絶望、終わりを待つ魂の崩壊を表現しようとしている。自然からインスピレーションを受けることが多い。

In her works she is trying to convey the atmosphere of the invisible obscure world of dark fantasies of female sensuality, beauty of oblivion, hopelessness, and the dissolution of the soul waiting for the end. She finds inspiration in nature.

dihaze.deviantart.com

↑ Everything I Need is Someone's Shoulder for to Cry 誰かが慰めてくれさえすればいい（部分）
デジタル・アート / 2013

→Mermaids Nightmare 人魚の悪夢
デジタル・アート / 2013

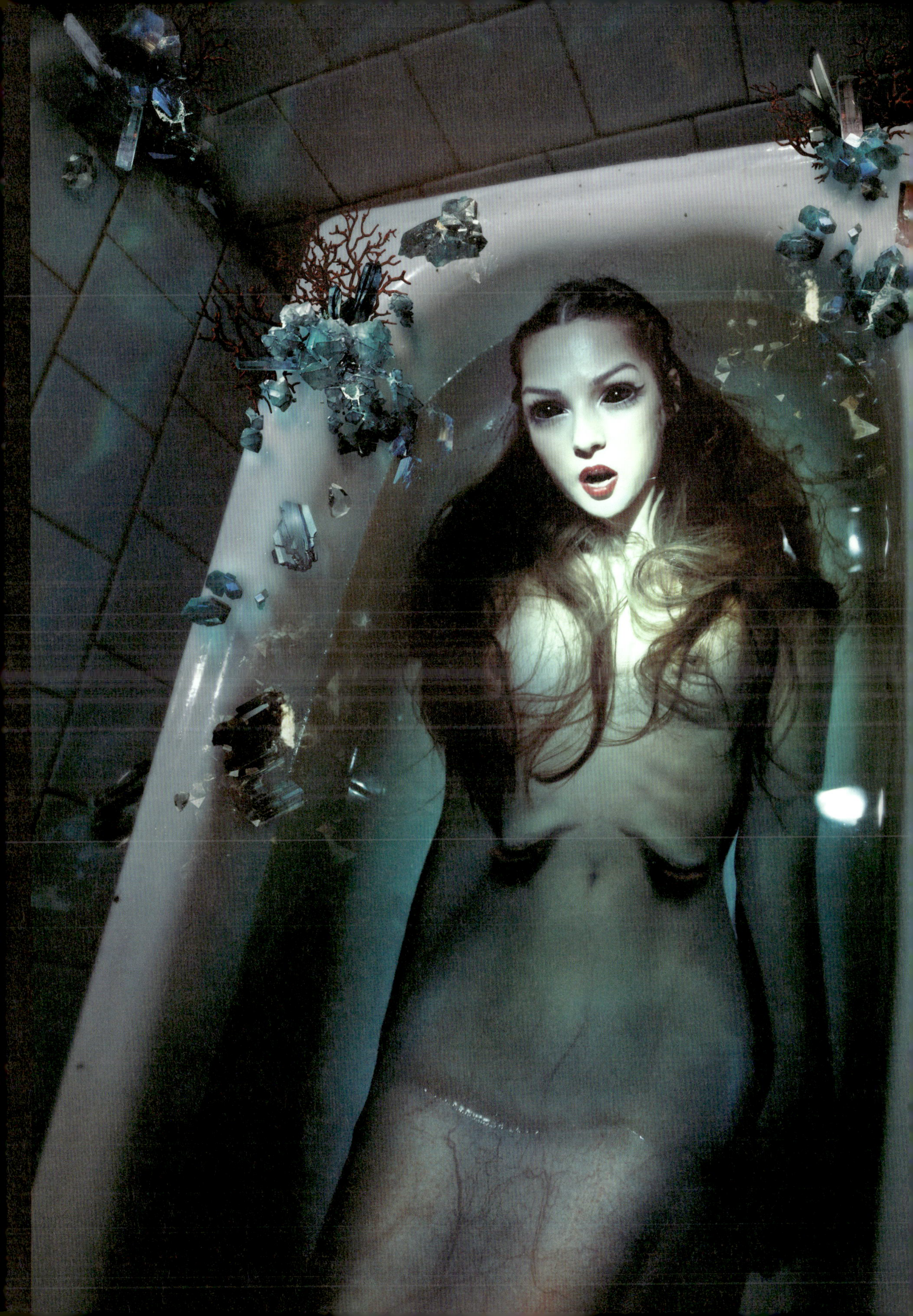

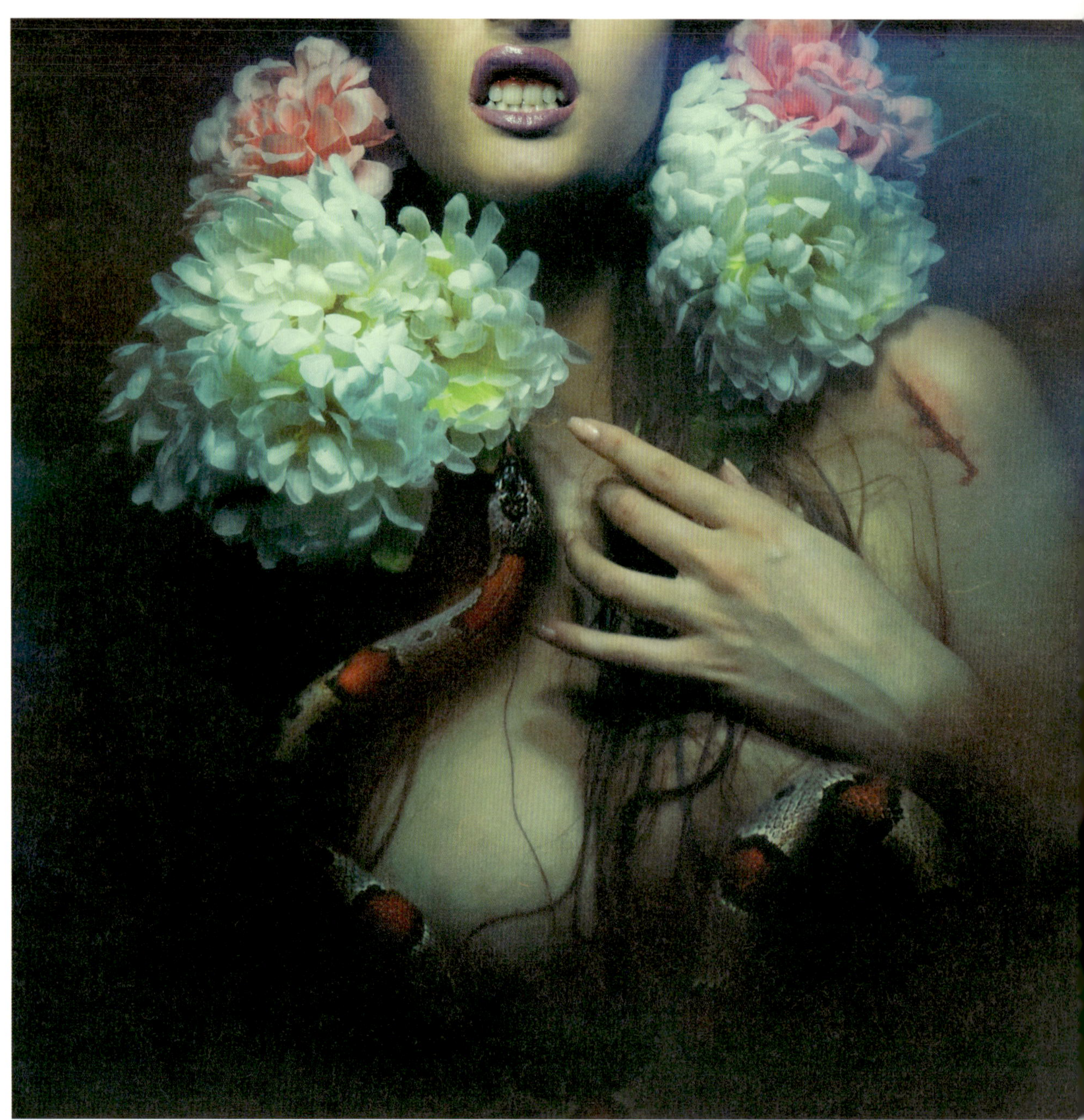

Thrill is Gone スリルがない
デジタル・アート / 2013

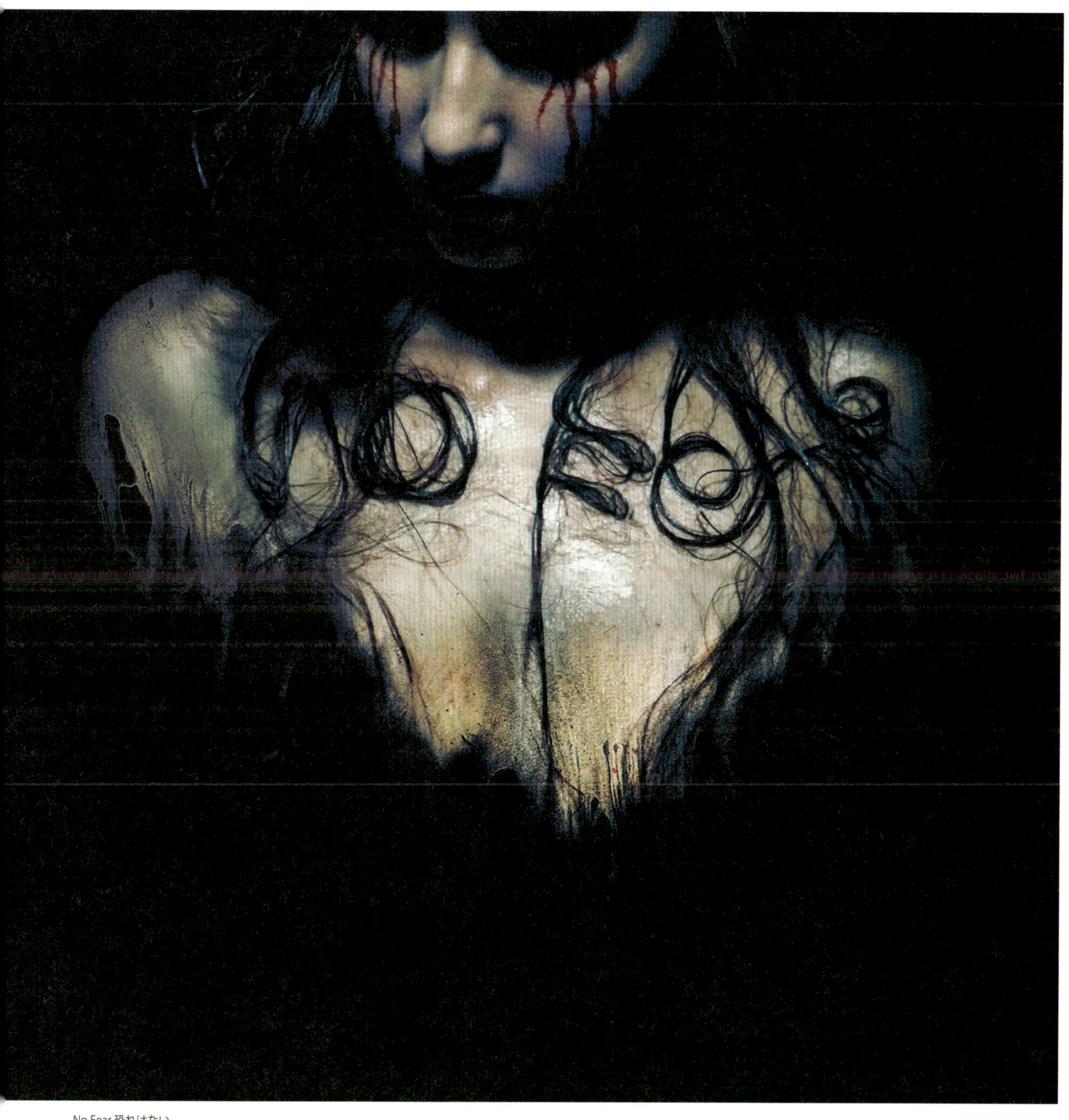

No Fear 恐れはない
デジタル・アート / 2013

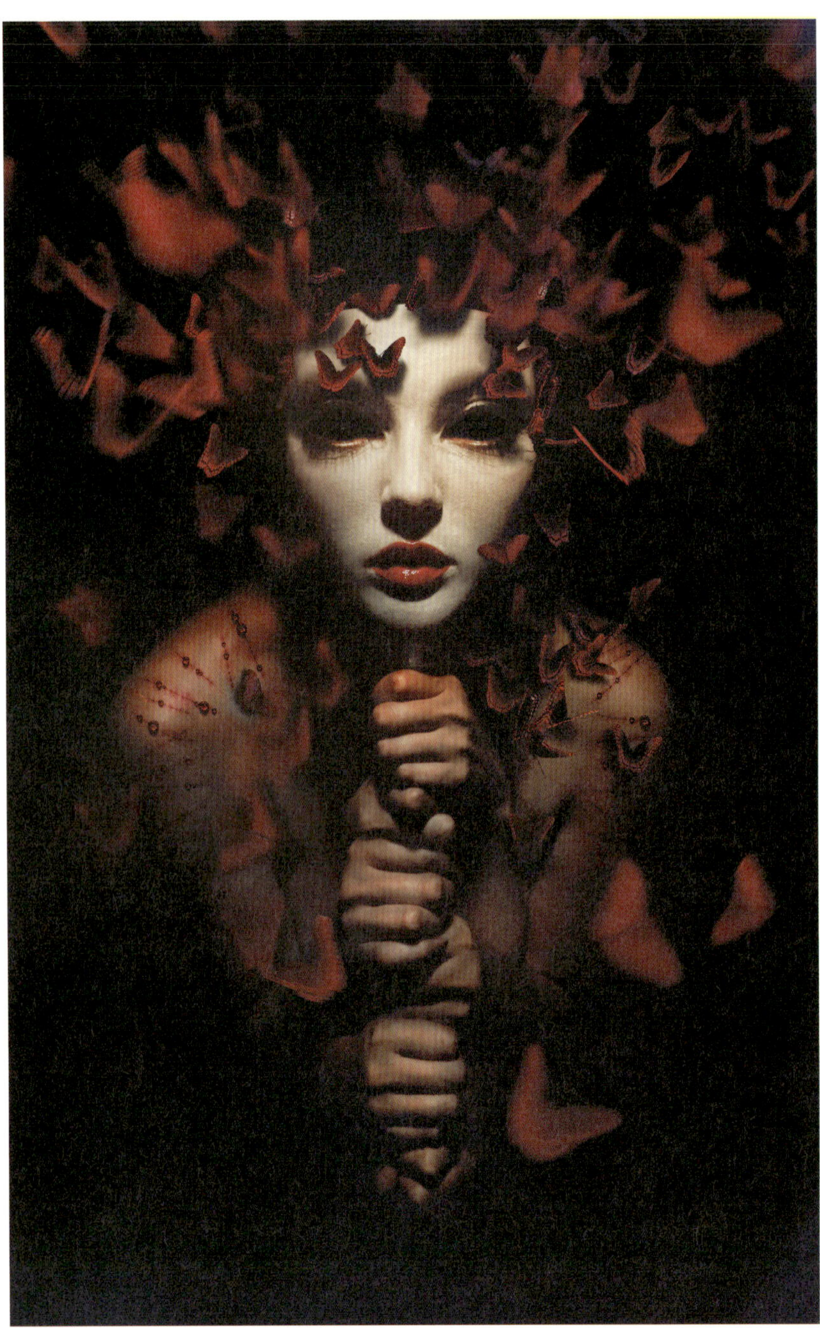

Don't Look to the Eyes of Empty Mask 空のマスクの目をのぞきこまないで
デジタル・アート / 2013

Serpentarium サーペンタリウム（ヘビの飼育所）
デジタル・アート / 2012

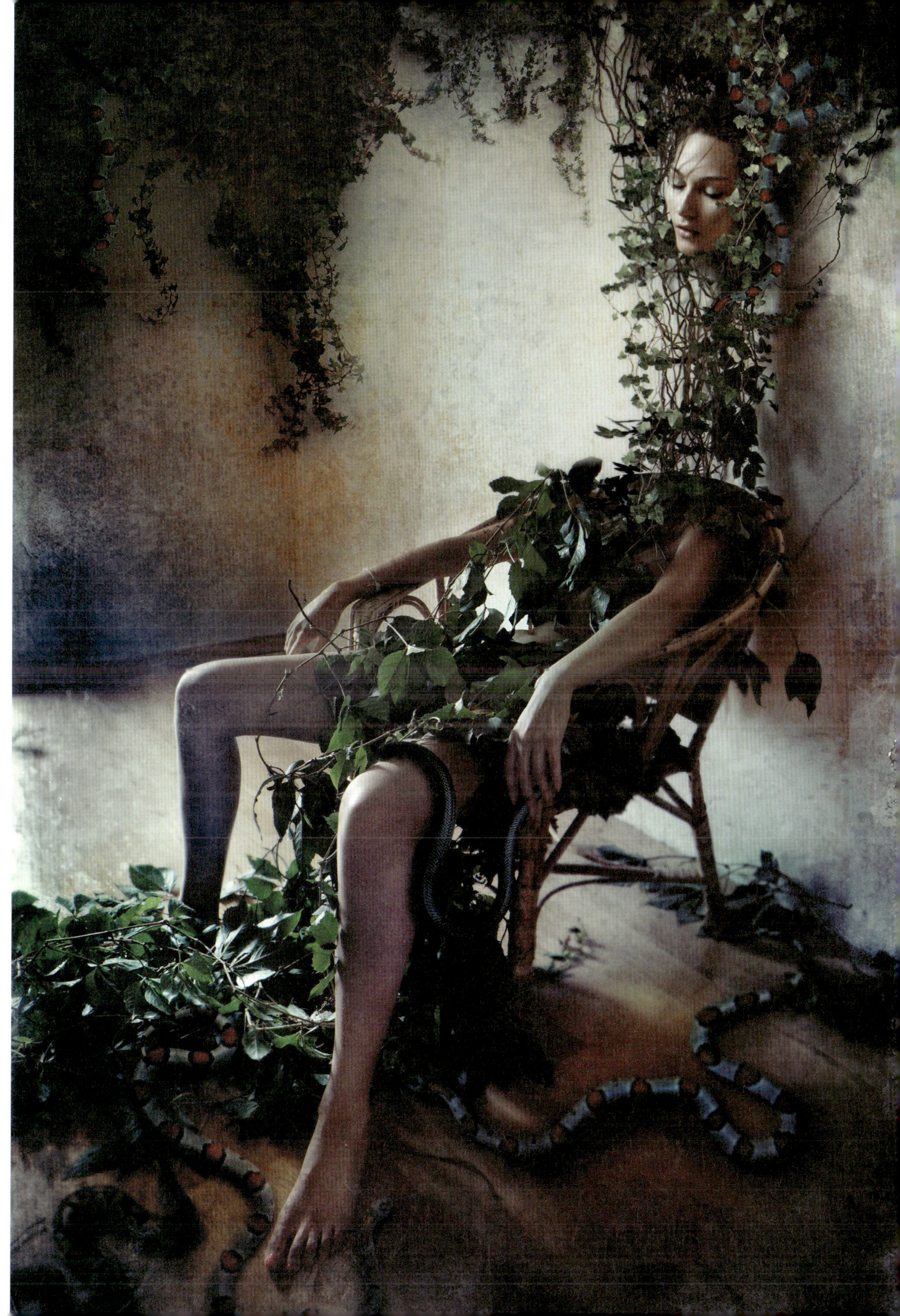

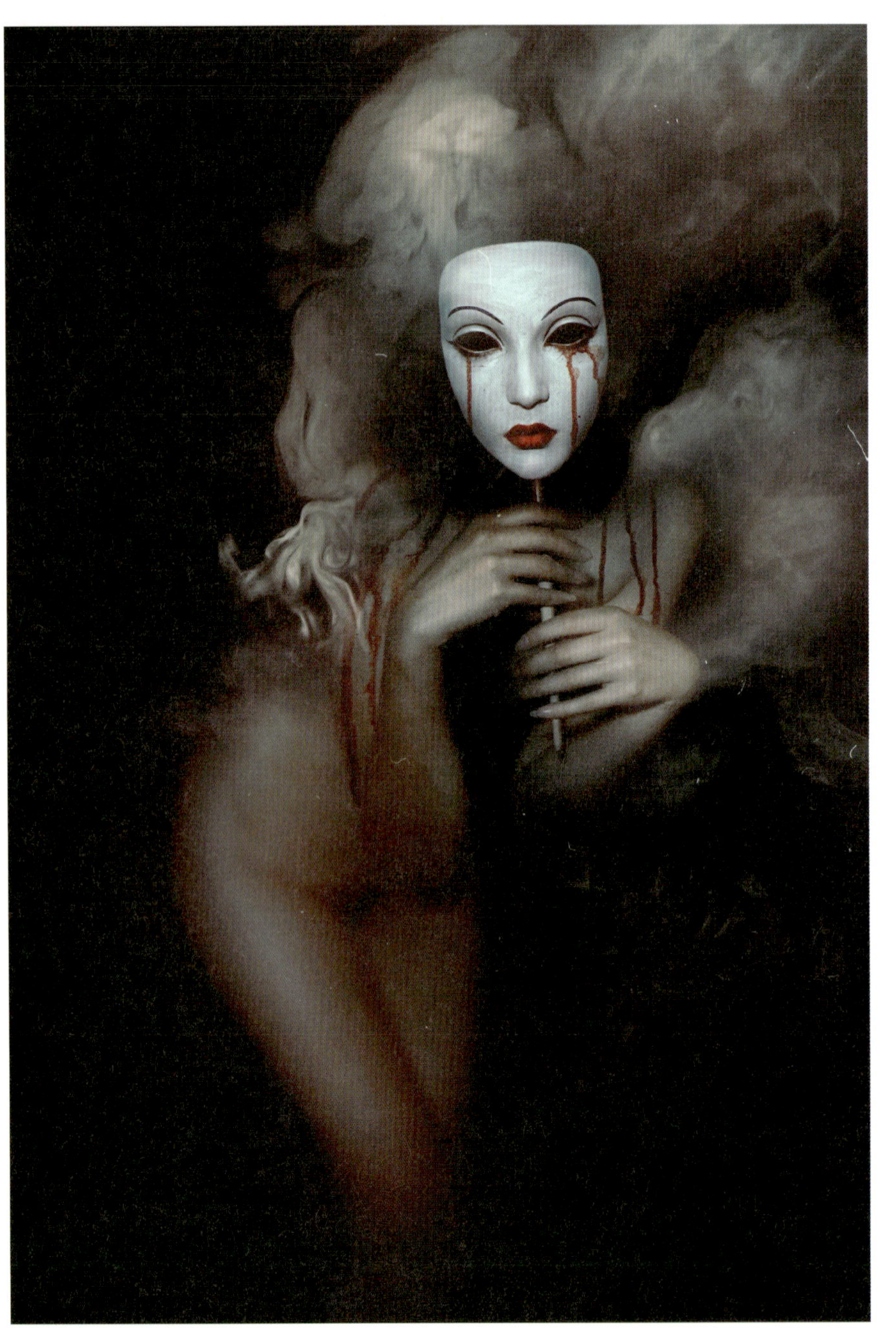

Silencio 沈黙
デジタル・アート / 2013

Not Falling 落ちてはいない
デジタル・アート / 2012

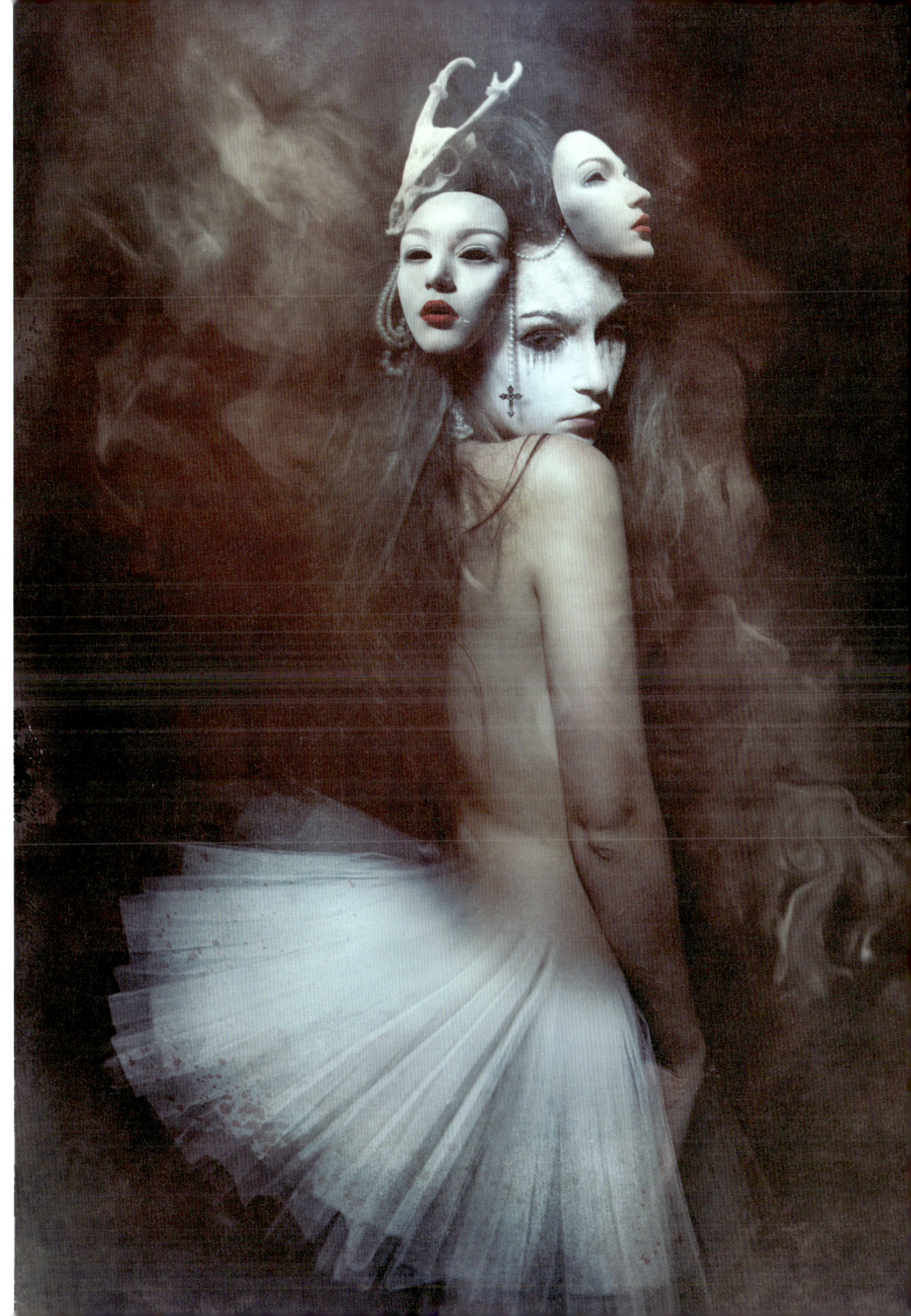

Karen Hsiao

カレン・シャオ（アメリカ USA）

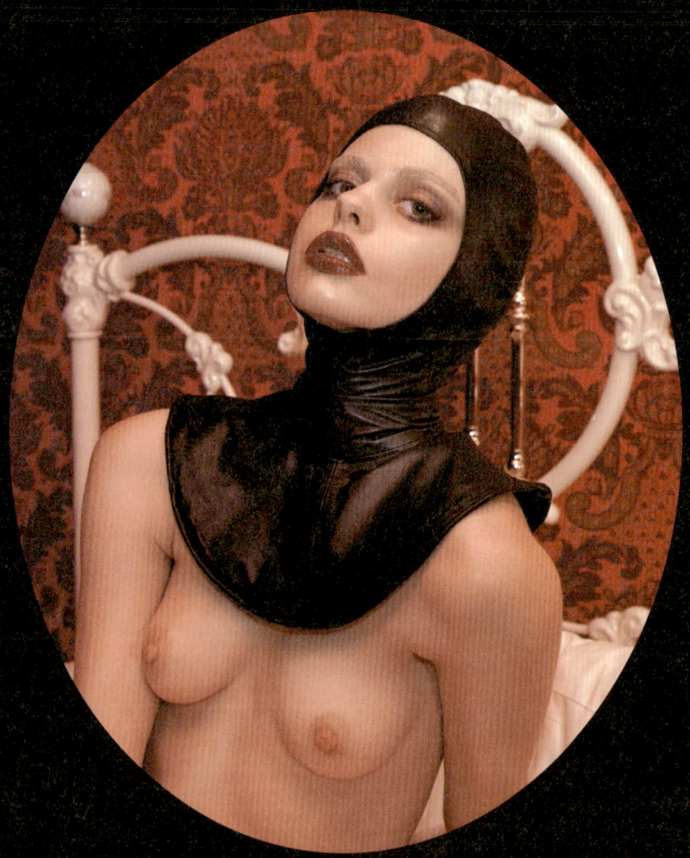

アート・センター・カレッジ・オブ・デザインを卒業し、イラストレーションの学位を取得。独学のファインアート・フォトグラファーで、独創的な方法で強烈な主題を扱う。初期は造形画家として、様々な素材を用いて形や空間を探究し、立体的で直感的な作品を制作した。写真は、彼女が追い求めた理想の延長線上にあった。彼女の作品はその主題とユニークなアプローチで多くの注目を集める。時には独創的なメイクアップ・アーティストやヘアスタイリス、オート・クチュールのファッション・デザイナーなどのチームが、彼女のコンセプトの具体化に一躍買っている。シャオは多くの出版物で紹介され、全世界のギャラリーに作品が展示されている。

Graduated from Art Center College of Design with a BFA in Illustration, Karen Hsiao is a self taught Fine Art photographer who uses intense subject matters in an unconventional way. Firstly a figurative painter in her early years, Hsiao has since explored the figure and its space through various mediums, creating pieces that are both tactile and intuitive. Photography was a natural extension of that process which Hsiao has sought to perfect. Her work has captured the attention of many primary because of her unique approach to her subject, sometimes with a team of ingenious makeup artist, hairstylists, and couture fashions designers to help materialize Hsiao's concept. Hsiao has been featured in published works and shown in galleries both nationwide and abroad.

karenhsiaofinearts.myshopify.com

↑"If Wallpapers Talk" Series「壁紙がしゃべるなら」シリーズ（部分）
モデル：ミカ・ジョーンズ、衣裳：クリストファー×シャオ／2017

→"If Wallpapers Talk" Series「壁紙がしゃべるなら」シリーズ（部分）
モデル：ユロリン・ヴェックス、衣裳：クリストファー×シャオ、ジェーン・ドウ・レイテックス／2017

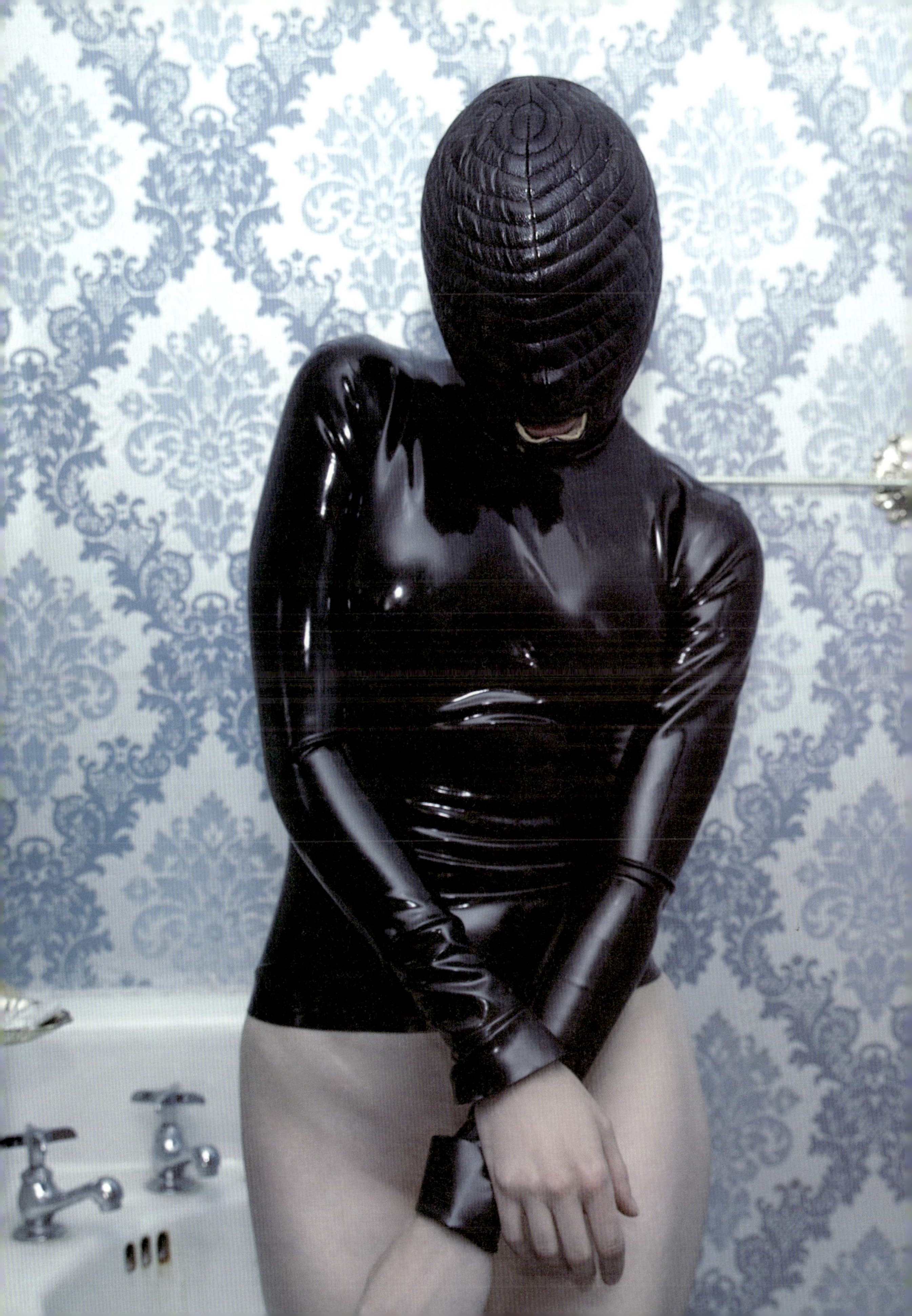

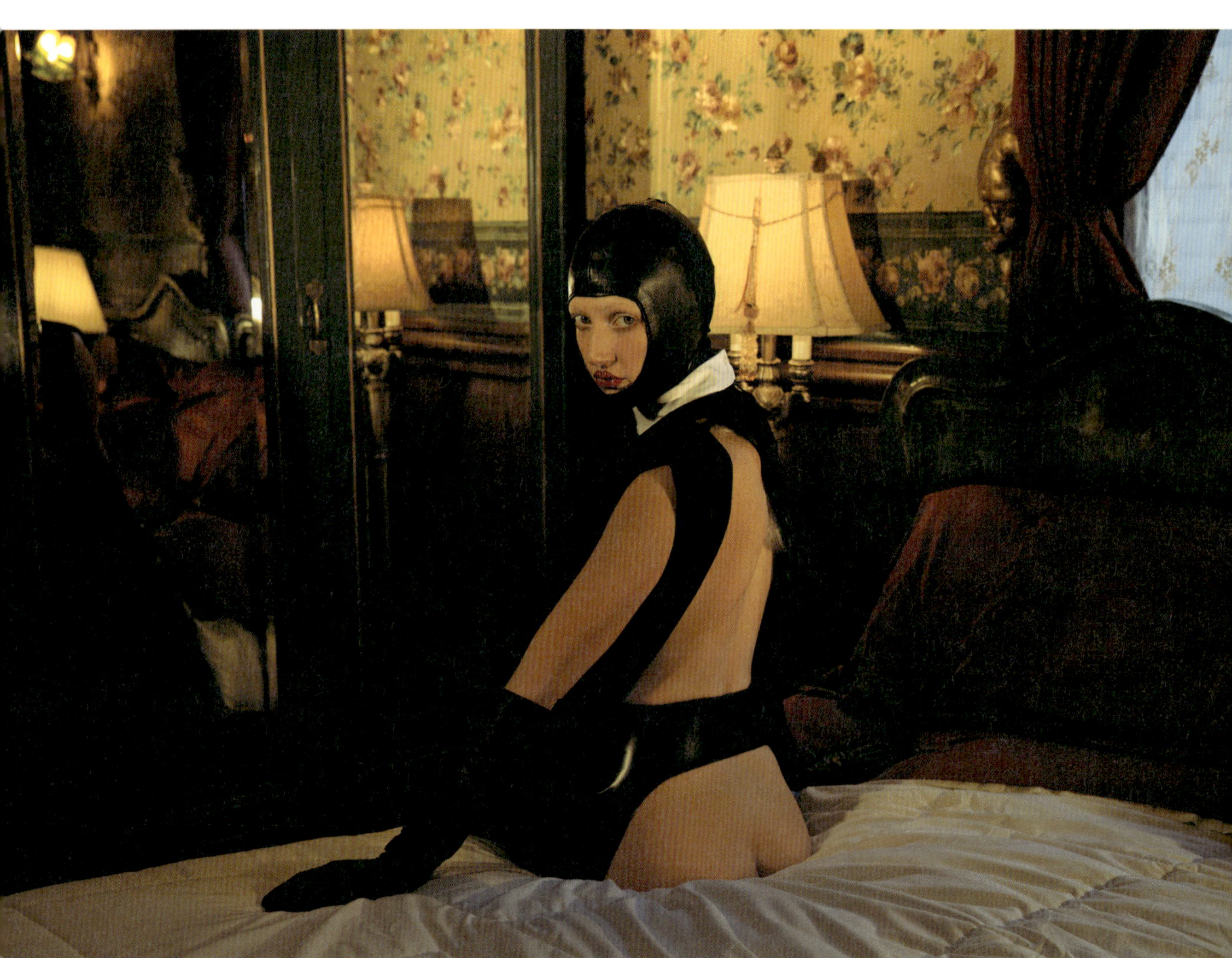

"If Wallpapers Talk" Series 「壁紙がしゃべるなら」シリーズ
モデル：ニッキー・ジーン、衣裳：クリストファー / 2017

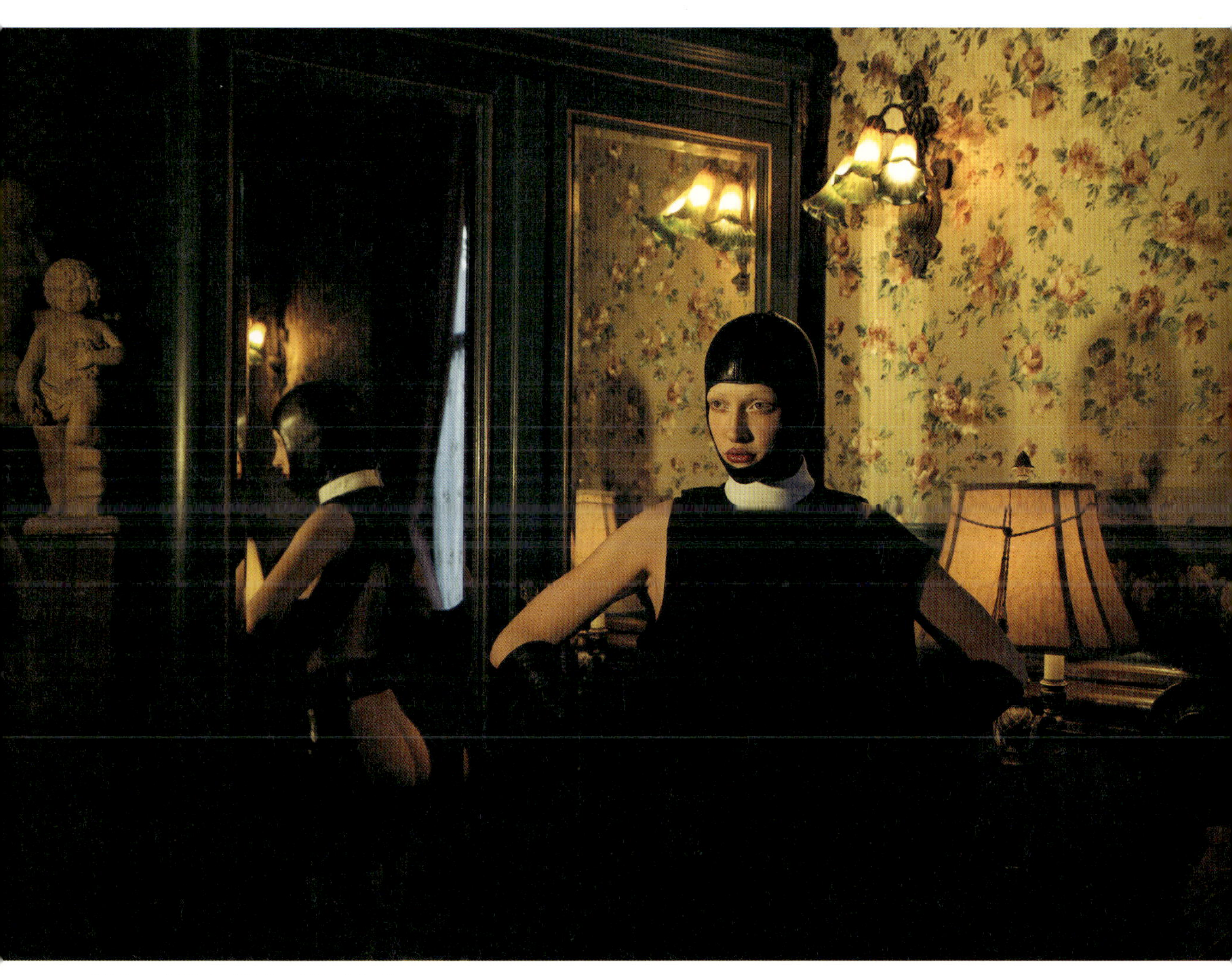

"If Wallpapers Talk" Series 「壁紙がしゃべるなら」シリーズ
モデル：ニッキー・ジーン、衣裳：クリストファー / 2017

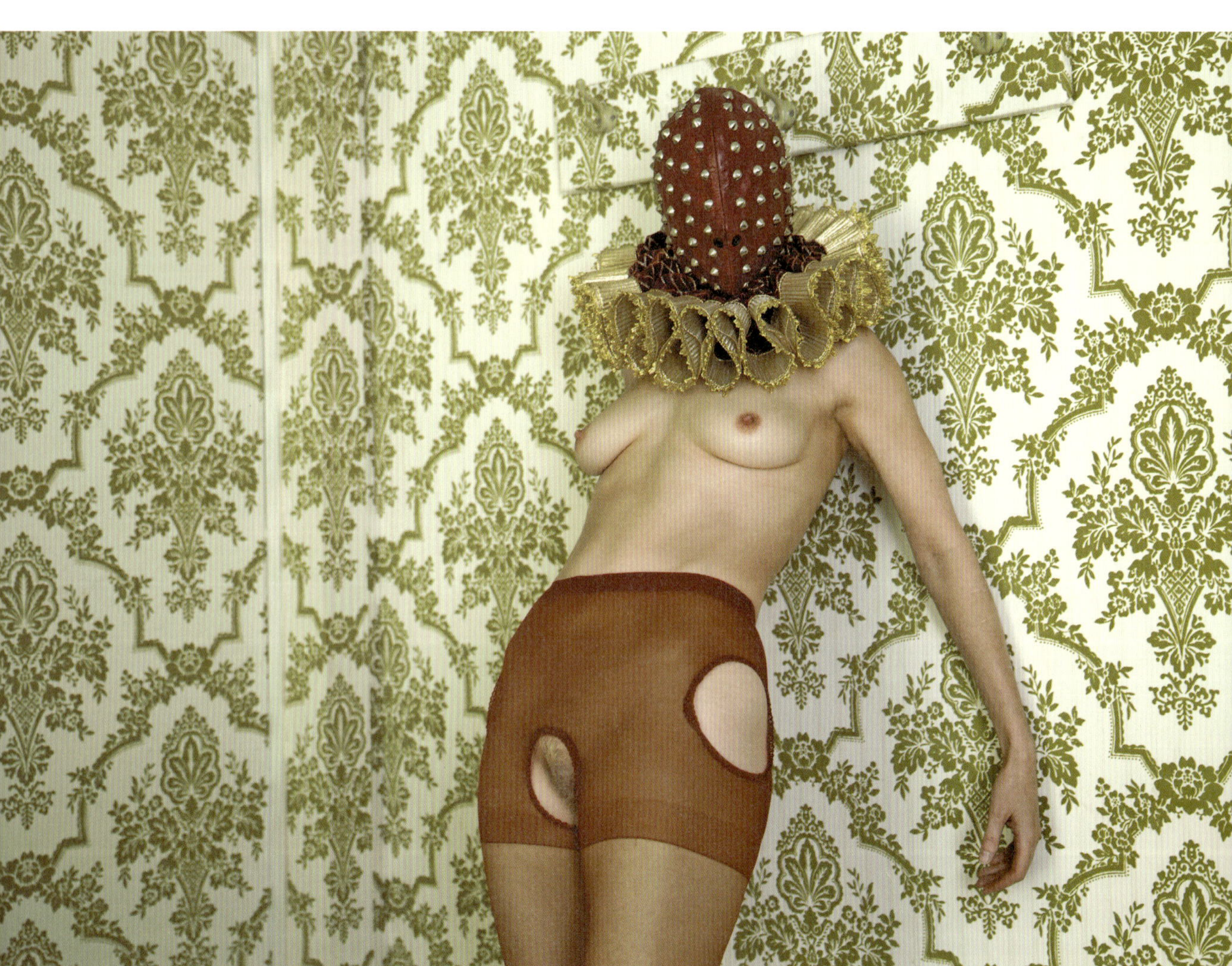

"If Wallpapers Talk" Series 「壁紙がしゃべるなら」シリーズ
モデル：ユロリン・ヴェックス、衣裳：クリストファー×シャオ、ジェーン・ドウ・レイテックス / 2017

Chapter 4
Three-Dimensional Art

立体アート

Popovy Sisters	ポポワ姉妹
Willy Verginer	ウィリー・ヴェルジネル
Danny van Ryswyk	ダニー・ファン・リズウィック
Seiko Kato	セイコ・カトウ
Elizabeth McGrath	エリザベス・マクグラス
Fiona Roberts	フィオナ・ロバーツ

Popovy Sisters (Elena Popova and Ekateria Popova)

ポポワ姉妹（エレーナ＆エカテリーナ・ポポワ、ロシア　Russia）

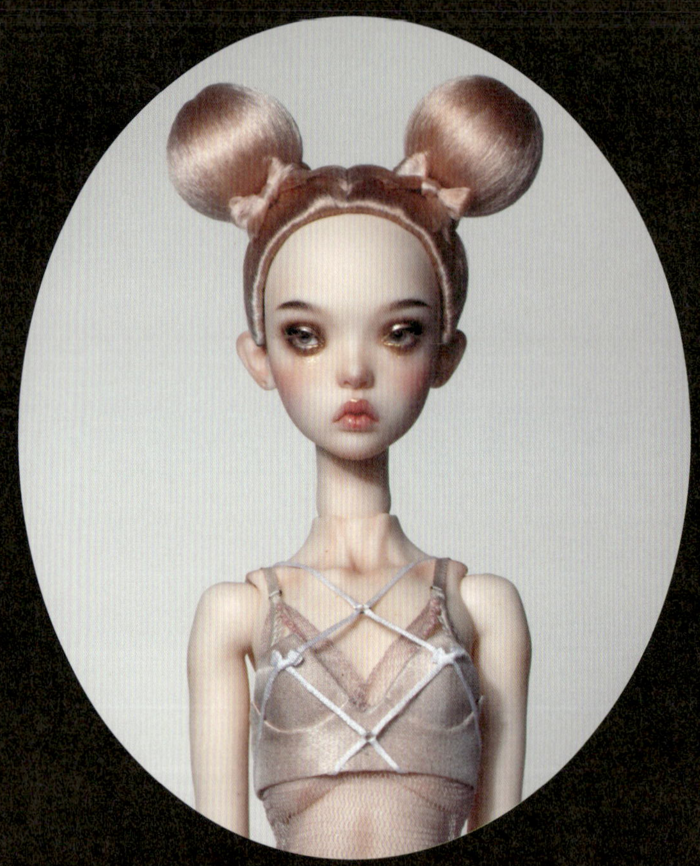

2004年からファイン・アート・ドールを制作。人形制作は、いつしか自分たちにとって特別な芸術表現となる。アート・ドールとそのファッションは、国籍や人種にとらわれない現代の美しさというものを自由に表現できる。1体1体の人形にストーリー性を持たせ、見る人に夢を与え、自由に想像をふくらませられるようにするのが姉妹の使命。歴史や自然から発想を得て、退屈な毎日を忘れられる夢の世界を創り上げる努力をしている。

Popovy Sisters have been making fine art dolls since 2004. And for them this activity has transformed into a special thematic kind of art. Together with fashion it has given us a freedom to express our contemporary and cosmopolitan vision of beauty. Popovy Sisters believe that our mission is to tell you a story and each time it should be a new one allowing to dream and escape into a world of unfettered imagination. Inspired by history and nature Popovy Sisters always try to transcend the humdrum and commonplace.

popovy-dolls.com

↑ → Lena & Katya Popovy

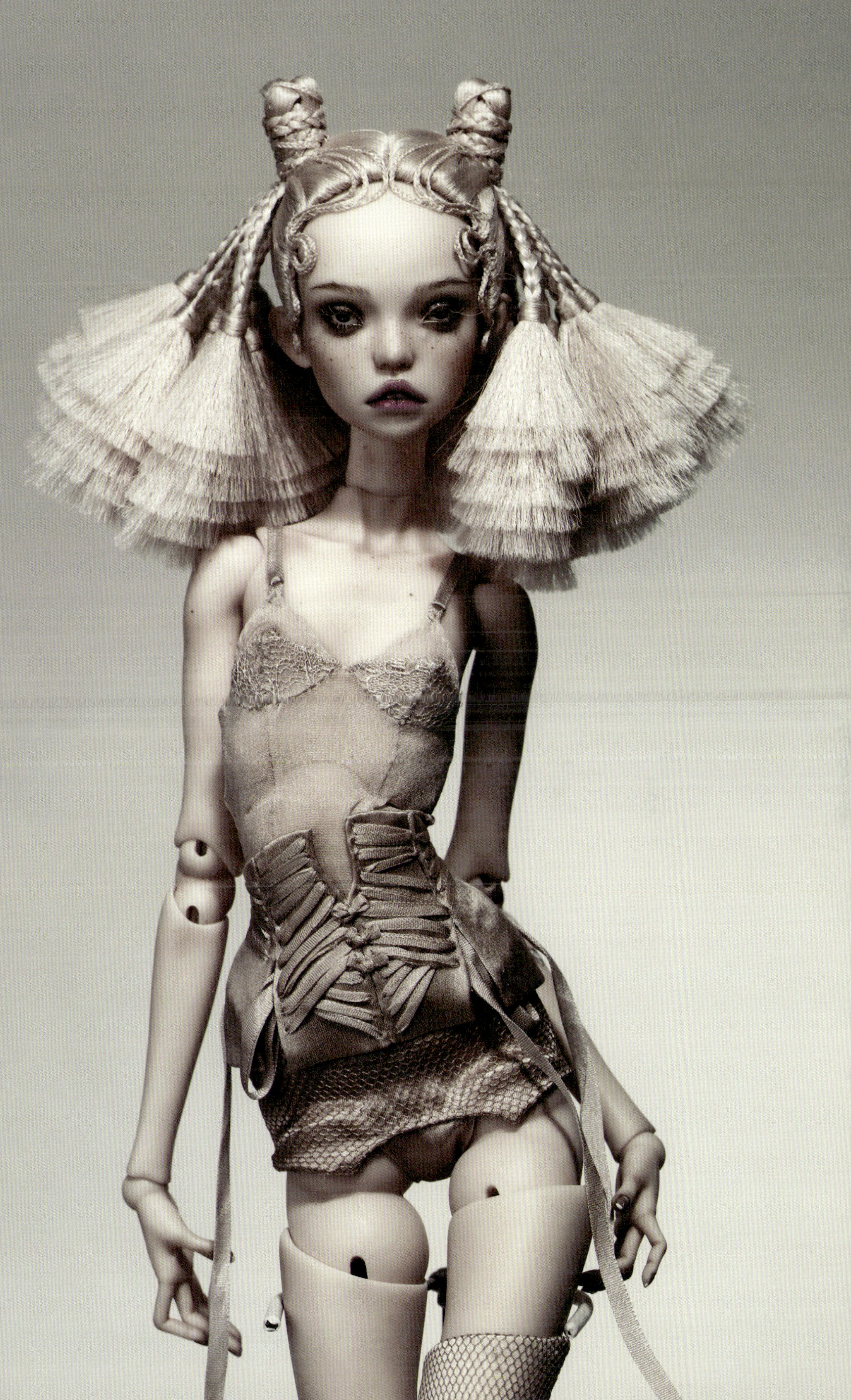

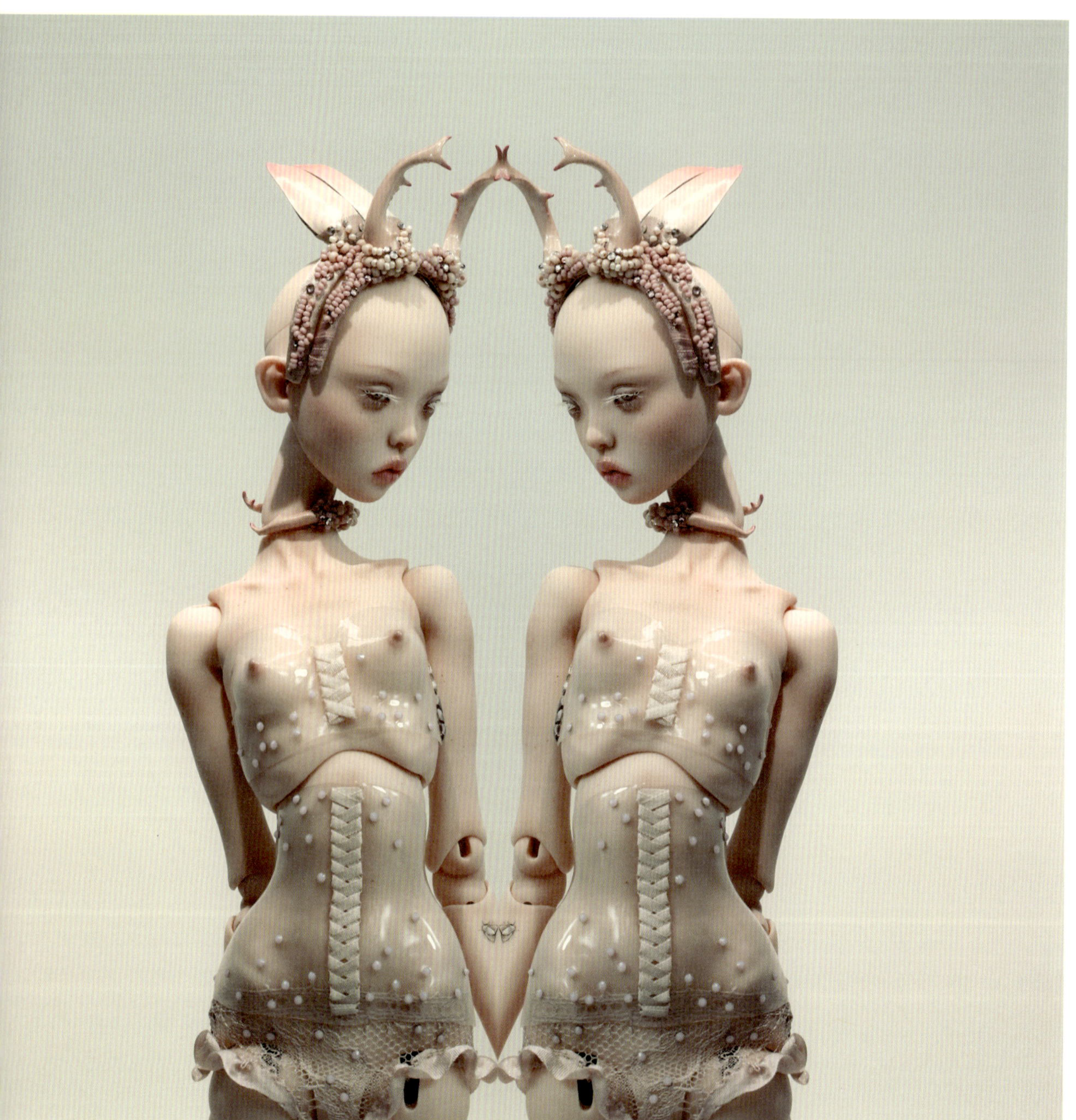

Lena & Katya Popovy

Lena & Katya Popovy

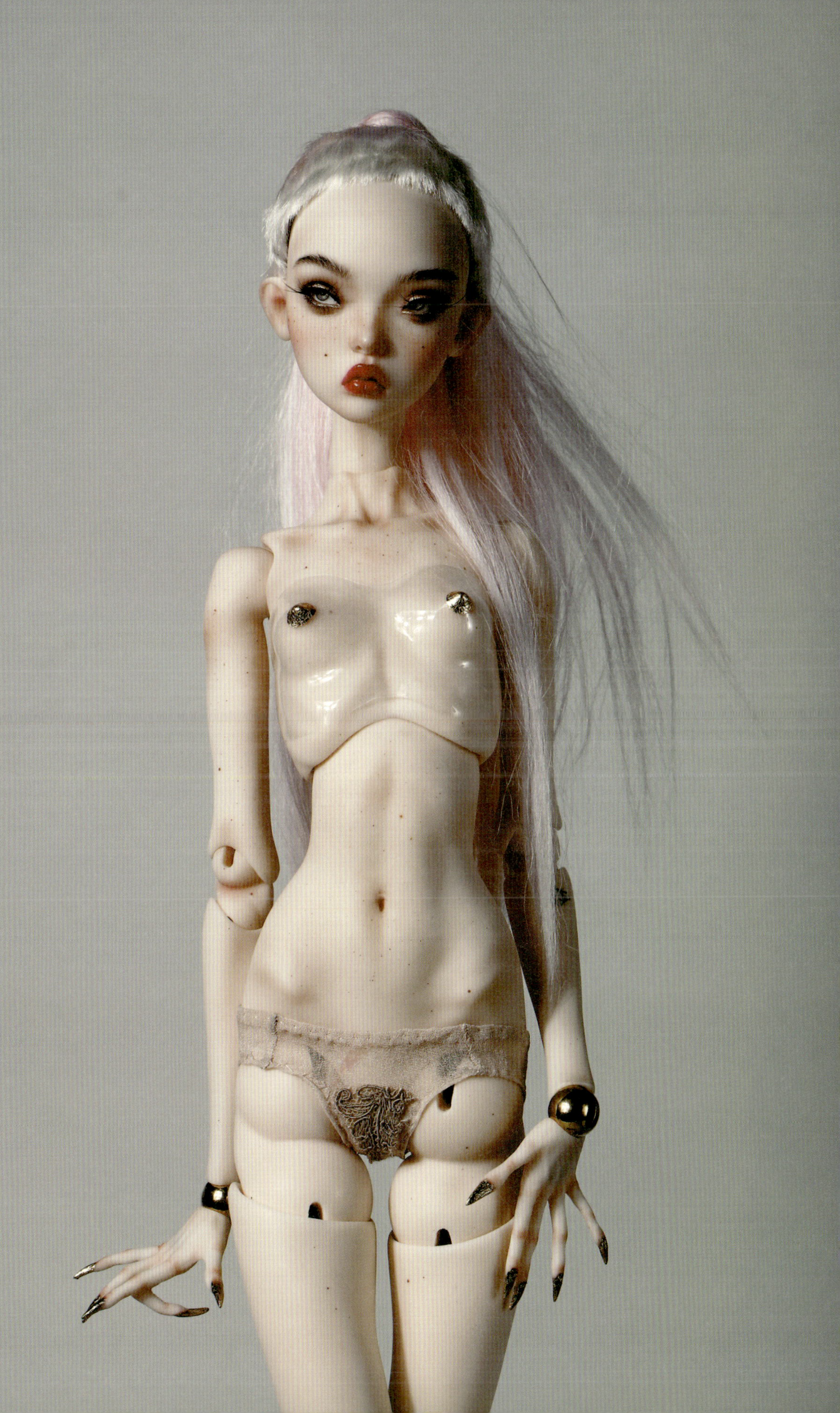

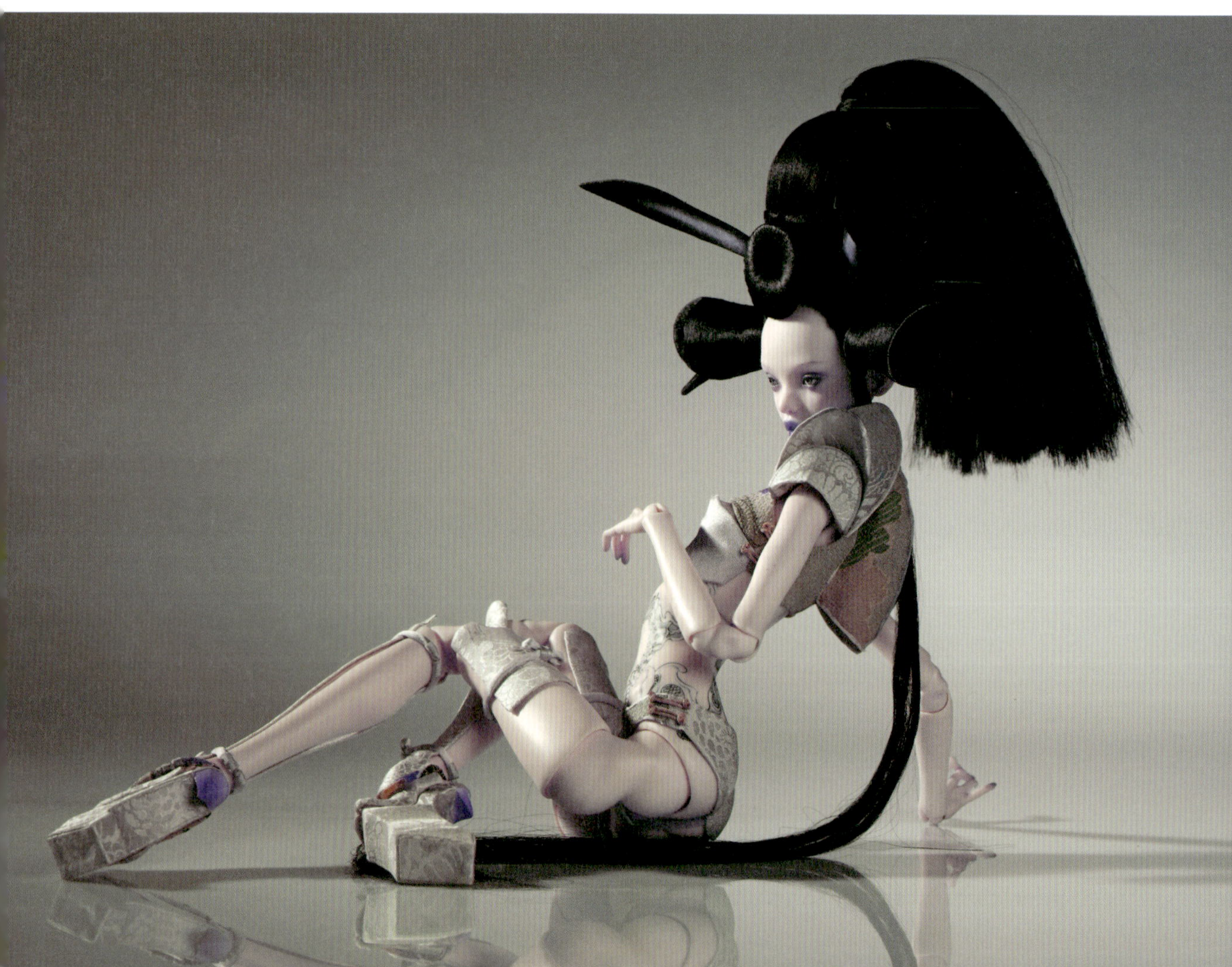

Lena & Katya Popovy

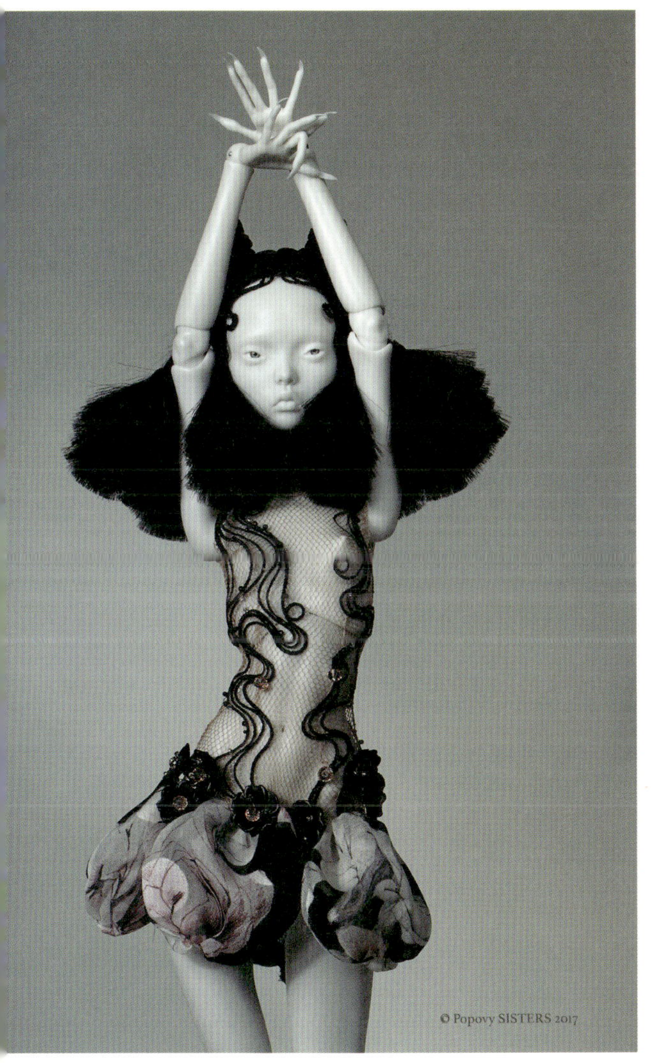

Lena & Katya Popovy

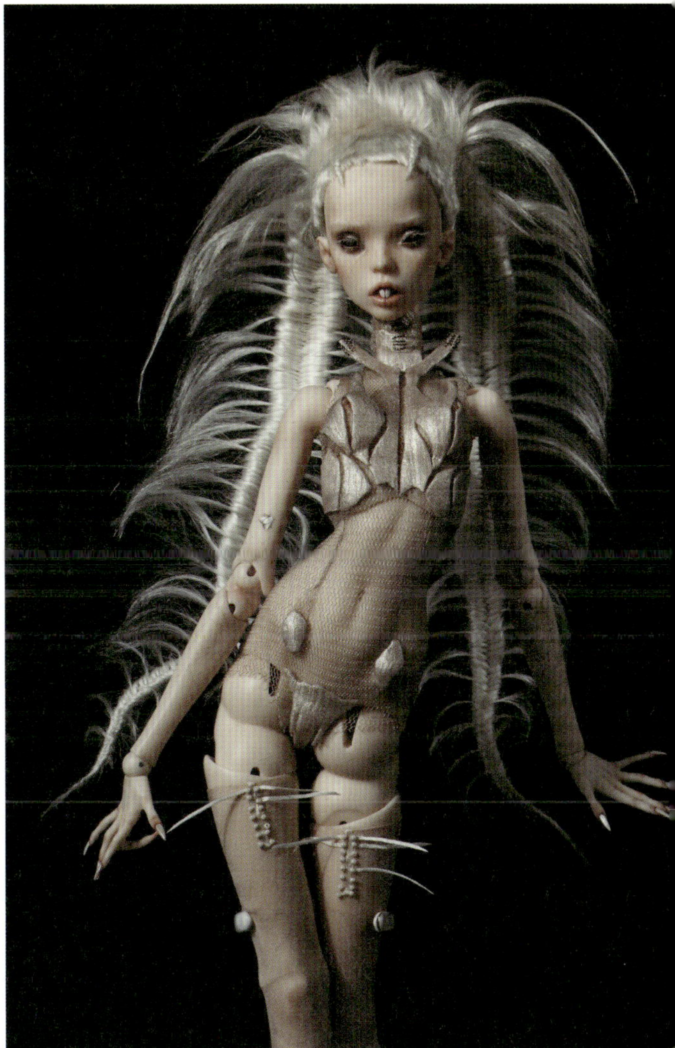

Lena & Katya Popovy

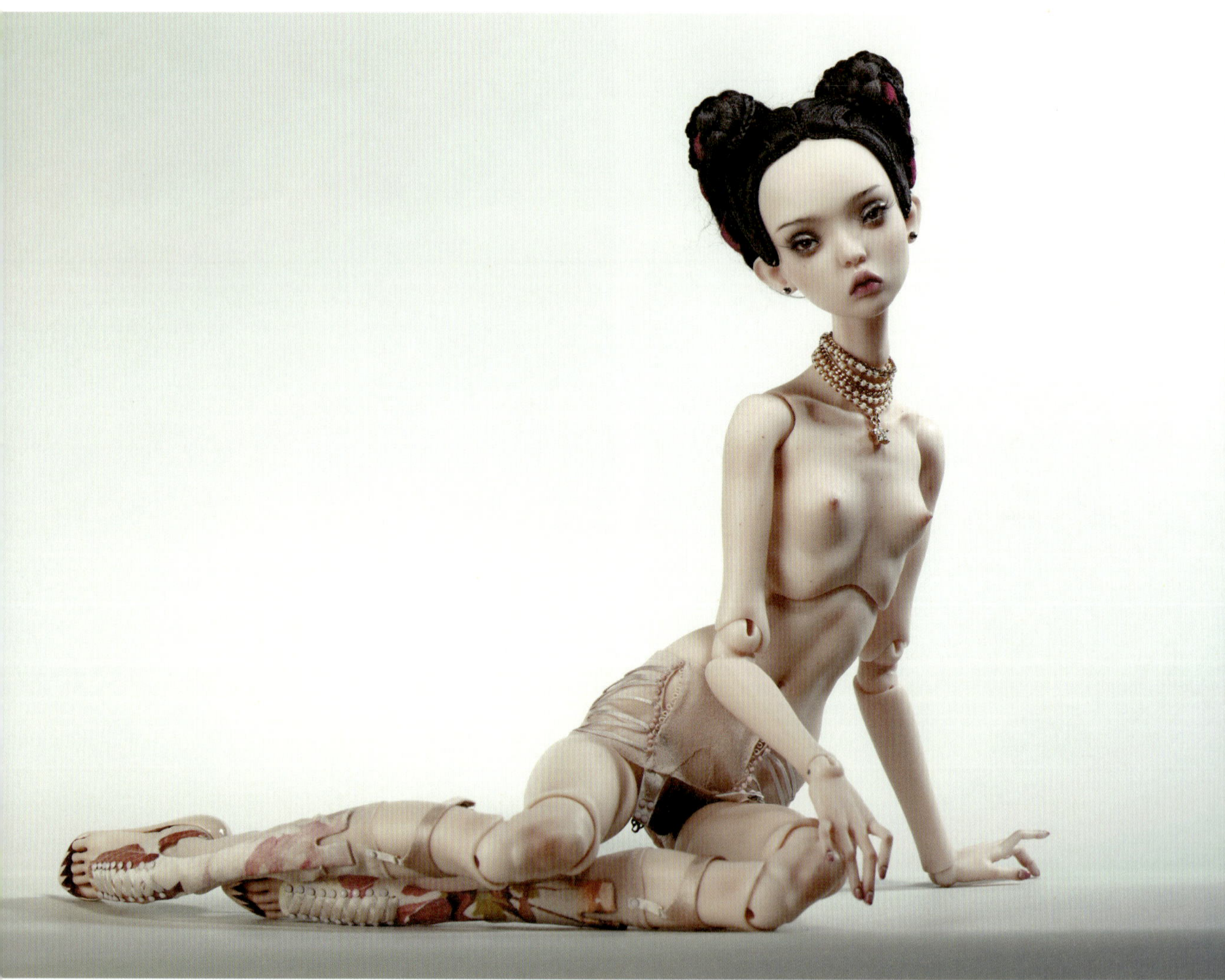

Lena & Katya Popovy

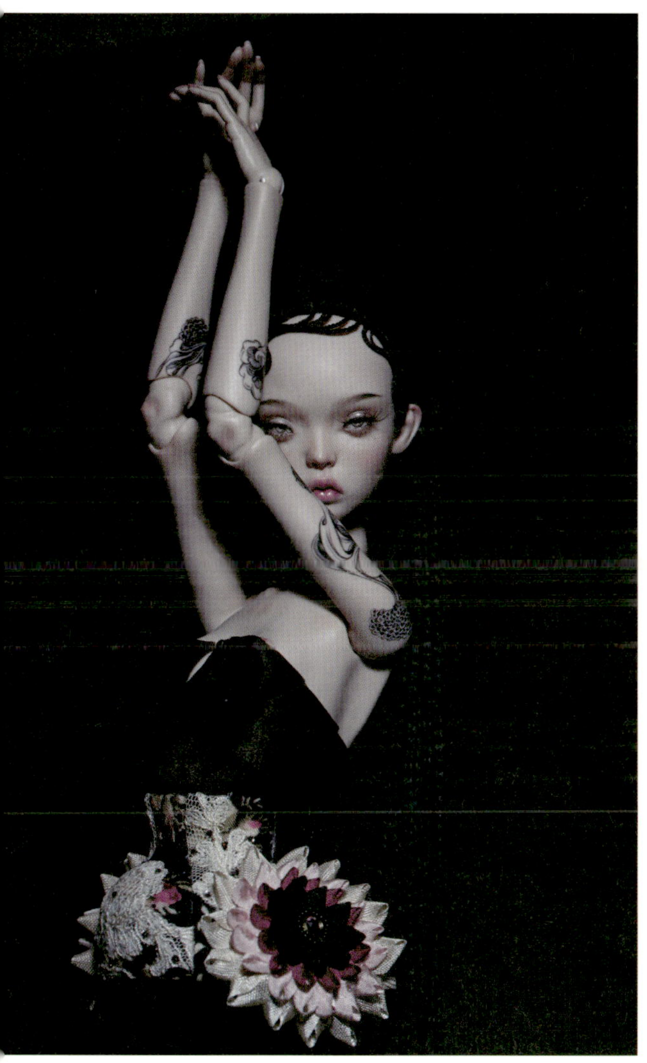 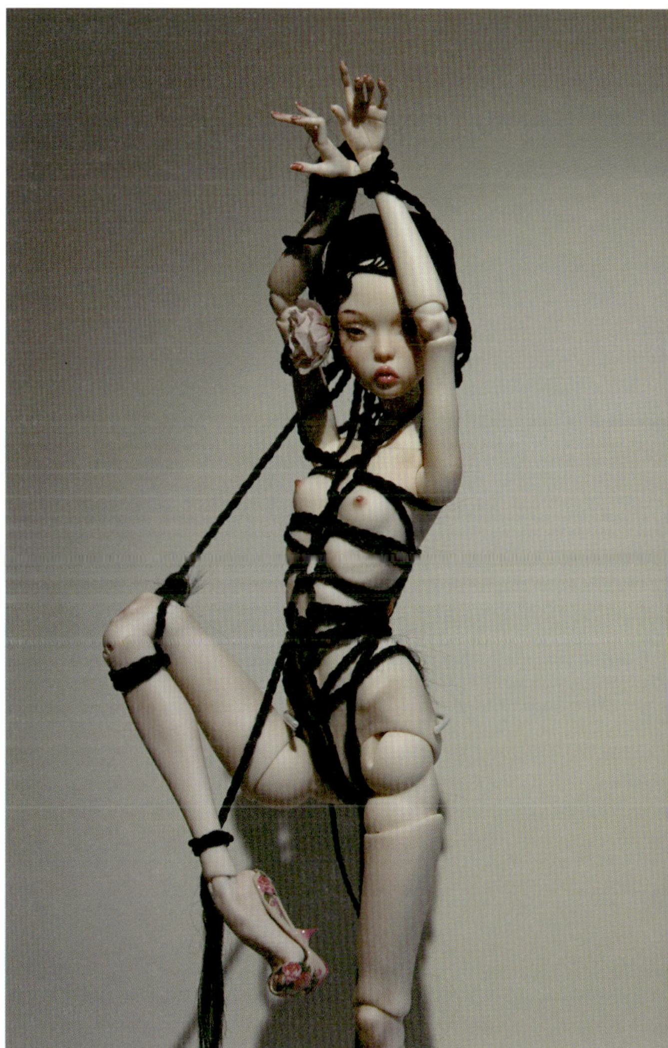

Lena & Katya Popovy

Lena & Katya Popovy

36

Willy Verginer
ウィリ・ヴェルジネル（イタリア　Italy）

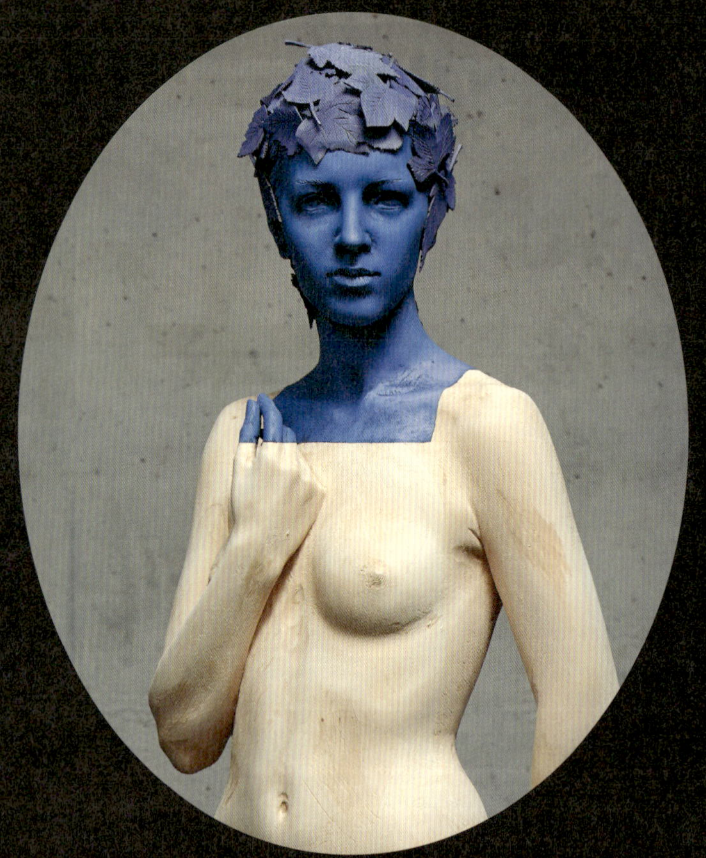

1957年イタリア、ブレッサノーネ生まれ。南チロル、ボルツァーノ自治県オルティゼーイ在住。主要な公立、私立の美術館、イタリア国内外の一流アート・ギャラリーにて、個展、グループ展を開催。木の幹から掘り出された等身大の人間像は、細部に至るまで本物そっくりに造られ、まるで生きているかのようだ。像は単体で展示されることが多いが、物や動物を組み合わせたメッセージ性の高い作品もある。伝統に縛られることなく、貪欲に新しい手法を取り入れ、社会問題にも関心が高い。環境問題を提起したインスタレーションは見る者をはっとさせる。

Born in 1957 in Bressanobe Italy. Lives and works in Ortisei BZ - South Tyrol Italy. Solo and group exhibitions made in the most important public and private institutions, in prestigious Italian and foreign art galleries. The sculptor carves ultra-realistic characters in human dimensions out of tree trunks. With remarkable precision and attention to detail, he showcases ordinary individuals sometimes combined with significant objects or animals. The artist has been able to move away from the traditional approach to sculpting with wood, preferring to adopt a totally contemporary process. By observing the world around him, the artist conceptualises social questions, including environmental concerns in particular, in installations that are often incredibly imposing.

www.verginer.com

↑ Ciüria de föies（Cap of Leaves）葉の帽子
シナ彫刻材、アクリル彩色 / H179cm / 2014

→Pe d'or（Golden Step）黄金の一歩
シナ彫刻材、アクリル彩色、金箔 / H91cm / 2013

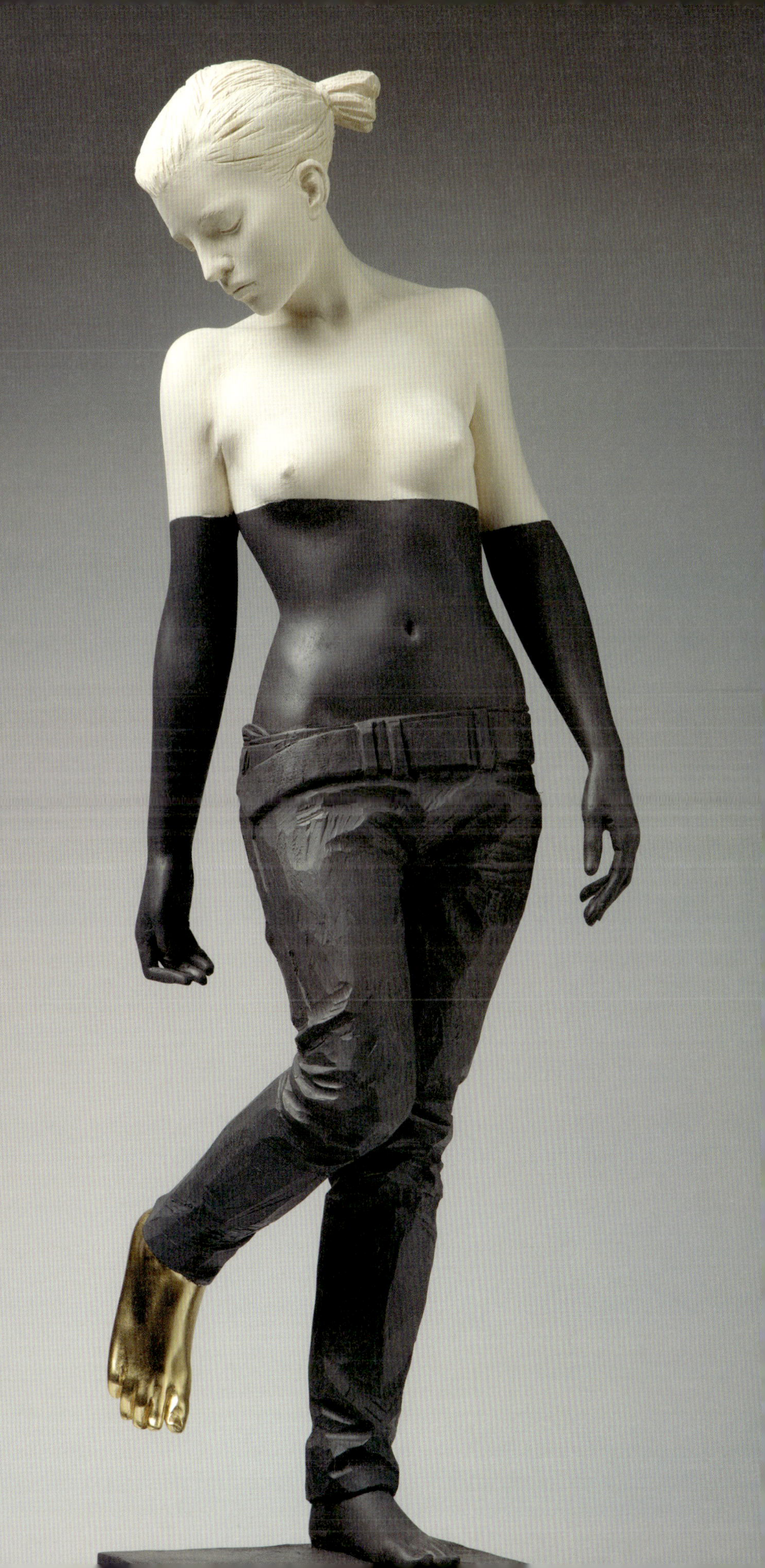

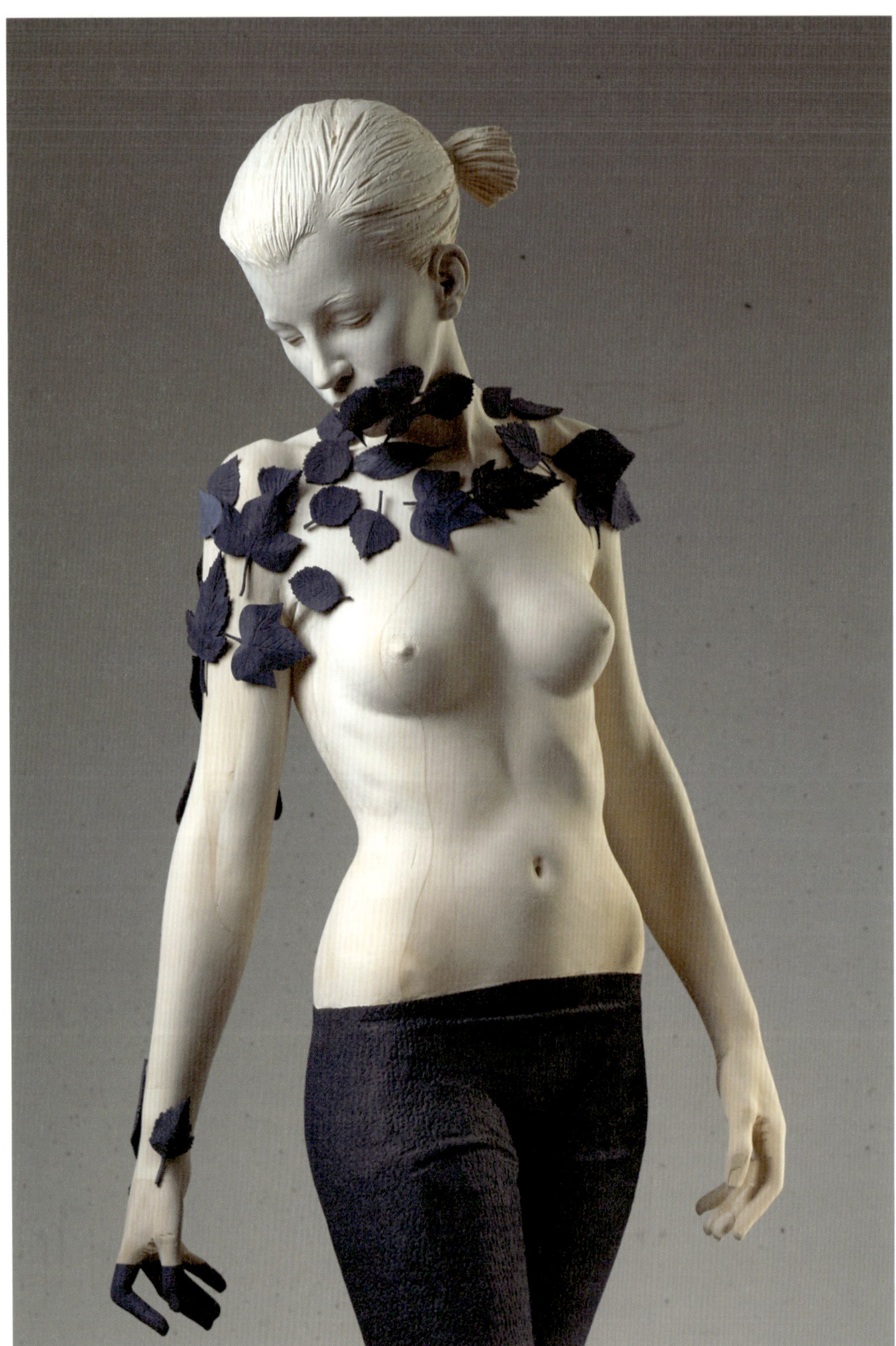

Ballare in Controluce（Dance against the Light）逆光のダンス
シナ彫刻材、アクリル彩色 / H175×W55×D50cm / 2015

Il vento di sera la invita（The Evening Wind Invites Her）夜風が彼女を誘う
シナ彫刻材、アクリル彩色 / H172cm / 2012

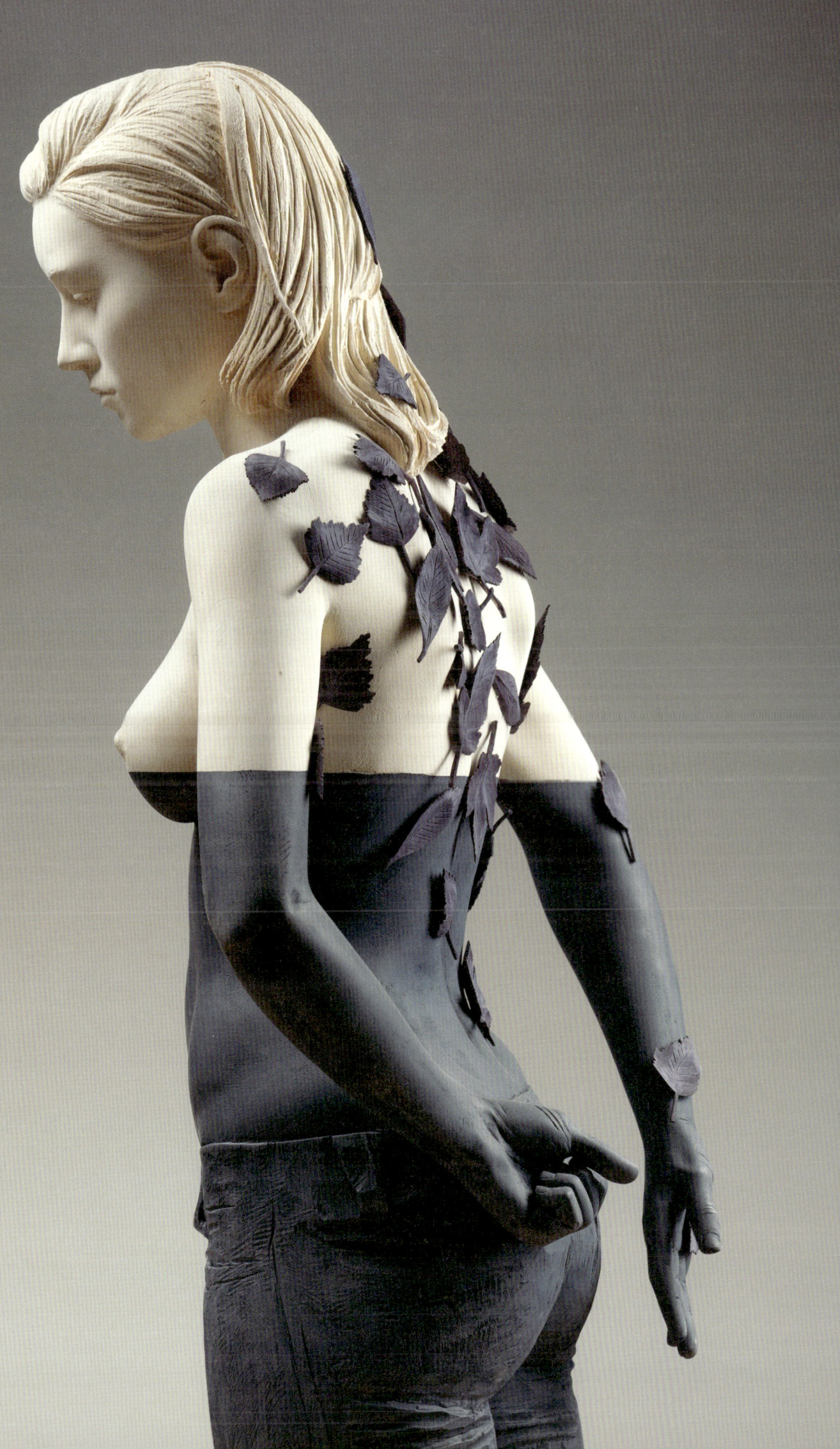

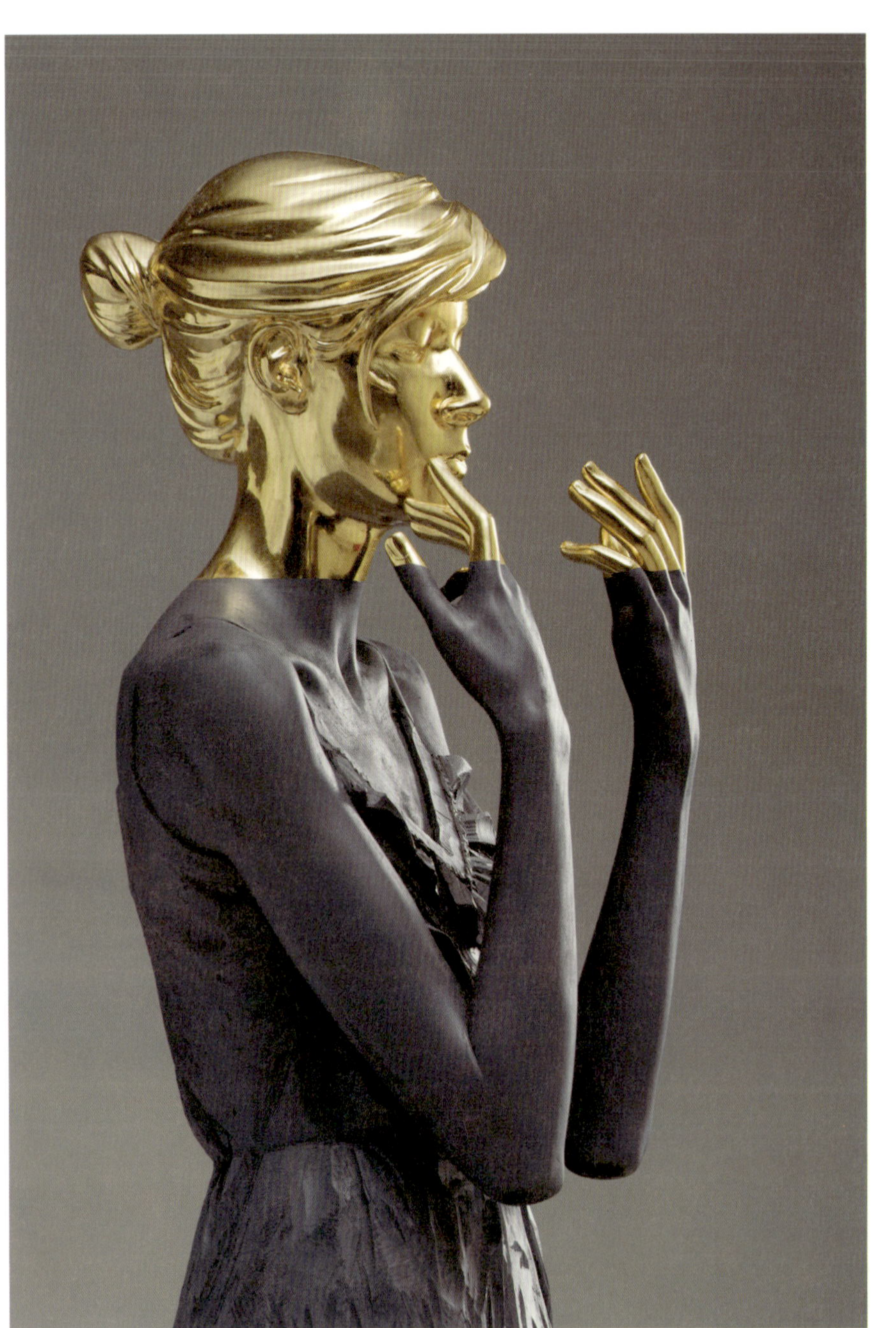

Shine on Me 私を輝かせて
シナ彫刻材、アクリル彩色、金箔 / H190cm / 2012

Ciüria de föies（Cap of Leanes）葉の帽子
ブロンズ、アクリル彩色 / H181×W63×D49cm / 2017

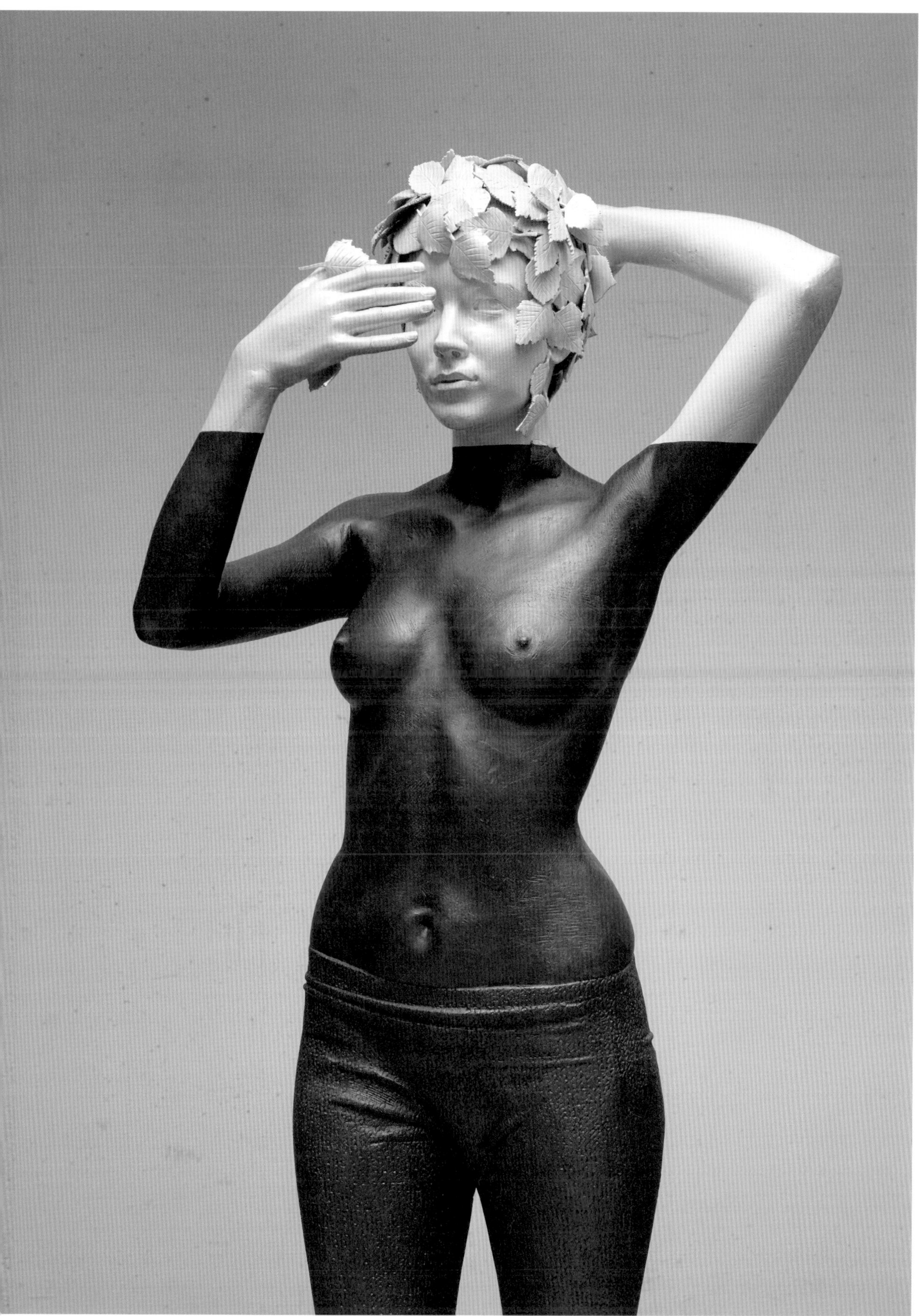

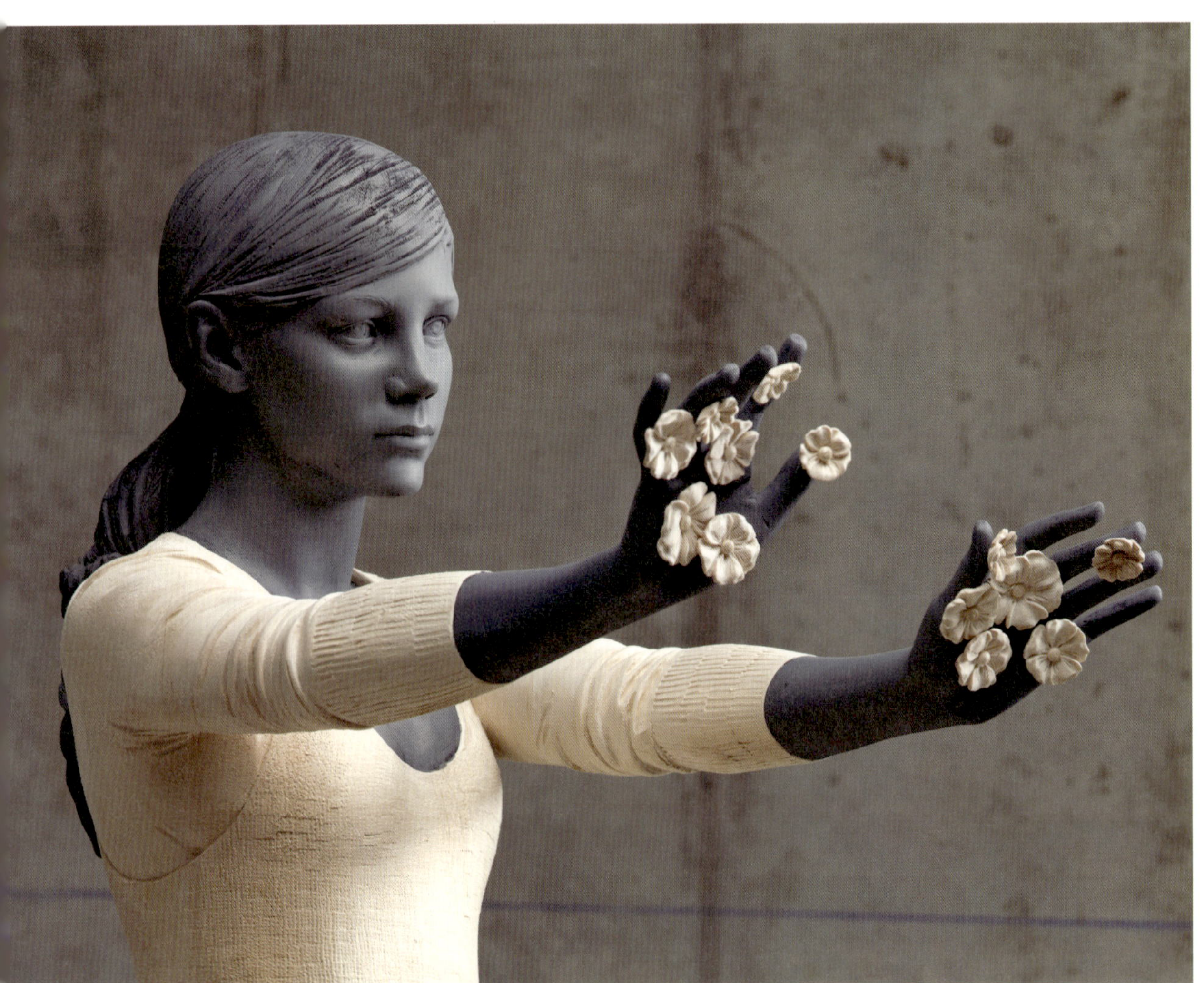

Eppure è primavera（And It's Spring yet）それでもまだ季節は春
シナ彫刻材、アクリル彩色 / H170cm / 2011

La pel dl vënt（The Skin of the Wind）風の肌
シナ彫刻材、アクリル彩色 / H172cm / 2013

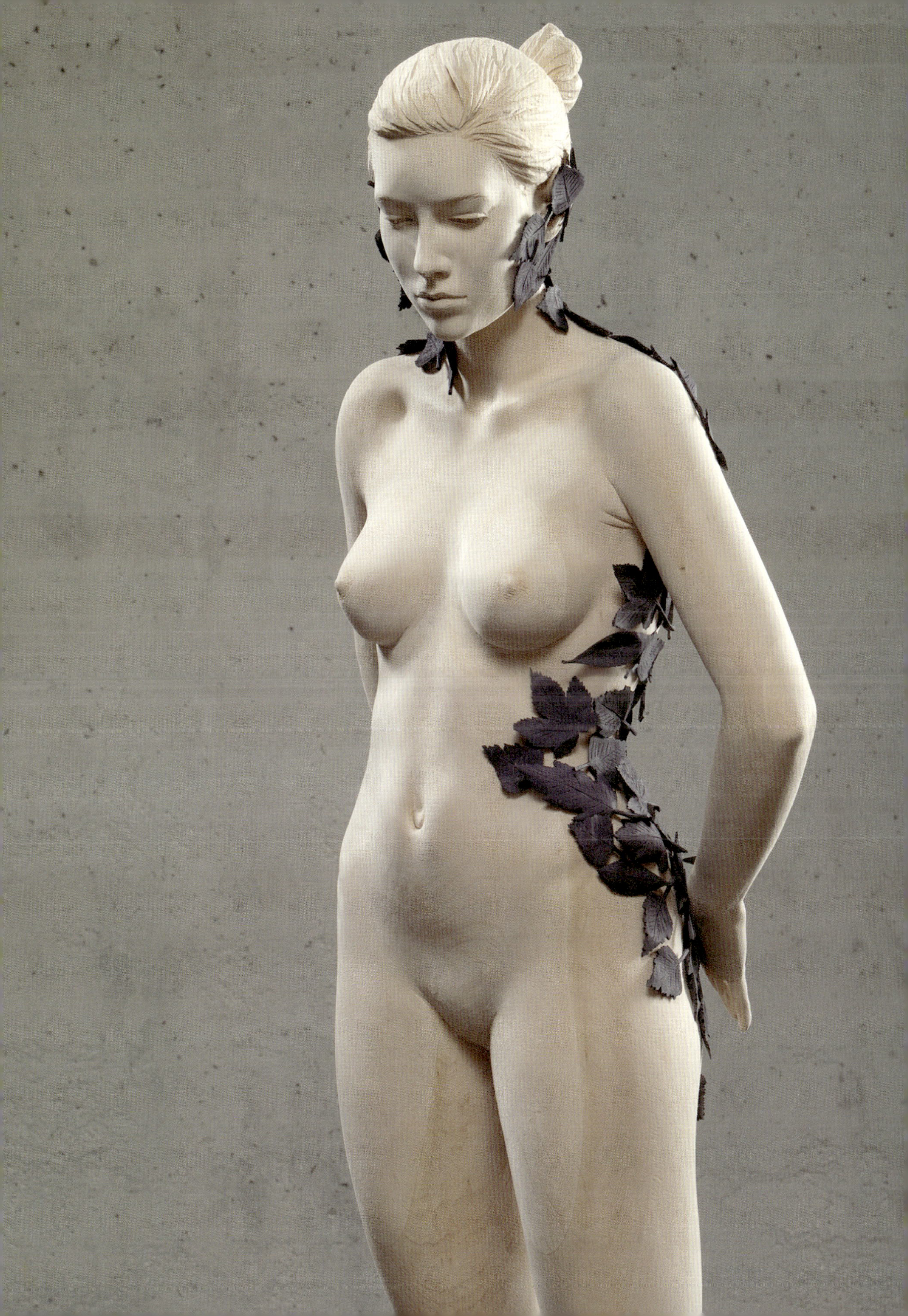

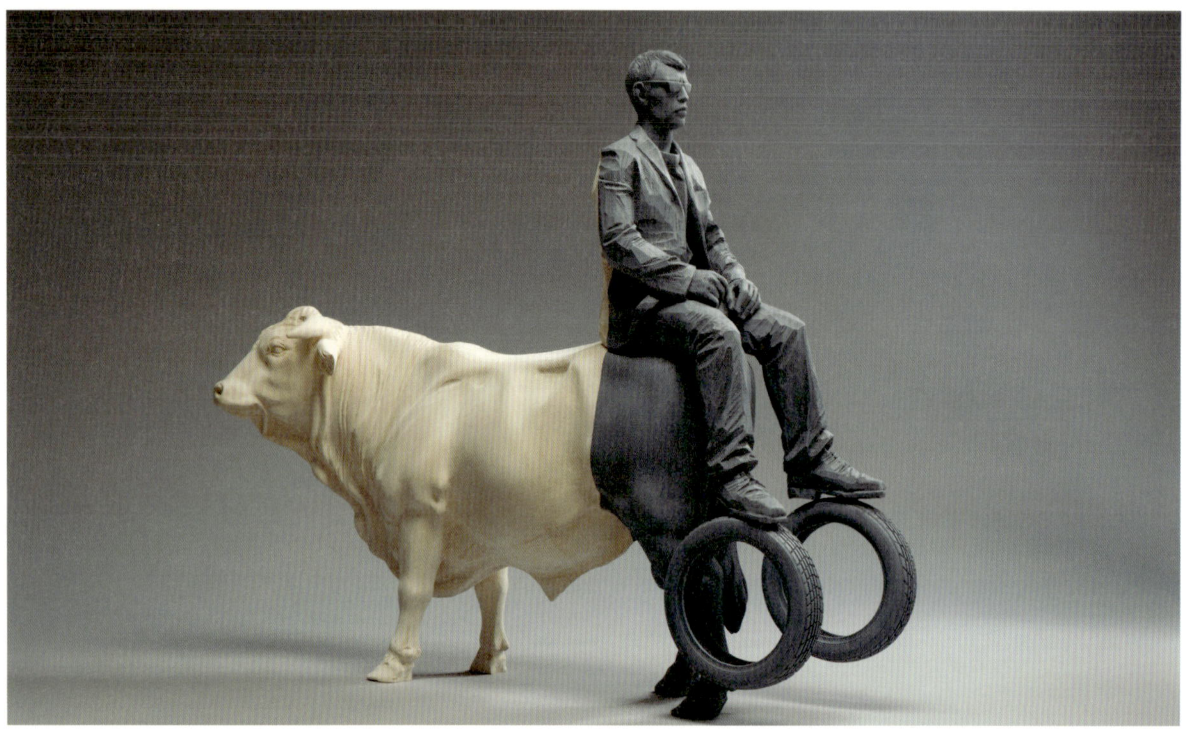

The Dark Side of the Bull 雄牛のダーク・サイド
シナ彫刻材、アクリル彩色 / H60×W74×D21cm / 2013

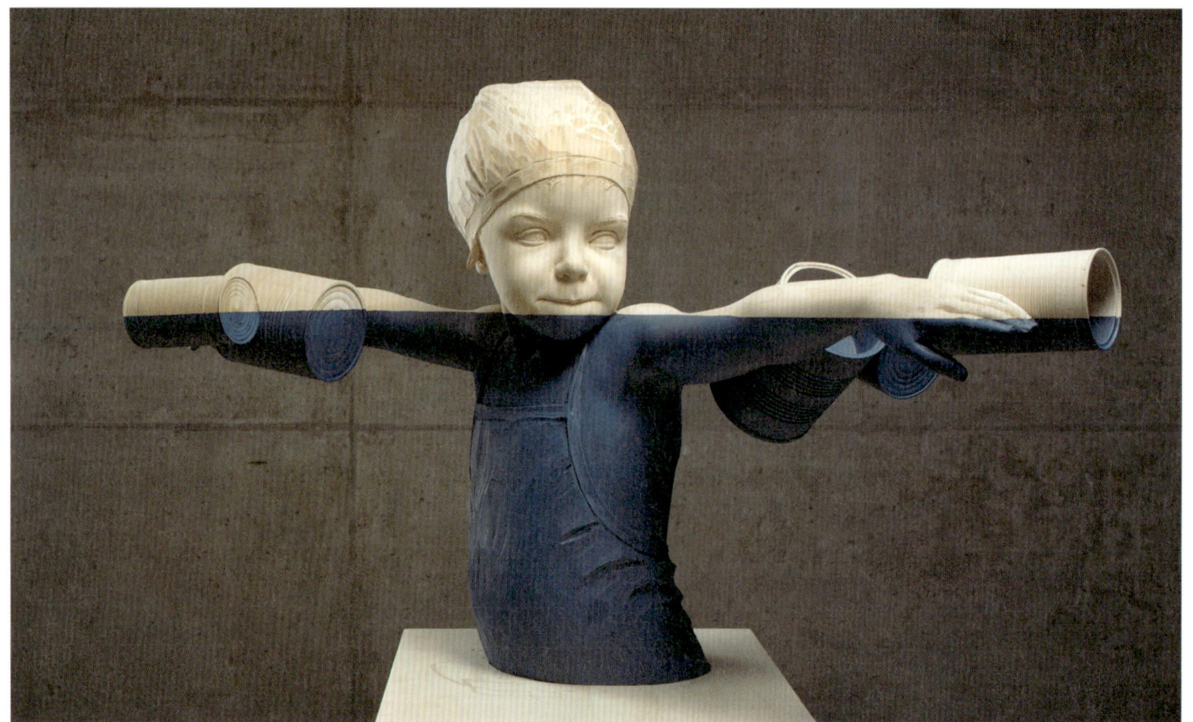

Ombre nell'acqua（Shadows in the Water）水の中の影
シナ彫刻材、アクリル彩色 / H175×W190×D80cm / 2016

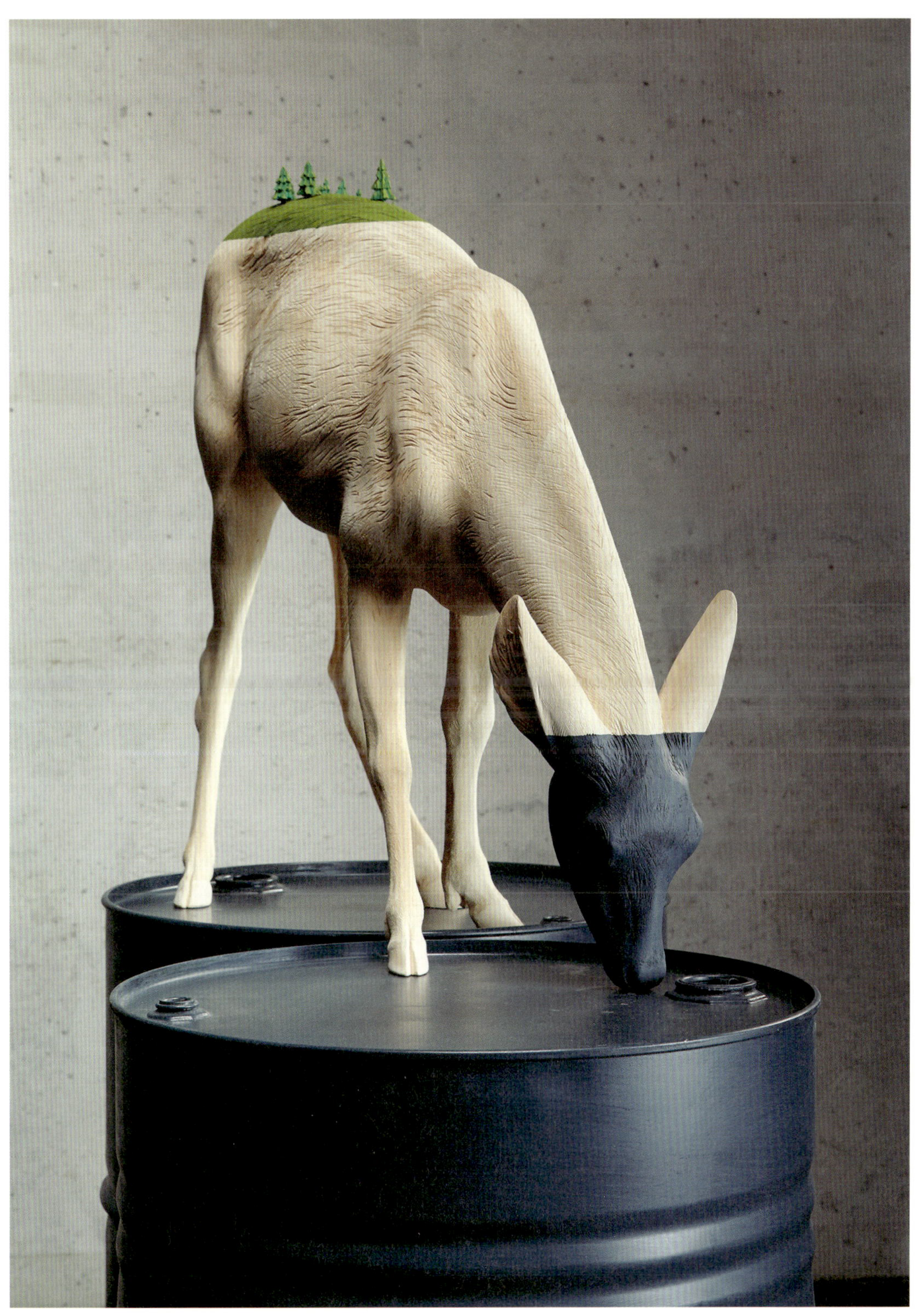

Tra idilico e realtà（Between Idyllio and Reality）のどかさと現実の間で
シナ彫刻材、アクリル彩色、鉄 / H160×W60×D120cm / 2014

37

Danny van Ryswyk

ダニー・ファン・リズウィック（オランダ Netherlands）

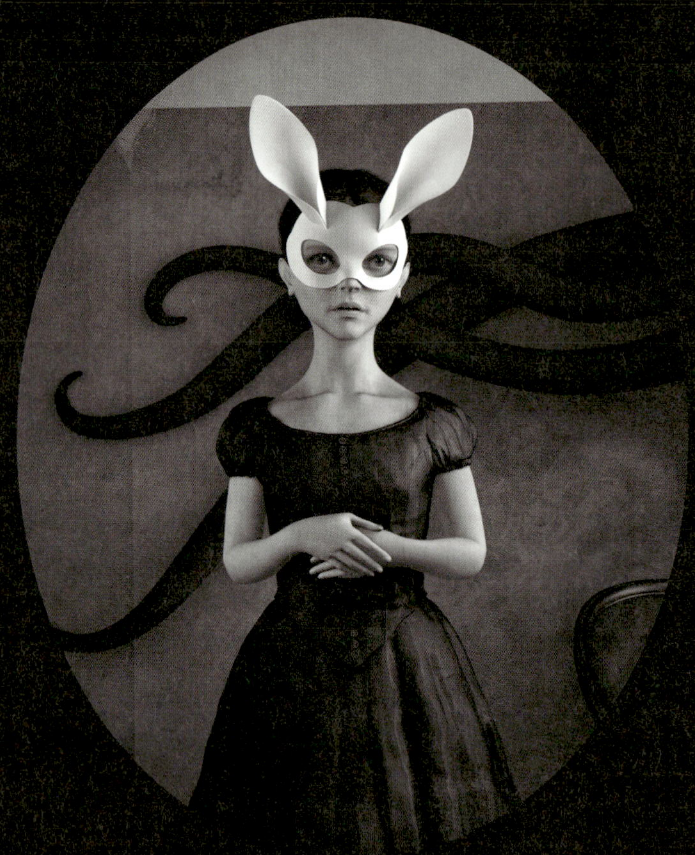

デジタル3D技術を駆使し、不機嫌で思い詰めたような表情のキャラクターの絵や彫像を制作。ガラスドームの
ケースに収められた作品は、古びた標本のようなノスタルジックな味わいがある。彼の作品の魅力は、アートの
本質がみごとに反映され、見る者の心を揺さぶる点にあるだろう。恐ろしいもの、神秘的なものに惹かれる人間
の心理が、神秘の本質を犠牲にすることなく、最先端のアートに投影され、見る者の心をざわつかせ、人間の心
に潜む闇や、宗教の暗部を覗きたい気持ちにさせる。

Danny van Ryswyk works digitally, producing 3D sculptures and paintings of moody and contemplative
characters. Sometimes encased in glass domes, they have a feel of scientific specimens from another era.
The fascinating thing about his work is that he perfectly reflects the essence of art, namely the generation of
emotional responses. He brings morbid fascinations and the metaphysical mysteries that lives in human life
to a modern decor without sacrificing the essence of the mystery. The work of Danny van Ryswyk not only
touches the spectator's emotion, it makes you think about the dark side of ourselves, religion and life.

www.dannyvanryswyk.com

↑White Rabbit 白ウサギ（部分）
アーカイバル・カラー印刷、コットン紙 / H29.7×W21cm

⇒The World Within 世界の中で
アーカイバル・カラー印刷、コットン紙 / H30×W21.4cm

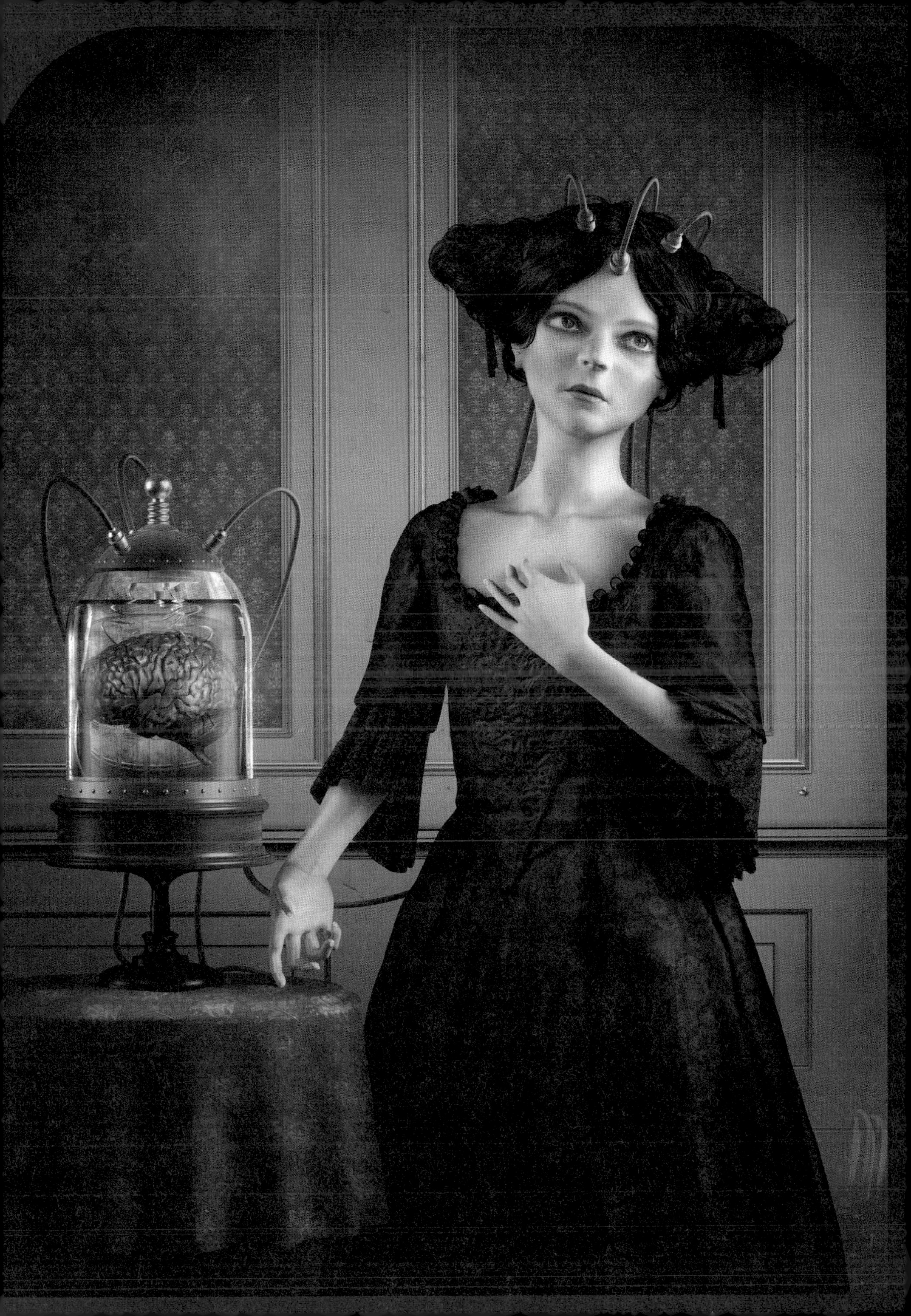

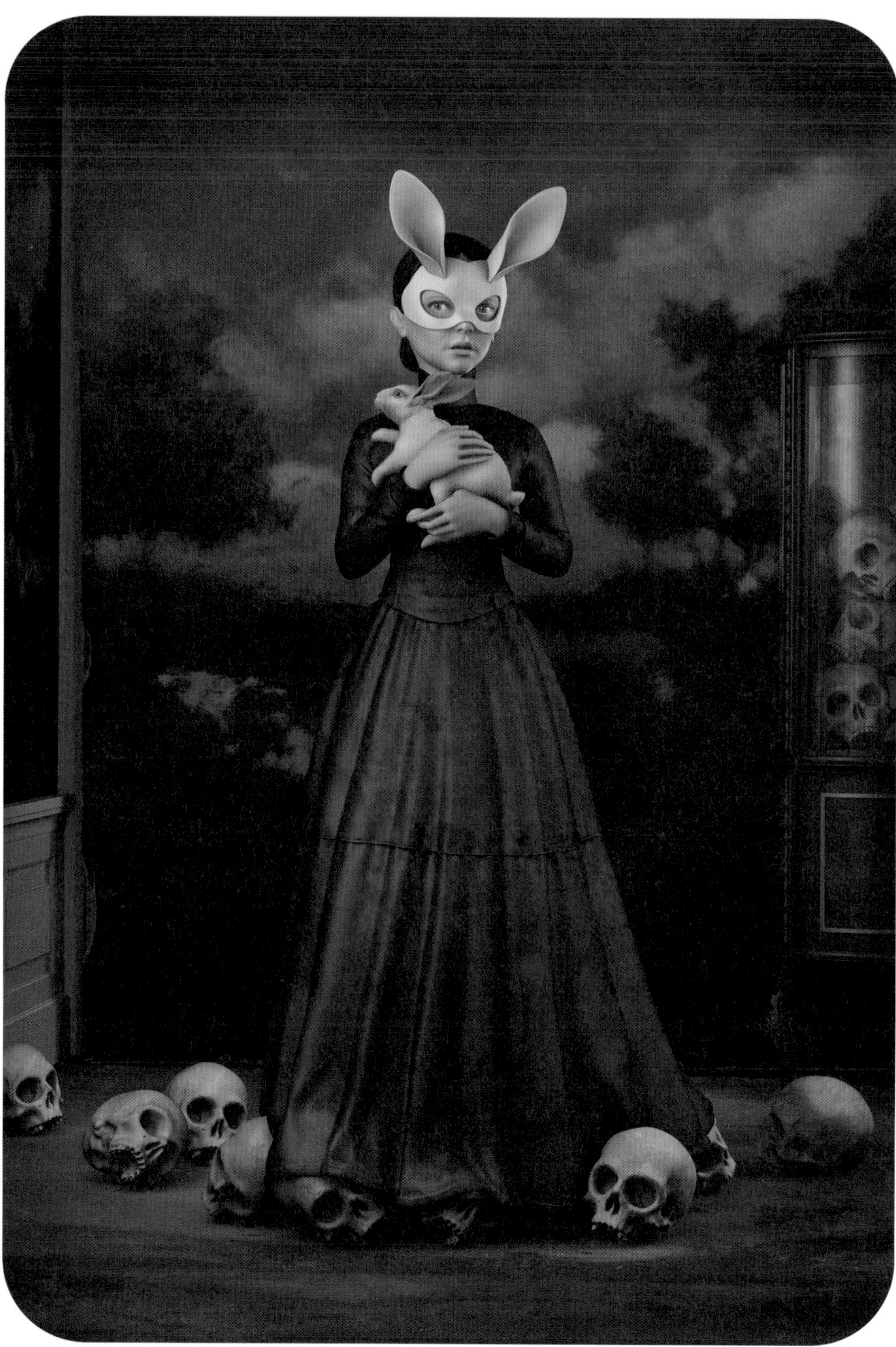

Tender Loving Darkness 闇を愛する番人
アーカイバル・カラー印刷, コットン紙 / H47.3×W31.9cm

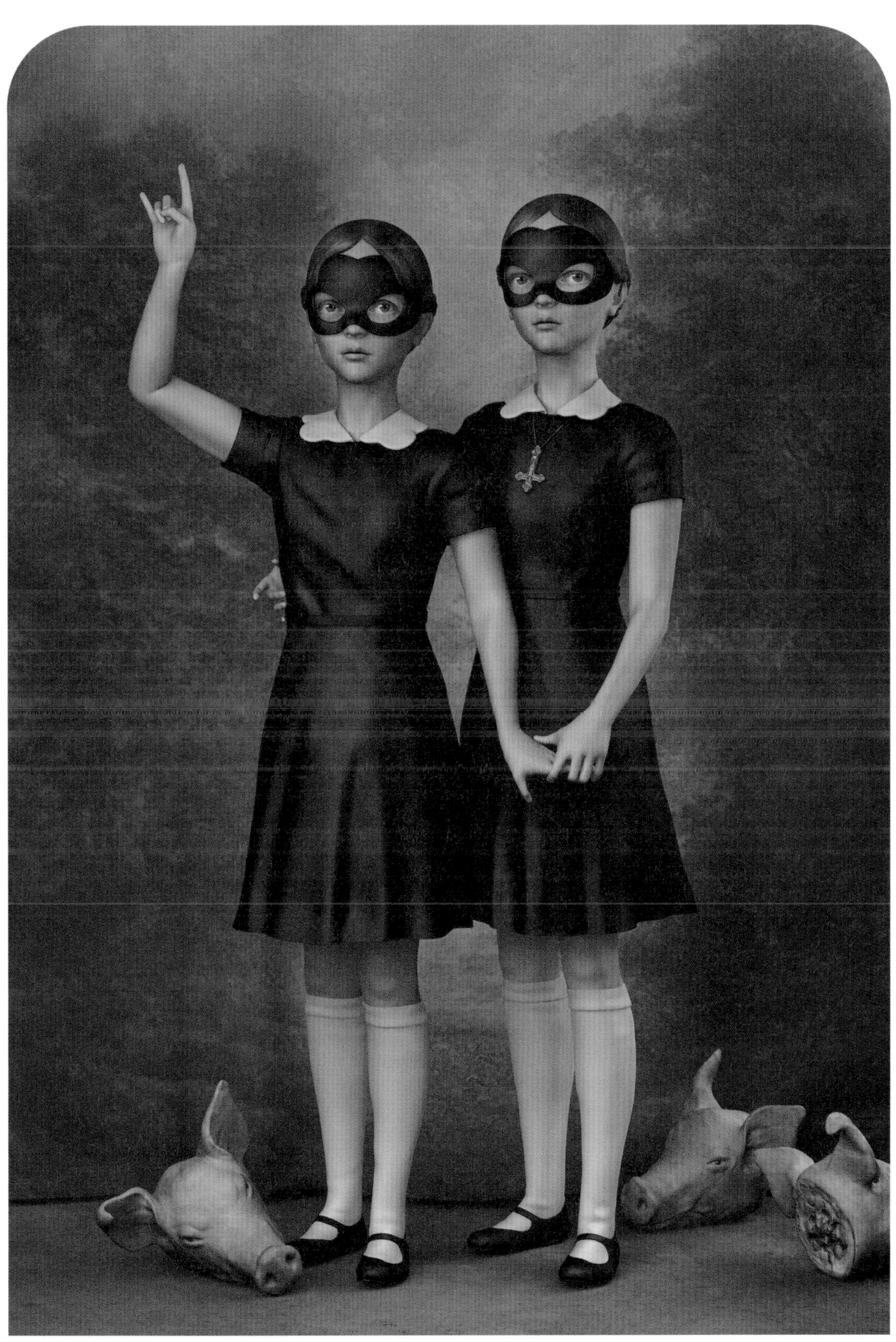

In the Name of Lucifer 悪魔の名のもとに
アーカイバル・カラー印刷、コットン紙 / H47.3×W31.9cm

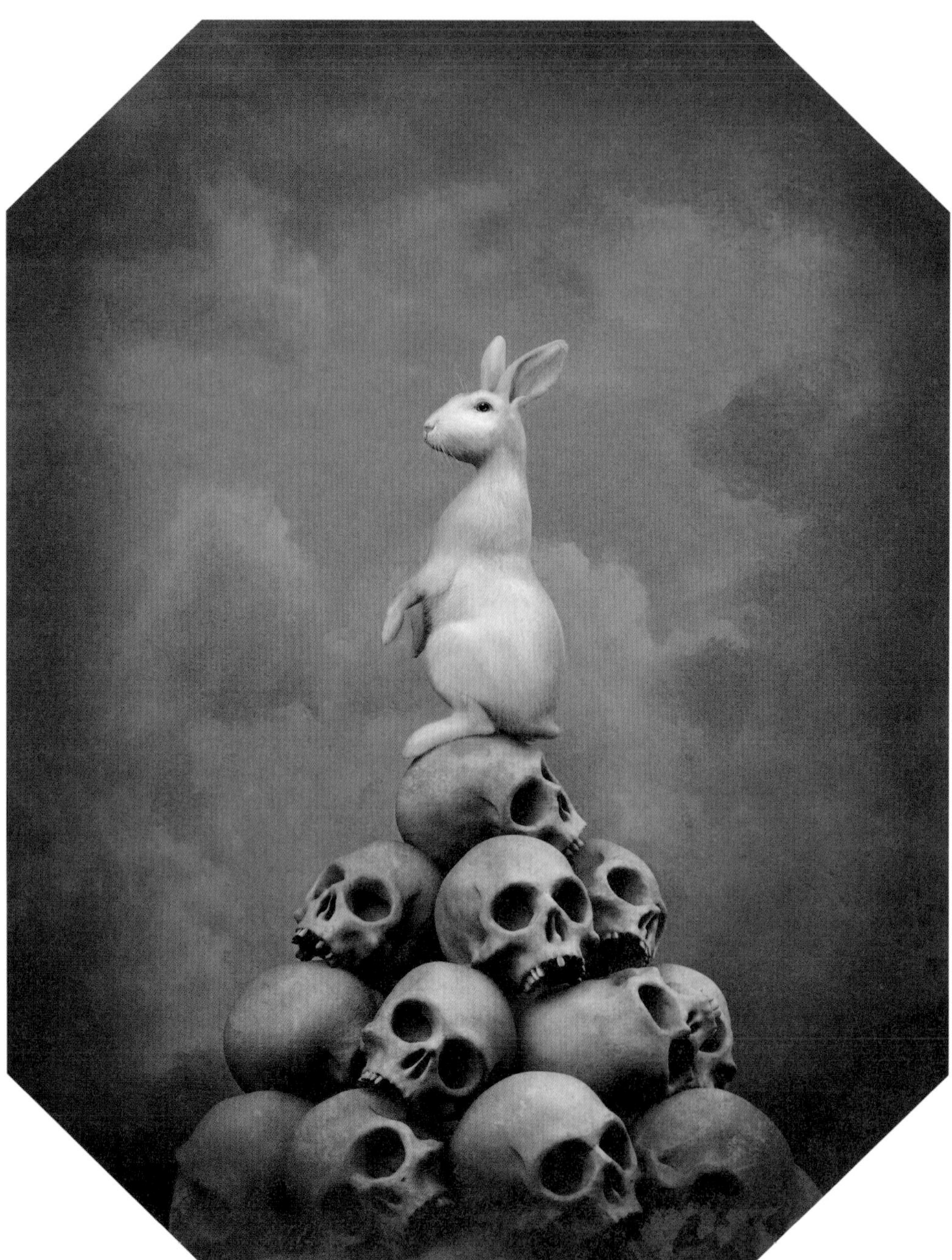

Deleted Souls 消された魂
アーカイバル・カラー印刷、コットン紙 / H18.5×W14cm

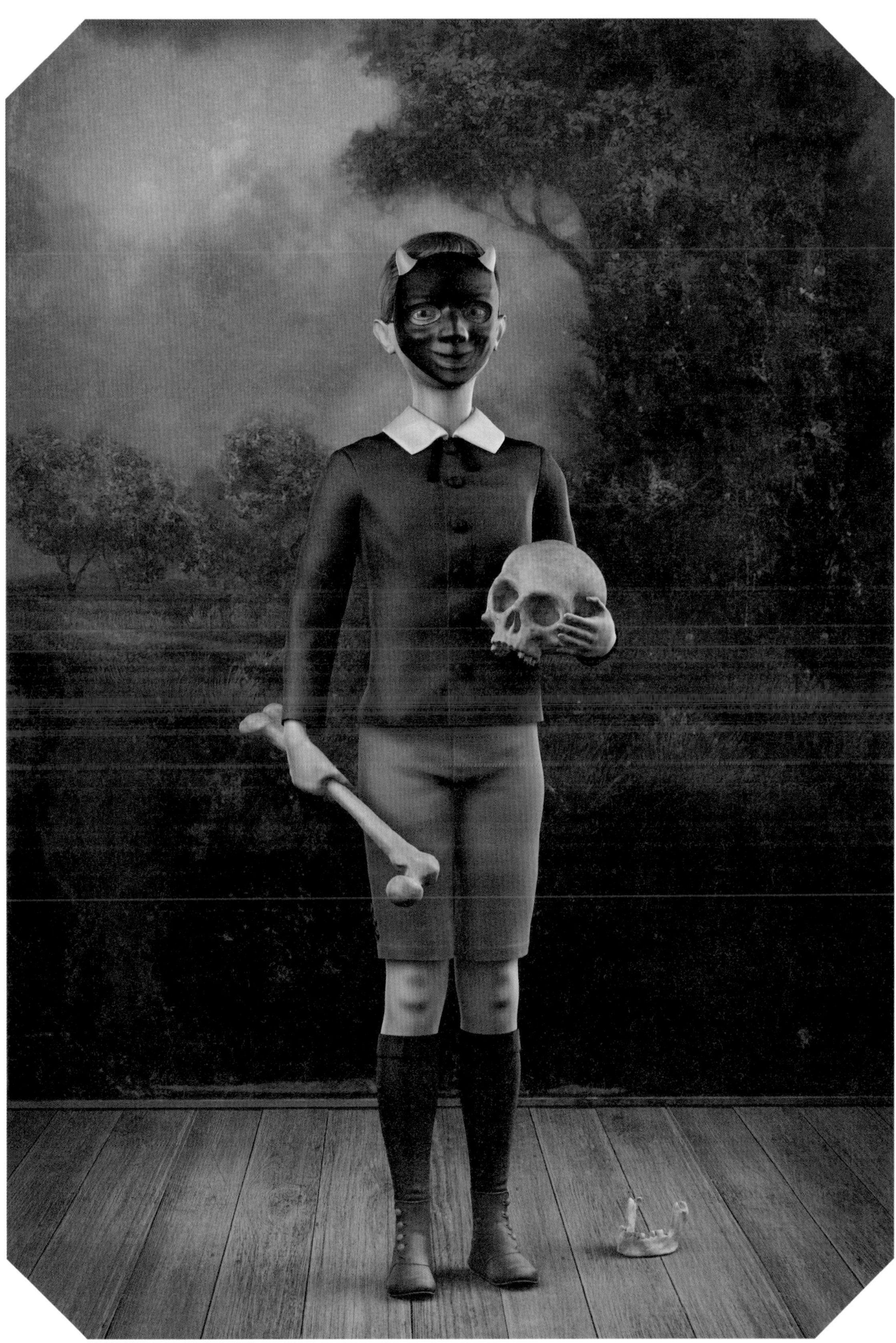

The Untitled 無題
アーカイバル・カラー印刷、コットン紙 / H47.3×W31.9cm

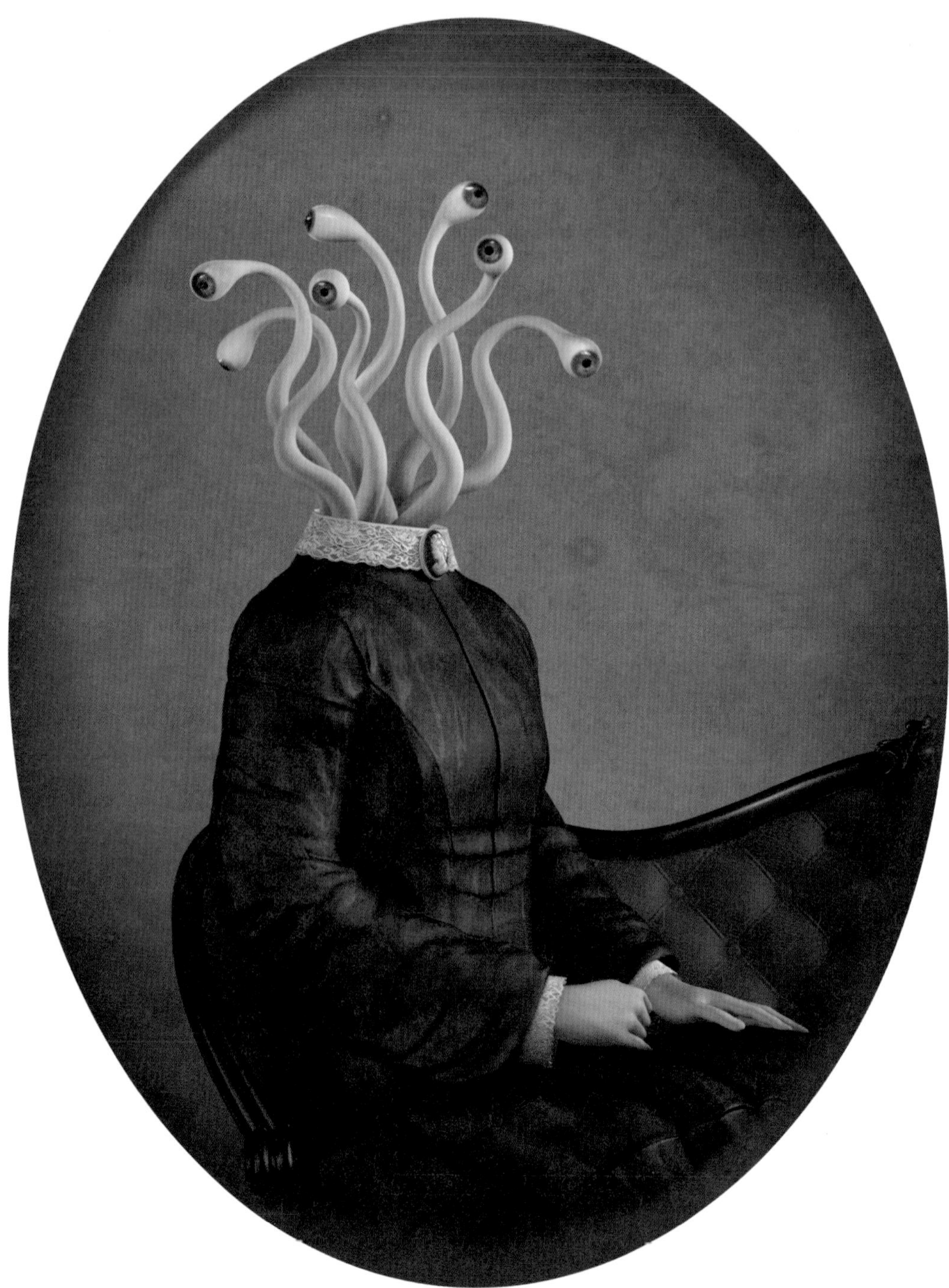

Strange Days Have Found Us 奇妙な日々が私たちを見つけた
アーカイバル・カラー印刷、コットン紙 / H23×W16.8cm

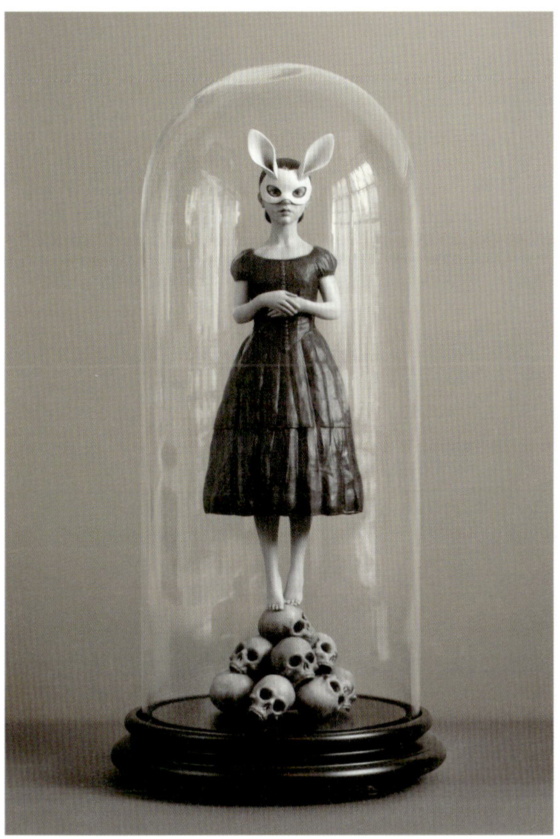

White Rabbit（3D sculpture）白ウサギ（3D彫刻）
アクリル彩色、ポリミアド3D彫刻、ガラス・ドーム /
彫刻：H35cm、ガラス・ドーム：H44cm

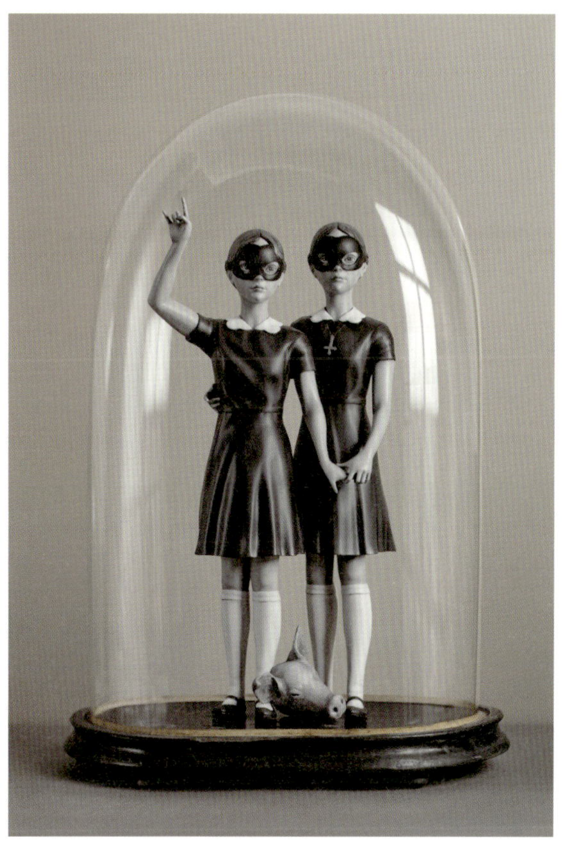

In the Name of Lucifer（3D sculpture）悪魔の名のもとに（3D彫刻）
アクリル彩色、ポリミアド3D彫刻、アンティーク・ガラス・ドーム、ローズウッド板台＆寄木パネル /
彫刻：H36.5cm、アンティーク・ガラス・ドーム：H51cm

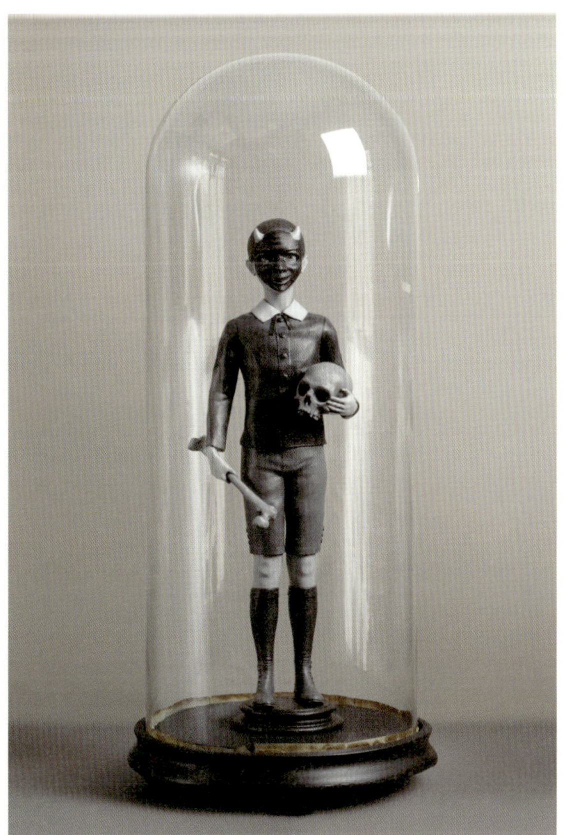

The Untitled（3D sculpture）無題（3D彫刻）
アクリル彩色、ポリミアド3D彫刻、アンティーク・ガラス・ドーム /
彫刻：H38cm、アンティーク・ガラス・ドーム：H55cm

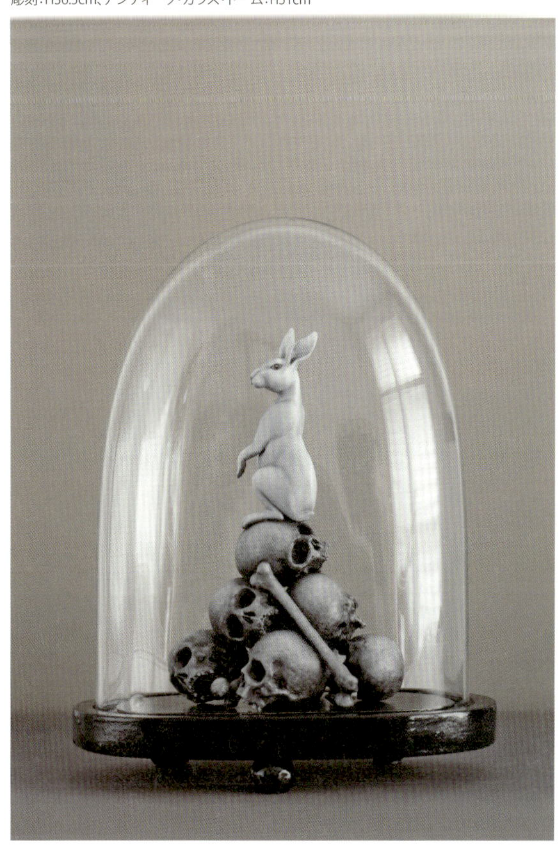

Deleted Souls（3D sculpture）消された魂（3D彫刻）
アクリル彩色、ポリミアド3D彫刻、アンティーク・ガラス・ドーム /
彫刻：H17cm、アンティーク・ガラス・ドーム：H25.5cm

38

Seiko Kato

セイコ・カトウ（日本 Janan）

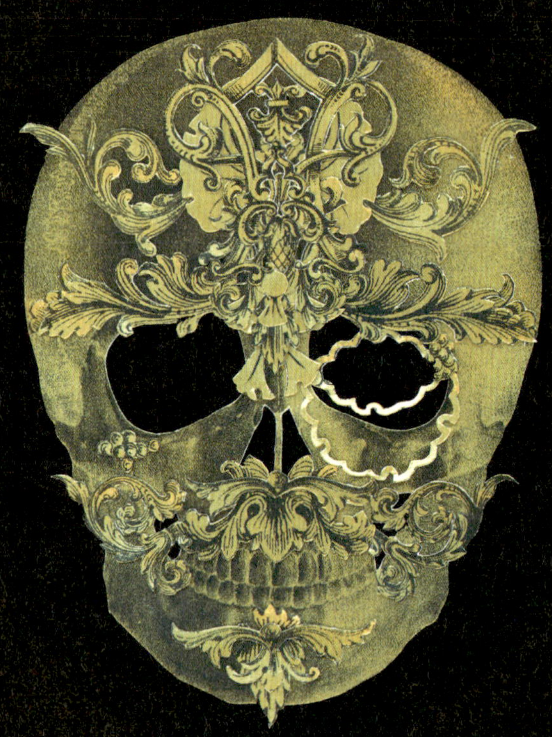

日本人のコラージュ作家。イギリス、ブライトン在住。古書、アンティークの装身具、漂流物の熱心なコレクターで、ヴィクトリア朝時代の医学書、銅版画、百科事典から強いインスピレーションを受けている。古い挿絵を分解しつなぎ合わせてつくられた作品は、独創的で美しい。小さなハサミでコラージュ素材をカットしていく。生と死をテーマにした作品は幻想的で不気味さを感じさせながらも遊び心があり、見る人を惹きつける。

Seiko Kato is a Japanese collage artist living in Brighton, U.K. An avid collector of vintage books, antique trinkets and interesting found objects, she finds particular inspiration in Victorian medical books, old Victorian etched drawings and encyclopaedia of things. Seiko deconstructs old illustrations and reconstructs them in a beautiful and unique way. She cuts out all of her collage materials using a tiny pair of scissors. Her intricate work shows a fascination with the macabre and surreal, mixed with playful elements that explore life and death

www.seikokato.com

↑Golden Skull ゴールデン・スカル（部分）
切り絵コラージュ、紙 / H12.4×W9.8cm / 2012

→Audrey オードリー
切り絵コラージュ、紙 / H39.8×W29.2cm / 2009

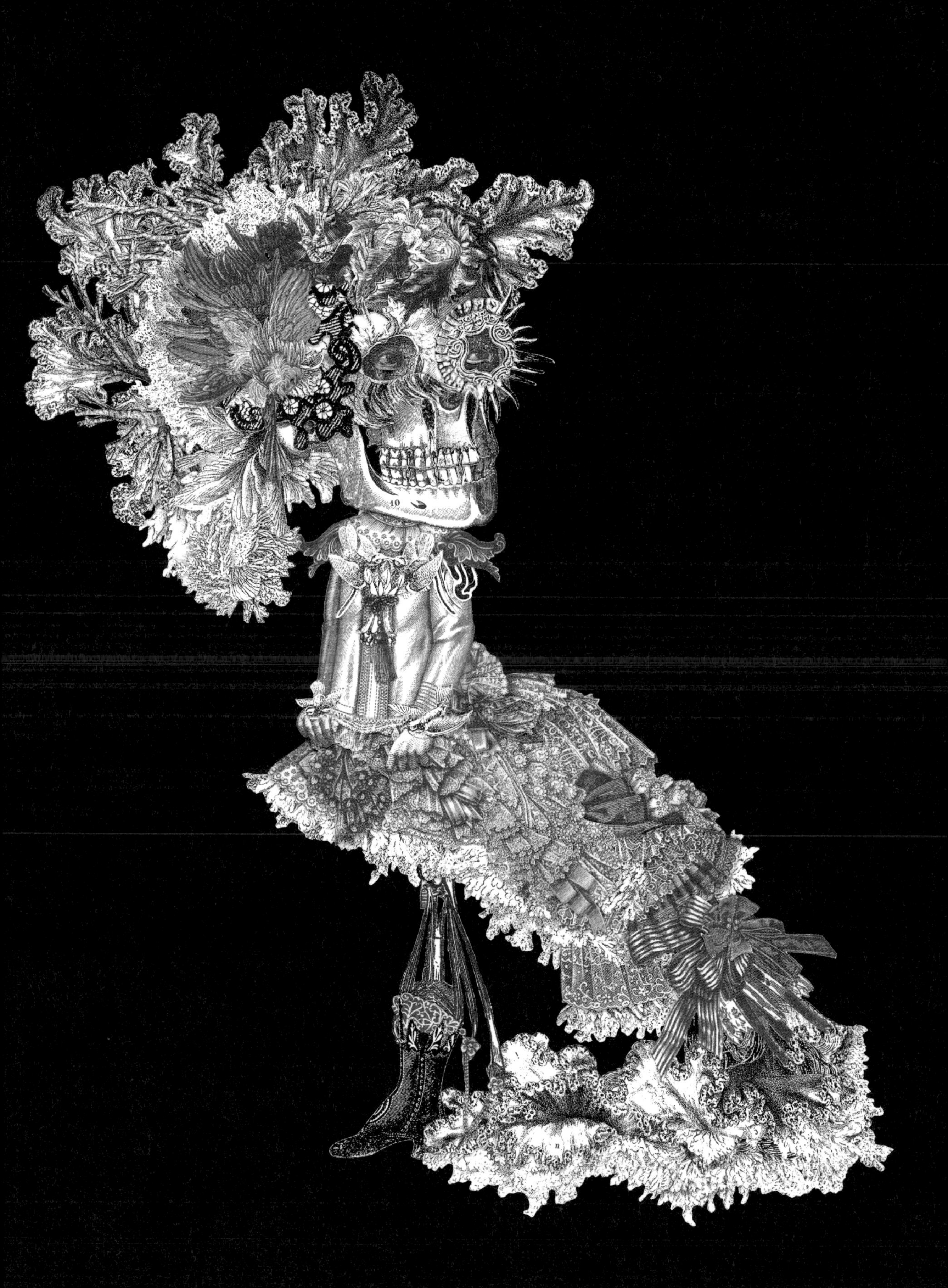

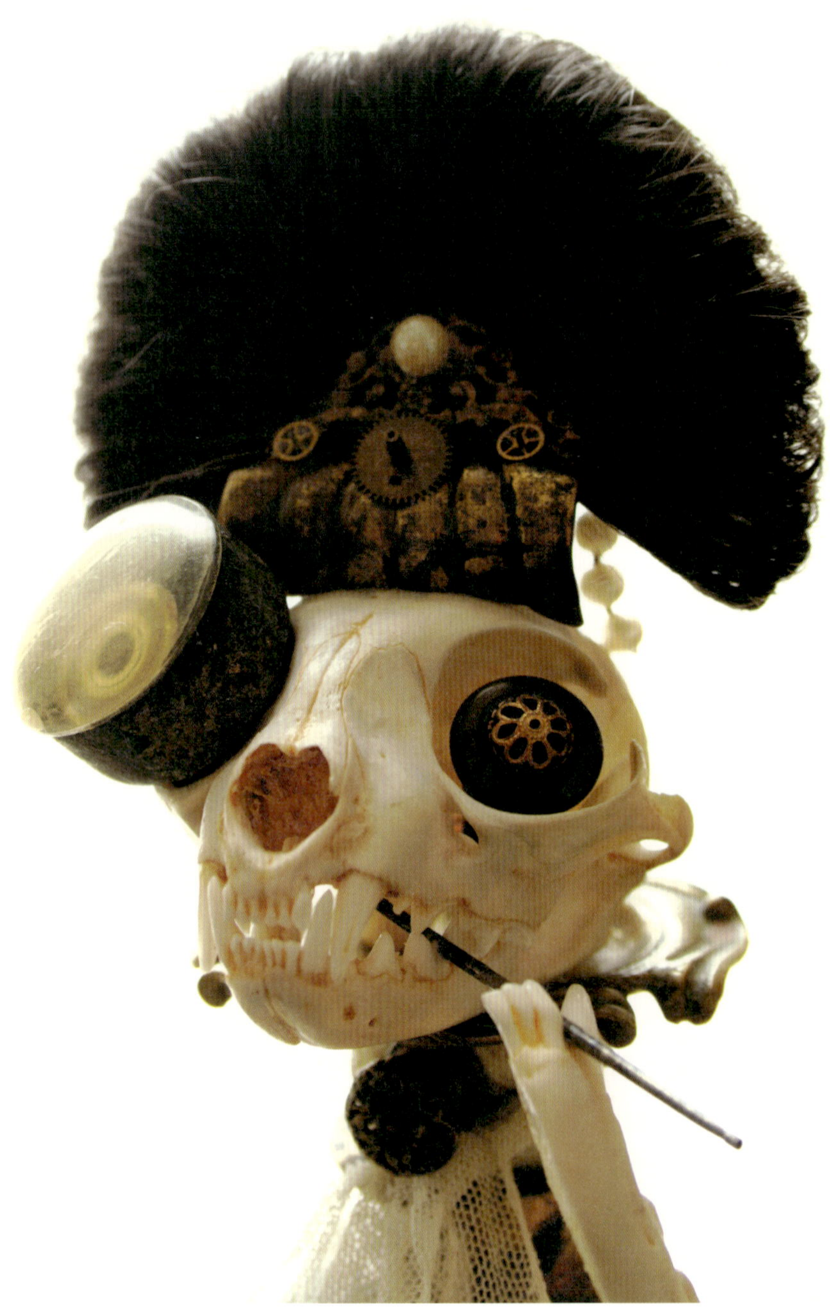

Antoinette アントワネット
猫の骸骨、人毛、鹿の顎の骨、ドール・ドレス、アンティーク・レース、カフスボタン、パール、アンティークのミシン針、金属製スタンド、ファウンド・オブジェ /
H28×W17×D15cm / 2008

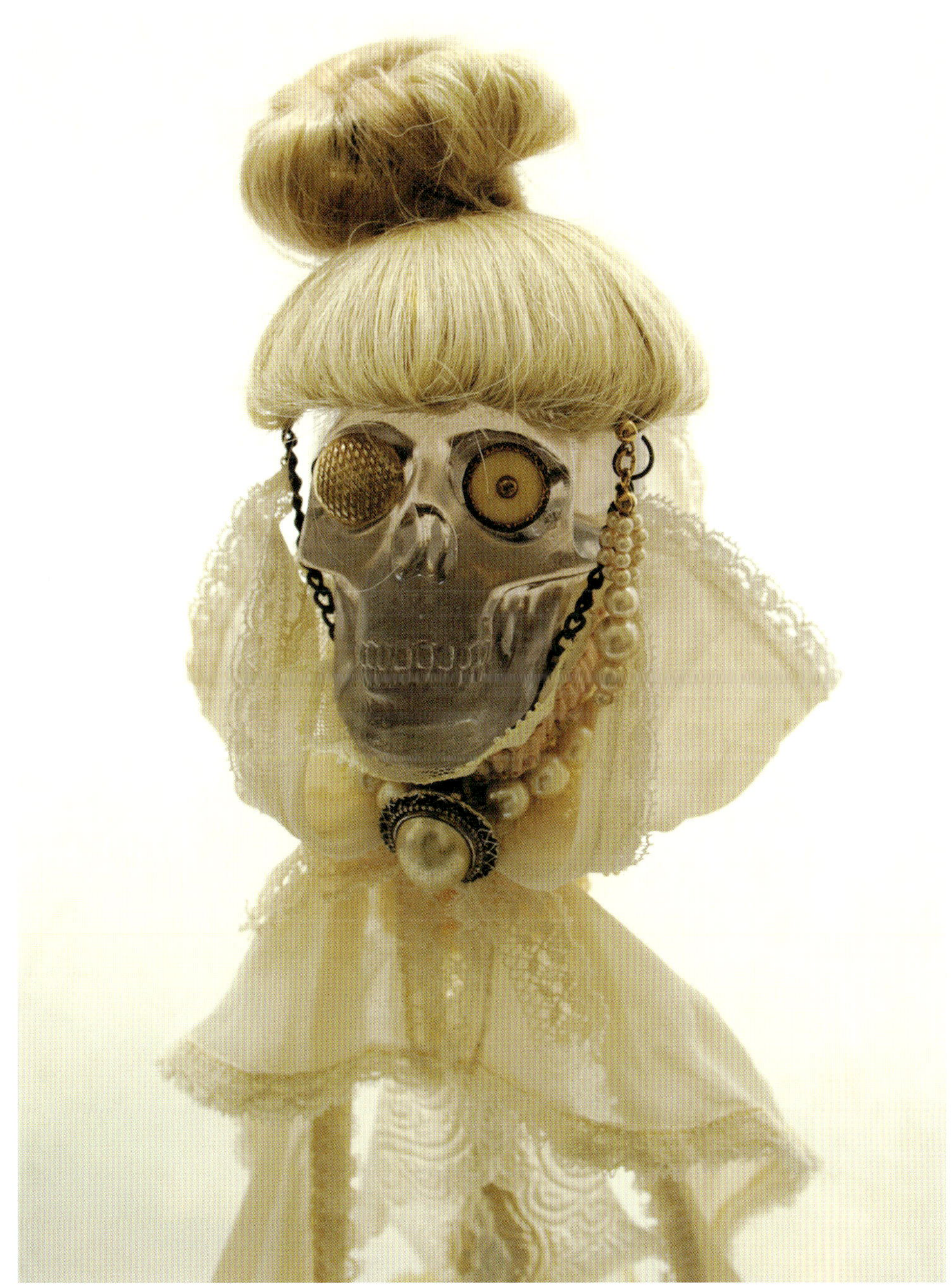

Ernest アーネスト
樹脂加工の骸骨、人毛、アンティーク・レース、シリコン素材のレース、イヤリング、ブローチ、パール、カフスボタン、金属製キャンドル・スタンド、ファウンド・オブジェ /
H33×W11×D8cm / 2008

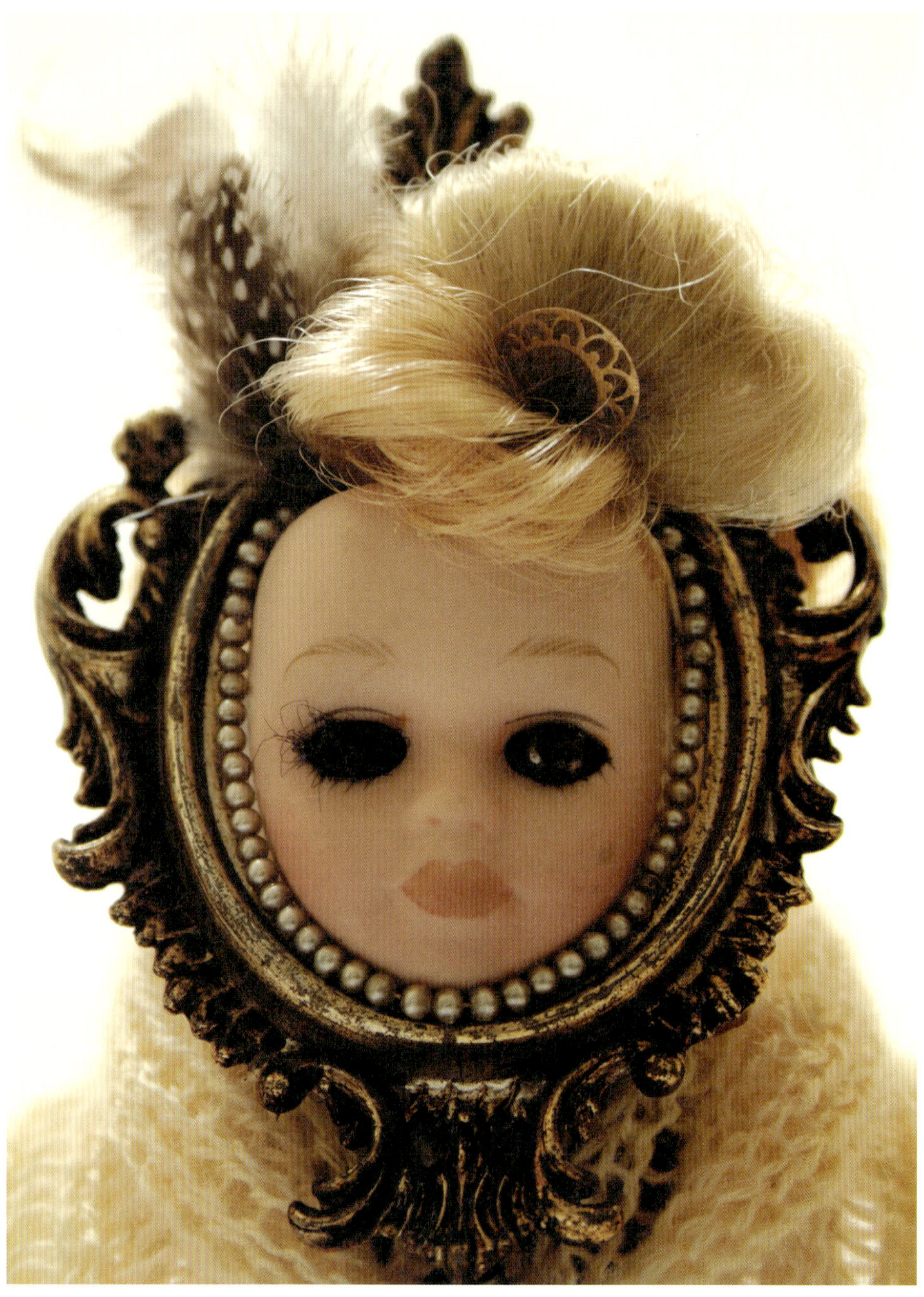

Valencia ヴァレンシア
ビスクドールの頭、人工毛、人毛、ビーズ、パール、手編みのウール、プラスチック・フレーム、木製糸巻、羽毛、ファウンド・オブジェ / H21×W11×D6cm / 2008

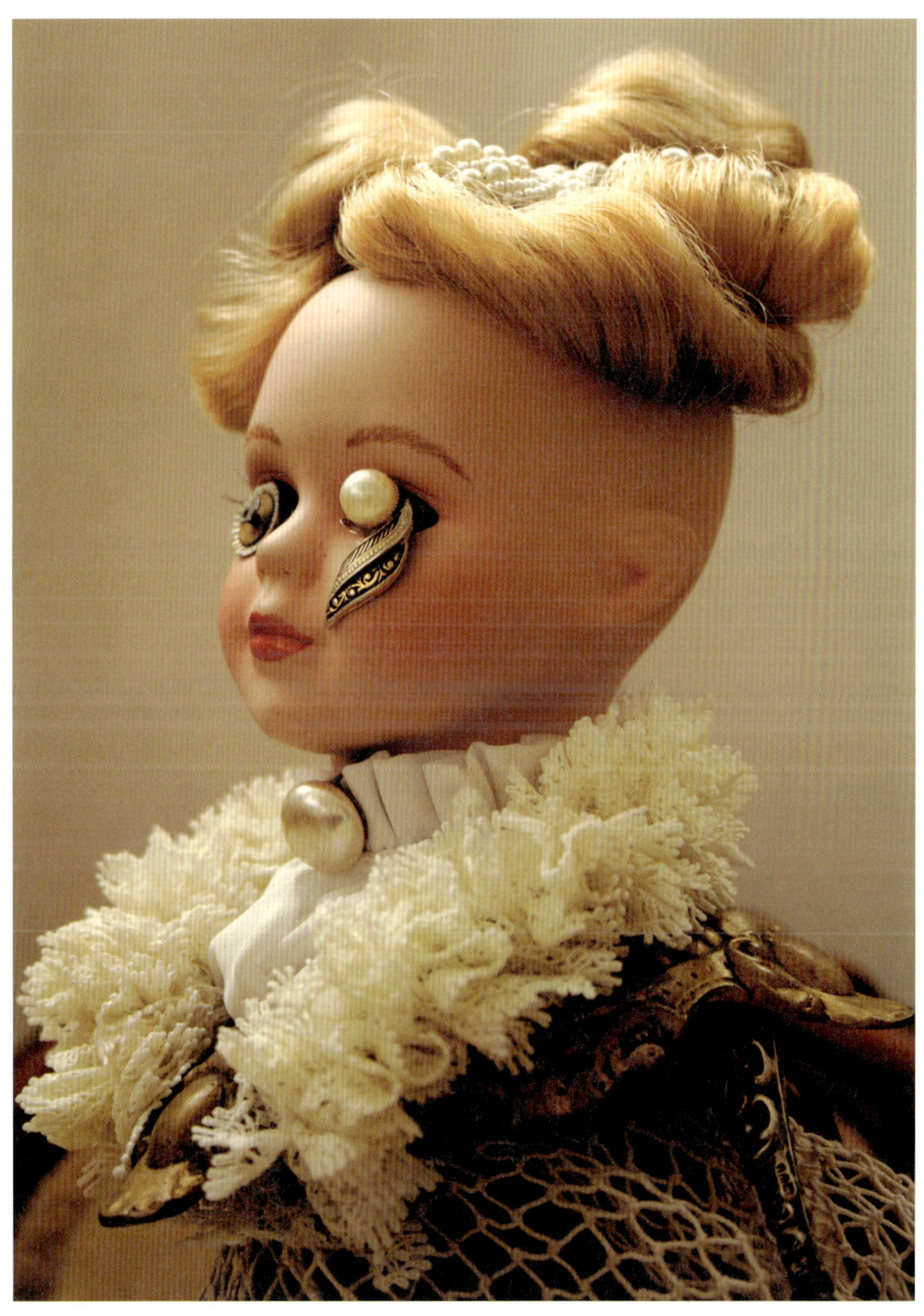

Scarlette スカーレット
ビスクドールの頭、人工毛、アンティーク・レース、パール、パール・イヤリング、パール・ブローチ、金属製スタンド、ファウンド・オブジェ / H27×W18×D13cm / 2008

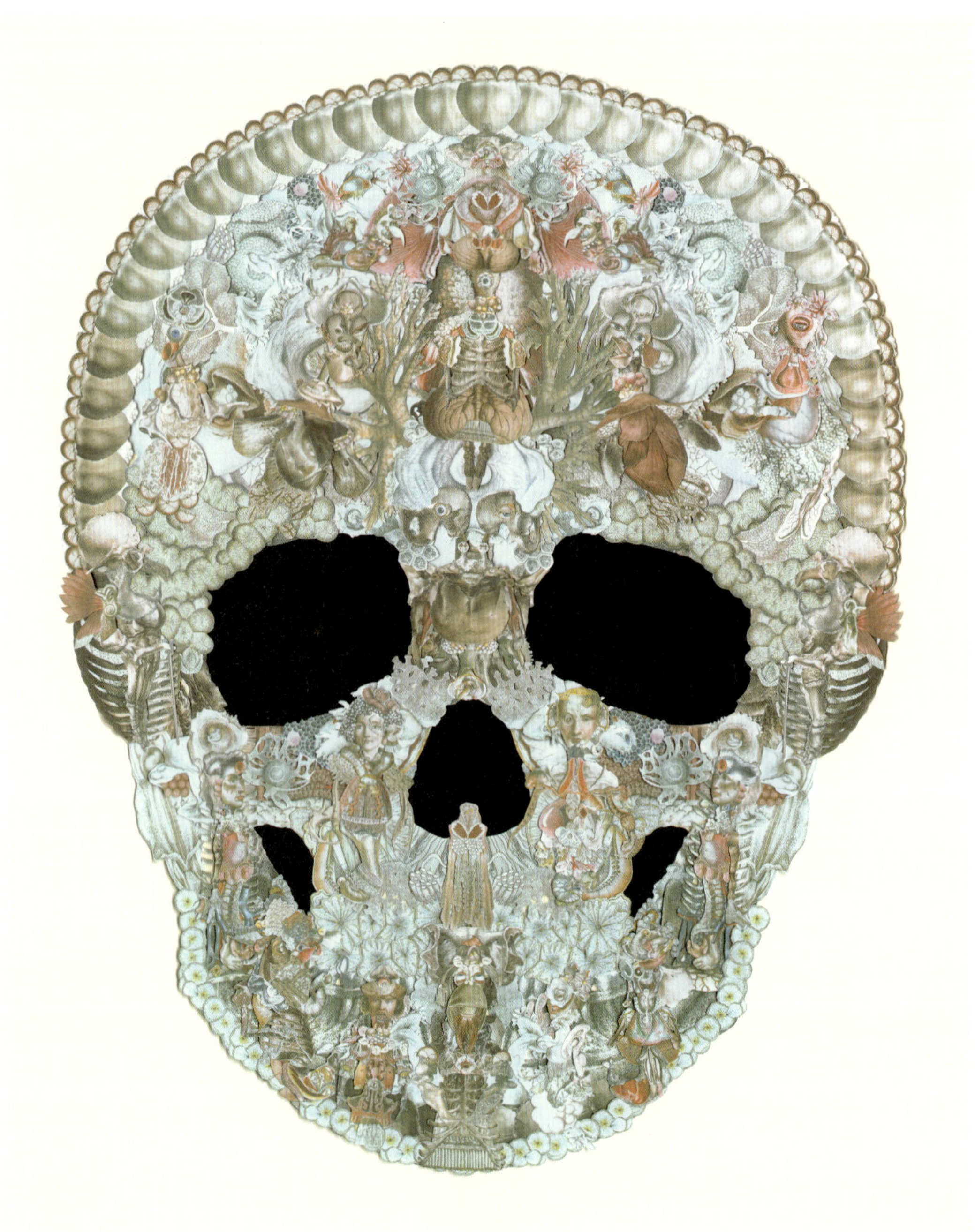

Subterranean 目に見えないもの
切り絵コラージュ、紙 / H84.1×W59.4cm / 2008

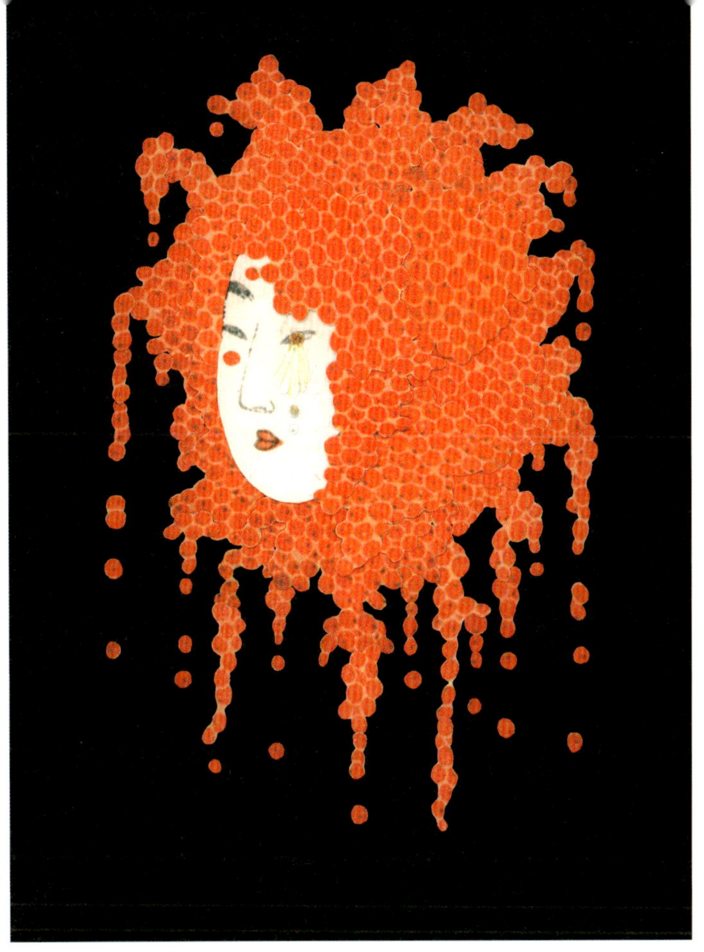

Sekirantou 赤卵頭
切り絵コラージュ、紙 / H13.6×W12cm / 2017

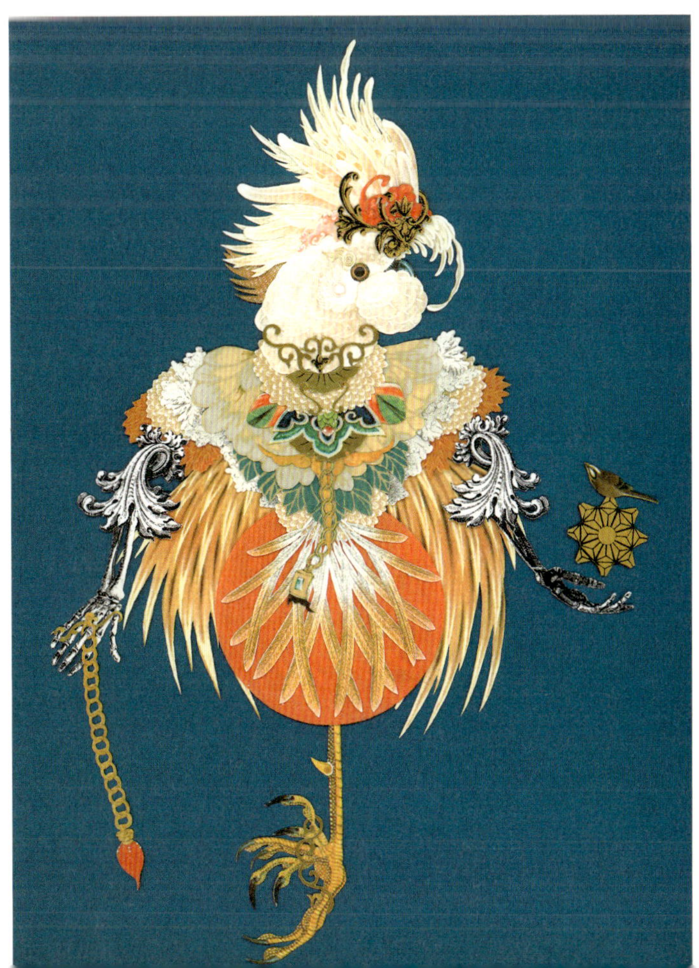

Acceptance 受容
切り絵コラージュ、紙 / H33.5×W33.5cm / 2017

Elizabeth McGrath

エリザベス・マクグラス（アメリカ　USA）

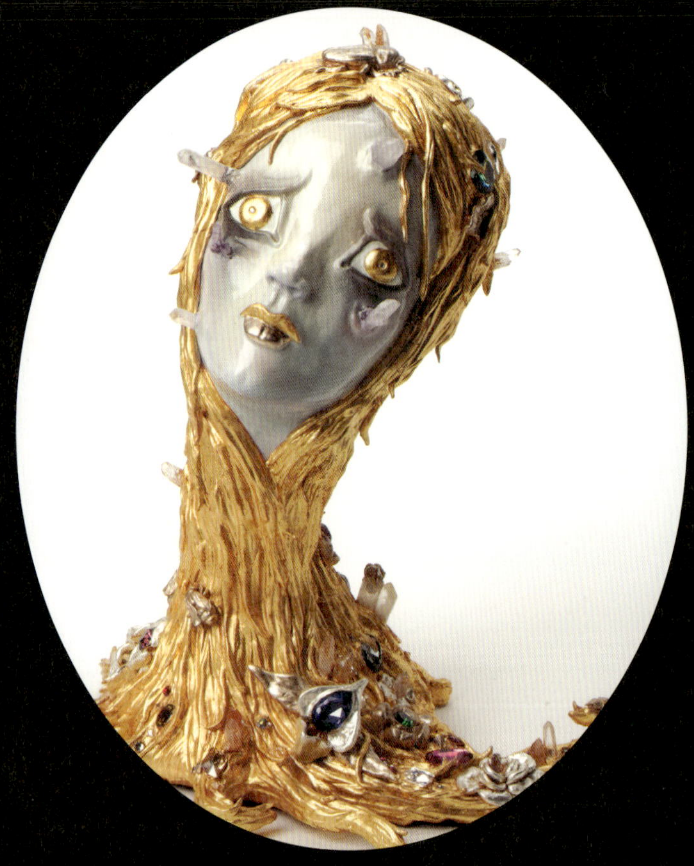

ロサンゼルスの郊外、母親の母国であるシンガポールで育つ。独学で美術を学び、アーティスト、ミュージシャンとして30年以上活動している。いつか人間がほかの惑星に住み、パラレルワールドを発見することを願っている。それまではこの仮の世界で精一杯生き、多くの人に楽しんでもらえる作品を作るつもりだ。

Self-taught artist and musician, who grew up in different suburbs near Los Angeles California and Singapore where her mother is from. She has been making art and playing music for over 30 years. She hopes that the world will one day respectfully inhabit other planets and discover parallel universes. Until then she will do her best to build her version of an alternate reality for your enjoyment.

lizmcgrath.com

↑ The Eyes of the Crystal Parasite ザ・アイズ・オブ・ザ・クリスタル・パラサイト（部分）
マジックスカルプ、樹脂、ワイヤーアーマチュア、粘土、24K & 18K金箔、スワロフスキー・クリスタル / H40×W63×D30cm / 2010
→White Beaver. Mr. Beavers Sweet Shoppe ホワイト・ビーバー ── ミスター・ビーバーのスイーツ・ショップ
マジックスカルプ、木、ポリマークレイ、サテン、フェイクファー、24K金箔 / H48×W43×D27cm / 2016

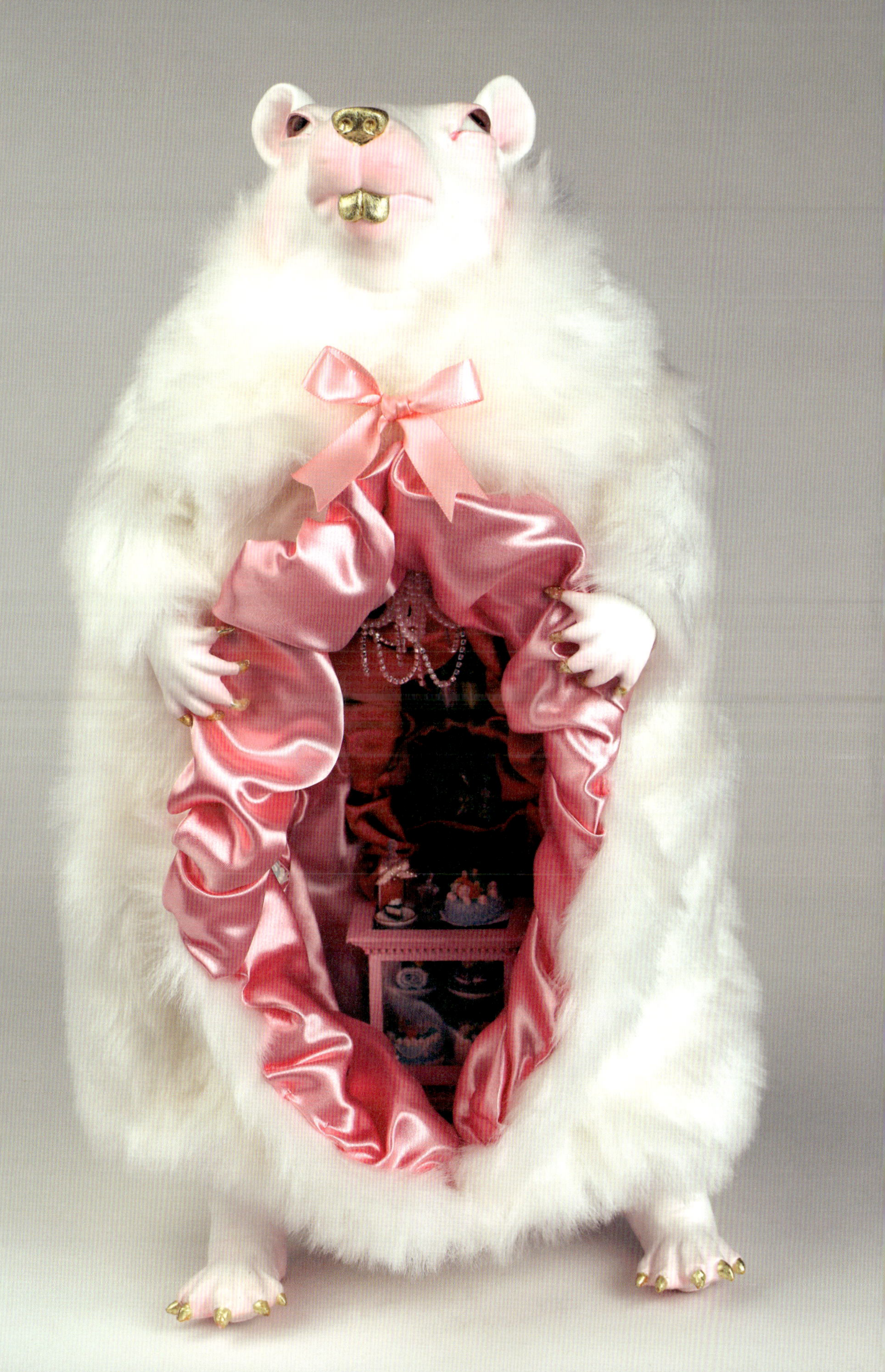

→Folley of St. Hubertus フォリー・オブ・セント・ウベルトゥス
マジックスカルプ、50000個以上のスワロフスキー・クリスタル＆24K金箔 / H60×W50×D40cm / 2006

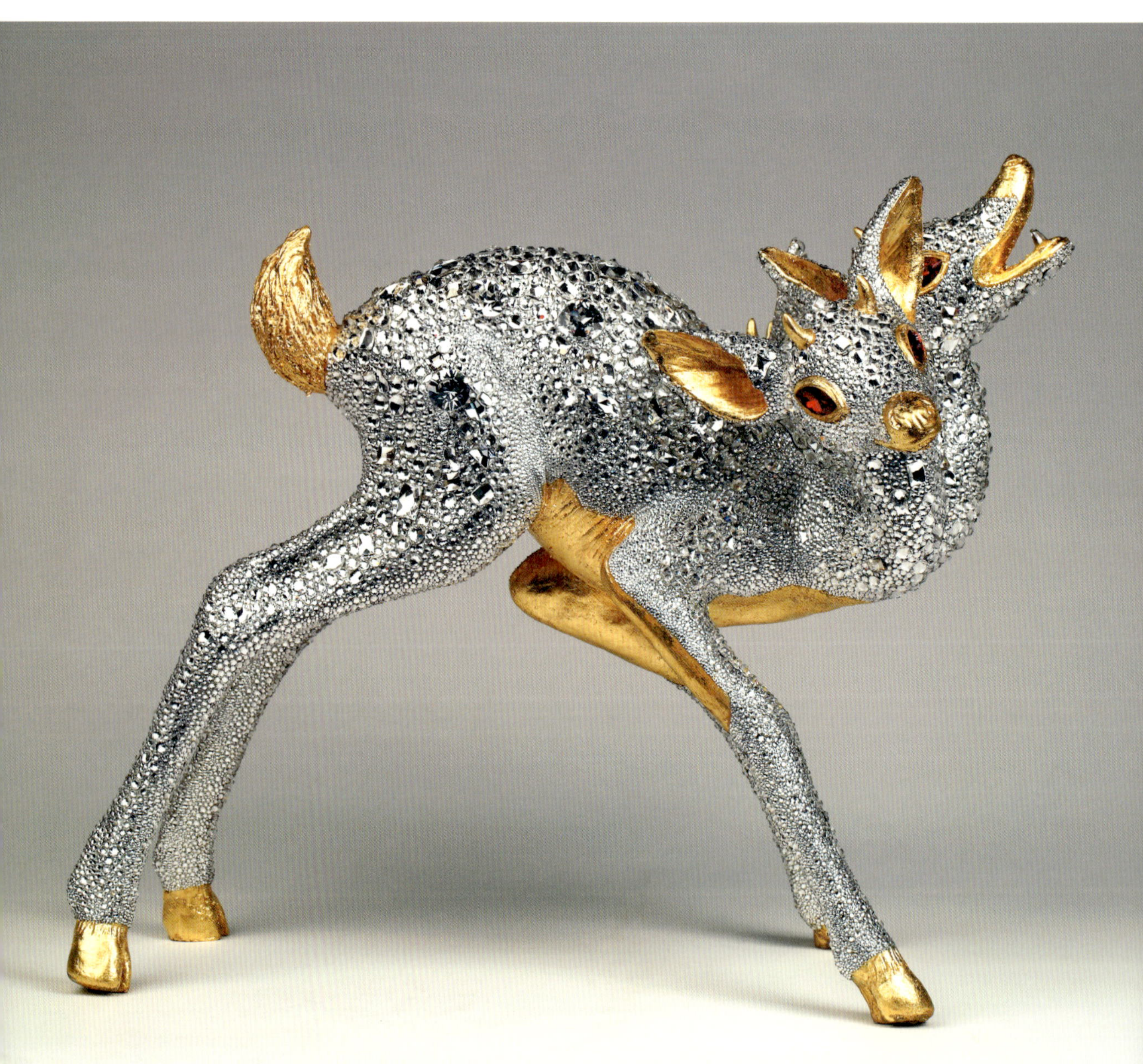

Fur Fur ファーファー
マジックスカルプ、50000個以上のスワロフスキー・クリスタル＆24K金箔 / H55×W48×D43cm / 2016

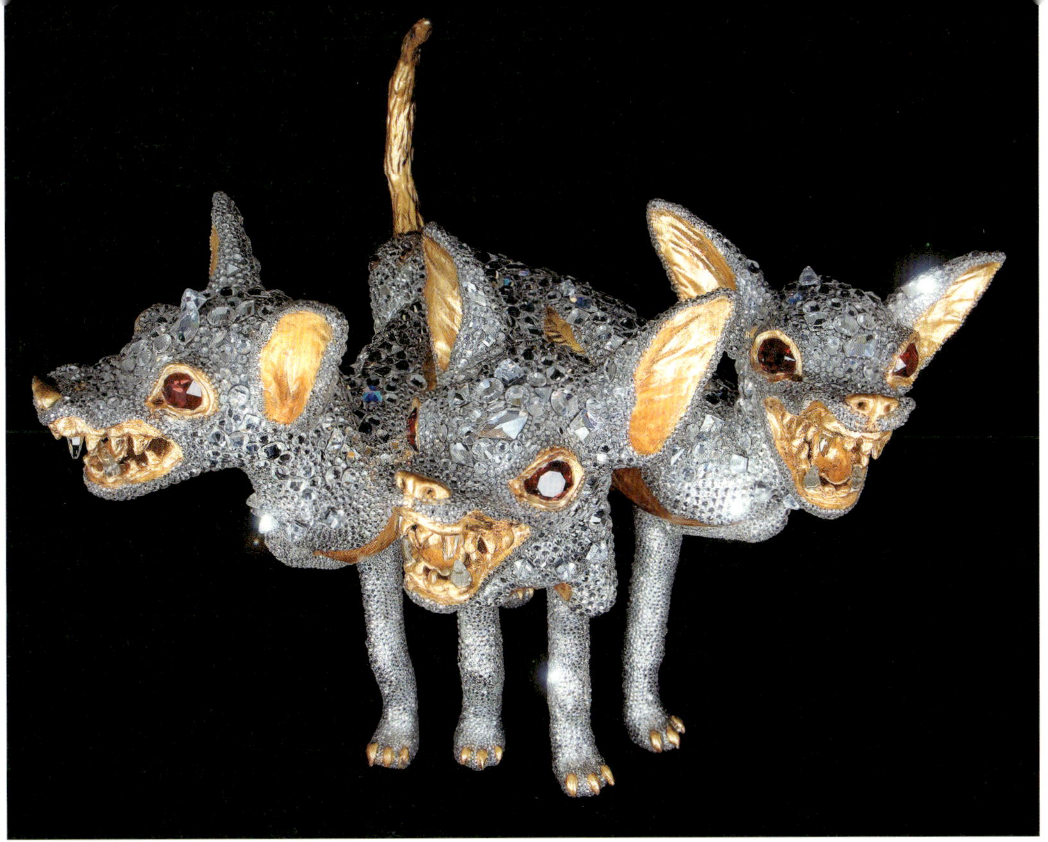

↑Cerebus セラバス
マジックスカルプ、50000個以上のスワロフスキー・クリスタル＆24K金箔 / H58×W50×D55cm / 2008

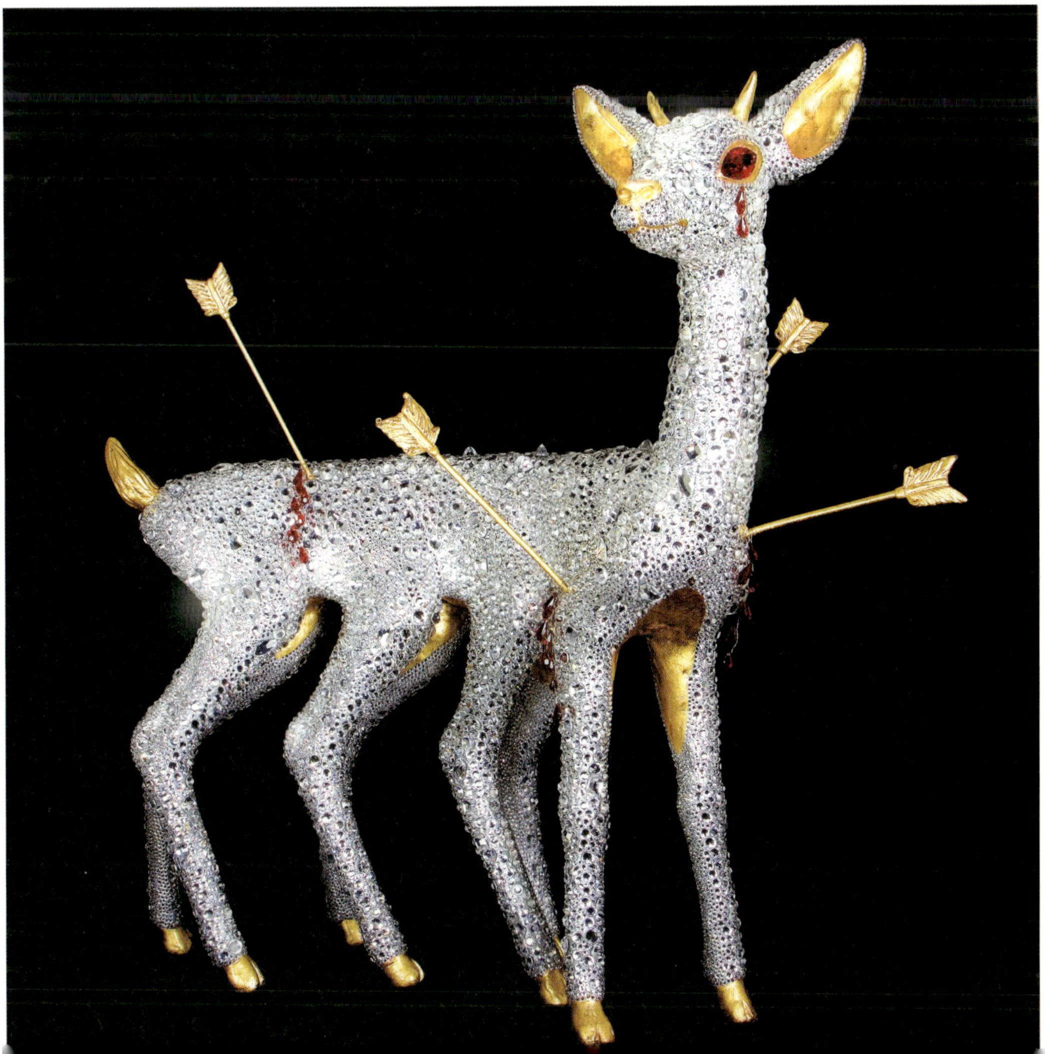

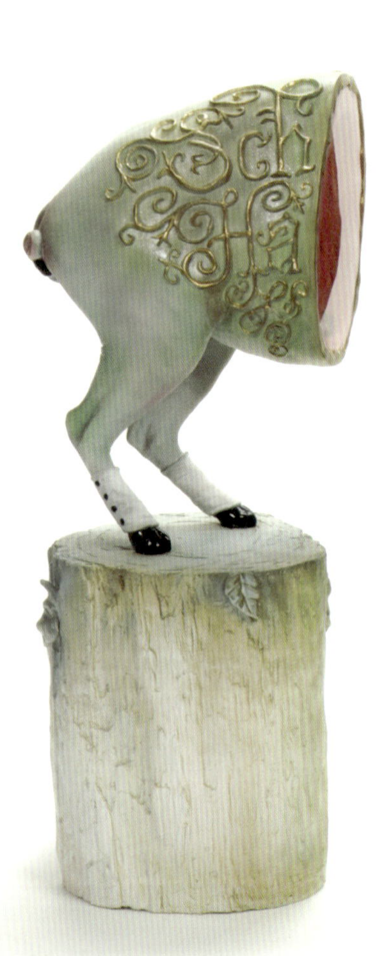

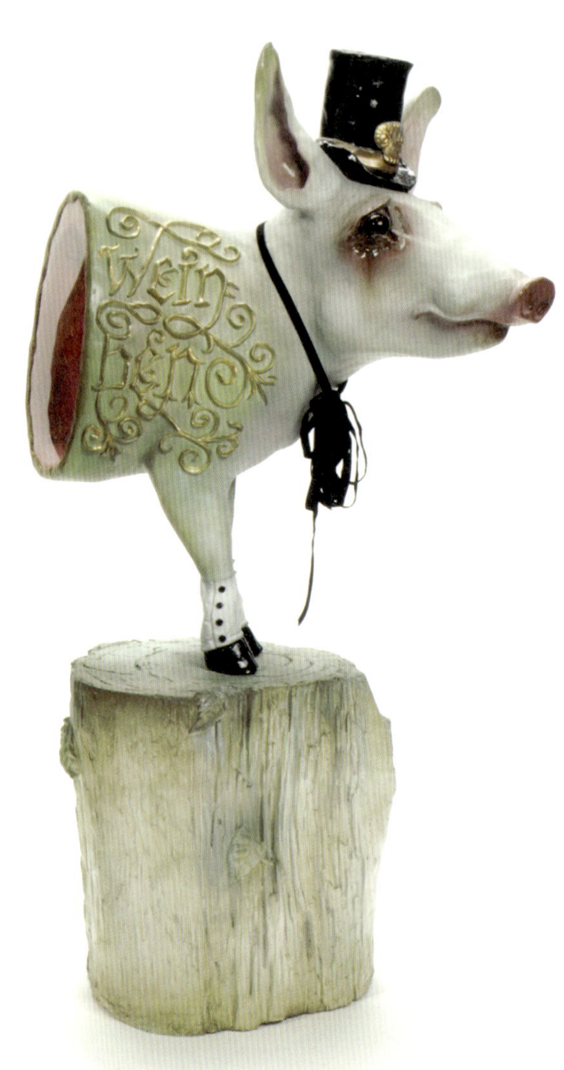

Schwein Haben シュヴァイン・ハーベン（動物虐待ではありません）
マジックスカルプ、小型模型、樹脂、彩色したワイヤーアーマチュア、石こう、ペンキ / H103×W45×D70cm（両側の概算サイズ）/ 2005

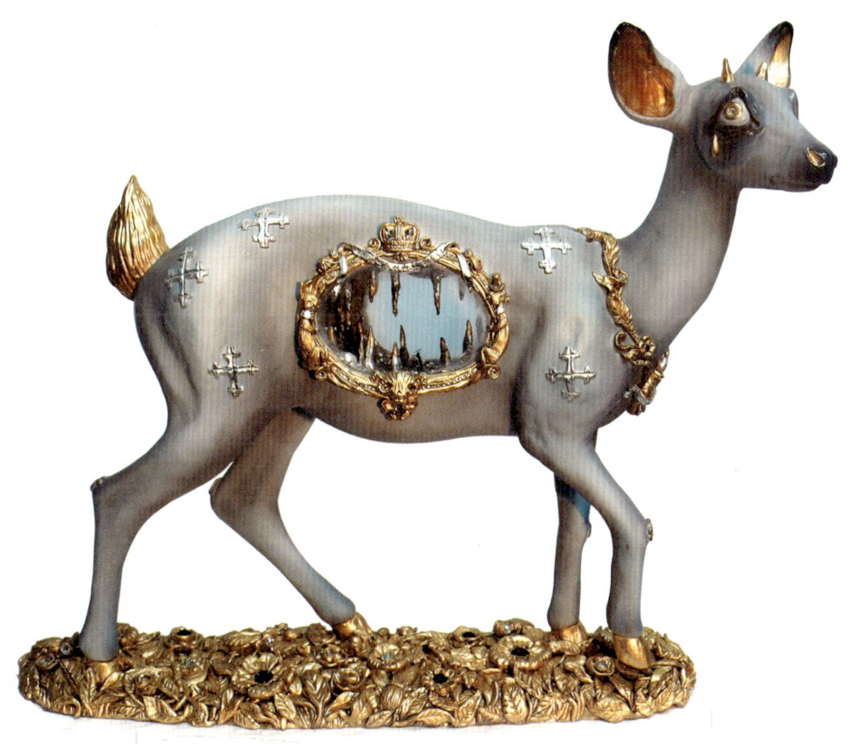

The Dik Dik ディク・ディク
マジックスカルプ、小型模型、樹脂、彩色したワイヤーアーマチュア、石こう、ペンキ / H60×W40×D38cm / 2005

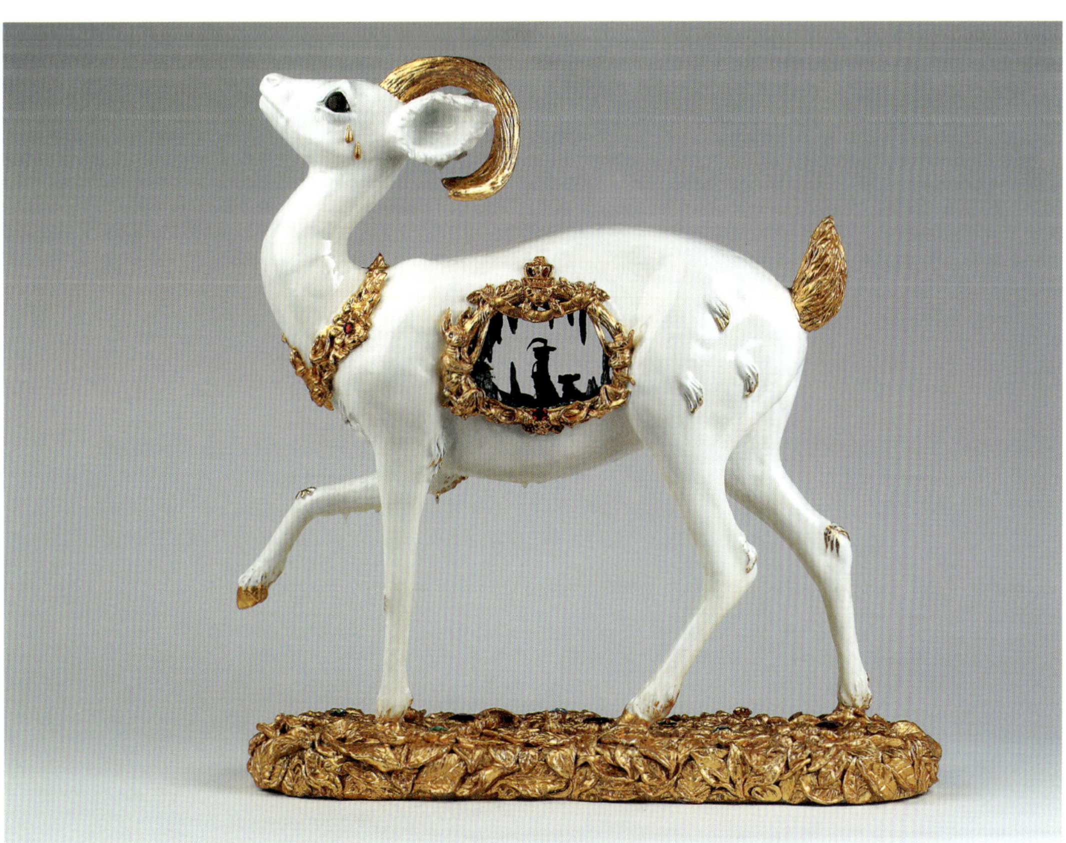

Psychopopms: the Valiant Goat 死後の世界に霊魂を導く者——勇敢なヤギ
マジックスカルプ、金箔、クリスタル、天然アメジストの塊、スワロフスキー・クリスタル、樹脂、エポシキ樹脂、高密度カービング・フォーム、ガラス繊維 / H66×W63×D20cm / 2016

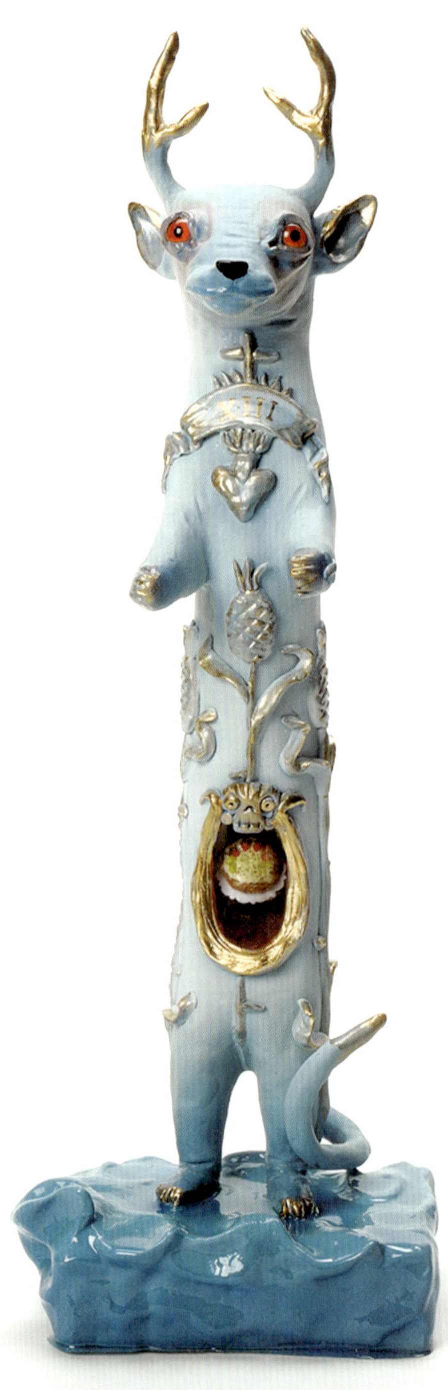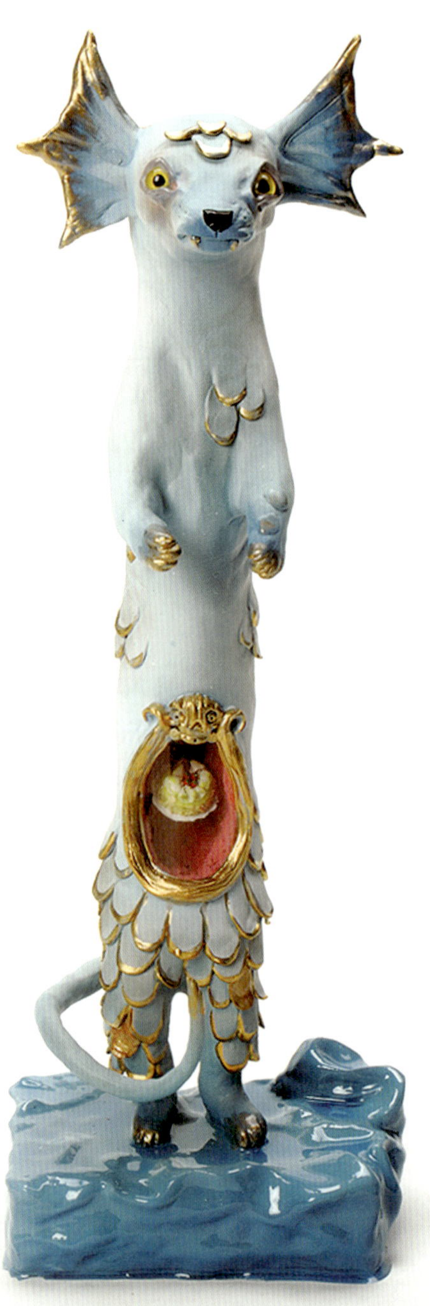

The Weasels イタチ
マジックスカルプ、ポリマークレイ、さまざまな彩色と艶出し / H27×W12×D13cm / 2003

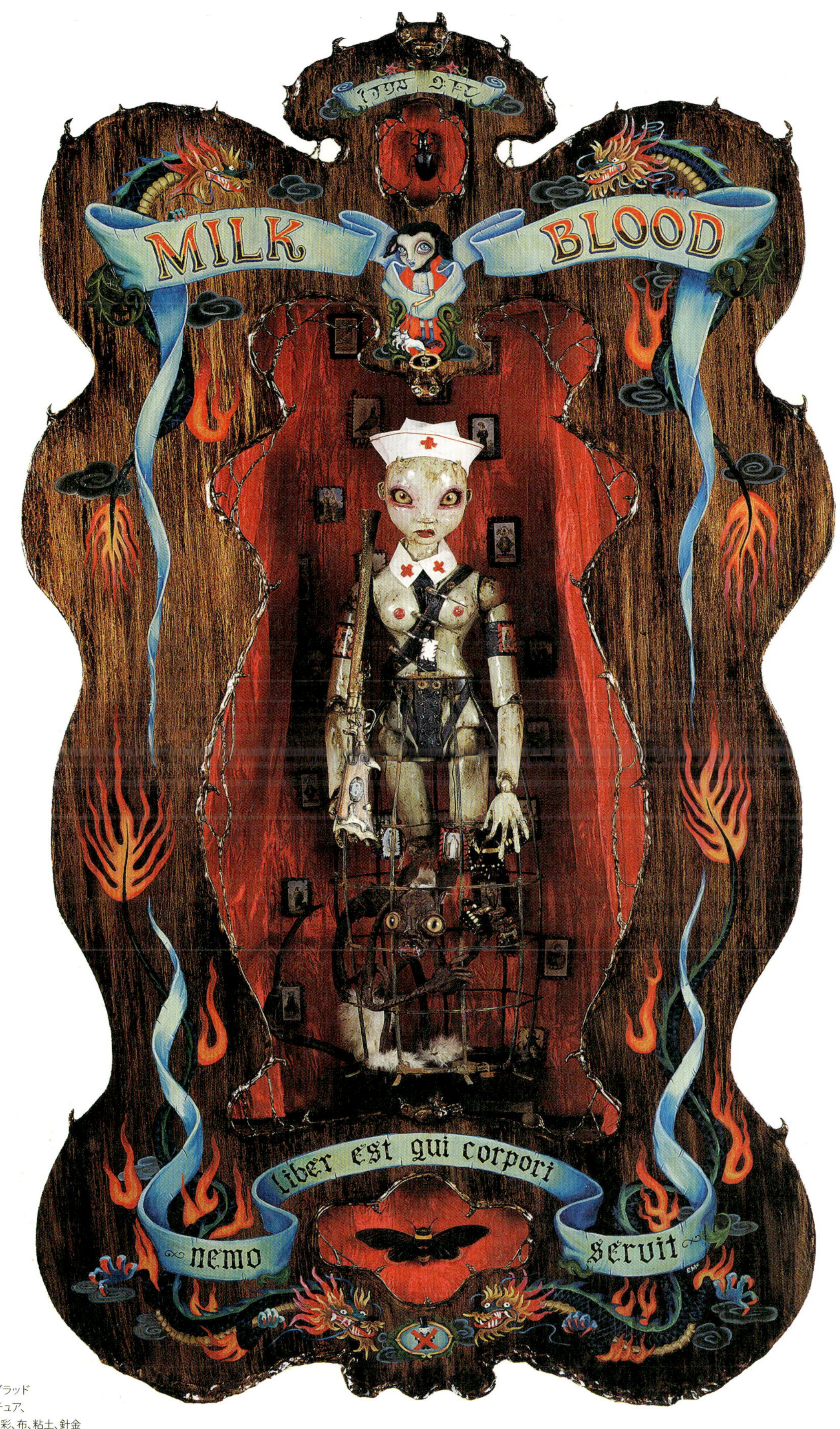

Milk Blood ミルク・ブラッド
木、ワイヤーアーマチュア、
マジックスカルプ、油彩、布、粘土、針金
（日本人形のつくり方を紹介するウェブページの制作写真がとても参考になりました）/ H213×W121×D25cm / 1997

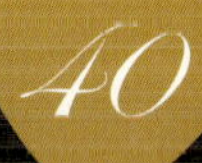

Fiona Roberts

フィオナ・ロバーツ（オーストラリア　Australia）

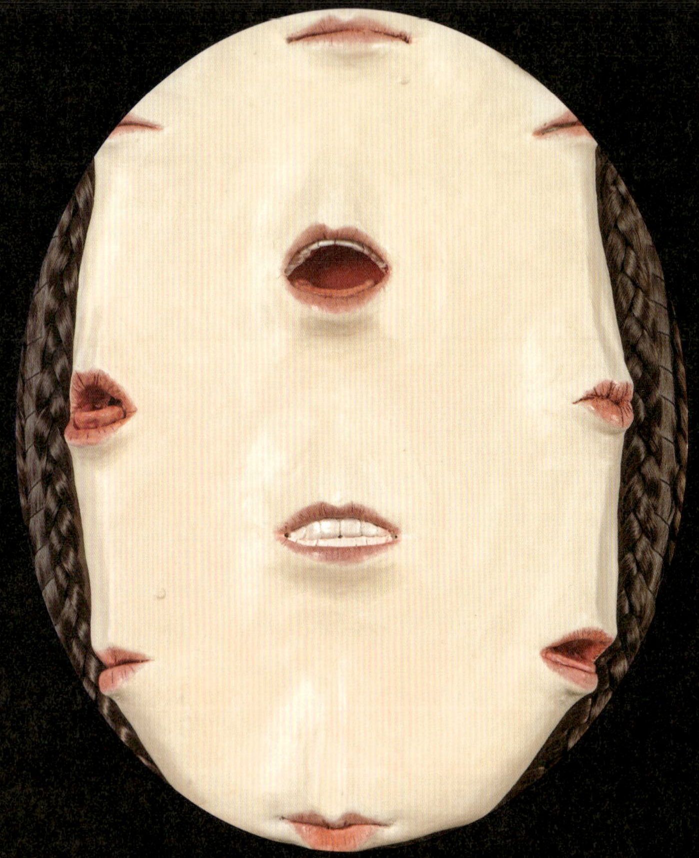

オーストラリア出身のインスタレーション・アーティスト。心と体、そして家との複雑な関係を探求している。ヴィクトリア朝時代の家を思わせる空間を用いることが多い。家は安らぎと安全の場であるという常識を覆し、住む人の弱さや不安を強調する場として表現。人間の体のパーツが家具やインテリアの一部になった作品は、見る者の予想を裏切り、はっとさせる。

Fiona Roberts is an Australian installation artist who explores the complex relationship between the mind, the body and the home. Her installations are often based on domestic spaces with a Victorian-era aesthetic. Roberts transforms the idea of a home from what is traditionally considered to be a place of comfort and safety to a space that accentuates the occupant's vulnerabilities and insecurities. Roberts' work actively subverts the audience's sense of familiarity and expectation by concealing a variety of bodily forms and textures through pattern, repetition, and traditional ornamentation in household objects and furnishings.

fiona-roberts.com

↑ The Chair 椅子（部分）
写真：マイケル・マージック／ミクスト・メディア／2014-15

→The Chair 椅子
写真：マイケル・マージック／ミクスト・メディア／2014-15

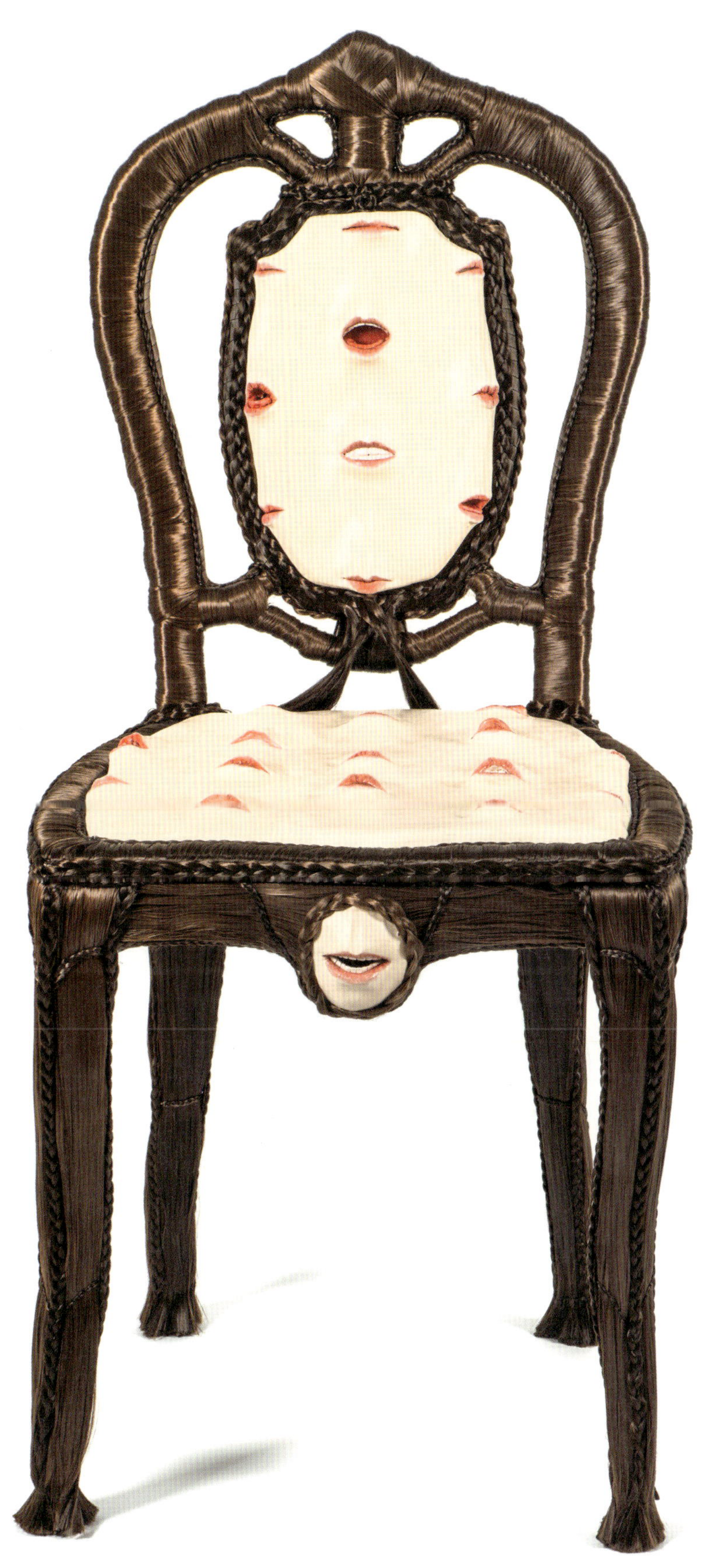

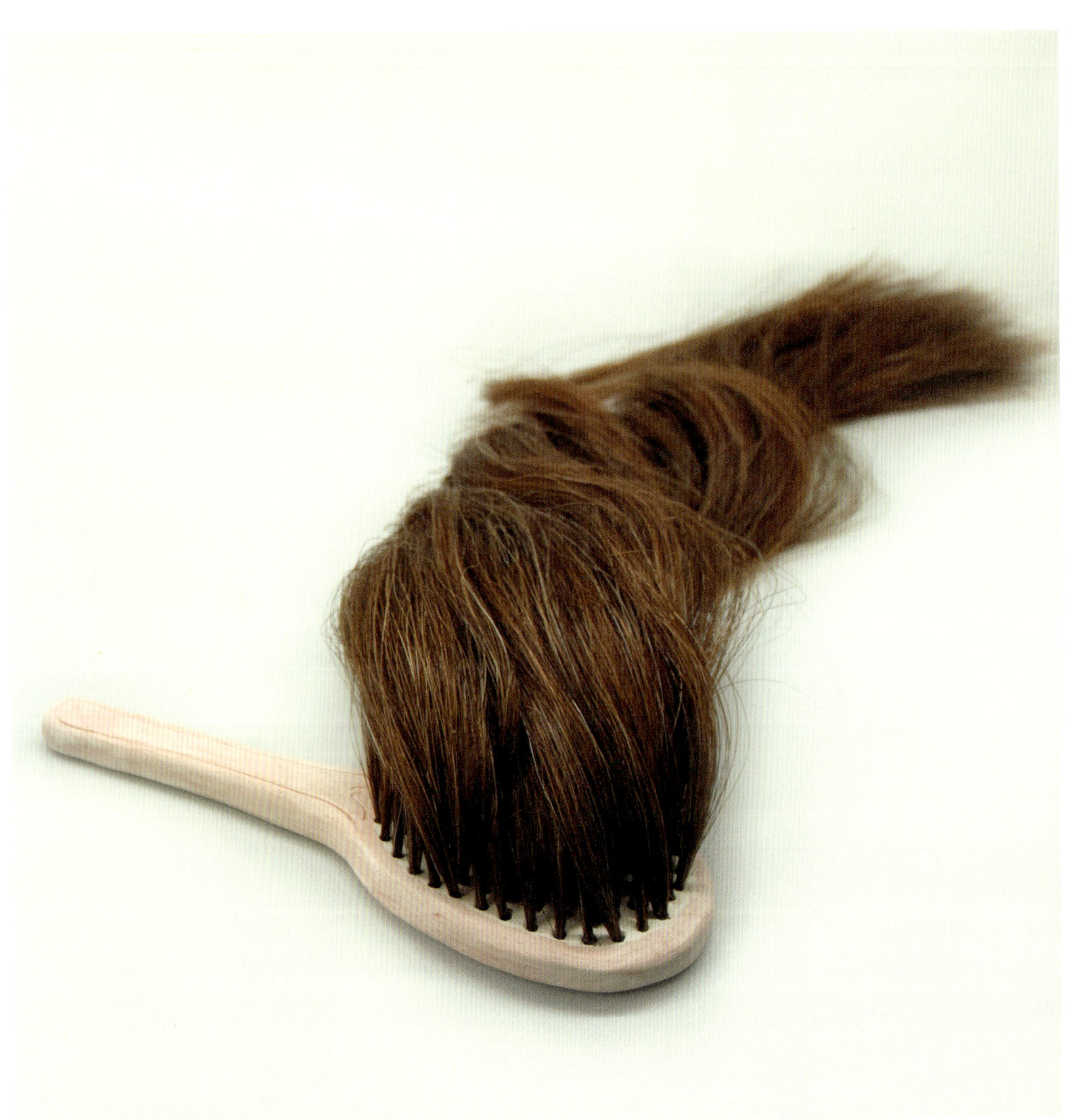

Hairbrush ヘアブラシ
セラミック、馬毛 / さまざまなサイズ / 2015

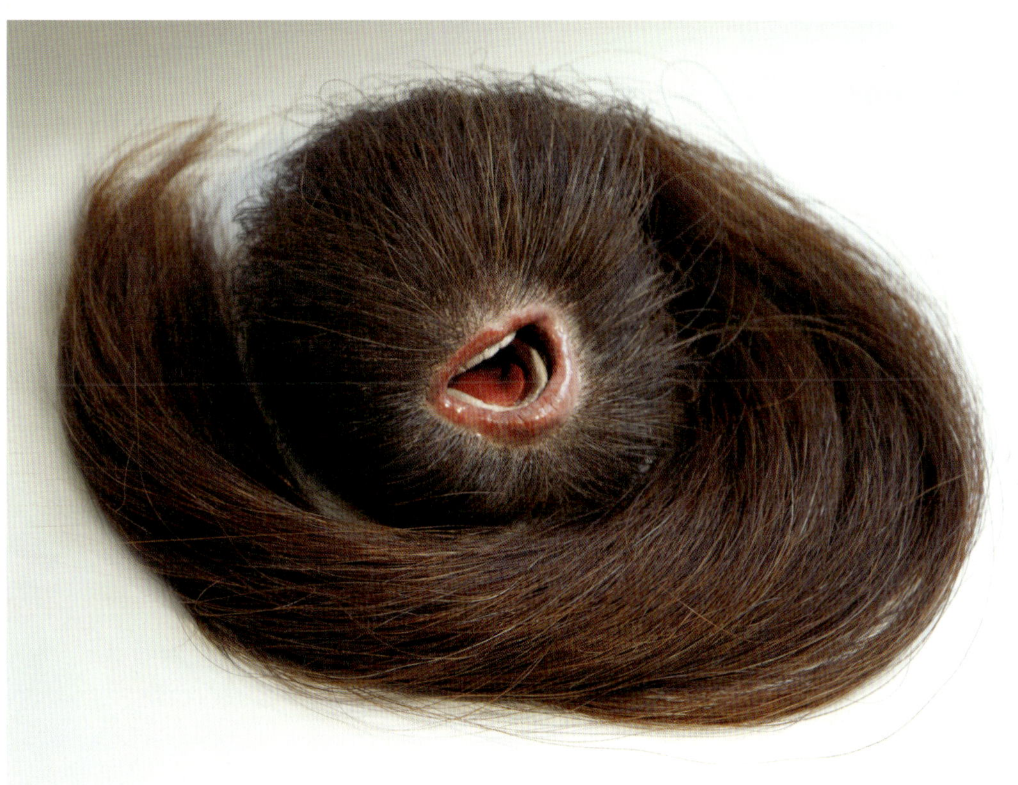

↑ In Knots ふさの中
ミクスト・メディア / さまざまなサイズ / 2012

↓ Chimera キマイラ
磁器、人毛 / さまざまなサイズ / 2016

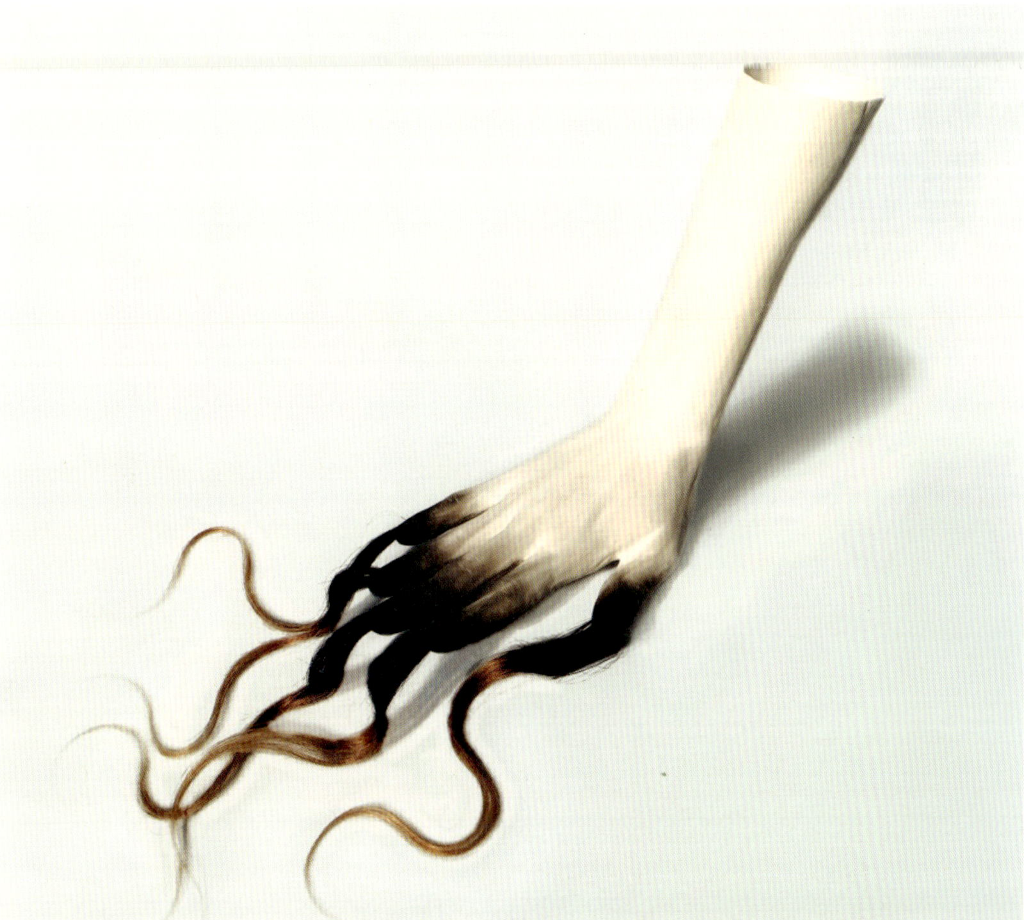

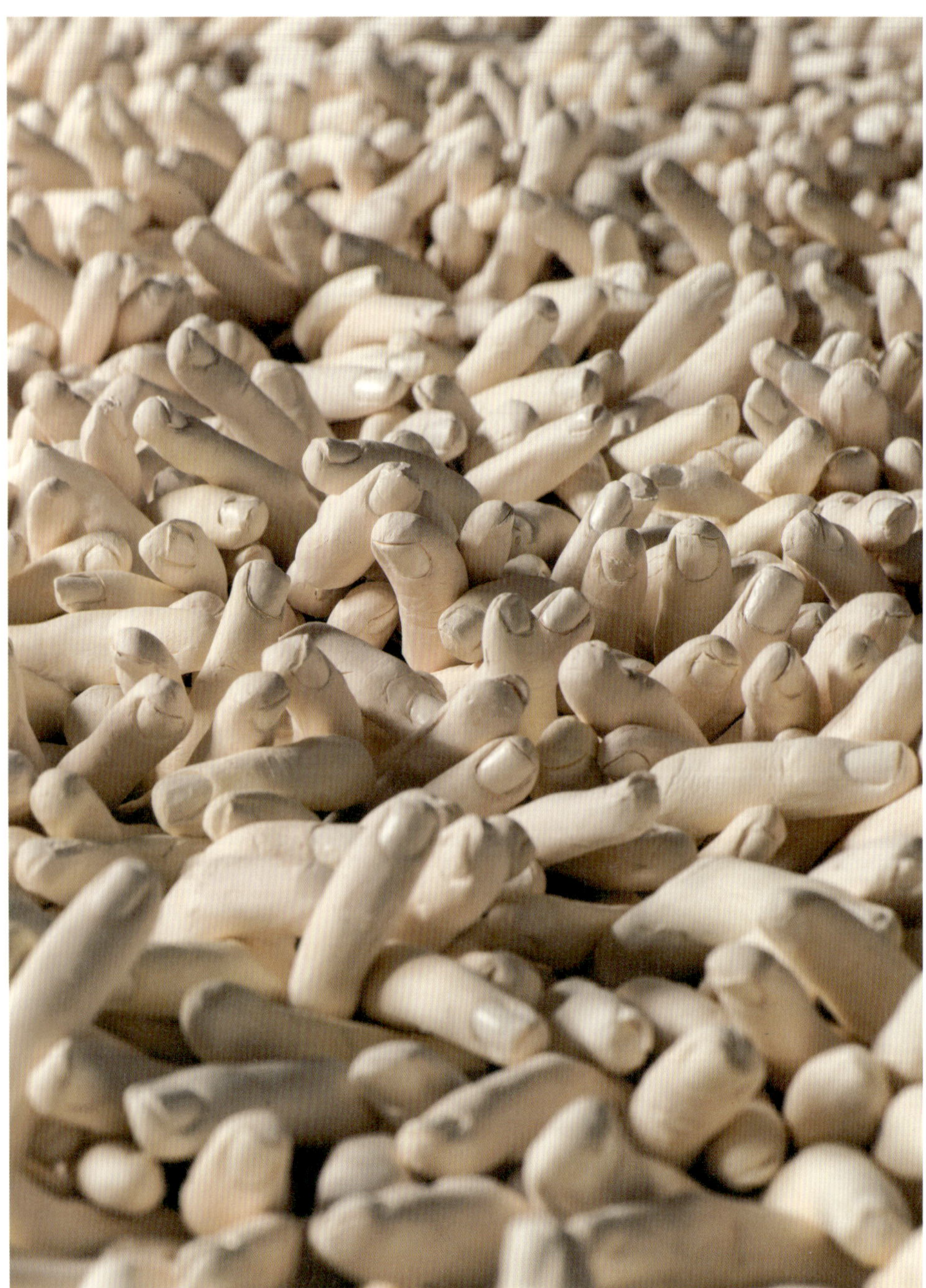

The Rug ラグマット
写真：マイケル・マージック／セラミック、糸、カンヴァス／H185×W125cm／2014-15

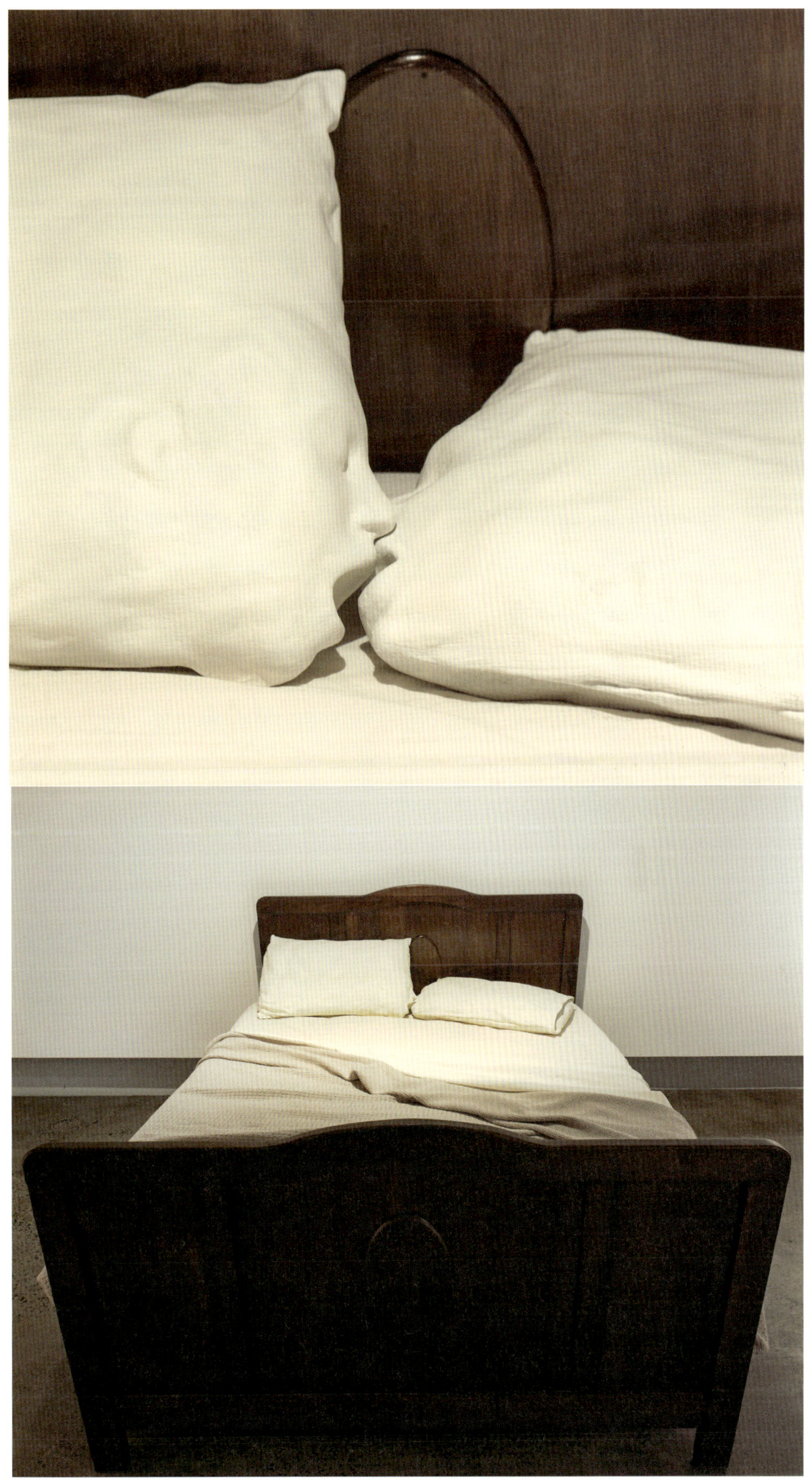

Passion Pillows パッション・ピロウズ
写真：マイケル・マージック /
ミクスト・メディア /
H180×W200cm / 2015

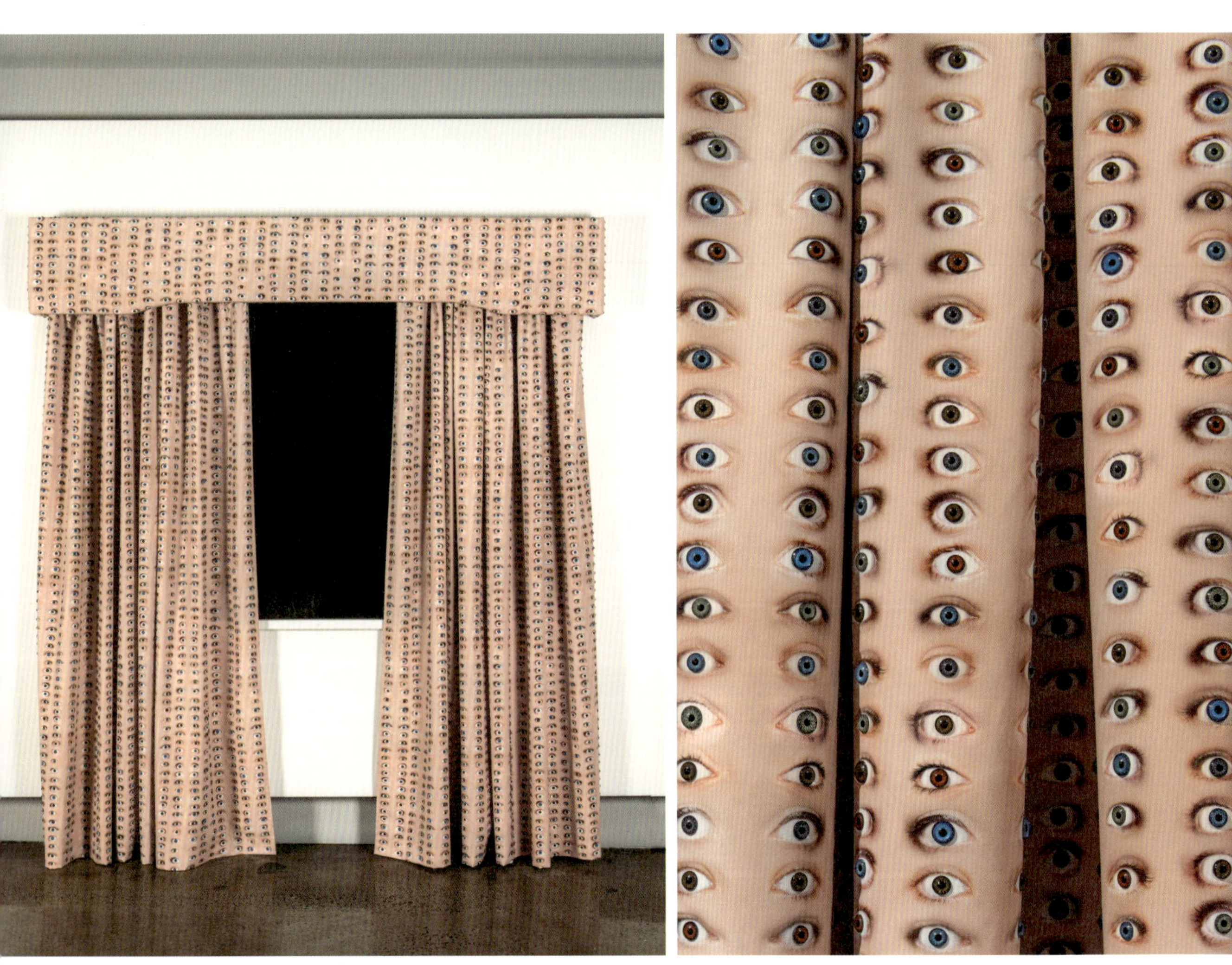

The Dark Window 暗闇の窓
写真：マイケル・マージック／布、アクリル・シート、木、虹彩ガラス、カーテン棒、留め具／H220×W200cm／2015

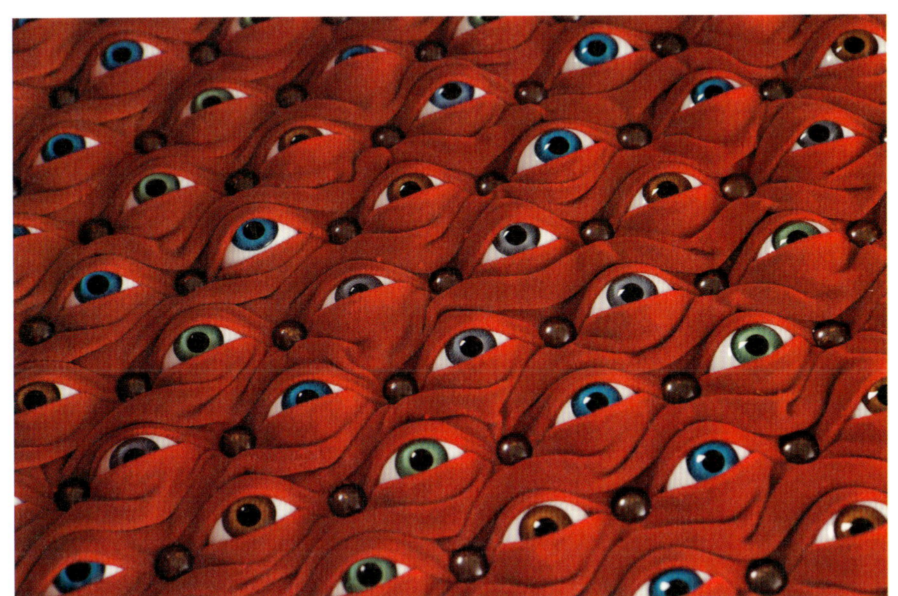

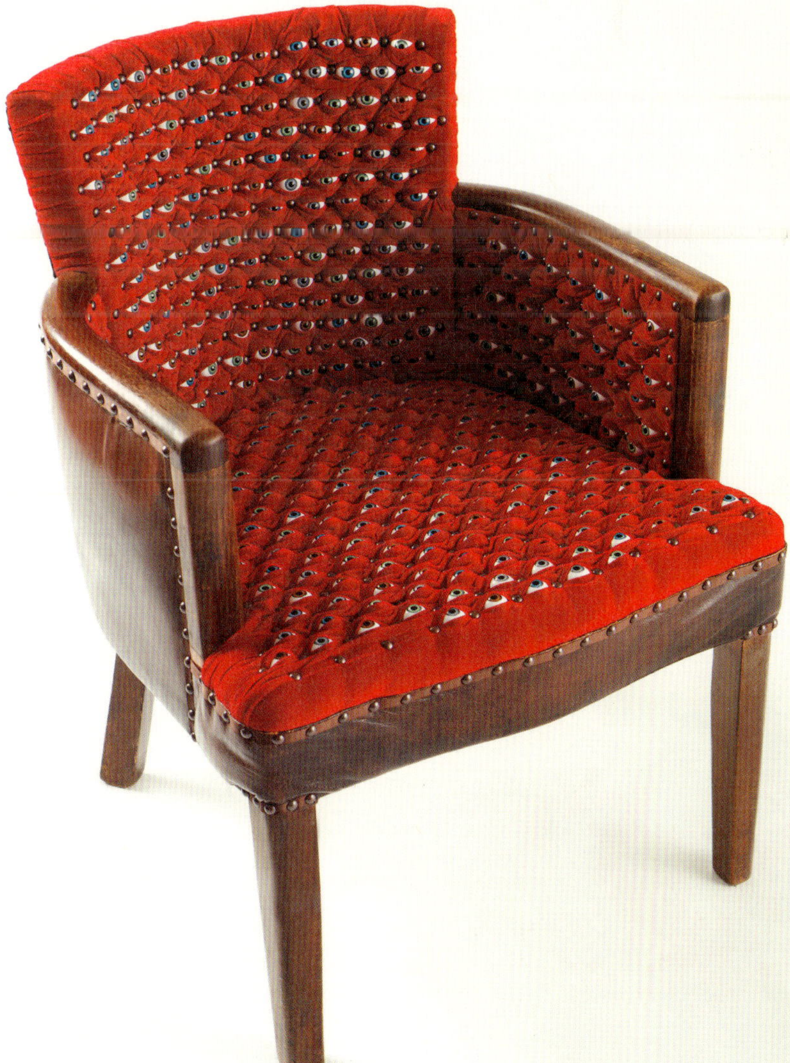

Scopophilia 窃視症
写真：ジェームス・フィールド ／
椅子、ヴェルヴェット、目、フォーム、椅子張り用ピン ／
2011

あとがき

ダーク・アートやデカダンスは絵画史から見てもその存在は古に遡ります。
そして今、また密かにその領域の盛りあがりを見せています。
なぜ人は、あえてダークを描き、かつそれを見たがるのでしょう。
ダークとは勿論、単にイメージが暗いのではなく、
反道徳、反正義、反社会、反体制など、
あえて世に背を向けた視点の表現であり、非主流でもあります。
だからといって、社会の暗部を暴き出して光明をあてようという、
ジャーナリズムの精神でもありません。
むしろ、仮想の世界を前提としているから、
その闇を肯定すらしているのです。
〈幻想〉は仮想現実や空想のことをいいますが、
アートの世界ではなぜか、それは明るくはありません。
しかし、そこに、〈耽美〉とつけば、それはもはや闇ではなく神秘です。
パイ インターナショナル既刊の『幻想耽美』、『幻想耽美II』と続き、
ここにきて海外に目を向け、ダークとフェティシズムのアートを探ってみました。
どちらにも共通しているのは、そこに分け行って身を委ね、陶酔する、
あるいはその世界へ逃避する、といった志向も根底にあるのかもしれません。
仮想現実であればこそ得られる、〈耽美〉への執着なのです。
本書の制作にあたってはこういった視点で、
現在注目を集めている魅力的な海外の作家の作品を集めました。
鑑賞することを超えて、その世界に身を遊ばせてもらえれば嬉しく思います。

高橋 善丸（アートディレクター）

Special Thanks　協 力（敬称略）

Elisa Ancori	Seiko Kato
Tom Bagshaw	KCN
Federico Bebber	Garth Knight
Antoine Bernhart	Zoe Lacchei
Alessandro Sicioldr Bianchi	Rodrigo Luff
David Bray	Elizabeth McGrath
Ray Caesar	Soey Milk
Nicoletta Ceccoli	Mira Nedyalkova
Neil Craver	Popovy Sisters
Diana Dihaze	Dan Quintana
DMOCHOWSKI GALLERY	Raimondi & Campbell
Sam Ectoplasm	Fiona Roberts
Jel Ena	Danny van Ryswyk
Daria Endresen	John Santerineross
Camilla d'Errico	Schilte & Portielje
Gallery House	Kristin Shiraef
Alex Gross	Studio Helnwein
Naoto Hattori	Miss Van
Gottfried Helnwein	Willy Verginer
Karen Hsiao	Katarzyna Widmańska
James Jean	Hannah Yata
Kahmann Gallery Amsterdam	

本書をまとめるにあたり、
上記の方々をはじめたくさんの皆様にご協力いただきました。
誠にありがとうございました。心より感謝申し上げます。

Credits of Artworks on Cover Jacket

"Self Examination" by Ray Caesar
「自省」レイ・シーザー画 / デジタル・ウルトラクローム印刷、印画紙 / H76.2×W76.2cm / 2011
Ray Caesar/Gallery House

【左上 Upper left】
"Hairball" (detail) by Camilla d'Errico
「ヘアボール」(部分) カミラ・デリコ画 / 油彩、木製パネル / H35.56×W27.94cm / 2012

【右上 Upper right】
"The last Days of Pompeii Ⅱ" (detail) by Gottfried Helnwein
セルフ・ポートレート「ポンペイ最後の日Ⅱ」(部分)
ゴットフリート・ヘルンヴァイン画 / 写真、ミクスト・メディア / 1987

【左下 Lower left】
"Veruna's Rainbow" (part) by John Santerineross
「ヴァルナの虹」(部分) ジョン・サンテリネロス作 / 印画紙にプリント / H71×W55cm

【右下 Lower right】
"White Rabbit" (3D Sculpture/detail) by Danny van Ryswyk
「白ウサギ」(3D彫刻、部分)　ダニー・ファン・リズウィック作 /
アクリル彩色、ポリミアド3D彫刻、ガラス・ドーム / 彫刻：H35cm、ガラス・ドーム：H44cm

【背表紙 Spine】
"Dulcis Agatha" (detail) by Nicoletta Ceccoli
「ダルシス・アガサ」(部分)　ニコレッタ・チェッコリ画 / アクリル、紙 / 2014

Dark & Fetish Art

PIE International Inc.
2-32-4 Minami-Otsuka, Toshima-ku, Tokyo 170-0005 JAPAN
international@pie.co.jp
www.pie.co.jp/english

ISBN: 978-4-7562-5038-4 (Outside Japan)

Printed in Japan

世界の幻想耽美　Dark & Fetish Art

2018年3月20日　初版第1刷発行
2023年1月15日　　第2刷発行

アートディレクション、デザイン　Art Director & Designer
高橋 善丸　Yoshimaru Takahashi

翻　訳　Translator
マクレリー・ルシー（ザ・ワード・ワークス）　Ruth S. McCreery（The Word Works）
ラパン　LAPIN-INC

編集協力、コーディネーション　Editor & Coordinator
CN International Inc.
岸田 麻矢　Maya Kishida
撫本 美樹　Miki Nademoto
田中 基晶　Motoaki Tanaka
清 あゆむ　Ayumu Sei

編　集　Editor
荒川 佳織　Kaoru Arakawa

発行人　　三芳 寛要

発行元　　株式会社 パイ インターナショナル
　　　　　〒170-0005　東京都豊島区南大塚 2-32-4
　　　　　TEL 03-3944-3981　FAX 03-5395-4830　sales@pie.co.jp

印刷・製本　株式会社東京印書館

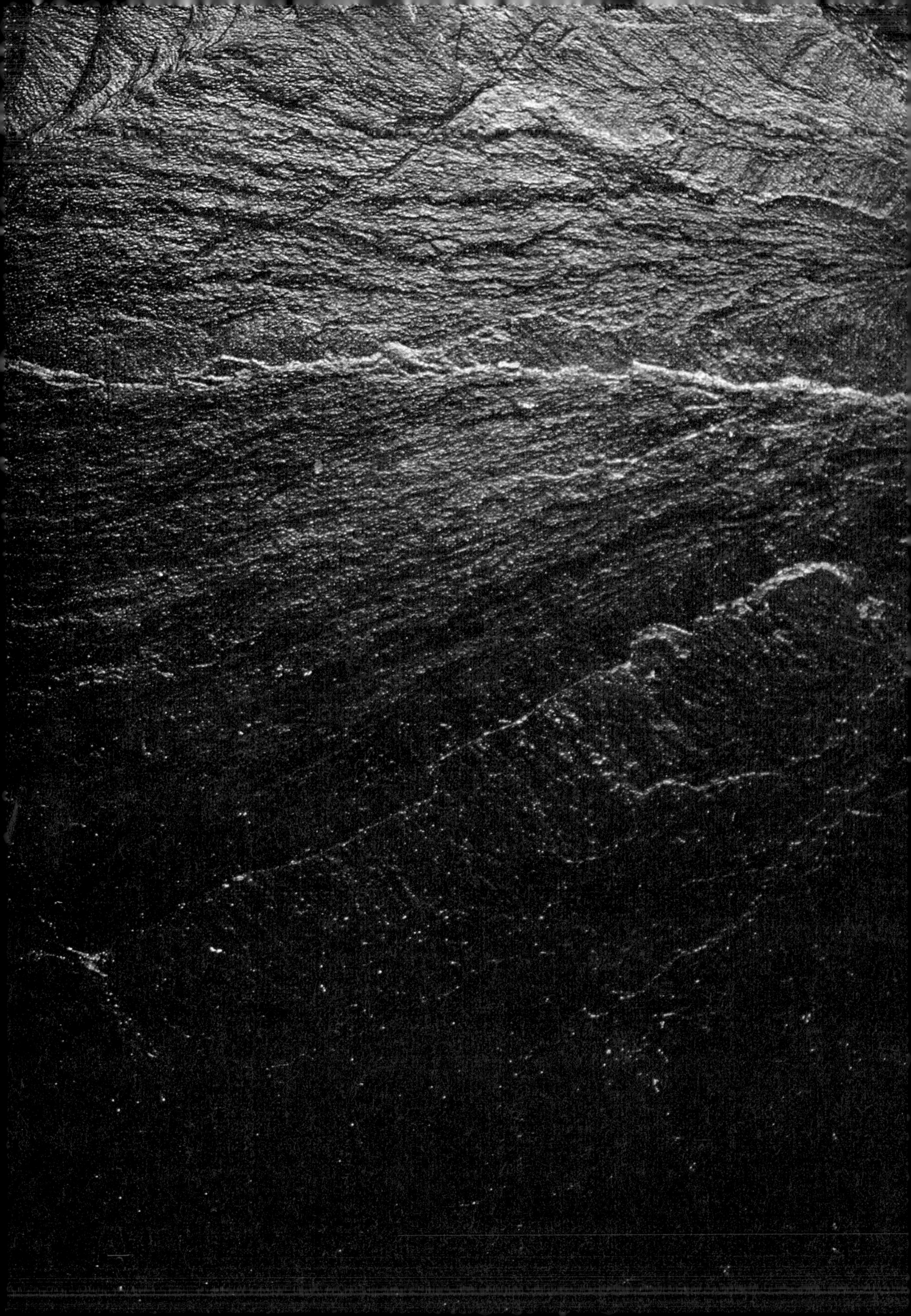